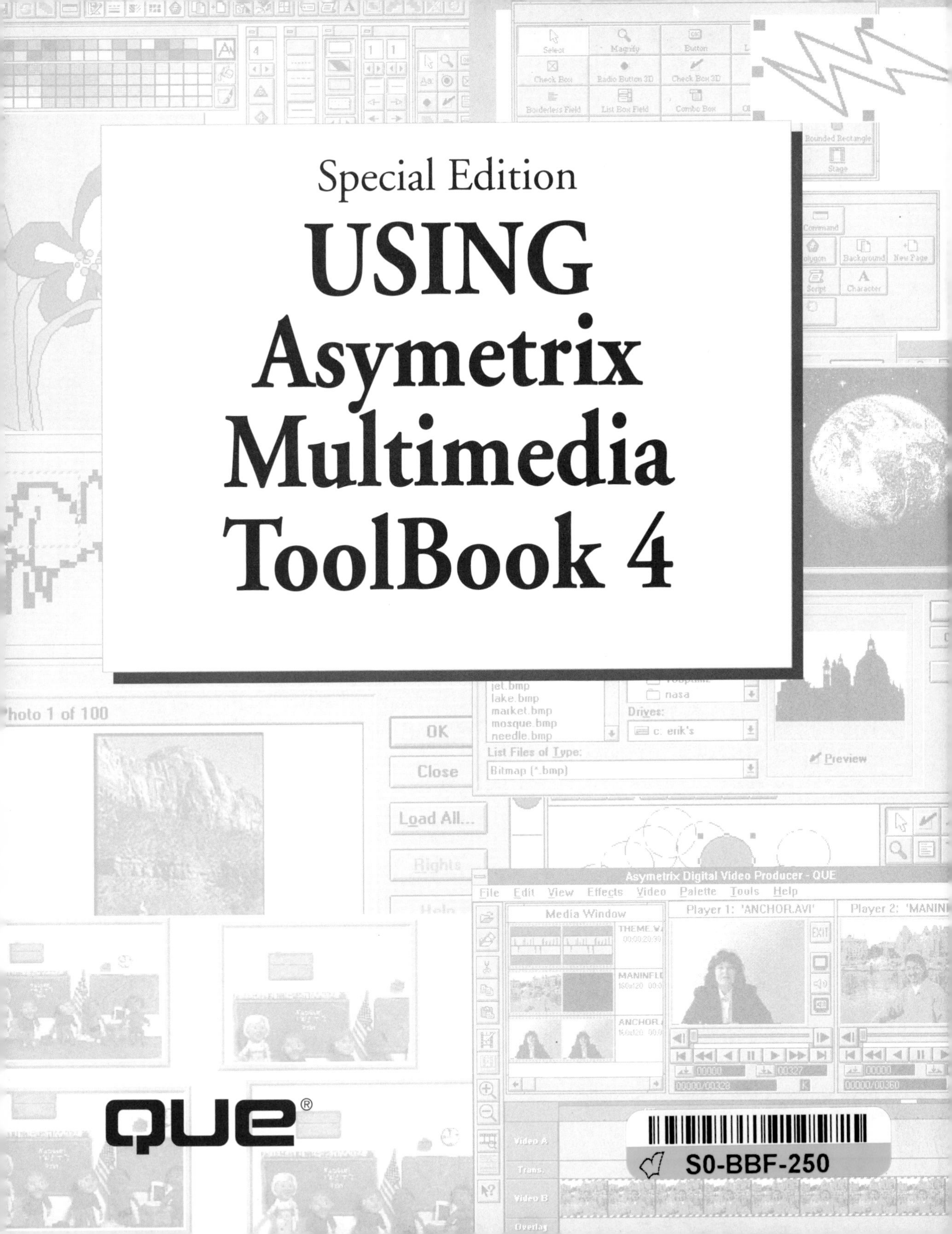
Special Edition
USING
Asymetrix
Multimedia
ToolBook 4
QUE®
S0-BBF-250
Select
Magnify
Button
Check Box
Radio Button 3D
Check Box 3D
Borderless Field
List Box Field
Combo Box
Rounded Rectangle
Stage
Command
Polygon
Background
New Page
Script
Character
Photo 1 of 100
OK
Close
Load All...
Rights
jet.bmp
lake.bmp
market.bmp
mosque.bmp
needle.bmp
nasa
Drives:
c: erik's
List Files of Type:
Bitmap (*.bmp)
Preview
Asymetrix Digital Video Producer - QUE
File Edit View Effects Video Palette Tools Help
Media Window
Player 1: 'ANCHOR.AVI'
Player 2: 'MANINI
THEME.W
MANINFLD
ANCHOR.
EXIT
Video A
Trans.
Video B
Overlay

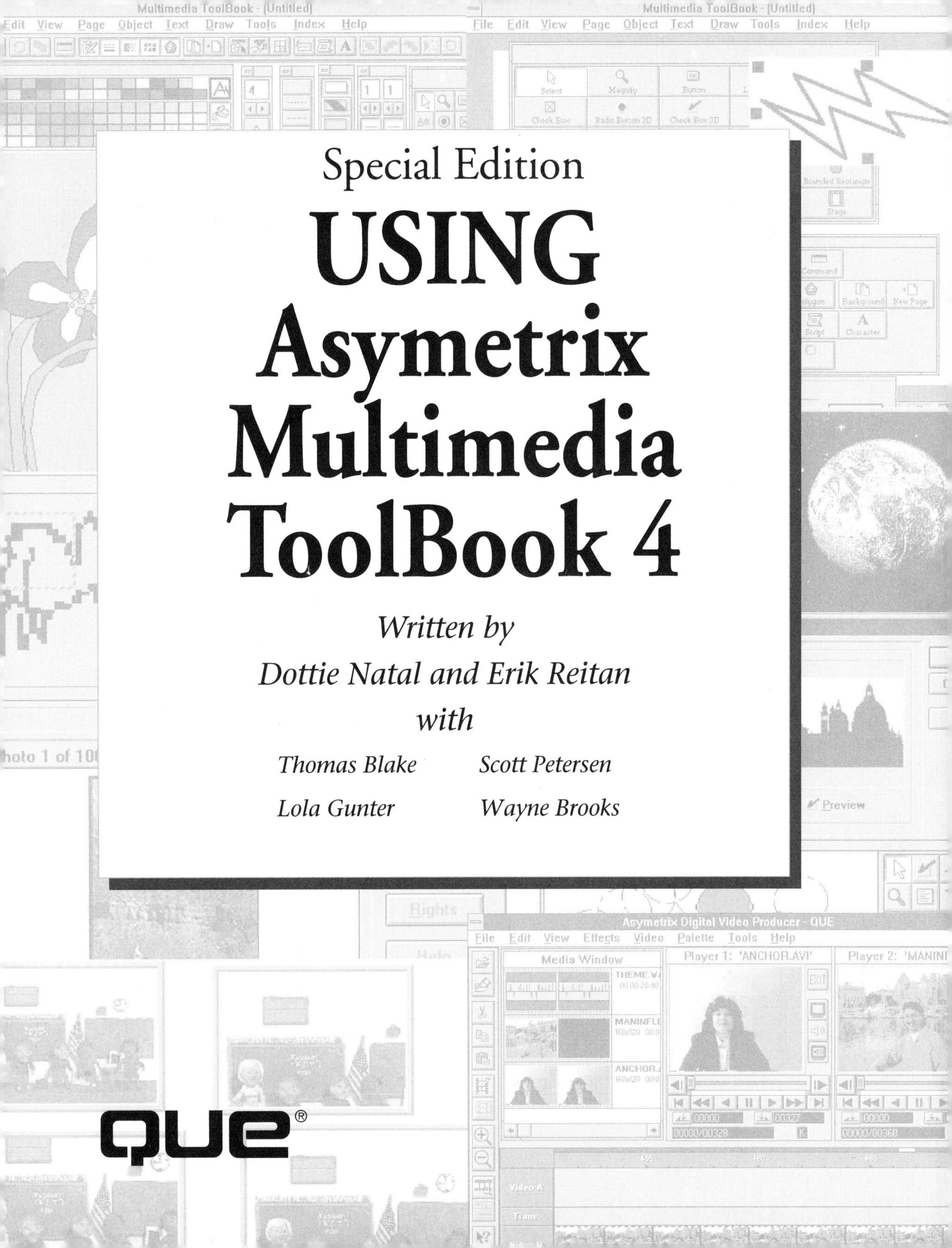

Special Edition

USING Asymetrix Multimedia ToolBook 4

Written by

Dottie Natal and Erik Reitan

with

Thomas Blake *Scott Petersen*

Lola Gunter *Wayne Brooks*

que®

Special Edition Using Asymetrix Multimedia ToolBook 4

Library of Congress Catalog No.: 95-78877

ISBN: 0-7897-0291-6

97 96 95 6 5 4 3 2 1

Interpretation of the printing code: the rightmost double-digit number is the year of the book's printing; the rightmost single-digit number, the number of the book's printing. For example, a printing code of 95-1 shows that the first printing of the book occurred in 1995.

Screen reproductions in this book were created using Collage Plus from Inner Media, Inc., Hollis, NH.

Composed in *Stone Serif* and *MCPdigital* by Que Corporation

Credits

President and Publisher
Roland Elgey

Associate Publisher
Joseph B. Wikert

Editorial Services Director
Elizabeth Keaffaber

Managing Editor
Sandy Doell

Director of Marketing
Lynn E. Zingraf

Senior Series Editor
Chris Nelson

Title Manager
Bryan Gambrel

Acquisitions Editor
Fred Slone

Product Director
Forrest Houlette

Production Editor
Maureen A. Schneeberger

Editors
Kelli Brooks
Kathy Simpson
Thomas Cirtin
Susan Dunn
Mike LaBonne
Nanci Sears Perry

Assistant Product Marketing Manager
Kim Margolius

Technical Editor
Wayne Brooks

Acquisitions Coordinator
Angela Kozlowski

Operations Coordinator
Patty Brooks

Editorial Assistant
Michelle Newcomb

Book Designer
Kim Scott

Cover Designer
Dan Armstrong

Production Team
Chad Dressler
Bryan Flores
Trey Frank
Amy Gornik
Damon Jordan
Daryl Kessler
Michael Thomas
Kelly Warner
Jody York
Karen York

Indexer
Gina Brown

About the Authors

Dottie Natal has been programming for over 20 years and works in a variety of programming languages. She uses a wide range of tools to create complete computer applications, including Asymetrix ToolBook, Autodesk 3D Studio, Macromedia Director, and Microsoft C++. She has a B.S. degree in mathematics, and spent five years programming computer simulations in theoretical nuclear physics. She has taught computer programming, science, and math courses from elementary school through college and currently teaches multimedia programming courses for various colleges. She has a Master's degree in Educational Psychology and is just about to file her Ph.D. dissertation titled, *Computer Mediated Hands-On Science for Bilingual Elementary Students in Cooperative Groups*. She is a frequent presenter at educational conferences on educational technology topics, and has published research articles on this topic.

Erik Reitan currently works for Asymetrix moderating the Asymetrix forum on CompuServe, instructing both the Introduction and Advanced Multimedia ToolBook courses at Asymetrix, and has been involved in creating sample applications for the Multimedia ToolBook release. Erik's predominant professional interests include programming in Windows and OpenScript to control video, sound, and database information. He is an avid OpenScript programmer and enjoys developing multimedia applications that are well-planned, unique, and have excellent user interfaces.

Thomas C. Blake comes from a professional recording background. After some years of designing audio-for-video and digital video post-production facilities for broadcast content, during which he programmed in C++ for the most part, he decided to move into interactive development. His company, Systems TCB Interactive Services, has reconstructed the Voyager Company's CD-ROM entertainment title *Comic Book Confidental* under Windows using Multimedia Toolbook 3.0, and is presently converting two other Voyager titles to Windows. He has also consulted on projects for Real World Multimedia, including the Windows version of *Xplora 1: Peter Gabriel's Secret World*, and is currently working with them on a new CD-ROM project.

Scott Petersen is an information technology consultant working in both the PC and Macintosh worlds. He provides clients in the public and private sectors with programming, systems analysis, and networking services. Scott is a long-time resident of beautiful Victoria, British Columbia, on Canada's west coast where he lives with his wife Myra and their two cats Mathew and Marilla.

Lola Gunter is a technical consultant in Raleigh, NC. She has worked in multimedia software development as a computer consultant and as a manager of technical documentation. She has a Bachelor's degree in Computer Science from the University of North Carolina at Asheville. Other than multimedia and the Internet, her interests include working with stained glass, roughhousing with her German Shepherd, and traveling.

Wayne F. Brooks is an independent consultant, technical writer, entrepreneur, and Multimedia ToolBook enthusiast. He has over 14 years experience in the areas of software development and quality assurance, and is president of Interactive Learning Technologiez (ILT). ILT produces and publishes interactive educational software in the areas of small business development, success education, and quality management. He is author of *ISO 9000 Questions and Answers—An Interactive Tutorial*, and the CD-ROM *Seminar CD: How To Start Your Own Homebased Multimedia Publishing Business*.

We'd Like to Hear from You!

As part of our continuing effort to produce books of the highest possible quality, Que would like to hear your comments. To stay competitive, we *really* want you, as a computer book reader and user, to let us know what you like or dislike most about this book or other Que products.

You can mail comments, ideas, or suggestions for improving future editions to the address below, or send us a fax at (317) 581-4663. For the online inclined, Macmillan Computer Publishing has a forum on CompuServe (type **GO QUEBOOKS** at any prompt) through which our staff and authors are available for questions and comments. The address of our Internet site is **http://www.mcp.com** (World Wide Web).

In addition to exploring our forum, please feel free to contact me personally to discuss your opinions of this book: I'm **75230,1556** on CompuServe, and I'm **bgambrel@que.mcp.com** on the Internet.

Thanks in advance—your comments will help us to continue publishing the best books available on computer topics in today's market.

Bryan Gambrel
Product Development Specialist
Que Corporation
201 W. 103rd Street
Indianapolis, Indiana 46290
USA

Contents at a Glance

Preparing for Distribution

Contents

Introduction

Until recently, computer programming was a skill few could hope to master. To force the computer to perform the feats of magic you knew it was capable of required many hours of patience and years of practice. Sure, anyone could write a simple program in Basic to perform calculations, but to create a front-end for the program that was both "user-friendly" and attractive required multiple skills and a great deal of programming time.

But those of us who programmed because we were enthralled with the power of the technology to assist people in their daily endeavors, who saw the implications for human interaction and communication through technology, were waiting for the day in which programming would be made easier, perhaps even accessible, to non-programmers.

When Asymetrix shipped its first version of Multimedia ToolBook (MTB), many were very excited. At last, a programming environment easy enough for a beginning programmer to use, yet so powerful that most multimedia application could be written with it! MTB is an excellent example of an exciting trend in the development in programming environments—a powerful programming environment that makes it easy to create a simple multimedia application, yet powerful enough that it can be extended to do even very complex applications.

Multimedia ToolBook is not perfect. It is, even after years of revision, still somewhat buggy. There are limitations to what you can get it to do in many cases. Sometimes things that seem obvious and straightforward take lots of time and fiddling to get to work properly. It is, however, the easiest to use prototyping tool for multimedia software on the market today, one of the very best possible tools for developing multimedia training materials, and an incredible bargain for the purchase price.

What is Multimedia ToolBook?

ToolBook is the programming environment of choice for many multimedia software developers. ToolBook can be used to create complete multimedia applications that can be freely distributed. As of the writing of this book,

ToolBook is a "Windows-only" program, with no Macintosh release announced or anticipated.

One reason that Multimedia ToolBook is so popular and such a bargain for the price is that the software contains everything you need to have when creating a multimedia application. Really, everything. The software ships with a bitmap editor (for creating and editing bitmap images), an icon editor, a cursor editor, and a digital video editor (which is excellent). ToolBook contains tools for vector-based drawing of objects, and import filters for practically any type of graphic file or multimedia element.

ToolBook ships with DLLs that let you interface with a variety of database file formats such as dBase and Paradox, allowing you to read, write, and manipulate these files (and you don't even need to have dBase or Paradox to do this)! It even ships with a "packager" that makes the process of creating setup and distribution files quite painless, including modules for runtime code, Video for Windows runtime, and modification of the users' `WIN.INI` or other `.INI` files. All of these features are described in this book, and these features taken together make ToolBook one of the most powerful and least expensive products on the market today.

Many programmers use Multimedia ToolBook as a prototyping tool, creating a complete "mock-up" of the title they will eventually create in a high level language, such as C++. ToolBook provides many tools that make rapid prototyping possible; an added plus is that the resulting application is easy to modify during the revision process. Other programmers use ToolBook to create complete titles, never finding a need to rewrite the program in a lower level language once it has been completed as a ToolBook application.

Many kiosk designers think of ToolBook as a kiosk designing program, because the tools it provides are especially useful for this type of application. ToolBook supports full color and all multimedia data types at all resolutions. This kind of use includes kiosks for museums, shopping centers, and so on.

ToolBook is used by business application programmers as a "front-end" for accounting and other data manipulations. ToolBook provides a wide range of tools that make interfacing with data bases easy to handle and makes creating interactive data entry screens a simple exercise.

ToolBook is also successfully used by non-programmers in a variety of settings, most notably in the education field where many instructors use it to design interactive software for classroom use. ToolBook is very well-suited to this setting, providing tools that make it simple to create interactive CBT (computer-based training) materials.

Who Should Use This Book

This book was written by experienced ToolBook programmers who have taught others how to use ToolBook and have created software applications using ToolBook under the stringent pressures of multimedia software development in the "real" world. Because of the experience of the authors, they are able to provide you with the "do's and don'ts" of development with this tool.

This book is not intended for a person new to computers. A basic familiarity with Microsoft Windows, as well as an understanding about files and directories, is assumed. Also, there is an assumption that the reader will know something about programming, if only from creating macros for his or her word processing program or spreadsheet.

Special Edition Using Asymetrix Multimedia ToolBook is perfect for the programmer who has been using other programming languages and wants to learn how to use ToolBook. It is perfect for a beginning multimedia enthusiast who has experience with other environments and wants to learn about multimedia elements. And it is perfect for anyone who has been using ToolBook for some time and wants to find out the answers to those nasty "why does it do this?" and "how can I get it to do that?" kinds of questions.

Use this book as a companion book for the ToolBook software, alongside the reference manuals provided by Asymetrix. It is not a replacement for the manuals, but instead covers in more detail the topics that are briefly touched upon in the manuals. This book is crammed full of the myriad of details that were left out in the Asymetrix manuals. It will save the programmer many hours by answering both the basic questions as well as the more complex questions that may occur as application development proceeds.

The CD-ROM that accompanies this book contains all of the examples shown in the book, and these examples can be cut and pasted into your own applications as needed. In addition, the CD-ROM contains tutorial files in Lotus Screen Cam format (controlled by a ToolBook menu system, of course). These files provide a tour of the more complex aspects of creating multimedia applications, providing the reader with a narrated walk-through of the process they will use to create their own applications.

How To Use This Book

This book is divided into seven sections. The earlier sections are intended for a general audience, and the later sections require understanding of the previous sections.

Part I—Introduction to MTB 4.0

In Part I, the basic nature of the software is discussed, and an overview of the development interface is presented. In this section, you find out the basics of how ToolBook is used. This is light reading, but recommended, even for the veteran programmer new to ToolBook. In Chapter 1, "Overview," you are introduced to the concepts of working in Author and Reader modes, and will learn about the tool palettes. In addition, this chapter discusses the multimedia software development cycle. In Chapter 2, "Touring the Development Interface," you are introduced to the components of the MTB programming window and the menus.

Part II—Anatomy of a ToolBook Book

In Part II, you learn the basic building blocks used in constructing a ToolBook application. Here, you also learn ToolBook terminology and how the media management and scripting tools work. If you are already an experienced ToolBook programmer, you may want to skim through these sections for new tips and tricks. In Chapter 3, "Understanding Objects," we introduce you to types of objects and their properties, including graphic items, buttons, and fields. In Chapter 4, "Understanding Books, Backgrounds, and Pages," we discuss how to add backgrounds and pages and how to navigate in a MTB application. Chapter 5, "Understanding the Media Management Tools," introduces you to the "managers" that are used in MTB to organize multimedia elements. And, Chapter 6, "Scripting Tools," walks you through the basics of creating, editing, and debugging scripts.

Part III—Customizing Tools and Techniques

In Part III, the real work begins. In Chapter 7, "Adding Multimedia Elements," you discover how to add multimedia elements to an application. Viewers—windows that can be created to be opened at the same time—are explored in detail in Chapter 8, "Working with Viewers." The art of creating menus (much easier than it sounds) is discussed in Chapter 9, "Creating Custom Menus," and the details of using graphic elements are explained in Chapter 10, "Using Graphics." Asymetrix manuals omitted the details of displaying and printing text, a topic that the authors of this book think is essential. These topics are covered in great detail in Chapter 11, "Working with Text," and Chapter 12, "Printing from ToolBook."

Part IV—Using OpenScript

Until this point in the book, you can create an application from the descriptions provided without writing any computer codes. In this section, we tempt you to begin trying your hand at programming. This part explains all you need to know to begin using the tools you need to master in order to gain complete control over the actions of the computer.

In Chapter 13, "OpenScript Fundamentals," the basics of OpenScript programming are explained. Chapter 14, "Messages, Objects, and Properties," offers an explanation of how messages are passed (the message hierarchy) and how to write handlers. Chapter 15, "Understanding Variables, Values, and Text," explains details such as the typing of variables, system and local variables, arrays, and constants. Control structures and functions are discussed in Chapter 16, "Statements, Functions, and Expressions," while Chapter 17, "Data and File Management," provides details on getting information into and out of your applications.

Part V—Enhancing Applications

Part V begins by discussing special effects in Chapter 18, "Using Special Effects." In this chapter, you learn how to create drag-and-drop applications, and how to create simple animations. Next, in Chapter 19, "Using Dynamic Link Libraries (DLLs) and Dynamic Data Exchange (DDE)," you learn how to use these important Windows features to add unlimited extensions to your ToolBook application. This is followed with a complete discussion of the tricky topic of dealing with color palettes and an explanation of the use of a range of multimedia elements in Chapter 20, "Fundamentals of Multimedia." The next chapter—Chapter 21, "Using Multimedia Elements"—discusses sound and video and the important issues of how to get sound and picture synchronized. Chapter 22, "MCI Devices and Multimedia," discusses how to use MTB to control other devices and introduces the MCI command set. The final chapter of this section, Chapter 23, "Digital Video Producer (DVP)," discusses the details of editing video in this program that is bundled with MTB.

Part VI—Troubleshooting

As you develop a multimedia application, you will certainly find that you need this section of the book. In Part VI, you learn about how to correct any problems that occur and how to use the debugging tools. Chapter 24, "Debugging Tools and Techniques," focuses on how to trap errors and trace code execution. Chapter 25, "Frequently Asked Questions," examines the questions that are most commonly asked by new users as well as veteran users of the software. You are sure to find answers to some of your own questions here!

Part VII—Preparing for Distribution

A big part of creating a software application is properly preparing for distribution. ToolBook's distribution software is discussed in the chapters in Part VII. Here we discuss those issues that you should be most concerned about as you prepare a title for distribution. In Chapter 26, "Preparing for Delivery," important considerations for successful distribution are discussed. This chapter should be considered before spending a lot of time in development on a product that is intended to be sent out to consumers. The final chapter—Chapter 27, "Distribution Tools"— provides details on how to create an installable program.

Conventions Used in This Book

Que has over a decade of experience writing and developing the most successful computer books available. With that experience, we've learned what special features help readers the most. Look for these special features throughout the book to enhance your learning experience.

Several type and font conventions are used in this book to help make reading it easier.

- *Italic type* is used to emphasize the author's points or to introduce new terms.
- Screen messages, code listings, and command samples appear in `monospace typeface`.
- Code the user needs to enter appears in **`bold monospace`**.

Note

Notes present interesting or useful information that isn't necessarily essential to the discussion. A note provides additional information that may help you avoid problems, or offers advice that relates to the topic.

Caution

Cautions serve to warn you about potential problems that a procedure may cause, unexpected results, and mistakes to avoid.

Troubleshooting

Troubleshooting sections anticipate common problems in the form of questions.

The response provides you with practical suggestions for solving these problems.

Tip

Tips present short advice on a quick or often overlooked procedure. These include shortcuts that will save you time.

▶▶ See "Using WordPerfect's QuickList Feature," p. xx

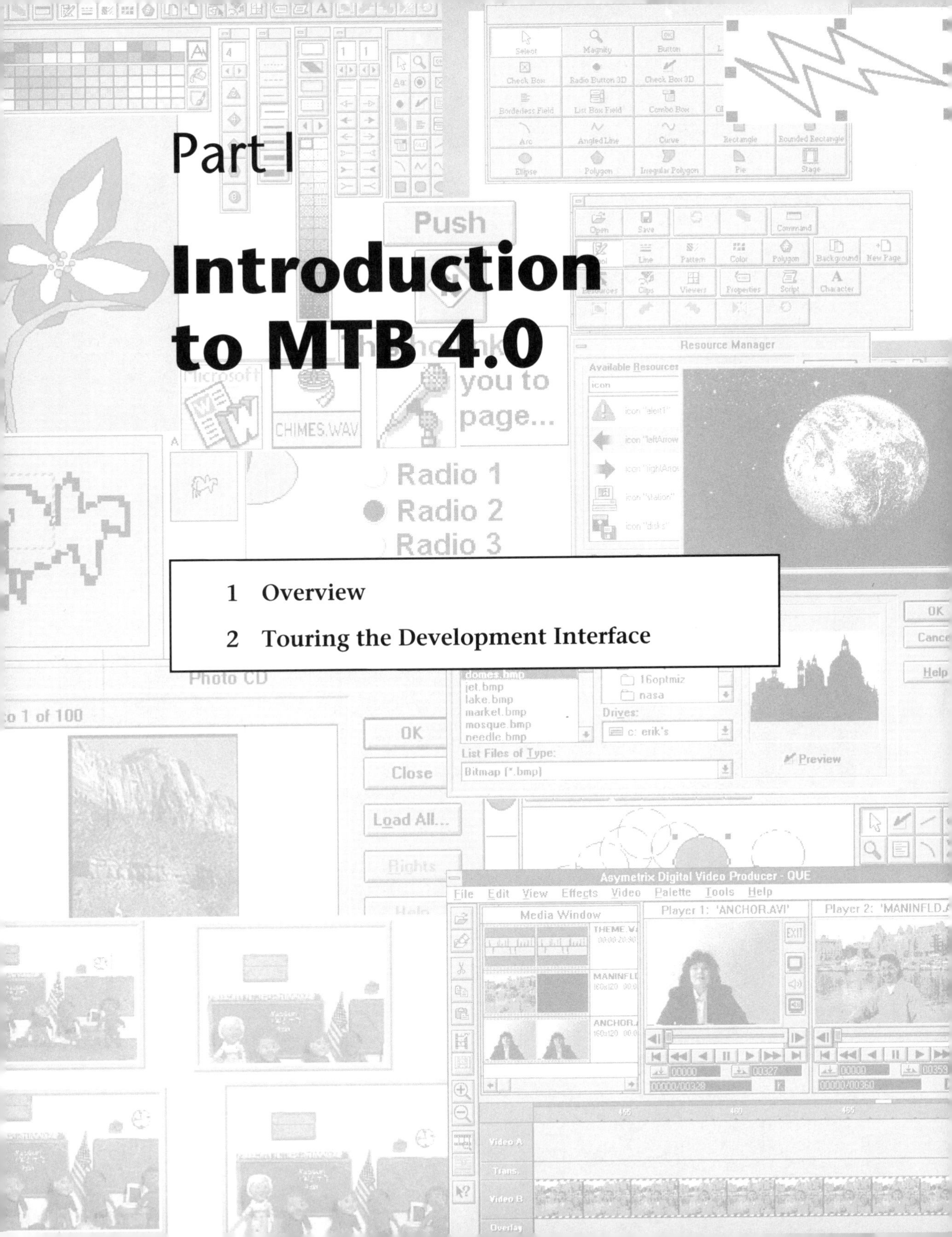

Part I

Introduction to MTB 4.0

1 Overview

2 Touring the Development Interface

Select
Magnify
Button
Check Box
Radio Button 3D
Check Box 3D
Borderless Field
List Box Field
Combo Box
Arc
Angled Line
Curve
Rectangle
Rounded Rectangle
Ellipse
Polygon
Irregular Polygon
Pie
Stage
Push
Open
Save
Command
Tool
Line
Pattern
Color
Polygon
Background
New Page
Resources
Clips
Viewers
Properties
Script
Character
This hotlink
you to
page...
Microsoft
CHIMES.WAV
Resource Manager
Available Resources
icon
Resource Properties
Radio 1
Radio 2
Radio 3
Undo To:
Import Graphic
File Name:
domes.bmp
Directories:
c:\...\clipart\bitmaps
coast.bmp
columns.bmp
domes.bmp
jet.bmp
lake.bmp
market.bmp
mosque.bmp
needle.bmp
clipart
bitmaps
16optmiz
nasa
Drives:
c: erik's
List Files of Type:
Bitmap [*.bmp]
Preview
Photo CD
Photo 1 of 100
OK
Close
Load All...
Rights
Asymetrix Digital Video Producer - QUE
File
Edit
View
Effects
Video
Palette
Tools
Help
Media Window
Player 1: 'ANCHOR.AVI'
00000
00327
00000/00328
00000/00360
Video A
Trans.
Video B

CHAPTER 1

Overview

In this chapter, you are introduced to the following:

- A brief description of the additions to Asymetrix Multimedia ToolBook with release of versions 3.0a and 4.0, of interest to users of previous versions of ToolBook
- A discussion of the general concepts of multimedia (what is it, how can you use it?), of interest to those new to the concepts of multimedia
- An overview of the application development life cycle, of interest to those new to multimedia application development

New Features in Multimedia ToolBook 3.0a

Multimedia ToolBook (MTB) has been in use by a large number of programmers for more than four years. The original version of MTB contained an impressive set of features; the 3.0a upgrade added many more features. The following list briefly describes the added features:

- New interface tools, including a second tear-off toolbar for easy access to graphic items
- Ruler shadows, which (especially when combined with the grid) make positioning objects on-screen easy
- Status bars at both Reader and Author levels, allowing you to obtain and display information about the current application
- Right-click pop-up menus that enable you to see or change an object's attributes
- New features, such as startup preferences, set tab order, add 3D style, import and export text, find and replace
- Spell checking

- Enhanced color support, including solid colors, RGB values along with HLS values, assignable shared palettes, 16- and 24-bit color support, automatic color dithering, and conformity to the colors set in the Windows Control Panel with the `useWindowsColors` property
- Easier resource management using embedded objects as resources available everywhere in a book, including menu bars, icons, cursors, bitmaps, and color palettes
- Installation packager, which enables you to create a distributable copy of your application
- Drag-and-drop support for graphics
- Added button types and features, including graphic labels
- Easier group editing features, which allow you to select and operate on components of a group
- Additional hotword support, including capability to import hotwords from a text file
- Additional field and record field support, including Rich Text Format (RTF) support and embedded graphics within text
- Multimedia widgets for video and animation control
- Path animation tools
- Improved programming tools, including changes to the Debugger, AutoScripting utility, improved Command Window (allowing you to scroll commands), notify handlers, better OpenScript efficiency and performance, new functions, messages and properties, and added DLL functions
- New operators, including assignment (=) and bitwise operators (such as `bitAnd`, `bitOr`, etc.)
- New functions, including menu-related, coordinate conversion, financial, and many other functions

New Features in Multimedia ToolBook 4.0

The recent upgrade to Version 4.0 of Multimedia ToolBook added many additional new features:

- Shared scripts, permitting objects in a book to share the same script
- An Object Browser, which permits you to examine the objects on a page or background and visually see the parent/child relationships between objects in the book
- A property editor that permits easy access to the properties of an object (user defined as well as system properties)
- Two object styles simultaneously supported: Windows 95 and Windows 3.x (for viewers, pushbuttons, checkboxes, fields, scroll bars)

- Custom Control support, permitting the use of objects created outside of ToolBook (such as Visual Basic Extensions)

Fundamentals of Multimedia Technology

Multimedia technology is a powerful way to present information so that it is easily navigated and easily understood. One of the reasons multimedia has gained popularity is because information that appeals to multiple senses is more easily assimilated and is generally more interesting than that presented in one format. However, before you can create effective multimedia applications, you must have a clear understanding of the steps involved in producing the user interface. This section provides you with an overview of the fundamental aspects of multimedia technology that is important to understand before undertaking a large multimedia project.

Multimedia Defined

What is multimedia? *Multimedia* is a relatively new term used to describe computer programs that combine multiple mediums, including graphics, text, video, animation, and sound. Although there are some applications that contain all of these elements, an application containing only a few of these elements is still considered multimedia. *Interactive* multimedia was a term coined to differentiate multimedia applications that were relatively passive in nature (sit back and watch) to those that require active input and interchange with the user. This term, however, has come to mean a number of different things to different people; some software is advertised as "interactive" when the main form of interaction is clicking to turn the page!

For all practical purposes, an application is referred to as a multimedia title if it is delivered on a CD-ROM disc and incorporates text with some kind of sound and graphics. CD-ROM is the preferred form of delivery because the large amounts of disk storage required for multimedia (especially sound and video) makes hard disk drive installation of elements impractical.

Practical Uses for Multimedia

Multimedia is the best media for delivery of information that requires:

- Graphical representation of information
- Support for multiple types of users
- Sound and video animation as well as text and still graphics
- Hypertext links

Asymetrix Multimedia ToolBook is one of the best known multimedia software production environments for the Windows platform. MTB is particularly well-suited to large multimedia projects because it is based on a structured programming model, providing features that make it easy to break down a large project into modules so that different parts can be assigned to different teams. It provides an incredibly powerful prototyping environment, and is simple enough for beginning programmers to learn to use while including features making it fully extensible for even the most demanding applications.

Overview of the Application Development Life Cycle

A multimedia product follows a predictable line of development, whether the project is a minor, short-term development or a large, full-scale project. The essential questions that must be answered at each stage in the development process are the following:

- Concept development—Who is the product intended for? What components should be included? How will it be developed?
- Requirements definition—How will the project proceed? How many people and what type will be required to complete the project?
- Interface design—What should the interface consist of? How should it look, how should the user interact with the product?
- Scripting—What is the best possible way to program the application?
- Testing—How well does the product work? How well does it meet the design requirements? Is it bug-free on the platforms it is meant to run on?
- Delivery—How will the product be reproduced and distributed? Updated?

Concept Development

The concept development phase is the very first step in the product development cycle. At this point, you will be making basic decisions about the project. Who is the intended audience? How will they find out about the product? Why would they want it? Once these basic questions have been answered, you will begin assembling the team needed to complete the project.

The basic plan for the amount and types of information that will be presented by the product must be explored. For example, let's suppose you are creating a "wine-tasting multimedia interface." How many wines will you include? How will you classify/group the different wine types? What kind of information will you present about each type of wine?

Requirements Definition

Next, based on the beginning concepts developed in the concept phase, you will begin assembling the people needed to complete the project. You will need to figure out who will be collecting and collating information, who will be in charge of keeping the production within time, who will market the product, how will the beta testing be handled, and so on.

One approach to providing a good requirements definition is to work the project out into an expected timeline. What is the target date that you are shooting for? How many hours do you expect it to take to gather the data needed for the product? How many to organize it? How many hours to design the interface? Program the interface? Don't forget the time it requires to create original artwork (if you are using it), secure copyrights to materials (if necessary), create sound or music, animate sequences, or shoot video, etc. Break the production down into as many component parts as you can, and look at who is available to work on each part.

Once the project has been divided into its component parts, it is much easier to look at your estimates for projected time of completion. Have each person involved review their expected contributions.

Tip

A good rule of thumb on programming time is "the last 10% of the work takes 90% of the time."

In an interactive prototyping cycle, which is only possible with powerful tools like Multimedia ToolBook, it becomes very easy for anyone to fool themselves about the time that the final product will take. Perhaps this is because the product really *looks* like it is done almost from the first prototype!

Interface Design

A big key to an effective multimedia program is careful attention to the interface design. The multimedia elements need to be logically placed and essential to the program, or they will be perceived as superfluous by the user of the product. The time taken at the beginning of the production cycle to create an effective interface will pay off handsomely by resulting in an effective, usable application. If you cannot afford the up-front time it takes to plan and test the design of the interface, then you cannot afford the project; these steps are essential, and prevent wasted time late in the development cycle.

An interface design team should be assembled. A team is a much better way to approach the interface design problem, because it is unlikely that one person will be able to think through the design issues from the multiple perspectives necessary to make the end product most useful. Any individual will approach the design process with his or her preconceived notions about how people think, how software should work, what information should be presented and how.

The interface design team should consist of a group of people that can work together without fear of their ideas being ridiculed. Preferably, one person will act as the team leader, keeping the discussions on track and productive, but without imposing undue restrictions on the creativity of the team as a whole. The initial stages of the design should be open-ended discussion, with the "no idea too crazy" rule. Later, these ideas will need to be tamed and reduced to a reasonable set of features. However, these initial brainstorming sessions can produce some very effective ideas.

The design team should be composed of a variety of different types of people. Usually it is a good idea to have a programmer, a computer novice, one or more people that are (or represent) end-consumers of the product, a graphics designer, one or more subject specialists. The team should meet for a period of time sufficient to discuss the kinds of information that will be presented in the application, ways that the information should be accessed, and benefits and pitfalls of the multimedia approach to presenting the information. This time period will vary according to the overall scope of the project, and may range from one or two short meetings up to a few weeks of meetings.

Ideally, the design team should consist of approximately four to eight people. Too many, and the conversation might bog down on irrelevant details or split into factions; too few, and the range of ideas and counter-ideas may be too limited to be useful.

Begin your design effort with a strong focus on the intended audience. What are their interests? Needs? If they already use the information you are supplying in a different format, focus on these issues: How do they access the data now? How will the interface build on the strengths of their current access of the data and remove the weaknesses?

For example, let's suppose you want to build the "killer recipe card" multimedia application. How do users already access recipes? You would begin by building on the metaphor that they are using—index cards. What are its strengths—ease of access, quick reference, simplistic filing system, predictable format. What are the weaknesses—lack of graphics, changes in portions require calculations that have to be done by hand, instructions for tricky details must be written out in words.

Obviously, these are all things that could be improved upon by using computer technology. A computer is well suited to showing pictures of the completed dishes, recalculating ingredients for change portion sizes, displaying with video tricky preparation steps, and so on. Now, concentrate on the new drawbacks introduced by the application: difficult to use in the kitchen, recipes are hard to send in the mail, etc. These drawbacks will need to be seriously considered in the design phase of the project.

Keys to Designing an Effective Interface

Employ the KISS principle (keep it simple, stupid!). Keep the number of steps that a user will need to do to handle any function to the minimum necessary. Design for the ease of the user, not the programmer. A well thought-out "home" screen that allows the user access to all of the main features of a program is well worth the thought process put into designing it. This keeps down the number of screens that need to be designed, as well as making the interface easier to use.

Tip

Invest in the services of a good graphic artist. Just because you *can* do it does not mean you *should* do it. A well-thought-out interface that is also aesthetically pleasing is the key to a successful interface design.

Checklist for Design Issues

Your interface design should be examined against this checklist to be sure that you have considered these important aspects of interface design:

- The product provides multimedia elements to explain, emphasize, or illustrate (and not merely because they *can* be included).
- All types of end users are supported, including those with thinking/interaction styles that are predominately visual, auditory, or kinesthetic, whenever possible.
- Multiple means of accessing data are provided; for example, cascading lists, data searching, table of contents, indexes, visual maps to the application.
- Organization of the product is clearly visible to the end user; that is, it is clear how much data is contained, what is the depth and breadth of the data, and where the user is located in the data at any given time.
- Data is available to the end user in the most efficient way possible. Data needed most often is always available with the minimum amount of keystrokes or clicking possible.
- Navigation buttons and other key features of the interface are "intuitively" placed (that is, where they would be expected by users), and do not change from screen to screen.
- Basic rules of graphical page layout are followed (such as not mixing too many fonts on a page, allowing for plenty of white space, appropriate and tasteful use of color, and so on).

As you design, keep in mind that one of the difficulties in using hyperlinked information is that the user tends to get lost in the data. You must provide a wide range of devices to help the user situate him/herself. In a book, you have many points of references; by the size of it, you know about how much text is in it. By flipping through the pages, you get a good idea about the quantity of graphical information. You know where to find the index, table of contents, references, glossary. You can remember where you found information last time you used the book.

In a multimedia application, you, as the programmer or interface designer, need to provide the user with the same quality of reference points. Your user needs to be aware of how much information is in the application, how it is organized, how to get to desired parts, where they have been, and so on. If you can design your interface so that it at *least* provides these types of information, it will be perceived as useful and usable.

Scripting

The scripting part of the cycle can vary in effort and overall time from project to project. An experienced, good programmer can often code subroutines at a much faster pace than an inexperienced programmer. A factor of 25 to 1 is not that uncommon! So, as you assemble the programming crew, keep that issue in mind. If you have a programming group that has used a lot of other tools but have not had experience with MTB, make sure you factor that into the estimates for completion time; as with any programming language, the "obvious" skills take some time to learn.

Because MTB provides so many pre-scripted functions and so many example scripts to work from, the job of coding a program can be significantly shortened (when compared to product development in other languages).

Good programming in ToolBook is like good programming in any computer language. You will want to keep the scripting as "clean" as possible—that is, logically easy to follow. Also, as in any programming language, maintain good documentation practices by providing lots of comments and reasons for doing things right in the scripts. An experienced MTB programmer will have enough experience to know at what level to put a code (object versus page, versus book, versus system book.) A new programmer will require some help or time to learn these concepts.

ToolBook is a great programming environment for multiple programmers, as it is quite easy to separate sections of a project into separate books, bringing them together again later as one book (or, for that matter, leaving them separate and having one call another).

Testing

The testing phase can be very important if the application is expected to run on a variety of systems. Later sections of this book warn you about some of the difficulties that you will run into (color palette problems, display device differences, problems with a variety of printers, and so on). Keep these in mind as you develop your product, and certainly take the necessary time to test the completed project on a range of machines that represent your expected audience. It is a good idea to schedule alpha tests (tests of the incomplete interface on a variety of machines with a variety of audiences) as often as practical along the development cycle, preventing any unpleasant major surprises at the end of the development cycle!

When you do begin your beta testing (testing the completed product with a wide-spectrum of end-users), make sure that you target the same range of users that your final product is expected to be delivered to, including novice users to test your documentation and instructions.

Delivery

Prior to delivery, you will be going through the mastering process of the development cycle. If you are delivering product on CD-ROM, you will want to take the time to read Chapter 26, "Preparing for Delivery," very carefully. The installation routines that Asymetrix ships are excellent, making it unnecessary to purchase another product for this purpose. When you are at the point of creating your installation disks, be sure to read through Chapter 27, "Distribution Tools."

Maintenance

ToolBook software makes the maintenance and upgrading of your delivered software much easier than might be the case for many other products. If you need to send out an update of your main programs, you can often just send the ToolBook file for installation (and not the runtime codes needed). If you are creating a product for which you intend frequent updates, you can design the product in a modular way so that very little needs to be sent out. For example, you could have your ToolBook file be an interface only, with the actual data stored in a database file. Then, as you update materials, you need only send the updated data file or even a script that reads the old data file, deletes outdated records, and adds in the new records. This modularity can make the maintenance issue an easy one for MTB programmers.

Applications Best Suited to Multimedia Implementation

Any application that is used for data transmission or retrieval is probably a candidate for successful multimedia implementation. The human brain is complex. We know that information that is introduced and reinforced using a variety of mediums is both easier to understand and also easier to retain.

There are a wide variety of multimedia programs out on the market today. These include reference materials such as encyclopedias and atlases; educational titles such as children's storybooks, games, and learning titles; business applications such as multimedia databases of information; and entertainment titles such as games, simulations, how-to titles, and travel guides.

Choosing the Most Appropriate Multimedia Programming Environment

When beginning a project, you must be careful to choose the multimedia programming environment best suited for your final application. MTB is an excellent choice for some applications but a poor candidate for others. It is important to keep in mind the bottom line cost of your project, which will consist of the following:

- The up-front expense of the software used to design the application.
- The runtime royalty fee for the distributed application.
- The expense of the time required to design the user interface.
- The expense of the time for programming the application.

- The direct and indirect expense for the content for the title.
- The expense for the beta test and debug cycle of the title.
- The cost of materials and time for mastering the final product.

The overall investment in the project will be mostly in time. It is important to weigh carefully different aspects of a project before deciding the programming environment to use. Table 1.1 summarizes a benefit/drawback comparison of Multimedia ToolBook with some of the other popular solutions for multimedia programming.

Table 1.1 Benefits/Drawbacks Comparisons of MTB with Other Multimedia Environments

Environment	Best For Applications That...	Benefits	Drawbacks
Low level programming languages such as Assembly, C++, Pascal, and other compilers	Require speed, low memory machines requiring optimum use of RAM, need to be completely customized.	No runtime fees. Complete customization. Possible cross-platform development (depends on compiler).	Much longer development time than with MTB. Expensive to train new programmers on project.
Macromedia Director	Consist of scenes with simple interactions. Requires timing of events such as synchronizing graphics and sound.	Cross platform (Windows, Mac). Relatively low overhead (disk space and RAM) for runtime. Popular, easy to find programmers. No runtime fees.	Requires XCMDs or DLLs for many features that are standard in MTB, such as text handling.
Multimedia database programs (FoxPro, Oracle, etc.)	Consist of data that needs to be sorted, retrieved, linked, replaced, or changed often.	Specifically designed to handle data and sorting. Many such environments are multiplatform.	Usually have runtime fees. Limited feature sets. Often high overhead (disk space and RAM).
Multimedia ToolBook	Complex applications that use multiple data types (video, sound, animation, text), requires quick production cycle, does not need to run on low level systems.	Quick prototyping. No runtime fees. Complete program including CD-ROM optimization coding and installation packager. Easy to learn.	Somewhat high overhead (disk space and RAM). Windows only. Older versions somewhat "buggy" when pushing the development limits.

From Here...

In this chapter, you found out about the new features that have been added to the Multimedia ToolBook interface. We defined multimedia for you, and discussed some uses for multimedia. We also provided a "roadmap" for the basic steps that are required when designing an interface. This chapter provides you with a sound conceptual understanding of product development issues. Now, you are ready to move forward and find out more:

- Chapter 2, "Touring the Development Interface," provides you with the background that you will need to begin to effectively program in Multimedia ToolBook.
- Chapter 4, "Understanding Books, Backgrounds, and Pages," discusses how to find out more about how a ToolBook file is organized.
- Chapter 6, "Scripting Tools," shows you how to find out more about how to script (or program) in ToolBook.

CHAPTER 2

Touring the Development Interface

Multimedia ToolBook is a powerful authoring environment, providing tools that are not available in many other authoring systems. For this reason, it can take some time to become familiar with the tools that are included in the system.

This chapter provides you with some of the information needed to gain this familiarity. This chapter describes the following:

- MTB's Author and Reader modes, which permit you to edit and test your application
- The metaphors used to describe programming in MTB
- Details of working in ToolBook's main window work area

Highlights of Key Features of MTB's Programming Environment

Highlights of some of the key elements and features of Multimedia ToolBook's programming enviroment include the following:

- Tool palettes—which contain the "tools" you will use when constructing an application—can be positioned anywhere on the screen and can be redimensioned for convenient placement during editing.
- Menus—both at Author (programming) level as well as Reader (runtime) level—can be configured for complete flexibility in customizing the working environment.
- A *Command Window* permits you to try out or execute commands interactively.
- A *status bar* along the bottom of the main Window provides feedback during development, including the name of the object your cursor is positioned over, the current screen location of your cursor, and your current page number.
- *Viewers*, which are windows that can be placed anywhere on the screen, can be easily created and displayed. Viewer types include pop-up text windows, palettes, main windows, dialog boxes, and button bars.

As you create applications in Multimedia ToolBook, you will not only use menus and dialog boxes with interfaces familiar to you from other Windows applications, but will also encounter features that may be new to you. One of these features is the use of the right mouse button to initiate actions. Clicking an object with the right mouse button will provide a shortcut to many of the menus. Other features that may be outside of your previous experience include the use of "tabs" in dialog boxes, as illustrated in figure 2.1. Using a dialog box with tabs requires you to click the tab, which is like a tab on a file folder, to flip to the "page" representing the desired section of the dialog.

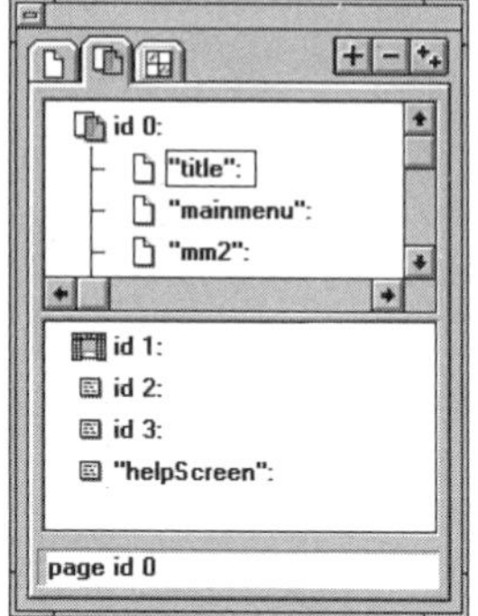

Fig. 2.1

The property browser, which presents a graphical representation of the objects in the current book, uses tabs to display different types of information.

About Author and Reader Modes

There are two modes of operation that you use when working in MTB—Reader mode and Author mode. The Reader mode is used when running or testing the application, and the Author mode is used while creating the application. As you develop your application, you can toggle between the modes by pressing the F3 button on the keyboard or choose Edit, Reader or Edit, Author from the main menu.

Working in Author Mode

In Author mode, your work environment will appear something like that shown in figure 2.2. The exact layout of the tools, palettes, and status bar may vary depending on the preferences that you have set, and also on where you have dragged the palettes and how you have resized them (they are meant to be easily reconfigured).

Until you are more familiar with the tools that are on the tool palette and the toolbar, you might want to display captions for the tool icons. You can do this by right-mouse–clicking the palette (that is, click the palette with the right mouse button—a technique you will become familiar with in short order when using ToolBook). Select Graphics and Palettes from the choices shown. The palettes will appear something like those in figure 2.3.

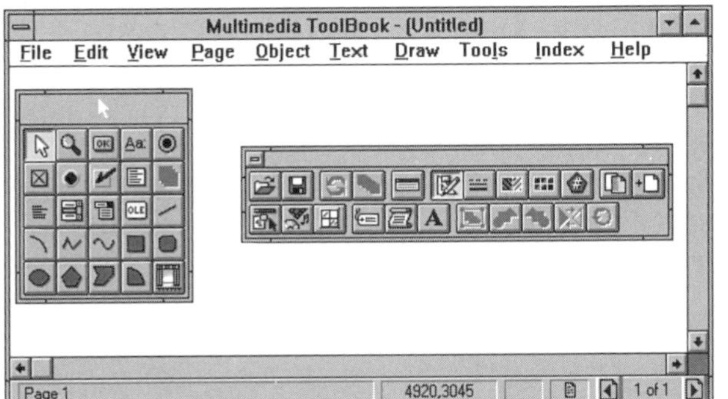

Fig. 2.2

The Author level working environment includes a main working window and tool palettes.

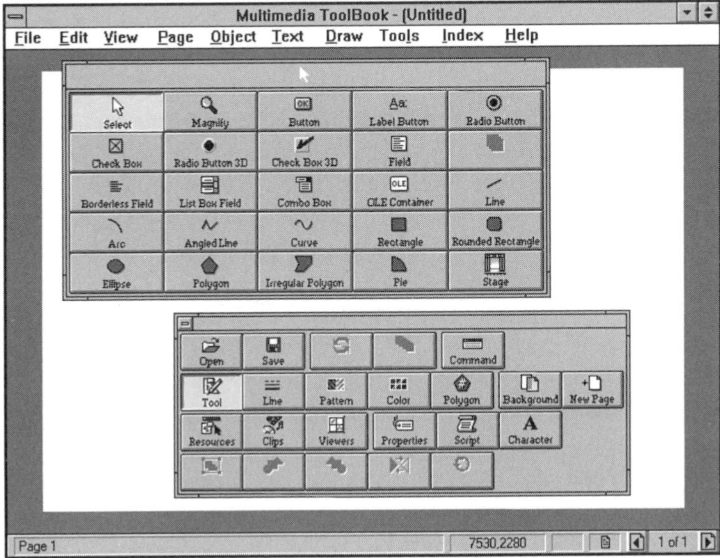

Fig. 2.3

The Author level working environment with button captions.

Additional details about the Author level working environment are found later in this chapter in the section titled, "ToolBook's Main Window Work Area."

Working in Reader Mode

When you start up a new, blank book in ToolBook and switch to Reader mode, what you will see is a blank screen displaying the default reader menu bar (File, Edit, Text, Page, and Help). Like a blank word-processing page, the first page of the interface will remain empty until you add something to it.

When you have completed an application, you distribute it to end users without the ToolBook programming tools. You substitute the ToolBook editing program with a runtime program that will permit the end user to run the application in Reader mode only. Using the Reader mode while authoring simulates the environment that your code will run in when completed.

Metaphors Used in ToolBook Programming

In order to make sense of programming in Multimedia ToolBook, it is helpful to understand the basic metaphors that describe the ToolBook development system. This section gives you an overview of the metaphors used in MTB's visual programming environment. These include:

- Books and pages
- Foreground and background
- Scripts, messages, and objects
- Event-driven programming

Books and Pages

The primary metaphors used in ToolBook are those of "book" and "page." A ToolBook application is referred to as a *book*. A book consists of a number of *pages* (where a page is the basic unit in a ToolBook application). This metaphor is useful for understanding the construction of a book, but should be understood to be the metaphor used to refer to constructing an application rather than the intended structure of the application. In the realization of a book, most multimedia authors break away from this basic metaphor. The terms *page* and *book* imply a relative linear organization of information; although you can certainly create a linear application in MTB, one of the most appealing aspects of multimedia applications is their ability to break out of the limiting bounds of linearity.

Creating nonlinearity in a ToolBook application is not difficult but may require you, as an author, to release preconceived notions of order. What comes first in a multimedia application? The notion of "first" may not make sense here. For example, you may want to determine the page to display first by examining what page was last displayed by the user the prior time he or she used the application. Or, commonly, you may want the first displayed screen to be a graphical table of contents that provides a quick jumping-off point for the user to get to other areas of the program. Nonlinear devices used in applications include buttons that link the user to other areas of the screen, hotwords that provide hypertext links to other regions of the interface, and pop-up windows (or *viewers*) of various sorts.

Unlike the pages in a physical book, pages in a ToolBook application can be any size, and you can mix and match page sizes within the application. And also unlike a physical book, you can even display more than one page of a ToolBook application at a time. This is accomplished by displaying one page over another as a viewer, as demonstrated in figure 2.4.

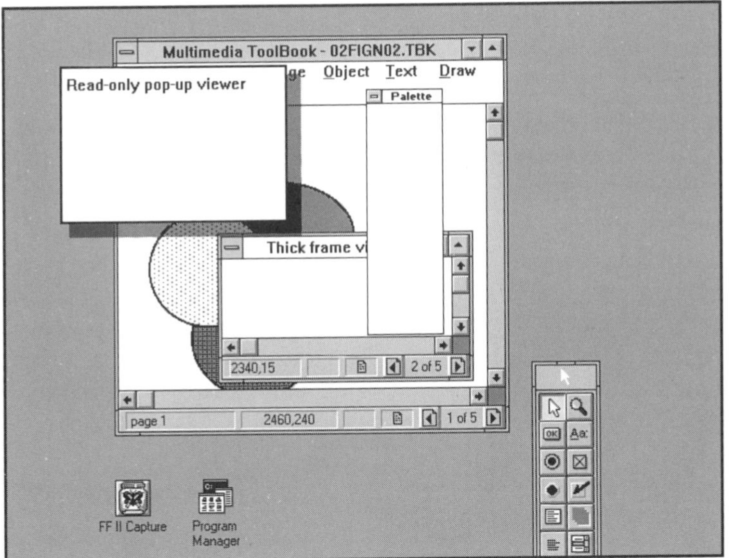

Fig. 2.4

Four different viewers are displayed on this page—a thick frame viewer, a read-only pop-up viewer, a palette, and the ToolBook main window viewer.

Foreground and Background

Another basic metaphor that MTB shares with many other applications are those of *foreground* and *background*. The *foreground* is like a transparent sheet of plastic on which you place objects that you want to display in front; while a *background* shows through the foreground and may contain objects that are on more than one page of the book. Figure 2.5 provides a visual representation of this concept. When creating a ToolBook application, it is often effective to use a single background on many pages of the book, while displaying a different foreground on each page.

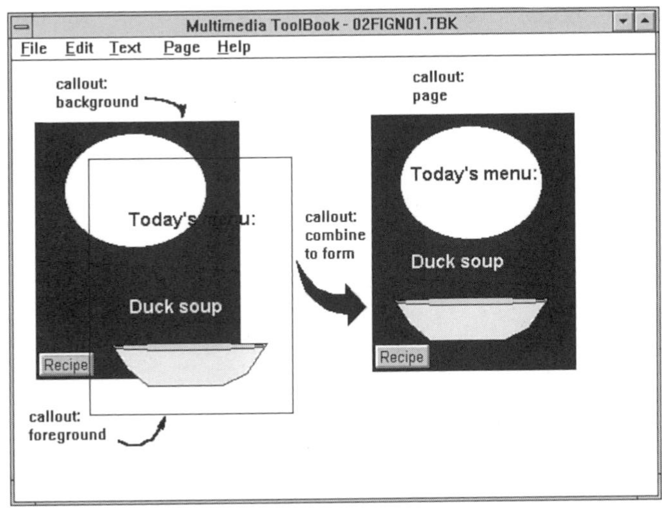

Fig. 2.5

The foreground is a transparent overlay that will be displayed over the objects in the background.

Scripts, Messages, and Objects

In ToolBook, a page consists of a number of *objects*—the basic elements in ToolBook. Examples of objects include buttons, graphic items such as rectangles and ellipses, pictures, and fields (areas of text). Any object in MTB can contain a *script*—codes that tell the objects what to do. Scripting in ToolBook is done in the OpenScript language, a Basic-like structured programming language.

Scripts for objects are triggered by some sort of event, such as the user clicking the object. If the object has been scripted to handle the particular event that occurs, then the instructions in the script are carried out in ToolBook. For example, if you create a button in ToolBook, you might want to handle the event `mouseUp` (`mouseUp` is defined as the event that occurs when the left mouse button is released after being pressed). An example of this is a button that causes the page of a ToolBook application to be "turned" to the next page. The script for this event would be the following:

```
to handle mouseUp
    go to next page
end
```

Any object in ToolBook can be scripted. When a handler is executed, it passes a message to other objects. The order in which messages are sent is referred to as the *object hierarchy*. The message will attempt to handle each object that is passed. If it does not have a handler for the event, then it will send the message up to the next object in the hierarchy. For example, if you script a button with the following code:

```
to handle buttonDown
     send twinkle
end
```

then the button will first attempt to handle the message. If no message handler for `twinkle` exists in the button, it will pass the message up to the group that the button belongs to (if any), then the page, and so on up the hierarchy. The message hierarchy is as follows in order of highest level to lowest level:

- ToolBook System
- System Books
- Book
- Background
- Page
- Group
- Object

This method of passing messages along a hierarchy permits you to create scripts that can be placed at their most logical level. For example, if you have an event that you want more than one object on the page to trigger, then you would put the handler for the event in the page itself. If there are events that may be called from anywhere within the application, then the handler might be placed in the book script instead. And, of course, many events happen one time and can be placed within the script of the object itself.

Event-Driven Programming Modes

MTB is an event-driven programming environment. That is to say, a ToolBook application sits there waiting for the user to trigger an event. An event might be clicking a button or object on the screen, moving the mouse over an object, or pressing a key on the keyboard. The event is "handled" by a scripted *handler*—lines of code that you write to tell the application what to do when that event occurs. For example, if you had an application where you wanted items to "light up" when the user placed the cursor over the object, you might choose to follow these general steps:

1. Create a backdrop picture (in a paint program external to ToolBook).
2. Create versions of each of the objects that are "lit up" in the Paint program, and save them as separate files.
3. Place the backdrop picture into the ToolBook page.
4. Place each of the lit-up pictures into their proper places on the backdrop.
5. Create transparent objects over each area that you want to use to trigger the event of showing the lit-up graphic object.
6. Script the transparent objects so that they would cause the lit-up graphic object to appear when the cursor was over them with a script such as the following:

```
to handle mouseEnter
     show paintObject "lit1"
end
to handle mouseLeave
     hide paintObject "lit1"
end
```

You should understand that the event-driven nature of MTB need not limit your programming because you can use a timer as the triggering event, allowing you to create time-driven codes. For example, you can have a timer begin at time equal to zero each time the mouse is moved or a key is pressed, and then check this timer periodically to see if the user is interacting with the program. After a specified period of inactive time has passed, you can trigger another event (such as displaying the opening screen in a kiosk). As you read through this book, you will find many other methods of creating time-driven events in ToolBook.

ToolBook's Main Window Work Area

MTB is a visual programming environment. This section introduces you to the basic tools and features of the environment, orienting you towards the different parts of the window that constitute the development environment.

The process of creating a ToolBook application is accomplished primarily within the ToolBook programming windows. The windows you will use most include the main ToolBook window work area, the Debug window, and the Scripting window (see fig. 2.6).

Fig. 2.6

During the development process, you will be using a variety of window types, as displayed in this figure.

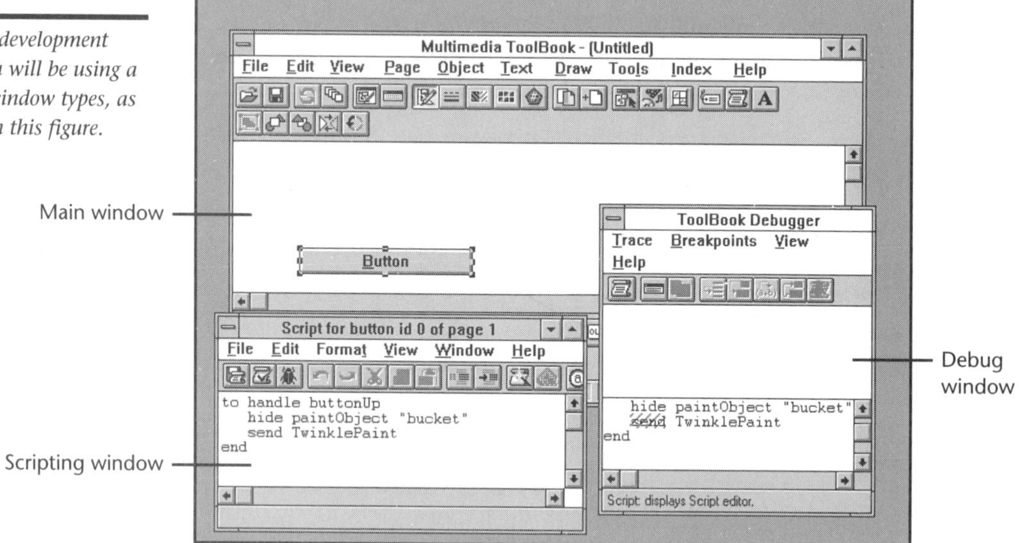

In the main window, there are these five main regions (see fig. 2.7):

- Work area—the (initially blank) window that contains objects added to the background and foreground of your application.
- Toolbar—a movable palette that contains icons representing commonly accessed menu items.
- Tools palette—a movable palette that contains "click-and-drag" tools that cannot be accessed from menus.
- Menus—the commands that can be accessed from the menu bar.
- Status bar—the region at the bottom of the screen that provides information about the interface status.

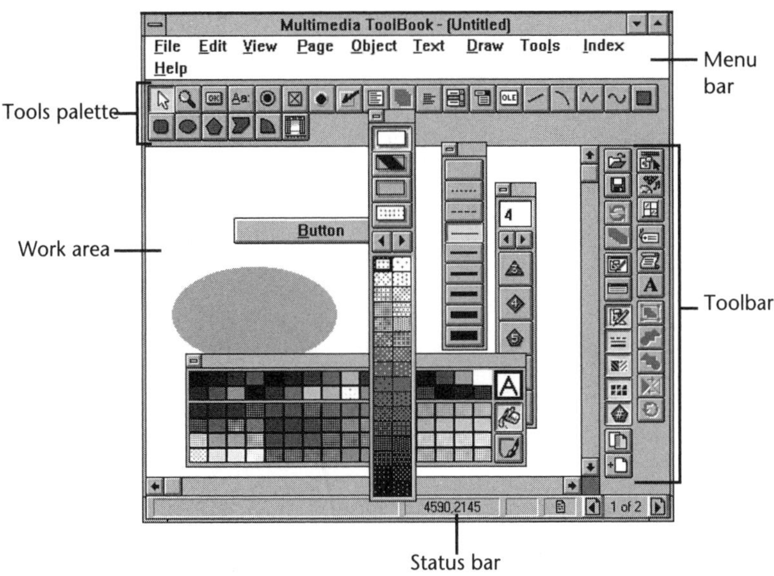

Fig. 2.7

The regions of the main window provide tools used during development and feedback on the status of objects in the current book.

The Toolbar

The toolbar icons include items that are frequently accessed in ToolBook, providing a convenient means of performing file manipulation (save, open), common actions (duplicate, switch to foreground/background, insert a new page, etc.), hide and show palettes, and access dialogs and resource managers. The toolbar icons are shown in Table 2.1.

Table 2.1 Toolbar Icons

Icon	Command	Description
Open	Open	Opens an existing ToolBook file
Save	Save	Saves the current book
Undo	Undo	Undoes the last action
Duplicate	Duplicate	Makes a duplicate of selected item
Command	Command	Shows the Command Window
Tool	Tool	Shows (or hides) Tool palette
Line	Line	Shows (or hides) Line palette

(continues)

Table 2.1 Continued

Icon	Command	Description
Pattern	Pattern	Shows (or hides) Pattern palette
Color	Color	Shows (or hides) Color palette
Polygon	Polygon	Shows (or hides) Polygon palette
Background	Background	Switches to editing background
New Page	New Page	Creates a new page
Resources	Resources	Shows the Resource Manager
Clips	Clips	Shows the Clip Manager
Viewers	Viewers	Shows Viewer dialog box
Properties	Properties	Shows the Object Properties dialog box
Script	Script	Opens Script Editor for selected item
A Character	Character	Shows Character dialog box
Group	Group	Groups (or ungroups) selected objects
Front	Front	Brings selected item to front
Back	Back	Sends selected item to back
Flip	Flip	Flips selected item horizontally
Rotate	Rotate	Rotates selected item to the left

Many of the icons in the toolbar, when clicked, will bring up a palette with the available functions for the feature. Unless you have a very large workspace, you will most likely toggle this palette on and off of your desktop. Figure 2.8 demonstrates a desktop with many of the available palettes showing.

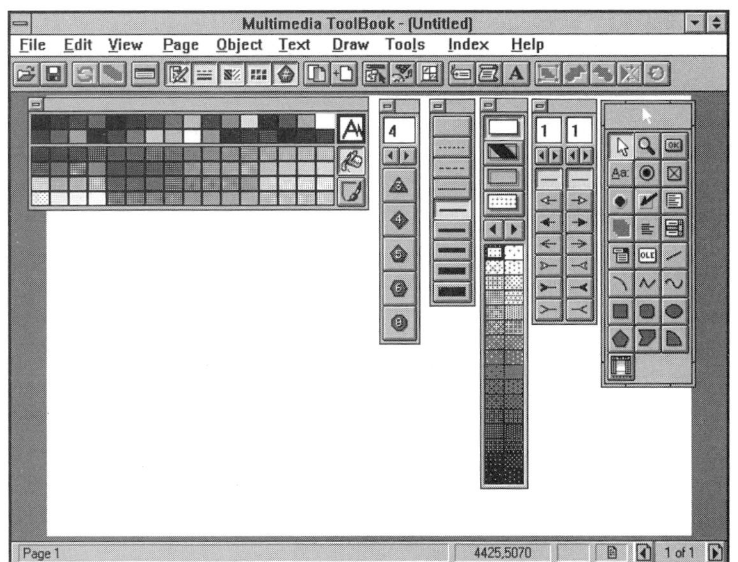

Fig. 2.8

The desktop can be arranged to permit access to a range of palettes used to create objects.

The Tools Palette

The Tools palette is one that you will use often as you construct your pages. It contains tools that cannot be accessed from the menus. These tools are all used to create drawn objects in your interface, including buttons, fields, stages, graphics, and OLE objects (see Table 2.2). To use one of these tools, click the icon representing the tool, and then click and drag the object into the space you want it to appear in the work area.

Table 2.2 Tools Palette Icons

Icon	Command	Description
Select	Select	Selects an object
Magnify	Magnify	Magnifies an object
Button	Button	Draws a button
Label Button	Label Button	Creates a label-style button
Radio Button	Radio Button	Creates a radio-style button
Check Box	Check Box	Creates a checkbox-style button
Radio Button 3D	Radio Button 3D	Creates a 3D-style radio button

(continues)

Table 2.2 Continued

Icon	Command	Description
Check Box 3D	Check Box 3D	Creates a 3D checkbox-style button
Field	Field	Creates a field
Record Field	Record Field	Creates a record field (background only)
Borderless Field	Borderless Field	Creates a borderless field
List Box Field	List Box Field	Creates a list box field
Combo Box	Combo Box	Creates a combo box
OLE Container	OLE Container	Creates an OLE container
Line	Line	Draws a line
Arc	Arc	Draws an arc
Angled Line	Angled Line	Draws an angled (connected) line (double-click to end)
Curve	Curve	Draws an adjustable curve (double-click to end)
Rectangle	Rectangle	Creates a four-sided (filled) object
Rounded Rectangle	Rounded Rectangle	Creates a four-sided (filled) rounded figure
Ellipse	Ellipse	Draws a (filled) ellipse
Polygon	Polygon	Draws an *n*-sided (filled) polygon
Irregular Polygon	Irregular Polygon	Draws an irregular (filled) polygon (double-click to end)
Pie	Pie	Draws a part of a circle
Stage	Stage	Draws a stage

The creation of an application in ToolBook consists of using the basic building blocks represented by these tools to construct the objects in the foreground and the background of the page. These constructed objects are then scripted to perform actions, based on what the program is intended to do. For example, if your goal was to construct a simple "memo pad" application that consisted of a page with a picture on it and a text box next to a drawn graphic, constructed so that the end user could type information into the text box and save it for the next time he or she entered the application, you would follow these steps:

1. Begin with ToolBook in Author mode.
2. From the Tools palette, choose the Field tool. Click and drag the field so that it fills the space on the screen that you want it to fill.

   If you make a mistake, click the Select tool, drag the field to the position you want, resize it by grabbing the corners and dragging them, and so on until the field is just as you want it.
3. Draw a graphic using the Irregular Polygon tool, Ellipse, Lines, etc., and the Color Selection palette.
4. Save the file. That's it! Now test it, running in Reader mode (click the F3 button). The resulting application will look something like figure 2.9, which is contained on the CD-ROM.

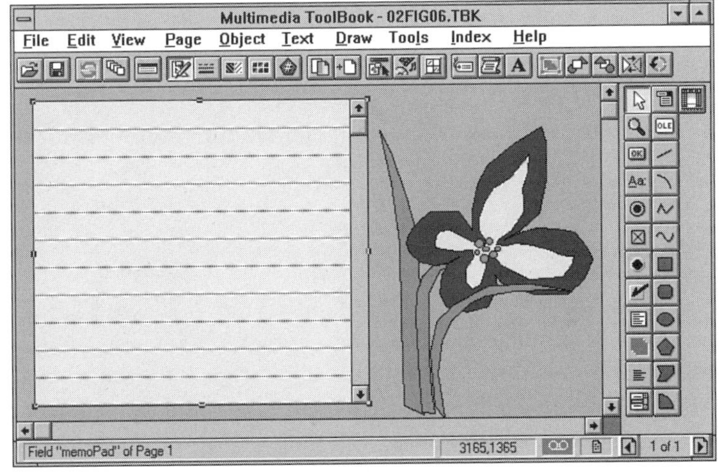

Fig. 2.9

A simple "memo pad" application can be developed with very little programming using the basic objects available in MTB.

Of course, as time goes on you will want to add more and more to your applications, learning how to create multiple pages, import pictures, play animations, and so on. Begin small, trying out a few of the tools, and before you know it you will have mastered the basics of using ToolBook to create complex applications.

The MTB Menu System

The ToolBook environment provides you with many different means of accomplishing the same goal. For example, to add a new page to your book, you could choose Object, New Page from the main menu; you could click the New Page icon in the Tool Bar; you could type `send newPage` in the Command Window; or, you could press the accelerator keys Ctrl+N. Any one of these methods would insert a new page after the current page.

These different means support different types of users; for the graphically oriented programmer, clicking an object in a palette is ideal. For those that use ToolBook often, the quick accelerator keystrokes that have been memorized can save considerable time. And, for an infrequent or inexperienced ToolBook programmer, using the menus may be the easiest way to recall the different programming elements that are available in this sophisticated environment.

There are two things about the ToolBook menus that you should be aware of. The first is that the menus are context-sensitive. This means that the entries in a menu will change depending on the objects that are currently selected. For example, if you have more than one item selected on a page, the Object menu will display Group as one of its options. If you have selected a group, the Object menu will instead show Ungroup as an option. And, if you have selected fewer than two items on the page, the Group option will be disabled (displayed in gray text).

The second feature of ToolBook menus that you need to understand is that they are completely modifiable by you, the programmer. This means that you can change the items that appear in the menus at either Reader or Author levels. This allows you complete control over the way the interface operates. For more information on changing the menus, see Chapter 9, "Creating Custom Menus."

The Status Bar

The status bar is the gray bar at the bottom of the ToolBook screen. It is used to display information about the page and objects on the page, and allows for easy navigation between pages. The caption area shows information about the object that the mouse is currently positioned over (such as the name of the object) or help text of a menu item, tool, or button.

The mouse position indicator displays (in page units) the coordinates of the pointer. The macro recording indicator has three states:

- *Blank* indicates that no recording is in progress and no recording is stored.
- *On* indicates that a recording is in progress (see fig. 2.10).

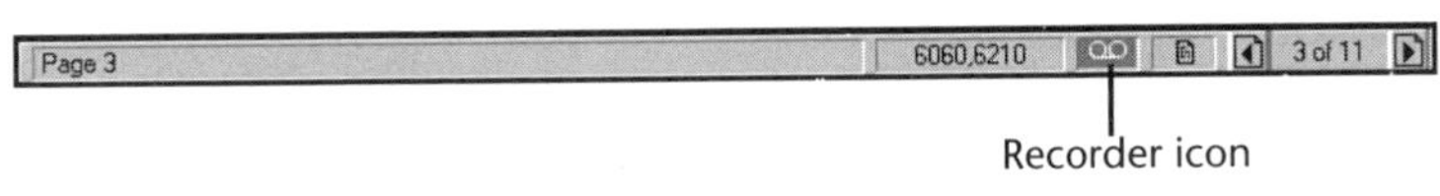

Fig. 2.10

This Recorder icon indicates the recorder is currently on (in recording mode).

- *Off* indicates that a recording has been stored (see fig. 2.11).

Fig. 2.11

This Recorder icon indicates that a recording has been stored.

The page selection indicator shows a blackened page if the page is selected (for example, prior to deleting the page). The status box provides the name of the object that the mouse is currently over.

The navigation control buttons allow you to move forward or backward through the pages, and you can click the status box between the controls in order to select a specific page to navigate to. If you are in the background, this will be indicated in the status box.

The status bar can be shown at Reader level, if you want. A "user-friendly" code uses the status bar to display information about the process that is occurring (such as defining the icons or displaying help text).

From Here...

In this chapter, you have been introduced to some of the basic concepts about ToolBook and how a ToolBook book is structured. You have also been introduced to the commands contained in the ToolBook menus. To find out more about the topics discussed in this chapter, refer to the following:

- Chapter 4, "Understanding Books, Backgrounds, and Pages," enables you to find out more about the components of a book.
- Chapter 6, "Scripting Tools," shows you more details about the scripting tools you use to create and debug your codes.
- Chapter 9, "Creating Custom Menus," explains the magic of how to configure menus so that they contain the entries that you want in your final application and explains how to link your menus to the customized scripts that you create.
- Chapter 13, "OpenScript Fundamentals," explains what you need to know in order to begin writing scripts to control your interface.

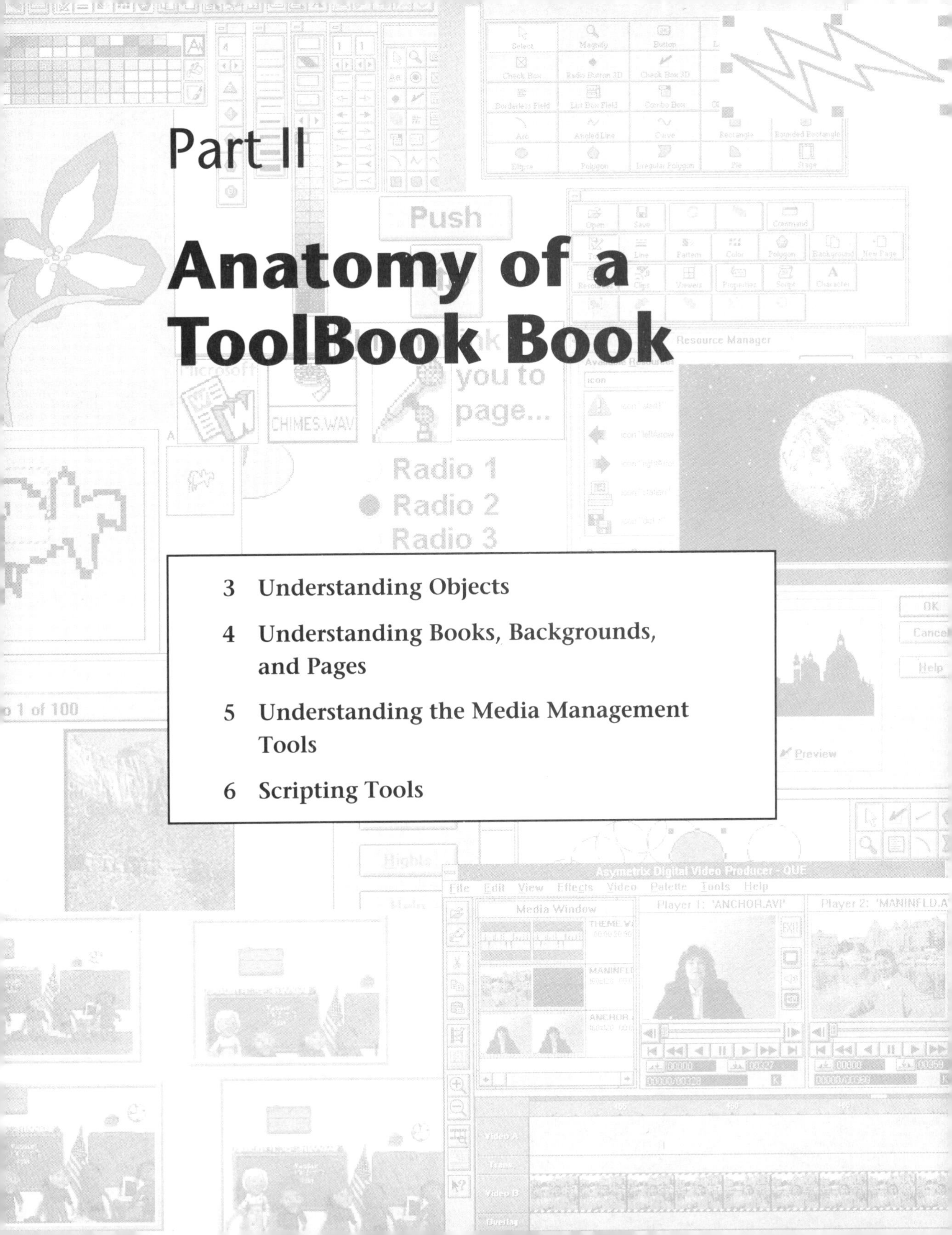

Part II

Anatomy of a ToolBook Book

Select
Magnify
Button
Check Box
Radio Button 3D
Check Box 3D
Borderless Field
List Box Field
Combo Box
Arc
Angled Line
Curve
Rectangle
Rounded Rectangle
Ellipse
Polygon
Irregular Polygon
Pie
Stage
Push
This hotlink
you to
page...
Microsoft
CHIMES.WAV
Open
Save
Command
Tool
Line
Pattern
Color
Polygon
Background
New Page
Resources
Clips
Viewers
Properties
Script
Character
Resource Manager
Available Resources
icon
Resource Properties
Radio 1
Radio 2
Radio 3
Undo To:
Photo CD
Photo 1 of 100
OK
Close
Load All...
Rights
Import Graphic
File Name:
domes.bmp
coast.bmp
columns.bmp
domes.bmp
jet.bmp
lake.bmp
market.bmp
mosque.bmp
needle.bmp
Directories:
c:\...\clipart\bitmaps
clipart
bitmaps
16optmiz
nasa
Drives:
c: erik's
List Files of Type:
Bitmap (*.bmp)
Preview
Asymetrix Digital Video Producer - QUE
File
Edit
View
Effects
Video
Palette
Tools
Help
Media Window
Player 1: 'ANCHOR.AVI'
Video A
Trans.
Video B

CHAPTER 3

Understanding Objects

This chapter describes some of the objects that you will use in the construction of your ToolBook applications. A ToolBook application consists of pages and backgrounds that contain the objects that you added to perform various functions.

Objects are items that you add to your interface to produce a visual effect or create interactivity for your user. A picture on the page is an object; a text field that the user can edit is an object; a stage that displays a video is an object. As you design your interface, you add a variety of objects. Objects can be manipulated later as you make changes in the interface.

This chapter provides you with the basic framework for creating interfaces with MTB, introducing you to the tools that you will use. This chapter explains:

- How to create and place various types of objects
- How to manipulate objects (move, align, delete, and group)
- How to create fields
- How to change properties of objects

Working with Objects

Many of the objects that you place in the foreground or background are generated directly from tools obtained from the Tool palette. (See Chapter 2, "Touring the Development Interface," for more details on the Tool palette.) These objects include lines, arcs, angled lines, curves, rectangles, ellipses, polygons, irregular polygons, pies, buttons, fields, and record fields.

In general, the act of drawing an object involves these steps:

1. Click the tool that you want to draw with.
2. Click the page to start a corner of the object that you want to draw.
3. Drag the mouse to create the object in the size that you want.
4. Release the mouse button.

Moving and Changing Objects

As you design your interface, adding objects to the page, you will need to move and change objects continually. MTB provides several useful features that make this process simple. To become an efficient MTB programmer, you will need to understand how to select objects and how to determine which objects are selected.

Selecting. As soon as you release the mouse button at the end of the drag operation that defines the object's boundaries, you can press the space bar. This action activates the Selection tool (the arrow in your Tool palette) and displays selection handles around the drawn object. Alternatively, you can click the Selection tool and then the object that you want to select.

Most likely, selection handles are familiar to you, because they are common to most drawing programs. Selection handles are represented by squares that appear on or around the object that is selected. Figure 3.1 shows some examples of selection handles.

Fig. 3.1

Selection handles allow you to change the bounds of an object.

Moving and Resizing. Any object you create in MTB is enclosed within a rectangular region referred to as its *bounding box*. Each selected object has a single handle at each corner of its bounding box, and a single handle at the center of each side of the bounding box (see fig. 3.2). Clicking and dragging a corner selection permits you to stretch the object up, down, left, or right, keeping the object anchored at the diagonal corner opposite the corner that you are dragging.

Fig. 3.2

Resize an object using the corner selection handles of the bounding box.

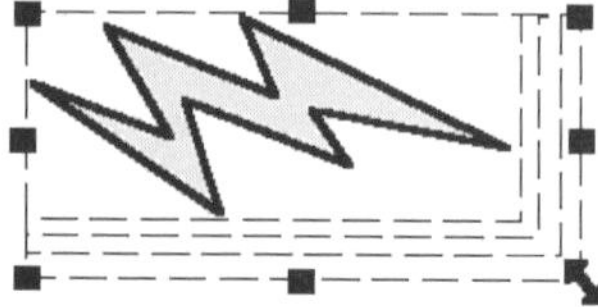

If you click and drag a side handle of the bounding box, the object will stretch only in one dimension—left–right (for a side handle) or up–down (for a top or bottom handle). Dragging from a corner handle will resize the figure in both dimensions.

To move the entire object without resizing it, click the Selection tool and then click the object itself and drag it to its new location.

Reshaping. Most of the objects that you create are defined by a few variables (such as radius and center) and can be fully resized by means of the selection handles, as described in the preceding section. Other objects, such as irregular polygons and angled lines, have vertices defined by the user and may need to be modified on a point-by-point basis. To resize these irregular shapes, you can select the entire object and stretch it as described in the preceding section, which provides scaling of the object. Alternatively, you can move specific vertices in the object using *reshape handles,* similar to the resize handles described previously, but which affect only one vertex of the figure at a time. To reshape an object, follow these steps:

1. Select the object.
2. Pull down the Draw menu and choose Reshape.
3. Grab the "reshape" handle that appears at the vertex you want to move and drag the vertex to its new position (see fig. 3.3).

> **Note**
>
> Watch your cursor shape. When you position the cursor over a reshape handle, it will switch to "crossed-arrows" indicating that you are in "reshape" edit mode. If you accidentally click anywhere except on a vertex of the object, the cursor will switch back to a normal arrow and you will lose your reshape handles!

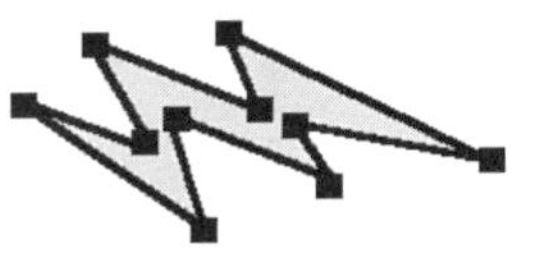

Fig. 3.3

Using reshape handles allows you to reshape an irregular object by moving single vertices.

Grouping. Often, it is convenient to group a set of objects so that they can be treated as one object. If you are drawing a face, for example, you may draw the eye as the eye opening, the iris, and the pupil. When you drag this eye around, you do not want a part to stay behind. The solution is to select all three parts, either by clicking and dragging a box around all three items, using the Selection tool; or by selecting one item, holding down the Shift key, and then selecting the other two items. You will be able to see that all three items are selected when three sets of selection handles are active (see fig. 3.4).

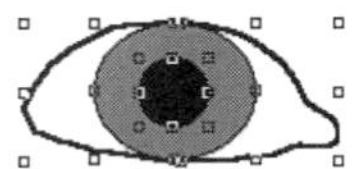

Fig. 3.4

Use a shift-click to select more than one object for grouping; these objects are ready to be grouped.

To group the three items, choose Object, Group (or press Ctrl+G). This results in the selected objects being grouped together. If you select a grouped object, selection handles apply to the entire group. When you resize a grouped object, all its components scale proportionately. If you want to move or resize only one object in a group, you can double-click the object. You will see the selection handles for that object as well as a dashed line that represents the boundary of the group (see fig. 3.5).

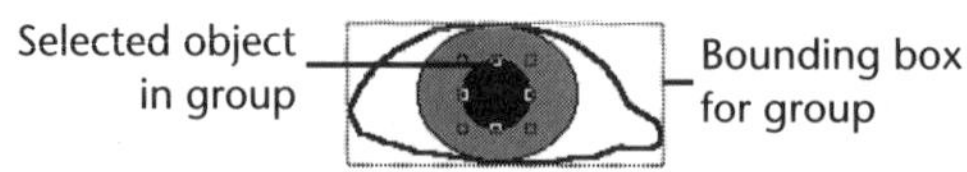

Fig. 3.5

A single object within the group is selected.

To ungroup objects, select the group and then choose Object, Ungroup.

Caution

Ungrouping destroys any scripting that you have created for the group but not for individual items within the group.

Layers. Every object that you create on a ToolBook page or background is assigned to a *layer* on the page or background. You can think of layers as being sheets of clear plastic that are lying on top of your ToolBook page. Each time you create a new object, you lay that object on another sheet of plastic. In figure 3.6, for example, the white of the eye occupies layer one of the foreground; the iris, layer two; and the pupil, layer three.

To move an object behind another object, you must switch the layers of the objects. You can perform this task in a few ways:

The layer is a property of the object and, as such, can be manipulated directly. This method of changing the layer is discussed later in this chapter in the section, "Properties Common to Objects."

You also can use menu commands to change the layer of an object. First, select the item that you want to move forward or back in the layers. Then pull down the Draw menu and choose Bring to Front, Send to Back, Bring Closer, or Send Farther. When you move an object from one layer to another, you are shuffling the layer numbers just as if you pulled a piece of plastic out of a stack and moved it to another layer. Bringing an object forward increases the layer number by one and shuffles the object that formerly occupied that layer back one layer.

When objects are grouped, the group itself has a layer number associated with all the objects on the page, and the objects within the group have a layer number relative to the other objects within the group.

In general, the layer of an object determines how it appears on the page; higher-numbered objects appear in front of lower-layer number objects. To avoid frustration, however, you must understand the following exceptions to this rule:

- Objects in the foreground appear in front of objects drawn in the background.
- Objects in a group appear in the layer defined by the layer number for the group, not the layer number for its individual elements.
- Objects with `direct draw` property set to `true` appear in front of any objects with `direct draw` property set to `false`.
- An object within a stage always appears in front of all other objects (stages, which are multimedia objects used to display video and other clips, are described in Chapter 7, "Adding Multimedia Elements").

Are you having layer problems? Items you know are there have disappeared beneath other objects? Objects not moving to the layer that you want them to occupy? Read on!

If you have an object hidden behind another object, select the object in front and choose Draw, Send to Back. Did the hidden object appear? If not, select the object in front, choose Draw, and examine Draw Direct. Is it checked? If so, uncheck it (by selecting it from the menu). Does that fix the problem? If not, the object may be part of a group. Double-click the object that needs to be moved, and choose Bring Closer or Send Farther from the Draw menu. Still having a problem? Choose each object that is in front, and select Send to Back from the Draw menu until the items are appearing as desired. Remember, if you created a "transparent" object, you will not be able to see it! It will, however, still occupy a layer.

Deleting. The act of deleting an object is simple; select the object and then press the Delete button on your keyboard. If you make a mistake, you can recover the object by choosing Edit, Undo (as long as you do perform another operation before choosing this command).

Aligning. As you begin designing pages, you will want to align objects in different ways, according to object types and space constraints. ToolBook has several built-in tools to assist you.

As you begin laying out the page, you may find it useful to turn on the rulers and the grid. The ruler and the grid are the two most common tools used for aligning objects.

The ruler can be used to place objects at specific locations on the page. Turn on the ruler by selecting View, Rulers in the main menu or by pressing Ctrl+R. As you draw objects on the pages, "shadows" of the objects will appear on the rulers, indicating their placement on the page.

The grid also assists in placing objects exactly on the page. Turn on the grid by selecting View, Grid from the main menu or by pressing Ctrl+Shift+G. The Grid dialog box will prompt you for the grid spacing (in inches), with checkbox choices for Show the Grid and Snap to Grid (see fig. 3.6). If you turn on Snap to Grid, any object you draw will be forced to conform to the grid, placing vertices at the grid point closest to where you begin or end the drag operation. When the Snap to Grid is turned on and you move an object that is already created, the vertices will not change, but the object will be lined up with the grid points. See figure 3.7 for an example of using the grid.

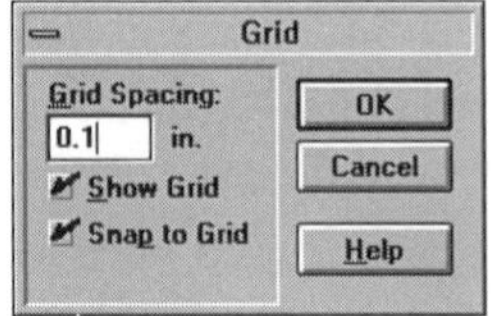

Fig. 3.6

The Grid dialog box permits you to specify the grid spacing (distance between dots), show grid, and snap to grid.

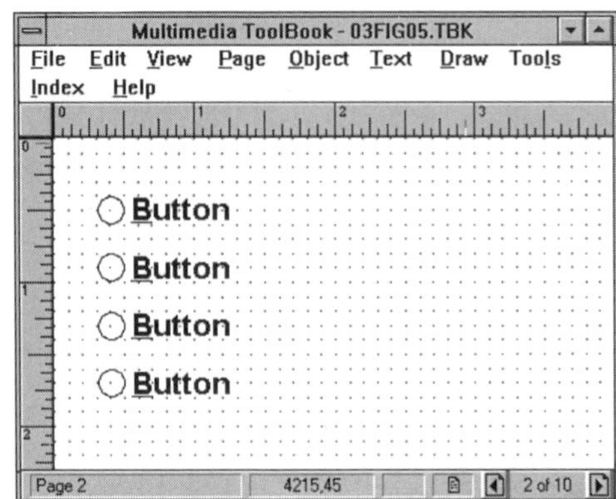

Fig. 3.7

The rulers and grid assist in lining up figures on the page.

Other means of aligning objects are useful when you are trying to space objects on a page. Suppose that you want to align a line of circles. Choosing Tools, Center gives you three choices in the cascading menu: Between Sides, Between Top and Bottom, and Both Ways (see fig. 3.8). Each of these commands centers the set of objects that you selected.

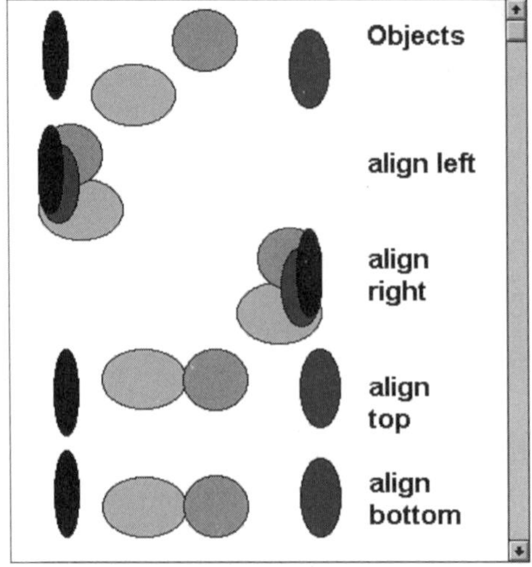

Fig. 3.8

This is an example of alignment options from the Draw and Tools menus.

Another way to standardize a set of objects is to choose Tools, Size and then Shrink to Smallest or Grow to Largest.

Caution

Be careful—this operation cannot be undone. Save your book before initiating the action. The operation results in resizing the selected objects to match the smallest or largest object in the set.

Choosing Tools, Spread Horizontally lines up the selected objects by their horizontal centers and spreads them left to right. Choosing Tools, Spread Vertically lines up the selected objects by their vertical centers and spreads them top to bottom.

Choosing Draw, Align provides you additional means of aligning objects. Choose Left, Right, or Horizontal Centers to align objects without changing the top–bottom spacing; choose Top, Bottom, or Vertical Centers to align objects without changing the left–right spacing.

Constraining While Drawing. As you draw objects, you can constrain the shape of the object by pressing the Ctrl key while you drag the mouse. A rectangle or rounded rectangle is constrained to a square while you draw if you hold down the Ctrl key. Pressing Ctrl also constrains a ellipse to a circle, a line or curve to multiples of 45 degrees, a rotation to multiples of 45 degrees, and a pie wedge to a quarter-circle.

Properties Common to Objects

A property of an object is an attribute that explains how the object should appear or respond to actions. For example, properties of a button include border (pushbutton, checkbox, rounded, etc.) and bounds (where it lies on the page.) All objects have properties and some are particular to an object type.

Because setting object properties are a key part of creating an interface, MTB provides many different ways to examine and change the properties of an object. The three most common means are:

- Select the object, pull down the Object menu, and choose the first item in the menu; what this item is depends on the object selected.

  For example, if an ellipse is selected, the first item in the Object menu is Graphic Properties. Choosing Graphic Properties will bring up the Properties dialog box. A short-cut method to display this dialog is to double-click the object.

- Right-click the object. The resulting shortcut menu shown in figure 3.9 provides various options. Click the Property Editor button to bring up the Property Editor which is a pop-up window that provides a list of the properties for the selected object (see fig. 3.10). Or, click the Select Properties button to display the Properties dialog box as described in the previous bullet.

Fig. 3.9

To set properties, use the right mouse-click shortcut menu.

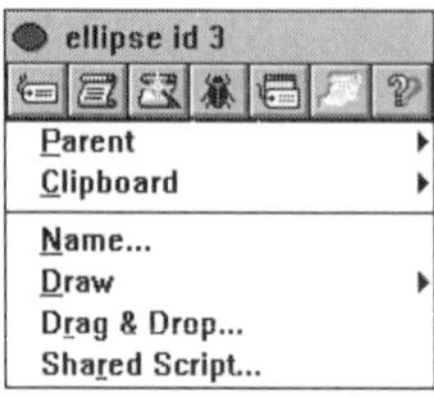

Fig. 3.10

The Property Editor for a rectangle can show both Object properties and User properties.

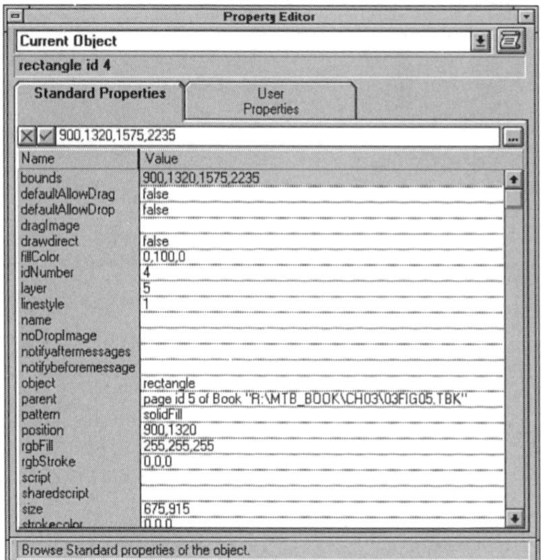

- Change the value of a property through use of OpenScript commands. For example, in the Command Window (described in Chapter 13, "OpenScript Fundamentals"), you could type the following:

```
set lineStyle of rectangle "blueBox" to none
```

The following table describes properties that you can set for most or all objects. Properties that are particular to an object type are discussed in the section under that property type heading.

Property	**Description**
`Bounds`	This property sets the size and location of an object's bounding box. For graphic items, the bounds are specified as the top-left coordinate (X,Y) and the bottom-right coordinate, in page units.
`Drag & Drop`	There is a set of properties for objects that define whether or not the object can be dragged and whether or not another object can be dropped on it. These properties are discussed in Chapter 6, "Scripting Tools."
`DrawDirect`	If `DrawDirect` is true, the object is drawn directly on the screen. If `false`, the object is drawn first off-screen.

Property	Description
`ID`	The ID number is assigned automatically by MTB when you create the object. You cannot change the ID number of an object.
`Layer`	This property (discussed in the section titled "Layers" earlier in this chapter) specifies where an object lies in the layers of objects on the page or background.
`LineStyle`	This property specifies the width of the line that surrounds the object (none, 1, 2, and so on).
`Name`	This property is set to null by default. You should name objects so that you can refer to them by name in your scripts.
`Position`	This property specifies the X,Y position for the object, in page units relative to the upper-left corner of the viewer for graphics items.
`rgbFill`	The three integers that define this property set the red-green-blue (RGB) color value for the fill of the object (such as the color inside a rectangle).
`rgbStroke`	The three integers that define this property set the RGB color value for the stroke of the object (such as the characters in a field).
`Script`	The script of the object, which defines its actions (such as what happens when the object is clicked, when the mouse pointer is positioned on it, or when an object is dropped on it).
`Transparent`	When set `True` for an object, the object is transparent.
`UseWindowsColors`	When this property is set `True` for an object, the object uses the colors specified in the Windows Control Panel.
`Visible`	This property specifies whether the object is displayed (visible) or not. This property is not to be confused with transparency, which specifies whether objects behind an object can be seen through the object.

Applying Colors and Patterns to Objects

All objects are displayed in two colors: *stroke color*, which is the color that is applied to an object's text and borders; and *fill color*, which is the color that fills in the background of an object. By default, an object that you draw uses the same colors that you used to draw the preceding object. To change an object's color, select the object and then click the Color Tray. (If the Color Tray is not displayed, choose View, Palettes, Color.) The current stroke and fill colors are displayed in the sample boxes at the right end of the Color Tray (see fig. 3.11). To change the fill color of the selected object, click the Fill Color button and then click the desired color. To change the stroke color of the selected object, click the Stroke Color button and then click the desired color.

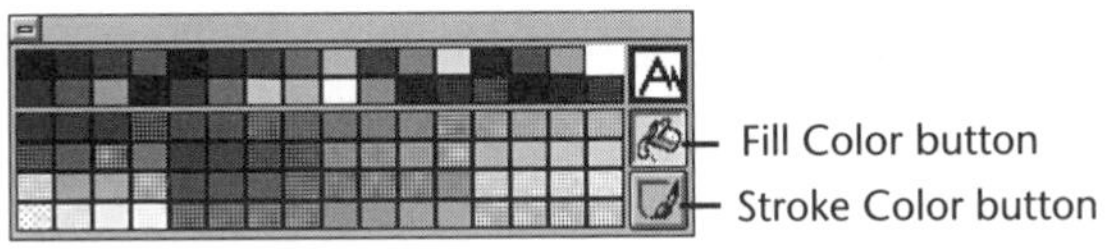

Fig. 3.11

The Color Tray is used to set stroke and fill color for objects.

Alternately, you can set a particular fill- or stroke-color value by displaying the Property Editor for the object and then typing the desired numeric values (refer to fig. 3.10 for an example of a Property Editor).

ToolBook also provides a palette of fill patterns that you can use with objects. These patterns are especially useful when you are constructing items that will be printed on a black-and-white printers. Even if your application will be displayed on a machine which uses a 16-color graphics driver, you can achieve great variation and interest in graphics by using the stroke and fill colors, along with patterns, when you create objects.

To display the Pattern palette, choose View, Palettes, Pattern. You may want to experiment with colors and patterns for the effect that you want. The Pattern palette contains the following buttons (see fig. 3.12):

- Fill color button—applies the current fill color to the selected object.
- Stroke color button—Applies a solid fill using the current stroke color to the selected object.
- None button—Removes any pattern and applies the current stroke and fill colors to the selected object.
- Pattern button—Applies the currently selected pattern to the selected object.
- Pattern select buttons—Displays more patterns from the 128 supplied patterns.

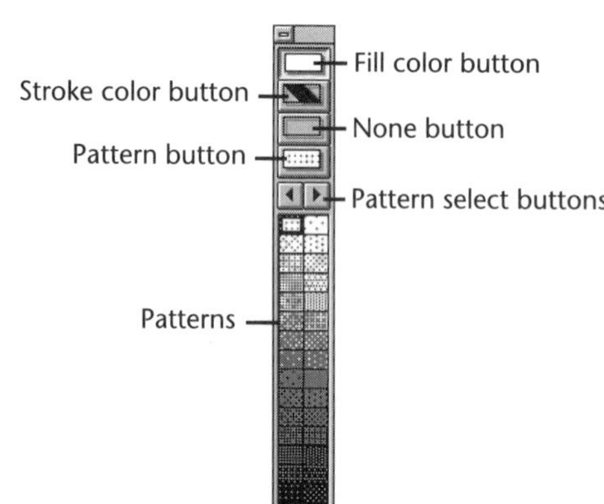

Fig. 3.12

The Pattern palette provides a wide range of patterns to choose from when creating images.

Understanding Buttons

Buttons are objects that are useful in practically every type of application that you script for Windows. Buttons can be used for a variety of tasks, including indicating choices, navigating to other sections of an application, and triggering events. In MTB, you can create any type of button that you can imagine. The ToolBook interface also provides many predefined button types that make your scripting job easier.

Button Types

Five basic types of buttons are commonly used in computer interfaces: pushbuttons, graphics buttons, hotwords (hypertext buttons in text), radio buttons, and checkboxes (see fig. 3.13). Hotwords are covered in detail in Chapter 7, "Adding Multimedia Elements." Figure 3.15 shows examples of the button types.

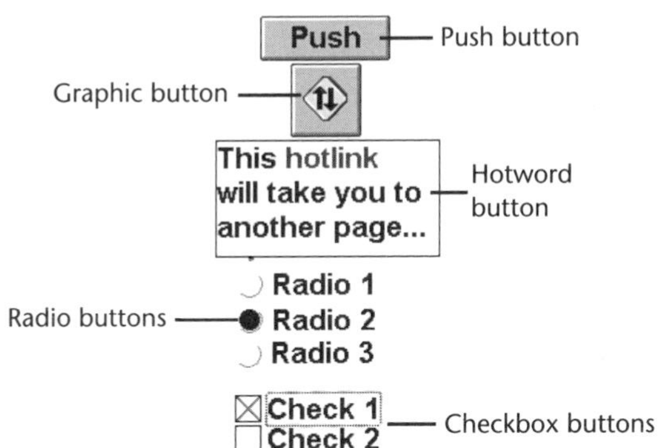

Fig. 3.13

These are examples of all different types of buttons that you can use in your interfaces.

The following guidelines can help you choose the type of button to use:

- *Push buttons*—Buttons of this type generally are used to initialize some action, such as "next page" or "yes" and "no" choices.
- *Graphic buttons*—These buttons are used when it is obvious what will happen when the button is clicked, such as a right arrow linking to the next page.
- *Hotword button*—These buttons are used in text fields to link to pop-up definitions, text fields on similar topics, or multimedia elements.
- *Radio buttons*—These buttons require the user to make an exclusive choice of one item in a set of items. When one button is selected in a set of radio buttons, the other buttons are inactive.
- *Checkbox buttons*—Checkboxes indicate nonexclusive choices to be made by the user.

You can create most of these button types easily by using the appropriate tool in the Tool palette. You can always draw a button of one type and then convert it to another type by resetting the button properties.

Button Properties

As you create buttons, you may need to change their properties. Figure 3.14 shows the Button Properties dialog box obtained by selecting the button and then choosing Object, Button Properties from the main menu.

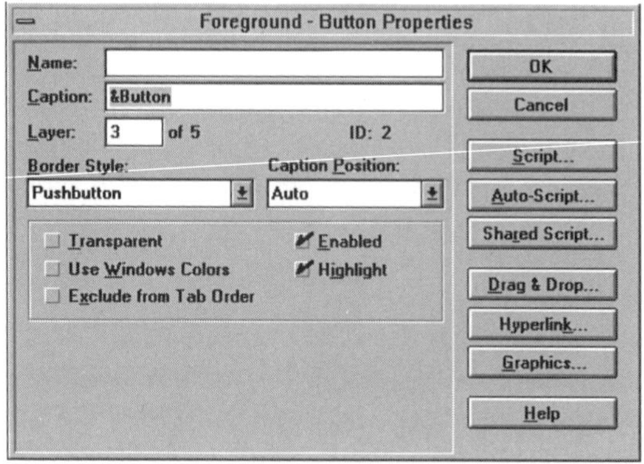

Fig. 3.14

The Button Properties dialog box allows you to set many of the basic properties of buttons.

If you intend to refer to a button in scripts, you should name the button. You can use any name; just use one that's short (32 characters or less) and easy to remember. The name of the button will not be apparent to the end user, so choose a convenient, descriptive name for your buttons.

The Caption property of a button is the text that appears on the button. Use the ampersand (&) to indicate what shortcut key can be pressed to depress the button. Using the caption `Bi&g`, for example, results in a button labeled Big, and the user can press Alt+G to depress the button (the underline of the *g* indicates the keyboard shortcut).

The Layer property refers to the current layer of the button in the background or foreground. (See the section, "Layers," earlier in this chapter, for details on setting and using layers in ToolBook.) You can change this number to move the button up or down through the layers.

The ID property is assigned to the button when it is created and cannot be changed.

The Border Style determines how the button will be displayed; the choices are shown in figure 3.15.

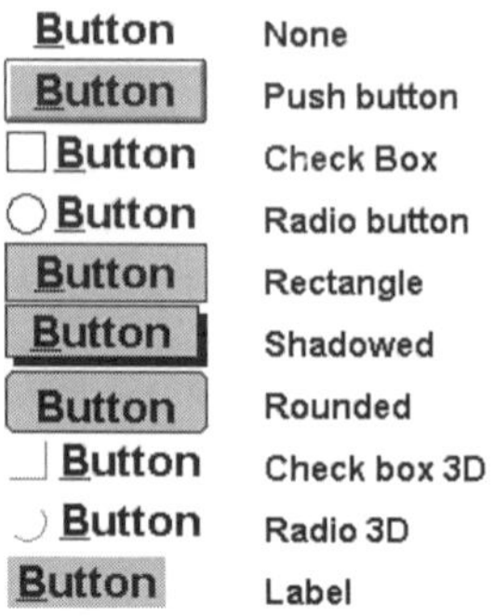

Fig. 3.15

The button styles you choose for your interface can be chosen from these supported styles.

The Caption Position property determines how the graphic and caption are displayed. The options are as follows (see fig. 3.16):

- Auto—This is the default position which places the caption below the graphic or centers the text if there is no graphic.
- Top—The caption appears centered above the graphic.
- Bottom—The caption appears centered below the graphic.
- Left—The caption appears to the left of the graphic.
- Right—The caption appears to the right of the graphic.
- Center—The caption is centered over the graphic.

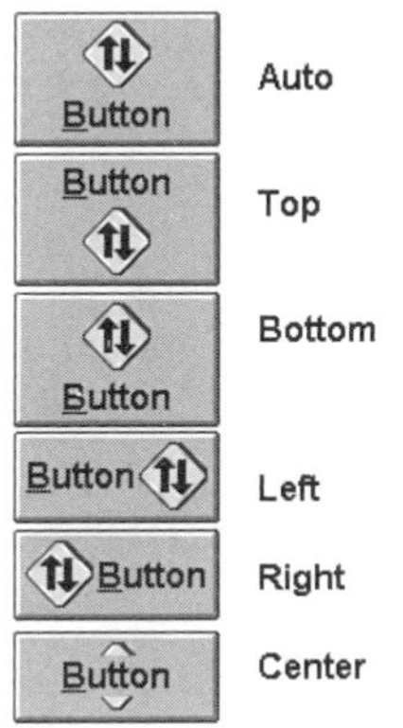

Fig. 3.16

These are button-caption positions for buttons that include graphics.

The Enabled property, when checked, determines whether a button can be selected. When a button is disabled, it appears dimmed, as shown in figure 13.17, and will not execute its script when clicked by the user.

Fig. 3.17

A disabled button is used to prevent the script from being executed and to let the user know that this button is inactive.

Usually when you create a button, you will want it enabled; if the option or feature the button represents is not available, you might write a script that disables the button. For example, if you have a button bar in an application that is on each page and is used to navigate to these pages, you might disable the button representing the current page that the user is on.

Transparent is another property of a button. You can use transparent buttons for special effects or to hide a button from the viewer, as in some children's games. These buttons can be useful when you want to place a button over a drawn object to create a custom button.

Tip

If an object does not look like a button, do not assume that the user will know that it is a button; this is not user-friendly programming.

Tip

In some scripted environments, you must use buttons to initiate actions. This is not true in ToolBook, in which you can script any object, including all graphics. Therefore, you need not create transparent buttons over every object that you want to script; instead, script the object itself to perform the action.

The buttons on the page become part of the tab order of items on the page. The *tab order* determines which item receives the focus when the tab key is pressed. Usually, you want to set the tab order for items on the page in some logical order, such as from the top of the page to the bottom. If a button should not be tabbed to, check the Exclude from Tab Order box in the button's Properties dialog box.

Fields

Fields are objects that contain text. This section discusses the various types of fields that you can create in ToolBook. The section also discusses record fields and combo boxes, which share many properties and features with fields.

Understanding Fields

One way to classify field types is from the perspective of the end user of the application. Any field on the page can serve as a label—a text item that is used to identify something on the page and that the user cannot modify. Other fields may contain scrollable text that the user can read but not modify. Some fields may include options that the user can select; other fields may be text "boxes" in which the user can type information.

Field Properties

In addition to the properties listed in the "Properties Common to Objects" section, earlier in this chapter, fields and record fields have the properties described in the following list:

- `Activated`—This property specifies whether the user can type text in the field (`True` means that typing is disabled).
- `Baselines`—When this property is `True`, dotted lines appear between lines of text in the field.
- `BorderStyle`—This property specifies the border style for the field. The options are `none`, `rectangle`, `scrolling`, `shadowed`, `raised`, and `inset`.

- `Enabled`—This property specifies whether the field can receive the focus (for example, to be tabbed to for data entry) and mouse-button messages (for example, selecting a text line in a single-select list field) at reader level.
- `FieldType`—The property determines how text is displayed in the field. The options are `wordWrap`, `noWrap`, `singleLineWrap`, `singleSelect`, and `multiSelect`.

`FieldType` properties are set to determine how the text appears and how the user interacts with the text. The settings are:

- `wordWrap`—This property specifies that text wraps from line to line within the field. If characters are inserted into a line and the line gets longer than can be displayed, text wraps to the following line.
- `noWrap`—This property specifies that text that does not fit on a line does not wrap, but disappears off the right edge of the field.
- `singleLineWrap`— This property specifies that only a single line of text is displayed.
- `singleSelect`—This property specifies that the user can select only one line in the text field. When the user clicks a line of text, it becomes selected. Clicking a second time on the same line of text will deselect it. Selecting another line of text will also deselect the previously selected text. Text does not wrap.
- `multiSelect`—This settings specifies that the user can select more than one line of text.

Figure 3.18 shows some of the types of fields discussed in the preceding list.

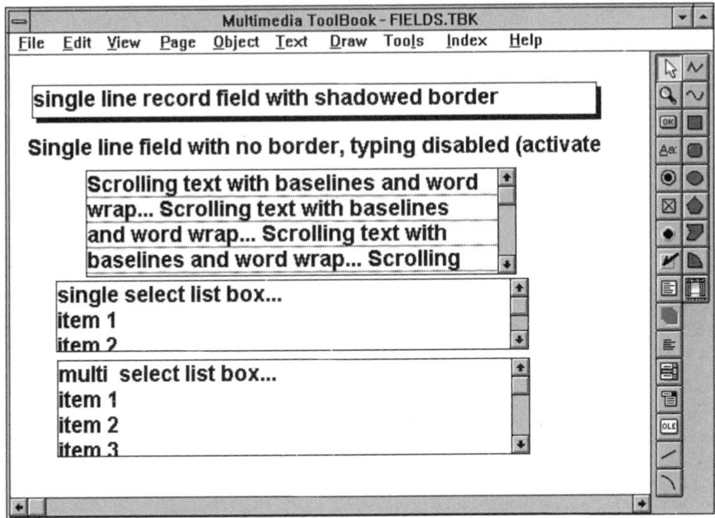

Fig. 3.18

Examples of fields that are supported by MTB.

List Boxes. List boxes are used to present a set of choices to the user. A single-select list box can be used as an alternative to radio buttons for exclusive choices; a multiselect list box is an alternative to check boxes for nonexclusive choices. Usually, buttons are used when the set of choices is limited (six or fewer options). A list box, however, can be used for any number of choices.

List boxes also are used to save screen space when there is not enough room to include all options. Also, buttons are most appropriate for information that does not change between times when the user accesses the screen, whereas list boxes are more appropriate for cases in which the options depend on other factors. For example, in a program in which you allow the user to specify when something occurs, if they have selected `Month` as their unit of time, the list box might contain `Once each week, Once at the beginning of the month, ...`; but if they had chosen `Week` as the unit of time, the list might contain `Monday, Tuesday, ....`

To create a list box, click the List Box tool in the Tool palette. As with other tools, drag to define the bounds of the list box. You can display the field properties using one of the usual techniques (double-clicking the field, right-clicking and selecting properties, or selecting the field and then choosing Objects, Field Properties from the main menu.) The Field Properties dialog box appears (see fig. 3.19).

Fig. 3.19

The Field Properties dialog box has many of the same properties as the Button Properties dialog box.

For Field Type, choose Single-Select List Box or Multi-Select List Box (depending on how you want the user to interact with the text).

To add text to a list box, double-click the field and type the text. Make certain that you use a carriage return at the end of each line.

Caution

Do not place a carriage return after the last item in a list box, or you will have a nonselectable blank line at the end of the list box.

In your scripting, the `selectedTextLines` property of the field is used to determine what line(s) the user has selected. (See Chapter 11, "Working with Text," for more details on scripting for combo boxes.)

Combo Boxes. Combo boxes provide features similar to those of single-select list boxes, in the sense that the user selects one option from a group of options. Combo boxes have the advantage of being compact, capable of fitting into a small area of the screen.

Combo boxes are commonly used to enable the user to select items (such as a disk drive in a list of drives), preference settings, and so on. If you have a large number of choices, you probably should use a single-select list box instead of a combo box, because it is easier to compare choices in a list box than in a combo box, which generally displays less information. In addition, users are accustomed to combo boxes that display a few predetermined choices, whereas a list box is not limited in this way.

A combo box has two parts: the edit box and the drop-down list (see fig. 3.20).

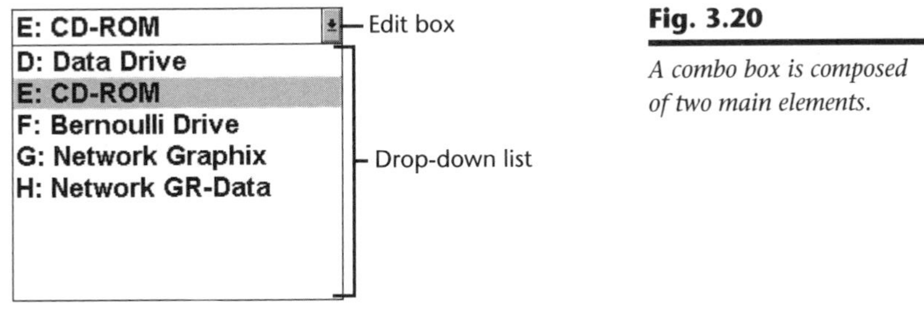

Fig. 3.20

A combo box is composed of two main elements.

In addition to the properties previously discussed that are common to all ToolBook objects, combo boxes have these properties:

- `Editable`—This property indicates whether the user can change values in the edit box.
- `Enabled`—This property specifies whether the field can receive the focus (such as being tabbed to) and mouse-button messages (such as being clicked on) at reader level.
- `LineCount`—This property specifies the number of items that are displayed in the drop-down list.
- `Scrollable`—If this property is set to `True`, a scroll bar is used in the drop-down list.

To add text to a combo box, switch to Author mode (press F3), double-click the down arrow in the combo box, and type text in the drop-down list box.

By default, a combo box displays five lines of text in the drop-down list box. You might want to change the number of lines displayed, for example to match exactly the number of lines of text that you have entered into the drop-down list box. To change the number of lines that appear in the drop-down list box, display the Combo Box Properties dialog box (by either double-clicking the field, right-clicking and selecting properties, or selecting the field and choosing Objects, Combo Box Properties) and change the value in the Line Count box (see fig. 3.21).

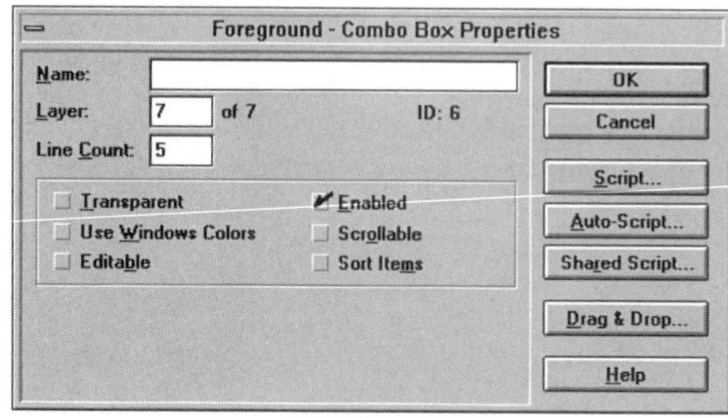

Fig. 3.21

The Combo Box Properties dialog box permits you to set many of the properties of the combo box.

If you want to sort the items in the drop-down list box in alphabetical order, choose Sort Items. You also can designate text in the drop-down box as scrollable by choosing Scrollable. Generally, if a drop-down list contains six or fewer items, it is preferable to make the box nonscrollable and to set the line count (the number of items in the drop-down list) to exactly the number of items in the list.

In your scripting, the `selectedItem` property of the combo box is used to determine what the user has selected. (See Chapter 11, "Working with Text," for more details on scripting for combo boxes.)

Record Fields. Record fields are very similar to other types of fields, but they have additional features that make them valuable resources for programming. These fields are background items and are used to display the same type of information in the same location on each page of the book. Typical uses of record fields include applications such as recipe cards, where the pages are displaying the same information in the same location. You can easily import, export, and format records for printing in ToolBook.

A record field is like a data field in a database or spreadsheet program. Each page in the book displays one record.

Record fields are drawn in the background of the page. To draw a record field, switch to the background (choose View, Background from the main menu or press the F4 key), and then click the Record Field tool in the tool menu. As with the other tools, drag to define the bounds of the record field.

> **Note**
>
> Remember, as with other objects drawn on the background, the record field will continue to appear on each page that you add to the book. To begin a new background that will not include this record field, you must select Object, New Background from the main menu.

The record field can contain different text for each page that shares the background, unlike other fields, which share the text of the field as well as the field itself.

Record fields can be used to produce reports. (See Chapter 12, "Printing from ToolBook," for more details on this topic.)

Record fields also can be used to import and export data. In fact, you can use a data file and record fields to create pages automatically in ToolBook. This topic is covered in Chapter 17, "Data and File Management."

A record field can be used to sort pages of a book. Assuming you have a book with more than one page in the background, follow these steps:

1. Create a record field by switching to the background (press F4), selecting the record field tool from the Tool palette, and dragging to draw the record field.
2. Name the field that you want to use to sort the pages. Double-click the record field to display the Record Field Properties dialog box, and type a name in the Name box.
3. Switch back to Reader mode (F3) and enter some data into the record field on each page.
4. Choose Page, Sort from the main menu. A Sort dialog box, such as that shown in figure 3.22, will appear.

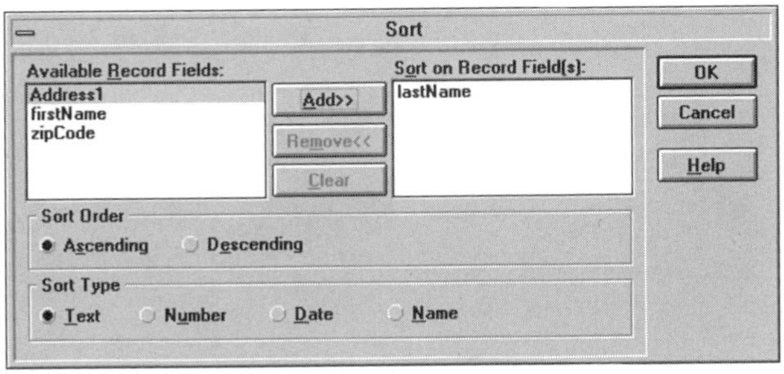

Fig. 3.22

The Sort dialog box provides a powerful interface for changing the order of pages in your ToolBook application.

5. From the list of Available Record Fields on the left, choose the field you want to sort by. Click the Add button to copy it to the Sort on Record Field(s) list box.
6. Choose the sort order (Ascending or Descending) and the Sort Type: Text for alphabetical sorting, Number for numerical sorting, Date for sorting by date, or Name to sort by the last word in the field.
7. Click OK to begin the sort.

Inserting Graphics into Text Fields

You can insert a graphic item into a text field. If the graphic item is already in the Clipboard, place the insertion point where you want the graphic item to appear and then paste it from the Clipboard. If the graphic is on disk, follow these steps:

1. Place the insertion point into the field where you want the graphic to appear.
2. Choose Text, Insert Graphic from the main menu. The Import Graphic dialog box will appear (see fig. 3.23).

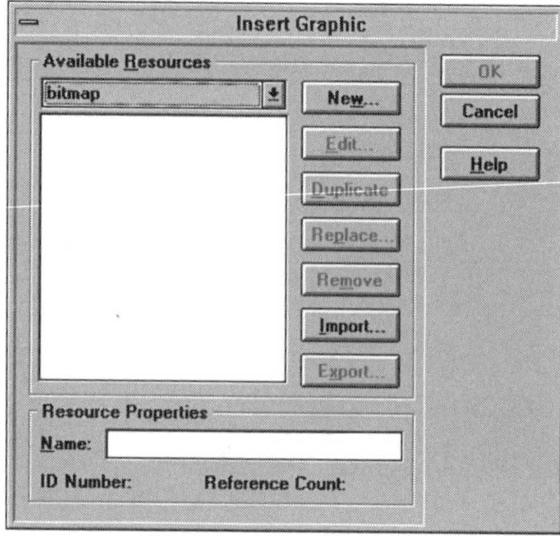

Fig. 3.23

The Insert Graphic dialog box allows you to specify the graphic item that you want to insert into the field.

3. Click the Import button and use the standard file dialog to choose the file to paste.

This action inserts into the text field a graphics item that can be scrolled along with the text, as shown in figure 3.24.

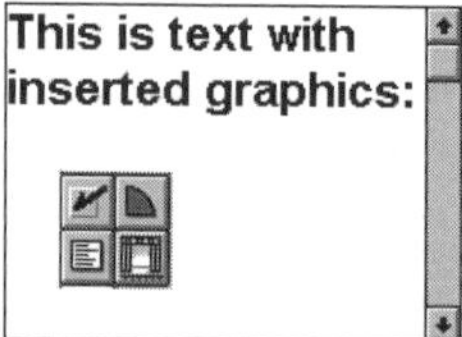

Fig. 3.24

A graphic within a field adds a great deal to the presentation of information.

Using Rich Text

You can use text that has been formatted as rich text (RTF) within a field in ToolBook. This format, which provides a way to maintain formatting of text between applications, is supported in many word processing programs.

To insert text in RTF, copy the text to the Clipboard in the application that you are using and then paste the text from the Clipboard into the field.

You can format text in a field and then output it to a file in RTF. This topic is covered in detail in Chapter 17, "Data and File Management." More information about formatting and working with text appears in Chapter 11, "Working with Text."

From Here...

This chapter introduced objects and their properties. The chapter demonstrated the basics of constructing graphic objects, fields, and combo boxes. As you begin working with fields, however, you will find that this chapter does not answer all your questions, such as how you get two list boxes to scroll together and how you set the default for a combo box choice. The answers to these questions require an understanding of scripting, which is covered in subsequent chapters:

- See Chapter 11, "Working with Text," for more information on using, formatting, and printing text in your applications.
- See Chapter 13, "OpenScript Fundamentals," for an overview of scripting.
- See Chapter 15, "Understanding Variables, Values, and Text," for more information on manipulating text in fields.

CHAPTER 4

Understanding Books, Backgrounds, and Pages

You can use Multimedia ToolBook to create applications which combine text, graphics, video, and animation. Some typical applications you might see and/or create include the following:

- Interactive training—Develop on-line tutorials, and computer-based training.
- Online presentations—Construct interactive slide shows, kiosks or other visual aids.
- Hypermedia documents—Design information applications such as online encyclopedias and help systems, each with links to help users explore topics.
- Application prototypes—Build prototypes for Windows applications to try out an application's interface before creating the "guts."
- Databases—Make flat-file databases in Multimedia ToolBook, or create a front-end for data from an external source.
- Other types—Create games, simulations, utilities, and other unique graphical applications.

All ToolBook applications are called *books*. The window on which you see information displayed in a book is called a page. Together with other key concepts in ToolBook such as objects, events and messages, you can start creating your own applications.

In this chapter, you get an introduction to the following:

- Objects, events, and messaging
- How to create books
- How to create pages
- How to create backgrounds
- Book design basics

Behind the Scenes

Books, pages, and backgrounds are objects. Because they are objects, they have characteristics which you can customize, and you can write scripts which detect messages sent to objects.

An *object* is a self-contained collection of data and routines. Specific objects in ToolBook include a book, page, background, viewer, field record field, button, hotword, draw object, graphic, group, or OLE container object. You can set the appearance and behavior of any object in ToolBook by changing its *properties*. Properties allow you to specify how the object looks and behaves. For example, you might make the color of a button gray with blue text, or you might add the title of the book in the book properties.

Multimedia ToolBook is an *event-driven* system. This means that all actions occur in response to events. An *event* is any action a person takes in a window. In other words, when you do something in a window, such as clicking a mouse button, pressing a key, or choosing a menu option, an event is generated. Events can occur in random order, and the application must respond to them.

So how does the application "know" when an event has occurred? Every event generates a *message*. A message tells objects what event has occurred. This means all programming in ToolBook is essentially a matter of detecting and responding to messages. For example, an `enterBook` event is caused when you open a ToolBook application. You can then write a handler which detects the `enterBook` message and performs some action.

A *handler* is a self-contained chunk of ToolBook code which detects and responds only to messages being sent to it. In Listing 4.1, the handler is in the book script of a book and causes a custom menu to appear when the book is opened at the Reader level; the menu is not present at the Author level. At Reader level, development tools are not available. At Author level, development tools are available. Reader level is how users will use the application.

Listing 4.1 Handler Example: Adding a Custom Menu to a Book

```
to handle enterBook
--Freeze the screen until all updates are done
     sysLockScreen = true

-- Creates a custom menu called "Dog" when you are at Reader level
--     "&" creates the keyboard shortcut character in the menu
--     To add a separator (line) in the menu, add a blank menu item,
and specify its position
--    NOTE: You must write handlers for custom menu and menu items
--
     add menu "&Dog" at Reader
        add menuItem "&Add Breed" to menu "Dog" at Reader
        add menuItem "&Remove breed" to menu "Dog" at Reader
        add menuItem "&Edit breed" to menu "Dog" at Reader
```

```
        add menuItem "" to menu "Dog" position 4 at Reader
        add menuItem "&Compare Breeds" to menu "Dog" at Reader

    -- Unlock the screen
    sysLockScreen = false

    -end enterBook
```

Figure 4.1 shows how this menu looks when you open the book. The custom menu looks and functions like a regular menu item (after you've added the handlers for the custom menu items).

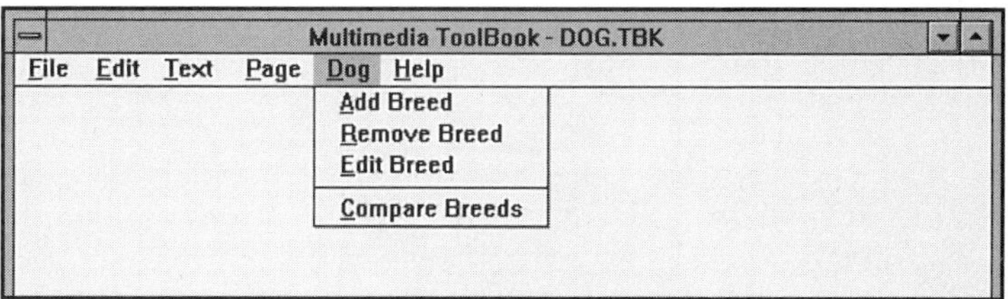

Fig. 4.1

This menu is the result of adding a custom menu.

Although events can occur in any order and in any combination, messages travel in predictable directions. Messages are sent to objects within a book. A handler within an object then determines what happens.

Note

When you create an object, it typically doesn't contain a script. Only default behaviors are active. For example, when you create a button, you can "click" it (the button seems to depress), but nothing happens. To make something happen, the button needs a script. When the button is "clicked," a `buttonUp` message is sent. You can detect this message and make something happen—for instance, flipping to another page.

Handlers do not have to be in the object they handle. For example, a `buttonUp` message sent when the left mouse button is clicked could have a handler in a page script, rather than in the button itself. Messages are forwarded from object to object until a handler for that particular message is found. If no custom handlers are found, the message passes up to the ToolBook system, which responds with a built-in behavior. The direction a message is forwarded is based on the object hierarchy. As you can see in figure 4.2, messages travel up the object hierarchy in search of a handler.

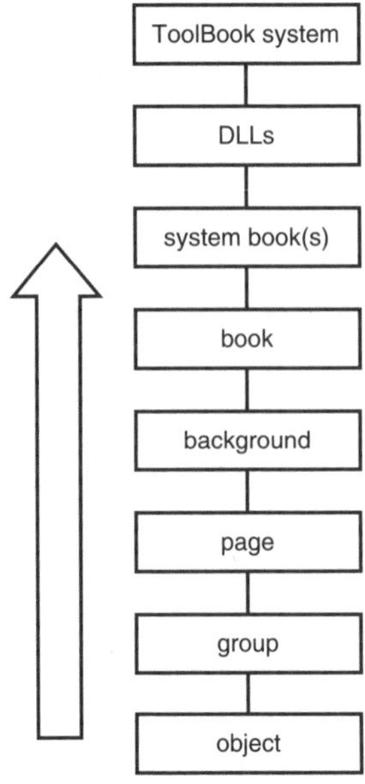

Fig. 4.2

ToolBook object hierarchy showing how messages pass from the lowest to the highest objects.

> **Note**
>
> When you use OpenScript (ToolBook's programming language) to intercept a message that normally triggers a built-in event—such as `enterBook`, `leaveBook`, `enterPage`, or `leavePage`—the message is not sent up the message hierarchy to perform its normal function. However, if you include a `forward` statement in the handler, the message will then be passed up the object hierarchy. A forward statement sends a message to the next highest object in the object hierarchy or directly to the ToolBook system.

Understanding Books

Real life books, like this one, contain words and pictures on pages. This is similar to a ToolBook application, which is also called a *book*. A ToolBook book is stored as a DOS file, just like any other Microsoft Windows application. As you might expect, a ToolBook book contains one or more *pages*. Pages contain text, graphics, and other objects which people will see and use. Depending upon how you have arranged it, users can "flip" back and forth between pages to see different information.

When you are producing a book, you will typically work in Author mode. Author mode means you can manipulate all objects in the book. You can add buttons, set properties, change the size of text fields, create and edit scripts, and so on. To actually use the book you've created, switch to Reader mode. This is the mode users will be in when they use your book. In Reader mode, you cannot change or edit objects in the book. To switch between Author and Reader mode, you can select the last item in the Edit menu or use the F3 key.

A book is a file containing a collection of pages and all the objects and scripts they contain. A book is also a type of ToolBook object. This means that it has specific properties, some of which can be customized, and that you can create custom behavior using scripts. A book has two important functions:

- It is the file which contains all of the objects and scripts which make up your application.
- Because it is an object, books have customizable properties which allow you to define how the application looks to users. Each page in the book may be different, but the characteristics set in the book properties generally remain the same—these are things like how large the window for the application is, the caption in the title bar, and so on.

Creating a Book

There are two stages to creating a book. The first stage involves planning what you want to put into the book. You can do this in your head, on a piece of paper, or you can create a "test" book to try out ideas. The second stage involves creating the book file and writing the handlers.

A complete application may be one book or several. Just like Microsoft Windows, or a real book for that matter, a ToolBook book is essentially a *graphical user interface* (*GUI*) for your information. Therefore, creating an application in ToolBook is a process of defining and refining a user interface. This involves adding, sizing, and setting the properties of the objects, like buttons, fields, and graphics which are used in the application. See the section "Effective Book Design" later in this chapter for more information.

When you start ToolBook, it will automatically open a book with a single empty page and background. You can save this book by choosing File, Save As. You can create a new book by doing any of the following:

- Choose New from the File menu
- Use the `send new` message

When you save a book, it will automatically be saved with the ToolBook `.TBK` filename extension. When you choose Open while working in ToolBook, only file names with `.TBK` extensions appear in the list. If you want to see other files in the list, you can type an asterisk (*) plus another filename extension in the Open Filename dialog box. Or you can type `*.*` to see all files in the current directory.

A special type of book is called a system book. It usually has a `.SBK` filename extension, and is saved as "System" with the Save or Save As menu item in the File menu. System books contain book scripts which can be shared by many different books. This means if you make a change in the system book script, any books which use this script will automatically pick up the change.

Figure 4.3 shows the Book Properties dialog box which appears when you choose Object, Book Properties. Just like any other ToolBook object, you can change a book's appearance and behavior by modifying built-in properties or customize its behavior using scripts. This figure also shows some of the built-in properties you can change. These include adding a name for the book (which shows up in the title bar), how the book is saved, what the page size is, and whether or not a password is needed.

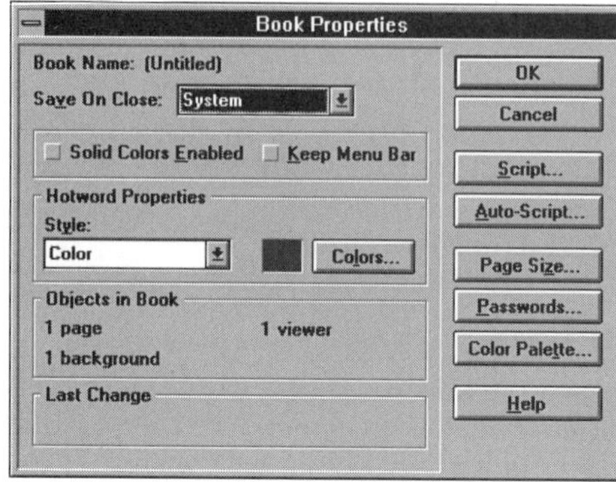

Fig. 4.3

Use the Book Properties dialog box to customize a book's appearance and behavior.

While no built-in messages are sent directly to a book, messages can travel up the hierarchy or be sent from scripts. The `enterBook` and `leaveBook` messages are sent to the current page. Other commands which can directly affect a book are `edit script`, `forward`, `get`, `save`, `save as`, `save changes`, `send`, and `set`.

> **Note**
>
> Include a `restore system` statement as the first statement in an `enterBook` handler and as the last statement in a `leaveBook` handler. This will set ToolBook to a known configuration, providing a predictable environment for opening and closing the book.

A book script is a good place to do the following:

- Add handlers for user-defined functions, messages, and properties that are used throughout a book.
- Define general behaviors for objects in a book.
- Create custom menus or remove standard menus.

When you want to refer to a book in your scripts, the way you do it depends on where the book is located. For example, if you want to refer to the current book you have open, you would say "this book." In a script, you might say:

```
go to page 4 of this book
```

or

```
send save to this book
```

How you talk about a book depends on where it's located. If you talk about the book you're in, you refer to it as "this book." If you refer to another book, you give it the name and location for that book. See Table 4.1 for more information.

Table 4.1 How to Refer to Books

To Refer To	Syntax to Use
The book you are currently in	`this book` `parent of this background`
A book in the current directory	`book "dog.tbk"`
A book in a different directory	`book"c:\example\dog.tbk"`

Performance Tips

Decisions you make about how your book looks, such as page size, backgrounds, number of items per page, and so on, also affect how fast the book runs. To get better performance, the following are some general suggestions to keep in mind when you plan and code your book. As always, you have to balance the way your application needs to look and work with reasonable speed:

- Make the book's page size as small as possible so that it displays faster.
- Use as few objects as possible and delete unused objects.
- Use as few pages and backgrounds as you can.
- Compact the book. To compact a book's file size, save the book under a different name with the Save As command from the File menu or the saveAs message from the Command Window.
- Send a message directly to a book with the `send` command rather than letting the message travel up the hierarchy.
- For faster display of the first page in a book, put as few statements as possible in the `enterBook` handler and handle other setup tasks in the `enterBackground` handler while `sysLockScreen` is `true`.
- Keep the number of font sizes and font styles down. A book's properties, including its script and font table, are stored in the book's 64K memory segment. Because the font table is stored in the book segment, a book that includes many font sizes and styles takes more memory than a book that uses fewer fonts.

Working with Pages

The simplest book you can create consists of a blank page with a blank background. This is what you would have if you saved your work immediately after choosing File, New. Obviously, this isn't a useful application at this point—it doesn't do anything. But it does illustrate the fact that the page and the background are fundamental book parts.

You will probably need more than one page in your book. You can create a new page by doing any of the following:

- Choosing New Page from the Page menu
- Sending the `newPage` message from the Command Window or a script
- Clicking the New Page button on the tool bar

Note

A new page is also added automatically when you add a new background. If you want to change the background of an existing page, select the page, go to a blank page containing the new background, do a pasteSpecial, and only paste the page onto the background.

Foreground and Background

A page is made up of two main parts, a *foreground* and a *background*. They are separate, but work together to form the page you see on-screen. The first part, the foreground, contains most of the objects with which users interact. The second part, the background, also contains objects. However, anything that is on a background page can be seen or used by any page that has that same background. Many pages can share the same background. Backgrounds are described in more detail later in this chapter.

The foreground and background are *layered*. What is layering? You can think of the foreground as a clear sheet of plastic lying on top of the background. Because it's clear, you can see any object on the background that hasn't been covered up by an object in the foreground. This also means that if you need to move an object on the background, you need to change to the background layer to do it and vice versa. Change back and forth between layers by pressing F4.

You can tell which layer you are working with by looking at the first menu item on the View menu—it will be either Foreground or Background. If you can't change an object you've created, make sure you're in the same layer as the object.

Page Properties

Just like any other ToolBook object, you can change a page's appearance and behavior by modifying built-in properties or customize its behavior using scripts. Figure 4.4 shows some of the built-in properties you can change in the Page Properties dialog box. These include adding a name for the page (which you can refer to in scripts), the page number, and how certain objects are handled.

Place an `enterPage` handler in a page script if you want that handler to execute each time ToolBook displays the page. Place other handlers in the page script if you want a message to be handled the same way for several objects on the page. Table 4.2 shows commands that can directly affect pages. You can use these in scripts or from the Command Window.

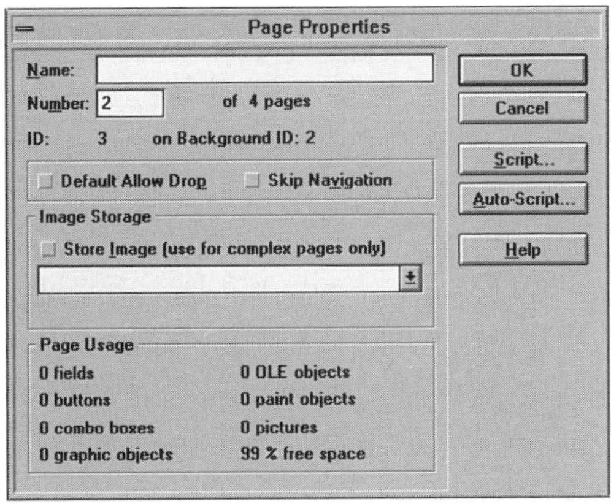

Fig. 4.4

Customize page properties in the Page Properties dialog box.

Table 4.2 Commands Affecting Pages

Command	Description	Example
`edit script`	Opens the script of an object in the Script editor.	`edit script of page 5`
`flip`	Displays the number of pages specified in the current book, starting from the page where you issue the command.	`flip`
`forward`	Sends a message to the next highest object in the object hierarchy. Generally used in a handler which overrides default behavior for a built-in message.	`forward`
`fxDissolve`	Visual effect for "dissolving" to another image.	`fxDissolve fast to page "shepherd"`
`fxWipe`	Visual effect to "wipe" to another image.	`fxWipe slow to page 3`
`fxZoom`	Visual effect to "zoom" to another image.	`fxZoom to the next page`
`get`	Evaluates an expression and places the value in `It`, a local variable. You can see the value of `It` by using the `put` command.	`get uniqueName of page "shepherd"` (returns the page ID number)
`go`	Used to move to a specific page in any book. If a `go to next page` is encountered on the last page of a book, the first page will be displayed. If a	`go to next page`

(continues)

Table 4.2 Continued

Command	Description	Example
	`go to previous page` is encountered on the first page, the last page will be displayed.	
`magnify`	Enlarges the view of the current page.	`magnify 2`
`print`	Prints all or selected pages in a book.	`print all`
`push`	Adds an item to a list (the stack). Items are retrieved from the list using the `pop` command. If you want to add pages to `sysHistory`, you must use the unique name for the page you want to add.	`push this page`
`search`	Searches for a string of characters you specify in fields and record field. You can limit the search to a single page, or make the search much broader.	`search for "Typical dog weight"`
`select`	Selects objects on the current page or background. You can also select the current page.	`select page "shepherd"`
`send`	Sends a message to an object. You can send built-in or user-defined messages to objects.	`send background`
`sort`	Sorts pages with the same background by a key you specify. You can use as many keys as you want, and can include any expression that can be used with a page. For example, you can sort pages according to their names.	`sort pages 1 to 5 by ascending text name of this page`
`transition`	Performs a transition from one page to the next or changing a page to a color.	`transition puzzle`

When something happens in ToolBook—opening a book, flipping to a page, and so on—a message is generated saying what just happened. You can create handlers to intercept these messages and perform an action. For example, you might want to cause something to happen when the user opens the book. The handler would look like this:

```
on enterBook
...put what you want to happen here
end enterBook
```

Table 4.3 shows messages that can be sent to the current page. Each time you start a book, an `enterBook` event is sent. Each time you flip to a page, an `enterPage` message is sent. This means you can create handlers that respond when that particular event happens in ToolBook.

Table 4.3 Messages Sent to the "Current" Page

Built-in Enter- and Leave-event Messages	Built-in Notification Messages	Other Messages
activateInstance	destroy	All menu event messages, including user-defined items
enterBook	idle	All DDE messages
enterPage	make	selectPage
enterSystem	*moved	
leaveBook	*shown	
leavePage	*sized	
leaveSystem		
enterBackground		
leaveBackground		
enterApplication		
leaveApplication		
* For Viewers		

Note

Messages sent to record fields are not forwarded to pages, because record fields are on backgrounds.

At the Reader level, the following built-in messages are automatically sent to the page:

- The keyboard-event messages, if `focus` is `null`.
- The mouse-event messages, if the mouse cursor is not pointing to an object on the page or the background.

The size of a page is defined by the book's `size` property. This sets the default page size for all new pages added. To change individual page sizes that share the same background, follow these steps:

1. From the Object menu, select Background Properties. The Background Properties dialog box appears.
2. Select the Page Size button.
3. Enter or select the new page size and press OK.

Performance Tips

Page design affects not only how the book looks, but also how it functions. One important book function to keep in mind is speed. That is, how fast will the book run? If it's too slow, your users will become frustrated. So what can you do to have better performance? One way is to design pages for better performance. The following are some general suggestions:

- Make pages as small as possible.
- Use the same background on similar pages. However, try to limit the number of backgrounds used.
- Wherever possible, put large objects—such as groups, paint objects, pictures, or complex draw objects—on the background, not on the page. ToolBook does not redraw background objects when navigating between pages of the same background.
- Try not to overlap objects and record fields. Overlapping causes ToolBook to redraw the record field and its text when the page is changed.

Page Navigation

There are many ways to move through the pages in a book. You can use the options in the Page menu, or you can move to pages by using scripts. Table 4.4 shows how you refer to various pages in scripts.

Table 4.4 How to Refer to Pages

To Refer To	Syntax to Use
Currently displayed	`this page`
In the current book	`page "shepherd"` `page ID 28`
In a viewer	`currentPage of viewer "dog_video"`
In another book	`page "shepherd" of book "dogs.tbk"`
A relational page	`next page` `previous page of book "dogs.tbk"`
	`first page [of this book]` `last page of this background`

An ordinal page	`first page of background "kennel"`
	`third page of this book`
	`seventh page of book "dogs.tbk"`

A page number	`page 2 of this background`
	`page 3 of this book`
	`page 7 of book "dogs.tbk"`

When you design your book, don't forget to allow your users a way to move between pages. These may include creating a Table of Contents to send readers to the correct section, or using buttons which "flip" pages back and forth.

Moving and Deleting Pages

When you add a new page, it is automatically added with the background of the page from which the new page command (Crtl+N or Options, New Page) was made. To "mix" backgrounds in a book, you can create a page with the background you want, then move the page where you want the background to appear.

Moving a page is also useful when you need to relocate a page for content reasons. To move a page, follow these steps:

1. Go to the page you want to move and then choose Select Page from the Edit menu.
2. Choose Cut or Clear from the Edit menu.
3. Go to the place in the book you want to add the page, then select Paste from the Edit menu or press Ctrl+V.

What about deleting pages? You might want to get rid of a page altogether. You can delete a page by doing any of the following:

- Go to the page you want to remove, choose Select Page from the Edit menu, then choose Cut or Clear from the Edit menu.
- Use the `select` command and then `send` the `cut` or `clear` message. When you use these commands, you can either enter them from the Command Window or from a script. For example:

```
select this page
send cut
```

Working with Backgrounds

A *background* is essentially a template shared by pages in a book. Every book has at least one background, whose objects all appear in the same position, style, and size on every page sharing that background.

You can create a new background by doing one of the following:

- Choose New Background from the Page menu
- Send the `newBackground` message

Backgrounds can hold graphic objects, buttons, fields, and record fields. The `activated` property of fields on the background is always `true`. Record fields can be placed only on backgrounds, although the text of a record field is unique to each page that shares the background.

> **Note**
>
> The objects on the background and their properties are stored in the background's 64K memory segment. When a paint object, picture object, or script is larger than 1K of memory, ToolBook moves the item to its own memory segment and stores a pointer to it with the background. The properties of the paint object or picture remain on the background.

When you first open a book, it automatically contains a blank page and a blank background. When you add a new page, it has the same background as the page where the new page command was issued. In other words, the page you are on when you add a new page determines the background the new page uses.

To select a background object, send the `background` message before selecting the object. If you don't want users to see what happens, you can conceal toggling between the foreground and background, by setting `sysLockScreen` to `true` first. When you've finished on the background, set `sysLockScreen` to `false`.

Background Properties

Just like any other ToolBook object, you can change a background's appearance and behavior by modifying built-in properties or customize its behavior using scripts. Figure 4.5 shows the Background Properties dialog box where you can change some of the built-in properties. These include adding a name for the background (which you can refer to in scripts), setting the background color, and how other objects are handled.

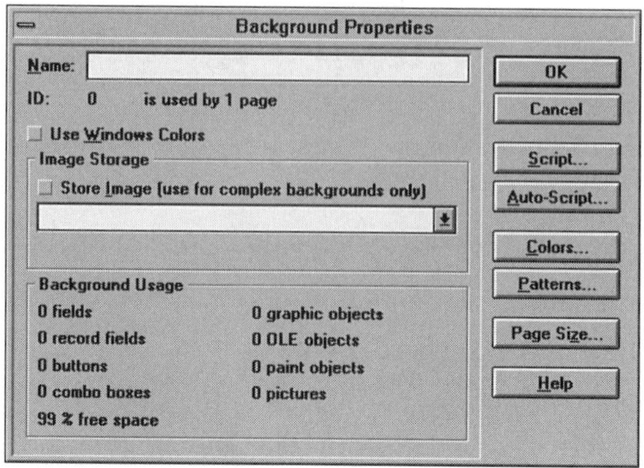

Fig. 4.5

These are background properties you can change.

These commands can directly affect backgrounds: `edit script`, `find`, `forward`, `get`, `send`, and `store`.

The `enterBackground` and `leaveBackground` messages are sent to the background when the user navigates between pages with different backgrounds. The `destroy` and `make` notification messages are sent to the background when it is created or deleted.

Performance Tips

Background design affects not only how the book looks, but also how it functions. One important book function to keep in mind is speed. That is, how fast will the book run? If it's too slow, your users will become frustrated. So what can you do to have better performance? One way is to design pages for better performance. The following are some general suggestions:

- Use as few backgrounds as possible. If your application has several similar pages, design the pages so they can share a common background.
- Place as many objects as possible on the background, especially large paint objects and pictures. This can improve navigation speed in your books, because ToolBook does not redraw the background when navigating between pages that share the background.
- Avoid placing foreground objects over background objects if the objects change; otherwise, ToolBook has to redraw both the foreground and background areas to update the screen image.
- Place a handler in a background script to define a general behavior for pages that share the background, or for objects on those pages and the background.

Moving, Changing, and Deleting Backgrounds

Each book must have at least one background, although it can have more than one. Backgrounds are closely associated with a particular page. If you create a new page and create a new background for that page, you must delete the page in order to delete the background. Similarly, if a background is used on several pages, all of the pages that refer to the background must be deleted in order for the background itself to actually be deleted.

For example, let's assume that you want to delete a background that you have created, and that three pages in your book use this background. You will need to delete each of the three pages that refers to the background, in order for the background to be deleted. How do you do this? From a Command Window or a script, execute the following two commands for each page that you need to delete:

```
send selectPage
send cut
```

You can also delete a page by using the ToolBook menus. From the Edit menu, choose Select Page. Then from the Edit menu, choose Cut.

Effective Book Design

When something is well-designed, you usually don't notice it. For example, when you need to write something down, you don't think, "Gee, this pencil and paper are well designed!" You just write your note. Someone else designed these items so that they are easy to use, and you can concentrate on what you want to do with them. Designing effective books has a similar goal. You want people to focus on what they can do with your application, not how they have to use it.

So how do you go about designing a book? Well, design involves planning. Planning involves thinking about what you want to do in your application, and who will use the application when it's done. Based on what and who, you can better define what kind of content is needed—such as text, graphics, animation, video, and so on—and how to present that information.

Note

To create a book, decide what you want to accomplish, what the application should contain, and how it should be organized. Then, create pages in one or more books to accomplish those goals.

You can create successful books by jumping right in, trying out all sorts of ideas, and experimenting with how things work together. ToolBook is great for this. However, you'll usually save time and see a better result by planning what you're going to do, and then trying out your ideas. You want to avoid jumping into a project, getting halfway done, and then having to redesign the whole thing from scratch. Some general questions you might consider are:

- Why am I creating this application? What does it do for users? Identify the purpose of the application. This helps you to figure out what you want to do, as well as what you'll need to actually create the application.
- Who will use my application? How can I design this book so that they get the most out of it? Think about who will use your application, and ways they might better understand how to use the application. Getting a fairly clear picture of "who" helps when you actually design the book interface.
- What do I need to include in my application? Decide what text, graphics, and/or video are needed to support the book's topic.
- How should my book look? Think about how to clearly present your information. Do you need to add custom menus? Do you need navigation buttons? Where should you place text fields? You might sketch ideas on paper, or test out ideas directly in ToolBook. In any case, you should also consider how the design will affect performance. For example, larger pages are easier to read, but also affect how big the file will be and require more memory.

Note

A common mistake in designing multimedia applications is to forget who will be using the application when it's done. It's easy to jump right into a project without really considering who will use your book and how they might get the most out of it.

Organizing and Presenting Information

When you open an application developed in ToolBook, what you're really seeing is the graphical user interface (GUI) for the application. In a GUI, words and graphical objects like buttons and icons represent the input and output of a program. A GUI is not only the way in which the information is presented—the "attractiveness" of the application—it also determines how the person will interact with your application. In other words, the way you put objects on a page determines not only how attractive the page is, but how easy it is to use. Ideally, pages should work the way the user works. Keep the people who will be using your application firmly in mind, especially during the planning stages, so you make the best design choices for them. A good application is both attractive and usable.

People are more comfortable with things that are familiar, and behave the way they expect. When you create your book, use existing standards for GUI applications. Try to put items where people expect to find them. For example, most Windows applications have a File menu with a Print command. If you're customizing printing for your ToolBook application, put the command on the File menu rather than in another menu.

After you have thought about the possible ways to organize information in the book, diagram your ideas either on a blank ToolBook page or on a piece of paper. Draw the book's overall flow and organization. Note on each page where you want fields, buttons, and graphics to appear and which fields you want to contain hotwords. Think about what kind of scripts you might need, and how they should be coded.

> **Note**
>
> A hotword is a special area of text. Like a button, when you make text a hotword and add a script, something happens when a user clicks on that text. Again, like a button, the "something" depends on the script in the hotword. Hotwords are commonly used to take a user to a related topic.

After planning, test how these ideas work in practice by implementing them in ToolBook. In most cases, you'll need to tweak your book. You may build several versions of a book before it reaches final form. You may find you don't like the way a particular design works, or you may think of a better way to do things. Create a few pages of typical information and establish backgrounds and scripts. Then you can either expand the prototype or cut and paste the pages and objects into the final book.

Designing Text and Graphics

Text and graphics play an important role in an application's look and feel. In a ToolBook application, *text* is the contents of a field. *Graphics* are pictures imported from other programs or shapes drawn in ToolBook. Thoughtful design of text and graphics improve a page's readability and usefulness as well as adding interest to the book.

As you've probably found out for yourself, the human eye tires more quickly reading from a monitor than from a printed page. Therefore, try to eliminate as much unnecessary text as possible. You can do this by maximizing graphics and minimizing text on pages. Good graphics can eliminate the need for a lot of text.

In applications requiring a lot of text, like a data entry book, you can make text more readable by using short text lines, displaying the text in easy-to-read fonts, and keeping the layout simple and uncluttered.

Note

Look at the design of other applications, and see how they are put together. You can also get ideas by looking at magazines—you'll notice that text is broken up by graphics and/or blank areas to make the page more readable.

Navigation and Controls

Navigation is the way readers find their way around in a book. A *control* is the means to navigate, for example, a button or menu command. A book's organization and navigational controls should be intuitive, so readers can easily find the information they need. The type of navigation needed will vary depending on the type of book you're creating. Try to look at applications that are similar to what you want to create and see if the navigation makes sense to you. In general, you want to make it easy for users to get to your pages and use them.

Testing a Book

Testing is an essential step in building a book. Test each part of your book as you complete it. Switch to Reader level to see how the page will look to users, and try out buttons and hotwords to make sure they work. Try to put yourself in the place of the person who will be using the book. Is it easy to use? Do your eyes follow the flow of the page, or do they get tired from trying to figure out what's going on? Do the buttons and other objects work the way they're supposed to? Testing the book as you build it will help you catch errors right away.

After the book is complete, test it as a whole. Go through it yourself to see if the overall design and organization work well, then get someone else to try it. A fresh perspective can be invaluable. Things which may seem obvious to you may not be to another person.

If you are building a book for others to use, it's especially important to find typical users to test it both during and after development. Carefully note the questions they ask and the errors they make. Make the effort to listen rather than explain why you designed the book in a particular way. What makes sense to you may not make sense to others, and testing is the only way to discover how you can improve the book.

From Here...

Now that you've seen how to create a book, you're ready to continue on with creating your application. Some chapters you may find helpful include the following:

- See Chapter 6, "Scripting Tools," for information on how to use the scripting tools.
- See Chapter 8, "Working with Viewers," for how to use viewers.
- See Chapter 13, "OpenScript Fundamentals," for the basics of OpenScript programming.
- See Chapter 14, "Messages, Objects, and Properties," for information about messages in ToolBook and how to create user properties.

CHAPTER 5

Understanding the Media Management Tools

This chapter discusses how you can add multimedia elements to your application using the media management tools. These tools are the *Resource Manager,* which keeps track of the resources such as icons and menu bars in your application, and the *Clip Manager,* which can be used to keep track of audio and visual clips of various sorts.

The Resource Manager

The Resource Manager provides a convenient means of adding resources to your application. Once added to the Resource Manager, the saved resources are easy to access when creating your application and can easily be copied from one application to another. Asymetrix not only provides the Manager, but also bundles tools that make it simple to create new resources. This section explores the resources that can be added and modified in ToolBook: bitmaps, cursors, fonts, icons, menu bars, and palettes.

Adding a resource to the Manager is accomplished by choosing Object, Resources from the main menu or clicking the resource manager icon in the Toolbar palette. This will bring up the Resource Manager dialog box (see fig. 5.1).

From the Available Resources drop-down list, choose the resource that you want to add or manipulate. Resources are used for a variety of purposes as you build a ToolBook application. For example, you might add all of the photos and backdrops that are part of your application into the Resource Manager. Although there are many other ways to store and use objects in ToolBook, the Resource Manager has the following attributes that make it a very convenient tool:

- All similar resources are displayed and catalogued, making them easy to find.
- A single copy of a resource can be stored and then accessed throughout the application, wherever needed, saving disk space.
- A change to a shared resource causes the change to occur anywhere the resource is used, making global changes simple.
- Named resources are easy to reference in OpenScript, simplifying the process of writing complex routines.

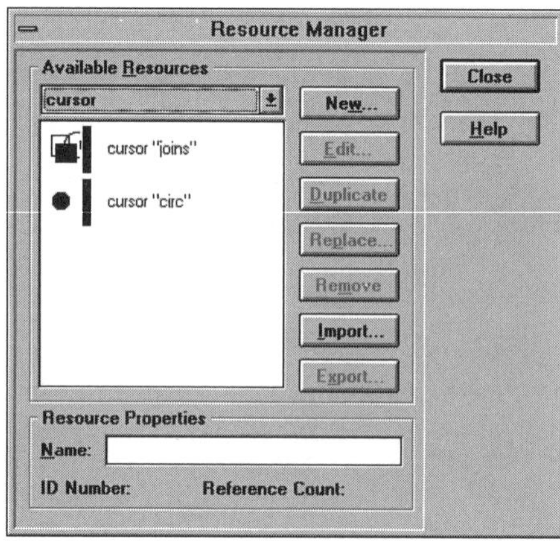

Fig. 5.1

The Resource Manager dialog box.

Keep in mind, however, that there are limits to how many resources can be added to a ToolBook application. In a book, the maximum number is 8,192 individual resources. No resource can exceed the size of 64K. Thus, there are times that you won't want to use the Resource Manager to handle your graphics or other resources. Other more effective techniques for manipulating large amounts of data are discussed throughout this book, in various examples provided. For example, a more general means of referring to picture files from the disk is given in Chapter 7, "Adding Multimedia Elements."

Icon and Cursor Resources

You use icon resources to store icons that represent functions (such as those found in most Window program Toolbars) or button graphics. Cursor resources are used to store custom cursors that you create for your application. For example, suppose you want a cursor that is a finger with a bow tied to it (representing a "reminder"). You would add this reminder cursor to your cursor resources. This is accomplished by following these steps:

1. Choose Object, Resources from the main menu.
2. Choose Cursor from the Available Resource drop-down list.
3. Click Import and use the file browser to select the cursor file.
4. Click OK. If the cursor is not already on the drive, you can use the cursor editor to create a new icon. This process is described in the following section titled "The Icon/Cursor Editor."
5. After you locate the cursor, it will appear in the cursor resource list. Type a name for the cursor into the Name field and then click Close.

Changing cursors using OpenScript programming is a simple process.

The Icon/Cursor Editor. The Icon/Cursor editor can be used to create new icons or cursors for your applications (see fig. 5.2).

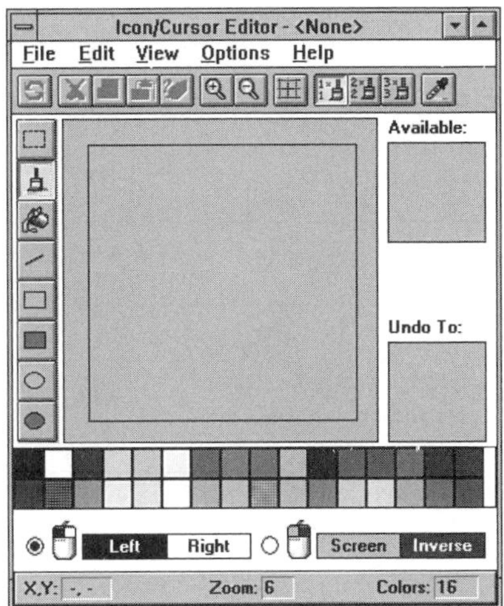

Fig. 5.2

The Icon/Cursor editor.

To create a new icon, follow these steps:

1. Choose Object, Resources from the main menu.
2. Choose Cursor from the Available Resource drop-down list.
3. Click the New button.
4. Using the drawing tools (described in Table 5.1), create the icon. Remember to set a "hot spot" and place it where the user would expect it to be (such as the tip of the paintbrush or the tip of the pencil).
5. Choose File, Save As, Cursor in Current Book from the menu bar. When prompted, enter a name for the cursor and exit the editor.
6. To use the cursor, you will need to script whatever object is resetting the cursor with a line, such as:

   ```
   syscursor = cursor "myHand"
   ```

   where `myHand` is the name of the cursor as assigned in step 5.

To edit a cursor in the Icon/Cursor editor, choose New in the Resource Manager dialog box. This brings up the editor. When you invoke the editor, you are asked to select a type (cursor or icon) and a color depth (B&W, 8, or 16 colors). Your choice depends on your needs for the given application, which will depend on whether color is essential for the icon or cursor, what type of graphics card will be available on the end-user's system, and how the icon or cursor will look displayed on the current background. Use the draw tools provided to create an icon or cursor. These tools are shown in Table 5.1.

Table 5.1 Icon/Cursor Editor Tools

Icon	Tool	Function
	Select	Selects an area for Copy or Clear
	Paintbrush	Paints 2 × 2, 3 × 3, or 4 × 4 pixel areas (depends on brush size)
	Paint can	Fills an area
	Line	Draws a line
	Rectangle	Draws an unfilled rectangle
	Filled rectangle	Draws a filled rectangle
	Ellipse	Draws an unfilled ellipse
	Filled ellipse	Draws a filled ellipse
Left Right	Color selections	Chooses a color in the color bar—click with the left mouse button to set left mouse draw color, and right button for right mouse button draw color
	Undo	Undoes the last action
	Cut	Cuts the current selection
	Copy	Copies to the Clipboard the current selection
	Paste	Pastes from the Clipboard
	Clear	Erases
	Zoom in	Changes the zoom factor (value displayed in the status bar)
	Zoom out	Changes the zoom factor (value displayed in the status bar)
	Grid	Shows a grid to help alignment in drawing

Icon	Tool	Function
	Small paintbrush	Sets paintbrush size to 1 pixel by 1 pixel
	Medium paintbrush	Sets paintbrush size to 2 pixels by 2 pixels
	Large paintbrush	Sets paintbrush size to 3 pixels by 3 pixels
	Pick up color	Picks up a color and assigns it to the left or right mouse button
	Set cursor hotspot	Sets the active hotspot for the cursor
	Test cursor	Tests the cursor resource currently being edited (position displayed in status bar)
Screen Inverse	Screen and inverse	Sets screen color (which is the color colors that allows whatever is behind it to show through) and inverse color (which shows the inverse of the color behind it to show through)

The Icon/Cursor editor provides a simple editor useful for creating icons and cursors for your applications.

Caution

The Icon/Cursor editor does not work properly on all machines. If you use the editor and it creates a streak in your cursor or icon, you are running into this problem. In this case, I suggest that you use a different editor.

Bitmap Resources

Bitmap resources are picture files that you can use in your application. For example, if you insert bitmapped images into your fields to represent different kinds of links to other pages in the application or to sound and video files, you can store these as bitmap resources in the book.

To create a new bitmap, follow these steps:

1. Choose Object, Resources from the main menu.
2. In the drop-down list box for Available Resources, choose bitmap.
3. Click the New button.
4. The New Bitmap dialog box appears, prompting you to enter the Width and Height of the bitmap as well as the color depth (see fig. 5.3). Click OK when you have made your choices.

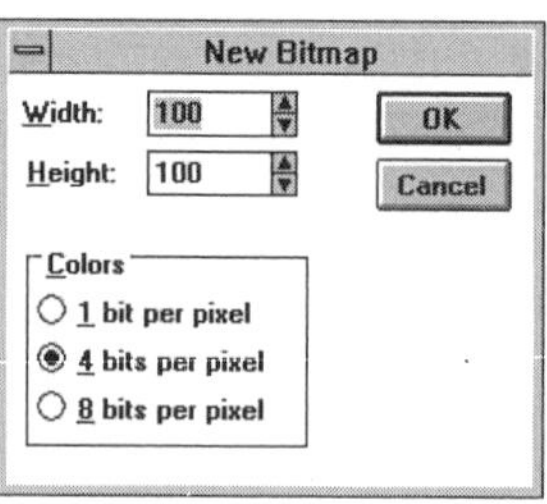

Fig. 5.3

Create a new bitmap with the New Bitmap dialog box.

5. Now, use the paint tools to create your bitmap picture. The tools are described in Table 5.2.
6. Choose File, Save As, Bitmap in Current Book from the menu bar. When prompted, enter a name for the bitmap and exit the editor.

Table 5.2 BitEdit Bitmap Editor Tools

Tool	Function
Select	Selects an area for Copy or Clear
Paintbrush	Paints with the currently selected color
Rectangle	Draws a rectangle using the current draw and fill colors (use transparent fill color for outline only)
Rounded rectangle	Draws a rounded rectangle using the current draw and fill colors (use transparent fill color for outline only)
Ellipse	Draws an ellipse using the current draw and fill colors (use transparent fill color for outline only)
Line	Draws a line using the currently selected line width
Eye dropper	Sets the current color to that selected with the eye dropper
Fill	Fills with the current foreground (left mouse button click) or background (right mouse button click)
Erase	Erases to background color
Select color	Changes the current color selections (left mouse button changes foreground, right mouse changes background)
Line width	Changes the current line width
Brush shape	Changes the current brush shape
Zoom in	Zooms in on the graphic art

As with any paint program, you will use these tools to edit or create the graphic image. The work space is shown in figure 5.4.

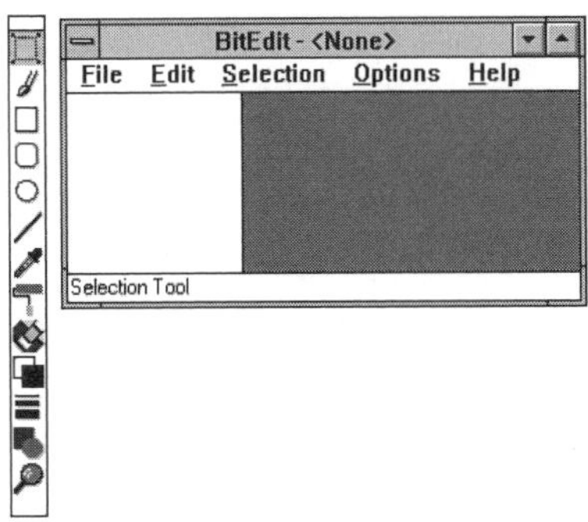

Fig. 5.4

The BitEdit window provides a simple paint program for creation of bitmap images.

You will want to choose a palette that is appropriate for the bitmap. If your application is going to be used on 256-color graphic cards, then you should strongly consider using only colors from the "identity palette" for all of the resources that are to be used on more than one page. This way you can selectively adapt the remaining colors for other images on the page and avoid concern about color shifts occurring in your icons. (This topic is covered in greater detail in Chapter 20, "Fundamentals of Multimedia.")

To make an identity palette, if you are creating a new image choose Options, Show Palette, Make Identity Palette from the BitMap Editor menu bar. If you are editing a previously created image, choose Options, Show Palette, File, Apply From File, and choose the appropriate palette. Then, choose Options, Show Palette, Make Identity Palette to force the identity palette colors. The identity palette includes the colors needed by windows for displaying menus, menu bars, and other windows items. Now, as you draw, use only the first ten and the last ten colors in the palette.

After you have created the bitmap, save it by selecting File, Save As, Bitmap in Current Book as in step 5 of the procedure described in the preceding section. Now this resource will be available to be used throughout the application.

Menu Bar Resources

In the applications you create, you will want to have control over the items and placement of items that appear in the menu bar. Asymetrix has provided a menu bar editor that allows you to interactively create the menu bar items and control placement, appearance, initial states, and so on (see fig. 5.5).

More details about creating and using menus can be found in Chapter 9, "Creating Custom Menus."

Fig. 5.5

The Menu Bar Editor.

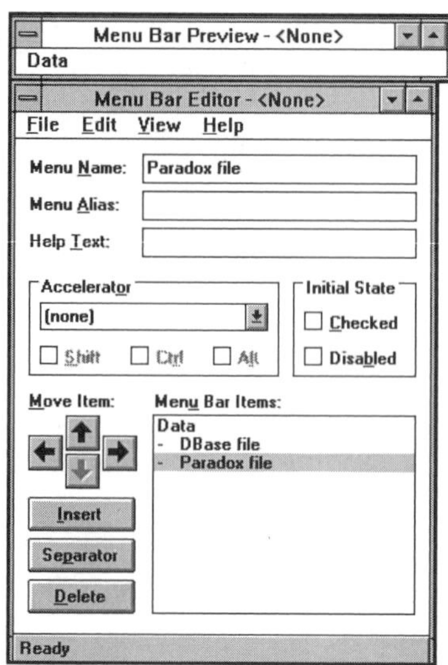

To create a new menu, follow these steps:

1. Choose Object, Resources from the main menu.
2. In the drop-down list box for Available Resources, choose menuBar.
3. Click the New button.
4. Type in the name of the menu or menu item in the Menu Name box.
5. You can set menu items as entries on the menu bar or as submenus using the Move Item keys (refer to fig. 5.5).
6. As you edit the menu bar, you can interactively test it in the Menu Bar Preview window that will appear on the screen as you edit.
7. Choose File, Save As, MenuBar in Current Book and enter a name for the menu bar, then exit the editor.

Palette Resources

If your final application is designed to work in full-color modes only, palette management will not be a big issue for you during the design process. If, however, you are using colorful images and intend the final product to be used in 256-color mode, you need to learn techniques for palette management. ToolBook provides a very well-designed Palette editor (see fig. 5.6). With the editor, you can manipulate the colors in a palette so that the palette is optimal for your application. As discussed in the "Bitmap Resources" section of this chapter, it is recommended that you use colors from the identity palette when creating buttons, icons, and other resources that will appear on more than one page of the application. This will minimize the undesired color shifts that occur on computers that have 256 colors or less available from their graphics cards.

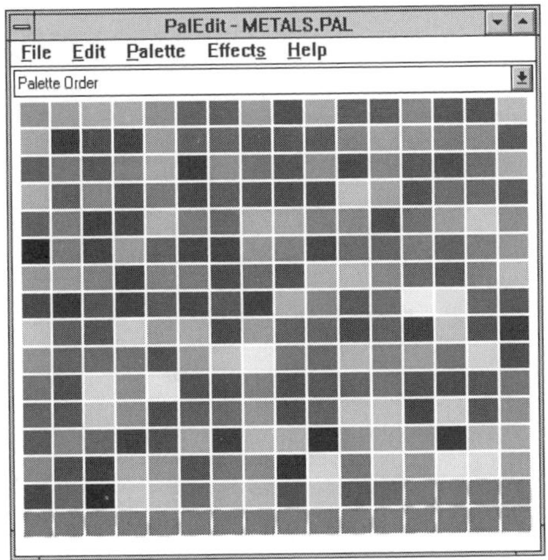

Fig. 5.6

The Palette editor permits you select the colors that are best for the pictures that you use or create for your application.

The menus in the Palette editor are listed in Table 5.3.

Table 5.3 BitEdit Menus

Menu Item	Entry	Usage
File	New	Starts a new palette
	Open From	Opens a palette from the disk (`*.pal`)
	Save	Saves the palette
	Save As	Saves the palette to a new filename (`*.pal`)
	Apply From File	Applies the currently opened palette file to the currently opened bitmap file in the bitmap editor
	Save to File	Saves the palette from the currently opened bitmap file as a palette file
	Exit	Exits the program
Edit	Undo	Undoes the last command
	Cut	Removes the selected cells to the Clipboard
	Copy	Copies selected cells to the Clipboard
	Paste	Pastes from the Clipboard
	Delete	Deletes selected cells
	Select All	Selects all cells in the palette
	Select Similar Colors	Selects cells with RGB values similar to the selected cell
	Select Unused Colors	Selects the colors that are not in use by the currently displayed bitmap

(continues)

Table 5.3 Continued

Menu Item	Entry	Usage
	Flash Selected Colors	"Flashes" or inverts the selected colors in the bitmap image, providing reference to where these colors are in use
	Merge Similar Colors	Blends two or more selected colors and replaces the used colors in the image with the blended color
	Preferences	Permits you to set Single or Dual Views and Delay Updates (to prevent delays while new palette is drawn)
Palette	Edit Color	Displays view of all available colors for changing a selected cell
	Add Color	Displays colors to allow you to add a new color to the end of the palette
	Copy View	Copies the view
	Make Identity Palette	Adds the 20 Windows reserved colors to the palette
Effects	Adjust Brightness	Adjusts the brightness of the palette
	Adjust Contrast	Adjusts the contrast of the palette
	Add Selected Color	Adds a selected color to the palette
	Fade to Selected Color	Fades all items in the palette a specified amount towards a specified color
	Fade to Palette	Adjusts all the colors in a current palette towards similar colors in another palette
	Cycle RGB	Cycles all of the color definitions in the palette through all of the hues of the color wheel by a selected amount
	Cycle Palette	Cycles color definitions among the specified cells

Once you have created a palette and stored it in the Resource Manager, it is easy to refer to that palette for different pages and images, permitting greater control over color in your application.

Caution

Do not invest a lot of time in perfecting a ToolBook application on a single machine with the intention of testing it on several machines late in the development cycle. It is important that you constantly review how the application looks on a variety of machines with different graphics cards before you invest a great deal of time in the interface, unless you have complete control over where the application will be displayed.

You might choose to handle color by having three or four different palettes (e.g. forest colors, indoor colors, and skin and hair colors), and then apply the appropriate palette to each bitmap that you bring into your application. This technique can eliminate the need for a large number of palettes.

Font Resources

Font resources are a means of handling the fonts that are used in a ToolBook application. You can include TrueType fonts (the most common font type used on Windows-based machines) with your application depending, of course, on whether you own the copyright or have negotiated for license of the font in your application.

Caution

Do not use fonts in your application if you cannot be certain they will be in place on the machine that the application will be installed upon. You may end up with happy faces and hearts where you intended meaningful text.

There are some fonts that you can count on being installed on the end users Windows systems; these include Arial, Courier New, and Times New Roman. System fonts, which are not TrueType, are always available but will appear differently on different machines. ToolBook does not provide a font editor, but there are many such programs available in the market today.

Fonts can be imported into the font resources. To import fonts, follow these steps:

1. Choose Object, Resources from the main menu. The Resource Manager appears.
2. In the drop-down list box for Available Resources, choose font.
3. Click the Import button. The Import Font dialog box appears (see fig. 5.7).
4. Select the font that you want to embed from the list of available fonts on your system.
5. Select the Import and then Close buttons.

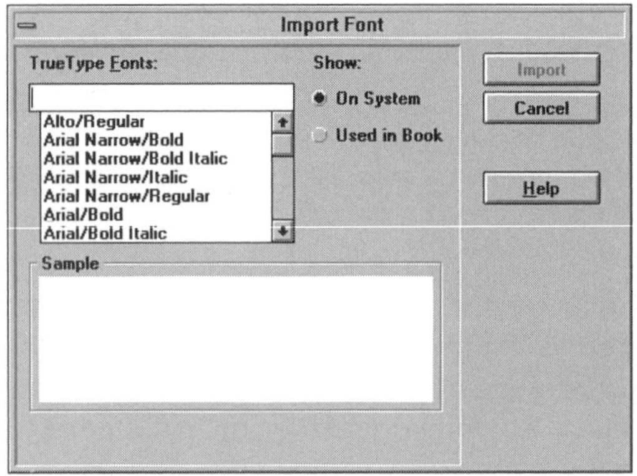

Fig. 5.7

The Import Font dialog box permits you to choose fonts to install as system resources in your book.

Fonts and related issues are discussed in more detail in Chapter 11, "Working with Text," and in Chapter 26, "Preparing for Delivery."

Using Resources

Once you have defined bitmaps, cursors, fonts, icons, menu bars, and palettes, you will be able to use them throughout your application. The Resource Manager maintains the list of these objects along with thumbnail images of them that will allow you to choose the correct object. Figure 5.8 shows a list of icon resources that have been installed in the Resource Manager window.

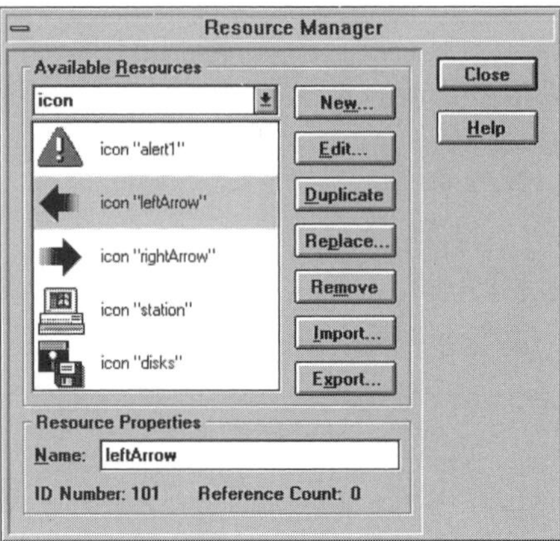

Fig. 5.8

Icon resources in the Resource Manager.

The means of applying resources varies. For example, to apply an icon to a button, follow these steps:

1. Draw a button using the button tool from the Tool palette.
2. Select the button and choose Object, Button Properties from the menu.

3. Click the Graphics button and then the Choose button. The Resource Manager will be displayed as shown in figure 5.8.
4. Select the graphic for the button that you want to use.
5. Click OK in each of the three dialogs to close them.

Within the Resource Manager, you have the option to edit, duplicate, replace, remove, import, or export. The processes for editing, importing, and exporting vary for each type of resource.

The Clip Manager

The Clip Manager provides a convenient way to catalog and maintain various animation, video, and still clips. Like the Resource Manager, the Clip Manager provides a means of maintaining and cataloging resources that you might need to access from different parts of your application. Figure 5.9 shows the Clip Manager dialog box, which can be accessed by choosing Object, Clips from the main menu or by clicking the Clip Manager icon in the Toolbar palette.

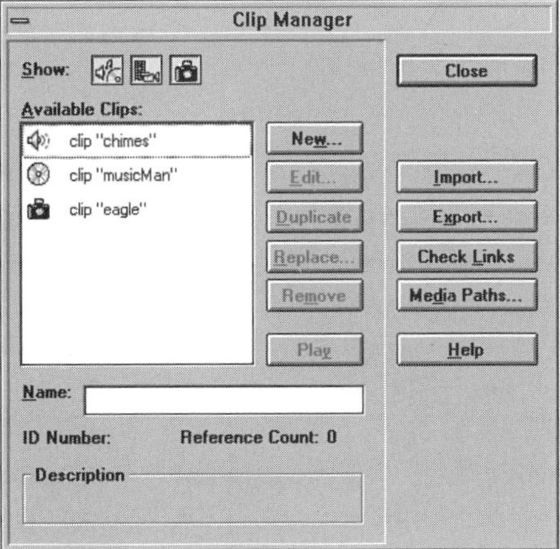

Fig. 5.9

Clip Manager dialog box.

Defining Clips

To define a clip in the Clip Manager, follow these steps:

1. Open up the Clip Manager by selecting Object, Clips.
2. Click the New button.
3. The Choose Source Type dialog box will prompt you to choose the source type (see fig. 5.10). Click the source type you want to add and then click the OK button.

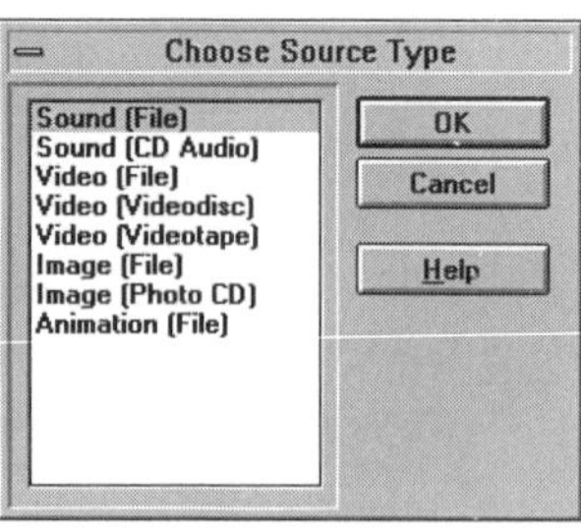

Fig. 5.10

The Choose Source Type dialog box enables you to choose the clip media data type.

Once the source type has been chosen, the Clip Editor dialog box will be available for you to set the parameters for the clip. The details of source types and clip settings are described in the following sections.

Choosing a Source Type. There are eight types of clips that are supported in MTB. Some of these clips are digitized multimedia elements that are played from the computer hard drive or CD-ROM drive including sound files, video files, still images, photo CDs, and animation files. Others clips are defined as sections of media that are played from devices controlled by the computer, including CD audio, videodisc, and videotape.

The types of clip media that are supported in the Clip Manager include the following:

- **Sound (File)**—bitmapped sound files (currently WAVE support only) and MIDI support
- **Sound (CD Audio)**—sound played directly from a CD audio CD-ROM disc
- **Video (File)**—digitized video in any format supported by the drivers on the machine in which the application is created (of course, these drivers must also be installed at the site that the final application will be run), including Microsoft Audio-Video Interleave (AVI), Apple QuickTime, Motion Picture Experts Group (MPEG), JPEG, and other formats
- **Video (Videodisc)**—pass video through to be displayed on a region of the screen (utilizing video overlay) or to a separate monitor from a videodisc player, typically controlled through a serial port
- **Video (Videotape)**—pass video signal through to be displayed on a region of the screen (utilizing video overlay) or to a separate monitor from a videotape player, typically controlled through a serial port (for example, to a Sony VBox)
- **Image (File)**—still images in any of the supported formats including `.BMP`, `.DIB`, `.WMF`, `.GIF`, `.TIF`, `.PCX`, and others
- **Image (Photo CD)**—Kodak Photo CD still graphic files
- **Animation (File)**—digital animation clips (`.FLI`, `.FLC`, `.MMM`)

The Clip Editor Source Tab. Fill in the Clip field with the name you want to use to refer to the clip (up to 32 characters).

In cases where the clip reads files from the disk, you will need to specify the location of the file. You do this by choosing the Source tab. For example, figure 5.11 shows the specifications for an animation file. You would click Choose in the Source box in order to identify the file to be played in the clip.

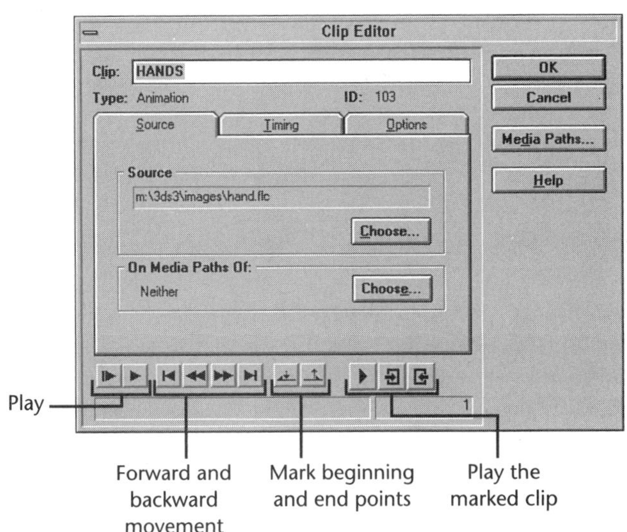

Fig. 5.11

Select the source file for an animation file in the Source tab of the Clip Editor.

In the On Media Paths Of box, you can choose the media path—the locations for the files for the clip—for the specific clip. Media paths are described in more detail later in this chapter.

The buttons across the bottom of the screen allow you to test out the animation file. The choices groups, from left to right, include play, forward and backward movement through the file, mark beginning and end points of the clip, and play the marked clip.

The Clip Editor Timing Tab. The Timing tab of the Clip Editor provides you with means of accurately specifying the time for a clip (see fig. 5.12). The Start, End, and Length boxes permit you to set numerical values that define the clip in various time formats.

Digital media is often measured in *frames*. A frame is one of the pictures played in succession to create a video or animation. Often it is convenient to refer to these explicitly by frame number, but other times it is more useful to reference in time format. The available formats are listed in Table 5.4. A mixed way of referencing time and frame numbers is the *HMSF format*, which uses hours, minutes, seconds, and frames. So, for example, a clip playing back at 15 frames per second that is 1 and 1/3 seconds long could have an endpoint defined as 0:00:01:05 in HMSF format (0 hours, 0 minutes, 1 second, 5 frames).

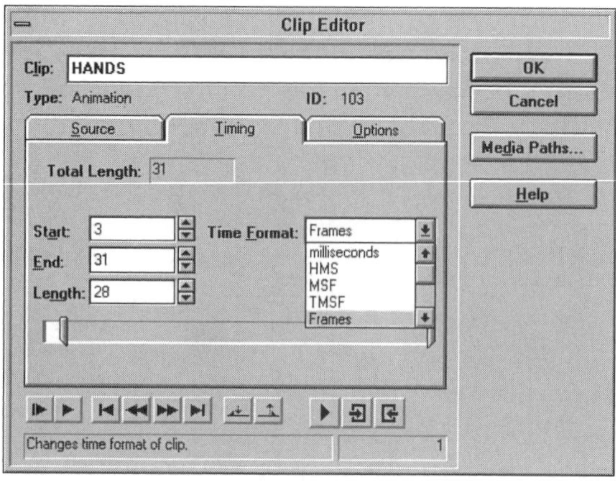

Fig. 5.12

Set the timing for an animation file in the Timing tab of the Clip Editor.

Table 5.4 Time Formats for Clip Lengths (*mmTimeFormat* Property Values)

Format	Description	Example
Frame	Frame number	2345
HMS	Hours, minutes, seconds	0:03:22
HMSF	Hours, minutes, seconds, frames	0:00:23:04
milliseconds	milliseconds	5676
MS	Minutes, seconds	2:34
MSms	Minutes, seconds, milliseconds	1:20:312
TMSF	Tracks, minutes, seconds, frames	0:00:22:003

The Clip Editor Options Tab. The final tab of the Clip Editor is the Options tab (see fig. 5.13). Here, you specify options such as the volume level for the clip, and the clip priority. *Clip priority* refers to what level of priority the clip will be given in relation to other clips that may be played simultaneously. This is only important when the clips need access to the same device channel. For example, you will not be able to hear the output from an `.AVI` file at the same time a `.WAV` file is played if the system is using a single sound card. Setting the clip priority allows you to specify which clip is to be given precedence. When you start a clip with a higher priority than a currently playing clip, the playing clip will be stopped (and closed, if it was not preloaded).

In the Options tab, you can specify whether the color palette of the book itself (also known as the background color palette) or of the clip that is playing takes precedence (except for sound files which have no color palette). To use the background color palette, select the Use background palette checkbox.

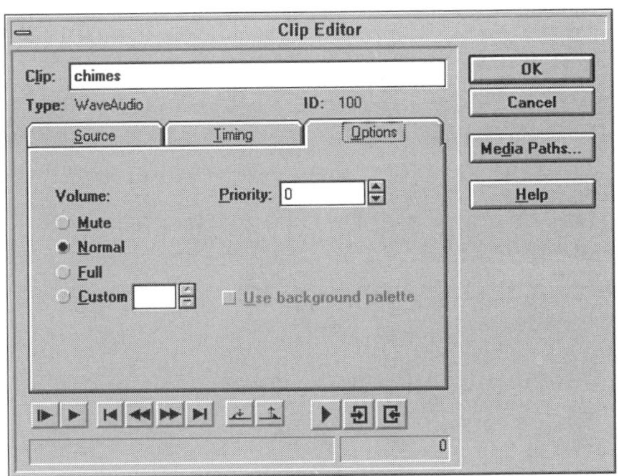

Fig. 5.13

Select options for a sound file in the Options tab of the Clip Editor.

The priority for the clip can be set in the Clip Editor or through explicit OpenScript commands, as discussed in later sections of this book. The OpenScript variable for this is `mmPriority`. See the examples in the help file provided by Asymetrix under the topic "Setting Clip Priority" for ways to start and stop clips (such as stopping a background audio track while a video is played, and then starting the audio back up when the video is complete). The volume control options specify volume as a fraction of the system volume.

The Photo CD media has its own special dialog box, somewhat different than the other clip definitions (see fig. 5.14). Use this dialog to specify the photo, the CD-ROM drive letter, and the requested size for the photo from those on the disk.

Fig. 5.14

Select photos from a Photo CD in the Clip Editor.

The Media Path

Clips that you use in your application will remain external files to your application. Unlike a graphic file that is imported into the page of your application and becomes part of the program, clips are maintained as pointers to external files. Thus, it is important to specify these items in such a way that they can be found when they are installed on the end user's machine. This is accomplished by setting the *media path* for the clips, which is specified on the Source tab of the Clip Editor by clicking the Choose button in the On Media Paths Of box.

It is very important to understand the options for specifying the media path for the clips that are used in your application. *Media* refers to the files themselves (video clips, sound files, etc.) and *path* refers to the search path that the computer uses to find the media clip that is requested.

Figure 5.15 shows the Media Paths dialog box, which allows you to specify the media paths to the Hard Disk and the CD-ROM drive. The current choices are shown in the field below the Path to Edit radio buttons.

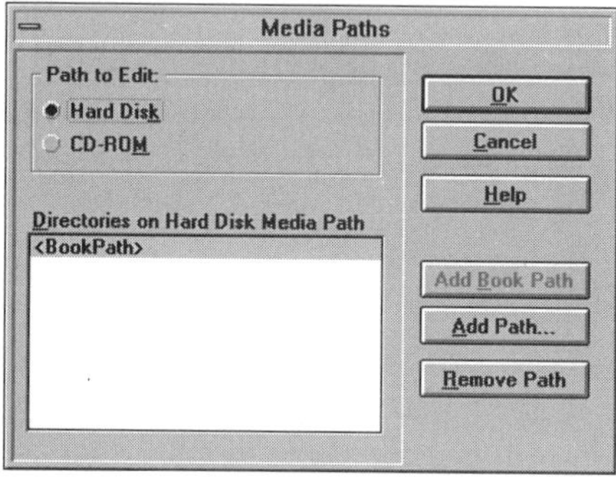

Fig. 5.15

You can change the media path in the Clip Manager.

The `<BookPath>`, which is the location of the currently running book, is automatically added to the list of paths. You can specify other locations for the search path by clicking the Add Path button and specifying the path using the standard file dialog.

Remember that some objects—such as text and pictures—can be embedded in your application, while others—such as sound or video clips—are read off the hard drive or the CD-ROM. After you have moved files around or done a test installation of your application, you may want to check to see if all of the files referenced are actually there. This might be a tedious process if done by hand. This can easily be accomplished from the Clip Manager by clicking the Check Links button.

At the time you are ready to distribute the application, you will want to make these links path-independent. Path independence is important because you will not know the exact path that the user will choose for installing the application. Setting up path independence can be accomplished by using the Media Packager found in the Tools menu (see fig. 5.16). Click the start button, and MTB will check the links and convert explicit paths to relative paths. If a link is found that is explicit, you will be prompted to either Move the clip to a location in the path, Copy it to a location in the path, Add its current location to the paths, or Skip this media reference (see fig. 5.17.)

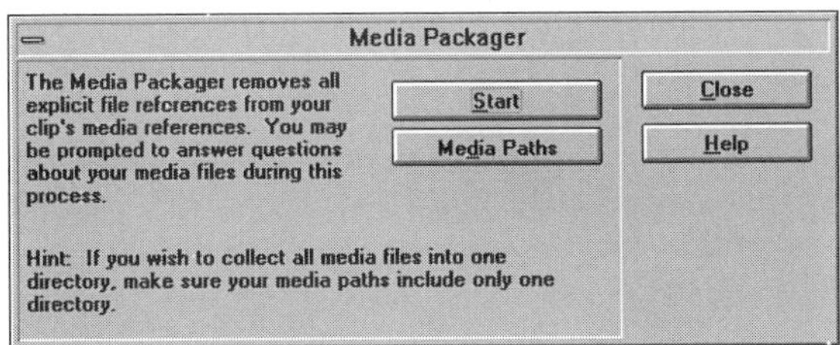

Fig. 5.16

Using the Media Packager.

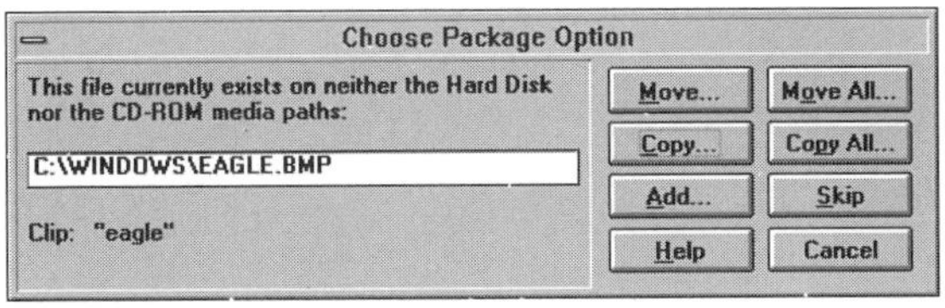

Choose Package Option

This file currently exists on neither the Hard Disk nor the CD-ROM media paths:

C:\WINDOWS\EAGLE.BMP

Clip: "eagle"

Move... Move All... Copy... Copy All... Add... Skip Help Cancel

Fig. 5.17

Change an explicit path to a relative path in the Clip Editor.

From Here...

This chapter has provided the basic outline for adding media resources and clips to your application and touched briefly on some of the topics that are important to completing an application that can be distributed to a wide range of users. To find out more information about the topics discussed in this chapter, refer to the following chapters:

- Chapter 9, "Creating Custom Menus," contains details of how you can create and use custom menus.
- Chapter 26, "Preparing for Delivery," provides more information about setting up paths for delivery of an application.

CHAPTER 6

Scripting Tools

This chapter explores the tools that you use in scripting your application. *Scripting* refers to the computer programming that you perform to customize your application. To do this scripting, you use the computer language OpenScript, the language of ToolBook. OpenScript shares many features of other programming languages, permitting typical looping structures such as `do while` and branching structures such as `if/then`.

To begin scripting in ToolBook, you first need to understand the scripting environment. This chapter discusses the elements of the scripting environment that you use in writing OpenScript commands. These elements are:

- The Command Window, used for quick tests of code
- The Script editor, which is the programming environment in which you enter scripts
- The Script recorder, which provides an automatic method of generating code
- Auto-Script, which allows you to save and reuse segments of code that you use often
- Shared Scripts, which permits you to create one script that is shared between different objects in the book
- The OpenScript Library, an application shipped with ToolBook that contains many examples of scripts
- The Debugger window, which contains the tools that you use to fix problems with your scripts

Command Window

The ToolBook Command Window provides a convenient notepad for trying out code fragments, sending messages, testing the current contents of variables, and displaying information. As you use ToolBook, you will rely on the Command Window often. To display the Command Window, click its icon in the toolbar or choose View, Command.

The Command Window consists of a viewer that is split horizontally (see fig. 6.1). You enter a command in the bottom half of the window. The top half of the viewer contains the previously typed commands and holds up to 20 lines of scripts.

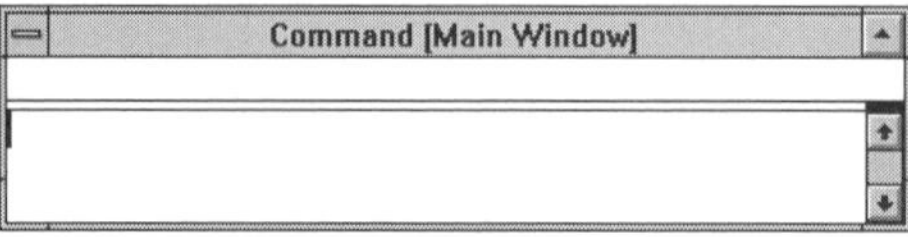

Fig. 6.1

The Command Window provides a convenient means of interactively testing scripts.

The Command Window refers the scripts to the current *execution context*—that is, the last active ToolBook window or viewer. The context appears in the Command Window's title bar. In figure 6.1, the context is the main window.) References such as `this page`, `this book`, and so on result in messages being sent to the execution context.

Figure 6.2 contains an example of how you might use the Command Window. In this example, you step through a series of color values for a field to choose the color that you like best.

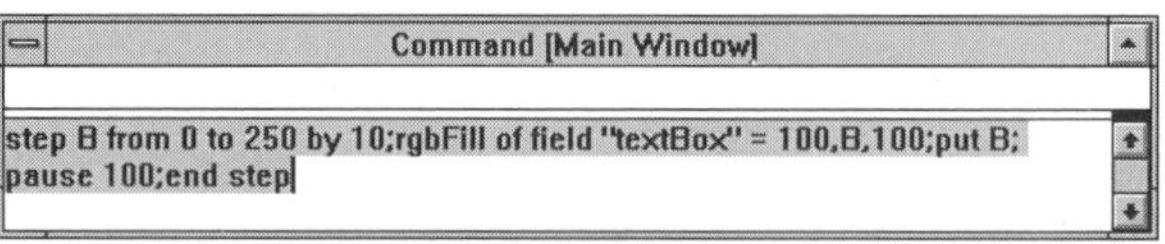

Fig. 6.2

Choosing a color is a typical use of the Command Window.

Although you can type and test a complex script in the Command Window, it is generally easier to create a temporary button or field for that purpose. The Command Window is best used for short fragments of code that you do not necessarily intend to use in a script, as in figure 6.2. Type the line of script, and instead of pressing Enter to specify a new line (as you would do in other scripting environments in ToolBook), use a semicolon to separate commands. The command executes when you press Enter.

Following are some ways that you might use the Command Window:

- To quickly run through the scripts of all the pages in your books (to make a small change, for example, or to look for a routine that you lost), use the following:

  ```
  step p from 1 to 20; edit page p of this book; end step
  ```

- To look at the script of another book, perhaps to copy a few lines for the current book, use the following line:

  ```
  edit the script of book "c:\data\datasort.tbk"
  ```

- To find out what objects are on the current page, use the following:

```
put the objects of this page
```

- To move a palette to the top-left corner of the desktop, use the following line:

```
move toolpalette to 0,0
```

- To see whether a problem occurred in the last executed command, use:

```
put syserror
```

- To examine the value of a system variable, use the following line:

```
system myVar; put myVar
```

The top half of the Command Window is separated from the bottom half by the Split bar. The area above the Split bar contains previously entered commands. You can copy a line from above the Split bar to the area below the Split bar by selecting it. This procedure makes it easy to reuse a command line that you just tried—for example, to modify a script that didn't work as expected. You can resize the top and bottom windows by dragging the window border and change the relative size of the top section (containing previously typed lines) and the bottom section (current test code) by dragging the Command Window's Split bar between them (see fig. 6.3).

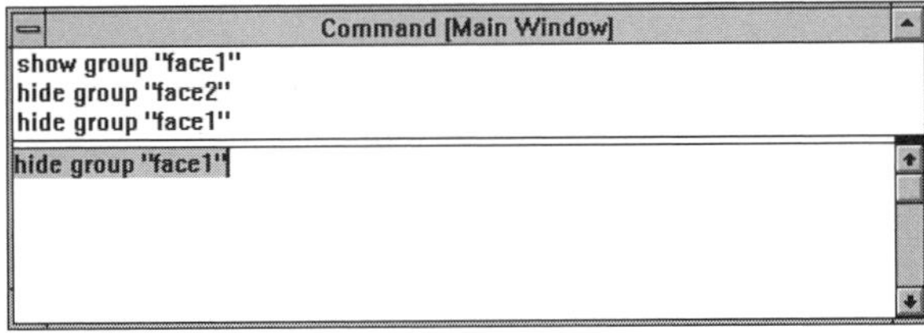
Command [Main Window]
show group "face1"
hide group "face2"
hide group "face1"
hide group "face1"

Fig. 6.3

The Command Window's Split bar is adjustable.

If you make an error when you type a script in the Command Window, ToolBook flags the error, as shown in figure 6.4.

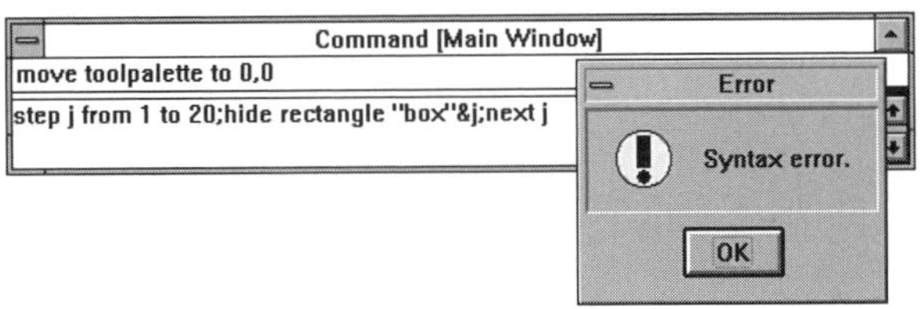
Command [Main Window]
move toolpalette to 0,0
step j from 1 to 20;hide rectangle "box"&j;next j
Error
Syntax error.
OK

Fig. 6.4

Errors in scripts in the Command Window are flagged immediately, making the Command Window a useful place to test experimental scripts.

The Command Window also provides a convenient place to display messages from scripts during the testing phase. Suppose that you have a loop in a button and want to examine the values of the variables as you run through the loop. Use the `put` command, as follows:

```
to handle buttonUp
while n < jMax
 send wiggle
```

```
 put "n="&n&&"jMax="&jMax
end
end buttonUp
```

The put command uses the Command Window to display results. In this example, the Command Window would continuously display the results of each loop and provide an ending display that looks something like this:

```
n=5 jMax=6
```

Script Editor

The *Script editor* is the window in ToolBook that you use to write, edit, and check scripts. Any object in ToolBook can contain a script, including the book itself, a background, a page, a graphic item, buttons, and fields.

Scripting is done at Author level. To open a Script editor window for an object, use one of the following methods:

- Select the object; then click the Script Editor button in the toolbar.
- Right-click the object; then click the Script Editor button in the toolbar of the Properties Browser.
- Select an object; then choose Objects, (for example, field, graphic, or button) Properties to edit the script of the object.
- Hold down the Ctrl key and then double-click the object.
- Choose Objects, Page Properties, Script to edit the script of the page.
- Hold down the Ctrl key and then click the page icon in the status bar to edit the page script.
- Choose Objects, Background Properties, Script to edit the script of the background.
- Choose Objects, Book Properties, Script to edit the script of the book.
- Hold down the Alt key and then click the page icon in the status bar to edit the book script.

Although it is beyond the scope of this chapter to explain OpenScript syntax, this section explains certain features of OpenScript to enable you to understand the remaining sections of this chapter. Listing 6.1 provides a typical example of OpenScript coding.

Listing 6.1 Example of OpenScript Language

```
to handle buttonUp
 -- myCurrentNumber is current number of games played
 system myCurrentNumber
 if myCurrentNumber > 10 then
 request "Are you sure you want to continue?"
 put it into myAnswer
```

```
get moreGames(myAnswer)
 end if
end buttonUp
```

This example of scripting contains typical programming features. The first and last lines of the script bound the script, defining the handler, and provide the context under which it is executed. A *handler* is the part of a script that defines responses to a message. For example, a `buttonUp` handler responds to the message sent when the mouse button is released. For more information on handlers, see Chapter 13, "OpenScript Fundamentals."

The second line in the script is a comment. A *comment* is a nonexecutable line of code that the programmer inserts to make the code easier to follow or to remind herself later of her reasons for doing things in a particular way.

Standard programming practice is to indent lines of code that are contained within a structure, which is why all the lines within the `buttonUp` handler are indented. Then, when the `if` statement is introduced, all the text within that block is indented to the next indent level.

Note

The mouse event message `buttonClick` is introduced with MTB 4.0. `buttonClick` accomplishes the same action as `buttonUp` and is the preferred message to use in when writing scripts, unless the use of `buttonUp` serves some special purpose.

Enter your OpenScript statements in the Script editor. With the Script editor, commands are typed, cut, and pasted from other windows, pasted from the Script Recorder, or pasted from the Auto-Script Library of pre-written scripts. When you finish entering the script, save it. The script for any object is available to be edited at any time. As you save the script, it is checked by the compiler for syntax errors, and any errors found will be immediately brought to your attention.

Figure 6.5 provides an example of the Script editor. In this example, the OpenScript coding was created for a button named `next` that the user clicks to move to the next page of the application.

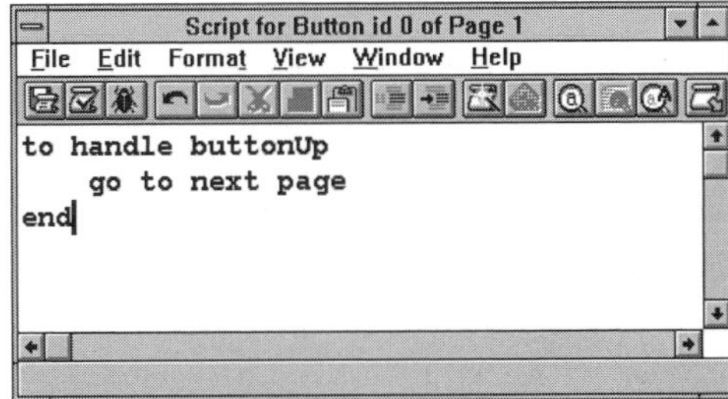
Script for Button id 0 of Page 1
File Edit Format View Window Help
to handle buttonUp
go to next page
end

Fig. 6.5

The Script editor window is used to enter OpenScript handlers.

The Script editor is much like a word processing program, in terms of the functions that it offers. The typical cut, copy, and paste functions are supported, as well as find and replace operations. Also, the window contains options for indenting text, commenting and uncommenting text, and checking syntax.

You can access most of the functions by clicking buttons in the Script editor toolbar. Table 6.1 describes these buttons.

Table 6.1 Script Editor Toolbar Buttons

Icon	Name	Action
	Update Script & Exit	Compiles, saves, and leaves current script
	Check Syntax	Checks current script's syntax
	Debug	Displays the debugger
	Undo	Reverses the effect of up to the last 10 actions
	Redo	Reverses the effect of the Undo command
	Cut	Places the selected item in the Windows Clipboard
	Copy	Copies the selected item to the Windows Clipboard
	Paste	Pastes the contents of the Windows Clipboard
	Comment	Formats the selection as a comment
	Indent	Indents a line or selection to the next tab stop
	Insert Auto-Script	Inserts predefined handlers
	Paste Recording	Pastes a recording from the script recorder
	Find	Finds specified text
	Find Next	Finds specified text again
	Replace	Replaces specified text
	Parent	Edits parent-object scripts

In addition to using the toolbar buttons, you can access the same features (and more) with menu commands, as described in Table 6.2.

Table 6.2 Script Editor Menus

Menu	Command	Action
File	Print	Displays the Print dialog box
	Debug	Displays the debugger
	Check Syntax	Checks the syntax of the script
	Update Script	Updates the script in the book
	Update & Save Book	Updates the script and saves the book
	Update Script & Exit	Updates the script and exits the editor
	Import File	Imports a text file into the script
	Export Script (Text)	Exports the script file as text
	Export Selection	Exports the currently selected script as text
	Exit	Exits the script and requests a save if changes are found
Edit	Undo	Undoes the latest changes (up to 10)
	Redo	Reverses the effect of the latest Undo operation
	Cut	Cuts the selected item to the Clipboard
	Copy	Copies the selected item to the Clipboard
	Paste	Pastes from the Clipboard at the current insertion-point position
	Clear	Clears the selected text
	Select All	Selects all the text in the script
	Find	Searches for a specified word or phrase
	Find Next	Repeats the preceding Find operation
	Replace	Replaces one specified text string with another
	Insert Auto-Script	Inserts a predefined script
	Paste Recording	Pastes the last recorded script into the window
Format	Comment	Turns the selected line(s) into comment lines (places two dashes at the beginning of the line)
	Uncomment	Removes the comment marks (double dashes) from the selected line(s)

(continues)

Table 6.2 Continued

Menu	Command	Action
	Indent	Indents the selected line(s)
	Outdent	Outdents (reverses an indent) of the selected line(s)
View	Toolbar	Shows or hides the toolbar
	Status Bar	Shows or hides the status bar
	Font	Displays a menu of fonts (limited choices)
Window	Parent	Displays a window for editing the script of the parent
Help	OpenScript Reference	Displays the OpenScript references help file
	Script Editor	Displays the Script editor help file

The usual process of creating a script includes these essential steps:

1. Create the object (book, page, background, or object) that you want to script.
2. Create the script in the script editor for the object, using a combination of cutting and pasting from other scripts, the Script recorder, the auto-script tool, and writing script from scratch.
3. Save the script.
4. Fix any syntax errors that occur.
5. Test the script.

Script Recorder

ToolBook provides a method for creating scripts that does not require much programming. This method is the *Script recorder.* When you need to automate a process and place it in a script, you can develop the code quickly by using the Script recorder.

To understand this process, consider a simple problem. Suppose that you have a red circle that you want to bounce off the bottom of the screen. The following steps walk you through the process of recording a "bounce" script and pasting it into a button:

1. Select the Ellipse tool from the Tool palette.
2. Drag out a circle.
3. Select the circle by pressing the space bar or clicking the Select tool in the Tool palette, and then selecting the circle.
4. Turn on the Color palette (if it is not already displayed) by clicking the Color Palette icon in the toolbar.

5. Click the Select Fill Color button on the Color palette and then click the red square in the Color palette to make the circle red.
6. Turn on the Script recorder by choosing Edit, Start Recording (or pressing F8).

> **Tip**
>
> To see whether the recorder is on, look at the Record button in the status bar. If the button is blank, the Script recorder is not recording, and no record is stored. If the button is dark gray, the Script recorder is recording. If the button is light gray, a recording has been stored.

7. Drag the circle a little bit of the way that you want it to bounce and then release the mouse button.
8. Drag the circle again and then release the mouse. Repeat the drag-release process as many times as you want, moving the ellipse a little each time. When it nears the bottom of the screen, begin dragging it upward (by drag-release) to define the bounce. Figure 6.6 shows movements you might choose for the exercise.

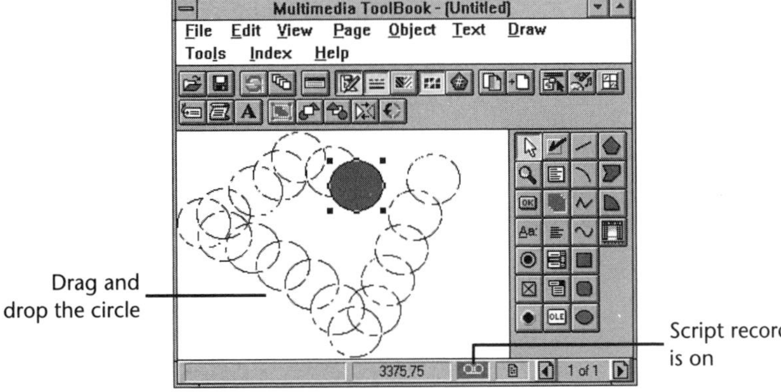

Fig. 6.6

Use the Script recorder to automate routine scripting tasks.

9. Choose Edit, Stop Recording, or press F8 to turn the recorder off.
10. The script is ready to paste. Create a button, selecting the Button tool from the toolbar and dragging out a button in the center of the screen.
11. Edit the script of the button; choose Object, Button Properties, Script, or hold down the Ctrl key and double-click the button to display the Script editor window.
12. Paste the recording by choosing Edit, Paste Recording. The resulting script looks something like that shown in figure 6.7.
13. Save the changes to the button script by choosing File, Update Script & Exit from the menu.

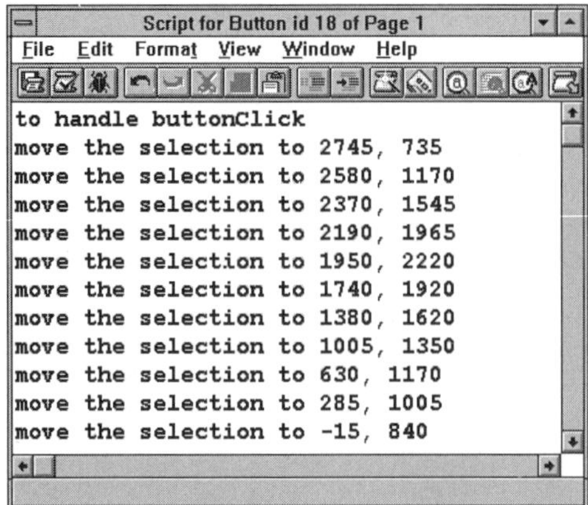
```
to handle buttonClick
move the selection to 2745, 735
move the selection to 2580, 1170
move the selection to 2370, 1545
move the selection to 2190, 1965
move the selection to 1950, 2220
move the selection to 1740, 1920
move the selection to 1380, 1620
move the selection to 1005, 1350
move the selection to 630, 1170
move the selection to 285, 1005
move the selection to -15, 840
```

Fig. 6.7

Paste recorded scripts in the Script editor.

14. Now test the script by switching to Reader mode (press F3) and clicking the button. Oh no! The button itself moves, but not the ellipse. The solution to this problem is to change the script slightly.
15. Switch back to Author mode (press F3 again), select the ellipse (click the Select tool and then the ellipse), and name it `redBall` (choose Object, Graphic Properties, and type the name **`redBall`**).
16. Edit the script of the button (click the Script button from the Graphic Properties dialog box), and insert the following line after the first line:

    ```
    select ellipse "redBall"
    ```
17. Move the button back to where you want it, switch back to Reader mode by pressing F3 yet again, and click the button. It works!

This simple example explains how to start using the Script recorder. This example, however, is not very useful, because an animation created this way may play too fast on some computers and too slow on others. A better way to create this sort of animation is to use the path-animation tool, which provides for timing using a timer internal to the computer. In general, you will find the Script recorder to be most useful in two contexts:

- When the process that you are attempting to automate involves printing (especially for record field reports)
- When you are attempting to do something but have no clue what commands to use

The Script recorder gives you a good starting point for writing the script.

Using Auto-Scripts

Auto-Script is a unique feature of ToolBook that can save you many hours of programming time. An auto-script is a predefined handler for a common action that you may want to perform. As you gain proficiency with ToolBook and develop your own routines for scripting, you can create auto-script files for them.

This section first describes the general actions that you perform to use auto-scripting and then addresses some advanced topics related to creating auto-scripts. You may not be able to use this section until you understand more about scripting itself and about the syntax and language of OpenScript; you may want to read the section briefly now and come back to it at a later date.

Inserting an Auto-Script

The auto-script icon is located in the script window's toolbar in the Script Editor window (refer to Table 6.1). Click this icon to display the Insert Auto-Script dialog box (see fig. 6.8).

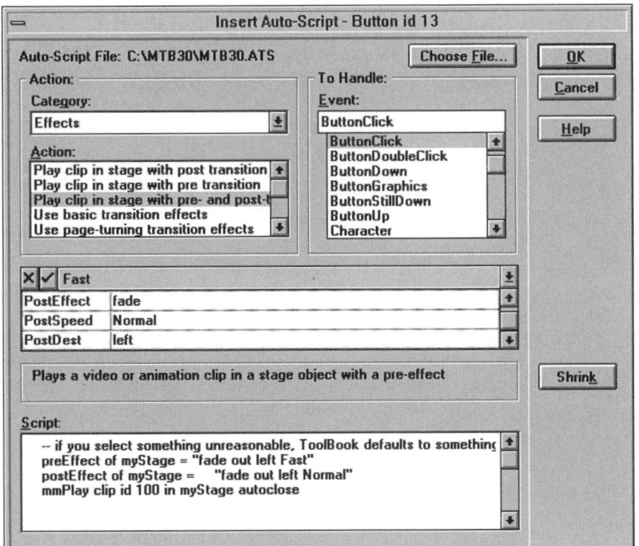

Fig. 6.8

The Insert Auto-Script dialog box provides preprogrammed scripts for a variety of common actions.

▶▶ See "Script Writing," p. 237

Auto-scripts are classified by general categories, such as animation, audio, clips, navigation, and resources. Within each category are a number of actions that you could perform. For example, in the category "multimedia" there is an entry for the action "Play a wave file." Many of the common programming tasks can be found in the auto-script entries.

For example, to create a button that will play a clip in a stage with a post-transition (transition effects as the clip stops), follow these steps:

1. Create a stage by choosing the stage tool and dragging out a stage.
2. Name the stage. Right-click the stage, choose Name from the pop-up menu, and type in a name such as **`PlayThis`**.
3. Add a clip to the clip editor to display in the stage. For this example, choose an `.AVI` file. To add a clip, select Object, Clips from the main menu. This will display the Clip Manager dialog box.
4. Select the New button, Video (File), and OK. Then select the name of the `.AVI` file that you want to display.
5. Give the clip a name (such as `myClip`) in the Clip Editor Clip field. Click the Close button to exit the Clip Editor.
6. Create a button by choosing the button tool and dragging out a button.
7. Name and caption the button. Select the button and choose Object, Button Properties.
8. Edit the script of the button; choose Object, Button Properties, Script, or hold down the Ctrl key and double-click the button to display the Script editor window.
9. From the Script Editor button bar, choose the auto-script icon. This will bring up the Insert Auto-Script dialog box (refer to fig. 6.8).
10. From the Category drop-down list, choose Effects.
11. From the Action choices, select Play clip in stage with post transition.
12. From the Event list, select the handler `buttonClick`.
13. Click the OK button to close the dialog box.
14. You will need to edit the script to specify the name of your stage and the name of your clip. Edit the following line:

    ```
    postEffect of myStage = "fade out left Normal"
    ```

    Replace `myStage` with `stage "PlayThis"` (or whatever name you gave the stage in step 1).

    Also, edit the following line:

    ```
    mmPlay clip id 100 in myStage autoclose
    ```

    Replace `id 100` with `"myClip"` (or whatever name you gave the clip in step 4) and `myStage` with `stage "PlayThis"` (or whatever name you gave the stage in step 1).

> **Note**
>
> It is important to include the quotes when you replace the name in step 12.

15. Save the changes to the button script by choosing File, Update Script & Exit from the menu.
16. Now, test the script by switching to Reader mode (press F3) and pressing the button.

Auto-Scripts Included with MTB

MTB ships with auto-script files defined for a variety of tasks. One included auto-script file is MTB40.ATS. The scripts included in the MTB40.ATS file include common actions for dealing with the following:

- Animation—to start an animation
- Clips—to play clips, play clips in stages with transitions, stop all clips, restart a clip, get the time format for a clip
- Devices—to find capability of the timer device, find all supported media
- Navigation—to go to next page, use page-turning transition effects

Another included auto-script file is ADVANCED.ATS. The scripts in this file perform some more advanced actions related to the following:

- Windows—to bring a ToolBook window to the front
- Clips—to build and play a wave clip, continuously play a clip, play an .AVI file as a clip
- Text and data—to convert textlines to a list, create a shuffled array, display 1D or 2D array values, find text in a list box, enable overwrite in a field, sort an array
- System information—to get the colors in the display, get the current version of DOS, get the resolution of the printer
- Miscellaneous—to compact a ToolBook file, exit and restart Windows, open a file using Common Open Dialog, resize a polypoint object

Another supplied auto-script file is the UTILS.ATS. The scripts in this file include basic utility actions related to the following:

- Dates—to determine if a year is a leap year, get the day from the date, get the days in a month
- Path and drive—to get free disk space on a drive, get the current drive letter, get the current path, search the path for a file
- Text—to put selected text into command window, remove trailing spaces from a string, clear the selected text, deselect a line of text

The DBASE.ATS contains scripts that are used to interface with dBase III data files. These actions include creating a dBase index, creating a dBase file, packing records, searching for a string, getting the total record count, and deleting a dBase field.

The auto-script file PARADOX.ATS provides scripts that encompass some of the basic programming techniques that you need to interface with Paradox data files. The entries include actions such as creating a Paradox table, navigating to a record, setting the value of a field, updating records, and adding a key.

Creating Your Own Auto-Script Files

The format for an auto-script file is well defined and easy to create. You can create an ATS file for any actions that you perform. ATS files are written in ASCII (text) format. You can create or edit these files in any word processor (be sure to save the files as text only), or read them into and export them from a field in ToolBook.

> **Caution**
>
> The format of an ATS file consists of several entries that ToolBook parses out when you invoke the auto-script tool. Be careful not to make errors; no debugging tools are available for auto-scripts.

You can easily create an auto-script file or modify one that Asymetrix provides. To do so, you need to understand how these files are structured. Auto-script files have two basic formats: scripts with arguments and without arguments. If your script has no arguments, use the following format:

```
SCRIPT "<short description of script>"
BEHAVIOR "<short description of behavior>"
CATEGORY <category>
{
<the OpenScript code lines>
}
```

Listing 6.2 is in the `ADVANCED.ATS` file.

Listing 6.2 Example of an Auto-Script Entry with No Arguments

```
SCRIPT "Insert a textline"
BEHAVIOR "Use if you need to insert a single line and maintain the
 field's sorted order."
CATEGORY Text
{
to get insertLine txt,newLine
 if txt is null
 return newLine
 end
 set start to 1 — first textline
 set tlc to textlinecount(txt)
 set ending to tlc — last textline
 local insertSpot
 while start <= ending
 set midPoint to (start+ending) div 2
 set middleLine to textline midPoint of txt
 conditions
 when newLine < middleLine as text
 -- start looking at values less than current midPoint
 set ending to midPoint-1
 set insertSpot to midPoint
 when newLine > middleLine as text
 -- start looking at values greater than current midPoint
```

```
 set start to midPoint+1
 set insertSpot to midPoint+1
 else
 -- the item already exists
 set insertSpot to midPoint
 break while
 end
 end
 if insertSpot > tlc
 put newLine before textline insertSpot of txt
 else
 put newLine&crlf before textline insertSpot of txt
 end
 return txt
end
}
```

If arguments are associated with the script, use the following format instead:

```
ACTION "<short description of script>"
BEHAVIOR "<short description of behavior>"
CATEGORY <category>
ARG <arginfo (see below)>
ARG <arginfo (see below)>
... (repeat for each argument)
ARG <arginfo (see below)>
{
<the OpenScript code lines>
}
```

The `ARG` lines shown previously take one of the following forms:

- `ARG <argument name> is "<value>" help <"help text">`—(when the argument has only one value)
- `ARG <argument name> oneOf "<list of choices>" is "<value>" help <"help text">`—(when the argument has multiple values)
- `ARG <argument name> FILE "<file list>" is "<default file>" help "<help text>"`—(when the argument contains specific file names)

Listings 6.3 and 6.4 provide examples of types of arguments in the context of the script.

Listing 6.3 Example of an Auto-Script Entry with Arguments

```
ACTION "Start an animation - complete"
BEHAVIOR "Starts an already defined animation. The script would
go in the animated object."
CATEGORIES Animation
ARG animation oneOf "1,2,3,4,5,6" is "1" help "Choose the animation
to play that you have already defined."
```

(continues)

Listing 6.3 Continued

```
ARG notifyObj is "self" help "Determine who will be notified when
the animation terminates. Leave blank for no notification."
ARG wait oneOf "TRUE,FALSE" is "FALSE" help "Set wait to true to
prevent the user from any action while the animation is going on."
{
 send playAnimation $$animation, $$notifyObj, $$wait
}
```

Listing 6.4 Example of an Auto-Script Entry with File Argument

```
ACTION "Image Command - Open"
BEHAVIOR "Initializes the displayer and associates the file with
 the alias"
CATEGORIES Images
ARG myBitmap FILE "Bitmap Files(*.BMP),*.bmp,(*.DIB),*.dib" is
"Cars.bmp" help "Find the bitmap file to display."
ARG alias is "myAlias" help "The alias you want associated with this
file. Keep your aliases consistent!"
ARG style oneOf "overlapped,popup,child" is "overlapped" help "Choose
the style of the window."
{
 get imageCommand("open $$myBitmap alias $$alias style $$style")
}
```

Perhaps the easiest means of becoming comfortable with creating your own ATS files is to examine the files provided by Asymetrix. These can be edited with any word processor—just remember *not* to save changes unless you are certain about what you are doing.

Using Shared Scripts

A feature new to ToolBook 4.0 is called *shared scripts*. The shared scripts feature of MTB allows you to create a single script that can be accessed by more than one object. To better understand shared scripts, you should first understand how the Object Hierarchy in ToolBook operates.

When a message is generated, it is passed along a hierarchy until a handler for the message is found. For example, if you create a button and then switch to Reader mode and click the button, ToolBook generates a `buttonDown` message. If the button itself has a `buttonDown` handler (which would happen only if you placed it there), then the message would be interpreted and stop there. If there was no `buttonDown` handler in the button, the message would get passed next to the group the button was in (if any). If there was no handler there, it would get passed to the page, and so on until a handler was located. If no handler was located, the message would get discarded (in the case of system generated messages) or generate an error (in the case of user-generated messages). The order of the hierarchy in ToolBook is as follows:

- object (such as button, graphic object, field)
- group
- background
- page
- book
- system book
- ToolBook system

When you create handlers, you normally place them at the level in the hierarchy in which they are needed. For example, if you were writing an application that interfaced with a database file and had a page in which the user could click a button and look up the name of a customer, then the handler would be placed in the button. If, on the other hand, the user might either click a button or click a "name" column in a field, you might place the handler at the page level, so it could be easily accessed by the handlers in the button or field. If at a later time, you expanded the interface, and added a data entry page, you might need the handler in more than one page, so you would move it up to the book script level. And if you had multiple books using the same routine, you would move it to the system book level.

There are cases in your scripting in which placing a handler high in the hierarchy is inconvenient. For example, you may want to handle a `buttonClick` message for certain hotwords that are scattered throughout the book. The problem is that you do not want to place the same handler in each of the objects. Not only does this waste space, but if you want to make changes in the script, you must edit it for each of the hotwords. However, if you place the handler at a high level, you will need to explicitly check the target (the object clicked) before executing the statements in the handler. This can cause problems if the target objects get changed (for example, renamed). Shared scripts are a solution to these dilemmas.

A shared script is stored as a resource of the book. When a shared script is run, it is as though it is in the script of the object that is sharing it. This permits you to write one handler and apply it to any object in the book. When you need to make changes in the handler, you can make the changes in one location and have them applied globally to any object that shares the script. In shared scripts, the keywords `self`, `this`, `my` apply to the object itself (the object which calls the shared script). The keyword `parent`, when used in a shared script, refers to the parent of the object (the group or page.) To forward a message from a shared script to the parent, you must forward it to the parent, like in the following:

```
to handle buttonClick
   forward to parent
end
```

Caution

Do not use the `forward` keyword in a shared script, use `forward to parent` instead. Using `forward` sends the message as though it had come from the object itself, resulting in an infinite loop.

Tip

If you get into an infinite loop in ToolBook, press down both shift keys simultaneously. This will break out of the loop.

Another difference between shared scripts and regular scripts is that when you use the `send` message, the message is first processed in the object, and then passed to the shared script.

Tip

You can create shared script that has default behaviors for different actions, and then script objects themselves determine the specific application of the action.

An example of this concept is if you have a shared script that presents a dialog for double-button click, you could let the shared script define the default dialog and script specific objects so that they make changes in the dialog that are appropriate for the object. Suppose the application is a children's game where the child can attach sounds to items on a page. The default dialog (as scripted in Listing 6.5) gives the child the choices of recording a sound or canceling.

Listing 6.5 Shared Script Attaching a Sound to an Object With a *buttonDoubleClick*

```
--shared script
to handle buttonDoubleClick loc
   send soundAttach
end buttonDoubleClick
to handle soundAttach
   request "Record Sound?" with "Yes" or "Cancel"
   if it is not "Cancel" then
      --sound recording commands here
   end if
end
```

However, when the child clicks a button on the page, you do not want them to be able to record sounds for the button, but maybe allow them to move the button to a new location.

This shared script would be shared by all of the objects on the page. The graphic items would have no additional script, but the buttons would contain this script in Listing 6.6.

Listing 6.6 Overriding a Shared Script in a Button Script

```
to handle soundAttach
   request "Move this button?" with "Yes" or "Cancel"
   if it is not "Cancel" then
      -- commands to move button
   end if
end
```

To create a shared script, follow these steps:

1. Choose Object, Resources from the main menu.
2. Select sharedscript from the Available Resources drop-down list.
3. Click the New button. The Script editor will be displayed.
4. Type your script in the Script editor.
5. Select Update Script & Exit from the File menu of the Script editor.
6. In the Resource Manager dialog box, select the script and type in a name.
7. Click the Close button.

To attach this script to an object, follow these steps:

1. Right-click the object and select Shared Script from the pop-up menu.
2. Select the desired shared script in the Choose Shared Script dialog box.
3. Click the OK button.

Using the Script Library

The script library is an application that Asymetrix ships with ToolBook. This tool is useful when you create scripts, because it includes samples of a wide variety of scripts. Like the auto-script tool, the script library can save you hours of programming effort. The examples that are included in the script library are as follows:

- Add number of days to date
- Auto-scroll field
- Binary insertion of textline
- Bring ToolBook window to front
- Bring up command window
- ButtonStillDown page navigation
- Changing the behavior of BACK
- Check for alpha non-numeric data

- Check for state abbreviation
- Controlling the volume of clips
- Convert textlines to list
- Converting to binary, hex, octal
- Create full-text search index
- Disabling task switching
- Display 2D array values
- Dragging objects
- Exit and restart Windows
- Get current path setting
- Get day of week from date
- Get free space on a drive
- Get number of days in a month
- Get path of current book
- Initialize Excel conversation
- Insert/Overwrite field
- isLeapYear( )
- itemOffset( )
- Limit length of entry string
- Making mmSource-path book relative
- Perform full-text search
- Play clip in a loop
- Play clip on enterPage
- Playing MIDI directly
- Playing random sounds
- Recording wave files from CD
- Remove given character from string
- Remove trailing spaces
- Search and replace in a string
- Search path for file
- Show all objects of page
- Sorting a 1D array
- Sorting a 2D array
- Spin controls
- Using a RECT structure
- Using system sounds
- Using Windows pointers

> **Tip**
>
> You can run a second instance (copy) of ToolBook by choosing File, Run from the main menu. Then you can cut and paste data between the two open applications.

The application provides not only the scripts, but also examples of how to use the scripts. To use the OpenScript library, open it in ToolBook—it should be found in the `MTB40\SAMPLES` subdirectory and named `LIBRARY.TBK`. Click a topic that you want to explore. Figure 6.9 shows an example of one of the pages.

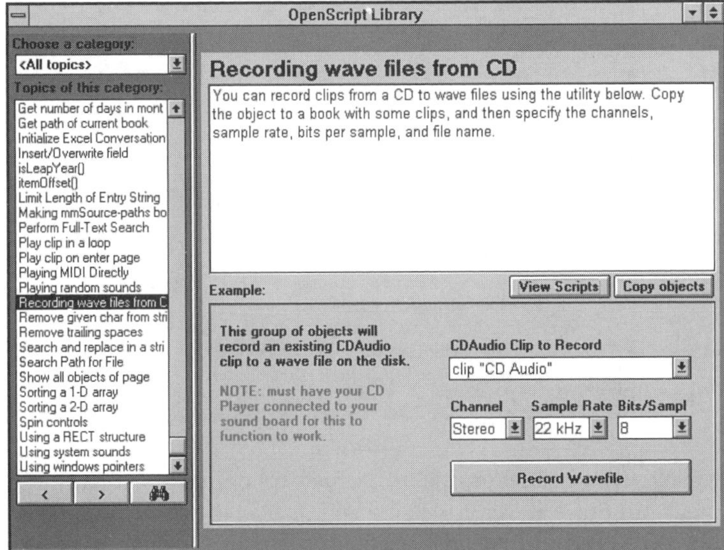

Fig. 6.9

The OpenScript library.

Each example in the OpenScript library explains the uses for the example in the explanation field at the top of the page. Below this explanation field are (usually) examples of the implementation. You can click the View Scripts button to see a list of all the scripts for the objects. You can copy and paste these scripts into your own objects. Click the Copy objects button to copy the selected objects to the Clipboard. Then you can switch to your application and paste the objects.

The OpenScript library is a good place to explore some of the more advanced scripting techniques. Beginning users may find the more complex and longer examples difficult to decipher. Don't disappear! Often, you can cut and paste the objects and use them as they are supplied. If you need to make changes, you can explore the script and make minor changes, observing how this effects the features of the example. And, later, when you have gained more experience in programming in OpenScript, these examples will become even easier to understand.

The ToolBook Debugger

The ToolBook Debugger window is the window in which you perform OpenScript code debugging (see fig. 6.10). In any programming environment, it is unusual for complex codes to run perfectly the first time. Debuggers were invented to aid programmers in perfecting their code.

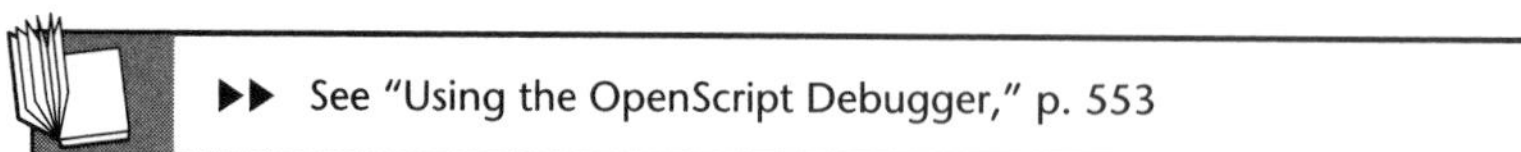
▸▸ See "Using the OpenScript Debugger," p. 553

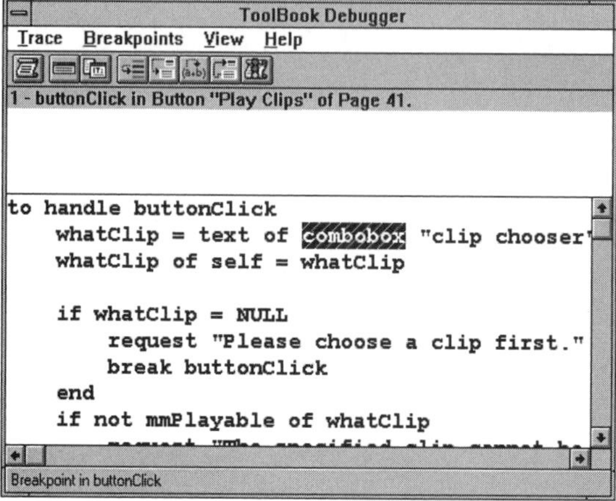

Fig. 6.10

The ToolBook Debugger window provides feedback on scripting errors.

The ToolBook debugger allows you to set *breakpoints*, which are points at which the code is instructed to break out of whatever it is doing and display the debugging tools. Debugging tools permit you to examine the values of variables, step through the script one line at a time, trace a subroutine call, and reset variables to see the effect on the result of the script.

Typical use of the debugger involves setting breakpoints and then examining the value of variables, often stepping through the lines of the script. Figure 6.11 shows the Variables window.

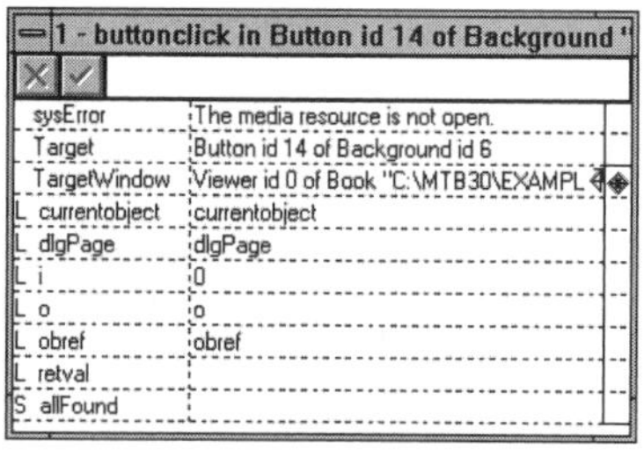

1 - buttonclick in Button id 14 of Background "

	Variable	Value
	sysError	The media resource is not open.
	Target	Button id 14 of Background id 6
	TargetWindow	Viewer id 0 of Book "C:\MTB30\EXAMPL
L	currentobject	currentobject
L	dlgPage	dlgPage
L	i	0
L	o	o
L	obref	obref
L	retval	
S	allFound	

Fig. 6.11

The Debugger Variables window.

In this Debugger Variables window, the first three lines contain selected system variables. Lines preceded by *L* are local variables; lines preceded by *S* are system variables.

From Here...

This chapter explored the mechanics of scripting, introducing the tools and useful sources for scripts. In addition to the sources listed in this chapter, you will want to explore more script examples in on-line resources (the Internet, CompuServe, and so on), as well as the example scripts that are shipped with ToolBook. Refer to the following chapters for additional information on the topics covered in the chapter:

- Chapter 13, "OpenScript Fundamentals," tells you more about OpenScript programming.
- Chapter 15, "Understanding Variables, Values, and Text," helps you make sense of variables.
- Chapter 24, "Debugging Tools and Techniques," discusses how to use the Debugger.

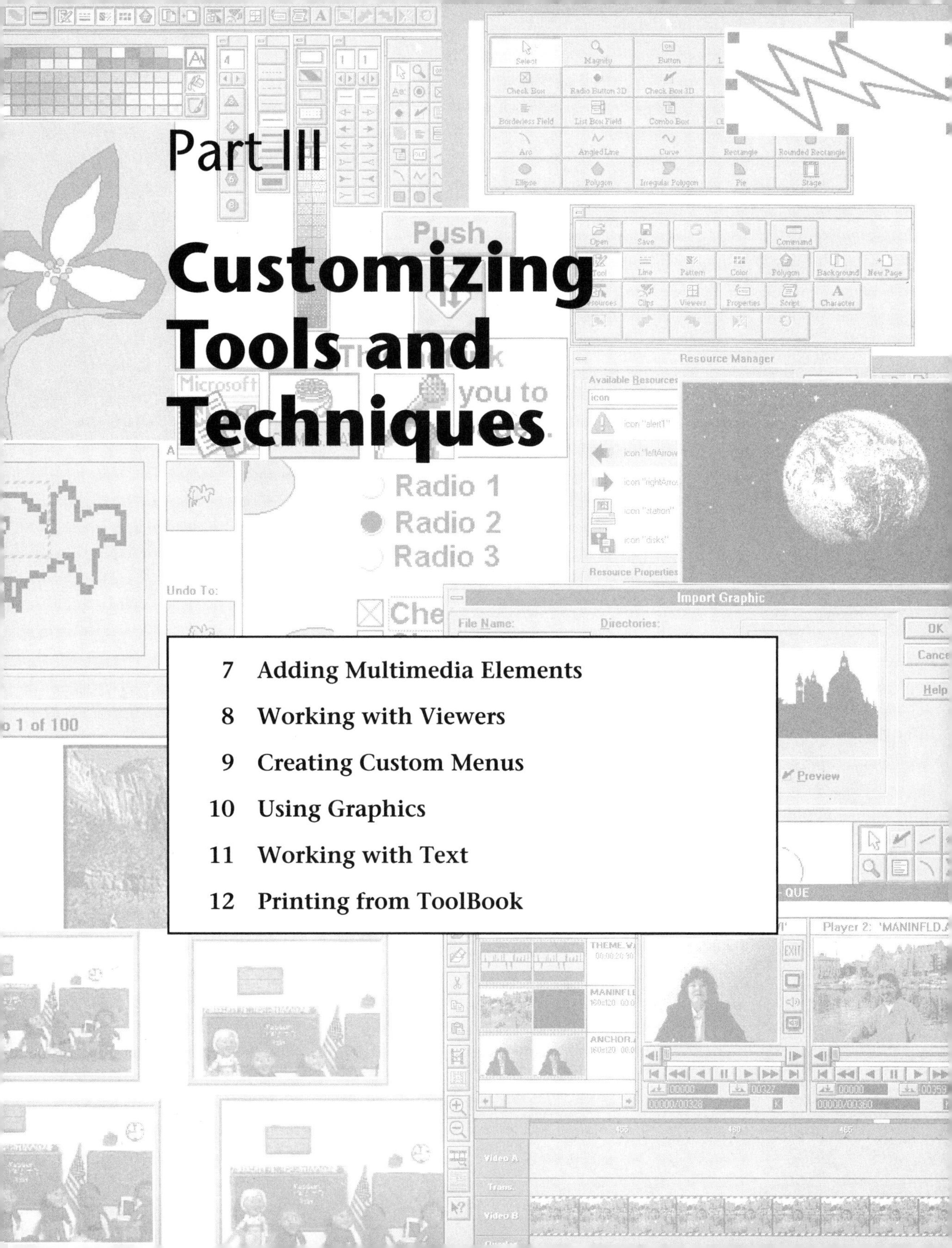

Part III

Customizing Tools and Techniques

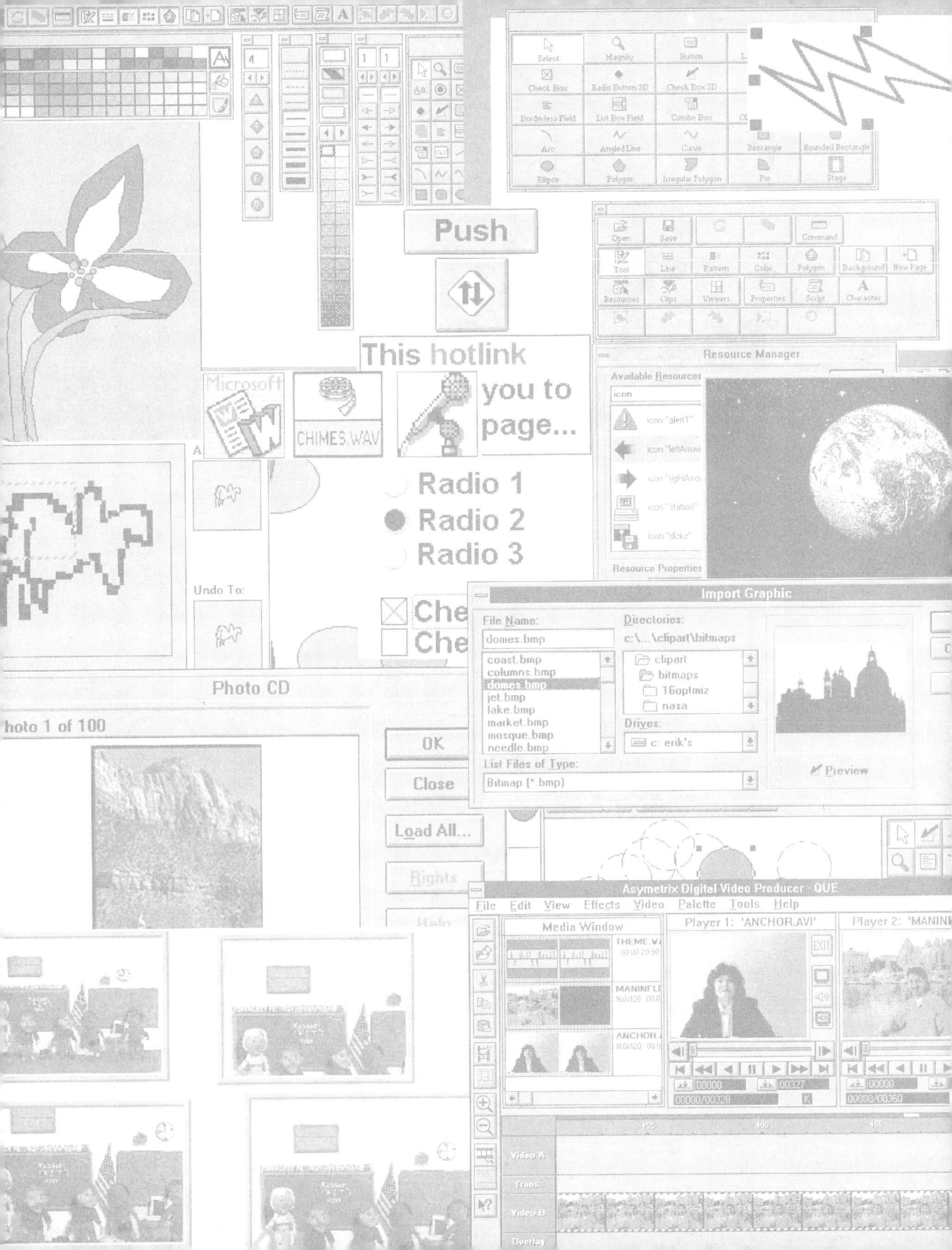

CHAPTER 7

Adding Multimedia Elements

This chapter discusses how you can add multimedia elements to your MTB applications. The multimedia elements discussed in this chapter include the following:

- Stages, which can be used to display animation clips, still pictures of all types, digital video clips, and video overlay.
- Hotwords, which can be used to add hyperlinking capabilities to fields or to pop-up text, video, or other elements.
- Object linking and embedding (OLE), which can be used to display elements from other programs within ToolBook applications.

Adding a Stage

Stages are used to add visual elements to the page, such as a video clip, animation, still image, or video overlay. ToolBook offers many other means of displaying these items; you can, for example, paste a still graphic directly into the page or background. The benefit of using stages, however, is that the properties you most likely will want to access are built into the stage objects. To change the way a picture is displayed (clipped or stretched), you simply change the value of one property.

You can use stages effectively to do the following things:

- Provide consistency in the application by displaying clips in the same format on each page
- Display a series of clips
- Display a series of images, using transition effects between them
- Display images that the user has added to the application (a slide-show application, for example)

Creating Stages

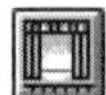

To create a stage, click the Stage tool; then drag the stage out until it is the size that you want. You can move and resize a stage, just as you can other objects. The size of the area for the image is displayed in the center of the stage (see fig. 7.1).

Fig. 7.1

The Stage tool is an enhancement introduced in MTB 4.0.

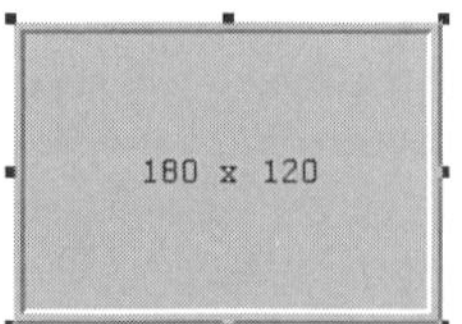

The size of a stage should be determined by the image that you want to display. Although you can stretch an image to fill an area larger than the stage (a digital video image, for example), this practice generally is not a good idea. Images that are stretched tend to lose their aspect ratio. This means they lose the resolution and clarity of their original size.

Setting Properties

To change the properties of a stage, select the stage and then choose Object, Stage Properties. You can set four classes of properties for stages: frame, display, pre-effect, and post-effect. As you can for all objects in ToolBook, you can set the properties for a stage by using the Stage Properties dialog box or through OpenScript commands. The following section discusses the dialog-box options; the OpenScript variables are discussed later in this chapter.

Frame Properties. Choosing Object, Stage Properties displays the Stage Properties dialog box (see fig. 7.2). You use the first tab of the dialog box, Frame, to specify the appearance of the frame for the stage.

Fig. 7.2

Adjust a stage's bevel in the Frame tab of the Stage Properties dialog box.

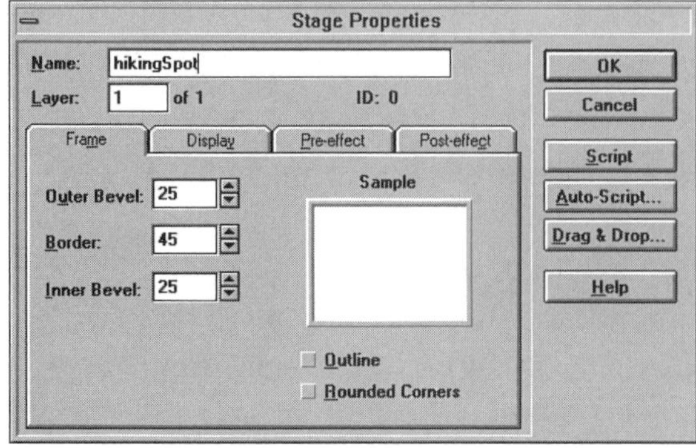

The frame consists of three parts: the outer bevel, the border, and the inner bevel. The *stage area*—the area inside the frame—is where image clips are displayed. The Frame tab of the Stage Properties dialog box allows you to set the width, in pixels, of each part of the frame. Figure 7.3 shows a stage with the inner and outer bevels set to 50 and the border set to 150. In general, setting the inner and outer bevels to the same value is best.

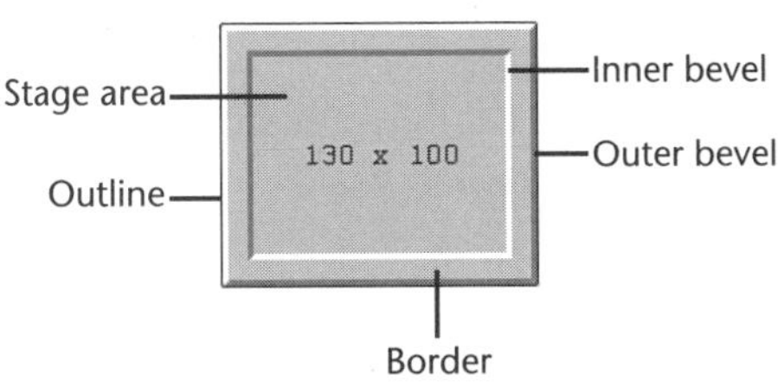

Fig. 7.3

Elements of a frame.

The Outline checkbox determines whether the frame has an outline (the thin line that surrounds the frame). The Rounded Corners checkbox specifies square or slightly rounded corners for the frame. The effects of changing the outline, corner, bevel, and border options appear in the Sample area of the dialog box.

Display Properties. The Display tab of the Stage Properties dialog box determines how the image is displayed within the stage (see fig. 7.4). If the Visible at Reader Level box is checked, the stage is visible at Reader level. Otherwise, the stage is not visible, but it still is an active area that can be used to display image clips.

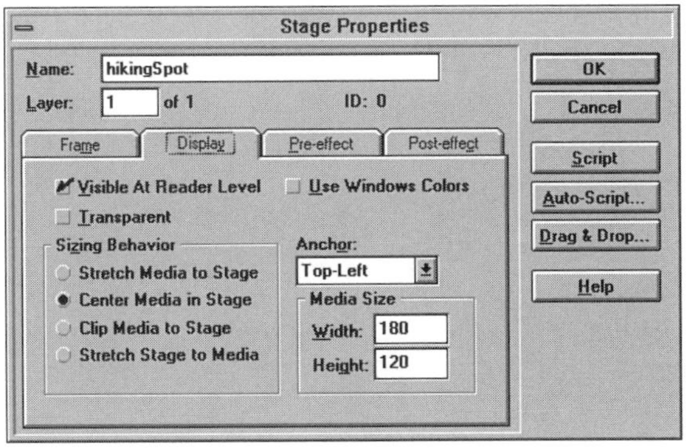

Fig. 7.4

Options under the Display tab control how a stage is presented on-screen.

When the Transparent box is checked, the stage becomes transparent—that is, any object behind the stage is visible. This option can provide interesting effects when the frame is placed on top of an image in the background.

> **Note**
>
> The image in a stage is *always* on top of any other objects on the page.

The Use Windows Colors checkbox indicates whether you want the stage to use the colors that you selected in the Windows Control Panel. In general, select this checkbox if you want the user to be able to control the appearance of the object. Don't check the checkbox if you want to be certain that the frame displays in exactly the colors that you specified.

The Sizing Behavior options indicate how the image will be sized within the frame. If the image and the frame are exactly the same size, these options have no effect. But if your image and stage are different sizes, you need to decide how you want to display the image.

Figure 7.5 shows an image that is slightly larger than the frame.

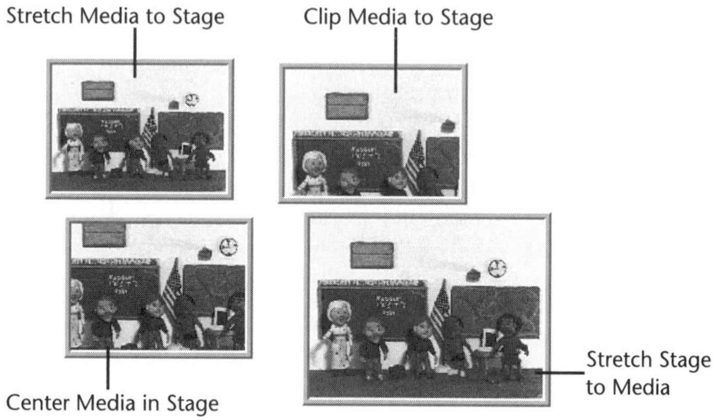

Fig. 7.5

Effects of changes in the sizing of stages.

Four settings are provided in the Sizing Behavior combo box in the Display tab of the Stage Properties dialog box. They are as follows:

- *Stretch Media to Stage*—The image is stretched or compressed to fit the proportions of the stage.
- *Center Media in Stage*—The image is centered and maintains its original size, however the user only sees as much of the image as the size of the stage will allow.
- *Clip Media to Stage*—The image is anchored at the top-left corner of the stage, and the image was clipped (in this case, on the right and the bottom).
- *Stretch Stage to Media*—By default, the stage stretches at the right and bottom edges, moving the frame so that the entire image can be displayed.

The options for anchoring the image within the stage are Center, Top-Left, Bottom-Left, Top-Right, and Bottom-Right.

The Media Size settings are the same as the stage-area size that you specified when you drew the stage. You can change these settings by typing new values. Units are pixels.

Pre-Effect and Post-Effect Properties. The Pre-effect and Post-effect tabs affect the way that transition effects are applied to images displayed in a stage (see fig. 7.6). You can use a variety of effects, including blind, dissolve, drip, fade, iris, push, puzzle, rain, slide, spiral, split, tear, turnPage, wipe, and zoom. These effects are applied when the image is displayed (pre-effect) and when the image is removed (post-effect).

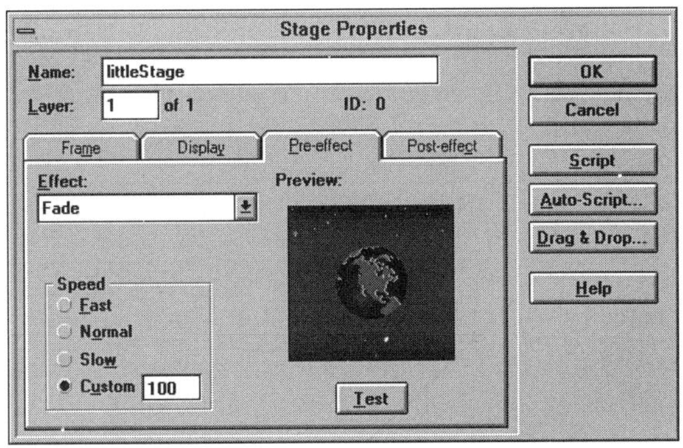

Fig. 7.6

Select an effect in the Pre-effect tab of the Stage Properties dialog box.

To use the effects, follow these steps:

1. Select the stage to which you want to apply the effect.
2. Choose Object, Stage Properties. The Stage Properties dialog box appears.
3. Click the Pre-effect or Post-effect tab.
4. From the Effect drop-down list, select the desired effect.
5. To see an example of an effect before applying it to your stage, click the Test button just below the Pre/Post-effect Preview window.
6. Choose the speed for the effect. Your choices are Fast, Normal, Slow, and Custom (measured in milliseconds).

You have created the stage, specified its frame and display formats, and indicated the pre-effect and post-effects that you want to use for the stage. Now you are ready to script the stage so that it is active.

OpenScript Variables for Stages. After you create the stage, you add the script that activates it. The means of activating the script depend on what you want to display, the manner in which you want to display it, and the effect that you want to achieve. Because this book has not yet discussed scripting formally, this section discusses the Media Widgets (prescripted media objects that use stages) that are provided with Multimedia ToolBook versions 3.0a and later. Later, the book provides more advanced scripting examples that may be most useful to you after you gain more experience in scripting.

> **Note**
>
> If you are currently using MTB 3.0, you can download the MTB 3.0a upgrade for free from the Asymetrix BBS. You need this version of the program to follow the examples in this section.

The CD-ROM included with this book contains all the examples from this section in the file named `STAGES.TBK`. This sample ToolBook application provides some of the most common uses for stages that you can adapt in your own programming efforts.

Using a Media Widget To Play a Video Clip in a Stage. To play a video clip in a stage, follow these steps:

◀◀ See "The Clip Manager," p. 93

1. Add the video clip that you want to use to the Clip Manager.
2. Choose Tools, Media, Media Widgets. The Media Widgets dialog box appears (see fig. 7.7).

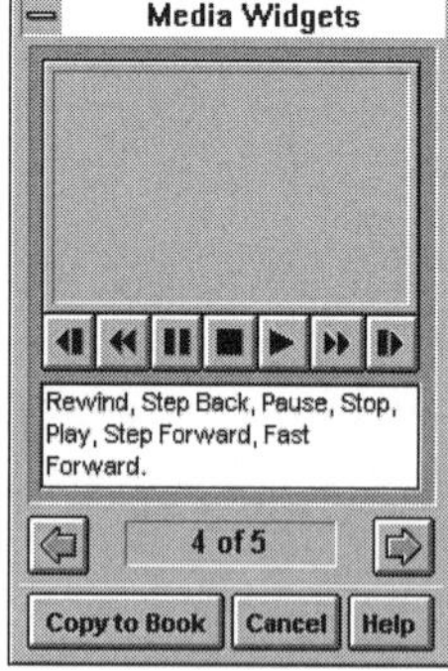

Fig. 7.7

Use media widgets to add a predefined stage with controls to a page.

> **Note**
>
> At this writing, not all the media widgets work properly. Don't let this problem stop you from using these handy widgets; just choose one that does not generate error messages.

3. Click the right and left arrow buttons to move through the selections. When you identify the widget that you want to use, click the Copy to Book button. The Media Widgets Properties dialog box appears (see fig. 7.8).
4. Click the Choose button to select the clip that you want to display in the stage.
5. Choose the properties you want for the `EnterPage` event. These properties are triggered whenever the user navigates to the effected page (see Table 7.1 for more information).

6. To set the stage properties, click the Stage button.
7. Click the Done button. You now have a fully functional, scripted media object.

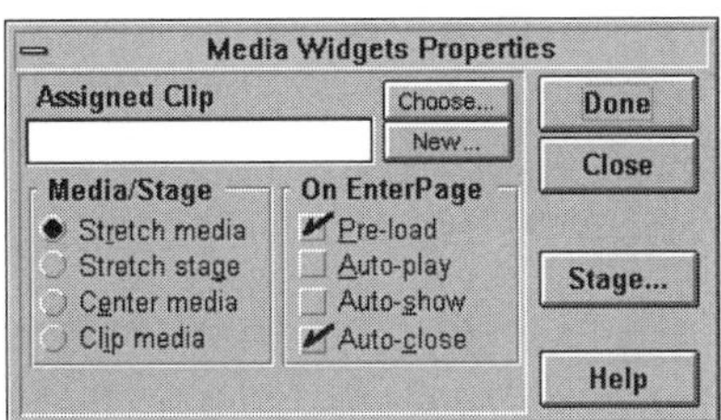

Fig. 7.8

Use this dialog box to set media widgets' properties.

Displaying a Still Graphic in a Stage. At many times, you will want to use stages to display still graphics. To create such a stage, follow these steps:

1. Add the graphic item that you want to use to the Clip Manager. Name the clip `pict1`.

◄◄ See "The Clip Manager," p. 93

2. Create a stage with the frame, display, pre-effects, and post-effects that you want to use, as described in the "Creating Stages" section of this chapter. Name the stage `showPicture` (or whatever you want, keeping track of the name for subsequent steps).
3. Create a button to hold the script for activating the stage by using the button tool and dragging out a button near the stage.
4. Select the button, and using the menu items Object, Button Properties, caption it `show picture`. Click the script button to activate the script editor.
5. Type the following script for the button:

```
to handle buttonUp
 mmPlay clip "pict1" in stage "showPicture"
end buttonUp
```

6. Save the script by choosing File, Update Script & Exit.
7. Test the script by pressing F3 to switch to Reader mode.

Figure 7.9 shows the completed stage and button.

Fig. 7.9

Use a stage to display a still image.

Displaying Video, Animation, Videotape, and PhotoCD Images in a Stage. You can use the same general technique to display other types of visual media in a stage, including video files, AutoDesk or Director animation files, videodisc clips, videotape clips, and PhotoCD images. Simply add the clip to the Clip Manager and reference the appropriate name for the clip in the script listed in step 4 of the previous example.

When you use stages, the scripting technique that you use depends on the application. You need to consider the following issues:

- Is the display of the clip controlled by the program or the user?

  If the visual element is meant to be displayed in a certain way, you want to retain control. In this case, you probably should place the script for displaying the image in the `enterPage` handler, so that the script executes as the user enters the page. If the display is controlled by the user, you will want to place the script in a button or other clickable object, like the button in the preceding example or in a combo box (refer to fig. 7.9).

- Will the user be able to display a limited number of specified images, or will the user be able to add images to the application?

  If the images are already specified, you can add them to the Clip Manager and include them in the application. If, on the other hand, you want to allow the user to add visual media (to create a slide show, for example), you need to use a more general technique.

- Does the image need to be preloaded?

  If you plan to display an image that has been preloaded into the book, stages are not the best choice, because they are always loaded when the stage is activated. This decision is important, because preloading the images requires more up-front time (at the time the book is opened, for example) but allows you to display images much quicker than loading them on-the-fly (as in stages).

  In many cases, preloading an image is preferable. For example, there are times that accessing an image will pause other processes that are occurring; in the case that you are playing a wave file from the disk, the delay can be unacceptable, resulting in a long "skip" in the sound. Another example is when the user needs to be able to see an image quickly, such as in a game application. In these cases, loading the image into a page at the time the book is opened or during a time that the delay can be disguised as a "feature" is preferable.

Loading an Image into a Stage at Runtime. If you are creating an application in which you want to allow the user to select an image from their system to be displayed, you can use the technique described in this section. Figure 7.10 displays a stage and a button that were created for just this purpose.

The stage was created, as described in the previous sections. Next, a button was created and the script provided in Listing 7.1 was typed into the button script.

Fig. 7.10

Use a single stage to display successive clips.

Listing 7.1 *buttonUp* Script for Adding and Displaying a Clip

```
to handle buttonUp
 -- link the DLL needed for standard file access
 linkDLL "TB30DLG.DLL"
 STRING getFileListDlg(STRING,STRING,STRING,STRING,INT)
 end linkDLL
 -- create the filter for the file types you are supporting
 filterList = "Bitmaps(*.bmp),*.bmp"
 -- send the standard file dialog box for requesting file names
 fileList = getFileListDlg("Which image file to display?", \
 null,null,filterList,1)
 -- the user pressed "cancel"
 if fileList is null
 request "User Canceled."
 else
 -- set the cursor to a wait icon
 syscursor = 4
 -- ignore error messages if the clip has not been added yet
 sysSuspend = false
 -- close the clip (just in case it is open)
 mmClose clip "playThis"
 -- remove the clip (just in case it has been added)
 remove resource clip "playThis"
 -- get the name that they selected
 pop fileList into fName
 if fileList is not null then
 -- they selected more than one file. In this example, we
 -- will ignore all but the first file chosen
 put "\" after fName
 pop fileList after fName
 end if
 -- add the clip to the clip manager
 new clip from fName
 -- name the clip
 name of It = "playThis"
 -- now, play it
 mmPlay clip "playThis" in stage "showThis"
 -- give the user their cursor back again
 syscursor = 1
 end if
end
```

If this listing is beyond your current level of understanding, don't despair! Copy the button from the page it is stored on (in STAGES.TBK) and paste it into your application. You can begin making changes when you are ready and you will learn to read this type of listing with practice. This example is well commented, providing a reference for each section. And, don't forget that you can position the cursor over an unfamiliar term and press the F1 key for instant help on the keyword.

The first line is the handler, telling ToolBook when to execute this script; in this example, using buttonUp, the script is executed when the user releases the mouse button. The next few lines link in the Dynamic Link Library (DLL) call that is used to bring up the standard Windows file dialog. You can specify the type of file that the user can add by choosing the appropriate filters in the next line. Another example is:

```
filterList = "Autodesk animations (*.flc),*.flc", "Video files
    (*.avi),*.avi"
```

The call to getFileListDLG() is where the linked file dialog is called for display. This is followed by an if/then block, sending the message User Canceled if the user presses cancel rather than selecting a file. This section of the code could be used to check for other conditions that might be reported to the user.

If the user has selected a file or files, the else part of the statement is executed. (This section begins with the closing of an open clip, which will be discussed later.) There are two possibilities: the user selected one file, or the user selected more than one file. To keep this example simple, when the user selects more than one file, the first file is used in the display and the other choices are ignored. The full path name of the file is loaded into the variable fName, which is then loaded into a clip in the following line:

```
new clip from fName
```

It is then named and played in the stage, and the user is given his/her cursor back. After the script has run once, the clip named playThis will be part of the Clip Manager, and will have been left in an open state. This means that executing the script a second time would result in another clip named playThis being created and opened. For this reason, the lines at the beginning of the block were added to close and remove the clip. First, sysSuspend is turned off, suppressing any error messages that would appear the first time the script is executed (because at that point there would be no clip to close and remove). Next, the clip is closed using the mmClose command. Finally, the clip is removed from the Clip Manager using the remove resource command.

This code listing provides you with some examples of how to use OpenScript commands for playing clips in stages. Other useful stage properties that you can use in your codes are listed in Table 7.1.

Table 7.1 Stage Properties

Command	Description	Example
borderWidth	Width of stage border in page units	borderWidth of stage "displC" = 25
bounds	Four corners of outside of stage in page units	bounds of stage "CC" = x1,y1,x2,y2
fillColor	Sets the fill color of the stage area in HLS	fillColor of stage "CC" = black
innerBevelWidth	Width of stage inner bevel in page units	innerBevelWidth of stage "displC" = 30
innerBounds	Bounds of stage area in page units	innerBounds of stage "lc" = x1,y1,x2,y2
mediaBounds	Bounds of media display in page units	mediaBounds of stage "lc" = x1,y1,x2,y2
mediaOpen	Specifies the media reference for the currently displayed media	if mediaOpen of stage "lc" is not null then...
mediaSize	Height and width in pixels for the stage's media display area	mediaSize of stage "xx" = 320,240
name	Name for the stage	name of selected = "myStage"
outerBevelWidth	Width of stage outer bevel in page units	outerBevelWidth of stage "displC" = 30
outline	Specifies whether a thin black line is drawn around stage	outline of stage "c" = true
overLayOpen	Specifies whether or not a video overlay device is open in the stage's display area	overLayOpen of stage "liveAction" = true
position	Specifies the position of the stage in page units relative to the upper left corner of the window	position of stage "lv" = x,y
postEffect	Specifies the post-effect for the stage	postEffect of stage "DV" = "dissolve fast"
preEffect	Specifies the pre-effect for the stage	postEffect of stage "DV" = "blinds slow"
readerVisible	Specifies whether stage is visible at Reader level	readerVisible of stage "DV" = true
RGBFill	Specifies fill color in RBG value for stage area	RGBFill of stage "DV" = 255,0,0

(continues)

Table 7.1 Continued

Command	Description	Example
`RGBStroke`	Specifies stroke color in RBG value for stage area	`RGBStroke of stage "DV" = 0,0,0`
`roundedCorners`	Specifies if the stage has rounded corners	`roundedCorners of stage "DV" = true`
`size`	Size, in page units, for the stage	`size of stage "DV" = stWidth, stHeight`
`stageAnchor`	Specifies the anchor point for the stage or media when it is stretched	`stageAnchor of stage "DV" = "topLeft"`
`stageSizing`	Specifies how to resolve difference between stage and media sizes (`centerMedia`, `clipMedia`, `stretchMedia`, `stretchStage`)	`if bigVideo = true and item 1 of mediaSize of stage "DV" < 320 then stageSizing of stage "DV" = "stretchStage"`
`strokeColor`	Specifies stroke color in HLS for stage area	`strokeColor of stage "ltv" = black`
`transparent`	Specifies whether the stage is transparent	`transparent of stage "hhh" = true`
`vertices`	Location of the stage's vertices in page units	`put vertices of stage "X" into text of field "stageCorners"`
`visible`	Sets whether the stage is visible. If `false`, the stage will not receive `keydown` and other events	`visible of stage "X" = true`

Adding Hotwords

Hotwords are words within a text field that are somehow indicated to the end user as being active, triggering some event when they are clicked. For example, in an encyclopedia, a word that is displayed in green might indicate that when the user clicks it, it will be pronounced, and a word in red might be indicative of a linking to an article about that topic.

Hotwords are normally indicated in the text by either color coding, underlining, reverse text, or a particular phrase ("Click here for more information"). Hot text is also usually associated with a change in the cursor state: the arrow turns into a pointing hand (or some other similar cursor).

Hotwords can be used to trigger any type of event that you can think of. For example, you can bring up a stage and play a video, link to another page, pop up a text box (e.g. with a definition), play a sound file, show a picture, etc.

MTB makes the creation and maintenance of hotwords simple. The process of adding hotwords to a field is described in the next section.

Creating a Hotword

The following steps describe how to add a hotword to a field in ToolBook and to create the script that causes clicking the word to link the user to another page in the application:

1. Create a field by using the field tool. Make sure that the Activated (typing disabled) checkbox is checked on the Field Properties dialog box, otherwise the field is editable by the user.
2. Type (or paste or import) the text you want into the field.
3. Select the word you want to link to another page in the book (double-click the word or click and drag to highlight it).
4. Choose Tools, Hyperlinks, Create HyperLink Hotword from the menu. This will bring up the Add Hyperlink Hotword dialog box shown in figure 7.11.

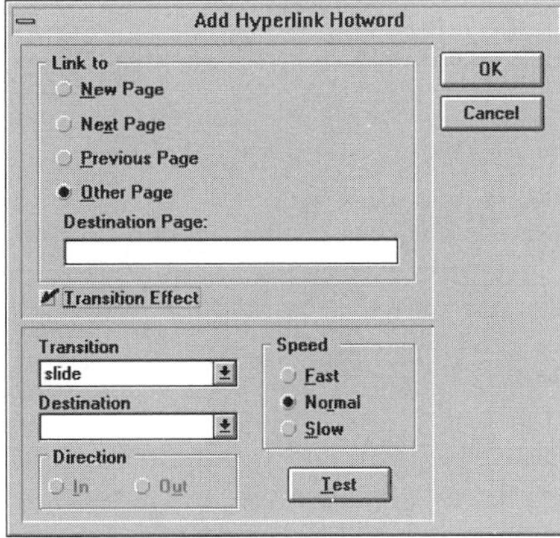

Fig. 7.11

Link hotwords with this dialog box.

5. Select the type of link (New Page, Next Page, Previous Page, Other Page) and the Transition Effect (the visual effect that is used for moving from one page to another, as described in Chapter 18, "Using Special Effects").

Once the link has been made in this manner, you can always edit it by selecting the hotword, then selecting Tools, Hyperlinks, Edit HyperLink Hotword. This will bring up the Edit Hyperlink Hotword dialog box permitting you to change the link.

The following steps are a more general method of creating scripts for hotwords:

1. Follow the previous steps one through three.
2. Select Text, Create Hotword from the main menu.
3. Select Object, Hotword Properties and click the Script button.

4. Type in your script. For example, to show the clip `myVideo` in the stage `littleStage`, you could use the following script:

```
to handle buttonUp
 mmOpen clip "myVideo"
 mmPlay clip "myVideo" in stage "littleStage" autoClose
end buttonUp
```

Hotword Properties

Hotword properties can be changed by selecting the hotword and choosing Object, Hotword Properties from the main menu. The Hotword Properties dialog box allows you to set the properties for hotwords (see fig. 7.12). Your choices for style are Book Default, None, Color, Frame, Dotted, and Underline. Book Default is the best choice if you are trying to maintain a consistent look and feel, and makes it quite simple to change the way all hotwords appear throughout the application by changing the book default hotword style. The `Invert` property displays the text in inverse style (see figure 7.14 for an example). The `highlight` property affects how the hotword behaves when clicked—`highlight` will make the hotword appear in highlighted form.

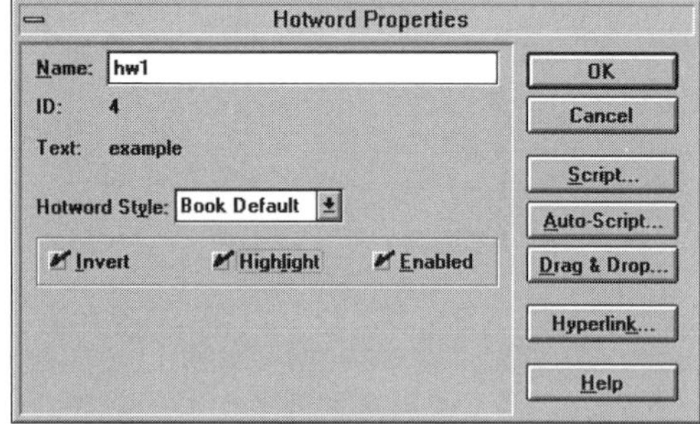

Fig. 7.12

Indicate hotwords with an underline via the Hotword Properties dialog box.

When you add a hotword, ToolBook uses the defaults that you have set up in the book properties for hotwords. To change the default properties of hotwords, choose Object, Book Properties from the main menu. In the Book Properties dialog box, shown in figure 7.13, change the hotword properties. You can choose any color for the hotwords, but only one color throughout the book. I recommend that you stay with the first sixteen colors in the palette so that you can be sure that the words will display properly on any machine. Standard hotword colors in most applications are red, blue, and green.

You can use a combination of hotword styles within any application, but do keep in mind the usual cautions about mixing too many styles of type in text to avoid "ransom note" style. Figure 7.14 shows some of the hotword style options in a text field.

When the user positions the cursor over a hotword, the cursor changes to a pointing hand. If the hotword has been disabled, the cursor will not change.

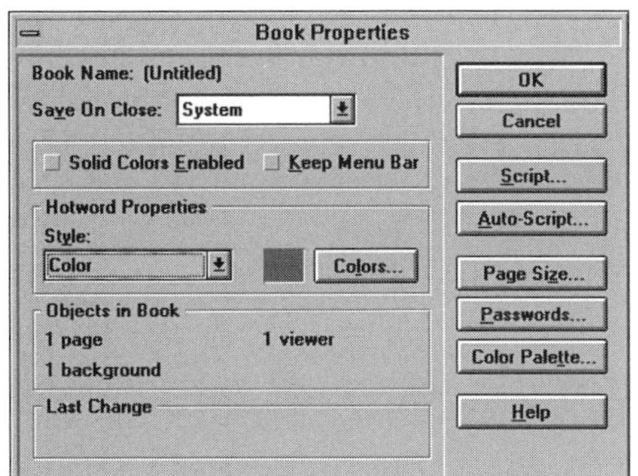

Fig. 7.13

Change the color of a hotword via the Book Properties dialog box.

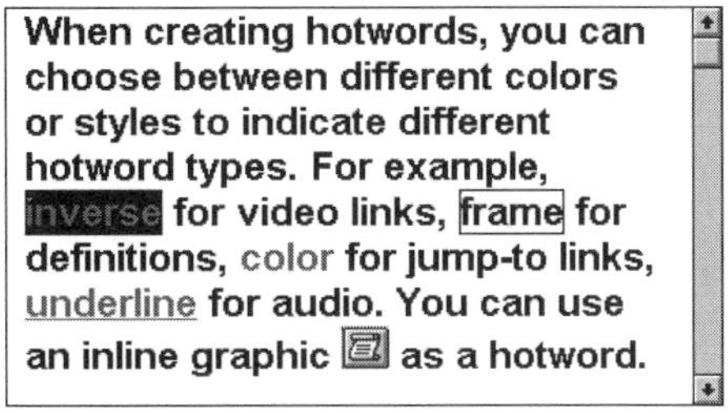

When creating hotwords, you can choose between different colors or styles to indicate different hotword types. For example, inverse for video links, frame for definitions, color for jump-to links, underline for audio. You can use an inline graphic as a hotword.

Fig. 7.14

Enabled hotwords change the cursor to a pointing hand.

Activating Hotwords

You can activate a hotword by clicking it. You must make the field property `Activated true` by selecting the field, and then choosing Object, Field Properties. The Field Properties dialog box in figure 7.15 shows the settings required.

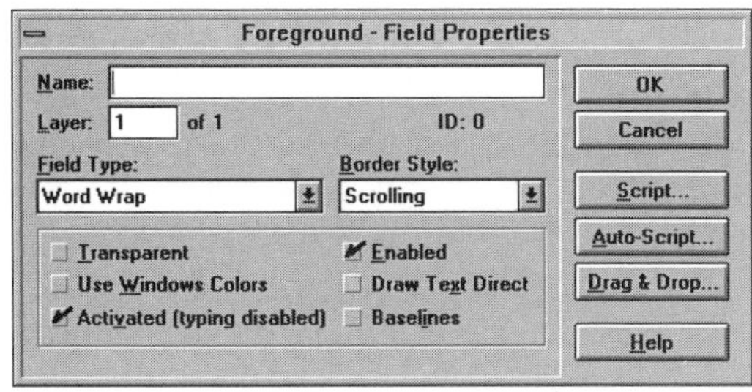

Fig. 7.15

Border Style for a text field is set from the Field Properties dialog box.

Removing Hotwords

A hotword can removed by selecting the hotword and then choosing Text, Remove Hotword. This will, of course, also remove any scripting for that hotword. If you want to temporarily deactivate the hotword without removing its scripting, you can choose the hotword and disable it in the Hotword Properties dialog box by deselecting the Enabled checkbox.

Using Object Linking and Embedding

Object Linking and Embedding (OLE) is a feature of Windows supported by ToolBook that can be very useful in a variety of applications. It enables you to embed an object into an application that, when double-clicked, will bring up the original application. For example, you can create a picture in the Windows Paint program, embed it into a ToolBook application, and then double-click it to activate the Windows Paint program.

ToolBook OLE containers can be one of two types: *linked* or *embedded*. A linked container refers to a source file external to ToolBook that is automatically updated in ToolBook each time it is changed by the application. An embedded container is a copy of a source file contained completely within the ToolBook file, which will be updated only when explicitly requested.

Creating an OLE Container

To create an OLE container, click the OLE tool in the toolbar and drag a shape that is the size you want the OLE object container to appear. Select the object, and choose Object, OLE Properties from the main menu. The OLE Properties dialog box appears (see fig. 7.16). From the Type list box, select Embedded or Linked. From the Class list box, select the class for the OLE object. The classes displayed will depend on the software that has been registered on your system.

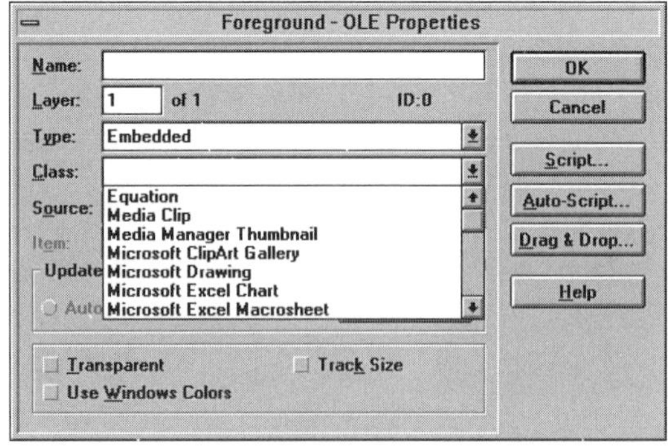

Fig. 7.16

Choose an OLE object class from the OLE Properties dialog box.

Next, choose the Source, the file that you are linking or embedding. You can use the Browse button to locate the file on your system. The Item text box is used for additional information about the item to be embedded, such as the column and row numbers in a spreadsheet.

In the case of embedded objects, the Update Options are not used. For linked objects, you must specify whether to use Automatic update—updating each time the source is changed—or Manual update—updated only when specified.

The Transparent and Use Windows Colors options are the same as for any other object in ToolBook. Track Size specifies that you want the size of the object maintained at the same size as it is in the OLE server application.

Using OLE Linking and Embedding

OLE linking and embedding is useful for a number of different types of applications. For example, you can use ToolBook to create custom programming applications for businesses that need a "user-friendly" front-end interface to applications when they do not want to invest training time for employees. Thus, for example, if your customer has an accounts receivable clerk that needs to create pie graphs of income by region on a monthly basis but does not understand how to copy the data from a database program into a spreadsheet program and then plot the data in the spreadsheet, you could write a custom application that would list the files, copy them, insert data into the spreadsheet, plot the data, and display the data in the ToolBook application.

Another useful application for OLE in ToolBook is in training modules where you want to link to specific examples for teaching purposes. In any case, the user must have the OLE server installed on their system for the OLE link to function. You will not want to use OLE in cases where the product is for general public use and you do not know if the end user will have the application or not.

When you link or embed an OLE object in ToolBook, it is displayed as an icon or graphic representing the data (see fig. 7.17). Double-clicking the object will display the data in the application. For example, double-clicking the Microsoft Word icon will display the file that is referenced within Microsoft Word.

Fig. 7.17

Double-click the icon to open the file associated with each icon.

You can, of course, use OpenScript commands for creating and updating links to OLE containers. When creating a general use ToolBook program that makes use of OLE, you will want to make "generic" references to the linked objects, rather than path-specific references. For example, the following line is too specific, and will cause a problem if the file has been installed on a different drive:

```
reference of selection = \
"linked,Microsoft Excel Worksheet, C:\DATA\BUDGET.XLS"
```

It would be preferable to use a more general reference, such as the following:

```
newSel = "linked,Microsoft Excel Worksheet,"& bDir
reference of selection = newSel
```

where `bDir` contains the full pathname to the spreadsheet data file, perhaps as specified in an `.INI` file.

An Example Application: The Picture Sound Link

This section walks you through the steps of using OLE to create a simple application. The steps in the process will stretch you a little beyond what you have already learned, but each step will be carefully explained. When you have completed this simple project, you will be ready to create your own applications using object linking and embedding.

The sample program is designed to be used by "novice" computer users who want a simple way to link a sound file and a picture file. Figure 7.18 shows the completed application. The program is intended to be used in this way: a user double-clicks the sound icon to hear a wave file. Double-clicking the picture brings up the Windows Paint program so that the picture can be edited. Changing the reference to the sound or bitmap file is done from the Data menu.

Fig. 7.18

The picture/sound link example application using OLE.

The name of the embedded OLE application is contained in a property of the container. This property is its *reference* (what it's referred to). In order to change the `reference` properties of the bitmap graphic and the wave file, you include a script at the book level. Rather than create a button to link to a different file, you create a new menu that accomplishes this task.

To create this application, follow these steps:

1. Open a new, blank book in ToolBook.
2. Using the OLE tool, create a large space for the bitmap graphic to be displayed.
3. Select the OLE container created in step 2 and choose Object, OLE Properties from the main menu.
4. In the OLE Properties dialog box, type in the name **`pictureFile`** for the container. From the Type list, choose Linked. From the Class list, choose Paintbrush Picture. Click the Browse button and select a bitmap graphics file from your computer. Under Update Options, select Automatic. Now click the OK button.

5. Use the OLE tool to create a smaller container below the first container (for the wave file). Open the OLE Properties dialog box for this object, and Name it `playWaveFile`. Under Type, choose Linked, and under Class, choose Sound. Use the Browse button and select a wave file (`*.wav`) from your system.

6. Now you are ready to tackle the coding. First, you'll want to change the menus so that the only menus the reader sees are the File menu and the Data menu. To do this, you create a script for the book. Get into the book script (choose Object, Book Properties, Script.) Enter the following script:

```
to handle enterBook
 remove menu "edit" at reader
 remove menu "text" at reader
 remove menu "page" at reader
 remove menu "help" at reader
 add menu "Data" at reader
 add menuItem "Select Wave File" alias \
 getWaveSound to menu "Data" at reader
 add menuItem "Select Bitmap File" alias \
 getBMPFile to menu "Data" at reader
end
```

As you will soon observe, this will eliminate the Edit, Text, Page, and Help menus from the reader level menu bar, while adding the Data menu with two entries—Select Wave File and Select Bitmap File.

7. Now you need to create the handlers that you called by the menu commands; these are `getWaveSound` and `getBMPFile`. Still in the script of the book, type in the following handler for `getWaveSound`:

```
to handle getWaveSound
 linkDLL "TB30DLG.DLL"
 STRING getFileListDlg(STRING,STRING,STRING,STRING,INT)
 end linkDLL
 filterList = "Wave Files (*.wav),*.wav"
 fileList = getFileListDlg("Wave sound
files...",null,null,filterList,1)
 if fileList is null
 request "No files selected!"
 else
 pop fileList into fName
 if itemCount(fileList) > 0
 pop fileList
 put fName & "\" & it into fName
 end
 reference of OLE "playWaveFile" = "linked,Sound,"&fName&","
 end if
end
```

The first lines of this code are similar to those explained in Listing 7.1 which link in the code needed to access the Windows file dialog. The "meat" of the code is the following line:

```
reference of OLE "playWaveFile" = "linked,Sound,"&fName&","
```

which will set the reference property of the OLE container `playWaveFile` to the wave file selected by the user.

8. Now, a similar handler is written for the bitmap file:

```
to handle getBMPFile
 linkDLL "TB30DLG.DLL"
 STRING getFileListDlg(STRING,STRING,STRING,STRING,INT)
 end linkDLL
 filterList = "Bitmap Picture Files (*.bmp),*.bmp"
 fileList = getFileListDlg("Bitmap files...",null,null,filterList,1)
 if fileList is null
 request "No files selected!"
 else
 pop fileList into fName
 if itemCount(fileList) > 0
 pop fileList
 put fName & "\" & it into fName
 end
 reference of OLE "pictureFile" = "linked,Paintbrush
Picture,"&fName&","
 end if
end
```

9. Save and name the book. Now you are ready to try it! Switching to Reader mode will not change the menus at this point—you need to enter the book for the change to take place. You can just use File, Open to cause the `enterBook` handler to execute. Switching to Reader mode will allow you to test the new menu items and to test the links. Double-click the microphone icon to hear the linked sound and the picture to edit it using Windows Paint.

From Here...

In this chapter, you have learned some about adding and using stages, creating hotwords, and using object linking and embedding. For more information on the topics discussed in this chapter, refer to the following:

- Chapter 9, "Creating Custom Menus," provides more details about adding and modifying menus.
- Chapter 11, "Working with Text," discusses hotwords in more detail.
- Chapter 18, "Using Special Effects," teaches you more about special effects, such as transitions.

CHAPTER 8

Working with Viewers

Viewers, which are windows that display pages, are a significant advantage to the Multimedia ToolBook developer. Many Multimedia ToolBook developers consider viewers to be the most beneficial aspect of this application development tool.

You can use viewers to display a wide variety of pages within a window, such as dialog boxes, tool palettes, status bars, and views of other books.

After completing this chapter, you should know how to do the following:

- Create, open, and display viewers
- Assign menus and icons to viewers
- Set and control properties of viewers
- Understand specific viewer examples

What is a Viewer?

A *viewer* is a window that displays pages as a rectangular area on your screen. You can display your pages differently within your viewers. For instance, you can create a dialog box viewer with your own custom-designed interface. Use a single viewer to navigate through several pages, or display several viewers on your screen, each displaying a different page.

You can also control and style your viewer in a number of different ways. Control of your viewer includes moving, opening, closing, and resizing. For instance, a viewer can be minimized to display an icon or maximized to fill the entire screen. Also, it is possible to display viewers inside other viewers. When selecting the style of a new viewer you can use a viewer template, such as a dialog box, a palette, a tool bar, a status bar, or a read-only popup text box. You can also create your own custom viewers to display the way you want.

Viewers simplify the development process. Setting the style of your ToolBook window would be difficult to accomplish without using viewer properties. It is extremely easy to change the properties of all of your ToolBook windows.

Note

When you open ToolBook, the Main window is displayed. In OpenScript, this window is known as viewer `ID 0` and `mainWindow`. As with any viewer, you can assign a name to the Main window.

Understanding What Viewers Display

The common use of a viewer is to display a page from the current book or another book. Figure 8.1 shows a popup viewer. Advanced OpenScript programmers can manipulate viewers to display other Windows applications or media, such as NotePad or video. When you first create a viewer, you can assign a page to the viewer, although the default is to automatically create and assign a new page and background. If you assign an invalid page, ToolBook will default to the first page of the book. To create a viewer, see the "Creating a Viewer" section of this chapter.

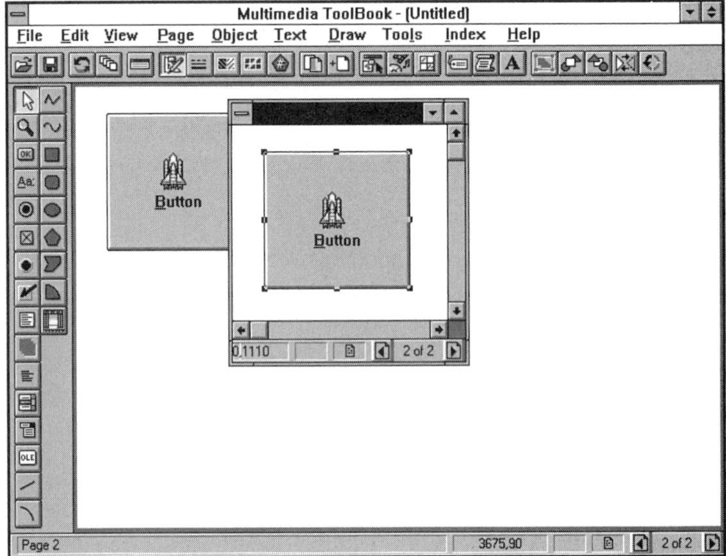

Fig. 8.1

The main viewer and the popup viewer are both displaying page ID 1.

Choosing a Type of Viewer

Not only can you set a viewer to a certain style, such as a dialog box or tool palette, you can also set the type of window for your viewer. You can display a viewer as either a child viewer or a popup viewer (see fig. 8.2). A *child* viewer is a window contained within a *parent* window. The Main window is displayed on top of the child viewer. The child viewer can be clipped by the Main window. A popup viewer is a window that can appear on top of the parent viewer. The popup viewer can also be displayed on top of the Main window. Both the child viewer and the popup viewer belong to the parent window. In most cases, the parent window will be the Main window. If the parent window is closed or minimized, the child and popup viewer will also be closed or minimized.

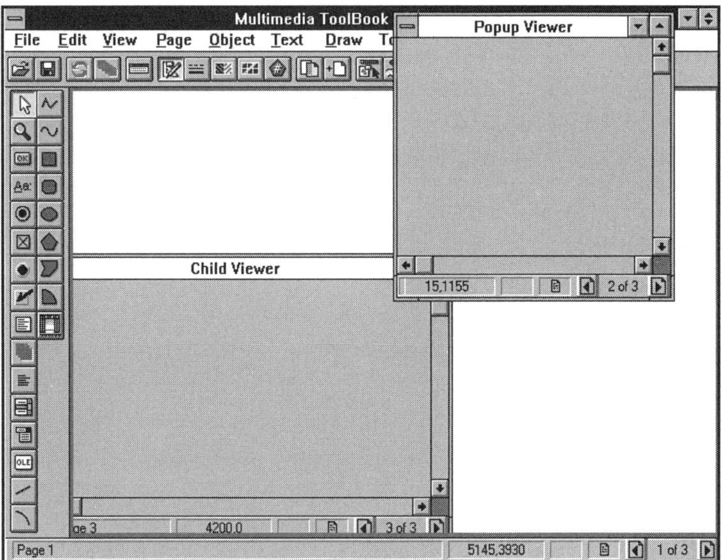

Fig. 8.2

Child viewers are commonly used from tool bars, whereas popup viewers are often used from dialog boxes and tool palettes.

When you need to display and manipulate information separately from the information in your Main window, such as displaying a dialog box or a customized NotePad, use a popup viewer. When information needs to be dependent on the display of your Main window, such as positioning your viewer relative to the Main windows title bar or minimized when the Main window is minimized, such as a tool bar, use a child viewer.

Understanding the Viewer's Place in the Object Hierarchy

In order to control a viewer using OpenScript, it is important to have an understanding of the viewers place in the object hierarchy.

In ToolBook, messages are sent from one object to another using a strict order of object progression. Messages follow this progression from one object to another. This is known as the ToolBook Object Hierarchy. If you have used ToolBook in the past, you may be familiar with the Object Hierarchy. Figure 8.3 displays a simplified view of the ToolBook Object Hierarchy.

There are essentially two important paths to follow in the Object Hierarchy: the path that progresses for standard objects and the path for viewers.

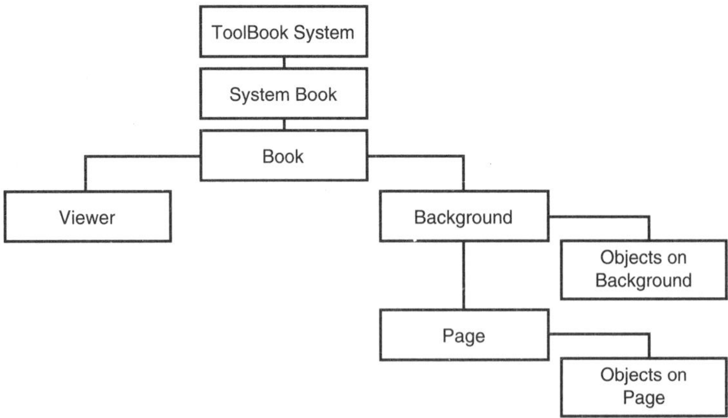

Fig. 8.3

Viewers have their own progression in the ToolBook Object Hierarchy.

Viewers have a different path within the Object Hierarchy. When a viewer receives a message, such as `enterWindow` or `leaveWindow`, the message progression begins. The message continues along the Object Hierarchy to the book script, the script of the system book(s), and then the ToolBook system.

The Object Hierarchy can be quickly understood for standard objects by following the progression of a `buttonClick` message. When a button is pressed in Reader mode, a number of messages are sent, such as `buttonDown`, `buttonUp`, and `buttonClick`. For instance, ToolBook will check the script of the button for a `buttonClick` handler. If such a handler is found within the script of the button, ToolBook processes the handler. If there is no `forward` command within this `buttonClick` handler, then ToolBook ends the progression through the Object Hierarchy.

However, if a `forward` command is included in the `buttonClick` script, then the next object in the Object Hierarchy with a `buttonClick` handler will process the `buttonClick` message. The `buttonClick` message will continue until the next object does not use the `forward` command within its `buttonClick` handler or until the ToolBook system is reached. Each object in the Hierarchy can contain a handler for the message. Therefore, you can use one handler at a higher level in the Object Hierarchy, such as a page, to define an action for several objects, such as buttons.

The script in Listing 8.1 can be used to demonstrate which object is currently processing the script. Place the handler into each object that you want to follow or check.

Listing 8.1 08MTB01.TBK Using *buttonClick* with the *forward* Command

```
to handle buttonClick
     request UniqueName of self
     forward
end buttonClick
```

This script is activated when the mouse button is clicked. The second line is used to request the ID of the object which also displays the type of object. Remember, use the `forward` command to send the `buttonClick` message to the next object in the hierarchy.

> **Note**
>
> It is important to understand that each object in the ToolBook Object Hierarchy can contain a handler for a particular message, such as a `buttonClick` handler or an `enterWindow` handler.

Creating a Viewer

There are two ways you can create a viewer. The first is to use the interface in Author mode. You can also use OpenScript to create a viewer.

Multimedia ToolBook makes it easy to create a viewer utilizing the interface in Author mode. To do so, follow these steps:

1. In Author mode, select Object, Viewers from the main menu. The Viewers dialog box appears.
2. Click the New button from the Viewers dialog box. The New Viewer dialog box appears (see fig. 8.4).

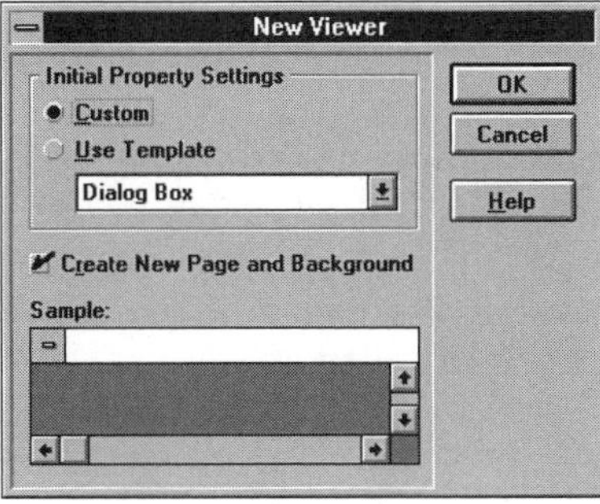

Fig. 8.4

The New Viewer dialog box allows you to create a customized viewer.

3. To create a customized viewer from the New Viewer dialog box, select Custom. The Viewer Properties dialog box appears (see fig. 8.5).
4. Enter or choose the properties of your viewer in the Viewer Properties dialog box, such as the Viewer Name, Default Page, Default Size, Style, Position, Size, Limits, and Options.
5. When finished, choose OK.
6. Choose Done from the Viewers dialog box.

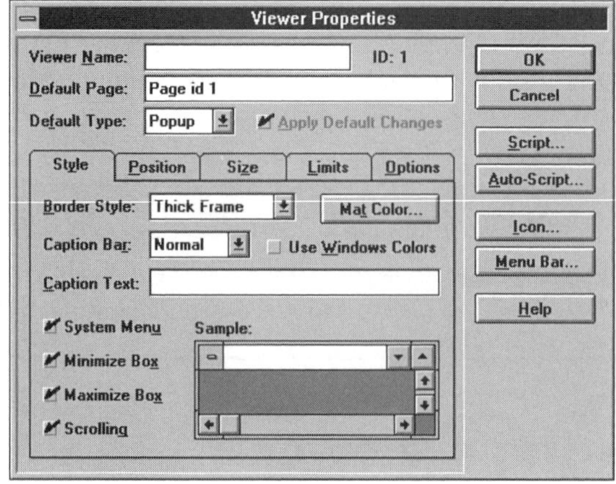

Fig. 8.5

The Viewer Properties dialog box allows you to set many of the properties of your viewer.

OpenScript can also be used to create a viewer. Place the script in Listing 8.2 into the script of a button.

Listing 8.2 08MTB02.TBK OpenScript Used to Create a Viewer

```
to handle buttonClick
     new viewer
     name of it = "Media Splash"
     defaultPage of viewer "Media Splash" = page "Mountain View"
     open viewer "Media Splash"
     show viewer "Media Splash"
end buttonClick
```

When the button that contains the above script is clicked, a new viewer is created, opened, and shown. When a new viewer is created using OpenScript, ToolBook assigns the default page that the viewer will display to the current page displayed in the Main window, unless you specify the `defaultPage` value of your viewer. Refer to the section "Setting Viewer Properties" later in this chapter.

Using Viewer Templates

Viewers can be styled in a number of different ways. You have the option to change the style of any viewer. In order to develop your application quickly, which is one of the main benefits of using Multimedia ToolBook, you can choose a predefined viewer style. There are six predefined styles of viewers, which are the following:

- Dialog Box
- Palette
- Tool Bar
- Status Bar
- Read-only Popup
- Thick Frame

To create a dialog box viewer, follow the steps in the "Creating a Dialog Box Viewer" section of this chapter. Other types of common viewers include palettes, tool bars, and popup text boxes. A palette viewer can be used to create a floating tool palette, similar to the color palette in Multimedia ToolBook. The tool bar generally contains buttons that are shortcuts for menu commands. A popup text box can be used to display descriptions, tips, or notes to the user.

Creating a New Page and Background

When creating a viewer using the interface, ToolBook creates a new page by default. You have the option to select the Create New Page and Background checkbox to enable or disable this feature in the New Viewer dialog box (refer to fig. 8.4). When creating a new viewer using OpenScript, no new page is created unless you specifically create the page.

Creating a Dialog Box Viewer

Creating a dialog box is one of the most common use of viewers. You can quickly create a dialog box viewer and add the contents to the page the viewer displays. A dialog box viewer can not be resized and has no minimize and maximize buttons.

In previous versions of ToolBook, before ToolBook supported viewers, a special process needed to be followed to create a dialog box. Now, using Multimedia ToolBook 4.0, the process is quick and simple.

You can use the viewer template to quickly create a dialog box viewer. Follow these steps:

1. Select Object, Viewers from the main menu. The Viewers dialog box appears.
2. Select New from the Viewers dialog box to create a new viewer. The New Viewer dialog box appears.
3. In the New Viewer dialog box, select Use Template and, from the drop-down list box, choose Dialog Box.

Viewer Management

Effectively controlling viewers often requires manipulating several aspects of viewer properties. Opening, displaying, and closing are the main actions involved when controlling viewers. Also, effectively setting viewer properties and managing viewer colors can help to properly display viewer information.

Setting Viewer Properties

Viewer properties are divided into persistent and nonpersistant properties. *Persistent* properties are the initial settings of the viewer when it is opened. *Nonpersistant* properties are changes that are not permanent, such as when the user modifies the viewer by moving, minimizing, or resizing the viewer. When you close your viewer, the persistent properties of the viewer remain but the nonpersistant properties do not remain.

The main properties contained in the Viewer Properties dialog box are the Viewer Name, Default Page, and Default Type (refer to fig. 8.5). The Default Page is the first page the viewer displays when it is opened.

> **Note**
>
> If you change the Default Page to an incorrect value or delete the reference, the viewer will default and display the first page of the book.

As previously mentioned, you can set the Default Type of a viewer to either Popup or Child. Popup is the true default viewer type. For a detailed description of both the popup and child viewers, refer to the section "Choosing a Type of Viewer" earlier in this chapter.

The other two main areas of the Viewer Properties dialog box are the tabs—Style, Position, Size, Limits, and Options—and the buttons, which include access to the Script and Auto-Script files, and Icon and Menu Bar for the viewer.

Setting the `Name`, `defaultPage`, and `defaultType` of a viewer can be accomplished using OpenScript. The script in Listing 8.3 sets these three viewer properties when the button is pressed. Create a viewer named `Startup Media Splash` and place the following script into the script of a button.

Listing 8.3 08MTB03.TBK Setting Up Viewer Properties

```
to handle buttonClick
     name of viewer ID 1 = "Startup Media Splash"
     defaultPage of viewer "Startup Media Splash" = page ID 4
     defaultType of viewer "Startup Media Splash" = popup
end buttonClick
```

Setting the Viewer's Style

The style properties of a viewer are used to determine how the viewer will appear, such as using a border or caption bar. The Style tab of the Viewer Properties dialog box allows you to set the border, the caption, and the mat color (refer to fig. 8.5)

The Border Style can be set to one of the following settings:

- **Thick Frame**, which is the default, is the border most developers find familiar. The viewer can be resized when using a Thick Frame.
- **Thin Frame** is most often used for tool palettes, such as volume or video control. Unlike a Thick Frame viewer, when a Thin Frame viewer is displayed, it can not be resized.
- The **Dialog Frame** has similarities to both the Thick Frame and Thin Frame border styles. Like a Thick Frame viewer, a Dialog Frame has a normal border, although the Dialog Frame can not be resized. Also, a Dialog Frame does not

have minimize and maximize buttons in the caption bar. Generally, developers display a dialog box viewer as centered on the screen.

- The **Shadowed** border displays a shadow along both the right side and the bottom of your viewer. This border style gives the effect of a raised viewer and is often used to display a popup text viewer. Also, this viewer cannot be resized or moved. Be careful when using this viewer; you may find that the shadowed area does not update the way you might expect.
- You can set the border to **None** if you want to display your application without a border.

Table 8.1 explains in more detail how the border styles can be used.

Table 8.1 Viewer Frames

Frame Type	Resizable	Movable	Common Uses
Thick Frame	Yes	Yes	Default
Thin Frame	No	Yes	Tool palettes
Dialog Frame	No	Yes	Dialog box
Shadowed Frame	No	Yes	Popup text
None	Yes	No	Graphics, etc.

> **Note**
>
> While you are setting the style properties, you can refer to the sample viewer for your viewer's basic look. The sample immediately updates as you choose each option.

OpenScript can also be used to set the border of your viewer. After creating a viewer named `My Palette`, enter the following into the Command Window:

```
borderStyle of viewer "My Palette" = thinFrame
```

Positioning the Viewer

You can select the default position of your viewer by using the Position tab of the Viewer Properties dialog box (see fig. 8.6). This tab contains five options related to positioning your viewer.

These options include the following:

- The **Tile** combo box specifies which side of the parent window your child window will be near. The options for positioning your child window include Left, Top, Right, Bottom, and None. The default Tile position is none. The tiling option is very useful when you need to position a Tool Bar viewer.

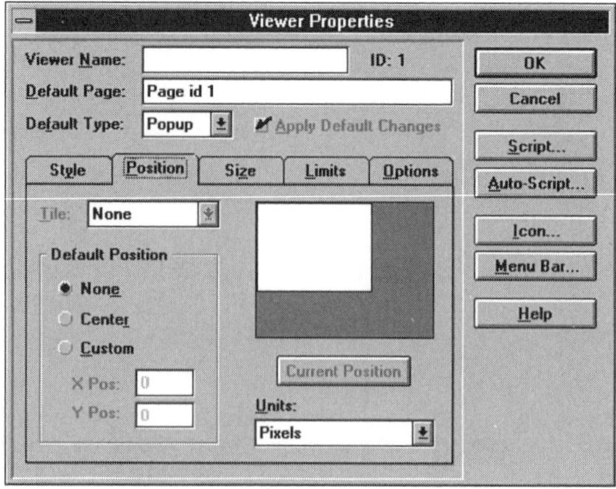

Fig. 8.6

The Position tab of the Viewer Properties dialog box allows you to quickly set your viewer's position.

- The **Default Position**, which is the way the viewer is displayed when opened, can either be None, Center, or Custom.

  If you choose Custom, you can set the position by entering your horizontal and vertical values in the X Pos and Y Pos boxes, respectively. The position relates to the top, left corner of the viewer.

- The **Current Position** is only active when the viewer has already been created. Use this button when you want to reset the position of the viewer.

- The **Sample** displays the way your viewer will display on the screen. If you choose Custom as the Default Position but don't know the exact coordinates you want, you can move the viewer to the desired location by clicking and dragging it in the position sample. When you position a popup viewer, the sample relates to the screen. When you position a child viewer, the sample relates to the parent window.

- When you select Custom as the Default Position, you can enter a horizontal and vertical amount in the **Units** that you prefer, such as Pixels, Page Units, Inches, or Centimeters.

You can set the position of your viewer using OpenScript as well. Place the following script into the script of a button and create a viewer named `Dialog1`:

```
to handle buttonClick
     position of viewer Dialog1 = 0,0
end buttonClick
```

Sizing the Viewer

The size of your viewer can be selected by using the Size tab of the Viewer Properties dialog box (see fig, 8.7). Much like the Position tab, the Size tab from the Viewer Properties dialog box contains five options. These options are Auto Size, Default Client Size, the Sample, Current Size, and Units.

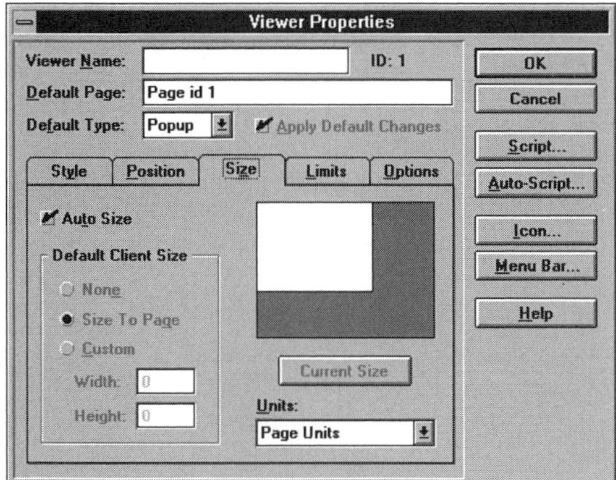

Fig. 8.7

Size your viewer using the viewer sample from the Size tab of the Viewer Properties dialog box.

When the Auto Size checkbox is selected, the client area of the viewer is automatically sized to the background of the page that the viewer displays. (This is the default setting.) If you deselect the Auto Size option, you can then set the Default Client Size to one of the following options:

- If you choose **None**, your viewer will be sized to two-thirds of the parent window. However, if the viewer is a child window and the Default Client Size is set to None, the viewer will be sized to two-thirds of the screen.
- Selecting **Size To Page** sets the client area of the viewer automatically to the size of the background. This is similar to **Auto Size**, although the viewer will not resize if a new page is viewed.
- The **Custom** option allows you to set your viewer to the size you want, using the **Units** of your choice—Pixels, Page Units, Inches, or Centimeters. You can either enter the **Width** and **Height** in their respective boxes or you can click and drag the viewer in the sizing sample.

The Current Size button is only active when the viewer has already been created. Use this button when you want to reset the size of the viewer. When you need to resize the page so that it covers your entire viewer, you can enter **`send sizeToViewer`** in the Command Window.

Setting the Limits of a Viewer

When users interact with your viewer, you can allow them to resize the viewer. The Limits tab gives you the option to set maximum and minimum viewer size and is similar to the Position and Size tabs (see fig. 8.8).

You can also set the limits of your viewer using script. Place the following script into the script of a button and create a viewer named `Example`:

```
to handle buttonClick
     maximumSize of viewer "Example" = size of mainWindow
end
```

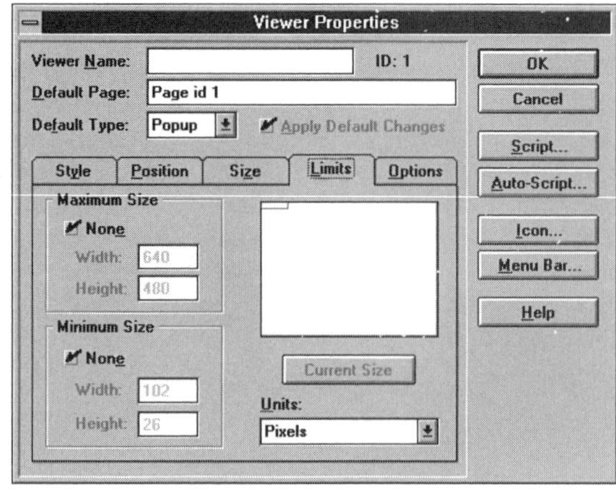

Fig. 8.8

To prevent the user from resizing your viewer, set the maximum and minimum limits of your viewer to the same size.

Setting the Options of a Viewer

There are essentially three sections of the Options tab of the Viewer Properties dialog box—the Default State, the Image Buffers, and nine checkboxes that include various capabilities (see fig. 8.9). These options, along with several of the style options, give you great control over your viewers without having to access the Window API.

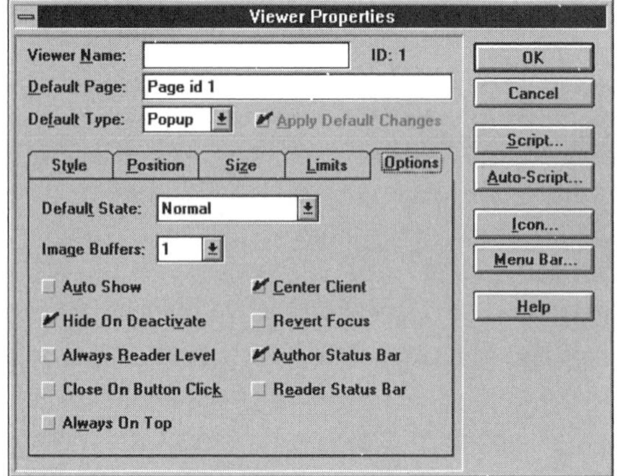

Fig. 8.9

The Options tab in the Viewer Properties dialog box gives you quick access to set various viewer properties, such as Always Reader Level.

There are several viewer options available. The four main options are the Default State, Image Buffers, Center Client, and Revert Focus:

- The **Default State**, allows you to set the default size of your viewer to Maximized, Minimized, LockMinimized, and Normal. Normal is the default state of a custom viewer. Maximized is often used when displaying full-screen applications.

- **Image Buffers** can either be set to 0, 1, or 2. Image buffers affect how quickly your page and background are drawn. The image buffers are explained in detail later in this chapter.
- The **Center Client** option, when checked, centers the viewer in the current window when the viewer is opened for the first time. Setting your Main window to be centered when opened is easy to accomplish and looks good, but too few developers take advantage of this option.
- Using **Revert Focus** sets the focus window to the previous active viewer. This option can be used to prevent a user from mistakenly navigating within a separate viewer which is used for simple display purposes.

Displaying Information Using Viewers

As previously mentioned, a viewer commonly displays the contents of a page from the current book or a different book. The interface allows you to set the default page that the viewer will display. Using OpenScript, like in Listing 8.4, you can first open a viewer, modify its properties, and then display the viewer the way you want.

Listing 8.4 08MTB04.TBK Example of OpenScript

```
to handle buttonClick
     open viewer "States"
     currentPage of viewer "States" = page "Washington"
     show viewer "States"
end buttonClick
```

You can choose to show the viewer in one of two modes. You can display the viewer as `notActive` or `modal`. A viewer that is shown as `notActive` simply doesn't receive the focus. A viewer that is shown as `modal` prevents other viewers from receiving the focus until the modal viewer is closed.

Opening a Viewer

There is a difference between showing a viewer and opening a viewer. A viewer can be opened without being shown. In Author mode, the simple way to show a viewer is to use the menus.

To open a viewer from Author mode, use the following steps:

1. Select Object, Viewers from the main menu. The Viewers dialog box appears.
2. Select a viewer to display from the Viewers dialog box and press Show Viewer.

In effect, these steps allow you to open and show a viewer.

You can also open a viewer using OpenScript. When you open a viewer using the OpenScript `open` command, the viewer is not yet shown. There are a few benefits from opening a viewer without showing it. You can modify properties of your viewer such as the size and position. If you use the OpenScript `show` command alone, the viewer is automatically opened and shown (see Listing 8.5).

Listing 8.5 08MTB05.TBK Using the *show* and *open* OpenScript Commands

```
to handle buttonClick
     open viewer "Media Splash"
     show viewer "Media Splash"
end buttonClick
```

To better understand the events that occur when a viewer is opened, it is helpful to understand the precedence of `enter` and `open` messages sent to the ToolBook system when entering the Main window (see Table 8.2).

Table 8.2 Enter and Open Messages

`enter` or `open` Message	Receiving Object
`enterSystem`	Main window upon opening an instance
`openWindow`	Viewer upon opening
`enterApplication`	Page upon opening an instance
`enterBook`	Page upon opening a book
`enterBackground`	Page upon opening a book
`enterPage`	Page upon opening a book
`enterWindow`	Viewer upon opening

Restricting Navigation

Often when you are using viewers to display information, you may not want the user to be able to navigate to a page, but rather have the page only visible from within a viewer. This way you can make sure the user of your application does not navigate to a particular page. Each page has its own Skip Navigation property. This property can easily be set for each page by using either the interface or OpenScript. To set the Skip Navigation property of the page, use the following steps:

1. Select Object, Page Properties from the main menu. The Page Properties dialog box appears.
2. Check the Skip Navigation option from the Page Properties dialog box.

You can use script to set the Skip Navigation property as well. For instance, the following script could be placed in an `enterWindow` handler within your viewer script to prevent the user from navigating to a particular page:

```
to handle enterWindow
skipNavigation of page "View Only" = true
end enterWindow
```

You can still navigate to the particular page using OpenScript. For instance, you could place the following script into the script of a button:

```
to handle buttonClick
go to page "View Only"
end buttonClick
```

Also, you can set the page the viewer will display using script. Place the following script into the script of a viewer:

```
notifyBefore enterWindow
currentPage of viewer "My View" = "View Only"
end enterWindow
```

Displaying Modal Viewers

You have the option to display a viewer as modal or nonmodal. A modal viewer retains the focus of the application until it is closed. Therefore, if you want users to recognize that they cannot continue until they have responded, use a modal viewer.

The following script is an example of showing a modal dialog box. Place the following script into the Command Window. Also, make sure you have a viewer named `Find Dialog`:

```
show viewer "Find Dialog" as modal
```

The viewer must have a default type of popup in order to be displayed as a modal viewer.

> **Note**
>
> If you set the `autoClose` property of a viewer to `true`, the viewer will not display as modal. `autoClose` can be set by selecting the Close on Button Click option from the Options Tab in the Viewer Properties dialog box.

Using Image Buffers

An *image buffer* is a portion of memory set aside to contain an image of the page and/or background. An image buffer is a persistent viewer property that can be set to one of the following three settings:

- Using 0 image buffers means that there is no saved image of the page or background; therefore, your images will display as if you set them all to draw direct, which means drawn directly to the screen.
- Using 1 image buffer stores the page image.
- Using 2 image buffers store both the page and the background. If you need quick navigation between pages, use two image buffers.

Use one image buffer when you need to animate objects on the page. For instance, if you have a viewer named `Media Splash`, you could set the `imageBuffers` for the viewer to `1` by entering the following script into the Command Window:

```
imageBuffers of viewer "Media Splash" = 1
```

Copying Viewers

Viewers can be copied within the same book, or from one book to another. Like other types of copied information within Windows, when a viewer is copied it is saved to the Clipboard. However, because viewers are unique to ToolBook, you do not use the standard Copy and Paste options from the Edit menu. The Copy and Paste options for viewers are located in the Viewers dialog box. Be sure to select the viewer that you want to copy from those listed in the Viewers of Book text box. The script of a viewer is also included when a viewer is copied.

To copy and paste a viewer, use the following steps:

1. Select Object, Viewers from the main menu bar. The Viewers dialog box appears.
2. Select the Viewer you want to copy from the Viewers dialog box.
3. Press Copy from the Viewers dialog box to copy the selected viewer to memory.
4. Press Paste from the Viewers dialog box to paste the viewer from memory to your application.

Working with Color

There are two ways color palettes are handled within a viewer. First, it is important to note that viewers cannot contain palette information. Palettes are either contained as part of the Paint Object, or as a book property. The viewer must be activated for the palette to be used. Only popup viewers can be activated; child viewers are displayed as part of the Main window. For more information related to palettes, see the section "Working with Palettes" in Chapter 10, "Using Graphics."

Viewer Menus and Icons

You can assign a menu and icon to a viewer. Popup viewers can display menus; child viewers cannot. If you assign a menu to a child viewer, the menu will be ignored.

Icons can be assigned to both popup and child viewers; however, each displays differently. The child viewer's icon will be displayed at the bottom, of its parent viewer. For instance, if you minimize a child viewer whose parent window is the Main window, the child viewer's icon will be displayed at the bottom left corner within the Main window. The popup viewer's icon will be displayed like other Windows application when minimized, at the bottom of the desktop in Windows.

Assigning a Menu Bar to a Viewer

To assign a menu bar to a viewer, you can either use the interface or use OpenScript. Using the interface to assign a menu bar to a viewer is easy by following these steps:

1. Select Object, Viewers from the main menu. The Viewers dialog box appears.
2. Select the viewer that you want to assign a menu bar.
3. Press the Properties button to display the Viewer Properties dialog box (refer to fig. 8.5).
4. Click the Menu Bar button from the Viewer Properties dialog box to display the Choose Menu Bar dialog box (see fig. 8.10).

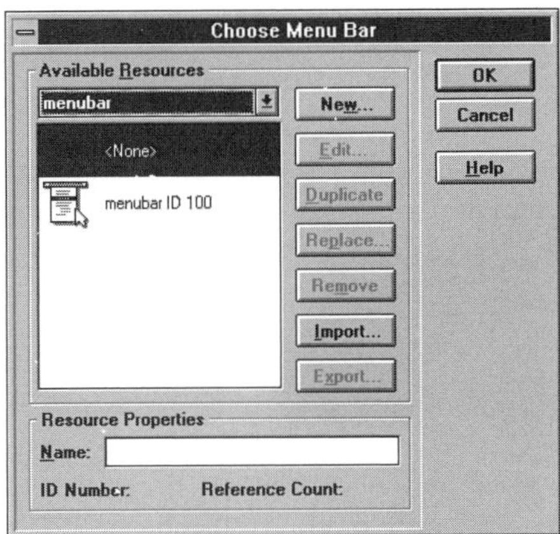

Fig. 8.10

The Choose Menu Bar dialog box allows you to assign a predefined menu bar.

5. Select a menu from the list of available menus.

You can also set the menu bar of a viewer from the Command Window, such as the following script does:

```
menuBar of viewer "Help" = menu ID 2
```

To create the menu itself, refer to Chapter 9, "Creating Custom Menus."

Determining an Icon for a Viewer

An icon can be assigned to a viewer as easily as a menu bar can. Follow these steps:

1. Select Object, Viewers from the main menu. The Viewers dialog box appears.
2. Select the viewer that you want to assign an icon.
3. Press the Properties button to display the Viewer Properties dialog box (refer to fig. 8.5).
4. Click the Icon button from the Viewer Properties dialog box to display the Choose Icon dialog box (see fig. 8.11).

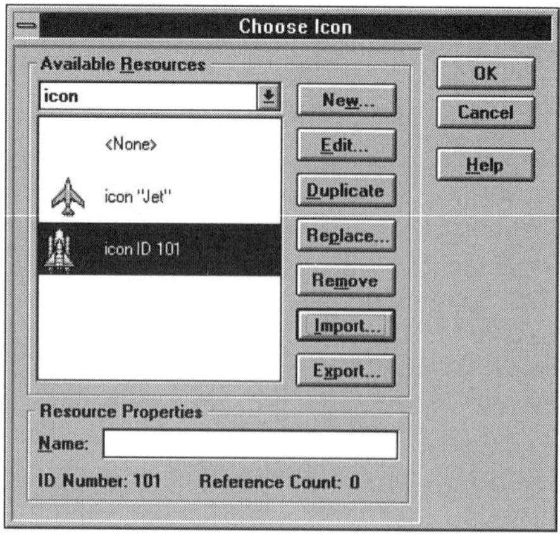

Fig. 8.11

Select New from the Choose Icon dialog box to create your own custom icon.

5. Select an icon from the list of available icons.

You can also use OpenScript to assign an icon to your viewer. For instance, you could enter the following script into the Command Window:

```
icon of viewer "Help" = icon ID 2
```

Advanced Viewers

There are many powerful features in Multimedia ToolBook, but at times it can be useful to review script examples of interesting methods to achieve certain effects.

Creating a Full-Screen Book

As a Multimedia ToolBook developer, you may find it necessary to create a full-screen application that draws the Main window without a border, caption bar, or menu bar. Also, you may need this application to fit to the entire screen resolution, no matter what resolution. Displaying a full screen book can be accomplished using the script in Listing 8.6.

Listing 8.6 08MTB06.TBK Full-Screen Book Script

```
to handle enterApplication
     forward
     linkDLL "user"
          INT lockWindowUpdate(WORD)
          WORD getDeskTopWindow()
     end
     deskTop = getDeskTopWindow()
     get LockWindowUpdate(deskTop)
     defaultState of mainWindow = maximized
     hide menuBar
     hide statusBar
     captionBar of mainWindow = none
     borderStyle of mainWindow = none
```

```
        show mainWindow
        send sizeToViewer
        get lockWindowUpdate(0)
    end enterApplication
```

Refer to Chapter 24 for details about the `lockWindowUpdate()` function and the `getDeskTopWindow()` function.

Creating a Transparent Viewer

Creating a transparent viewer may suggest to you the use of several API calls. In fact, a transparent viewer can be created using just a few simple settings. Follow these steps:

1. Create a new viewer with a new page and background.
2. Make certain the new background's color is set to white.
3. Set the pattern of the background to `none` using OpenScript, such as in the following:

   ```
   pattern of this background = none
   ```

4. Now, create a bitmap clip and name the clip `bmp1`. (For information related to creating clips, refer to Chapter 21, "Using Multimedia Elements.")
5. Create a viewer and name it `stage1`.
6. Create a button and add the following script to the button:

   ```
   to handle buttonClick
             mmPlay clip "bmp1" in stage "stage1"
             show viewer "Transparent Viewer" as notActive
   end buttonClick
   ```

From Here...

In this chapter, you have learned to manipulate viewers. For further information, see the following:

- Chapter 13, "OpenScript Fundamentals," explains how each object fits in the Object Hierarchy.
- Chapter 9, "Creating Custom Menus," explains how to create and add a menu to a viewer.

CHAPTER 9

Creating Custom Menus

If you are familiar with Windows, then you are no doubt familiar with menus and their components. Menus allow you to quickly access your applications' specific or more commonly used functions. You may have noticed that nearly all Windows applications have File, Edit, and Help menus. Not only do these common menus help add consistency among Windows applications, but they also allow users to feel more familiar and comfortable with new applications.

Multimedia ToolBook allows you to create and control menus in your applications with little difficulty. The Menu Bar Editor gives you a quick means to create and edit entire menu bars. These menu bars can be imported as resources into your application and referenced when you need them. In addition to adding and changing entire menu bar resources, you can also use specific OpenScript terms to modify all parts of a menu bar and menus.

ToolBook provides capabilities to create and edit menu bars with submenus and also popup menus. After completing this chapter, you will be able to:

- Create and edit a menu bar resource
- Use OpenScript to modify a menu while your application is executing
- Create popup menus using OpenScript

Using Menus

Menus are contained within a menu bar. Multimedia ToolBook applications can contain many menu bar resources; however, each viewer can display only one menu bar at a time. Switching the menu bar of a viewer gives you the ability to change the users' capabilities based on available menus.

> **Note**
>
> A viewer can have only one menu bar assigned to it at a time.

Before you use menus, you need to understand the different types of menus available in Multimedia ToolBook. Once you understand which type of menu you want to use, you need to know how you and the users can interact with the menu.

Menu Types

The three types of menus that you can create using ToolBook are *drop-down menus, submenus*, and *popup menus*. Each menu in your menu bar is commonly called a drop-down menu because it can contain several menu items. Submenus are additional menus displayed to the right of your selected menu item. Each submenu can contain an additional submenu. When you generate several layers of submenus, it's known as creating *cascading menus*. Popup menus are single menus that display at a specific location determined by you, the developer.

Drop-down Menus

A drop-down menu is created when you add one or more menu items to a menu. For instance, the Copy menu item is usually found in the Edit drop-down menu. Figure 9.1 displays a drop-down menu.

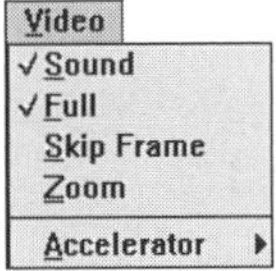

Fig. 9.1

A drop-down menu is created when you add one or more menu items to a menu.

Submenus

A submenu is an additional menu that is displayed to the right of your selected menu item (see fig. 9.2). The availability of a submenu is indicated by a triangle on the right side of the menu item that simply points to the right. Submenus allow you to have the availability of several quick selections, save space, and are visually easy to understand.

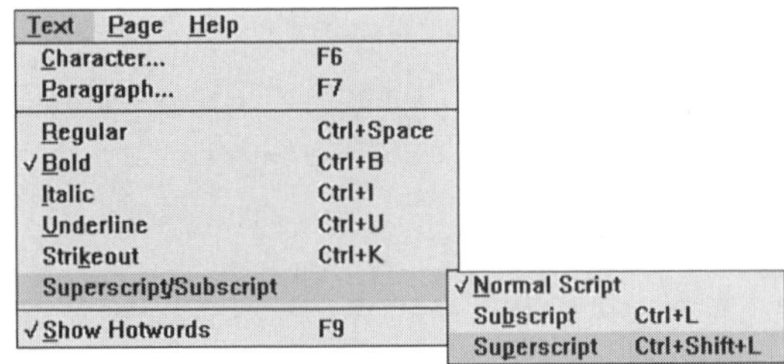

Fig. 9.2

A submenu is an additional menu that is displayed to the right of your selected menu item.

When you have an extensive number of options you can use several levels of submenus, commonly described as *cascading menus*.

Popup Menus

Popup menus allow you to display a menu at any location within the client area of your ToolBook application. At first look, popup menus may seem difficult to use, but are actually quite simple. There are two types of popup menus, each created a different way in Multimedia ToolBook. You can use the `popupMenu()` function, which requires no special DLL linking, or the `popMenu()` function from `TB3WIN.DLL`.

Popup menus can be displayed anywhere within your Main window or any other viewer. Figure 9.3 displays two types of popup menus.

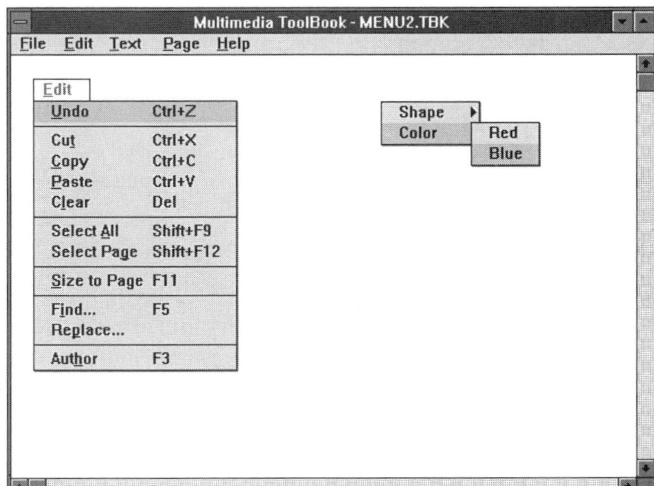

Fig. 9.3

Popup menus allow you to display a menu at any location within the client area of your ToolBook application.

Menu Interaction

Other than using a pointing device such as a mouse, you can select a menu and menu items using shortcut keys or OpenScript.

When creating a Computer Based Training application to demonstrate how to use certain menu items in your menu bar, you could control your menus and menu events using OpenScript.

Using OpenScript

Two OpenScript methods that can be used to access menu functionality are the `send` command and the `sendKeys()` function.

The `send` command executes the same handler that is executed when a menu item is selected. For example, rather than choosing Page, Next from the menu bar, you enter the following script from the Command Window:

```
send next
```

The `sendKeys()` function allows you to access a menu bar as if you were selecting each menu and menu item using a mouse. This function can be very useful for demos; however, it can also be difficult to use—once you begin executing a series of `sendKeys()` commands, it is difficult to ensure that the proper event is occurring.

Whenever you use `sendKeys()`, temporarily disable the user from adding additional key strokes by locking out the user. Use Windows API call called `enableHardwareInput()`. The `enableHardwareInput()` function can either enable or disable mouse and keyboard input. At times, you may find disabling input at the beginning of the process and enabling input after the process is completed a benefit.

Caution

The `enableHardwareInput()` function is fairly risky to use because it can prevent the user from controlling the computer. It's likely that this function wasn't included in OpenScript because of the dangers of its use. Therefore, you should be very familiar with OpenScript and using Windows API calls before using this function.

Using Shortcut Keys

Using shortcut keys to select menus and menu items can be very efficient compared to using a mouse; however, memorizing shortcut keys is not as comfortable or friendly as using a mouse. Generally, only power users use shortcut keys to select menus and menu items. Menu shortcut keys can be recognized by the underscored character of the menu or menu item name. This special character is called a *mnemonic character*.

◀◀ Mnemonic characters can be used to access buttons as well. Refer to Chapter 3, "Understanding Objects," for details.

ToolBook allows you to define a shortcut key for menus and menu items by placing an ampersand (&) in front of the character you want to define as the shortcut key, or mnemonic character. For instance, if you have a menu named `Multimedia` with a menu item of `Sound`, you could define the shortcut key as `o` by placing an ampersand in front of the `o`, such as `S&ound`.

To place an ampersand character within the name of your menu or menu item, enter two consecutive ampersands. For instance, if you want your menu to display as `Sound & Video`, you would name your menu `Sound && Video`. If you also needed to included a shortcut key you could name your menu `S&ound && Video`.

Using Menu Bar Resources

The Resource Manager allows you to manipulate many types of ToolBook resources. To access the Resource Manager, select Object, Resource (Ctrl+F10) from the menu bar, or select the resources icon from the toolbar. The Resource Manager gives you control of resources such as bitmaps, icons, cursors, fonts and menu bars (see fig. 9.4).

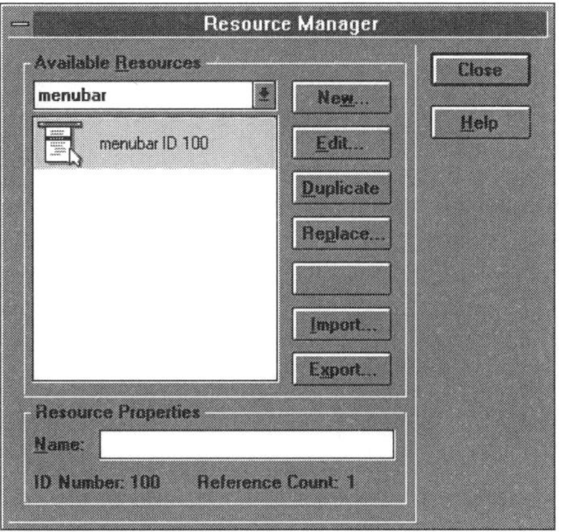

Fig. 9.4

The Resource Manager gives you control of several different types of resources, such as bitmaps, icons, cursors, fonts, and menu bars.

This section describes the Resource Manager when working with menus. For information related to applying a menu bar resource to a viewer, refer to the section "Applying a Menu Bar Resource," later in this chapter. For complete information about the Resource Manager, refer to Chapter 5, "Understanding the Media Management Tools."

Creating a Menu Bar Resource

At times, you may want to create a new menu bar resource rather than modify an existing menu. When you want to create a new menu resource, you can use the Menu Bar Editor.

The Menu Bar Editor is a development tool that allows you to quickly create and change your entire menu bar. The menu bar that you create can be included as a resource of your book. This menu resource can be saved with your book and applied to your viewers for use at both Author and Reader level. Also, a menu bar resource can be used with the Main viewer at Reader level. The Menu Bar Editor is a separate Windows program much like `BitEdit` and `PalEdit`. When you create a menu, you can save it as a file with the extension of `.MNU` or import it directly into your Multimedia ToolBook book.

Tip

The menu bar resources created with the Menu Bar editor can only be applied within a ToolBook application.

Creating a menu bar resource is an easy process using the Menu Bar Editor. The Menu Bar Editor allows you to enter your menu name, the alias of your menu, and any help text that you want to display in the status bar when you place your cursor over the menu and menu item. You can also add shortcut keys, set the initial state, and position each menu and menu item. The steps are as follows:

1. Within ToolBook, open the Resource Manager dialog box by selecting Object, Resources from the menu bar, selecting the Resources icon from the toolbar, or by pressing Ctrl+F10. (Also note that the Menu Bar Editor can be opened by selecting the Menu Editor icon from the Multimedia ToolBook group in the Program Manager.)
2. Set the resource type as menu bar by selecting `menubar` from the Available Resource list box.
3. Launch the Menu Bar editor by selecting New from the Resource Manager dialog box. The Menu Bar Editor is displayed (see fig. 9.5).

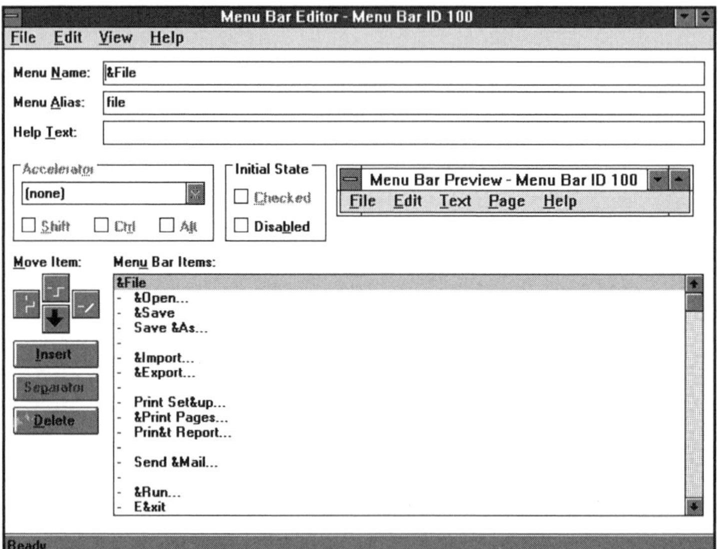

Fig. 9.5

You can use the Menu Bar editor to create a menu bar resource for your ToolBook application.

4. To add a menu or menu item, enter the Menu Name into the appropriate text box. Notice that the menu bar items are displayed at the bottom of the Menu Bar Editor. Click below the last line in the Menu Bar Items box to add more menus and menu items. Repeat this step to add even more.
5. Move each menu bar item within the Menu Bar Items box so that your menus and menu items are displayed as you want. Select one of the four directional arrows underneath Move Item. Reordering your menus and menu items is similar to adjusting lines in an outline. You can move menu bar items up or down the list, or to the right or left. Notice that there is a Menu Bar Preview window that displays your current menu bar.
6. If you want, you can add additional functionality to each menu item by adding an alias, desired help text, the initial state of each menu, and a shortcut key.

7. Select File, Save As, Menu Bar In Current Book from the menu bar of the Menu Bar Editor.
8. Enter a name for your menu bar resource in the Define Name dialog box to save it to your book.

Editing a Menu Bar Resource

Editing a menu resource allows you to make permanent changes to your menu bar resource rather than just temporary changes that can be made using OpenScript commands.

The Menu Bar Editor makes it easy to edit a menu bar resource. When you display a menu bar resource in the Menu Bar Editor, you will see the entire layout of the menu. Also notice that there is a Menu Bar Preview window. To edit a menu bar, follow these steps:

1. Within ToolBook, open the Resource Manager dialog box by selecting Object, Resources from the menu bar, selecting the Resources icon from the toolbar, or pressing Ctrl+F10. If ToolBook is not open, select the Menu Editor icon from the Multimedia ToolBook group in the Program Manager.
2. Set the resource type as Menu Bar by selecting `menubar` from the Available Resource list box.
3. Now select the menu bar resource that you want to edit.
4. Launch the Menu Bar Editor by selecting Edit from the Resource Manager dialog box. At this point, the Menu Bar Editor is displayed.
5. You can modify a menu or menu item by changing the Menu Name in the appropriate text box. Notice that the menu bar items are display at the bottom of the Menu Bar Editor in the Menu Bar Items list box.
6. Move each menu bar item within the Menu Bar Items box so that your menus and menu items are displayed as you want. Select one of the four directional arrows underneath Move Item. Reordering your menus and menu items is similar to adjusting lines in a outline. You can move menu bar items up or down the list, or to the right or left. Notice that there is a Menu Bar Preview window that displays your current menu bar.
7. If you want, you can add additional functionality to each menu item by adding an alias, desired help text, the initial state of each menu, and a shortcut key.
8. Select File, Update (Ctrl+S) from the menu bar of the Menu Bar Editor to update the menu in the Resource Manager.
9. Select File, Exit (Alt+F4) to exit the Menu Bar Editor.

Duplicating a Menu Bar Resource

Rather than creating a new menu bar, you may find it easier and quicker to duplicate a menu bar and edit it. If you want to copy a menu bar into another book, refer to the sections, "Exporting a Menu Bar Resource" and "Importing a Menu Bar Resource" later in this chapter. To duplicate a menu bar resource, follow these steps:

1. Display the Resource Manager by selecting Object, Resource from the menu bar, selecting the resources icon from the toolbar, or pressing Ctrl+F10.
2. Select `menubar` from the Available Resource list box from the Resource Manager dialog box.
3. Select the menu bar resource that you want to duplicate.
4. Press the Duplicate button from the Resource Manager dialog box.

Duplicating a menu bar is truly an authoring activity. There is no OpenScript command to directly duplicate a menu bar resource; however, you could export the menu bar resource and then import the resource as previously mentioned.

Replacing a Menu Bar Resource

You can also replace a Menu Bar Resource using the Resource Manager. Rather than resetting several viewers to use a new menu bar resource, you can simply replace your old menu bar from the Resource Manager. For instance, if you want to replace a specific menu bar resource from your current book with a menu bar resource from another book, follow these steps:

1. Display the Resource Manager by selecting Object, Resource from the menu bar, selecting the resources icon from the toolbar, or by pressing Ctrl+F10.
2. Select `menubar` from the Available Resource list box from the Resource Manager dialog box.
3. Select the menu bar resource that you want to replace.
4. Press the Replace button from the Resource Manager dialog box. The Replace Resource dialog box appears.
5. Choose a book (`.TBK`) that contains the replacement menu bar resource from the Replace Resource dialog box.
6. Select the replacement menu bar resource and press OK.

Script can be used to replace a menu resource from a menu bar file. For example, if you had a menu bar resource named `video` and menu bar file named `VIDEONEW.MNU`, you could enter the following script into the Command Window:

```
replace resource menubar "video" with "C:\MTB30\MENU\VIDEONEW.MNU"
```

Removing a Menu Bar Resource

When you no longer need a menu bar resource in your book, such as when you have duplicated a menu bar resource, you can remove it if you want. To reduce the size of your application, you can remove an unneeded menu bar resource as follows:

1. Display the Resource Manager by selecting Object, Resource from the menu bar, selecting the resources icon from the toolbar, or by pressing Ctrl+F10.
2. Select `menubar` from the Available Resource list box from the Resource Manager dialog box.
3. Select the menu bar resource that you want to remove.
4. Press the Remove button from the Resource Manager dialog box.

You can also remove a menu bar resource using OpenScript. For instance, if you needed to remove a menu bar resource during the execution of your application, you could use script. The following example could be placed into the script of a button to remove a menu bar resource:

```
to handle buttonClick
remove resource menuBar ID 101 of this book
end buttonClick
```

You could also reference a menu bar resource by the resource's name and the name of the book the resource is located. For instance:

```
to handle buttonClick
remove resource menuBar "video menu" of book "training.tbk"
end buttonClick
```

Note

If the menu bar resource is in use by a viewer, ToolBook will not allow you to remove the resource until the menu bar is no longer in use.

Importing a Menu Bar Resource

Rather than using the Menu Bar Editor to recreate a menu bar resource each time you need a new menu, you could import an existing menu directly into your book. You can import a menu bar resource from a menu file (`.MNU`) or a book. For instance, suppose you save all of your menu bar resources as `.MNU` files in a specific directory. You can use the following steps to import a menu bar resource:

1. Display the Resource Manager by selecting Object, Resource from the menu bar, selecting the resources icon from the toolbar, or by pressing Ctrl+F10.
2. Press the Import button from the Resource Manager dialog box to display the Import Resource dialog box.
3. Choose a menu bar resource file (`.MNU`) or enter a menu bar resource file name in the File Name box and select OK.
4. If you want, name your new menu bar resource by selecting it and entering a name in the Name box at the bottom of the Resource Manager dialog box.

The following script example imports the menu bar resource and also names the resource. ToolBook automatically assigns its ID reference. Enter the following script into the Command Window:

```
import menuBar  resource "c:\video.mnu"
```

The following example imports a menu bar resource and names it `Video`. Enter the following script into the Command Window:

```
import menuBar  resource "video.mnu" as "video"
```

Exporting a Menu Bar Resource

At times, you may want to manage your menu bar resources as separate menu bar files. Menu bar files are stored with the extension `.MNU`. You can export a menu bar resource to its own file from the Resource Manager dialog box. To do so, follow these steps:

1. Display the Resource Manager by selecting Object, Resource from the menu bar, selecting the resources icon from the toolbar, or by pressing Ctrl+F10.
2. Select `menubar` from the Available Resource list box from the Resource Manager dialog box.
3. Select the menu bar resource that you want to export.
4. Press the Export button from the Resource Manager dialog box.
5. Name the menu bar resource file, such as `BMPCTRL.MNU`.

Note

The resource will not be removed from your book when exported to a file. To remove a menu bar resource, refer to the earlier section "Removing a Menu Bar Resource."

The following example exports a menu bar resource from a book. Enter the following example into the Command Window:

```
export resource menuBar  "clock" as "c:\menus\clock.mnu"
```

Applying a Menu Bar Resource

Once you have designed your menu bar resource using the Menu Bar Editor, you can apply it to any viewer in your ToolBook application, except the Author menu in the Main window.

Note

A new viewer will not have a menu bar assigned to it unless you assign a menu bar resource to your viewer.

To apply a menu bar resource to a viewer, follow these steps:

1. Choose Object, Viewers from the menu bar or press Shift+F10.
2. Select the viewer that will display your menu bar from the list of viewers in the Viewers dialog box.
3. Press the Properties button in the Viewers dialog box.
4. Press the Menu Bar button in the Viewer Properties dialog box.
5. Select the menu bar resource that you want your viewer to display and press OK. (To create a new menu bar resource, refer to the section, "Creating a Menu Bar Resource," earlier in this chapter.)

The following example assigns a menu bar resource to a viewer using OpenScript:

```
menuBar of viewer "Video Display" = menuBar "video"
```

Using OpenScript to Modify Menus

When you want to temporarily modify a menu bar without changing the current menu bar resource or you need to modify the author menus—which cannot be done using a menu bar resource—use OpenScript.

OpenScript gives you the control you need to temporarily modify your menus and menu items. Also, using OpenScript is the only way you can modify the menus and menu items at the author level.

One important disadvantage of using OpenScript to modify your menu and menu items is that your menus and menu items are only temporarily changed. When you leave ToolBook, your menus will be restored to the default. Therefore, menu bar resources, which are saved as part of the book, can be easier than using several OpenScript commands to make menu changes.

Note

The `restore menuBar` command reverts all changes made to the menus and menu items made with OpenScript commands.

Adding to the Menu Bar

When you need to make changes to a menu bar during runtime or at the Author level menu, you can use OpenScript.

Note

Changes to the menu bar using OpenScript are temporary. To make permanent changes to a menu, you will need to use the Menu Bar Editor while authoring your application.

There are several OpenScript commands that are used to control menu bars within your book. Table 9.1 identifies each OpenScript menu command and purpose.

Table 9.1 OpenScript Menu Commands

Command	Purpose
`restore menuBar`	Reverts the menu back to it original resource state
`hide menuBar`	Removes a menu bar from sight
`show menuBar`	Displays a menu bar that was hidden
`Add menu`	Adds a menu to the menu bar or to another menu item as a submenu
`remove menu`	Removes a menu from the menu bar or from a menu item
`setMenuName()`	Changes the display name of a menu
`setMenuHelpText()`	Changes the help text assigned to a menu
`enable menu`	Enables a previously disabled menu or submenu (undims)
`disable menu`	Disables a menu or submenu (dims)
`menuEnabled()`	Checks if a menu or submenu is enabled or disabled
`add menuItem`	Adds a menu item to a menu
`remove menuItem`	Removes a menu item from a menu
`remove separator`	Removes a separator bar from a menu
`setMenuItemName()`	Sets the name of a menu item
`setMenuItemHelpText()`	Sets the help text displayed when a menu item is pointed to
`enable menuItem`	Enables a disabled menu item
`disable menuItem`	Disables an enabled menu item
`check menuItem`	Places a checkmark next to the selected menu item
`uncheck menuItem`	Removes a checkmark next to the menu item
`menuItemEnabled()`	Checks if a menu item is enabled or disabled
`menuItemChecked()`	Checks if a menu item is checked or not

Adding Menus Using OpenScript

When using OpenScript to add a menu to the menu bar, there are several parameters to include. The parameters for the `add menu` command include the menu name, the menu alias, the menu reference, the position of the menu, the menu level, and the help text of the menu. Only the menu name and menu reference are necessary when adding a menu, although you will no doubt use the additional menu parameters.

The following example adds a new menu named `Media` to the menu bar in the Main window at Reader level. Enter the following script from the Command Window:

```
add menu "Media" position 4 at reader \
with helpText "Select supported media"
```

The following example adds a new menu named `Properties` to viewer `Media Manager`. Place the script in Listing 9.1 into the script of a button.

Listing 9.1 Adding a Menu Using OpenScript

```
to handle buttonClick
     in viewer "Media Manager"
          add menu "Properties" alias "Media Props"
     end in
end buttonClick
```

As you can see in this script, the `in` structure can be very useful in relation to viewers. For more information about the `in` structure, refer to Chapter 8, "Working with Viewers."

Adding Menu Items Using OpenScript

Once you have successfully added your menu, you can begin to add your menu items. If you want, you can add menu items to existing menu items to create submenus. The script in Listing 9.2 adds a menu to a viewer.

Listing 9.2 Adding a Menu Item Using OpenScript

```
to handle buttonClick
     Open viewer "3DVideo"
     in viewer "3DVideo"
          add menuItem "&Video" to menu "Media" position 1 with helpText \
          "Displays properties of available Video clips" at both
     end in
end buttonClick
```

This script adds both a menu item to a menu and includes the help text of that menu item. The help text appears in the status bar when the user places the cursor over the menu item.

Adding Submenus Using OpenScript

You can also modify your menus by adding submenus. When you add several continuing submenus to your menu bar, you are creating cascading menus. For instance, if you needed to create cascading menus related to media control, you could use the following example to get started. Place the script in Listing 9.3 into the script of a button.

Listing 9.3 Creating Cascading Menus Using OpenScript

```
to handle buttonClick
     add menu "&Media" at author
     add menu "&Video" in menu "Media" at author
     add menuItem "&Control" to menu "&Video" in menu "Media" \
     at author with helpText "Modify Video options"
end buttonClick
```

This script creates a cascading menu by first adding the menu named `Media` to the menu bar at Author level. Then, a second menu is added to the `Media` menu called `Video`. Within the `Video` menu, the author will have one option called `Control`. As the author, you could add additional menu items to the `Video` submenu.

Controlling Menus

When you need to dynamically control your menu bar, you can use the OpenScript menu functions. Enabling, checking, restoring, removing and changing menus and menu items are all possible using OpenScript.

Enabling and Disabling Menus and Menu Items

At times, you may need to control the amount of access your user has to certain menus and menu items. To enable a menu that has been previously disabled, you can use the `enable menu` command, by entering script similar to the following into the Command Window:

```
enable menu "Video" in menu "Media" at author
```

> **Note**
>
> It is good OpenScript practice to enclose all names of objects and menus inside quotation marks. It is particularly important to enclose the name of a menu or menu item in quotation marks if the name contains spaces. Using quotes helps ToolBook correctly interpret the names of objects, resources, clips, files, and menus rather than misinterpreting the script as a variable.

You can enable a menu item almost as easily as enabling a menu. Enabling a menu item at reader level gives the use additional capabilities to control your application. To enable a menu item, use the `enable menuItem` command. For instance, if you had a menu named `Media` with a submenu of `Video` and a menu item named `Control`, you could enter the following script into the Command Window to enable the menu item:

```
enable menuItem "Control" in menu "Video" in menu "Media" at author
```

Disabling a menu or menu item at Reader level prevents the user of your application from using capabilities that you do not want the users to access. Disabled menus and menu items are dimmed. You can still see the menu or menu item; however, they will not respond when clicked. To disable a menu that is currently enabled, you can use the `disable menu` command. Enter the following script into the Command Window:

```
disable menu "Video" in menu "Media" at author
```

You can also disable a menu item by using the `disable menuItem` command, like the following:

```
disable menuItem "Control" in menu "Video" in menu "Media" at author
```

Hiding and Showing Menus

When you want to remove the menu bar from your users' view, you can use the `hide` command. Equally, the `show` command can be used to display a hidden menu bar. When you want to customize your application with your own controls, such as a navigation toolbar, you could hide your menu bar from the user of your application.

When you hide a menu bar, the shortcut keys, also known as mnemonic keys, no longer work for the menu; however, the function keys and control keys will work. Enter the following script into the Command Window:

```
hide menuBar
```

Upon hiding a menu bar, the client window will shift up to the position of the previously shown menu bar. It is not possible to create a blank menu bar; however, it is possible to use the `popupMenu()` function to simulate a menu bar. When the simulated menu bar is hidden, the client window remains in its original position.

At times you may want to show a menu bar that was previously hidden, such as when you change the interface, when you change from Reader to Author level, or when you want to give the user additional menu capabilities. To show a hidden menu bar, use the `show menuBar` command, like the following:

```
show menuBar
```

Removing Menus And Menu Items

When you want to reduce the number of menu capabilities available to your users, you can simply remove a menu from your menu bar. Use the `remove menu` command when you need to remove a menu from the menu bar or you need to remove a submenu from a menu item. For instance, you could remove the standard Page menu from reader level so that the user must use your customized navigation interface. Enter the following script into the Command Window:

```
remove menu "Video" in menu "Media" at author
```

You can also remove menu items from a menu. Use the `remove menuItem` command to remove menu items, like the following:

```
remove menuItem "Control" in menu "Video" in menu "Media" at author
```

> **Note**
>
> Submenus are recognized by the arrow that points to the menu items on the right. Although submenus are listed along with menu items, submenus must be treated as menus rather than menu items.

Restoring Menus

Use the `restore menuBar` command when you need to set all menus and menu items back to their original menu resource state. When you restore a menu bar, you can choose which level you want to restore. You have the choice of Reader level, Author level, or both levels. If you do not specify which level to restore your menu bar, the menu bar is restored in the target window at the current working level. For instance, you could have a viewer that displays media with a variety of options. These options could be changed by selecting different menu items. You could modify the available menus depending on the choice of media that you display. When the user closes this viewer, you could reset the displayed menu bar. The following script could be placed into the script of a viewer to restore the menu bar at both reader and author level:

```
to handle leaveWindow
     restore menuBar at both
     forward
end
```

This script, when placed into the script of a viewer, will reset the menu bar at both Reader and Author level.

Using Menus Between Books

If you set the `keepMenuBar` book property to `true`, your menu bar will not change when you navigate to a new book. By default, when you navigate to a new book, your menu bar will change to the menu bar assigned to the Main viewer of the new book.

All new books are automatically created displaying the Main window with `menuBar ID 100` assigned to the Main window. `menuBar ID 100` is simply the default menu bar resource.

Using Menu Item Checkmarks

When you have a specific feature and want to visibly indicate whether the feature is true or false, you can add a menu item that displays a checkmark when selected. For instance, you could create a timer function that automatically saves your book every ten minutes. When the menu item is checked, your book will be automatically saved. When the menu item is unchecked, you must manually save your book.

The example script in Listing 9.4 can be used to increase your authoring productivity. This script allows you to quickly add a name to each new object that is created in your book; this should be added to the script of your book.

Listing 9.4 Controlling Authoring Capabilities Using Menu Item Checkmarks

```
to handle make
     forward
     system autoMenu
     if autoMenu <> true
          add menuItem "Auto Name" alias "autoName" \
to menu "Object" position 1 at author
autoMenu = true
     end
     if menuItemChecked("Auto Name" in menu "Object") = true
          ask "Name of new" && object of selection
          name of selection = it
     end
end
```

```
to handle autoName
     if menuItemChecked("Auto Name" in menu "Object") = true
          uncheck menuItem "Auto Name" in menu "Object"
     else
          check menuItem "Auto Name" in menu "Object"
     end
end
```

This script can be used to automatically name any newly created object. Place this script into the script of your book or include it within a system book that you use for authoring. To activate this script, start by creating an object. When you create an object and this script is available, it will add a menu named `Auto Name` to your `Object` menu in Author mode. When you select the `Auto Name` menu item, the menu item becomes checked. While this menu item is checked, you will be prompted to name each newly created object, such as buttons, rectangles, stages, and so on. When you uncheck the `Auto Name` menu item, you no longer will be prompted for a name.

Changing Menu and Menu Item Names

You can change the name of a menu as it appears on the menu bar using the `setMenuName()` menu control function. Use the `setMenuName()` function to change a submenu's name as well. This function is used to change just the menu name, the menu alias does not change. For instance, you could use this function to set a menu name to `Video` whenever you enter the page that deals with video control. Enter the following script into the Command Window to change the `Help` menu to `MyHelp`:

```
get setMenuName("Help", "MyHelp", mainWindow)
```

This script contains `get` at the beginning of the script statement because you are "getting" a function named `setMenuName` with three parameters.

> **Note**
>
> For more information about using the `get` command, refer to Chapter 16, "Statements, Functions, and Expressions."

If you need to change a menu item name you can use the `setMenuItemName` menu control function. For example, if you needed to change a menu item named `Control` to `MyControl`, you would enter the following script into the Command Window:

```
get setMenuItemName("Control", "MyControl", mainWindow)
```

Adding Optional Menu Features

There are several options of the menu bar that you are not required to set, such as mnemonic access, menu aliases, and menu help text; however, these options are well worth understanding. To give the user a quick method to access menus, you can add shortcut keys. If you need to display the name of your menu differently than the handler you create for the menu, use a menu alias. When you want to give the user additional information when selecting a menu, add menu help text.

Adding Mnemonic Access

Adding mnemonic access to your menus and menu items has been mentioned throughout this chapter. Mnemonic access is simply the use of a shortcut key. Mnemonic access to a menu is available when you see an underscored character in the name of the menu or menu item. A mnemonic character allows you to access a menu or menu item using the keyboard, such as Alt+F.

You can designate which character is the mnemonic character when you create the menu or menu item. However, it is possible to set the mnemonic character by using the `setMenuName()` or `setMenuItemName()` functions. To add mnemonic access using OpenScript, you simply need to add an ampersand in front of the character within the name of your menu or menu item that you want to designate as the mnemonic access character.

To add mnemonic access to a menu, enter the following script into the Command Window:

```
get setMenuName("Help", "&Help", mainWindow)
```

The first parameter is the name of the menu you want to rename. The second parameter is where you add your shortcut key. In the example above, you designate the `H` as the shortcut key. The third parameter is the reference to the viewer. You are modifying the Main windows menu bar.

The process of renaming a menu item is similar to renaming a menu, although you use a different function. To add mnemonic access to a menu item, enter the following script into the Command Window:

```
get setMenuItemName("Control", "&Control", mainWindow)
```

Menu Aliases

A menu alias is an optional parameter used with the `add menu` and `add menuItem` commands that specifies the message to be sent when a user-defined menu or menu item is chosen. The same alias can be used for more than one menu or menu item. Also, if you need to use a DLL function that uses the same name as an OpenScript keyword, you can use a menu alias with `linkDLL` to specify a DLL function name or ordinal reference.

The alias parameter is used with the `add menu` and `add menuItem` commands. When a user-defined menu or menu item is selected, the menu alias is sent as an OpenScript message rather than the name of the menu or menu item. Using a menu alias allows you to have more than one menu or menu item with the same name. Also, you can use the alias to have the same handler executed when you choose different menus or menu items. To create a menu with an alias, enter the following script into the Command Window:

```
add menu "&Video" alias "mediaCtrl" in menu "Help" \
at reader with helpText "Shows supported media types"
```

Menu Help Text

In Reader mode, when you place your cursor over a menu, the help text that is assigned to the menu appears in the status bar of the viewer. The same is true when you place your cursor over menu items. The status bar appears at the bottom of your Main window. To set or change the help text that is assigned to a menu, use the `setMenuHelpText()` function. To change or set the help text of a menu, enter the following script into the Command Window:

```
get setMenuHelpText("Help","New Help text!", mainWindow)
```

You can also set the help text of a menu item. Use the `setMenuItemHelpText()` function to set the help text of a menu item. For instance, if you had a menu named `Contents`, you could enter the following script into the Command Window to set or change its associated help text:

```
get setMenuItemHelpText("Contents","New Contents text!", mainWindow)
```

In addition, you have the option to use the menu or menu item alias rather than using the name of the menu or menu item. Remember, a menu or menu item alias sends the name of the alias as an OpenScript message rather than the displayed name.

Separator Bars

A separator bar is a line between your menu items. These separator bars allow you to show a division between your menu items. To add a separator bar using OpenScript, you can use the `add menuItem` command. For example, if you had a menu named `Media` with a submenu of `Video`, you could add a separator bar to this submenu by entering the following script into the Command Window:

```
add menuItem "" to menu "Video" in menu "Media" at author
```

To remove a separator bar from a menu, you need to use the `remove separator` command:

```
remove separator 2 in menu "Media" at author
```

You can also remove your menu's separator bar using the menu alias rather than the menu name. Removing a separator bar is a bit easier than adding one. When you add a separator bar to a menu, you simply add a blank menu item.

Using the *popupMenu()* Function

The popup menu functions allows you to display a menu at any location within the client area of your ToolBook application.

The popupMenu() function is easier to use then the popMenu() function. popupMenu() doesn't require you to link to a DLL to use the function. It also is much easier to define the structure of a popupMenu() function because it makes use of a menu bar resource.

popupMenu() allows you to specify three parameters—the location of the menu, the menu bar resource reference, and the name of the menu within the resource that you need to reference.

popupMenu() displays the menu items of the menu your choose from the menu bar resource. The menu bar resource must be available in your book.

Note

You can only choose one menu from the menu bar resource because the popupMenu() function does not support multiple menus.

When the user chooses a menu item from the displayed menu using popupMenu(), the function returns the name of the menu item and its alias, separated by a comma. If the user makes no selection, the popupMenu() function returns null. To understand how the popupMenu() function can be used, place the following script into the script of a button:

```
to handle buttonClick
     myMenuChoice = popupMenu("0,0", menuBar ID 100, "Help")
     if myMenuChoice <> null
          send (item 2 of myMenuChoice)
     end if
end buttonClick
```

This script will display the menu items of the standard Help menu. A local variable named myMenuChoice is set to the value that the popupMenu() function returns.

Using the *popMenu()* Function

The popMenu() function is similar to the popupMenu() function, however the former is more customizable and also more difficult to use.

To make the popMenu() function available, you must link in the function using the linkDLL statement. Refer to Chapter 19, "Using Dynamic Link Libraries (DLLs) and Dynamic Data Exchange (DDE)," for information about linking to DLLs.

Note

Each window that is displayed in Windows has its own unique reference number called the windowHandle.

The `popMenu()` function has six parameters, which are the values used to determine what information will be returned. Only five of the six parameters are used in the `popMenu()` function. The last parameter must be set to `null`. The first parameter that the `popMenu()` function requires is the `windowHandle` of the window you want to display the menu. The `windowHandle` of a window is simply a unique number that identifies a specific window. In the script example displayed in Listing 9.5, notice that the first parameter of the `popMenu()` function is the `windowHandle` of the Main window.

Remember, when you use the `popMenu()` function, you must display the menu with in a viewer. Often you will display your menu within the Main window, also known as viewer `ID 0`. When using `popMenu()` and displaying the menu within the Main window, you can simply reference the `windowHandle` as `windowHandle of mainWindow`. Remember, `popMenu()` requires you to use the `windowHandle` as a parameter. When you are displaying the menu in a different viewer, you can reference that viewer, such as `windowHandle of viewer "Help"`. You can also refer to the current window as `windowHandle of this window`.

The second parameter that you need to enter when using this function is the `pageScroll`. The `pageScroll` is a set of two numbers that represent the horizontal and vertical position of a window. In order to have your menu displayed in the correct location relative to the position of your client window, you must specify the offset value of the scroll of the client window if it has been adjusted vertically or horizontally. The `clientWindow` is a window displayed separately from its parent windows border, caption bar, and menu. Normally the `pageScroll` of your window will be `0,0`, which is the default. Notice that the example in Listing 9.5 uses the `pageScroll` of the Main window.

On rare occasion, you may need to display a menu in a viewer that has its magnification greater than normal. The third parameter of the `popMenu()` function can be used to account for magnification—such as the magnification of the current window or the magnification of the Main window. Listing 9.5 uses the magnification of the Main window.

You also can specify the position where your menu will be displayed. The position is the location of the top left corner of the menu. The position is comprised of a set of numbers represented in Page Units. If this value is outside the window being referenced, Windows will adjust the position of your menu so that it is completely displayed.

An easy way to set the position of your menu is to use a place holder, such as a rectangle. You can easily move the rectangle to the position where you would like your menu to be displayed; however, you would need to reference the position of the rectangle as the position of the menu. In the example in Listing 9.5, a ToolBook object is used to position the menu. Before executing the script in Listing 9.5, you must first draw a rectangle object and name it `MenuMark`.

The fifth parameter of the `popMenu()` function is the most important. This parameter is used to specify your menu items. Notice that in Listing 9.5 a variable named `menuList` was created to hold your menu items.

The script in Listing 9.5 requires the following steps to implement:

1. Create a rectangle named `MenuMark`.
2. Create a button and add the script in Listing 9.5 to the button.
3. From Reader mode, press and hold the button down. While the button is still depressed, select a menu item.

Listing 9.5 Using the *popMenu()* Function

```
to handle buttonDown
     linkDLL "TB30WIN.DLL"
          INT popMenu(WORD,STRING,INT,STRING,STRING,STRING)
     end linkDLL
     menuList = "{Shape," & "Square," & "Round,}," & \
     "{Color," & "Red,Blue,}"
     put popMenu(windowHandle of mainWindow,\
     pageScroll of mainWindow, magnification of mainWindow, \
     position of rectangle "MenuMark", menuList, null)
     -- create a rectangle named 'markMenu' and position this
     -- rectangle at the location you need to display the menu
end buttonDown
```

From Here...

In this chapter, you learned about creating, editing, and controlling menus. For further information, see the following chapters:

- Chapter 3, "Understanding Objects," discusses mnemonic access to buttons.
- Chapter 5, "Understanding the Media Management Tools," explains the Resource Manager in detail.
- Chapter 8, "Working with Viewers," explains the `in` structure.
- Chapter 16, " Statements, Functions, and Expressions " discusses in more detail how to use the `get` command.
- Chapter 19, "Using Dynamic Link Libraries (DLLs) and Dynamic Data Exchange (DDE)," shows you how to link to a DLL.

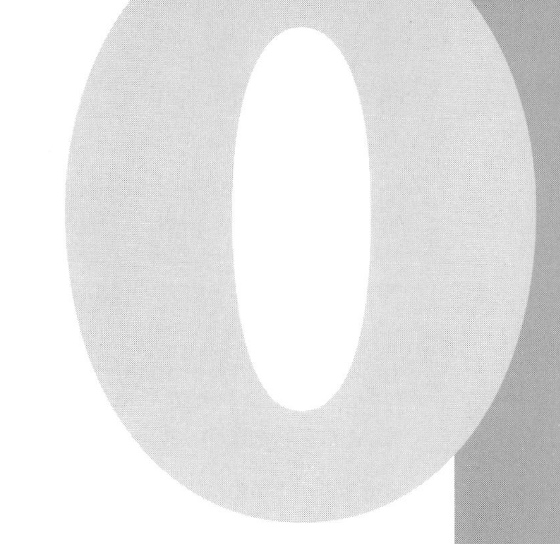

CHAPTER 10

Using Graphics

When you create multimedia applications, graphics become a necessity. You can display graphics in Multimedia ToolBook in six ways. These methods are as follows:

- Importing a graphic from a file to your page or background
- Using a graphic resource in a button, field, or stage
- Using a stage to display an image clip
- Using the `imageCommand()`
- Using an OLE object
- Pasting a graphic from another Windows application using the Clipboard

This chapter discusses importing and pasting bitmap and vector graphics into your applications. These graphics, like other objects in Multimedia ToolBook, have properties and a script. After completing this chapter, you will be able to do the following:

- Define a bitmap and vector-type graphic
- Import and display graphics in your applications
- Modify the properties of paint objects and picture objects
- Understand a specific graphic example

Graphic Object Types

Multimedia ToolBook has two graphic-object types: paint objects and picture objects. To display these objects, you need to import or paste the graphic into your page or background. Before you can decide which type of object to import, you must recognize the difference between these two types of objects.

Paint Objects

Examples of *paint objects* include photos and screen captures. To modify a paint object, you need a paint program.

A *bitmap* is an image composed of dots. Each dot is called a *pixel* (an abbreviation for *picture element*). A pixel is the smallest unit that your monitor can display. Pixels display different colors and intensities, which we can perceive as shading and depth. The bitmap file contains details about drawing each pixel that will be displayed. In essence, the image is a map of bits.

Bitmaps are referenced as paint objects in Multimedia ToolBook. A bitmap usually is captured from a video source or scanner, or created in a paint application such as BitEdit or Photoshop.

You should note that bitmaps contain a color palette. Color palettes are discussed later in this chapter.

Tip

To ensure that your bitmap image displays correctly on various systems, use an uncompressed bitmap format instead of a compressed bitmap format.

Paint objects have two major advantages: they draw fast, and they display great detail. These two benefits are the reasons why bitmaps are so commonly used. Bitmaps, however, have disadvantages: they require a great amount of disk space, they may display differently on different systems, and they are difficult to resize with true clarity.

Paint Object Properties. Other than allowing you to set the script and drag-and-drop options, the Paint Object Properties dialog box allows you to specify six main settings: the name; the layer; the transparent option; the Use Windows Colors option; and the Use Chromakey option, for which you also specify a color to see through (see fig. 10.1).

Fig. 10.1

The Paint Object Properties dialog box.

As you can for other objects in Multimedia ToolBook, you can set the name and the layer order of the paint object. Referring to objects by name rather than by ID can be beneficial. At times, you may copy an object and delete the original—an action that changes the object's ID.

Note

The layer number is ignored when using draw direct.

The transparent option allows objects behind your paint object, or on a higher-numbered layer, to be visible. You can set the `fillcolor` of the transparent object to white for complete transparency, or a color for partial visibility.

When you choose the Use Windows Colors option, you set the fill color and the stroke color to the colors specified in the Windows Control Panel.

The Chromakey option allows a selected color within the paint object to be transparent.

Picture Objects

Vector-type graphics (also known as draw-type graphics) are referred to as picture objects in Multimedia Toolbook. A vector graphic is created in a drawing program such as CorelDRAW!.

A *picture object* is a graphic that is not as detailed as a paint object. Picture objects are drawn based on instructions that define the details of the graphic. The details within the picture object (such as a circle or square) have their own dimensions, color, and style. The details can be as simple as four lines used to create a square. Essentially, the picture object is drawn based on an instruction map.

Note

A picture object cannot be modified within Multimedia ToolBook. You should make all modifications to your graphics—both picture and paint objects—before you place them in your application.

Picture Object Properties. Similar to paint objects, picture objects include such properties as Name, Layer, Transparent, and Use Window Colors. These are found in the Picture Properties dialog box (see fig. 10.2). Picture objects do not include a Chromakey option but do have a Convert button, which allows you to change your picture object to a paint object.

Caution

If you convert a paint object to a picture object, you cannot reverse the conversion.

Fig. 10.2

The Picture Properties dialog box.

The fastest way to edit paint and picture object properties is to right-click the object to display the shortcut menu. This menu is nearly the same for both paint and picture objects (see figs. 10.3 and 10.4). The paint-object menu includes the Chromakey option, which is unavailable for picture objects, although picture objects can be converted to paint objects. Also, picture objects can display the color white, much as a paint object can display the Chromakey effect.

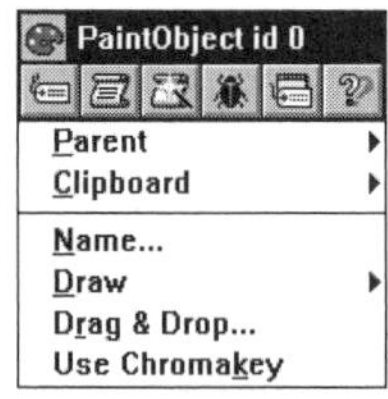

Fig. 10.3

The paint object shortcut menu.

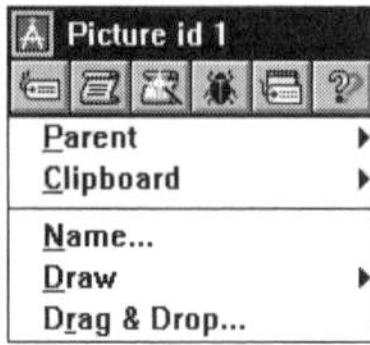

Fig. 10.4

The picture object shortcut menu.

Converting Picture Objects. Multimedia ToolBook gives you the option to convert your picture object to a paint object. Multimedia ToolBook essentially captures an image of your picture object.

You may want to convert a picture object to a paint object for two main reasons. The first reason is to gain imaging performance. If you want to drag an image, for example, use a paint object, because it will redraw faster and the movement will be smoother. The second reason for converting a picture object is to change the portion of the image that you want to display—a procedure that is called *cropping* the image. The anchor for the image is the top left corner.

Converting your picture object to a paint object is easy. Use the following steps:

1. Select the Picture object that you want to convert to a Paint object.
2. Select Object, Picture Properties from the menu bar. The Picture Properties dialog box will be displayed.
3. Now, select Convert from the Picture Properties dialog box. Note that a warning will be displayed stating that this conversion cannot be reversed.
4. Select OK to continue. Once the Picture object has been converted to a Paint object, the Paint Object Properties dialog box will automatically be displayed.
5. Select OK from the Paint Object Properties dialog box.

Importing Graphics

As you learned at the beginning of this chapter, you can use several methods to display graphics in Multimedia ToolBook. These methods are importing, using resources, displaying as a clip, using the `imageCommand` function, using an OLE object, and pasting from another Windows application. You should consider which method you want to use before you begin developing your application.

Importing or pasting graphics provides advantages and disadvantages. The advantages include palette control by means of a book palette, the capability to use the Chromakey effect for paint objects, the capability to crop paint objects, and the capability to scale picture objects. The disadvantages include the fact that you cannot scale imported paint objects. Both paint objects and picture objects become a permanent part of the book, thereby increasing the size of the book. You cannot make major modifications of an imported or pasted image within Multimedia ToolBook. The page or background memory limit that the image has been imported or pasted to is reduced in size.

You also can use *resources* to display graphics in Multimedia ToolBook. Resources can display images inside buttons, fields, or stages. The Chromakey option and scaling capabilities are both big benefits of using a graphic resource.

The most powerful, but not always the best way to display a graphic image, is to use the `imageCommand()` function. This function gives you great control of the image, and because the image is not contained in the book, it's easy to modify. The main drawback of using this function is its complexity.

Using a clip to display a graphic image gives you powerful control rather easily. In addition, you can add a transition effect to the stage that you use to display the image, control the palette easily, and modify the image quickly because it is not contained in the book. This method is the second in difficulty of use to the `imageCommand()` function.

The final way to display graphics in Multimedia ToolBook is to use an OLE object. This method allows you to modify a graphic easily if the image is linked to a Windows draw or paint application.

Filters and Formats

You can use several types of filters when you import graphics into Multimedia ToolBook. A *filter* is a definition of how a specific graphic file will be interpreted. When the graphic is imported with a filter, it is recognized as a paint object or a picture object, depending on the filter that you choose.

Multimedia ToolBook includes filters for importing a wide variety of graphic formats, including Bitmap (BMP), Macintosh QuickDraw Picture (PCT), ZSoft PC Paintbrush (PCX), Tag Image File Format (TIF), Windows Metafile (WMF), and Graphic Interchange Format (GIF).

You can add import filters by modifying the Graphic Import Filters section of the `ASYM.INI` file. Follow the line format, and make certain that the line points to a valid filter file.

If the Import Graphic dialog box does not include the filter that you need or does not support the desired format, you can use the Print Screen key or a capture program to capture the image. When the image is captured, you can paste it into your page or background.

To capture your image using the Print Screen button, refer to the following steps:

1. Display the image that you want to capture.
2. Press the Print Screen button on your keyboard.
3. Display your ToolBook book.
4. Select Edit, Paste from the ToolBook menu bar.

The Import Graphic Dialog Box

The Import Graphic dialog box allows you to select and preview the desired image (see fig. 10.5). You can select the image by file type or enter the file name. The preview displays a representation of your image. This feature is particularly time-saving when you are uncertain which image is contained in a file.

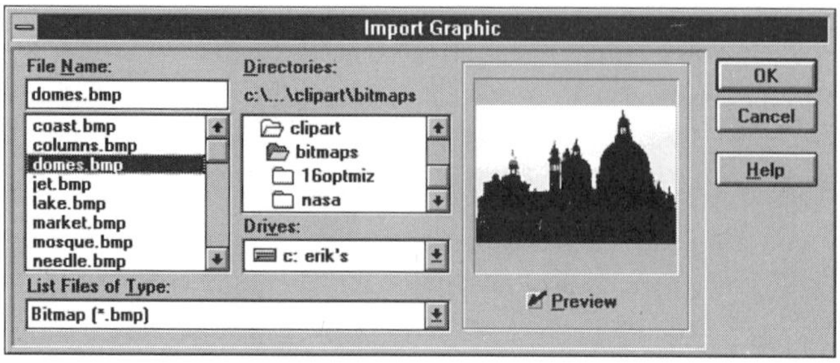

Fig. 10.5

The Import Graphic dialog box.

To import a graphic into your page or background, follow these steps:

1. Navigate to the page or background of where you want to place your graphic.
2. Select File, Import Graphic from the menu bar.
3. Select the graphic file type by choosing any of the types listed in the List Files of Type list box. For instance, choose Bitmap `(*.bmp)`.
4. Select both the Drive and Directory of where your graphic is located.
5. Also, select the File Name of your graphic. Note that you can click once on a displayed name to view the image in the Preview area.
6. Once you have successfully located your desired graphic, you can select OK to import it into your page or background.

It is possible to import a graphic using the OpenScript command called `importGraphic`. Enter the following script into the Command Window to import a graphic using OpenScript (note you may need to modify the file name and path):

```
importGraphic "c:\image\ranier.bmp"
```

Although it is possible to import a graphic using the `importGraphic` command, you may find controlling your image as a clip or using the `imageCommand()` function better methods for working with graphics.

Pasting Graphics

You can paste graphics into Multimedia ToolBook by copying them from other Windows applications. The Clipboard, which is a feature of Windows, allows you to temporarily store the image while switching from one Windows application to another. When you copy a vector graphic from a Windows application and then paste the image into a Multimedia ToolBook application, the image is a picture object. When a bitmap is copied and pasted from another Windows application, the image appears as a paint object in Multimedia ToolBook.

For example, let's import an image into your application from Paintbrush, using the following steps:

1. Open your ToolBook book and also Paintbrush. Paintbrush is commonly found in the Accessories group within Program Manager in Windows.
2. From within Paintbrush, choose File, Open from the menu bar.
3. Now select a Drive, Directory, and File Name from the Open dialog box within Paintbrush. For example, choose `256color.bmp` from the Windows directory.
4. Now, select the portion of the image that you want to import into ToolBook. Use the scissors tool from the tool bar at the left.
5. Select Edit, Copy from the menu bar.
6. Now display your ToolBook application. For instance, use Alt+Tab to quickly switch to your ToolBook application.
7. Select Edit, Paste from the ToolBook menu bar.

Display Management

In addition to importing your graphics to your page or background, you may need to modify the way that your graphics are displayed. When you work with graphics, you should consider the display of palettes, solid colors, draw direct, Chromakey, and ways to modify the appearance of your graphics.

Working with Palettes

Displaying palettes correctly can be the most difficult part of developing your application. Many developers create their applications to display in as many configurations as possible. Other developers create their applications for a specific computer system, because they know the limitations of the specific hardware and software.

The users of your Multimedia ToolBook applications generally will be running Windows 3.1 in 4-bit mode (16 colors), 8-bit mode (256 colors), 16-bit mode (65,536 colors), or 24-bit mode (16.7 million colors).

> **Note**
>
> The standard VGA driver for Windows displays at 640 x 480, using 16 colors. This driver works well for testing.

Palette conflicts are a concern when you are using an 8-bit driver, because only 256 colors are displayed at any time. When you display more than one bitmap at a time, you may see a distorted image or palette shift. A *palette shift* is a color flash that temporarily produces a distorted image when the display of bitmaps changes.

Windows can display a total 256 colors on-screen when you use a 256-color video driver. Each graphic that you display has its own color palette. If the image that you are displaying uses all 256 palette entries, any other image that you display at the same time will have distorted colors unless each image uses the same palette entries. In other words, if you use the same colors for different bitmaps, you will not display a palette shift.

When you create a 256-color bitmap, you should include the standard Windows colors. These palette entries will be the first 10 (0–9) and last 10 (246–255) in your color palette. PalEdit allows you to create a palette with the standard Windows colors.

◀◀ See "Advanced Viewers," p. 164

Displaying your application full-screen is beneficial so that you don't experience palette shifts as a result of displaying other Windows applications behind your application.

PalOpt. PalOpt is used to read the palette information of several graphic files and create one 256 color optimized palette. This palette can then be applied to each graphic file or used as the palette of your book.

PalEdit. PalEdit, is an application modified specifically for ToolBook and allows you to edit the colors of your bitmaps. You can use PalEdit to accomplish a variety of bitmap color tasks. One specific use is extracting your bitmap palette and importing it, as a resource, into Multimedia ToolBook. When you have imported this resource into your application and assigned it to your book, you can minimize or eliminate the occurrence of palette flashes.

Solid Colors

Multimedia ToolBook provides you a few options for keeping your graphics looking good. You can obtain additional control of the colors of your graphics by using the `solidColorsEnabled` book property. To use this property effectively, you must understand how Multimedia ToolBook controls palettes.

When the `solidColorEnabled` property of the book is set to `True` and is also set to `True` for your picture object, Multimedia ToolBook does its best to match the colors in the picture object's palette with the current palette.

When using OpenScript, enter the following lines consecutively into the Command Window:

```
solidColorsEnabled of this book = true
solidColorsEnabled of picture "mountain" = true
```

Draw Direct

You have the capability to draw your graphics directly to the screen. This option displays the image faster, although these objects will flash when entering the page. Also, layer control between draw-direct objects and non-draw-direct objects can be confusing. In most cases, controlling the layer order is very important. For simplicity, use draw direct only when needed.

> **Note**
>
> You can set the `sysDrawDirect` property to `true` or `false` upon entering the book by modifying the `startupDrawDirect` line in the `MTB30.INI` file.

Using OpenScript, enter the following line into the Command Window:

```
drawDirect of paintObject "mountain" = false
```

Chromakey

The Chromakey option is one of the most interesting effects used in Multimedia ToolBook. When the Chromakey option is applied, every color occurrence in the graphic that has an exact match with the color that you assign to the graphic, the fill color, appears as completely transparent. You can place another bitmap behind the Chromakeyed bitmap and clearly see the bitmap where the selected color is displayed.

> **Note**
>
> The Chromakey effect also is available for bitmap resources in Multimedia ToolBook.

Paint objects, which often display photos, may appear to use one solid color, such as a scenic photo of the sky. Such a photo often uses several colors to make the appearance realistic, such as several shades of blue to depict the sky. The Chromakey option allows you to select only one color—the fill color—as your transparent color. If you need to Chromakey an entire section of your paint object (in the example, the sky), you need to modify your graphic outside ToolBook. Photoshop allows you to make edits of this type rather easily.

Modifying Graphics

To modify a graphic, you often need to export the graphic to a paint or drawing program. If possible, you should finalize your graphics before bringing them into your ToolBook application.

You can make minor adjustments to your graphics after you import them into Multimedia ToolBook. Cropping and setting the border style are two ways to make minor modifications to your graphics.

Cropping. When you want to change the amount of the paint object that is visible, you can crop the image by selecting a corner and resizing the visible portion of the image. The image remains anchored to the upper left corner.

Using OpenScript to crop the image, place the following script into the script of a paint object and click the object when in Reader mode:

```
bounds of paintObject "mountain" = 150,200, 1200,1600
```

Border Style. The border style of your graphic can be changed by selecting the object, displaying the Line Palette, and changing the line style.

Using OpenScript, enter the following line in the Command Window:

```
lineStyle of paintObject "mountain" = 0
```

BitEdit. BitEdit, another Microsoft product modified by Asymetrix specifically for ToolBook, allows you to create and modify your bitmap. Using BitEdit and PalEdit in conjunction is beneficial. You can select a color that you want to modify in PalEdit and display where this color occurs on your bitmap in BitEdit.

Hiding and Showing Graphics

At times, when the user enters and leaves pages and backgrounds, you may want to hide or show graphics. You can accomplish these tasks by using the Show and Hide commands. For example, place the fololowing script into the script of your graphic:

```
notifyBefore enterPage
     sysLockScreen = true
     show self
end enterPage
notifyBefore leavePage
     sysLockScreen = true
     hide self
end leavePage
```

> **Note**
>
> When you use `sysLockScreen`, the screen is unlocked automatically at the end of the executing handler.

From Here...

In this chapter, you have learned about importing and using graphics within ToolBook. For further information, see the following chapters:

- See Chapter 3, "Understanding Objects," for more information about `fillColor`.
- See Chapter 5, "Understanding the Media Management Tools," for details related to image resources and clips.
- For more information about using OLE objects, refer to Chapter 7, "Adding Multimedia Elements."
- See Chapter 21, "Using Multimedia Elements," for more information about using the `imageCommand()` function.

CHAPTER 11

Working with Text

Text is a vital element of your multimedia application. You use text in your application to display labels, comments, instructions, and data, as well as to obtain information from your user.

In this chapter, you learn how to do the following:

- Add text to objects
- Format text
- Apply color to text
- Use rich-text
- Find and replace text
- Display text using OpenScript

Displaying Text

Other than using video, sound, still images and animation, many applications depend greatly on the presence of text to convey information. You can display text in a number of different ways in Multimedia ToolBook. The way text is displayed depends on which type of object you select. Objects that display text include, label buttons, combo boxes, fields and record fields. Also, you can use an OLE object to display text.

Adding Text to Objects

Adding text to objects can be an easy process. You can use the interface or OpenScript to add text to label buttons, combo boxes, fields and record fields.

Fields and Record Fields. *Fields* are objects that allow you to display, as well as gather, text information. There are several properties of a field which are combined to present text, such as the field type, the field border style, and the field's transparent property.

Record fields, which exist only on the background, are unique because the text you add is stored with the page, rather than with the record field (see fig. 11.1). When you change pages, the text displayed in the record field changes. However, if you include a field on the background, rather than including a record field, the text will not change when you navigate between pages of the background.

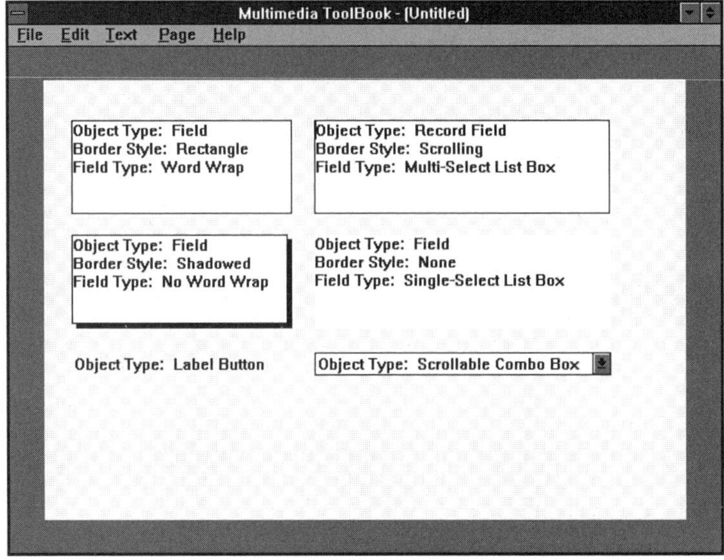

Fig. 11.1

Text can be displayed using different objects, such as Fields, Record fields, Combo Boxes, and Label Buttons.

> **Note**
>
> Both fields and record fields can display just under 32,000 characters for each page.

Fields and record fields allow you to add text the same way. There are four common methods used to add text to a field. To add text to a field you can:

- Type
- Import
- Paste
- Use OpenScript

Adding text can be describe for both fields and record fields, because both fields and record fields are similar. Before you type, import, or paste text into your field, you must display the insertion point within the field. Start by double-clicking the field. Setting the insertion point of your field also sets the focus to the field. The insertion point will begin blinking in the field. Now you can type, paste, or import your text into your field.

To type text into your field or record field, use the following steps:

1. Double-click your field or record field to display the insertion point.
2. Begin typing in your field.

Note

If you want to select a record field to edit the properties of the record field rather than edit the text, be sure that you are on the background by pressing F4, or right-click the record field to display the right-click menu.

Before pasting text, you must copy the desired text to the Clipboard. To copy text from most Windows applications, you first select the text, then select Edit, Copy. At this point your text is stored in the Windows Clipboard. To paste your text, display the ToolBook window, set the focus to your field by double-clicking it and select Edit, Paste.

To paste text into a field or record field, use the following steps:

1. Select the text that you want to import. For instance, your text could be in Windows Notepad.
2. After your text has been selected, copy the text to the Clipboard by selecting Edit, Copy from the menu bar of Notepad.
3. Display your ToolBook book and double-click inside the text field where you want to place your text.
4. Select Edit, Paste from the ToolBook menu bar.

Note

ToolBook also gives you the option to paste text in other formats. Select Edit, Paste Special for additional pasting options.

Other than typing and pasting your text into your application, you also have limited importing options. When you select File, Import from the menu bar of ToolBook, you can specify a text file to import. This importing option is designed to import comma delimited data, not documents. When the text file is imported into ToolBook, a record field and several pages are automatically created based on the number of items in the text file.

To import data into a new record field, use the following steps:

1. Select File, Import from the menu bar to display the Import dialog box.
2. Set the Import Type to Text Files (`*.TXT`) rather than ToolBook Files (`*.?BK`). The Import Type combo box is displayed at the lower-left section of the Import dialog box.
3. Select from among your Drives and Directories to locate your file. You also can enter the File Name of your text file.
4. After you have selected your text file, press OK to import the text file data into your ToolBook book.

> **Note**
>
> The Import menu item from the File pull-down menu limits how text is imported. For greater detail concerning the Import menu item, see the "Importing and Exporting Text" section of Chapter 17, "Data and File Management."

When you need to edit the text of your field or record field, you can simply make your changes by double-clicking inside your field and modifying the text how you want. To prevent the user of your application from modifying the text of your field, you can set the `Activated` property of your field to `true`.

To prevent users from modifying the text of your field, use the following steps:

1. Right-click the field in Author mode to display the right-click menu for the field.
2. Select Activate Scripts from the right-click menu.

> **Note**
>
> If you want to edit your field in Reader mode, you must make sure that your field is enabled and the script is not activated. Right-click the field to display the right-click menu and select the Enabled option. Also, make sure the Activate Scripts option is disabled.

It's also possible to add and edit the text in your field by using OpenScript. For example, if you need to prompt the user of your application for text, or change the second word of a field, you can use OpenScript to accomplish these changes.

Use the following steps to edit the text of a field using OpenScript:

1. Create a field and name it `Mountain`.
2. Display the Command Window by choosing View, Command or by pressing Shift + F3.
3. Enter the following line of script into the Command Window to set the entire text of the field named `Mountain`:

```
text of field "Mountain" = "Rainier"
```

You can also place additional text after the current text of a field. Use the following steps to edit the text of a field:

1. Make sure you can complete the steps in the previous example.
2. Enter the following script into the Command Window:

```
put "National Forest" after text of field "Address"
```

You will see that text has now been added to your field named `Mountain`, however there is no space in between the first and second word. To include a space using OpenScript, you can add the keyword `space` and a concatenation symbol (&) within the script such as:

```
put space & "National Forest" after text of field "Address"
```

To import and export text directly into your field or record field you can use OpenScript. Certain keywords such as `openFile`, `closeFile`, `readFile`, `writeFile`, and `seekFile` can be used to import as well as export text. For more information, see the "Reading and Writing Text" section of Chapter 17, "Data and File Management."

Combo Boxes. A combo box object allows you to display a list of items in a drop-down box. Combo boxes—which were described earlier in Chapter 3, "Understanding Objects"—consist of an edit box, a push button, and a drop-down list box. The edit box contains the text that is commonly seen before the user interacts with the combo box. The text displayed is one of the choices from within the drop-down list. The push button is used to display the drop-down list box. To select an alternative item for the edit box, you can select a line from the drop-down list box (refer to fig. 11.1, which displays a combo box as well as other objects used to display text).

Adding text to a combo box is similar to adding text to a field or record field. You can add text to two parts of the combo box: the edit box and the drop-down list box. You can add text by first double-clicking the edit box, and then typing the text. To add text to the drop-down list box, you need to select the push button, double-click in the drop-down list box and type your text.

Follow these steps to add text to a combo box:

1. To add text to the edit box, start by double-clicking the edit box to show the insertion point.
2. Type the text you want to display in the edit box. This text is displayed by default.
3. To add text to the drop-down list box, you must push the combo box push-button, which displays the drop-down list box.
4. Type items that will be displayed, pressing Enter after each item.

Label Buttons. When a simple description is needed for an object, a label button can be used.

Adding text to a label button is a little different than adding text to a field or combo box. You can add text to a label button using two methods. Using the interface allows you to quickly add a caption to your label button. You can change the caption of a label button by displaying the button properties dialog box. OpenScript also allows you to add or change the caption. Figure 11.1 displays a label button as well as other objects used to display text.

The limit to the number of characters you can add to a label button is 255. The default caption for a label button is `&Button`. The ampersand, which is included in the default label button caption, allows the character following it to be used as a mnemonic key, also known as a shortcut key. A mnemonic key, which appears underlined in the caption, can be activated by pressing Alt + the underlined character. You can set the mnemonic key of a button using OpenScript. The following steps are an example of setting the mnemonic key for a button:

1. Display the Command window by pressing Ctrl+F3.

2. Assuming that you have a button named `Mountain`, enter the following script into the Command Window:

```
caption of button "Mountain" = "&Rainier"
```

Formatting Text

It is important to present your text in a favorable and readable manner. By setting the font, style, and size of any text within your application, you can better convey or obtain information. For instance, when you need the user of your application to pay particular attention to certain text, change the text formatting. You can use the interface and OpenScript to modify the text of your objects.

Fields and Record Fields. Like all objects that display text, the text format of your field and record field can be changed. Paragraphs of fields and record fields also can be set and changed.

Character Formatting. You can format the characters of your field or record field by either using the interface or using OpenScript. It's very important to understand the difference between the default character formatting for your field and the format of the individual characters that you add to a field. The default formatting for newly created fields and record fields can be set using such OpenScript system properties as `sysFontFace`, `sysFontSize`, and `sysFontStyle`. These values set the font type, the font size, and the font style for all of your fields that you create after setting these values. For example, you can set the default character size for all newly created fields by entering the following script into the Command Window:

```
sysFontSize = 12
```

You can change the default character formatting for a field, so that when you begin entering text into the field, the text will display under the default formatting. When you want to set the default character format for an individual field that already exists, follow these steps:

1. Right-click the field or record field that you want to edit.
2. Select Character from the right-click menu to display the Character dialog box.
3. Set the Font, Font Style, Size, and the Effects for the field as you desire.

Now, when you type into the blank field, the text will display as you have formatted.

You can also format specific text within a field by selecting the text and changing the text's format. Note that simply changing the text of a field does not change the default format of the field. Also, it's important to know that when you add text onto other text, the new text takes the format of the existing text rather than the format of the field.

There are two ways to reach the Character dialog box using the interface. The first way is to select the field and then select Text, Character from the menu. Figure 11.2 displays the Character dialog box.

You can also display the Character dialog box by right-clicking the field and selecting the Character menu item. Figure 11.3 displays the right-click menu for a field.

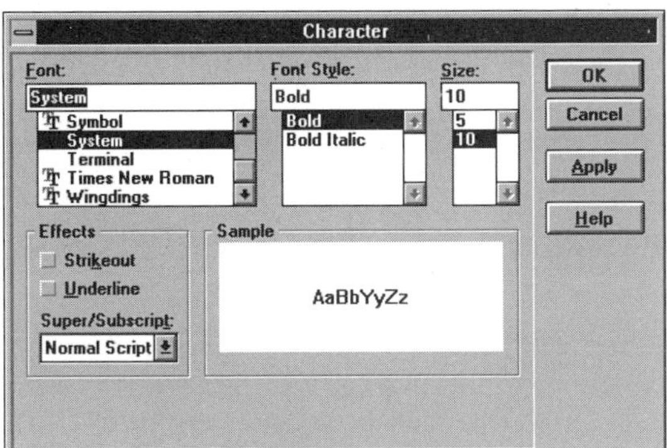

Fig. 11.2

The Character dialog box allows you to set the font type, style, size, and effect of your text.

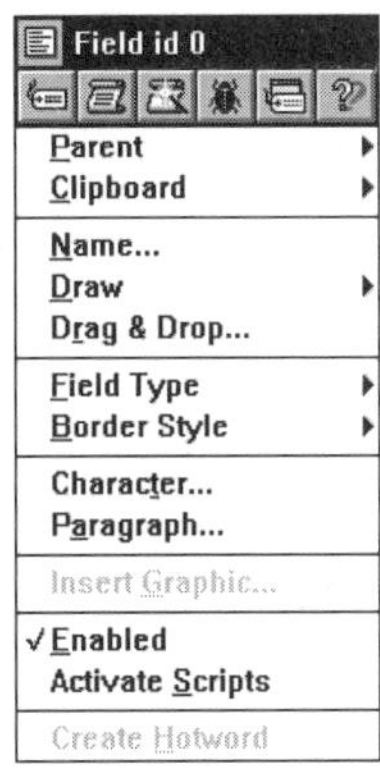

Fig. 11.3

The Character dialog box can be quickly displayed using the right-click menu for a field or record field.

Within the Character dialog box, you have several options to change the look of your text. There are four main areas in the Character dialog box. These areas allow you to change not only the type of font you use, but also the style, size, and effect of your font. When you choose a font, the specific style and size change based on the font type. Different fonts allow certain characteristics. You will find that TrueType fonts will give you the greatest amount of style and size options.

Windows includes a number of different fonts, such as Arial, Times New Roman, and Symbol. You can install a wide variety of additional fonts to Windows as well. However, the more fonts you add to Windows, the less memory you will have to work with in your application. This can be a concern when developing your application.

> **Note**
>
> Multimedia ToolBook includes a Widgets font as well. The characters in the Widgets font can be used to create special animation effects.

The Character dialog box also displays a sample of the specific font, with style, size, and effects displayed in the sample.

Note

TrueType fonts can be recognized by the TrueType graphic that appears to the left of the font name (refer to fig. 11.2).

The style of most fonts are fairly consistent. Most fonts can appear as Regular, Italic, Bold, and Bold Italic.

Font size can be successfully set to nearly any size when using a TrueType font. Generally you should limit regular fonts to the sizes that are given. When text is visible on screen but not visible when printed, resize your field or record field.

If you want to ensure the availability of a specific font, you can embed a font into your application. (Refer to Chapter 26, "Preparing for Delivery," for more on embedded fonts.) Embedded fonts are extremely useful because the developer can control which font type is displayed, rather than allowing Windows to substitute a font when a chosen font is unavailable.

The Effects section of the Character dialog box allows for three options, which include Strikeout, Underline, and Super/Subscript. Strikeout displays the text with a horizontal line through the center of the text. The Underline option simply underlines your text. Super/Subscript allows you to include text that displays smaller and to the top or bottom of the text line.

Paragraph Formatting. One way to make text more prominent, other than modifying the characters of the text, is to change the paragraph formatting of your field or record field. Formatting the paragraph of your text can be accomplished by either using the interface or by using OpenScript.

To use the interface, start by selecting the field, and then choose Text, Paragraph from the menu. Figure 11.4 displays the Paragraph dialog box.

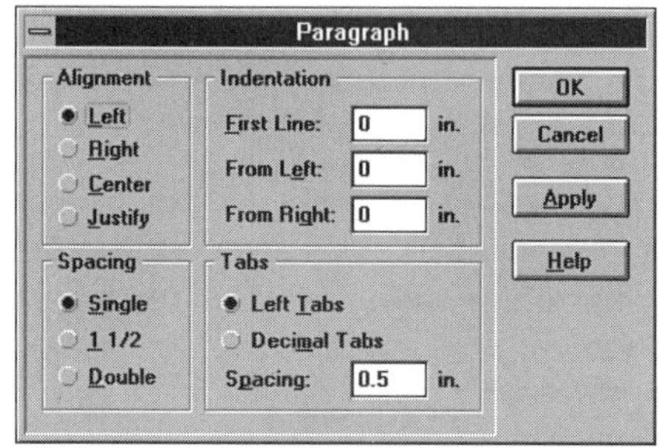

Fig. 11.4

The Paragraph dialog box allows you to set the alignment, indentation, spacing, and tabs of your field or record field.

You can also display the paragraph menu by right-clicking the field and selecting paragraph. The Paragraph dialog box contains four sections related to the text of your field. You can set the alignment, indentation, spacing, and tabs.

Tip

To include a tab in your field, select Ctrl+Tab.

Although the paragraph format of your field can be changed, your field can only support one type of paragraph format at one time.

You can select one of four alignment options for your field or record field. Alignment options are left, right, center, and justify. Note that you cannot have more than one type of alignment assigned to a field or record field.

You can also set the alignment of your field or record field using OpenScript. For example, if you create a field named `Mountain`, you could set the field's alignment by entering the following script into the Command Window:

```
textAlignment of field "Mountain" = center
```

To set the default alignment of all newly created fields and record fields, enter the following script into the Command Window:

```
sysAlignment = center
```

There are three options related to text indentation that you can apply to your field or record field. You can select the indention amount in inches for the first line, the left side of the text, and the right side of the text. OpenScript can be used to set the indents of a particular field or record field. Enter the following script into the Command Window to set the indents of field Directory:

```
indents of field "Directory" = 720,140,140
```

To set the default indents of all newly created fields and record fields, enter the following script into the Command Window:

```
sysIndents = 720,0,0
```

You can set line spacing within your field to 1, 1.5, or 2. The default is 1. If you change the `sysLineSpacing` system property from the default, any newly created field or record field will conform to this new value. For example, enter the following script into the Command Window to set the spacing for a field named `Directory`:

```
spacing of field "Directory" = 1.5
```

Regular and decimal tabs are the two types of tabs you can set within your field or record field. The default tab spacing is set to 720 page units, which equals 1/2 inch. To set the default tab for all future fields and record fields change the `sysTabSpacing` value.

Label Buttons. The look and style of a label button can be changed like other objects that support text. Label buttons support character formatting, although these objects do not support paragraph formatting, because they display only one line of text.

When you do not specifically set a character style, size, or font type to your label button, the system properties determine the look of the label button's caption and other attributes. The three system properties that relate to the text are `sysFontFace`, `sysFontStyle`, and `sysFontSize`.

Applying Color

ToolBook objects have two types of color settings, `strokeColor` and `fillColor`. The `strokeColor` allows you to set the border color of the object, and if the object is a field or record field, the text is set to the color as well.

Setting the `strokeColor` of a field sets the default color of the text. However, you can select a portion of your text, such as the first character of each paragraph, and change the color of the text.

> **Note**
>
> When selecting a color, use the left and right mouse buttons to change the `fillColor` and `strokeColor` of your field.

You can select a specific color for your text by using the Color Tray. The Color Tray displays 32 colors on the top and 64 colors on the bottom. You have a number of color choices available to you. If you do not see the color you need, you can modify any of the lower 64 colors. The top colors are Windows colors and can not be modified within ToolBook.

Using Rich Text Format

The Rich Text Format is a text formatting standard that allows easy transfer of formatted text among different applications, and from different platforms. Not only can you copy and import your Rich Text from another application or from an RTF file, but you can also pre-define hotwords that will be dynamically created when text is imported to your field or record field.

Rich Text is a text formatting standard that contains specific information about the text, such as the font, font size, and font style.

Including RTF Text. There are two main ways to bring Rich Text into your Multimedia ToolBook application. These methods are pasting and using OpenScript.

> **Tip**
>
> You can also use an OLE object to display Rich Text.

Cutting and Pasting RTF Text. The easiest way to include Rich Text into your application is to copy the text from another windows application, and paste the text into your field or record field. This method maintains the text format, such as font types, and character sizes and styles.

You can paste your text into a field or record field using the following steps:

1. Select the text within your other Windows application.
2. Copy the text to the Clipboard. You can select Edit, Copy from the menu bar in the other Windows application.
3. Display your ToolBook application and double-click your field or record field so that the i-beam is flashing in the field.
4. Select Edit, Paste from the ToolBook menu bar.

Creating Dynamic Hotwords using RTF Text. Multimedia ToolBook supports Rich Text and also allows you to include additional text related information. Hotwords can be defined in your Rich Text before you import the text to your application. A hotword is a selection of characters that you select and designate as an object.

Creating hotwords dynamically is an interesting Rich Text capability. You can implement this option when pasting Rich Text into a field or record field.

Before you import your text into your application, you can define your hotword by marking the text as double-underlined. To include hotword properties, such as a hotword name, style, and user property, you can include hidden text immediately following your desired hotword. There is a limit to the number of user properties that you can add this way. The total number of characters that can be used to define your hotword is 100.

The example of the format used to define hotwords in text is as follows, where the double-underlined text represents the desired hotword and the single underline represents hidden text:

```
NewHotword name=hotwordName; hotwordstyle=Frame; firstUserProp=Text
 of user property;
```

Note that the above format is in a word processing document that supports Rich Text. The format is used before importing your Rich Text into your ToolBook field.

Rich Text and OpenScript. The `richText` keyword can be used to convert pure RTF text, which displays all the special text codes, to regularly formatted text. For example, enter the following script into the Command Window:

```
text of field "Product Description" = richText of field
"Product Description"
```

Finding and Replacing Text

To quickly find or replace text, you can use the Find or Replace menu items in the Edit menu. The Find and Replace dialog boxes are fairly similar.

The Find dialog box is comprised of a text box that you enter your text to find and five checkboxes that allow you to specify the search parameters (see fig. 11.5). Also, when searching for text within record fields, you can select a record field from among all listed record fields.

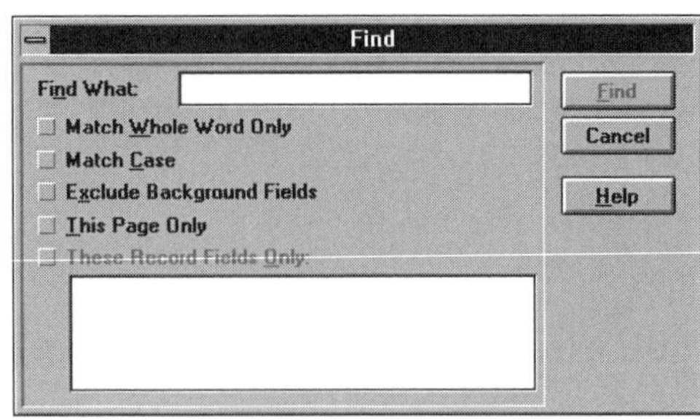

Fig. 11.5

The Find dialog box allows you to find text based on selected search options.

The first checkbox option, Match Whole Word Only, allows you to find only the specified word, rather than finding your text within another word. For instance, this option could be used to find the word "media" and ignore the word "multimedia."

At times, it is useful to search with case sensitivity enabled. The Match Case option allows you to search for the exact case as entered in the Find What text box.

Both the Exclude Background Fields and This Page Only options allow you to narrow your search. Remember that the text of a field on the background is part of the background field and the text of a record field is part of the page.

Replacing text using the Replace dialog box simply adds an additional text box to the dialog interface. Enter the text that you want to substitute for your original text in the Replace With text box (see fig. 11.6).

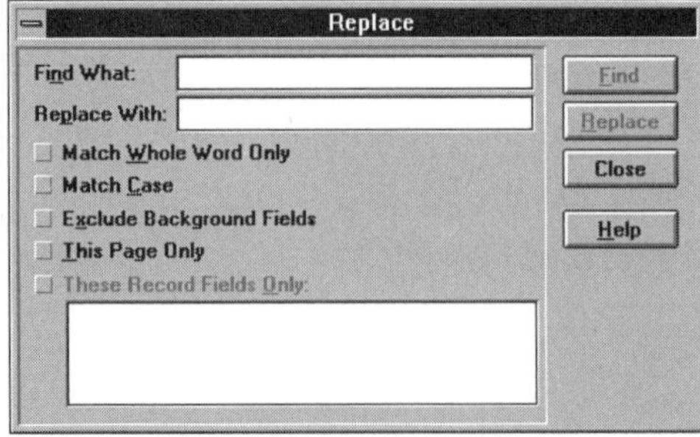

Fig. 11.6

The Replace dialog box allows you to find and replace text based on selected search options.

Displaying Text Using OpenScript

There are a number of different OpenScript functions and keywords in ToolBook related to text. Many of these functions are quickly understood, others are more difficult to use.

You'll find the most common way to display text is to use fields and record fields. However, at times you may want to prompt the user to enter text, or display text to give the user additional information or input.

You can use the commands `request` and `ask` to prompt the user for input. The `ask` command can be used to retrieve information from the user. Enter the following script into the Command Window:

```
ask "What is your favorite mountain?" with "Rainier"
```

The `request` command can be used to display information, although the user can only select specific responses. Enter the following script into the Command Window:

```
request "Choose a color for your car..." with "Red" or "Green"
 or "Blue"
```

The status bar allows you to give additional details or help to the user. Commonly, the status bar is used to describe a particular object or give hints as to what the user should do.

The text of a status bar can be set using OpenScript. For example, you could enter the following script into the Command Window to set the text of the status bar:

```
caption of statusBar = "Press F1 to display Help"
```

To show the status bar, enter the following script into the Command Window:

```
show statusBar
```

From Here...

In this chapter, you have learned the ins and outs of manipulating text. For further information, refer to the following chapters:

- For more information on objects that display text, applying color, and using Rich Text, see Chapter 3, "Understanding Objects."
- For more information on how to add hotwords, see Chapter 7, "Adding Multimedia Elements."
- For more information on the process of reading and writing to text files, see Chapter 17, "Data and File Management."
- For more information on the process of embedding fonts, see Chapter 26, "Preparing for Delivery."

CHAPTER 12

Printing from ToolBook

As a developer, you may find it useful to print your pages, script, and text to organize, modify, and update your application. Also, rather than use ToolBook's printing capabilities while you develop, you may want to include printing capabilities within your application.

ToolBook enables you to produce printed output of your pages, script, text, and viewers. After completing this chapter, you will be able accomplish the following:

- Print pages, reports, scripts, and viewers
- Understand many important OpenScript printing keywords
- Create printing scripts by recording your steps

Printing Pages

Although you can print viewers and script, ToolBook's printing is divided primarily between two types of output: pages and reports. Printing pages allows you to print what you see in the ToolBook window. Printing a report prints only the text in your record fields.

You can't put a computer in your back pocket, or make quick notes on your laptop screen. At times, printed information is more convenient than computer displayed information. You may have several reasons for printing the pages of your application. For instance, you may need to print your exquisite interface for later reference, or perhaps make handwritten notes on your printed pages to be reviewed by the graphic artist, or other members of your team. Although your application is your end product, printouts of your pages give you added flexibility, such as comparing several pages at one time.

When you print one or more pages of your application, you can choose among several print options. Select File, Print Pages from the menu bar to display the Print Pages dialog box. The main options in the Print Pages dialog box control the arrangement and page range of your printed ToolBook pages. The arrangement is simply how your pages will be displayed on the printed sheet of paper. The page range determines which pages of your application will be printed. Additional settings involve previewing your page, setting print options, setting the header and footer, and setting up the printer. The selected print driver is displayed at the bottom of the Print Pages dialog box (see fig. 12.1).

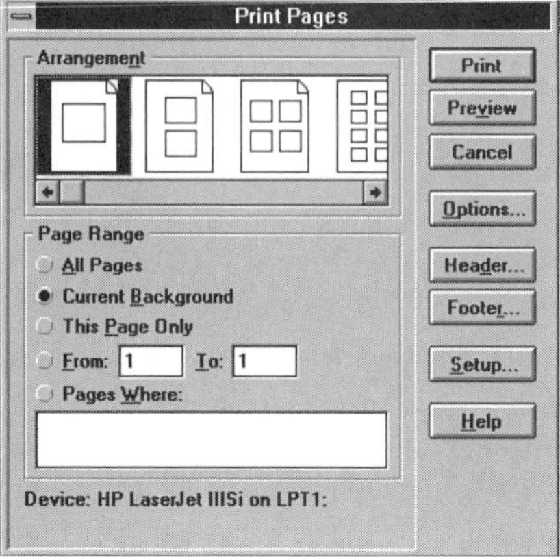

Fig. 12.1

The Print Pages dialog box allows you to easily set the print arrangement and range.

Using the menus available from ToolBook, you can easily print a page of your application. Use the following steps to print a page:

1. First, navigate to the page you want to print. There are several ways you can reach the page you want to print. One way to navigate is to select a navigate option from the Page menu of the menu bar.
2. Now select File, Print Pages from the menu bar. The Print Pages dialog box is displayed.
3. Select This Page Only from the Page Range section.
4. Press the Print button to print the page.

Page Arrangement

When you need to display more than one of your application's pages on a sheet of paper, you can change the arrangement of your print layout. This feature is especially useful when you need to check or compare the flow of your application. For instance, you may need to compare the interface of your application, such as the placement of your fields (or buttons) on the pages. Also, printing several of your application's pages on a few sheets of paper allows you to quickly follow the application's flow, reduces paper usage, and can be easier to manage.

The arrangement section of the Print Pages dialog box allows you to set the number of pages to be printed on each sheet of paper. You can print 1, 2, 4, 16, or 32 pages on one sheet. The Print Pages dialog box makes setting the arrangement for your printout easy; simply select the number of ToolBook pages that you want to appear on a printed page by selecting the page graphic in the Arrangement section of the

Print Pages dialog box. The Arrangement section displays the number of pages both vertically and horizontally that you can print per sheet of paper. Use the arrow keys or the horizontal scroll bar to choose your printer arrangement.

Rather than using the interface to set how the pages of your application will be printed on each sheet of paper, you can use OpenScript. You can set the arrangement of your pages to be printed using the `printerArrangement` system property.

> **Note**
>
> Don't let the name of the OpenScript `printerArrangement` property confuse you. We're still dealing with the number of pages printed on a sheet of paper.

The `printerArrangement` system property contains two positive integers, separated by a comma. The first integer sets the number of ToolBook pages to be printed on a sheet of paper. The maximum number of pages printed across the sheet is four. The second printer-arrangement number represents the number of ToolBook pages printed from the top to the bottom of the sheet. The maximum number of pages printed from the top to the bottom of the sheet is eight.

For instance, if you need your pages to be printed as two across and two down for a total of four pages per printed sheet, you could set the Arrangement option in the Print Pages dialog box or use OpenScript to set the `printerArrangement` to `2,2`. Refer to Listing 12.1 for an example of using the `printerArrangement` OpenScript keyword. To set the Arrangement in the Print Pages dialog box, use the following steps:

1. Navigate to the page where you want to begin printing.
2. Now select File, Print Pages from the menu bar. The Print Pages dialog box is displayed.
3. Select the number of pages of your application that you want to print on each sheet of paper by selecting from the Arrangement section of the Print Pages dialog box.
4. Select Current Background from the Page Range section.
5. Press the Print button to print the pages.

Page Range

You can specify the pages of your application that you want to print by selecting the appropriate options in the Page Range section of the Print Pages dialog box. The Page Range options include the following:

- All Pages—To print all the pages of a book (which developers commonly do to review the entire book), choose this option.
- Current Background—If you want to print all the pages on the background that you are viewing, choose this option.
- This Page Only—This Page Range option allows you to print the current page.

- From and To—You also can print from one page to another page, such as from 12 to 25.
- Pages Where—This option is the most complicated Page Range option. You can print pages that are specified by your OpenScript statement. Type the OpenScript statement in the text box below the Pages Where option.

To print a specific range of pages, you can select from one of these five Page Range options. Use the following steps to help you select and print specific pages of you book:

1. Select File, Print Pages from the menu bar. The Print Pages dialog box is displayed.
2. Select the number of pages of your application that you want to print on each sheet of paper by selecting from the Arrangement section of the Print Pages dialog box.
3. Select one of the five options from the Page Range section of the Print Pages dialog box. For example, choose Current Background from the Page Range section.
4. Press the Print button to print the pages.

At times, you may want to use script to print your application rather than the menu options. The efficient way to create script for printing is to use the Script recorder. For details about the Script recorder, refer to "Recording Scripts for Printing" later in this chapter.

When you record your printing script, which you can later place in an object, ToolBook hard-codes the number of pages to print. A *hard-coded value* is a specific name or number rather than a variable. Using a variable to specify which page to print allows you to easily reuse the script. Unlike a recorded script that in many circumstances can only be applied to a specific printing situation, the following script prints appropriately without having hard-coded printing limits. The example shown in Listing 12.1 sets several printing properties to ensure correct printed output for all pages. Place the following script example into the script of a button.

Listing 12.1 12LIST01.TXT Printing All Pages

```
to handle buttonClick
     printerStyle = pages
     printerMargins = 1440,1440,1440,1440
     printerGutters = 360,360
     printerScaling = custom
     printerBorders = true
     printerArrangement = 2,2
     printerPageBitmap = false
     rangeVar = pageCount of this book
     start spooler
          print rangeVar
     end spooler
end buttonClick
```

This script allows you to print all the pages of your book. The keywords that begin with `printer` all are involved in determining how the page will be printed. The unique part of this script is the line where the variable `rangeVar` is set. The variable was named `rangeVar` so that you could easily recognize what it means. Here you set the variable `rangeVar` to the total number of pages of this book. Once the printing range has been established, you print your page range.

To print all the pages of your current background, you can use the following script. The example shown in Listing 12.2 prints all the pages of the current background. Place the following script into the script of a button.

Listing 12.2 12LIST02.TXT Printing Pages of the Current Background

```
to handle buttonClick
     sysLockScreen = true
     printerStyle = pages
     printerMargins = 1440,1440,1440,1440
     printerGutters = 360,360
     printerScaling = custom
     printerBorders = true
     printerArrangement = 2,2
     printerPageBitmap = false
     rangeVar = pageCount of this background
     go to first page of this background
     start spooler
          print rangeVar
     end spooler
     send back
end buttonClick
```

In the above script, you start by locking the ToolBook window so the navigation is not displayed during script execution. Next, you set your page range variable. Then you navigate to the first page of the background in order to be certain to include all the pages of the current background. Then, you print your selected pages. Lastly, you return to our original page using `send back`.

> **Note**
>
> When you lock the ToolBook window using the `sysLockScreen` command, it automatically unlocks the screen when the script is completed.

You can also print just your current page. The example shown in Listing 12.3 prints only the current page. Place the following script into the script of a button.

Listing 12.3 12LIST03.TXT Printing the Current Page

```
to handle buttonClick
     printerStyle = pages
     printerMargins = 1440,1440,1440,1440
     printerGutters = 360,360
     printerScaling = custom
     printerBorders = true
     printerArrangement = 1,1
     printerPageBitmap = false
     start spooler
          print 1
     end spooler
end buttonClick
```

When you need to print from one page to another, you first need to navigate to the starting page. Then, print the pages and return back to the original page. The example shown in Listing 12.4 prints your pages from one page to another. Place the following script example into the script of a button.

Listing 12.4 12LIST04.TXT Printing From One Page to Another

```
to handle buttonClick
     sysLockScreen = true
     printerStyle = pages
     printerMargins = 1440,1440,1440,1440
     printerGutters = 360,360
     printerScaling = custom
     printerBorders = true
     printerArrangement = 2,2
     printerPageBitmap = false
     go to page 12
     start spooler
          print 14
     end spooler
     send back
end buttonClick
```

When you need to define specific pages to print based on certain conditions, such as when the page contains certain text or the page has a specific name, you can define when a certain page will print. Place the following script into the script of a button:

```
name of this page = "Drum Set" or name of this page = "Percussion"
```

Tip

To advance the printer to the top of the next page, use the `print eject` command in the `start spooler` control structure.

Page-Printing Options

To change or set layout properties of your page, such as scaling and borders, you can set the print page options. Click the Options button in the Print Pages dialog box to display the Print Page Options dialog box (see fig. 12.2). The options for printing a page allow you to change the margins, print the page as a bitmap, and include a border around your printed pages.

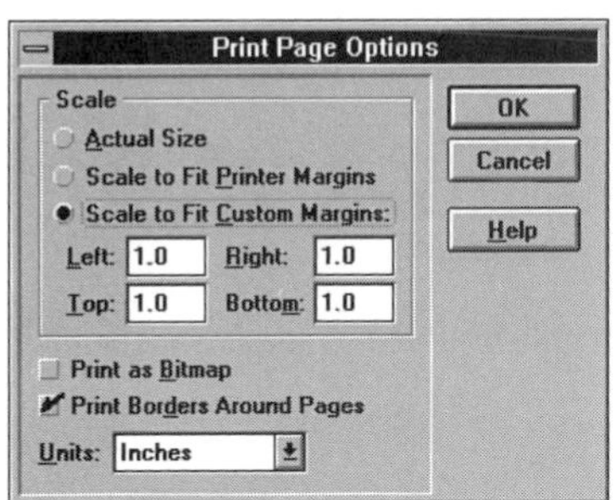

Fig. 12.2

The Print Page Options dialog box allows you to set properties, such as the margins, scale, and borders of the printed page.

To change the margins, you can modify options in the Scale section of the Print Page Options dialog box. The first Scale option allows you to scale your printout to the Actual Size of your ToolBook pages. This option is unique to pages and can not be applied to reports. The second Scale option, Scale to Fit Printer Margins, sizes the page proportionately to fit the printer margins.

When you choose Scale to Fit Custom Margins, you can select a specific margin for all four sides of your page. This scale option is selected by default. All four margins are automatically set to one inch. You can change the units used for margins to inches, centimeters, or page units.

Tip

Most printers require at least a half-inch border; otherwise, your page will be clipped.

The Print Page Options dialog box also allows you to print your page as bitmaps. To activate this option, click the Print as Bitmap checkbox. Printing as a bitmap ensures that your printout appears in the same layout as the ToolBook page on-screen. The bitmap may print with lower image quality, however.

You also have the option to include borders around your printed page by choosing Print Borders Around Pages. This option is selected by default.

OpenScript Page-Printing Example

This section contains an example of a button handler that is used to print four ToolBook pages on one sheet of paper. When you want to print pages, rather than record fields, you need to set the `printerStyle` property to `Pages`. Follow these steps to print four pages from a book on one sheet of paper:

1. Create a new book by selecting File, New from the menu bar.
2. Add three pages to your book by selecting Object, New Page (Ctrl+N) from the menu bar.
3. Add an object to each of the pages, such as a field with text, so that each page can be recognized. You will need to navigate between pages, such as going to the next page. Select Page, Next (Alt+Right) for example.
4. Enter the script in Listing 12.5 to a button on your first page to set several printing properties and ensure correct printed output for all four pages.

Listing 12.5 12LIST05.TXT Printing Four Pages on One Sheet

```
to handle buttonClick
     printerStyle = pages
     printerMargins = 1440,1440,1440,1440
     printerGutters = 360,360
     printerScaling = custom
     printerBorders = true
     printerArrangement = 2,2
     printerPageBitmap = false
     start spooler
          print 4
     end spooler
end buttonClick
```

5. Enter Reader mode (F3) and press the button containing the new script to print all four pages on one sheet of paper.

Printing Reports

Printing a report is the other common method of creating printed output from ToolBook. Reports are useful for printing information similar to database data. Report information is organized similarly to a flat-file database, because reports are created from *record fields*. Record fields exist only on the background, but are unique because the text you add is stored with the page rather than as a part of the record field.

You can print your reports from the ToolBook menus or by using OpenScript. To display the Print Report dialog box, choose File, Print Report.

> **Note**
>
> The Print Report menu item is not available unless your application contains at least one record field. Reports print the contents of record fields.

The Print Report dialog box allows you to select the record fields to print, the style of the report, and the range of pages to print (see fig. 12.3). Additional options enable you to set specific layout options for your report. The selected print driver is displayed at the bottom of the dialog box.

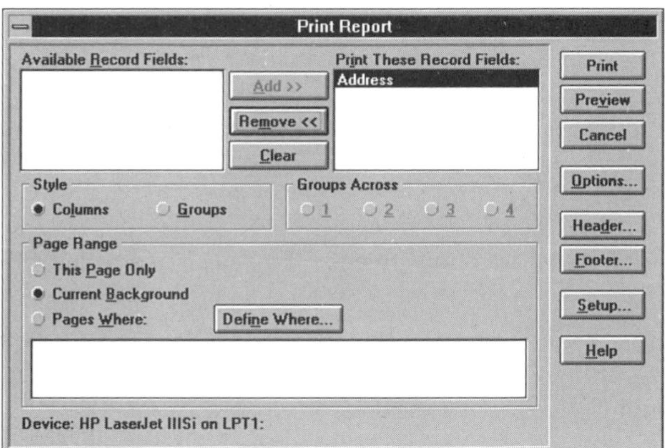

Fig. 12.3

The Print Report dialog box allows you to specify record fields to be printed, set the print style, and set the printed page range.

Using menu selections from ToolBook, you can print the record fields of your application. Use the following steps to print a report:

1. Select File, Print Report from the menu bar to display the Print Report dialog box. If your Print Report menu item is not available, it means you have not created a record field on your background. Refer to Chapter 3, "Understanding Objects," for details on record fields.
2. Select which record field you want to include in your report by selecting among the record fields listed in the Available Record Fields list.
3. After you have selected a record field, you can Add it to the Print These Record Fields list. Note that you can add several record fields to your print list if you want.
4. Set the other options that you want to include before printing.
5. Press the Print button to print the page.

Selecting Record Fields

To print one or more record fields from the Print Report dialog box, you first must select each record field in the Available Record Fields list box and then click the Add button. Each record field is listed by name or (if the record field is not named) by ID. The list box labeled Print These Record Fields displays each record field that is to be printed.

Report Layout

To display the data and text of your report in readable, useful format, you can specify the style of your report. A report can be displayed in columns or groups.

Tip

When you need to print a document, select Columns from the Style section of the Print Report dialog box.

Columns. If you need to print your report as columns, set the report style to Columns in the Print Report dialog box. For example, you could create a report used to list a directory or document. When you need to print a report rather than printing pages you need to select File, Print Report from the menu bar in ToolBook. Follow these steps to print a report:

1. Create a new book by selecting File, New from the menu bar.
2. Add two pages to your book by selecting Object, New Page (Ctrl+N) from the menu bar.
3. Add two record fields to your current background. First, select View, Background (F4), then draw two record fields on your background. Return to the Foreground when you are finished by selecting View, Foreground (F4).
4. Navigate to each page and add text to each record field. Select Page, Next (Alt+Right) to navigate between pages. Add text to each record field by double-clicking the record field.
5. Enter the script in Listing 12.6 to a button on your first page to print both record fields.

The example shown in Listing 12.6 prints the text of record field `ID 0` and record field `ID 1` as a report in columns. Place the script in Listing 12.6 into the script of a button.

Listing 12.6 12LIST06.TXT Printing a Report Using Columns

```
to handle buttonClick
     printerStyle = columns
     printerMargins = 1440,1440,1440,1440
     printerGutters = 360,360
     printerScaling = custom
     printerFields = "ID 0,ID 1"
     printerFieldWidths = 4208,4749
     printerFieldNames = true
     printerClipText = false
     start spooler
          print 3
     end spooler
end buttonClick
```

This script prints two record fields from three ToolBook pages. Both record fields are displayed side by side as columns. The record fields are recognized in this script by their ID numbers.

Groups Across. When you print a report, you have the option to print the text as a group. A group contains the text of a record field from one page. For example, you could print mailing labels as a group using five record fields. If you choose to print your report in groups, you can select the number of groups to be printed across the page (the default is 1). You can select 1 to 4 Groups in the Style section of the Print Report dialog box. The script in Listing 12.7 is an example of printing two record fields within a group. Follow these steps to print two record fields as a group:

1. Create a new book by selecting File, New from the menu bar.
2. Add two pages to your book by selecting Object, New Page (Ctrl+N) from the menu bar.
3. Add two record fields to your current background. First, select View, Background (F4), then draw two record fields on your background. Return to the Foreground when you are finished by selecting View, Foreground (F4).
4. Navigate to each page and add text to each record field. Select Page, Next (Alt+Right) to navigate between pages. Add text to each record field by double-clicking the record field.
5. Enter the script in Listing 12.7 to a button on your first page to print both record fields.

Listing 12.7 12LIST07.TXT Printing Both Record Fields

```
to handle buttonClick
     printerStyle = groups
     printerMargins = 1440,1440,1440,1440
     printerGutters = 180,360
     printerScaling = custom
     printerFields = "ID 0,ID 1"
     printerFieldWidths = 8057,8057
     printerFieldNames = true
     printerClipText = false
     printerGroupsAcross = 1
     printerSize = 0,0
     printerLabelWidth = 1080
     start spooler
          print 3
     end spooler
end buttonClick
```

Page Range

When you print a report, you generally will be using the default Page Range, which is the Current Background. However, there are three options for the Page Range. When you print a report, you can print the current page by selecting This Page Only, the pages of the Current Background, or the pages that meet certain conditions by selecting the Pages Where option. Setting the Page Range based on a condition may seem complex, but it's easy. For instance, you can print all pages where a certain record field contains the word "Total." Follow these steps when printing a report based on specific conditions:

1. Select File, Print Report from the menu bar. The Print Report dialog box is displayed.
2. Include the record fields you want to print from the Available Record Fields list box to the Print These Record Fields list box by pressing the Add button.

3. Set the Page Range by selecting the Pages Where option.
4. Press the Define Where button to specify which pages you will print.
5. In the Define Where dialog box, select a record field from the Available Record fields list box, such as `ID 0`.
6. Choose the Operator that will compare a record field with a particular value, such as `Contains`.
7. Type a Comparison value, such as **`Total`**.
8. Select a Compare As value, such as Text.

Report Printing Options

In the Print Report dialog box, you can click the Options button to set several report-layout properties, such as margin scaling, clipping text to prevent overflow, and printing labels of your record fields.

To change the margins, you can modify the Scale section of the Print Report Options dialog box (see fig. 12.4). The Scale section allows you to modify the printout of your report in two ways. The first option allows you to scale your printout to fit the printer margins. The second option, Scale to Fit Custom Margins, enables you to set the margin on all four sides of your report. This option is the default margin setting; all four margins are automatically set to one inch. You can change the units used for margins at the bottom of the Print Report Options dialog box by selecting Units. If you want to modify the margins of your report before you print, follow these steps:

1. Make sure you have a record field with text.
2. Select File, Print Report from the menu bar.
3. Add a record field from the Available Record Fields list box to the Print These Record Fields list box.
4. Select the Options button from the Print Report dialog box. The Print Report Options dialog box is displayed.
5. Select Scale to Fit Custom Margins from the Print Report Options dialog box. Also, change the Left, Right, Top, and Bottom margins so that they are all set to .5.
6. Press OK from the Print Report Options dialog box to set the margins of your report.

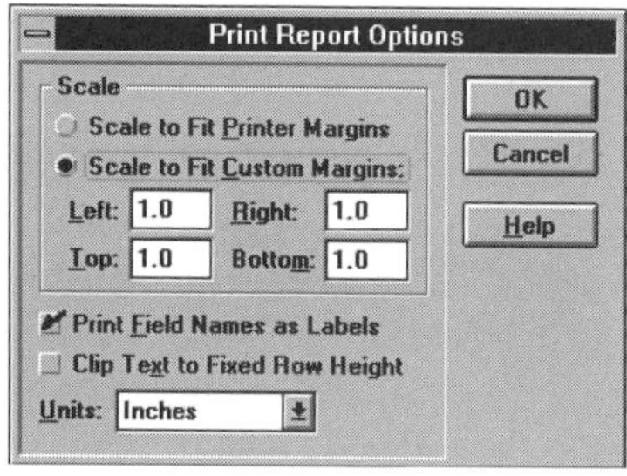

Fig. 12.4

The Print Report Options dialog box allows you to change the margin scale, include record-field labels, and clip the text to a fixed row height.

The Print Report Options dialog box includes the Print Field Names as Labels checkbox, which enables you to print the names of your record fields as labels positioned next to the record field text. To clip the text of your printed record field so that the row height is fixed, choose the Clip Text to Fixed Row Height option.

Print Preview and Layout

The Print Preview window allows you to check your page or report layout before printing (see fig. 12.5). In the Print Preview window, you can set the header, footer, margins, options, and zoom. To invoke the Print Preview window, you need to select the Preview button from either the Print Pages dialog box or the Print Report dialog box.

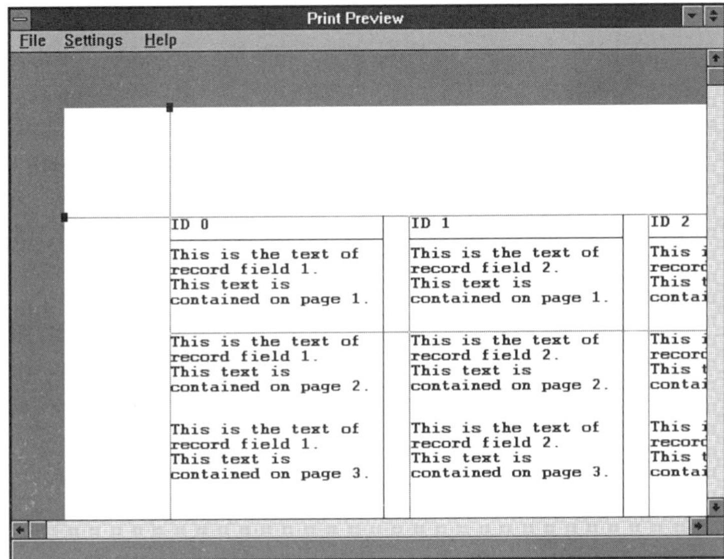

Fig. 12.5

To zoom in on the page or report in the Print Preview window, double-click the window.

The benefit of using Print Preview is to see how all the text on a page will display. If the text is cut off due to margin settings, you can zoom in and adjust the margins. When you adjust the margins, the margin measurements are displayed in the status bar.

Header and Footer

You have the option of adding a separate section of text at the top and bottom of each printed sheet of paper. At the top of your page, you can add a section of text called a *header*. At the bottom of the page, you can add another portion of text called a *footer*. The header and footer are visible when you preview the pages and report. Figure 12.6 displays the Header dialog box.

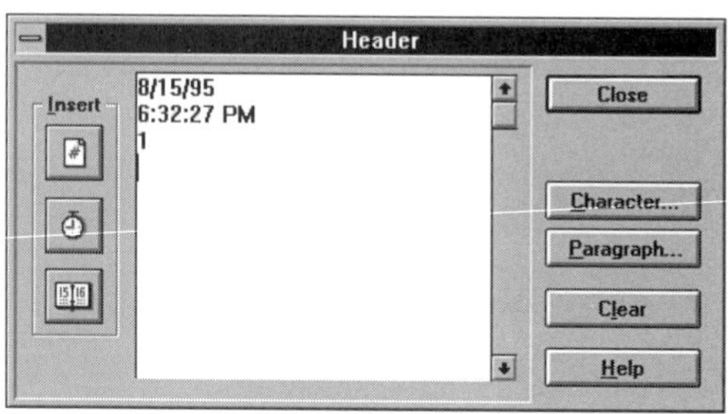

Fig. 12.6

The Header dialog box allows you to add text to the top of each printed page.

The header, which is placed at the top of the sheet, is easy to set. You can access the Header dialog box and the Footer dialog box from the Print Pages dialog box, the Print Report dialog box, or the Print Preview window. To access the Header from the Print Report dialog box, select the Header button. To select the Footer from the Print Report Dialog box, select the Footer button.

The Header and Footer dialog boxes are very similar. The three buttons on the left side of the dialog box allow you to add the page number, the time, and the date to the header (if you are in the Header dialog box) or the footer (if you are in the Footer dialog box). For instance, if you need to add a footer that displays the page number and a title in your printed report, follow these steps:

1. Make sure you have a record field with text.
2. Select File, Print Report from the menu bar. The Print Report dialog box is displayed.
3. Add a record field from the Available Record Fields list box to the Print These Record Fields list box.
4. Select the Footer button from the Print Report dialog box. The Footer dialog box is displayed.
5. Insert a page number by pressing the Page button on the left side of the Footer dialog box.
6. Press Shift+Enter to move to the next line.
7. Enter the title of your report in the footer field, such as **`Multimedia Project 1`**.
8. Press the Close button to close the Footer dialog box.

You also can set the character and paragraph styles of your header or footer text. See Chapter 11, "Working with Text," for details concerning character and paragraph styles.

Printer Setup

Although your printer setup is specific to the printer that you are using, the Print Setup option under the File menu is commonly used to change the printer, paper size, paper source, or page orientation.

You can display the Print Setup dialog box in several ways. The most direct way is to choose File, Print Setup. The Print Page, Print Report, and Print Preview dialog boxes also have an option to reach the Print Setup dialog box. To use the Print Setup dialog box, follow these steps:

1. Select File, Print Setup from the menu bar. The Print Setup dialog box is displayed.
2. Select the appropriate printer driver from the Printer options in the Print Setup dialog box. It is very likely that you already have the correct printer driver selected.
3. If you want, you change the settings of your specific printer driver by selecting Setup from the Printer Setup dialog box. For example, you can set the Paper Size, Resolution, and Orientation for most printer drivers.

Printing Viewers

To print a viewer, a window of your application, you must add the `PRINTWND.SBK` system book to your `sysBooks` property. When `PRINTWND.SBK` has been added, the Print Window command is added to the File menu in Author mode. For more information about Viewers, see Chapter 8, "Working with Viewers." Figure 12.7 shows the Print Window dialog box.

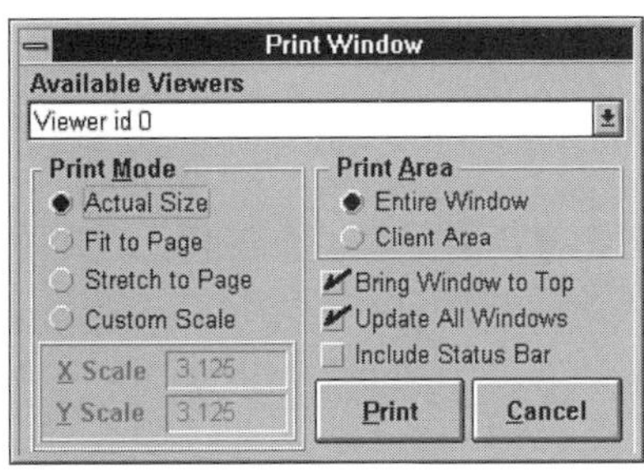

Fig. 12.7

The Print Window dialog box allows you to print an open viewer. You also can set the Print Mode and Print Area, as well as other options.

You can include the `PRINTWND.SBK` system book in your `sysBooks` property by using the `push` command, as follows:

```
push "C:\MTB40\PRINTWND.SBK" onto sysBooks
```

After you select a viewer, you can specify how to display it. To scale the printout of your viewer, select one of four options. Choose Actual Size to print the viewer as it appears on-screen. Choose Fit to Page to scale the viewer so that it is as large as possible but does not lose its proportion. The Stretch to Page option fits the viewer to the printed page. This option can distort the image. You also can scale the printed image to the X and Y values that you specify.

To print a viewer, follow these steps:

1. Select File, Print Window from the menu bar to display the Print Window dialog box. The Print Window dialog box contains options that control which viewer you print and how the viewer appears.
2. Select a viewer to print from the Available Viewers combo box in the Print Window dialog box.
3. Choose the Print Mode from the available options. For instance, select Actual Size.
4. Select the Print Area. Select the Entire Window to include the caption bar, menu bar, and window border.
5. Select the Print button to print the viewer.

> **Note**
>
> You can print only open viewers. A viewer does not have to be shown to be open. For more information about viewers, see Chapter 8, "Working with Viewers."

The Print Area options allow you to print the Entire Window, including the title bar, or just the Client Area. The Client Area is all of the window except the title bar, menu bar, and window border. For detailed information on the client window, refer to Chapter 8, "Working with Viewers."

Recording Scripts for Printing

Creating scripts for printing can be difficult because so many keywords are associated with printing in ToolBook. If you record your actions while printing, however, you can paste scripts of those actions into an object later.

> **Note**
>
> The Page Range values for pages and reports are hard-coded when you use the Script recorder. A hard-coded value is a specific name or number rather than a variable. Using a variable to specify which page to print allows you to easily reuse the script. Refer to the section "Page Range" early in this chapter for more information about printing pages using script.

Tip

At times, when a specific OpenScript keyword escapes you, you can use the Script recorder to create an example script by recording your actions.

Using the Script recorder to generate script is similar to defining a macro, although you can modify the script to customize it. For more information about modifying a script refer to Chapter 13, "OpenScript Fundamentals."

To record the script while you print a report, follow these steps:

1. In Author mode, choose Edit, Start Recording (F8). All actions that you make will be recorded until you stop recording.
2. Choose File, Print Report. The Print Report dialog box appears.
3. Select the recordfields that you want to print from the Available Record Fields list box to the Print These Record Fields list box by selecting the Add button in the Print Report dialog box.
4. Change the Style by selecting either Columns or Groups from the Style section of the Print Report dialog box.
5. Select the Page Range, such as the Current Background, from the Print Report dialog box.
6. Add a header and footer by selecting the Header and Footer buttons in the Print Report dialog box. For more details, refer to the "Header and Footer" section of this chapter.
7. Change any printing options by selecting Options from the Print Report dialog box.
8. Click the Print button within the Print Report dialog box to print your report.
9. When the report finishes printing, choose Edit, Stop Recording (F8).
10. Create a button by selecting the button tool and drawing a button. Refer to Chapter 3, "Understanding Objects," for details about drawing buttons.
11. Display the script of the newly created button. Select the button and then select Object, Button Properties. The Button Properties dialog box is displayed. Select the Script button to display the script window for the button.
12. Choose Edit, Paste Recording (F8) from the menu bar of the script window.

Printing Scripts

At times, you may need to view your script in printed form. Refining, improving, and reviewing your script are easier to accomplish when you work with printed script.

When you need to print your scripts, you have the option to do so from the script window. To print your script from the script window, choose File, Print (Ctrl+P). A ToolBook Script printing dialog box appears while the script is printing.

From Here...

In this chapter, you learned to print pages, reports, scripts, and viewers. For further information, see the following chapters:

- Chapter 3, "Understanding Objects," details record fields and drawing objects.
- Chapter 8, "Working with Viewers", explains how to work with the client window within a viewer.
- Chapter 9, "Creating Custom Menus", explains how to hide menus and menu items.
- Chapter 11, "Working with Text," deals with character and paragraph styles.
- Chapter 13, "OpenScript Fundamentals," explains how to modify a script.

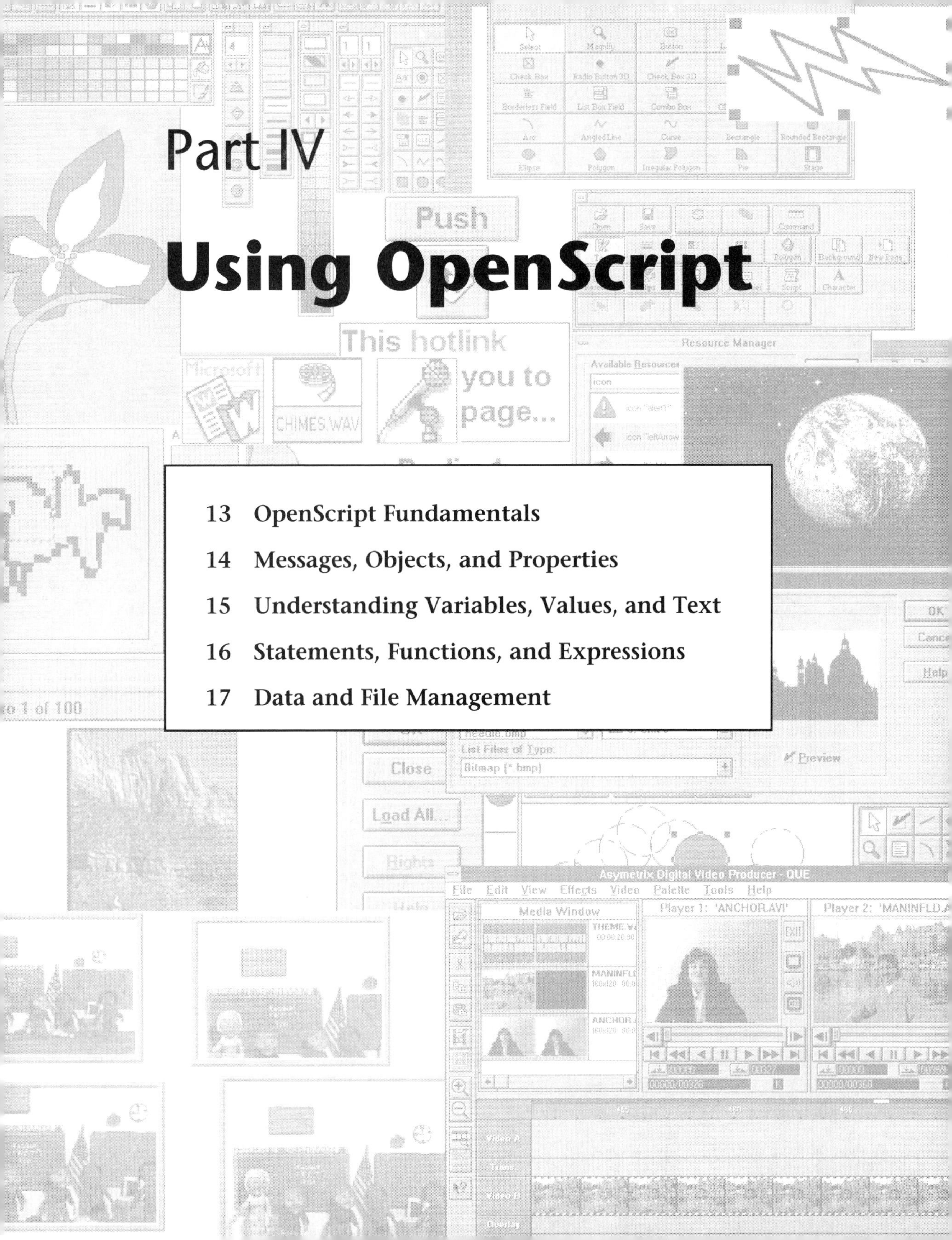

Part IV

Using OpenScript

Select
Magnify
Button
Check Box
Radio Button 3D
Check Box 3D
Borderless Field
List Box Field
Combo Box
Arc
Angled Line
Curve
Rectangle
Rounded Rectangle
Ellipse
Polygon
Irregular Polygon
Pie
Stage
Push
Open
Save
Command
Tool
Line
Pattern
Color
Polygon
Background
New Page
Resources
Clips
Viewers
Properties
Script
Character
This hotlink
you to
page...
Microsoft
CHIMES.WAV
Resource Manager
Available Resources
icon
Resource Properties
Radio 1
Radio 2
Radio 3
Undo To:
Import Graphic
File Name:
domes.bmp
Directories:
c:\...\clipart\bitmaps
coast.bmp
columns.bmp
domes.bmp
jet.bmp
lake.bmp
market.bmp
mosque.bmp
needle.bmp
clipart
bitmaps
16optmiz
nasa
Drives:
c: erik's
List Files of Type:
Bitmap (*.bmp)
Preview
Photo CD
Photo 1 of 100
OK
Close
Load All...
Rights
Asymetrix Digital Video Producer - QUE
File
Edit
View
Effects
Video
Palette
Tools
Help
Media Window
Player 1: 'ANCHOR.AVI'
Video A
Trans.
Video B
Overlay

CHAPTER 13

OpenScript Fundamentals

As powerful as Multimedia ToolBook's point-and-click navigational features and widgets are, its full elegance and power are expressed in its programming language, OpenScript. ToolBook works by sending one message at a time to a ToolBook object (or, via DDE, to another application). The object receiving the message may intercept and respond to the message or not, depending on the type of object involved and the values of its various attributes, or *properties*.

Most ToolBook objects have a `script` property, which is a container for OpenScript text statements which can utilize, modify, or create other attributes of that object and others. With OpenScript's built-in messages, properties, and functions, you can access every feature associated with a menu or dialog box button and much more, from turning a page to loading a font to exchanging information between books or between a book and a different application. As you learn to send and handle custom messages, define your own functions, and link functions from other libraries, the range of applications you can create becomes directly tied to your mastery of OpenScript.

In this chapter, you learn about the following topics:

- Scripting languages and structured programming
- Script writing
- The object hierarchy
- Shared script resources

Scripting Languages and Structured Programming

OpenScript, as its name implies, is a *scripting* language, using statements which can be more or less understood as phrases and sentences of English text.

One advantage of this approach to programming is that the language is easier to get started with than "traditional" languages such as C; another is that the inner workings of complex operations are automatically taken care of without need of user intervention.

However, scripts are often viewed as confining. For instance, you, the programmer, may want access to those very operations from which the script takes so much care to shield you. OpenScript is designed to allow access to the Windows API, functions called from dynamic link libraries, and all of ToolBook's functions and properties. In this sense, the objection disappears. Be aware, though, that certain API and DLL functions are more difficult than others to use through OpenScript calls.

A traditional disadvantage of scripts is the speed penalty paid for having the authoring system interpret high-level, natural-language instructions. OpenScript is no exception to this rule, and it really pays to learn or discover as many speed-optimizing tricks as possible. You will find out more about these throughout the rest of the book.

Given these facts, some programmers using "traditional" languages such as C do not consider scripted languages to be true programming languages at all, but simply "front-ends" for uninitiates and novices to produce a limited range of programs. However, such a position cannot be sustained for OpenScript. It is a true structured programming language, and therefore demands *structured programming*.

Structured Programming

The hallmarks of structured programming are use of self-contained structures to direct program flow and data encapsulation.

In OpenScript, the self-contained structures are blocks of statements known as *handlers*, described in detail later. In the previous example, the handler begins with the `TO HANDLE` directive followed by the message to be processed. The handler ends with an `END` directive. The handler as a whole is a *container*. All handlers are containers, but not all containers are handlers; variables, some properties, and the various kinds of looping or branching routines of a handler are also containers.

> **Note**
>
> Another property of a structured program is the extreme rarity or complete absence of `go to` or `jump` statements. Instead, *control structures* (or *flow structures*) are used to direct the program flow. Control structures are usually some form of conditional loop.

Data Encapsulation, as used in OpenScript, essentially means that a statement is not useful if it is not contained within a handler. Specifically, variables and functions can be (and must be) created within handlers. A newly created variable is, by default, *local*. This means that its content cannot be altered by any handler but the one in which it was created (declared). This feature makes debugging much easier. However, once the handler has finished its job, its local variables are destroyed; their values are not preserved. Optionally, you may declare a variable as a *system* variable, whose value is persistent through the ToolBook instance, but which is accessible to all handlers, making it subject to unintended change. Data contained in system variables is not encapsulated.

OpenScript provides for parameter passing so that local variables can be passed from one handler to another when required.

ToolBook also provides for a different method of "encapsulating" data—*properties*. Properties belong to objects (although they can be created by scripts) and are therefore global in nature like system variables. Then again, they can usually be used only when the specific object to which they are "attached" is named in the script, providing some protection against accidental change. Many objects have built-in properties—size, color, ID number, and so forth—but you can also create your own *user properties*. (The script itself is the "value" of the built-in `script` property of an object.) Properties are persistent between ToolBook instances. Close your book, exit Windows, switch off your computer; the next time you open your book, properties retain their values.

Script Writing

If you aren't familiar with scripting, a good way of creating scripts for your program is to let ToolBook do it for you. There are three tools available for automatic script creation. One of these is the Hyperlink button in the Button Properties dialog box (described in Chapter 4, "Understanding Books, Backgrounds, and Pages"), which provides simple navigational commands for page navigation. More powerful tools are the Script Recorder and the AutoScript feature.

Using the Script Recorder

The Script Recorder is a truly useful tool for recording actions. Unlike some other action recording devices, such as Windows' own Recorder accessory, ToolBook's Script Recorder records only actions that can be translated into OpenScript statements, such as creating objects, deleting and displacing objects, and changing object properties. There is no penalty for selecting the wrong menu by mistake, as long as no item is selected from that menu. It doesn't matter how fast or slow you move the mouse cursor. This means that the Script Recorder is not the tool of choice for path animation; while you can let it write a script that moves an object, that object always moves at maximum speed. Use the path animation feature if you want to animate an object or objects along a screen path.

As a simple demonstration of Script Recorder usage, you can have it write a script which responds to a click anywhere on the page by drawing a rectangle, filling it with a red color, and assigning it a name. (This script is the script of page 1 of `RECORD.TBK`, supplied on the disk accompanying this book.)

To invoke the Script Recorder, you must be at Author level. If you are at Reader level, select Edit, Author or press F3. Then follow this procedure:

1. Select Edit, Start Recording, or press F8. The Recording icon appears immediately to the right of the cursor position indicator of the status bar.
2. Select the Rectangle tool from the Tool palette.

3. Draw a rectangle from about 2820,1515 to about 5445,3795. The exact coordinates are not important, but do not click within the bounds of the rectangle at this time. The rectangle must remain selected, with the resizing handles visible.
4. Select View, Palettes, Color or select the Color Tray button on the toolbar to show the color tray. Click one of the shades of red that the palette offers. Your rectangle will become filled with the selected color. You may choose at this point to reduce screen clutter by clicking the close box on the Color Tray, but you may leave the colors visible if you want.
5. Select Object, Graphic Properties, press Shift+F6, or double-click the rectangle while holding down the Shift key. The Graphic Properties dialog box will appear.
6. In the Name field of the properties dialog, type **`Red Rectangle`**.
7. Close the Graphic Properties book by clicking the OK button or pressing the Enter key.
8. Choose Edit, Stop Recording or press F8 to halt the recording process. The Recording icon remains visible as an indication that a script is being held in memory. To paste the new script into the script property of an object, continue with the following steps:
9. Delete the red rectangle by pressing the Delete key.
10. Choose Object, Page Properties or press Shift+F7 to open the Page Properties dialog box. Click the Script button on the right side of the box. The Script Editor will open.
11. Select Edit, Paste Recording, press F8, or click the Paste Recording button on the Script Editor's toolbar. The script that you have made is now visible in the edit area of the Script Editor.
12. Close the Script Editor by pressing Alt+F4 or clicking the Save and Close button on the editor's toolbar.
13. Change to Reader level by pressing F3; then click anywhere on the page. Your rectangle is redrawn, colored, and named automatically.

For a beginning of an explanation of what the script statements actually mean, see the "Understanding Message Handlers" section later in this chapter.

Using the AutoScript Feature. *AutoScript* is ToolBook's term for its script storage and retrieval feature. AutoScript does not write scripts automatically, although a few small libraries of predefined scripts are supplied with the program. Rather, it eases the labor of script writing by allowing quick location and editing of frequently used scripts.

> **Note**
>
> An AutoScript script library is a file with the ATS extension. If you have reason to reinstall ToolBook, new or modified ATS files are not preserved. Back up your ATS files as you would any other valuable files.

To use AutoScript you must be at Author level. Suppose you want to navigate to the next page of your book when a button is clicked on any part of the page. Follow these steps to accomplish this task using one of the scripts supplied with ToolBook:

1. Create a new book by choosing File, New. A new book contains one page.
2. Add a second page by choosing Object, New Page.
3. Return to page 1 by choosing Page, Previous or Page, First, or by pressing Alt+left arrow. (Recall that the page number is displayed in the status bar at the bottom of the main window.)
4. Choose Object, Page Properties or press Shift+F7 to open the Page Properties dialog box. Click the Script button on the right side of the box. The Script Editor for the script of the page opens.
5. Choose Edit, Insert Auto-Script or click the AutoScript button on the Script Editor's toolbar. The AutoScript browser will appear.
6. Click the Choose File button on the browser. The standard Windows file selector appears. Select the default AutoScript file if it is not already the currently open ATS file. If you chose the default options during installation of ToolBook, the relative path to the basic library is `\MTB30\MTB30.ATS`.

   AutoScript needs a minimum of two additional pieces of information to complete the navigation request. The first is the description of what it is you want to do. The second is the event or message that causes the action to begin. The library of tasks is shown in the Actions list of the AutoScript browser. The library of events is shown in the Events list.
7. Scroll down the Actions list until the entry Go To Next Page is visible; then click that line to select it.
8. Scroll down the Events list until `buttonClick` is visible; click that line to select it.
9. Click the OK button. The stored script appears in the edit section of the Script Editor.
10. Go to page 2 by selecting Page, Next or by pressing Alt+right arrow.
11. Repeat steps 1 through 9 for the second page, but substitute the selection Go To Previous Page in step 7.
12. Switch to Reader mode by pressing F3.

Clicking anywhere on either of the two pages navigates to the other one.

Composing Scripts

You can inspect the scripts written by the Script Recorder or retrieved by AutoScript in order to gain a greater understanding of how script statements work. Nevertheless, mastery of the scripting process itself is essential to mastery of ToolBook and to the success of a complex program.

To see why this is true, consider the limitations of using the "automatic" script insertion tools. The Script Recorder's abilities are relevant only when dealing with processes that have a definite start and end. Except insofar as the programmer can script the appearance of a dialog box, choices of action are not supported. On the other hand, AutoScript can paste a script of arbitrary length and functionality into the Script Editor, but the supplied set of scripts is limited. You will have to write the scripts you need. Any complex script produced by either tool will require modification to run in your particular program, particularly if path names and variables appear in it.

Entering Scripts

Most scripts for normal purposes are entered into the edit area of the Script Editor. The Command Window is useful for entering tentative or diagnostic handlers and statements, at Reader as well as Author level, and for displaying results of such statements. Recall that the Command Window is available at Author level via the View, Command menu selection or the Command Window button on the toolbar. It does not close automatically when Reader mode is entered, so you may use Command Window statements to act on running programs, an invaluable debugging aid.

OpenScript, like many other structured languages, allows some stylistic freedom in the appearance of its source text. Except when breaking a source line into two or more lines to avoid the language's 80 character per line limit, it ignores "white space" (tab and space characters and blank lines). It is also case-insensitive. `TO HANDLE` and `END` are capitalized here only for visual compatibility with the AutoScript style. Similarly, neither the blank lines between statements nor the indentation of the script statement are necessary, but guide the eye from the highest level (the handler) through subordinate levels (statements and control structures). Feel free to develop your own style, but make it readable and use it consistently.

It is important to plan your scripts to take advantage of data encapsulation (parameter passing and local variables) as often as possible. The extra effort will pay off during the debugging process.

Understanding Message Handlers. ToolBook, like Windows itself, works by setting up an *event loop*. Most of the time, it is running in a loop which tests for the occurrence of an event. Typical events include keystrokes, mouse movements, button clicks, drag-and-drop actions, requests for data exchange by other programs, and so forth, but they can also be generated by internal processes or Windows. Each event generates a unique *message*; each message is processed by an OpenScript *handler*.

A *script* is made up of one or more handlers—a large multimedia project may have hundreds of handlers, with perhaps a dozen or two in each page script and the bulk of the rest in the book and system book scripts. There are actually several types of handlers used in OpenScript programming. They include the following:

- The `to handle` structure, which defines what happens when a particular message is received by an object.
- The `to set` handler, which sends a message that sets the value of a property of an object or creates a new property.

- The `to get` handler, which sends a message that retrieves the value of a property of an object or defines a function.
- The `notify` handler, which is actually a request for an object to receive and handle a message it would not normally receive.

Handlers must have the `TO HANDLE`, `TO SET`, `TO GET`, `NOTIFYBEFORE`, or `NOTIFYAFTER` statement in the first active line, followed by the message name, which is sometimes followed by additional arguments. The final line always begins with `END`.

Note

You may follow the `END` keyword (capitalization optional) with the name of the message. If you do not include the message name, the `END` keyword alone defines the end of the handler; that handler's script will compile properly assuming the absence of other errors. However, if you do include a message name after `END`, it must match the message name on the first line. Otherwise an error will be generated. In a long script with long handlers, placing the message name at the end as well as the beginning of a handler can enhance readability. Don't include any other arguments after the message name on the end line.

Correcting Scripting Errors

Unless you are a perfect algorithm designer, programmer, and typist, you are sometimes going to generate errors while programming in OpenScript.

Compile-time script errors, such as bad syntax, unmatched parentheses, unterminated text strings, and certain misspellings are caught at the time you check syntax or attempt to save the script. These must be corrected at once or your script will fail to compile. If the compiler encounters an error, it alerts you by displaying a message like that in figure 13.1.

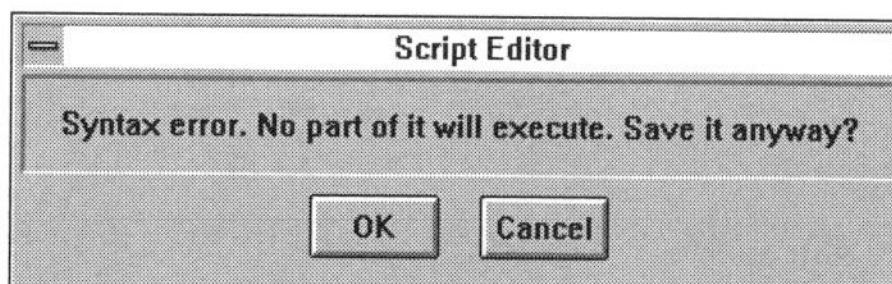

Fig. 13.1

Typographical and syntax errors must be corrected prior to an attempt to run a script or else you will get this—the compiler error alert.

Tip

A compiler error message which seems to make no sense in context can often be traced to a missing quotation mark in a literal string, to unbalanced parentheses, and particularly to missing end keywords in flow structures, many lines before the one at which the message is finally displayed. ToolBook's compiler often catches errors at the right place but is unable to do so when script statements following the actual mistake make sense in any context whatsoever.

Scripts for Navigation. To write a simple OpenScript handler for navigation between two pages using a button, follow these steps:

1. Make sure you are in Author mode. If you are not, select Edit, Author, or simply press F3.
2. Create a new book by selecting File, New, or press Ctrl+N. The new book has one background and one page. Name and save the book.

> **Note**
>
> The default style for the tool palettes is Graphics Only, meaning that only pictures are shown on the buttons representing the tools. Right-click anywhere in the palette to pop up a menu which allows you to select Captions Only or Graphics and Captions, each of which provides a short descriptive text string on each button. The advantage of the Graphics Only view is that its palette takes up less screen area than that of the other views.

3. Select the Field tool from the Tool Palette. Drag the mouse from about 3165,360 to about 4770,645. (Mouse position is displayed in the second box from the left on the status bar at the bottom of the screen. The exact coordinates are not critical.) You now have a text field that can be used to display the current page. Be sure to click the Selection tool after you draw the field to prepare the system for drawing other objects.
4. Enter the page number manually. Double-click inside the field you have just created. The cursor will become a blinking insertion bar. Type **`This is Page 1`**, and then click the Selection (arrow) tool to deselect the field.
5. Select the Button tool. Draw a button from about 3375,825 to about 4605,1245.
6. Disable the Button tool by clicking the selection (arrow) tool. The new button will be selected automatically, as indicated by the presence of sizing handles. Select Button Properties from the Object menu, or hold down the Shift key as you double-click the button.

> **Tip**
>
> If the Properties dialog does not appear after a Shift-double-click, you have probably moved the mouse inadvertently between clicks. Look at the Undo item in the Edit menu. If it is enabled (black), choose it immediately to restore the object to its original size.

7. Change the button caption to `Next`, then click the Script button to invoke the Script Editor.
8. Type the following lines in the Script Editor window. The line breaks are necessary. The indentation of the second line is not strictly necessary but improves readability:

```
TO HANDLE buttonClick
    go to next page
END buttonClick
```

9. Close the Script Editor by selecting Exit from the editor's File menu; by pressing Alt+F4; or by clicking the Update Script And Exit button. If an error alert appears, recheck your spelling and try again.
10. Once the editor is closed, dismiss the Button Properties box by clicking OK.
11. Choose Select Page from the Edit menu, press Shift+F12, or click the page selection icon on the status bar (in the fourth box from the left). Duplicate the page by choosing Duplicate from the Edit menu or by pressing Ctrl+D. The status bar's current page box (near the right end) should now say `2 of 2`. Notice that your field and button have been duplicated, but the field's text still reads `This is Page 1`. Select the field, double-click inside it to allow text entry (as indicated by the cursor's becoming the standard Windows edit cursor, a blinking I-beam), and change the 1 to 2.
12. Select the button and open its Properties dialog box by choosing Object, Button Properties. Change the caption to `Previous`. Click the Script button. Your button script should be intact. Alter the second line by changing the word `next` to `previous`, and then exit the Editor and Properties boxes.
13. Go to Reader mode by choosing Edit, Reader or pressing F3. The tools will disappear, and your buttons should switch the current page between 1 and 2 when clicked.

While this example may seem trivially simple, there are numerous variations which can be demonstrated with just these two pages. For instance, go to page 1, invoke the Script Editor as in steps 6 through 8 of the the procedure you've just followed, and enter each of the following lines, one at a time, as line 2 of your script:

```
go next page    --"to" is unnecessary

go to second page    --ordinals go up to "tenth"

go to page 2   --page number of book

--increment built-in ID number
go to page (IDNumber of this page + 1)
go to page 2 of this book  --specify the book
```

You may in fact just choose View, Command, click the Command Window tool, or press Shift+F3 to show the Command Window and simply type each line, followed by Enter, in it.

You may have inferred from the last line that it is possible to go to pages in other books, perhaps even closed ones. You are correct. The next-to-last statement works only if you have created the pages in order 1, then 2, with no deleted pages in between. The page ID number is available from the Page Properties dialog under the

Object menu. While you have the Properties for page 2 on-screen, give that page a name by entering **mySecondPage** into the Name field. Then use the name in the button script of page 1's button:

```
go to page "theSecondPage"
```

You can go to other books or pages of other books by specifying the book and (optionally) the page; the default is page 1.

Tip

Next/Previous navigation is fine for electronic books and other applications which have several ordered pages of text. However, in most other cases it is safer to give each page a name and use the name in navigation scripts. That way, if pages are added or subtracted, your navigation will be unaffected. (Using page ID numbers provides the same measure of safety, but these often become hard to remember if they get out of order—and they usually will. Using the page numbers does not affect your navigation, as you may rearrange pages freely.)

The following statement will work in your handler if there is no variable named `mySecondPage` in scope:

```
go to page mySecondPage
```

This kind of statement is not recommended, however, as ToolBook doesn't know at first whether the last word is a variable containing a number, a variable containing a text string, or a literal text string. You, however, know that it's a literal string; so use the quotation marks to tell that to ToolBook. Execution will speed up (though maybe not noticeably in this simple example).

Note

One of the features which gives ToolBook its great ease of use is the ability to use *untyped variables,* or variables whose type is unspecified. There will be more on this later, but, for now, understand that OpenScript slows down when it has to work out what type of variable it's dealing with. You should strive to specify the types of as many of your variables as possible to maximize speed and to disallow entry of data of the specified type. The previous example doesn't use any variables at all, but a page name or number could certainly be constructed from expressions containing variables. Don't set yourself up for confusion.

Any of these statements may be included in handlers within the script of a button, hotword, draw or paint object, or even a page (if you want to leave a page, such as a title page, click anywhere on it). Remember from the descriptions of objects that the distinguishing features of a button are that it has built-in responses to a mouse click. For instance, it changes its appearance to give the visual illusion of being pressed and released, and it can also navigate to a given page without explicit scripting if you desire. Other objects work just as well as buttons when it comes to scripted navigation.

Finally, a built-in or custom menu item message can be sent directly. The message `next` or `previous` is sent when you select Next or Previous from the Page menu item, but you may go to the next page from OpenScript by using the following:

```
send next
```

You may recognize this command as the one used in the earlier AutoScript example to turn a page. It isn't a very good choice for a navigation command. If your application has removed or altered ToolBook's built-in Reader-level menu bar, the `next` message will not be sent.

Tip

Having pointed out the potential pitfall, sending menu item messages from buttons and hotwords is nonetheless an excellent way of keeping code in one place (making maintenance easy) and of assuring that the result of a button click has the same "look and feel" as that of a menu selection.

From this point, you will not receive an explicit instruction for every step; entering other, more complex scripts into the Script Editor follows this blueprint.

Scripts for Text and Data Manipulation. OpenScript programming for text and data is a deep issue. It is somewhat misleading to separate text and numerical data in OpenScript. ToolBook has automatic type conversion abilities; you may mix text and numerals freely in many cases. String variables can contain text strings, which, if each character is a number, are numbers themselves.

Text in ToolBook is contained in combo boxes, fields, record fields, and variables. Text commands act on several subsets of a field's text—characters, numerals treated as characters, characters treated as numerals, words, groups of adjacent words, and individual lines of text.

OpenScript provides operators for algebraic and logical functions, as well as functions for some of the transcendentals. A few financial functions are also included.

User properties provide a means of saving data between ToolBook instances in the same way that the color of a square, for instance, is preserved.

Any combination of text and data entities that produces a result is an OpenScript *expression.*

Understanding Mouse and Keyboard Events. The mouse and keyboard are, in most cases, the primary means of user input for ToolBook books. Built-in OpenScript messages have many options for conveying information about keyboard and button input.

Consider the `buttonClick` message you intercepted (with a `buttonClick` handler) and processed in this section's first examples. It is actually the last of four messages that are sent automatically by ToolBook when the left mouse button is pressed and released. The `buttonDown` message is sent to the target (the button) when the button is pressed, and the `buttonUp` message when it is released. Each of these messages is followed by one of the following three arguments, which so far have been ignored:

- The location of the mouse when the button is pressed or released (two numbers which specify the mouse's current location in the current viewer).
- Whether the Shift key is depressed (`true` or `false`).
- Whether the Ctrl key is depressed (`true` or `false`).

Put the following handler in the script of a new page, and then click anywhere on the page:

```
--It doesn't matter what you call the parameters,
--but use the names consistently within the handler.
TO HANDLE buttonDown pLoc,isShift,isCtrl
     request "Button Down:" & CRLF \
     & "Position =" && pLoc & CRLF \
     & "Shift = " && isShift & CRLF \
     & "Control =" && isCtrl
END buttonDown
```

Note

Remember that the backslash character (\), as used at the end of a typographical script line, means that the next typographical line is a continuation of the OpenScript statement. You do this if you want to format your line to fit in the usable area of your screen or printer or, as here, to clarify the meanings of parts of the expression. This can go on for numerous (typographical) lines when writing a long statement. To OpenScript, the previous script contains one statement. Type it on one line if you want (omitting all backslashes). Comments do not require backslashes but do require the comment operator, `--`, before each line.

The text in the Request box, which is displayed upon execution of the `request` command, reports the cursor location at the time the mouse button is depressed (as a list of two coordinates in ToolBook page units), and reports the state of the Shift and Ctrl keys as `false` and `true` for up and down, respectively. Dismiss the dialog box and click again, this time with the Shift and/or Ctrl keys held down. Try substituting `buttonUp` and `buttonClick` for the message name. Substitute `buttonDoubleClick` and double-click the page. The analogous messages are automatically generated for the right mouse button by adding `right`, as in `rightButtonDown`.

Note

If you want to view the results of this script without having to dismiss a dialog box each time the mouse is clicked, replace the `request` command with a `put` command. The result of the expression now appears in the Command Window. You may have to resize the Command Window to show all four lines of text. The full syntax is `put` *`statements(s)`* `into commandWindow`.

What happens if you want to do something that is dependent on the motion of the mouse while a button is held down? Drag-and-drop features are included in ToolBook; but suppose, for example, that you want to scroll a picture by pushing it around with the mouse? You can set a flag in an idle handler to send a custom message when the mouse button is down, but OpenScript provides an easier way. The `buttonStillDown` message is sent repeatedly when either the left or right mouse button is depressed and held. This requires a fourth `LOGICAL` parameter to be passed with the message. This parameter is `false` when the left button is held down and `true` when the right one is.

The keyboard events are a little more complex, as there are two character sets relevant to ToolBook: the built-in character constants and the ANSI extended set. The ToolBook character constants are strings representing integer values; for instance, the constant `KeyA` represents the (decimal) integer 65. Some, but not all, of the ToolBook constants have values corresponding to the ASCII number of the key. The ANSI character set, on the other hand, starts with the 7-bit ASCII character set and uses the eighth bit to provide 128 additional characters. These previously undefined values above 127 represent special characters and letters specific to languages other than English. The ToolBook set and the ANSI set overlap, so it is best to use the ToolBook constants unless an ANSI value is specifically required.

Tip

If you are using a ToolBook constant and require its numerical value for a mathematical operation, get it with the `evaluate()` function. This is true of all ToolBook constants, not just key constants.

The concept of the focus needs introduction here. On a typical page, there may be any number of objects which are capable of receiving keyboard input. Whichever one is going to receive the message from the next keypress is said to have the *focus*. A blinking insertion point cursor in a text field is an indication that it has the focus. The sign of a button's having the focus may be a thin gray line encircling its caption or a thickening of the dark border surrounding the entire button. Other objects, including pages, may have the focus. If a modal dialog box is displayed, there may or may not be a text field to receive the focus, but there will always be at least one button present. It is often the case that the Tab key selects which button is ready to respond to an

Enter keypress or some other keyboard shortcut; that button has the focus. (The definition of "focus" will be extended in the discussion of viewers, but this is enough to go on for now.)

PC keyboards send a character code when a key is pressed and a different one when a key is released. OpenScript provides statements and functions to process the messages associated with each. Put the two handlers shown in Listing 13.1 into the script of a button or page.

Listing 13.1 13LST01.TXT Examples of Messages with Parameters

```
TO HANDLE keyDown k, s, c
     put "Key Down:" & CRLF \
          & "Key =" && k & CRLF \
           & "Shift = " && s & CRLF \
          & "Control =" && c
     END KeyDown

TO HANDLE keyUp k, s, c
     put "Key Up:" & CRLF \
          & "Key =" && k & CRLF \
           & "Shift = " && s & CRLF \
          & "Control =" && c
     END keyUp
```

Pressing a key displays the value of its ToolBook key constant and the states of the Shift and Ctrl keys in the edit box of the Command Window. Releasing the key provides similar information. The two messages are distinct. In most cases, the parameter values are the same for each message, but the Shift and Ctrl parameters need not be.

Using System Books

Most programming languages provide for the use of external libraries of functions or data. ToolBook's "native" kind of library is the system book.

What is a system book? The short answer is that a *system book* is a ToolBook book bearing the extension SBK (and a few restrictions), not the usual book extensions TBK or EXE. A system book is built to be used by one or more books as a library. System books are higher in the object hierarchy (discussed in the next section) than the main book and respond slightly differently to certain keywords. Use them when your application is composed of several books, each of which has some functions or data in common, or when the types of application you tend to write are focused on a narrow range of tasks.

There is no essential difference between writing a system book and a standard book, except that it is best to limit the content of a particular system book to related handlers, art, and controls which may be needed by multiple books. This keeps the sizes of both the system book and the main book down.

For instance, examine the system book `MTB30.SBK`. Here you will find much of the page art and scripts used to implement the standard behavior of Multimedia ToolBook's Author mode. For contrast, take a look at `MTB30MM.SBK`, a system book shipped primarily to maintain compatibility with the multimedia tools of prior versions of Multimedia ToolBook. This book has only one page. Its entire functionality is provided by the book script (available through the Book Properties dialog box or the Parent button on the Script Editor toolbar).

Caution

Do not change or edit any portion of any system book provided with ToolBook unless you are certain you want the change the behavior of every book which uses it. Even then, save the system book under another name and edit the copy.

The main book, in order to save time and space, must have information about which system books may be required if any. You are responsible for providing that information most of the time. To do this, use a built-in property of the system, `sysBooks`, which is a list of currently installed system books. You may add a book by inserting the name of the book into the list. Add the lines in Listing 13.2 to the book script of the book that you built earlier for page navigation.

Listing 13.2 13LST02.TXT Adding a System Book

```
TO HANDLE enterBook
--Make sure that the book is not already in the list.
--f it is not, add it:
if "MYSYSBK.SBK" is not in sysBooks
    push "MYSYSBK.SBK" onto sysBooks
end if
END enterBook
```

Save the book under any name you want and close it. Create a new book and save it under the name `MYSYSBK.SBK`. (The book doesn't need to have functionality, but it does need to be in the same folder as the original book.) Reopen the original book and type the following in the Command Window:

```
request sysBooks
```

Your `sysBook` should be the first filename listed in the text of the request box.

When the system book is not in the same folder as the main book, use the full path to the system book. Do not precede the name with the keyword `book`.

Once a system book is linked to one book of an application, its handlers are available to all other books of that application.

Note

The preceding handler pushes the book onto sysBooks only if it isn't already present. No actual harm is done if a book is pushed onto the stack more than once, but it is inefficient. What's more, if some process repeatedly pushes the same book(s) onto the stack, you'll eventually run out of memory. Always check for a system book's absence before adding it to the list.

The Push keyword implies that sysBooks is a variable of type `STACK`. A stack is a list of comma-separated elements. The elements themselves may be of any data type. The push keyword adds an element (in this case, a book name) to the stack, or `list`, as the first entry. The `request sysBooks` statement presents a dialog showing the list of `sysBooks`. In this example, the dialog text might read the following:

```
c:\mtb30\myBooks\mySysBk.sbk,c:\mtb30\mtb30.sbk
```

To have a particular system book added each time ToolBook is opened, push it onto `startupSysBooks`. Actually, you will find the startup system book list in the document `\WINDOWS\MTB30.INI`. While it is possible to edit this file directly, be sure to add a comment in your script, at the application or book level, that this has been done.

Tip

The *OpenScript Reference Manual* states that the document containing the list of startup system books is called `TOOLBOOK.INI`, rather than `MTB30.INI`. This is incorrect.

Here is a simple little system book which has only one handler, which turns pages. Create a new book by choosing File, New and put the following handler in the book script by choosing Object, Book Properties. The Book Properties dialog box appears. Click the Script button in the Book Properties dialog box and enter the handler in Listing 13.3.

Listing 13.3 13LST03.TXT Adding a System Book: Part 1

```
TO HANDLE pageTurn direction
--pageTurn is a custom message, not a built-in one. direction is a
--parameter passed to this handler by the calling handler.
--The use of a conditions flow structure is a little extravagant here,
--since-there are only two conditions, but it introduces its use and
--is shorter than two if statements.
      conditions
           when direction = "@next"
                go to next page
           when direction = "@previous"
                go to previous page
      end conditions
END pageTurn
```

Save the book as PAGETURN.SBK. Create another new book, name it TURNTEST.TBK, and add several pages to it by pressing Ctrl+N a few times. View the background by choosing View, Background. Click the polygon palette tool and select "3" so that the regular polygon tool draws triangles. Use the regular polygon tool to draw a triangle about 1/2" high and 3/8" or so wide on the background, with the vertex of the short sides on the left. Click the arrow tool to select the triangle and put the handler in Listing 13.4 into its script (not the page's script).

Listing 13.4 13LST04.TXT Adding a System Book: Part 2

```
TO HANDLE buttonClick
     if "pageTurn.sbk" is not in sysBooks
          push "pageTurn.sbk" onto sysBooks
     end if
--Send a custom message with the following parameter:
     send pageTurn @previous
END buttonClick
```

Duplicate this triangle (make sure you're still on the background), flip it horizontally, and position it to the right of the first triangle to form a pair of arrowheads facing left and right. Change the script of the triangle on the right so that the next-to-last script line reads the following:

```
send pageTurn @next
```

Go to Reader mode and click either of the triangles. The page number should increment when you click the right arrow and decrement when you click the left. To demonstrate that the sysBook's command is being called, try commenting it out by placing comment marks (--) before each line of the system book's script. You should then receive an Execution Suspended alert.

Note the use of parameter passing. You are sending the same message from each arrow, but followed by the parameter @next in one case and @previous in the other. Also, be aware that parameters and messages that you create (such as these) must have different names than ToolBook's built-in messages. This is why the @ is added to the next and previous parameters; those are both OpenScript menu item messages and therefore unsuitable for use in custom messages. Actually, you could use any unique message and parameter names you like as long as the target handler knows what they are.

Tip

While page navigation is an easy task suitable for a demonstration, be aware that this is not the type of function which is generally included in a system book, as its entire functionality is available from within OpenScript.

You discover as you settle into your own scripting habits that the handlers that you might want to put into system books are those that are not built-in but which are used repeatedly in your books. Multiple open books can access the handlers in a system book, as long as the books are running under the same instance of ToolBook.

When you close a book, its system books are closed as well. If you are keeping two or more books open simultaneously, there is no need to link a given system book in each subsidiary book as long as a system book is not unlinked by closing the book that linked it.

Application Initialization

ToolBook sends messages at various points during the startup of a book. Your handlers can intercept these messages and take the appropriate action for your needs.

The system sends an `enterSystem` message during startup of each ToolBook instance. Any initialization or customization of ToolBook that you want to affect all books running in under the current instance—and which may or must be handled before the first screen from your application is displayed—can be done here.

There is a particularly useful reason to trap this message. It is followed by a parameter that contains the command line used to start the instance. (This is true of the command line which Program Manager uses when a book's icon is double-clicked as well a line entered via the File, Run command from Program Manager or File Manager.) If arguments, switches, or filenames are added to the command line (or if the book name itself contains key letter combinations), OpenScript's text parsing statements can be used in a custom handler which tells the system to initialize itself in a certain way. For example, the main menu bar can normally show the menus allowed in normal book use, but allow the programmer to enter a command-line switch that adds additional menus while troubleshooting onsite.

The `enterApplication` and `enterBook` messages can be a little confusing at first, because the order in which they are sent depends on whether there are pages shown in the main window or not. `enterApplication` is sent immediately before a page of the newly opened book is shown in the main window. `enterBook` is sent if a page is shown in the main window or in any other viewer. Use the `enterApplication` handler only in the main book, not in system books or ancillary books. It is a good place to keep the initial declarations of system variables (if you want to collect these in one place) and an especially good place to show the opening screen, set up the look of the first page by making sure the correct objects are visible, and set the focus if there are one or more text fields or buttons. Use an `enterBook` handler for setting the initial color palette, page size, and other properties unique to a particular book if they differ from the ones set in the Book Properties dialog box.

As a practical matter, some end users feel that ToolBook applications in general take a long time to open. The ToolBook engine itself takes a subjectively long time to load compared with several popular spreadsheets and word processors. It is not the purpose here to benchmark ToolBook's speed, but to point out ways in which it can be improved. ToolBook applications are often highly visual. So, the faster you can get your book to do something on-screen, the better for your users. Yet you still need to initialize your book, as there are things which need to be done before the first page appears. The balance between startup speed and technical requirements is often a delicate one. The following are some rules of thumb for improving perceived performance:

- Get something on the screen as quickly as possible. Open a viewer onto an introductory page near the very start of your `enterApplication` or `enterBook` handler.
- If there are a lot of resources (especially fonts) or DLL function calls which are not used immediately, consider loading the resources or linking the DLLs later, preferably just before they are needed. It's true that this merely moves the associated load time to another part of the book, but if a background or page can be found with a short or nonexistent enter handler, the delay might be unnoticeable.

  You really have to take this on a case-by-case basis. It may help to put some book-scope handlers in an `enterBackground` handler for the first background, because the first page is visible at that point. But if your application repeatedly returns to the first background, be sure that your initializations are still wanted when returning to that background. If not, set a flag when the initialization is finished, then test it and skip the initialization portion. Clear the flag in a `leaveBook` or `leaveApplication` handler.
- Unless you are really uncomfortable with mathematical concepts or with traditional programming, use arrays rather than lists (stacks) or user properties for multi-element variables. The access time is faster for arrays. You save time initializing and gain speed throughout the book.
- If persistent values are required, it is a lot faster to get them from user properties (perhaps also assigning them to variables for faster access later) than to read them from an external file such as a `.INI` text file. In addition to the time required to open the file, find the needed text, read it, and close the file, there is an additional penalty when using sectionalized files in that the DLL must be linked and unlinked if you want to use the calls that directly support sections.

The following tasks should be performed (in any order) in the initialization phase:

- Determine the main window's behavior (presence or absence of a menu bar, screen centering, etc.) if it is different than that defined by the main window's Viewer Properties dialog box.
- If it is likely that the book will be run at different screen resolutions at different times, determine the current screen resolution so that objects can be sized properly.
- Define or determine the path(s) to external media files. While Multimedia ToolBook's Clip Manager can make sound, video, and pictures path-independent, you may elect not to use it (and often the drive letter needs to be found and substituted in the media paths).

- Assign values to variables and properties that will be used soon after initialization (including but not limited to those values which prevent divide-by-zero errors).

Other assignment statements may need to be performed at startup, but if you can place them elsewhere in the book, do so.

Correcting Script Execution Errors

Fatal runtime errors normally cause ToolBook to present the Execution Suspended dialog box. If you run across the Execution Suspend dialog box, the following are your options:

- Click Author to return ToolBook to the authoring mode. This is appropriate when the error description implies a problem elsewhere in the book or downward in the object hierarchy.
- Click Edit to edit the script directly from Reader mode. Save the script in the usual way, and your program will attempt to continue running with the modified script. You can reach the scripts of objects higher in the object hierarchy than the one in which the error was caught by using the Parent tool from the Script Editor.
- Click Debug to enter the ToolBook debugger. Use of the debugger is described in more detail in Chapter 24, "Debugging Tools and Techniques."
- Click Cancel to dismiss the dialog box. This option may be used when the error is a result of a purposeful trap in the script. It does cause the handler in which the error occurred to be skipped; it does not stop execution of the program as a whole.

> **Note**
>
> Script execution can be halted manually, and the script displayed at the current line, by pressing and holding both Shift keys at once. Be patient; you may have to hold them down for a second or longer. This feature is invaluable in that an infinite loop, which is not an error but is usually a mistake, can be halted. Failure of the Shift keys to halt execution and display the script is often the symptom of a serious system error.

ToolBook includes a built-in variable, `sysErrorNumber`, that is automatically set to a numeric value representing the nature of a fatal or nonfatal error. This number can be used by your script to implement custom error handling.

Tip

There is another built-in variable, `sysError`, which contains a string describing an error. Useful as this sounds, its use in a localized book (potentially, any book) is discouraged because the string is always an English-language statement. Few things are more embarrassing than an error handling system which displays the error's cause in the wrong language!

Note

A script error which inadvertently causes ToolBook to read from or write to memory allocated to another application (including Windows itself, as well as some library files) will cause a Windows General Protection Fault (GPF). A GPF may make your work impossible to save. In the event of a GPF; always exit and restart Windows, even if Windows seems to be running normally.

The Object Hierarchy

Very nearly every ToolBook entity can be described as an "object" under OpenScript. Formally, though, ToolBook defines several types of object which, along with their properties, lie at some level on the *object hierarchy* (see fig. 13.2).

While the concept of the object hierarchy can be approached from several different viewpoints, the definition to focus on at this time is based around the question "where do OpenScript messages originate and what happens to them if there is no script to handle them?"

Note

Messages are dealt with more fully in the next chapter. For now, know that messages are information passed from object to object as a result of user input or system intervention.

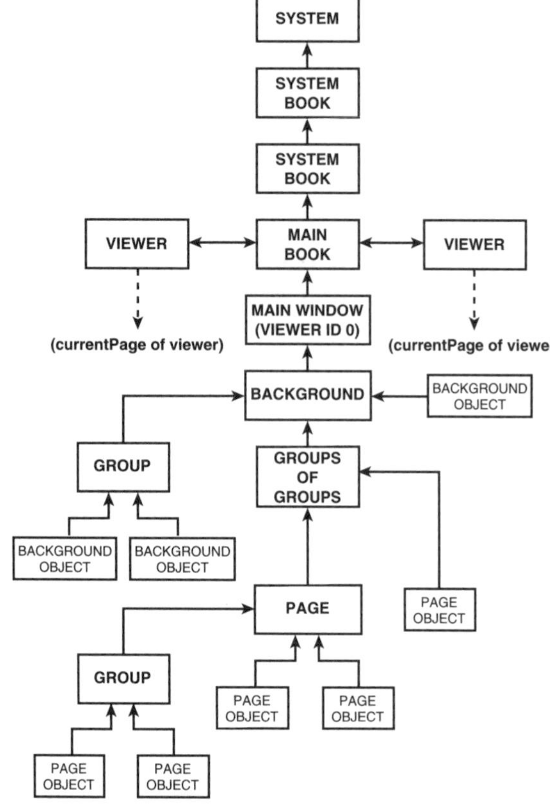

Fig. 13.2

The ToolBook object hierarchy is shown in its simplest form.

Message Origination

The *foreground* is the object upon which or through which you can see and control buttons, fields, and many other objects that respond to user input. Messages originate at the *target*, which is also the focus if the object is a button, field, or combo box. The target is basically just the object that received the most recent message; the focus is specifically the recipient of keyboard input. The two may be identical. For instance, when you click a button object, the button becomes the target. It sends the messages `buttonDown`, `buttonStillDown`, `buttonUp`, `buttonClick`, and, when appropriate, `allowDrag` and `allowDrop` with their attendant parameters. These messages originate at the button. The button may be on the foreground or background. If it is on the foreground, its messages may be intercepted by handlers in the script of the background; but if it's on the background, its messages are not automatically intercepted by handlers on the foreground (though messages may be sent to them by name). Except in the View menu, the foreground is almost universally called the *page*.

Objects on the Page. Viewed in this way, the base of the object hierarchy (that subset of objects which receive no system messages automatically) is the objects on the page. These include buttons, imported bitmaps, stages, draw objects of all kinds, and so on. Note that these objects are not intrinsically at the bottom of the "pecking order;" it is the fact that they are on the *page* that puts them in that position. These objects can receive user input (mouse events and keystrokes) and messages directly addressed to them from objects higher in the hierarchy or other objects on the page. They do not automatically receive system messages such as `idle`. Forwarded messages do not reach them.

Groups on the Page. Grouped objects on the page act very much like normal objects on the page. A complication arises when a group is itself part of a larger group. In this case, the group that contains the greatest number of other groups (which is the same as saying, "the most recent grouping of those groups") sits at the top of the group's own object hierarchy, as in figure 13.3. Next down are the groups that contain the second most numerous groups. This the case for each individual group of groups. Each object and group of objects (including groups of groups) has its own properties, including the `script` property. As groups can have a confusing hierarchy of their own, it is best to send messages to the specific object in the group (again emphasizing that an included group is an object) which handles the message. The keywords `my` and `self` may be used in a group's script to refer to its members.

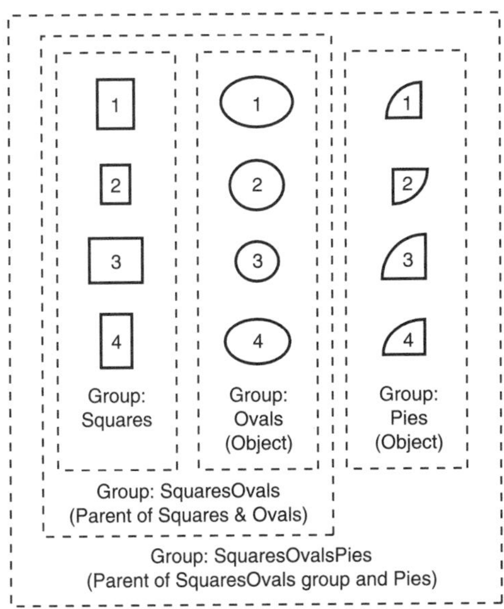

Fig. 13.3

A schematic diagram of a simple three-tier group. Each "parent" is higher in the object hierarchy than the objects that comprise it.

The Page. In most everyday use, the page is the object around which OpenScript activity revolves. Being one step up the hierarchy, it is proper to refer to it as the *parent* of the objects on it. It is the first object which automatically receives the `idle` message. User events that are not handled by an object on the page or forwarded messages from any object on the page, as well those directly addressed to the page, reach the page.

A handler in a page's script which calls another handler will first look for that handler on the page, searching farther up the hierarchy only if the target handler is not in the script of that page. A notify handler (described in the next chapter) functions only if the message to which it responds reaches the page on which it lies. Handlers that affect page behavior or the behavior of several objects on a page should be located in the script of that page.

The Background. Many pages can be associated with one background, and the background is the parent of each and all of those pages. Handlers (and other objects) that affect all or most of the pages of a background should be put into the script for that background.

References to objects on the background levels must be explicit. To refer to such an object, always add "of this background" to the reference. To see why, follow these steps:

1. Draw a rectangle on a page and name it r.
2. Enter the handler from Listing 13.5 into the script of the page.

Listing 13.5 13LST.05.TXT Using an Implicit Reference to a Rectangle

```
TO HANDLE buttonClick
     if fillColor of rectangle "r" <> green
          fillColor of rectangle "r" = green
     else
          fillColor of rectangle "r" = white
     end if
END buttonClick
```

3. Switch to Reader level by choosing Edit, Reader or by pressing F3.

   At this point, alternate mouse clicks should toggle the color of your rectangle from white to green and back.
4. Switch back to Author mode by choosing Edit, Author or pressing F3.
5. Select the rectangle that you drew in step 1 by clicking in it.
6. Delete the selected rectangle by pressing Delete.
7. Choose Open, Page Properties. The Page Properties dialog box appears.
8. Click the Script button in the Page Properties dialog box and select the entire page script by choosing Edit, Select All.
9. Choose Edit, Cut to remove the script. Cutting the selected text also places it into the Clipboard.
10. Save the now empty script by choosing the Save Script and Exit button on the Script Editor's toolbar.
11. Open the Background Properties dialog box by choosing Object, Background.

12. Choose the Script button on the Background Properties dialog box and paste the script that you cut in step 9 into the Editor.
13. Save the script by choosing the Save Script and Exit button on the Script Editor's toolbar.

    The pasted text is now the content of the Script property of the object of type Background.
14. Choose Edit, Reader to go to Reader mode. Click the page. You should get an Execution Suspended error box informing you that your rectangle (referred to by ID number) does not exist.
15. Return to Author mode by pressing F3 again.
16. Draw another rectangle on the page (not the background) which does not cover the rectangle on the background (so you can see at least part of each).
17. Choose Object, Page Properties to view the Page Properties dialog box for the current page. Enter **r** in the Name field of the dialog.

    There is now a rectangle named `r` on the foreground (the page) and a different rectangle with the same name on the background.
18. Return to Reader mode by pressing F3 and click the page. Rectangle `r` of the page should toggle in color from white to green.

What's going on? Well, it turns out that the page, in addition to being the lowest-level object that system messages are commonly sent to, has a special attribute—the ability to recognize an *implicit reference*. All other objects, below and above the page in the hierarchy, must be referred to explicitly. To demonstrate, change every reference to `rectangle r` in the preceding script to an explicit reference as in Listing 13.6.

Listing 13.6 13LST.06.DOC Explicit Reference to a Rectangle on the Background

```
TO HANDLE buttonClick
--use red for the background rectangle color for contrast:
if fillColor of rectangle "r" of this background <> red
          fillColor of rectangle "r" of this background = red
     else
          fillColor of rectangle "r" of this background = white
     end if
END buttonClick
```

Now the background's rectangle should toggle its color when the background receives a `buttonClick` message (sent when you click any part on the background that isn't hidden by a visible object on the page).

The necessity of explicit object references is not unique to the background. Nevertheless, it is convenient to include it here because you are likely to first encounter it at the background level when you start to write scripts for backgrounds that have more than one page. Try deleting the background script, then entering each of the previous handlers into the script of the book, which is another level up in the object hierarchy. As long as the references remain valid for a given page or background, and as long as there are no other handlers intercepting the same message without forwarding it, that object will get the message, causing the handler to execute.

It is good practice to always include an explicit reference whenever sending a message to an object, whether the object is on a page or not. A handler containing only explicit references can be moved up or down in the object hierarchy. For instance, if you discover that a handler in a page script needs to act on multiple backgrounds (perhaps to accommodate a change in the application feature specification), use of explicit references often makes the change as simple as cutting the text of the handler from the script of the page and pasting it into that of the book (the parent of backgrounds).

You will probably want to extend this concept even further by giving objects (including pages and backgrounds) meaningful names so you won't have to keep a record of object ID numbers. A reference to a name is as good as a reference to an ID.

Groups on the Background. Groups on a background are subject to the same considerations as are groups on a page, except that their internal hierarchies begin on the background. Again, an explicit reference to group members is recommended, in fact necessary, except that the keywords `my` and `self` may again be used in a group's script to refer to its members.

The Main Window. The main window, or viewer `ID 0`, is the only viewer in the main object hierarchy. It is the window in which all other objects (except, under certain conditions, other popup viewers) are displayed. The screen size of the main window is, by default, the size of the current background, though you may change its size by choosing Object, Viewers, choosing Main Window, clicking the Size tab, and changing the dimensions. The main window can spawn child windows (viewers) as described below. It is the parent of the backgrounds.

The Book. The next stop on the upward journey through the object hierarchy is the book. The book is the basic currency, so to speak, of ToolBook. It is, in the absence of system books, the parent of all other objects except the system, including viewers. (If a system book is in use, it is the main book's parent.) The handlers that affect the most objects in the greatest number of backgrounds or viewers should be put into the book script, as should the initialization and cleanup statements.

Viewers. Viewers can be confusing and infuriating objects to the OpenScript programmer. A viewer is nothing but a window onto the contents of a ToolBook book page. The book is the parent of all viewers, including the main window, but viewers other than the main window are not in the main object hierarchy; rather, the main hierarchy is defined by the presence of the main window, while other viewers are attached only to the book or to a system book and can have their own hierarchies (similar to the main one), but which have no direct connection with the primary message flow. The book script can often be used to process messages from child and popup viewers and pass corresponding messages down the main object message path. A system book is a useful place to handle messages that are common to several of these paths, as the system book resides higher than the main book. (System books themselves do not generally have viewers, but they certainly can if a certain viewer needs to be available to several other viewers.) There is also a flow structure, *in viewer*, that specifies which viewer's hierarchy is used to process messages.

The System. What actually calls Windows API and other functions to make ToolBook work is the system. The system has some properties, so it belongs in the object hierarchy as does any other object. The system properties are by default applied to all ToolBook instances, but the menu bars, color tray, palettes, controls, and indicators which define the normal ToolBook Author and Reader environments can be hidden and revealed (and sometimes modified). Typeface (such as font and style) and paragraph settings (such as justification and tab widths) are also system-wide.

When many variables are typed, objects are all named, and references are made explicit, your handlers will begin to take on the look of a file in a traditional programming language, and the time spent writing the script will be much greater than that spent writing the simplest script possible. But your script will outperform that simple script and you will be able to make many changes by cutting and pasting as described previously. Don't be discouraged by the seeming complexity; just think of the number of statements it would take to draw a rectangle and change its color based on user input if you had only the Windows API, not OpenScript, to use!

Shared Scripts

The script of an object is a property of that object. The script's value is the set of all of its message handlers. Whether a handler receives a message depends on the position in the object hierarchy of the object whose script the handler is part of (the script's parent). You have seen two ways of making a handler available to more than one object. The first is simply to duplicate the handler's text in the script of each of the objects for which its functionality is required; the other is to place the handler in an object, such as a book or system book, that lies high in the object hierarchy so that messages of the desired name "percolate" up from objects lower down until they encounter the handler. As only one message can be handled at a time, there are no conflicts among messages sent, for instance, by multiple buttons on a page. You might think that duplicating a script in many objects is wasteful of space. Worse, modifying the duplicated scripts is difficult or, at least, time-consuming as each must be changed separately. (Actually, you can write a temporary script to make all the changes at once, but what is gained in that case is consistency, not time, as it is also time-consuming to write the temporary script.)

But the method of sharing script statements by placing a handler high in the message path has its own problem: you can only share those statements that are relevant to common behavior of all of the objects that might send the handler's message. Sometimes you can get around this by writing statements in the high-level handler that makes message processing conditional on some other property's value, such as the name of the object that has sent the message. In general, though, you will be thrown back on the expedient of writing scripts in low-level objects which define specific behavior and then forwarding the message to a high-level handler that defines general responses to that message.

To allow access to a specific handler from any object at any level, OpenScript uses a resource type: the *shared script*. Using shared scripts is aided by knowledge of how to use the Resource Editor, but shared scripts may be created and used using OpenScript statements only.

To briefly illustrate the use of a shared script, follow these steps:

1. Make sure that your current folder (directory) contains PAGETURN.SBK. This book holds Listing 13.3 in its book script.
2. Open the Command Window by choosing View, Command. Enter the following series of statements in the Command Window's edit area (it doesn't matter where the text wraps in the window) and then press Enter:

   ```
   new sharedScript;name of it = "pageTurn";script of it
    = script of book "PAGETURN.SBK"
   ```

   Note the use of the ; operator to separate statements. You may also use Ctrl+Enter to make new statement lines in the Command Window. (If this script were part of a book, it would have been preferable to place each statement on one line for ease of troubleshooting.)
3. Change the script of the left triangle on the background of book TURNPAGE.TBK to read like the following:

   ```
   TO HANDLE buttonClick
       sharedScript of self = sharedScript "pageTurn"
       send pageTurn @previous
   END buttonClick
   ```

4. Change the script of the left triangle on the background of book TURNPAGE.TBK to read like the following:

   ```
   TO HANDLE buttonClick
       sharedScript of self = sharedScript "pageTurn"
       send pageTurn @next
   END buttonClick
   ```

   Do not link the system book PAGETURN.SBK.

Clicking the arrows now runs the shared script in the resource pageTurn to navigate between contiguous pages.

Note

The term `sharedScript` is used as the name of a built-in property of an object and as the name of a resource type. In the following line:

```
sharedScript of self = sharedScript "pageTurn"
```

the first occurrence of `sharedScript` refers to the property of a triangle, the second to the resource type.

From Here...

To summarize the central topic of this chapter, a script is a collection of one or more message handlers, composed of text and contained in the `script` property of a ToolBook object. You were introduced to the basic methods of script writing in ToolBook. You learned about ToolBook objects and the order in which they receive messages from a script or from the system. Additionally, you touched on the deep subject of program debugging.

- To find out more about the Script Editor, the Script Recorder, and the AutoScript tool, see Chapter 6, "Scripting Tools."
- To find out more about the object hierarchy and message passing, as well as about system books, refer to Chapter 14, "Messages, Objects, and Properties."
- To learn more about shared scripts, see Chapter 16, "Statements, Functions, and Expressions."
- To find out more about program debugging, see Chapter 24, "Debugging Tools and Techniques."

CHAPTER 14

Messages, Objects, and Properties

Objects, their properties, and the messages passed among them have been referred to in Chapter 13, "OpenScript Fundamentals." Now it's time to examine them in more detail. In this section, you'll have a brief review of what messages are, what events send them, and which objects receive them. This is good preparation for learning about some of the most commonly used messages and properties by examining a working script.

In this chapter, you learn about the following topics:

- Messages in Multimedia ToolBook
- Objects, system objects, and their properties
- Creating user properties
- Notify handlers and self-contained tools

Messages in Multimedia ToolBook

ToolBook operates by sending, or passing, messages among ToolBook objects or between ToolBook objects and another application via DDE. Additionally, messages may be passed between Visual Basic (VBX) and ToolBook (TBX) custom controls. Furthermore, Windows messages can be received and sent to the Windows API. While there are differences in the ways in which you send and handle the different kinds of messages, they are actually very similar; many OpenScript commands are just calls to a single Windows API function that accomplishes the same purpose as the command. The Windows functions are "wrapped" in code that converts ToolBook-compatible data types into Windows data types; then the entire wrapper is available to you via an OpenScript message.

When you are programming in OpenScript, you don't need to know much about object programming. OpenScript scripts are entirely procedural. ToolBook is written to shield the user from the most difficult object programming concepts. A graphical interface is provided for creating and modifying objects; ToolBook just presents the objects you choose to create as finished products, unless you build custom objects in another language. Messages and properties can then be used with or created for the objects.

An analogy to message passing is a vending machine. Putting money into a vending machine is a message to start the vending process; pressing each button for items in the machine is a message to a central decoding object; and when the transaction is finished, properties that keep track of how much money was inserted and how much the selected items cost are used to send a message to some other object that, if the machine is working properly, determines and dispenses the items and excess money. At no point is one concerned with whether the objects and message transmission paths are made of mechanical components or out of electronic devices; the meanings of the messages and the responses elicited are all that matters.

OpenScript Message Behavior

As explained briefly in Chapter 13, "OpenScript Fundamentals," a message is created by the ToolBook system in response to an event. It is then sent to an object and allowed to travel upward in the object hierarchy until it is intercepted by a handler for it. If there is no handler for the message, ToolBook either performs default processing on the message, or, if there is no default response, the message is ignored. An example of a built-in message that elicits a built-in response from the ToolBook system is `select`, for which the exact response depends on the parameters accompanying the message but which always causes objects or text to be selected. A message that has no default processing includes `buttonClick`, which simply disappears with no harm done if it is not intercepted by a handler. User-defined messages have no default system response.

How Messages Get Passed. ToolBook's built-in messages are initiated by the system as a result of an event. In many cases, the event is an external event, such as a mouse button click, a keystroke, a menu selection, or a DDE message from another application. Other messages are associated with the screen cursor's entering or leaving the bounds of an object. Some ToolBook and Media Control Interface (MCI) processes generate messages to report their status; these are *notification messages* sent to a specified object.

Custom Messages. You are free to send custom messages to handlers written specifically to receive them. You must name your custom messages so that none of the messages or message parameters ever have the same names as one of OpenScript's built-in messages. Asymetrix's recommendation is to prefix the name of each of your custom message with @.

Custom messages will often be sent to numerous objects. There is no essential difference between OpenScript's own messages and the many custom messages you will normally generate in your scripts, except that additional parameters or arguments normally can't be appended to the built-in messages. Your custom messages may have as many parameters as necessary, provided each handler for each message receives the correct number of parameters of the correct data type.

Using custom messages sent from built-in messages is, in fact, one way of making your application more maintainable. For instance, if you want to have a set of activities performed on `buttonClick`, you could send messages as in Listing 14.1.

Listing 14.1 14LST01.DOC Handlers May Be Nested

```
TO HANDLE buttonClick
    send @message1
    send @message2
END buttonClick
```

Then, you must handle each of the two custom messages. Suppose that you want to change the color and position of whichever rectangle on a page has been clicked. You would put a script something like that of Listing 14.2 in the script of the page, background, or book.

Listing 14.2 14LST02.DOC Handlers Called by Listing 14.1

```
TO HANDLE @message1
    --Make sure you're clicking on a rectangle:
    if object of target = "Rectangle"
        --rgbFill is an object property
        --which specifies red, green, and blue values.
        rgbFill of target = "50, 100, 70"
    end if
END @message1

TO HANDLE @message2
    --Make sure you're clicking on a rectangle:
    if object of target = "Rectangle"
        --position is an object property
        --which specifies horizontal and vertical values.
        position of target = "1440,1500"
    end if
END @message2
```

How does using these custom messages make maintainability easier? Listing 14.1 is a pretty basic example, but suppose that later on you want to add features to the handler for `@message1` or replace its functionality altogether. You could do so merely by replacing the body of the handler for `@message1`. If multiple objects send `@message1`, that message's behavior is altered for all of them; there's no need to go back and change the script of each object that sends the message.

Called and Calling Handlers. The "Custom Messages" section illustrates a case in which a handler for one message sends another message. The first handler is then said to *call* the other; the other is *called* by the first. In the case of Listing 14.1, a `buttonClick` handler calls the `@message1` handler; the `@message1` handler is called by the `buttonClick` handler. Such nesting may go many handlers deep, with each handler calling others by sending the appropriate messages. The originating handler is known as the *topmost calling handler*. All handlers in a running program must finish running unless the script includes specific commands to break out of one or more handlers. So even if a calling handler navigates to another book, it must navigate back to finish executing its statements. In such cases the values of `target`, `targetWindow`, `focus`, and `focusWindow` may change. For more information about `target`, `targetWindow`, `focus`, and `focusWindow`, see "The Target" section of this chapter.

Standard Messages. There are a number of messages, called *standard messages*, that bypass the message hierarchy and are processed directly and immediately by the system. Standard messages include the following:

- `autoscript` (not available in runtime ToolBook)
- `convertPicture`
- `customEdit` (if `TOOLS30.SBK` is loaded)
- `debugScript` (not available in runtime ToolBook)
- `editScript` (not available in runtime ToolBook)
- `pageSize`
- `previewHelp`
- `showGrid`
- `sizeToViewer`
- `snapGrid` (not available in runtime ToolBook)

Standard messages are sent in the usual manner; for instance:

```
send sizeToViewer
```

You will not be able to write handlers to implement additional or substitute behavior for these messages, though.

Any message can be sent directly to the system through the use of the `forward to system` command. When you forward a command to the system, handlers may exist between the forwarding handler and the ToolBook system, but they will not run. In fact, the reason for using `forward to system` is usually to prevent such intervening handlers from processing a message when the message is sent from a certain handler. Usage is straightforward, as in the following example:

```
TO HANDLE cut
    forward to system
END cut
```

The example using the `cut` menu event message actually works. You would use it if you had disabled `cut` to prevent the inadvertent removal of objects, but wanted a particular object to be cuttable. The example handler would go into the script of the cuttable object. Note that you could also have sent the message directly from a handler for another message, as in the following example:

```
TO HANDLE buttonClick
    send cut to system
END buttonClick
```

Again, the `send message to system` form is only required when there are other handlers for the message which you would like to skip. If there are no such handlers, it isn't necessary to send directly to the system and the second line of the example is simpler; just use `send cut`.

Viewer Messages. Viewers, including the main window, enter the object hierarchy just below the level of the book. They are not in the message hierarchy of the objects they show. Messages sent by the system to a viewer as the result of an event are the ones which specifically have to do with windowing activities. These include:

- `enterWindow`
- `leaveWindow`
- `openWindow`
- `closeWindow`
- `hidden`
- `shown`
- `windowMoved`
- `windowSized`

The messages `moved` and `sized` are also sent to viewers, but these messages are not unique to viewers. Other objects also automatically receive these messages when they are moved or resized.

To handle a viewer message for multiple viewers, the handler must be at the book or system book level, as the book is the parent of the viewers.

The Target. Suppose that you click the left button of your mouse. `buttonClick` is among the messages sent by ToolBook. To which object is the message sent? The answer depends on the type of message. The first recipient of a `buttonClick` message is normally the object within whose bounds the cursor lies when the button is clicked. That object, whether or not it processes the button message, is then the *target* object. There is a system property, `target`, that contains a text string which is the `uniqueName` property of some object. `target` is one of the most commonly used system properties in OpenScript programming, as its value may be used in scripts to control the properties or behavior of an object when it is not known in advance what that object is. To make a simple example that uses ToolBook predefined color constants in combination with `target` to create an object highlighting program, do the following steps, which make up the script of page 1 of `TARGET.TBK`, included on the accompanying disk.

1. If ToolBook is not already in Author mode, switch to it by choosing Edit, Author or pressing F3.
2. Create a new book using File, New. Choose File, Save and save the new book as `TARGET.TBK`.
3. Make sure that the Tool Palette is visible. If it is not, choose View, Palettes, Tools.

4. Choose the Rectangle tool from the Tool Palette and draw a small rectangle (perhaps 1440 × 1440 page units) on the page of your new book.
5. Click the Arrow tool on the Tool Palette to deselect the Rectangle tool.
6. Repeat steps 3 and 4, substituting different shapes such as Rounded Rectangle, Oval, and Pie for "Rectangle," until you have four to six shapes on the page.
7. Select Object, Page Properties or press Shift+F7 to reveal the Page Properties dialog box. Click the Script button and enter the code for the handler (see in Listing 14.3).

Listing 14.3 14LST03.DOC Simple Usage of *target*

```
TO HANDLE buttonClick
    fillColor of objects of this page = GREEN
    if object of target <> "page"
        fillColor of target = RED
    end if
END buttonClick
```

8. Switch to the Foreground (page) by choosing View, Foreground or pressing F4.

Because you performed no initialization, the colors of the shapes are unpredictable at this point. But as soon as you click anywhere on the page, all objects are filled with ToolBook's standard green. If you click a shape, that shape alone becomes the target and is filled with ToolBook's standard red. Note that the `fillColor` property can be applied to a list of several objects. The expression `object of target` contains the object type of the target and is used in Listing 14.3 to prevent a runtime error that would otherwise occur because a page, which is also an object you can click, doesn't have a `fillColor` property.

Using the `target` property in the manner of Listing 14.3 is a very common way of writing scripts that control the behavior of several objects at once. But the value of `target` persists at most through the lifetime of a handler, so keeping track of which object is the target can be tricky. You may understand this more fully by first creating a script in which the target seems to be one object and then refining the handlers until it's evident that the target is changing after each handler runs. To create a display of `target`, which is included as page 2 of `TARGET.TBK` on the disk supplied with this book, follow these steps:

1. Return to Author mode while on the page of `TARGET.TBK`. Select the page by choosing Edit, Select Page or pressing Shift+F12.
2. Create a new background (and thus a new page as well) by choosing Edit, Paste Special and selecting the list item, MTB40 Page and Background. Your page objects will be duplicated, but the background will be new.
3. Switch to the Background by choosing View, Background or pressing F4.
4. Choose the Field tool from the Tool Palette and draw a field on the background. Draw from about 1860,600 to about 6810,1140; the exact size isn't critical.

5. Choose Object, Field Properties to see the Field Properties dialog box. Alternatively, hold down the Shift key while double-clicking within the field.
6. In the Field Properties dialog box, name the field "f" and then click OK.
7. Choose Object, Page Properties to see the Page Properties dialog box. Click the Script button, delete the original handler, and enter Listing 14.4's code.

Listing 14.4 14LST04.DOC Simple Display of *target*

```
TO HANDLE buttonClick
    put target into text of field "f" of this background
END buttonClick
```

8. Switch to the Foreground (page) by choosing View, Foreground or pressing F4.
9. Switch to Reader mode by choosing Edit, Reader or pressing F3.

Click within any of the shapes you have drawn, or anywhere else on the page except within field `"f"`. The text of field `"f"` displays what the target was during the running of the `buttonClick` handler.

But isn't that still the value of `target`? In general, the answer is, "No." There are other messages besides those generated by user action which can, and almost always do, change the value of `target`. Page 3 of `TARGET.TBK` shows the effect of the `idle` message, which is repeatedly sent by the system to the page. To build this page yourself, follow this procedure:

1. Return to Author mode while on page 2 of `TARGET.TBK`. Select the page by choosing Edit, Select Page or pressing Shift+F12.
2. Duplicate the page by choosing Edit, Duplicate.
3. Choose Object, Page Properties or press Shift+F7 to see the Page Properties dialog box. Click the Script button and enter the code in Listing 14.5.

Listing 14.5 14LST05.DOC Continuous Display of *target*

```
TO HANDLE buttonClick
    system oldTarget
    oldTarget = target
    text of field "f" of this background = target
    pause 1 seconds
    forward
END buttonClick

TO HANDLE idle
    system oldTarget
    if target <> oldTarget
        text of field "f" of this background = target
    end if
    forward
END idle
```

4. Switch to the Foreground (page) by choosing View, Foreground or pressing F4.
5. Switch to Reader mode by choosing Edit, Reader or pressing F3.

The handler for `buttonClick` in Listing 14.5 declares an untyped system variable that holds the value of `target`. (The variable has been left untyped because `NULL` is a possible value for its contents, but variables of type `OBJECT` can't be set to `NULL`.) An object on the page still receives the `buttonClick` message when clicked, but the text of the field changes so quickly as a result of the `idle` handler, that a one second delay has been added so that the text is displayed long enough to read it. The `idle` handler itself compares the value of the system variable with that of the current value of `target` and updates the field's text when the two values don't match. You can see from the text display that the value of `target` is set to the current page whenever `idle` messages are being sent—that is to say, when no message is being handled at Reader level.

> **Note**
>
> In Listing 14.5, a value is stored in a system variable and then compared with an updated value before deciding whether to redraw the text of a field. The reason for using this decision procedure is that allowing each `idle` message to update the display would cause severe flickering of the on-screen text, as `idle` is sent repetitively.

It is, strictly speaking, not correct to say that an object is the target before it receives a message. `target` contains the name of an object; the next object to receive a message may be that one or a different one. There is, in general, no way for an object to know that it will be receiving a specific message. Rather, the target is defined as that object which received the current message.

The Target Window. After reading the previous section, it may still not be evident why it is so important to keep track of the target. After all, as long as the target object in Listing 14.5 received the `buttonClick` message, the value of `target` was preserved through the lifetime of the `buttonClick` handler and the script performed as desired. However, there is only one viewer open in the example. If there are additional viewers open, you must take into account their individual object hierarchies.

Suppose that you have a book in which you use the left and right arrow keys to navigate among pages. You want to have a window, such as a palette or help text document in a viewer, open on top of the pages. Such a book is `TARGFOCS.TBK`. To build the book yourself, follow this procedure:

1. If ToolBook is not already in Author mode, switch to it by choosing Edit, Author or pressing F3.
2. Create a new book using File, New. Choose File, Save and save the new book as `TARGFOCS.TBK`.
3. Make sure that the Tool Palette is visible. If it is not, choose View, Palettes, Tool.

4. Click the Viewers tool on the Toolbar or choose Object, Viewers to see the Viewers dialog box. Click the New button to create a new viewer. Set Border Style and Caption Bar to None. Set its default state to maximized. Leave the viewer open.
5. Go to page 2, which will have been created along with the viewer.
6. Choose the Field tool from the Tool Palette and draw a field on page 2. Type the words **`Help Text or Palette`** into the field and resize the field to the text if desired. Drag the field on the page until it's fully visible in the open viewer.
7. Click the Arrow tool on the Tool Palette to deselect the Field tool.
8. Go to page 1. Add several new pages after page 1 by repeatedly pressing Ctrl+N.
9. Choose Object, Book Properties or press Shift+F8 to show the Book Properties dialog box. Click the Script button to open the Script Editor and enter the following script, which intercepts keystrokes and navigates between adjacent pages if the key pressed is the left or right arrow key. The script is Listing 14.6.

Listing 14.6 14LST06.DOC Arrow Key Navigation Script

```
TO HANDLE keyUp k
    if k = keyLeftButton
        go to previous page
        break
    end if
    if k = keyRightButton
        go to next page
        break
    end if
    forward
END keyUp
```

10. Close the Script Editor by clicking the Save Script and Exit button on the Script Editor toolbar. Exit the Book Properties dialog by clicking the OK button.
11. Save the book by selecting File, Save.

Click anywhere in the main window. The caption bar highlights to indicate that the main window is the active window. Press the right arrow key; the page turns to the next page. The left arrow key turns to the previous page.

Click anywhere in the viewer you created in step 4. Its caption bar highlights to indicate that the viewer is the active window. Press the left or right arrow key. The page number in the viewer decrements or increments so that your help text disappears, while the page in the main window does not turn. This is not the desired behavior.

The reason each viewer changes its own current page when you navigate is simply because you haven't told it not to. Since the navigation script (refer to Listing 14.6) is at the book level, it affects all viewers. But the keystroke enters the focus window, which is by default the target window, which in turn defaults to the active window. There is no focus (see the next section, "The Focus," for a description of the `focus` property), but by clicking in each window, you activate it. The target is the page of the viewer you're clicking in, and, once that is established, messages travel up the message hierarchy for that specific target window.

So why not put the navigation handler in Listing 14.6 lower in the main window's message hierarchy, say at the background level, so that the other viewer's message path would never receive the navigation commands? This tactic would, in fact, prevent the viewer's current page from changing as a result of pressing an arrow key. But it isn't a completely satisfactory cure. If you click the viewer, the main window's message path no longer receives the keystroke messages, and no pages turn in either window. Clicking in the main window again, or writing an `enterWindow` handler to activate the main window when the cursor enters it, is necessary to reestablish arrow key navigation in the main window. But there is an easier way; simply embed the script in Listing 14.6 in an `in viewer` structure. (For more on control structures, see Chapter 16, "Statements, Functions, and Expressions.") Using the `in` structure involves adding two lines to the navigation script, as shown in Listing 14.7.

Listing 14.7 14LST07.DOC Arrow Key Navigation Script with *in*

```
TO HANDLE keyUp k
    --Add the "in" structure:
    --You could use "viewer id 0" instead of "mainWindow"
    in mainWindow
        if k = keyLeftButton
            go to previous page
            break
        end if
        if k = keyRightButton
            go to next page
            break
        end if
        forward
    --Close the "in" structure.
    end in
END keyUp
```

Now the arrow keys navigate between adjacent pages in the main window regardless of which window contains the target and focus. This is the desired behavior.

The Focus. The *focus* is the object that is ready to receive keyboard input. While one normally associates keyboard activity with fields and recordfields, combo boxes and buttons can also respond to keystrokes and can have the focus in a viewer. `focus` is a viewer property that holds the value of the `uniqueName` of the object that has the focus. Each viewer has its own focus property. The focus, unlike the target, can be set. (In fact, setting the focus is what you're doing when you tab among fields or buttons.)

Fields that have typing enabled can have the focus but cannot be the target because such fields don't handle messages. Combo boxes and buttons may be both target and focus.

The Focus Window. The focus window is that viewer which displays the object that has the focus. Its value is contained in a system property called `focusWindow`. The active window is usually the focus window as well, the exception being when a child viewer is the focus window. The focus window (the value of `focusWindow`) is also the same as the value of `targetWindow` except when a script running in the target window explicitly changes the focus and the new focus is in another window.

Redirecting Messages

A message that is traveling up the message hierarchy may be intercepted ("trapped") by a handler in the script of an object in order to define or modify the behavior of that object. Specifically, a message may be sent to another viewer or book or sent downward to an object lower in the pecking order. Often the message will be built-in and a response is desired which is an addition to or a substitute for the message's normal one.

Tip

Sometimes you can write handlers to divert or reorder built-in messages to get a desired behavior without using custom messages.

`REDIRECT.TBK`, which is on the disk accompanying this book, demonstrates an example of message redirection. It uses the model of page flip animation, which is the easiest way to animate in ToolBook, though hardly the most economical in terms of book size. This example simply shows a rectangle skittering across the screen; you can get more creative if you want. Follow these steps to create the example yourself:

1. If ToolBook is not already in Author mode, switch to it by choosing Edit, Author or pressing F3.
2. Create a new book using File, New. Choose File, Save and save the new book as `REDIRECT.TBK`.
3. Make sure that the Tool Palette is visible. If it is not, choose View, Palettes, Tool.
4. Choose the Rectangle tool from the Tool palette and draw a rectangle of size 1440 × 1440 on the book page.
5. Choose View, Command or press Shift+F3 to show the Command Window. Enter the following script into the Command Window:

   ```
   fillColor of selection = red
   ```

6. Click the Arrow tool on the Tool palette to deselect the Rectangle tool.
7. Enter the following script into the Command Window:

   ```
   step i from 1 to 99;select rectangle "r";send copy;send newPage;send
   paste;move selection by 60,0;end step
   ```

   The Command Window script makes 99 new pages and pastes 99 copies of the rectangle that you drew in step 4.

> **Note**
>
> The preceding script is not part of the book. It's a script to build the book. You may put it in a `buttonClick` or some other handler if you want, either in a button or on the first page. But putting it in the Command Window makes editing very easy if something is not quite right. In fact, during the design of the example, the fill color was not set. That was easily remedied by the following Command Window script:
>
> ```
> step i from 1 to 100; fillColor of
> rectangle "r" of page i = RED;end step
> ```

8. Put the following handlers in the background or book script. The `buttonDown` handler is simply a navigation tool:

```
TO HANDLE buttondown
    go to next page
END buttonDown
```

The other handler is for a message, buttonStillDown, which is sent repeatedly, as fast as the system can, while the left or right mouse button is pressed and held down. There is a short delay between the time the button is pressed end the time that buttonStillDown messages start, to allow time for double-clicking. The second handler has this form:

```
TO HANDLE buttonStillDown
    send buttonDown
END buttonStillDown
```

9. Go to Reader level by selecting View, Reader or pressing F3.

Hold the left mouse button down. The `buttonClick` message causes a page to turn. The position of the animated object on the page is slightly shifted to the right, giving the illusion of motion. When `buttonStillDown` messages start, each one sends an additional `buttonClick` message. Then each `buttonClick` message repeats the page-turning sequence, giving the illusion of continuous motion on the part of the animated rectangle. The "animation" runs as long as the button is depressed because the repetitive message `buttonStillDown` is simply being used to produce repetitions of `buttonDown`.

Sending one OpenScript built-in message as the result of another is common when duplicating menu commands with on-screen buttons. Send the menu command in the body of a button event handler.

The *forward* Statement. If there is one command that can be singled out as that which gives beginning OpenScript programmers the most trouble, it's the `forward` command. Once grasped, though, the statement is a powerful tool, allowing messages to be processed by more than one object, or, just as importantly, blocking a message from traveling on its appointed path up the object hierarchy.

The following example is included as pages 3 and 4 of `FORWARD.TBK`, and illustrates a handler in which `forward` should be included and one in which it should be omitted.

Suppose that you want the screen to be covered by a viewer onto a black page during a navigation that would otherwise cause a visible palette flash. In this case, a grayscale display of a picture is compared with a color version. In addition, you want the "hourglass" cursor to appear during the transition, and a pointing finger cursor to appear when the page is ready to be used, but only on the current background. To do so, follow these steps:

1. If ToolBook is not already in Author mode, switch to it by choosing Edit, Author or pressing F3.
2. Create a new book choosing File, New. Choose File, Save and save the new book as `FORWARD.TBK`.
3. Make sure that the Tool Palette is visible. If it is not, choose View, Palettes, Tool.
4. Press Ctrl+N twice to create two additional pages (for a total of 3).
5. Select View, Background or press F4 to work on the background. Click the Script button to enter a script that turns the cursor to a pointing finger when the various handlers have finished running:

```
TO HANDLE firstIdle
    sysCursor = 44
END firstIdle
```

6. Click the Color button; the Color Tray appears. Select a black square in the Color tray. The background turns black. Click OK.
7. From page 3, choose Object, Page Properties or press Shift+F7 to view the Page Properties dialog box. Enter **Black** as the page name.
8. To add a script to page 3 that blocks the `firstIdle` message, click Script and enter the following into the script handler:

```
TO HANDLE firstIdle
END firstIdle
```

9. Select Object, Book Properties or press Shift+F8 to view the Button Properties dialog box. To add a script to page 3 that will show and hide a viewer, click Script and enter Listing 14.8 into the script handler.

Listing 14.8 14LST08.DOC Book Script for *FORWARD.TBK*

```
--goPage is a custom message and thePage is a parameter
 --representing the destination page; these messages are
 --meaningless to the system, so the names aren't critical.
TO HANDLE goPage thePage
    --Put statements here to make showing
    --the viewer dependent on the color depth if desired.
    sysCursor = 4  --This is the hourglass cursor
    show viewer "@black"
    go to page thePage
END goPage

TO HANDLE firstIdle
    if isOpen of viewer "@black"
        close viewer "@black'
    end if
END firstIdle
```

10. Go to page 1. Click the button to select it. Choose Object, Button Properties or press Shift+F6 to view the Button Properties dialog box. Enter the caption of page 1's button as **"Next"**. Click OK.
11. To add a script to page 1's button that will navigate to page 2, click Script, enter the following handler, and then click the Save Script and Exit button on the Script Editor toolbar:

```
TO HANDLE buttonClick
    send goPage 2
END buttonClick
```

12. Click OK in the Button Properties dialog box.
13. Go to page 2. Click the button to select it. Choose Object, Button Properties or press Shift+F6 to view the Button Properties dialog box. Enter the caption of page 2's button as **"Previous"**. Click OK.
14. To add a script to page 2's button that will navigate to page 1, click Script, enter the following handler, and then click the Save Script and Exit button on the Script Editor toolbar:

```
TO HANDLE buttonClick
    send goPage 1
END buttonClick
```

15. Click OK in the Button Properties dialog box.
16. Choose Object, Page Properties or press Shift+F7 to view the Page Properties dialog box. Click Script, and then enter the two handlers in Listing 14.9, which assign a palette when navigating onto page 2 and remove the palette when navigating away from page 2.

Listing 14.9 14LST09.DOC Script of Page 2 of *FORWARD.TBK*

```
TO HANDLE enterPage
    palette of this book = palette "grays"
END enterPage

TO HANDLE leavePage
    palette of this book = NULL
ENDleavePage
```

17. Click the Save Script and Exit button on the Script Editor toolbar. Click OK in the Page Properties dialog box.
18. Choose File, Import Graphic to import one copy of a color picture onto each of the first two pages. The picture in the example is taken from the bitmaps supplied with Multimedia ToolBook. The relative path to them is normally `\MTB40\CLIPART\BITMAPS\`.
19. Use `PALEDIT` to create a 256 level grayscale (you don't want an identity palette in this particular case). Name the palette `GRAYS.PAL`.

20. Click the Resource tool on the toolbar or choose Object, Resources to open the Resource Editor. Choose Palettes and then click the Import button in the Resource Editor dialog box. A standard file selector appears.

21. Use the standard file selector to import `GRAYS.PAL`. In the Resource Editor Name text box, name the palette **`Grays`**.

22. Click the Viewers tool on the Toolbar or choose Object, Viewers to show the Viewers dialog box. Click the New button to create a new viewer. Set Border Style and Caption Bar to None. Set its position to Center. Set its default state to maximized. Set its default page to page 3. Click the Close button and then click the Done button.

23. Save the book by choosing File, Save.

24. Go to Reader mode by choosing Edit, Reader or selecting F3.

The `goPage` handler opens a viewer onto a black page to cover the palette shift that would be visible in the main window. The built-in `leavePage` message can't be used instead of the new custom message `goPage` because the black viewer has to be shown before the `currentPage` of the main window changes. The palette change begins before a `leavePage` handler could run. The `firstIdle` handler informs you that the navigation is complete, as it is sent only after the page is ready to receive other messages. At this point, it is usually safe to show the screen again without danger of displaying a palette flash. The `firstIdle` handler closes the black viewer. Since there may be navigations that do not require the use of the black viewer, check to make sure that the viewer is open before closing it. Attempting to close a closed viewer results in an `Execution Suspended` message at runtime.

Tip

An `idle` or `firstIdle` message is the best indication that the topmost calling handler has returned after a navigation.

Note

A good place to take care of things which requires that the background is ready to receive messages is in an `enterBackground` handler at `book` or `sysBook` level. Remember that normally the farther up a handler is placed in the object hierarchy, the later it runs. You could also use the `firstIdle` message, but the handler would want to ensure that the current page is the first one of that background.

Be sure to have the Command Window visible before you run this script; it makes execution easier, and it will allow you to extricate yourself from the predicament that you will find yourself in. (To show the Command Window, switch to Author mode, select Command Window from the View menu, press Shift+F3, or click on the Command Window button of the toolbar. The Command Window remains visible and usable after changing to Reader mode.)

From Reader mode, click anywhere on the first page to run the `goPage` handler to navigate to page 2. If the viewer `Black` has been set up correctly, you will find that the screen goes black and stays that way. This is because the `firstIdle` handler in the script of the background is blocking the passage of the `firstIdle` message to the `firstIdle` handler in the script of the book.

At this point, you are in a dilemma; you can't show anything but a black screen. Execute the statement `close viewer "Black"` from the Command Window to close the viewer onto the black page and reveal the second page. (The `goPage` handler did run, so the current page number is now the value of `thePage`, which you set at 2.) You may, if the menu bar is visible, choose Edit, Author and then choose Objects Viewers. Select viewer `@black` from the resulting Viewer Properties dialog box and then click the Close Viewer button.

The proper way around this dilemma is to change the background's `firstIdle` handler to include a `forward` command, like the following:

```
TO HANDLE firstIdle
    sysCursor = 44
    forward
ENDfirstIdle
```

The `forward` statement tells OpenScript to pass a copy of a message, in this case `firstIdle`, up the message hierarchy. Thus, the book's `firstIdle` handler gets the message. From Reader mode, click page 1 as before. The screen should black out during a the page transition and clear to reveal page 2 since the book's `firstIdle` handler closes the black viewer for you.

Why is the handler with no statements present in the script of page 3? This is an illustration of the other side of the coin—a case in which it's necessary to stop a message from travelling up the message hierarchy. What is not obvious at first about opening and closing a viewer is that, as the viewer is always a window onto a page, opening or closing a viewer counts as a page navigation and that page's default messages are sent. If there were no `firstIdle` handler on page 3, or if its `firstIdle` handler contained a `forward` command, the message would travel through the background level to the book level and not only restore the cursor prematurely but also close the `@black` viewer immediately—not the effect desired! (In fact, you wouldn't even be able to keep the viewer open from the Viewer Properties dialog's Show Viewer button.) The page that hides the palette changing mechanisms from view must have `firstIdle` disabled. A `firstIdle` handler with no statements accomplishes just that—no more, no less.

The example in `FORWARD.TBK` has a couple of extra buttons which do the navigation without hiding the palette flash, just to increase your enthusiasm for hiding it! The situation is often worse when two or more different color pictures are involved.

Note

This example assumes, as stated earlier, that you want the cursor changes to happen only on the current background. If you want something to happen on all backgrounds, skip the background handlers altogether and write all the functionality at book level.

Generally, `enterPage`, `enterBackground`, `leavePage`, and `leaveBackground` messages should be forwarded, though there are exceptions. It's up to you to determine whether other messages are forwarded. To send a message directly to an object, `send it`.

Note

When there is no handler for a message at a level higher than the one on which that message originated, the message is forwarded automatically. There is no reason to write a handler that contains only a `forward` command.

While the `forward` statement is more often than not the final statement in a handler, as in this example, it is also imperative to use it before breaking out of a handler if the message is to be used higher up. Suppose you want to filter characters from the keyboard so that the left and right arrow keys navigate among pages. You can use a variant of Listing 14.6. In that listing, you weren't concerned with whether there are any handlers higher in the message path. Listing 14.10 shows one way to write an arrow-key script with forwarded keystrokes.

Listing 14.10 14LST10.DOC Arrow Key Navigation Script

```
TO HANDLE keyUp theKey, isShift, isControl
    if theKey is not in (keyLeftArrow,keyRightArrow)
        forward
        break
    end if
    conditions
        when theKey = keyLeftArrow
        go to previous page
        when theKey = keyRightArrow
        go to next page
    end conditions
END keyChar
```

(The `if` and `conditions...when` flow constructs are discussed in Chapter 15.) This script is as complex as it is only because two goals are accomplished. (It's contained in the group script of the page-turning widget in `PROGRESS.TBK`.) Functionality is being assigned to two keys and the other keys are disabled—their messages aren't forwarded.

The key is tested to see whether it is a right or left arrow key. If it's neither, the key message is forwarded so that normal processing may continue on the remaining keys, and a `break` statement abandons the handler. In practice, you'd probably also filter the `keyDown` and `keyChar` messages, and perhaps `cut`, `copy`, `paste`, `clear`, and other commands that have keyboard shortcuts as well.

Tip

Make sure that a message isn't unintentionally forwarded more than once.

Objects and Properties

ToolBook objects are often defined as a list of specific items. Because ToolBook has the ability to use custom controls, a potential for a very large number of object types exists. It is often more convenient to think of an object as any entity that has properties. All objects have a `script` property, which is actually the container for the text that makes up the OpenScript handlers you write.

Note

The images displayed by the Clip Manager and `callMCI()` functions are not ToolBook objects and have no properties.

Properties are containers that tell the ToolBook system what attributes, such as color or size, the object that owns the property has. Changing the value of a built-in property changes the corresponding attribute of the owner object. Properties may be related in the sense that changing the value of one modifies another as well. For example, the unformatted text of a field is contained in a property of the field; the property is called `text`. The formatted text of the same field is stored in Rich Text Format in a field property named `richText`. Changing the text of a field modifies the contents of both `text` and `richText`.

Object Properties

Table 14.1 shows some important properties and the objects for which they are built in. The table is by no means a comprehensive list; each object type has many additional built-in properties, as well as user properties (see the "User Properties" section in this chapter). Rather, Table 14.1 is a compendium of some of the most commonly used object properties as well as a few properties that are useful but little-understood.

Table 14.1 Typical Properties for Common Object Types

Property	Description	Objects with Property
`uniqueName`	ID number, object type, books	all
`script`	Container for message handlers	all
`drawDirect`	`TRUE` or `FALSE`; Draw offscreen?	Buttons Combo boxes Graphic objects OLE Containers Fields, Recordfields
`fillColor`, `rgbFill`	List of 3 numbers: fill color	Background Buttons Combo boxes Graphic objects OLE Containers Fields, Recordfields
`strokeColor`, `rgbStroke`	Color of pen stroke	Background Buttons Combo boxes Graphic objects OLE Containers Fields, Recordfields
`name`	User-supplied string	Backgrounds Buttons Combo boxes Graphic objects Groups OLE Containers Fields, Recordfields Pages Viewers Books
`size`	List: height, width	Backgrounds Buttons Combo boxes Graphic objects Groups OLE Containers Fields, Recordfields Pages Viewers Books
`bounds`	List: upper left, lower right	Backgrounds Buttons Combo boxes Graphic objects Groups OLE Containers Fields, Recordfields Viewers

(continues)

Table 14.1 Continued

Property	Description	Objects with Property
`vertices`	List of four to many numbers	Combo boxes Buttons Graphic objects Groups OLE Containers Fields, Recordfields Viewers
`position`	List: right offset, down offset	Combo boxes Buttons Graphic objects Groups OLE Containers Fields, Recordfields Viewers
`caption`		Buttons Viewers
`windows` `transparent`	List of the book's viewers TRUE or FALSE	Book Combo boxes Buttons Graphic objects Groups OLE Containers Fields, Recordfields
`visible`	TRUE or FALSE	Combo boxes Buttons Graphic objects Groups OLE Containers Fields, Recordfields
`object`	String: type of object	Backgrounds Buttons Combo boxes Graphic objects Groups OLE Containers Fields, Recordfields Viewers
`objects`	List: other objects in object	Backgrounds Groups Pages
`pageNumber`	Page number in book order	Pages
`parent`	Next object up in hierarchy	Backgrounds Buttons Combo boxes Graphic objects Groups OLE Containers Fields, Recordfields Viewers

Property	Description	Objects with Property
`shownBy`	Windows that display a page	Pages
`"text,richText"`	Containers for field text	Combo boxes Fields, Recordfields
`textOverflow`	Characters scrolled below object	Buttons Fields, Recordfields
`textRightOverflow`	Characters scrolled off edge	Buttons Fields, Recordfields
`textUnderflow`	Characters scrolled above object	Fields, Recordfields
`notifyBeforeMessages`	List of message names	Buttons Combo boxes Graphic objects Groups OLE Containers Fields, Recordfields
notifyAfterMessages	List of message names	Buttons Combo boxes Graphic objects Groups OLE Containers Fields, Recordfields

Here are a few suggestions for working with built-in properties of objects. With practice, you'll undoubtedly discover dozens of other so-called tricks.

- It isn't generally necessary to get both `bounds` and `position` of an object even if both are needed in a handler. The bounds of an object contain a comma-separated list of four numbers, which represent two points. The first point is the position of the upper right corner of the smallest rectangle that can enclose the object (the object's *bounding rectangle*). The second pair of numbers represents the bottom left corner of the object's bounding rectangle. If you're already using `bounds` in a script, the first pair of numbers in `bounds` is the object's position. That is, `item 1 of bounds = item 1 of position` and `item 2 of bounds = item 2 of position`.
- Objects in a group are visible if, and only if, the group's `visible` property is `TRUE` and the object's `visible` property is also `TRUE`. Such behavior not only means that you can hide individual objects in a group without disturbing the visibility of other members of the same group, but also means that showing a group does not necessarily show all of its members. You have to explicitly show everything.
- Some properties can be set simultaneously for multiple objects. `visible` is one of them. So one way of making sure that all of a group's objects are shown when the group is shown is simply to include the following lines at the point in a handler where you want to show the whole group:

```
visible of objects of group "g1" = TRUE
visible of group "g1" = TRUE
```

(Remember that assigning an object's `visible` property to `TRUE` is equivalent to using the command `show <object>`; setting `visible` to `FALSE` is the equivalent of using `hide <object>`.) Among the other properties which can be set for multiple objects include `transparent`, `fillColor`, and `strokeColor`.

- The `objects` property, built into backgrounds, groups, and pages, contains object references and group references for objects on the page or background but no references to any group members. To make sure you list all the objects on a page, background, or group when you desire to do so, get the objects of each group and push each one onto the list along with the rest of the items. If you use groups of groups, you must get the objects of each group grouped individually.
- Using the `parent` property, which is built into each object except the system, is the proper way to refer to objects one step up the object hierarchy. It works with ungrouped objects, group members, and nested groups. You may navigate the message hierarchy by using `parent` in statements such as `parent of parent of parent` if you need to refer to an object whose reference is unknown; in the case of `parent of parent of parent`, the resulting reference is to an object three steps up in the object hierarchy with respect to the original object.
- Viewers have parents. The main window's parent is the book whose pages are displayed in the main window. At those times when you are working with multiple books and want to refer to "the book displayed in the main window, whatever it is," use `parent of mainwindow`. (Even if your application has only one book, you may use different revisions of that book, with different names, during the development process. Referring to the current book as the parent of the main window makes the rest of your code, such as full-text search indices, independent of your version names.)
- The existence of the properties `notifyAfterMessages` and `notifyBeforeMessages` in an object's property list indicate that the object can divert messages to itself which it would not otherwise receive. See the "Self-Contained Tools" section in this chapter for examples of how to use these properties.
- The `textRightOverflow` property, applicable to button caption text, fields, and recordfields, is really the only way to count lines of wrapped text in ToolBook. To get the total number of lines, ignore the contents of each member of the list contained in `textRightOverflow`. Get the number of items of that list by calling `itemCount()`; each item represents a line of text (not necessarily an OpenScript textline terminated by CRLF). A code line which puts the line count of a recordfield into `It` looks like the following statement, assuming a recordfield named `"rf"`:

```
get itemCount(textRightOverflow of recordfield "rf")
```

Objects and properties are evidently inseparable. There can be, in addition to the long built-in property list associated with each object, a number of user properties, which you create. User properties may be used to hold data of any type in the same manner as the native object properties. In addition, the ToolBook system has properties of its own, which provide information about the application environment as a whole, as described in the next section.

The System Object

The Multimedia ToolBook system owns fourteen types of object. The values of the properties of these objects control the "look and feel" of ToolBook, allowing a great deal of customization of its Author and Reader environments. You can get, and in some cases set, these properties with OpenScript statements.

The objects that belong to the system are, generally speaking, tools and indicators. Many of these are not available in runtime Multimedia ToolBook, but there are ways to mimic some of the objects' properties using OpenScript (see Table 14.2).

Table 14.2 OpenScript Messages to Substitute for Runtime MTB

System Messages	Object Messages

`colorTray`	`fillColor`
	`rgbFill`
	`rgbStroke`
	`strokeColor`

`commandWindow`	none
`lineEndsPalette`	`lineEndStyle` `lineEndSize`
`linePalette`	`lineStyle`
`patternPalette`	`pattern`
`polygonPalette`	`sysPolygonShape`
`scrollBar`	(usable)
`statusBar`	(usable)
`statusBox`	(usable)
`statusControls`	(usable)
`statusIndicators`	(usable)

`toolPalette`	`draw`
	`select`
	`magnify`

Caution

Even if you are developing focused applications for use with full versions of Multimedia ToolBook, avoid manipulating these system objects if there is a chance that they will be distributed with runtime Multimedia ToolBook because an attempt to send a message to a system object causes the `Execution Suspended` alert to appear. Use viewers to make palettes instead.

The `toolbar` message (for the object type `toolBar`) can be made visible only at Author level. The other system object types are available at Reader level.

The substitute OpenScript statements in Table 14.2 are meant for use in the scripts of individual objects. The runtime engine provides no references whatever to the fourteen system commands in the table.

System Properties

You have already used some of the properties of the system objects: `target`, `focus`, `targetWindow`, `focusWindow`, and `selection`. All of these are concerned with the object that has received the immediate previous message, whether it is handled or not.

There are many other system properties. Most, but not all, of them begin with the helpful letters `sys`. The Multimedia ToolBook online help and release notes explain these interactively.

User Properties

As used in OpenScript, user properties are similar to built-in properties. They are actually properties that you create for an object. While user properties have some of the attributes of system variables and may sometimes be used instead of system variables, user properties have all the attributes of built-in properties. They stay associated with their owner object when the object is copied or pasted. They are persistent between ToolBook instances, which makes them good candidates for storing relatively small amounts of permanent data of any type, though a large amount of data stored in user properties noticeably increases the size of the book.

Creating User Properties

The processes for calling a new property into being are very much like those for creating undeclared untyped variables. In short, you just enter the name and owner object of the user property in the body of a handler, set the value of the property to anything other than `NULL`, and the property is automatically created.

Direct Assignment. Recall how untyped local variables can be created: just enter the name of the new variable in an OpenScript expression. User properties are created in an analogous manner, but a reference to the object is inserted after the name:

```
newProperty of page "contents" = "Varda"
```

The assignment operator creates the user property `newProperty`, associated with the page named `contents` just as the name or ID number of the page is. But watch out for typographical errors, as in the following:

```
newProperly of page "contents" = "Olorin"
```

You are certainly free to assign a number of user properties to the same object, but in this case that's not what was intended. The misspelling of `newProperty` created an additional user property rather than changing the value of an existing one. Don't forget to double-check the object reference as well; if it is incorrect and the object doesn't exist, you will be duly warned by an error message. But if an incorrect existing object is used as the reference, the new property will be assigned to it. If the object reference is omitted, the syntax reduces to that used to declare a new untyped local variable, and no property will be created or modified at all.

The *to set* Handler. `set...to` is the "classic" OpenScript assignment expression, and you may still write this expression as the following:

```
set newProperty of page "contents" to "Varda"
```

However, ToolBook handles this statement in a slightly different manner. Instead of immediately creating a new property, it looks for a built-in property with the given name. If it doesn't find one, it then searches for a handler, which informs it how to set the property. If no such handler exists, ToolBook creates a user property of the target object with the specified name and value. You can write a handler to set the value of the property. Use this kind of structure when the property's value depends on the result of a series of calculations involving the values of other properties or variables, especially when the property may be set for more than one object in the same script.

Don't worry if this type of handler is a little unclear at first. It's really just an equals sign that can set one or more values for a specific object. To the ToolBook system, the chief difference between a `to set` handler and a normal assignment statement is in the way the system interprets the `set` command. If the `set` command really finds no object reference or `to set` handler, it reduces to the simple assignment operator.

To retrieve the value of a property whose value has been defined by a `to set` handler, use the `to get` structure.

> **Note**
>
> The syntax of a `to get` handler for a property is identical to that for a function. Functions are introduced in Chapter 16, "Statements, Functions, and Expressions."

A simple `to set` handler and `to get` handler can be found in `TO_SET.TBK`, which is supplied with this book. This script uses a bitmap from the ToolBook clipart collection. You can type the bitmap's path in a field, set its position in another field, and read its position in a read-only field. The book, if you want to build it yourself, requires one page, two single-line fields, and two buttons, as in the following script:

```
TO HANDLE enterPage
    get imageCommand ("open" && text of field "fn" of \
        this page && "alias a style child parent" && windowHandle \
        of this window)
    get imageCommand ("play a")
END enterPage
```

Clips are not used in this example. You have just asked the `imageCommand()` functions to show a bitmap, whose path is contained in the text of field `"fn"` and whose window is a child of the current window (the main window, in this case).

The following is the script for one of the buttons, which you should label `Move`:

```
TO HANDLE buttonClick
    set bmapPosition ("a") to (text of field "mt" of this page)
END
```

Field `"mt"` is where you enter the coordinates for the picture position. These are in pixels—not ToolBook page units! An example is `"20,20"`.

The second button should be labeled `Close`. Its script contains the following statement:

```
TO HANDLE buttonClick
    get imageCommand ("close all")
END buttonClick
```

This script does pretty much what the button label says. If you find `close all` a little sloppy, you may use `close a`.

The `TO SET` handler itself is in the script of the button or any higher object. Put the following handler at page level:

```
TO SET bmapPosition theAlias to thePoint
    get imageCommand("window" && theAlias && "position" \
        && thePoint && "wait" )
END bmapPosition
```

Arguments to `imageCommand()` and `callMCI()` functions are literal strings, but the parameters passed to this handler are embedded through the use of the text concatenation operators `&` and `&&`.

Compare this construct with the message handler used for setting the position of the bitmap in the "`translateWindowMessage`" section of Chapter 16, "Statements, Functions, and Expressions" (from which this example was adapted). They each do the same job, though perhaps the `TO SET` version is a little more elegant.

Getting the value set by a `to set` handler may not refer to objects or containers in the `to set` handler. Getting a value is an independent process that may require independent calculation. In the case of `TO_SET.TBK`, the `to get` handler is simple:

```
TO GET bmapPosition
    return imageCommand("status" && theAlias && "position")
END bmapPosition
```

Notification and Notify Handlers

A number of OpenScript's messages are generated by the system to inform the user that some process has reached a certain point (usually the end). You can write handlers to act on these messages; ToolBook as a rule does nothing with them.

Note

The distinction between notification messages and messages that are normal responses to events is to some extent an artificial one. The techniques that are useful in writing a `buttonStillDown` handler, for instance, are equally valid in creating an `idle` handler, and for the same reason: both messages are repetitive. The difference is that "commands" such as `buttonStillDown` travel from objects to the system, while the standard "notification" messages are sent by the system to object(s) and cannot be used as commands.

A *notify handler* is a distinct name for a special structure which is quite different from the standard handler structure for a notification or other message generated by a normal event. This type of structure is discussed later in this chapter.

The Notification Messages

A *notification message* is sent to a specific object (see Table 14.3). It is not a command, and can't be used as an argument to a `send` statement. Often it is a reply to a `send` statement which is sent in addition to any other messages.

Table 14.3 Multimedia ToolBook's Notification Messages Alert Objects to Certain Events

Notification Message	Message Is Sent To
`destroy`	Page or Background
`hidden`	Page or Background
`make`	Page or Background
`menuItemSelected`	Page or Background
`moved`	Page or Background
`pageScrolled`	Page or Background
`selectChange`	Page or Background
`selectionChanged`	Page or Background
`shown`	Page or Background
`sized`	Page or Background
`textScrolled`	Page or Background
`closeWindow`	Viewer
`moved`	Viewer
`openWindow`	Viewer
`stateChanged`	Viewer
`linkSysBook`	System Book
`unlinkSysBook`	System Book

(continues)

Table 14.3 Continued

Notification Message	Message Is Sent To
`MCINotify`	User-Specified Object
`MCISignal`	User-Specified Object
`mmNotify`	User-Specified Object
`systemRestored`	User-specified Object
`timerNotify`	User-Specified Object

Most of the messages in Table 14.3 are not used by the system. They are useful information that is available for you to intercept and handle. For instance, if you wanted a shorter than normal viewer caption when a viewer is minimized, you would write a handler for `stateChanged` that gets the `state` of the window; if it is `minimized`, assign a short text string to the `caption` of the viewer; otherwise, assign a long string.

Of course, a notification message enters the message hierarchy at the level of the object to which the message is sent (the target object). The message may be handled in the target object's script or higher. Many of the messages in Table 14.2 can be requested by objects on the page or background through the use of the notify handlers, described in the "Notify Handlers" section of this chapter.

The *idle* Message. The `idle` message deserves a more thorough discussion than most of the other notification messages in that it, instead of notifying you that something has happened, notifies you that nothing is happening. At Reader level, the system sends an `idle` message on each iteration of the event loop when no message is being handled. The result is a constant stream of `idle` messages whenever the system is ready to process another message.

> **Note**
>
> The `idle` message is sent by the system to the current page. It can be handled at page level or above in the usual way. Objects below the level of the page may be manipulated by explicit reference from an `idle` handler; but a more elegant way of trapping `idle` is with the aforementioned notify handler construct.

`idle` messages are not sent when another handler is running, including an `idle` handler or a notify handler.

Listing 14.11 is an example of using `idle`.

Listing 14.11 14LST11.DOC *idle* Handler to Restore a Cursor

```
TO HANDLE idle
    system lastCursor --Contains the desired cursor
    if sysCursor <> lastCursor
        sysCursor = lastCursor
    end if
    forward
END idle
```

Why the system variable? As you know, a local variable is lost each time a handler finishes running; but the whole purpose of this structure is to restore a cursor that is absent when the handler isn't running. A system variable is called for here to preserve the cursor until `idle` messages begin again. A user property would also work, but for a value that is likely to change many times during your application's runtime, the variable is faster. The conditional structure is necessary to prevent the cursor's changing to itself at each `idle` message. While allowing that to happen doesn't directly break the application, it causes the cursor to flicker on the screen as a result of the repeated redraws. Such redraws also enormously degrade the execution speed of the application.

Note

It is very bad practice to allow an `idle` handler's statements to act on an object when the action is redundant. (Comparisons and conditional statements are fine.) Good practice in this regard can lead to many nested control structures and a daunting script as various properties' values are checked. Consider testing sequentially rather than nesting; even though the script will have a lot of typographical redundancy, it will be easier to troubleshoot than a nested form.

The example handler using `firstIdle` is cleaner than the example using `idle`. `firstIdle`, as its name implies, is sent once before the first `idle` message each time a page is entered. Refer to Listing 14.12.

Listing 14.12 14LST12.DOC *firstIdle* Handler to Restore a Cursor

```
TO HANDLE firstIdle
    system lastCursor --Contains the desired cursor
    sysCursor = lastCursor
    forward
END firstIdle
```

This handler is usable as is in the script of any object at page level or higher. The handler's function is to set the current screen cursor to a value previously stored in a system variable when `firstIdle` is received (meaning that the page is ready to receive messages—that is, the page is ready to be used). So that the handler may be used with many pages, placing it at book level is often desirable.

Notify Handlers

Notify handlers are among the most exciting features of OpenScript, and, in the context of building freestanding objects, among the greatest timesaving devices. Besides, they're fun!

***NOTIFYBEFORE* and *NOTIFYAFTER*.** The two directives `NOTIFYBEFORE` and `NOTIFYAFTER`, with a message name as a parameter, define a notify handler. Effectively, a notify handler is a request to the system to send a special message to run a handler just before or just after the "normal" specified message is sent. The object containing the script requesting notification is lower in the message hierarchy than the object that receives the actual message, so not all objects are allowed to have notify handlers. A `NOTIFYBEFORE idle` handler in the script of a group will run just before `idle` is sent, even though the actual `idle` message is sent to the page. (Note that no `idle` messages are sent while the notify handler is running, as the system is no longer idle!)

Among many other uses, `idle` handlers are convenient for triggering events based on media position. However, if the event acts on a property of an object on the page or background, a notify handler may be more convenient.

Self-Contained Tools. Using notify handlers, you can build self-contained objects that can be copied and then pasted onto pages and backgrounds, after which they perform a task without any further manipulation at all.

As a basic example which you can build upon, put together a group consisting of a rectangle (for a backdrop) and three thinner rectangles to form a gauge-like drawing with two horizontal bars for indication and one for contrast, as shown in figure 14.1.

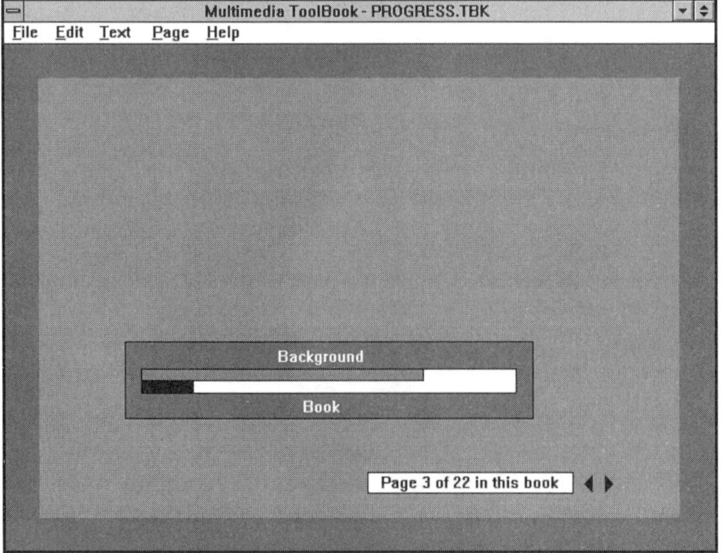

Fig. 14.1

Draw and group these objects for the standalone progress bar example.

The top progress bar is nominally green; name it `greenBar`. Name the bottom one `blueBar`. Name the bar upon which they rest `whiteBar`. Add the captions using a transparent field, then group all of the objects in the drawing. If you don't want to go to that trouble, you'll find the example on the disk accompanying this book as `PROGRESS.TBK`.

Enter Listing 14.13 as the script for the entire group.

Listing 14.13 14LST13.DOC Group Script for Progress Bar

```
 NOTIFYAFTER enterBook
    item 1 of size of rectangle "blueBar" of this background \
         = (item 1 of size of rectangle "whiteBar" \
         of this background)/(pageCount of this book)
    item 1 of size of rectangle "greenBar" of this background \
         = (item 1 of size of rectangle "whiteBar" \
          of this background)/(pageCount of this background)
END enterBook

NOTIFYBEFORE enterBackground
    item 1 of size of rectangle greenBar of this background = 0
END enterBackground

NOTIFYAFTER enterPage
    item 1 of size of rectangle "blueBar" of this background = \
        (item 1 of size of rectangle "whiteBar" of this background \
        /(pageCount of this book/pageNumber of this page)
    pageNumBG = ( pageNumber of this page \
                - pageNumber of first page of this background) + 1
    item 1 of size of rectangle "greenBar" of this background \
         = (item 1 of size of rectangle "whiteBar" \
         of this background)/(pageCount of this background/pageNumBG)
END enterPage
```

The `enterBook` script initializes the width of the page progress bar and the bar that you are comparing it against. It's necessary to calculate what proportion of one of the book's pages is to the total count because the book always opens at page 1; if there were only two pages, the progress bar would already be half as wide as the comparison bar when the book opens. The `enterBackground` handler simply initializes the width of the bar that shows your progress through the background; it is nominally zero. The `enterPage` handler does the individual page calculations. For progress through the book, it simply compares the current page number with the total page number and sets the width of the blue bar accordingly. The progress through a background has to account for pages in the backgrounds that came before the current one. Subtracting the page number of the first page of the background from itself accomplishes this, but since the result is 0, you need to add 1 to the calculation to represent page 1 of the background.

This is the entire script. The individual objects in the group need names but not scripts.

Make a book with three or four backgrounds with several pages in each background. Paste the progress object onto each background. (It could be made self-replicating; but there would need to be a means of allowing it to replicate only onto the desired backgrounds. That's a good job for a user property of each background.)

Now the top bar tracks the page count through each background, while the bottom bar measures the progress through the entire book, updating at every page turn.

The page turning arrows and the page counter at the bottom right are widgets as well. (Actually, the two arrows are part of a group, which in turn is part of the group that also contains the field.) The script for the page turning widget is the script of the group of two arrows, embedded inside the larger group. It doesn't matter; the notify handler still gets the message.

To build a page number display and page turning widget, follow these steps:

1. If ToolBook is not already in Author mode, switch to it by choosing Edit, Author or pressing F3.
2. Create a new book using File, New. Choose File, Save and save the new book as `PAGES.TBK`.
3. Make sure that the Tool Palette is visible. If it is not, choose View, Palettes, Tools.
4. Work on the background by choosing View, Background or pressing F4.
5. Choose the Recordfield tool from the Tool Palette and draw a small recordfield (perhaps 1440 × 1440 page units) on the background of your new book.
6. Choose Object, Graphic Properties or press Shift+F6 to see the Graphic Properties dialog box. Name the recordfield `r`, and then mark the Draw Text Direct checkbox.
7. Click the Script button on the Graphic Properties dialog box and enter the following `buttonClick` handler to navigate to the previous page:

```
TO HANDLE buttonClick
    go to previous page
END buttonClick
```

8. Close the Graphic Properties dialog box by clicking the OK button.
9. Click the Arrow tool on the Tool Palette to deselect the Recordfield tool.
10. Choose the Regular Polygon tool from the Tool Palette and draw a triangle on the background of your new book. When you are done, the triangle will be selected. Leave it in the selected state.
11. Double-click the Regular Polygon tool from the Tool Palette and click the 3 button on the resulting Polygon palette.
12. Select Object, Graphic Properties or press Shift+F6 to see the Graphic Properties dialog box. Name the triangle `p`.
13. Click the Script button on the Graphic Properties dialog box and enter the following `buttonClick` handler to navigate to the previous page:

```
TO HANDLE buttonClick
    go to previous page
END buttonClick
```

14. Close the Graphic Properties dialog box by clicking the OK button.
15. Choose Object, Graphic Properties or press Shift+F6 to open the Graphic Properties dialog box. Change the name of the triangle to n.
16. Triangle n should still be selected. If it is not, select it by clicking it once. Press the right arrow key repeatedly until there are about 10 pixels (10 presses of the right arrow key) separating triangle n and triangle p.
17. Click the Script button in the Graphic Properties dialog box. Change the text of the buttonClick handler to read:

```
TO HANDLE buttonClick
    go to next page
END buttonClick
```

18. Close the Graphic Properties dialog box by clicking the OK button.
19. Triangle n should still be selected. If it is not, select triangle n by clicking it once. Hold down a Shift key and click triangle p and recordfield r. The two triangles and the recordfield should all be selected.
20. Group the three selected objects by choosing Objects, Group. The selection handles should now appear around the entire group.
21. Choose Object, Group Properties or press Shift+F6 to reveal the Group Properties dialog box. Name the group g.
22. Click the Script button on the Group Properties dialog box. Enter the code of Listing 14.14.

Listing 14.14 14LST14.DOC Script for Page Indicators

```
NOTIFYBEFORE enterPage
--prevent activity from updating the screen
    sysLockScreen = TRUE
--"self" refers to the group, as this is the script of the group.
--Show both triangles in case one or the other is hidden:
    show polygon "n" of self
    show polygon "p" of self
--The text "Page (x) of (y)" must already be in recordfield "r"
    conditions
        when word 2 of text of recordfield "r" of self = "1"
            hide polygon "p"
        when word 2 of text of recordfield "r" of self \
        = word 4 of recordfield "r" of self
            hide polygon "n"
    end conditions
END enterPage
```

23. Close the Group Properties dialog box by clicking the OK button.
24. Switch to the Foreground (page) by choosing View, Foreground or pressing F4.

When recordfield `r` contains text of the form `Page` *`number`* `of` *`total number of pages`*, the navigation buttons, which in this case are triangles containing a `buttonClick` handler in the script of each, disappear as necessary to prevent navigation to a page before `Page 1` or after `Page` *`total number of pages`*. Note that this widget is dependent only on the text of the recordfield so that it can be used with any number of contiguous pages on the same background.

The usefulness of this widget is not really very evident. If you must enter all of the text in the page number field, you might as well hide the navigation buttons manually as well. You need a way of automatically entering the page numbers into the text field, and perhaps a way of calculating the page numbers. Consider the following two ways of filling the page number field (recordfield `r`) with text in the proper format:

- Write a temporary script in the Command Window or in a temporary button to fill in the text directly.
- Extend the functionality of the widget's script to use some property of the pages for page number calculation.

Method 1 has the advantage of speed of navigation since no calculation has to be performed while the program is running. This method doesn't work if pages are to be added or removed while the program is running. Method 2 makes adding and removing pages possible, because the page numbers are calculated at runtime, but slows the navigation speed a bit. Assume that you want to navigate among 23 contiguous pages. Follow these steps to implement Method 1 of filling recordfield `r`:

1. Add at least 22 pages to the book `PAGES.TBK`, in which you built the page widget by pressing Ctrl+N at least 22 times.
2. If the Command Window is not open, go to Author level if necessary by selecting Edit, Author. Then click the Command Window tool on the toolbar, select View, Command, or press Shift+F3 to open the Command Window.
3. Go to the first page of the group of 23 pages you want to number.
4. Enter the following script into the Command Window and then press Enter:

   ```
   step i from 1 to 23; text of recordfield "r" of page
   ((pageNumber of this page) + (i - 1)) = "Page" && i
   && "of 23";end step
   ```

   The script may wrap differently in the Command Window than on the printed page.
5. Save the book by clicking the Save tool on the toolbar, choosing File, Save.

The pages are now numbered in sequence, 1 to 23 of 23, and the navigation widget will operate properly. The script in step 4 requires a little explanation. You are manipulating the text of a recordfield for each of 23 pages using a counter variable, `i`. The first word of the text is always `Page` and the last two words are always `of 23`. The second word is the value of the counter. You compensate for the fact that you may not be on the first page of the book by referring to the page's number and adding

0 to 22 to it to obtain the 23 page references. Then you fill in the text of the recordfield for each of the 23 pages. It is not necessary to navigate to a page to change the text of a recordfield on that page, so there's no need to actually turn the pages.

> **Note**
>
> While a recordfield object resides on the background, its text appears on the foreground (page). Send messages to `Recordfield` *`recordfield reference`* `of` *`background reference`*, but manipulate record field text on a page by referring to the text as `text of recordfield` *`recordfield reference`* `of` *`page reference`*.

To use Method 2 of filling in page numbers for your widget to use, it's best to have a separate background for each group of navigable pages. Follow these steps:

1. If you have not already done so, add 22 pages to the book `PAGES.TBK`, in which you built the page widget, by pressing Ctrl+N at least 22 times.
2. If the Command Window is not open, go to Author level if necessary by selecting Edit, Author. Then click the Command Window tool on the toolbar, choose View, Command, or press Shift+F3 to open the Command Window.
3. Enter the following script into the Command Window and then press Enter:

   ```
   edit script of group "g" of this background
   ```

4. Modify the group's script to read as Listing 14.15.

Listing 14.15 14LST15.DOC Group Script for Page Numbering

```
NOTIFYBEFORE enterPage
--prevent activity from updating the screen
    sysLockScreen = TRUE
--"self" refers to the group, as this is the script of
--the group.
--Show both triangles in case one or the other is hidden:
    show polygon "n" of self
    show polygon "p" of self
    text of recordfield "r" = "Page" \
         && ((pageNumber of this page \
         - pageNumber of first page of this \
         background) + 1) && "of" \
         && pageCount of this background
    conditions
        when this page = first page of this background
            hide polygon "p"
        when this page = last page of this background
            hide polygon "n"
    end conditions
END enterPage
```

5. Save the book by clicking the Save tool on the toolbar or choosing File, Save.

Now the group is a full-blown widget, capable of being cut and pasted onto different backgrounds. If you have to perform automatic page numbering and button hiding for pages that span multiple backgrounds, you can't use a widget; you'll need to write a book-level handler for one of the messages associated with page navigation—the most common message to handle is `enterPage`.

The number and quality of the standalone objects in the `WIDGETS.TBK` file provided with Multimedia ToolBook is impressive. Have a good look at them—many of them will be useful as your needs grow. The Program Manager icons are called Widgets and Script Library. If you have not built a Multimedia ToolBook group, the usual relative path to these books is `MTB30\SAMPLES\`; the book names are `WIDGETS.TBK` and `LIBRARY.TBK`.

From Here...

In this chapter, you've been through most of what makes OpenScript work. You have seen that messages are sent from one object to another to change the behavior of the target (the object receiving the message). You know that messages may originate from user events, script statements, the ToolBook system, other applications, or Windows itself. You've been introduced to the various kinds of properties and learned how to create and set user properties by direct assignment and by using the sequential search behavior of the `set` command. Finally, you've used messages in combination with properties to build composite objects that are self-running.

To find out more about the topics discussed in this chapter, refer to the following:

- For more on control structures in handlers, see Chapter 16, "Statements, Functions, and Expressions."
- For more on `imageCommand()` and `callMCI()` handlers, see Chapter 22, "MCI Devices and Multimedia."
- To find out more about script debugging, see Chapter 24, "Debugging Tools and Techniques."

CHAPTER 15

Understanding Variables, Values, and Text

OpenScript has a rich variety of commands, messages, and functions to manage variables and their contents. Text in Multimedia ToolBook can, and sometimes should, be contained in variables, but you also have a number of tools for manipulating text directly.

In this chapter, you are introduced to the following ToolBook scripting techniques:

- Creating and assigning values to variables
- Creating and using arrays
- Using constants and literal values
- Using text strings and their parts

Using Variables

One of the types of OpenScript container is the *variable*. A variable is a word in a script which represents the data contained in a certain section of memory. The content is known as the value of the variable. A variable can contain data of any valid type and is generally used for a nonpersistent value, such as the result of computations or concatenations.

Scope of Variables

It's important to distinguish between a variable whose content is available to all handlers and one whose value is available only to the handler in which it is created or declared. The first is a *system variable*, which has global scope—its value can be read and set from anywhere in the book—and which exists for as long as the book is open. The other is a *local variable*, which has local scope; it is available to a single handler and exists for only as long as the handler is running. The value of a local variable is not preserved until the next time that handler is run; the variable must be initialized each time that handler is called.

Creating Variables

A system variable requires a *declaration* in each handler which uses it. A declaration is a statement which tells the ToolBook system that you want to create a system variable with a given name. The type of data which the variable will contain may optionally be included. Follow these steps to create and initialize a system variable:

1. Create a new book by opening the ToolBook program by double-clicking its Program Manager or shortcut icon.
2. Open the Script Editor to the script of the page by selecting Object, Page Properties or pressing Shift+F7, then clicking the Script button of the resulting Properties dialog box.
3. To create a system variable named `splunge`, which holds data of type `INT`, and assign to it a value of `44`, enter the handler in Listing 15.1 in the script of the only page of the newly created book.

Listing 15.1 15LST01.DOC Handler for Declaring and Initializing a System Variable

```
TO HANDLE enterPage
    system INT splunge
    splunge =44
END enterPage
```

4. Select File, Save, then enter **SPLUNGE.TBK** as the book's name. Save the book by clicking OK or pressing Enter.
5. Reopen the book by selecting File, Open, choosing `SPLUNGE.TBK`, and clicking OK or pressing Enter.

   The reason for closing the book and reopening it is that the `enterPage` message must be sent in order for your handler to intercept and process it. The `enterPage` message is sent when the page appears as the book opens. Another way of sending the message is to change pages. This book has only one page; but clicking one of the page navigation arrows on the status bar, or selecting Page, First, causes the `enterPage` message to be sent nonetheless. Also, recall the object hierarchy introduced in Chapter 13, "OpenScript Fundamentals." The `enterPage` message handler may be entered into the script of an object higher in the hierarchy, such as the background or book, and the message will reach it if there are no handlers in between that intercept that message without forwarding it.
6. Without closing ToolBook, make a new, untitled book by selecting File, New.
7. Open the Script Editor to the page level as in step 2, and enter the handler in Listing 15.2.

Listing 15.2 15LST02.DOC Handler for Displaying the Contents of a System Variable

```
TO HANDLE buttonClick
    system INT splunge
    request "splunge = " && splunge
END buttonClick
```

A local variable can be created simply by assigning a value to a previously unused name, but must be declared if a type is specified.

The `request` statement, as used in Listing 15.2, constructs a text string from a block of text inside quotation marks, separated from the contents (value) of the system variable `splunge` by the "concatenate with space" operator. The statement simply tells ToolBook to put the contents of `splunge` after the literal text with a space in between and display the result as a text string in a dialog box.

Because you entered this `buttonClick` handler into the script of the page, it will run when you click the left mouse button at any point on the page object which isn't covered by other, opaque objects. At this point, your untitled book has no objects obstructing any part of the page. However, the button messages are not sent to the page unless the system is at Reader level.

8. Switch to Reader mode by selecting Edit, Reader or pressing F3.

   Click anywhere on the page of the current untitled book and the Request box pops up, which bears the message, `splunge = 44`.

   To see what happens if the system variable is not declared in each handler which uses it, continue with the following steps.

9. Return to Author mode by selecting Edit, Author or pressing F3.
10. Open the Script Editor, as in steps 2 and 7, to Listing 15.2.
11. Delete the following line:

    ```
    system INT splunge
    ```

12. Return to Reader level as in step 8.

Now, sending a `buttonClick` message to the page results in a quite different message:

```
splunge = splunge
```

The ToolBook system doesn't know that `splunge` is meant to be a system variable, so it determines that there are no local variables of that name and interprets the variable name as a string instead. Put the handler back into working condition by restoring the line you removed in step 11:

```
system INT splunge
```

You have actually done a lot so far. You have:

- Created a variable
- Declared the new variable as a system variable

- Told the system what kind of data to expect when it retrieves the value of the variable
- Assigned an initial value to the variable. Initialization is often an important step in manipulating variables
- Retrieved and displayed the variable's value

In the example presented in Listings 15.1 and 15.2, you used the equals sign as the means of putting the number `44` into the variable `splunge`. The assignment and retrieval of its value, or contents, is the reason for a variable's existence. The various ways to place values into OpenScript variables and take them out again are numerous.

> **Note**
>
> A system variable may be declared anywhere in a handler. There is some contention (as in other languages) over whether it's a better practice to gather all declarations in a group at the beginning of the handler for easy reference, or to declare each at the point at which it is needed—for easy reference. Use your own judgement.

So what about local variables? Well, it's not necessary to declare a local variable at all; you may just choose a name, use it for the first time in an assignment statement, and OpenScript does the rest. Of course, this is not the most efficient way to create variables; it takes time for OpenScript to work out what sort of meaning should be assigned to each typographical word. You can help the system out by declaring and typing local variables. To do so, simply substitute the keyword `local` for `system` in the declaration. For instance, if you had wanted to delare the variable `splunge` as a local variable, you would have entered the following statement in your handler:

```
local INT splunge
```

Note, however, that this variable is available to another handler only if sent specifically as a parameter of a message. This is good. Use system variables when parameter passing is truly impractical (as when you need to pass a value to a handler for a built-in message), but keep as many variables local as possible in order to prevent unwanted access by other parts of the script.

As with system variables, the type specification for local variables is optional but desirable.

Putting Values into Variables

Once you create a variable, it is necessary to make it represent a desired value. There are three primary ways of putting a value into a variable:

- **The assignment operator.** The standard method for setting the value of a variable is to use the assignment operator, =. This is the method used in Listing 15.1:

  ```
  splunge = 44
  ```

- **The `set...to` statement.** This is the classic method of assignment in Openscript:

```
set splunge to 44
```

- **The `put...into` statement.** This syntax is often used when assigning to containers other than variables, but works with variables as well:

```
put 44 into splunge
```

Try each of the variant assignment statements by entering it in place of this line (in Listing 15.1):

```
splunge = 44
```

Assignment statements replace the previous value of the variable and calculations are performed before assignment, so that it is perfectly valid for a variable to assign a new value to itself. By analogy with the preceding expressions, the following expressions are valid also:

```
splunge = splunge + 12
set splunge to splunge + 12
put splunge + 12 into splunge
```

Try substituting the `set` and `put` forms as the assignment statement in Listing 15.1. In each case, the Request box should display `splunge = 56`.

Retrieving Values from Variables

Having assigned the contents of a variable, you'll need ways of getting that value out of the "variable" container to put into another container for manipulation, display, and other purposes. The commands provided by OpenScript for retrieving variable contents are essentially the same commands used for assigning variable values. This is not surprising; moving data among any OpenScript containers takes essentially the same form. In the example scripts of Listings 15.1 and 15.2, you use the `request` command to retrieve and display the value of the variable `splunge`. In an extension of that exercise, you retrieved the value of a variable, manipulated that value by adding a number to it, and placed the resulting value back in the original variable container.

There is a specific command for obtaining the value of a container: the `get` command. Used alone, `get <variable name>` places a copy of the variable's contents into the built-in local variable `It`. This can be illustrated very simply using the book, `SPLUNGE.TBK`, which you constructed with the script from Listing 15.1. (A copy of `SPLUNGE.TBK` is found on the disk accompanying this book.) Follow the steps of this short example:

1. If you have not exited the ToolBook program since `SPLUNGE.TBK` was opened, skip to step 3.
2. Start ToolBook and open `SPLUNGE.TBK` via File, Open. Or, simply double-click that book's shortcut or Program Manager icon.
3. Show the Command Window by choosing View, Command or pressing Shift+F3.

4. Enter the following line in the edit area of the Command Window:

```
system INT splunge;get "splunge = " && splunge
```

The command is accepted and the statement is placed into the Command Window's history area, but nothing else changes on-screen. The variable `It`, however, now contains the text string to be displayed.

5. Enter the following line in the edit area of the Command Window:

```
request it
```

The request is for the contents of `It`, so the message `splunge = 44` is displayed in a dialog box.

6. `get` is an example of an OpenScript retrieval command which has a default container. `put` is another such command. Used alone, `put` displays the contents of a container such as a variable in the Command Window itself. Without changing anything else, change the command in step 4 to the following:

```
put it
```

Now, upon pressing Enter, the message which had appeared in the Request box takes the place of the text in the Command Window. If the Command Window is not open when a script encounters a `put` statement of this form, it's opened automatically.

> **Note**
>
> The `put` command has two advantages over the Request box when used to view intermediate values, as might be done during debugging. First, the `put` command does not require that a dialog box be dismissed each time it's used. More important is the fact that `request` puts a value into `It`, destroying the original value; `put` doesn't.

Variable Types

A variable may have a type specifier which essentially is a way of telling OpenScript how much memory to reserve for that variable's contents and how to manipulate it in an expression (see Table 15.1).

Table 15.1 OpenScript Data Types Include Object Types

Data Type	Size	Used For
`INT`	16 bits	General calculation
`LONG`	32 bits	General calculation
`REAL`	64 bits	Floating-point calculation
`WORD`	16 bits	General calculation
`DWORD`	32 bits	General calculation
`STRING`	User defined	Text and numeral manipulation

Data Type	Size	Used For
LOGICAL	Variable	Boolean true/false states
POINT	User defined	Two-item stack
COLOR	3 bytes	Color specification
STACK	User-defined	User-defined
DATE	Variable	Date calculations
TIME	Variable	Time calculations
PAGE	Variable	Explicit page reference
BACKGROUND	Variable	Explicit background reference
LAYER	Variable	Explicit page or background layer reference
GRAPHIC	Variable	Explicit graphic reference
FIELD	Variable	Explicit text field reference
OBJECT	Variable	Explicit reference to object types
BOOK	Variable	Explicit book path reference (for an explanation of quirks in the numeric types, see the section headed, "Numeric Types" later in this chapter)

To type a variable, put the type name before the variable's name in a declaration statement, like the following one:

```
system STACK theList
```

The primary use of the `time`, `date`, and `object` type variables is in forcing an error to occur when an invalid assignment is made. Specifying a variable of type `time` causes an error if you attempt to set it to a value which is not in the format specified by the system property `sysTimeFormat`. Analogously, specifying type `date` checks for conformance with `sysDateFormat`. The variable types `page`, `background`, `field`, `layer`, `graphic`, `object`, and `book` contain page references of the form `Page id 0 of Book "ch15.tbk"` (for a variable of type `page` or `object`). Enter the following script into the Command Window and press Enter:

```
system page p; p = this page; request p
```

The page ID number appears in an alert box. Change the script to read:

```
system page p; p = this background; request p
```

This time you receive an alert box warning you that a background is not a page.

Note

Recall that you can use the semicolon character (;), rather than a new line, as a script statement delimiter in the Command Window or in a script.

Page 1 of the ToolBook book `CH15.TBK`, on the accompanying disk, demonstrates the `date` type. Select a date format from the combo box, enter a date in the Enter a Date field, and press Enter. You receive an alert telling you whether your entry is acceptable or not. See the entire script on that page or in Listing 15.3.

Listing 15.3 15LST03.DOC The Handler for Page 1 of *CH15.TBK* uses a *DATE* Variable

```
TO HANDLE keyDown k
    local DATE d
    local STRING s
    if k <> keyEnter
        forward
        break
    end if
    sysDateFormat = text of combobox "dbox" of this page
    sysSuspend = false
    sysErrorNumber = 0
    d = text of field "dfield" of this page
    if sysErrorNumber <> 0
        s = "Your date entry must be in the" \
            && sysDateFormat && "format."
    else
        s = "Your entry is in the correct format."
    end if
    request s
    sysSuspend = true
    forward
END keyDown
```

It is not necessary to specify a type for an OpenScript variable, but doing so can improve performance and help trap errors.

Automatic and Explicit Typing of Variables. The reason it's unnecessary to type a variable is that ToolBook contains mechanisms for determining the data type of a variable and applying it automatically. Such a determination must be made each time an attempt is made to assign a value to an untyped variable.

Obviously ToolBook spends some time ascertaining the type of data contained in a variable of unspecified type. This is time ill spent when the program is trying to complete its event loop. It is time thoroughly wasted when a handler is executing an iterative control structure (described in Chapter 16, "Statements, Functions, and Expressions"), especially if the structure loops hundreds or thousands of times.

Another drawback to automatic typing is that it allows the programmer to enter data of an undesired type. Many feel that this argument is even stronger than the argument from wasted time, and with reason. Debugging a script whose problem lies in applying integer arithmetic to real values, for example, can be frustrating in the extreme, and it may not be immediately obvious that there is a problem at all unless rigorous testing reveals it in time.

This is an issue which is especially relevant to system variables. A system variable must be declared in each handler in which it appears, and may be typed or untyped at each occurrence; there is nothing except experience to prevent you from assigning a value typed as, say, `DWORD` to a system variable in one handler while another handler uses the contents of the very same variable as a `STRING`. There is no error; it's not even a mistake in some cases. Nevertheless, when you have 20 or 30 handlers using the same variable, only a very organized programmer, to say the least, can predict what values a given handler uses during the lifetime of a book instance. A corollary of this feature of system variables is that they usually take a little longer to access.

While the following points have been stressed already, they are worth making again:

Specify a data type:

- **When a variable is expected to hold the same type of data throughout its lifetime.** Remember that the lifetime of a local variable is from its creation until the handler in which it was created is finished running. The lifetime of a system variable is from its creation until the book is closed.
- **When speed is of great importance.** A typical interactive content title or CBT project can easily have hundreds of variables and looping control structures. Explicit typing eliminates the overhead of automatic typing.
- **When maintainability is of great importance.** It is easier to finish and modify a project if you have the assurance that your data will prevent the compilation if it is of the wrong type. This gives you one less thing to worry about.

While automatic typing of variables sounds like, and is, a powerful tool, you should take advantage of it only when necessary. Situations in which automatic typing is useful include the following:

- **When a variable is expected to hold different types of data at different times.** An example would be reading the contents of a cell of a spreadsheet.
- **When numbers are embedded in text.** This is a very common occurrence. Automatic text-to-number and number-to-text conversion is the archetypical use of untyped variables. (However, see the discussion of variables of type `STRING` in the next section.)
- **When file and resource names are coded to direct program flow.** This is merely an extension of the previous example. Say that you have two bitmap files, `S0001.BMP` and `L0001.BMP`. The "S" stands for "small" and the "L" for "large." Perhaps you use the large bitmap when the screen resolution is 800 × 600 pixels, and the small one when it is 640 × 480 pixels. You may then want to use the initials S and L along with the numerals 0001 and so forth to construct the name of the proper file to open. An untyped variable would be useful to hold the filename, although a `STRING` variable is usually sufficient.
- **When using a variable to hold an object type which could at any time be `NULL`.** The `OBJECT` data type does not accept `NULL` as a valid value.

Variable Name Restrictions and Reserved Variables. The earlier statement that the name of a variable must consist of a previously unused letter combination is a necessary but not sufficient rule for choosing the name. Two restrictions apply. The first is that the name must begin with a letter, underscore (_), or at symbol (@); the other is that it must not be any OpenScript keyword. For example, `ask` is not an acceptable variable name, but `@ask`, `_ask`, and `askTheQuestion` are suitable.

There are two variables, `argCount` and `argList`, which ToolBook uses to hold the number of parameters passed to a handler and their names, respectively. Get the values of these variables when needed, but don't attempt to assign values to them. You have already encountered `It`, the variable which automatically receives the result of a `get` statement, in the preceding two chapters. These three variables are reserved for ToolBook's use and their names must never be used as your variable names.

Working with Arrays

Arrays are daunting to some beginning programmers, though most intermediate to advanced programmers are very comfortable with them. They are among the least intuitive constructs of a scripted language (although game writers would be lost without the two- or three-dimensional arrays called *matrices*). OpenScript suports arrays of up to 16 dimensions; the number of elements in a given dimension must not exceed 65,536.

Declaring Arrays

Arrays aren't really much different to use than standard variables. An array must be declared because ToolBook needs to know that it is an array, how many dimensions are involved, and often how many data entries are reserved in each dimension.

Fixed Arrays. A *fixed array* is one for which the number (or at least the maximum number) of data elements is known and specified at the time the array variable is declared. A typical declaration of a two-dimensional array of 32 elements in the first dimension and 16 in the second, used as an untyped system variable, looks like the following:

```
system svArray[32][16]
```

The number of bracket pairs, two in this case, equal the number of dimensions declared. The fact that numbers are within the brackets indicates that this is a fixed array. If it is an array of 32-bit `LONG` integers, the amount of memory allocated in bytes is 4 (per `LONG`) times 32 (element count of the first dimension) times 16 (element count of the second dimension), or 2,048 bytes. Extend this declaration to three dimensions; assume that you need 16 elements in the following third dimension:

```
system svArray[32][16][16]
```

The amount of memory allocated is now 2,048 times 16, or 32K. It doesn't take many dimensions to use up a fair amount of memory, and the situation is worse if the elements consist of text strings of arbitrary length.

Note

It's easy to get bogged down worrying about memory. Unless you've considerably overestimated the required number of elements per dimension, you would have had to allocate that much memory to variables in any event.

An advantage of using arrays is the fact that you can carry around that much data in one container; pass it as a parameter, just like any other variable; and, if your taste and skill lies this way, you can perform array-based calculations which leave analogous single-element variable algorithms far behind in speed. In fact, what arrays mean to the average user is speed. Accessing an element of an array is faster than getting a comma-delimited list item, and a lot faster than getting a textline (described later in this chapter).

OpenScript also supports dynamic arrays for those cases in which the array size is modified by the script.

Dynamic Arrays. A *dynamic array* is one for which the maximum number of elements per dimension is unknown or alterable. The number of dimensions must be known and specified. The syntax for declaring a dynamic array is analogous to that used in declaring a fixed array; for two dimensions, the declaration would take the following form:

```
system svArray[][]
```

Once again, `svArray` has been declared as a `system` variable, but `local` may be substituted for `system` if a nonpersistent variable is desired. Note that in a dynamic array, none of the dimensions can be of fixed size.

The maximum number of elements in any one dimension of a dynamic array is still 65,536. The amount of memory claimed by a dynamic array varies with the number and size of elements added or subtracted. Unless you have taken special precautions to check the maximum amount of memory available and limit your dynamic array size accordingly, you are in some danger of writing to other applications' memory partitions, causing a General Protection Fault. It is poor programming practice to assume that an array will always be small enough for available memory.

Tip

It is always desirable to use fixed arrays if there is any means of determining the maximum array sizes. The fixed declaration allocates enough memory to hold the array. Additionally, elements of fixed arrays can be accessed faster than those of dynamic arrays.

As with any variable, data typing improves performance. When the data type of an array is `STRING`, the actual memory usage varies with the length of the strings contained by the array elements. This is the case whether the array has been declared as fixed or dynamic.

Tip

ToolBook printed documentation states that the data type WORD is appropriate for text operations. This is erroneous; the type is STRING.

A one-dimensional array is the fastest type of "list." Declare it as a variable followed by one set of brackets, with or without an element count.

Manipulating Data in Arrays The value of an array element can be assigned to another variable, used in calculations, and modified just like the value of any other variable. All that is necessary is to tell OpenScript which element you want to use, as in the following statement:

```
get svArray[1][2] --The element's value is now in It
```

Arrays as User Properties and Parameters. An array may be assigned as a user property like any other variable. An array may be passed as a parameter to another handler in the same manner. In each of these two cases, omit the reference to the number of array dimensions. The following script fragment illustrates the declaration of a three-dimensional array, and the syntax for passing the same array as a parameter of the user-defined message `theMessage`:

```
local theArray[3][6][4]
send theMessage theArray
```

A handler can accept an array as a parameter, but the syntax is slightly different from that used with the basic data types. In the preceding code fragment, the variable `theArray` is passed with the message `theMessage`. The corresponding message handler then begins in this manner:

```
TO HANDLE theMessage theArray[][][]
...statements...
```

Note that the called handler needs to know the number of dimensions expected (three, in this case) but not their sizes.

Using Literal Values and Constants

Many of the considerations which apply to variables also apply to constants. In fact, it can sometimes be difficult to decide when to use built-in constants and when to use variables instead.

Using Literal Values

If your variables have been declared to contain a certain data type, OpenScript performs the appropriate typechecking when an assignment is performed. Typechecking catches a number of problems which can arise while assigning literal values. Due to OpenScript's ability to interchange numerals appearing within text constructs with their actual numerical values, assigning literal numerals to variables of type STRING can be extremely useful.

Numeric Types. Nevertheless the typechecking offered by OpenScript for numeric data assignments is idiosyncratic and allows some mismatches to occur without errors, and some to compile but not run. For instance, draw a button on a page and put the following handler into the button's script:

```
TO HANDLE buttonClick     --Line 1
    local REAL a      --Line 2
    a = 4.49          --Line 3
    put a             --Line 4
END buttonClick           --Line 5
```

This and the following scripts are demonstrated on page 2 of the book `CH15.TBK` on the included disk. In that book, the results of the assignments are put into a field instead of into the Command Window.

Return to Reader mode and click the button. The result is `4.49`; the data types match.

Substitute the following lines, one at a time, into line 2 of the previous script, return to Reader mode, and press the button:

```
local INT a       --Line 2
```

The result is `4`; the data types don't match, but this fact isn't recognized; the script runs, but the real number is replaced by the signed integer nearest it. Try another type:

```
local WORD a      --Line 2
```

The result is again `4`. A `WORD` is an integer value; it acts like an unsigned `INT`. Using the `DWORD` type yields the same result, as `DWORD` doesn't accept real values either.

Now replace lines 2 and 3 with the following statements (replace both of the lines at the same time):

```
local INT a       --Line 2
a = -4.49         --Line 3
```

The result is now `-4`; the `INT` data type is signed, but only integer values are allowed, so truncation still occurs. For contrast, change line 2 again (leave the negative number in line 3):

```
local WORD a      --Line 2
```

The `WORD` and `DWORD` data types are unsigned, so you would expect the compiler to catch the attempted assignment of a negative integer. It does not; the script compiles, but at the button press, the Execution Suspended runtime alert informs you that the number is out of range.

Finally, replace lines 2 and 3 again:

```
local INT a       --Line 2
a = 60000         --Line 3
```

The `INT` data type has a range of `-32767` to `32767`, so the assignment of `60000` to the variable a is clearly erroneous. This time the compiler catches the error; the handler can't be run.

> **Note**
>
> While this section on literal values provides a convenient place to demonstrate assignment quirks, don't forget that the demonstration is valid for any expression or container which evaluates to a number.

Text Types. *String* is the generic term for any subset of a body of text ranging from one to all of its characters; as such, it is very broad. The only direct reference to strings in OpenScript is the data type `STRING`, which is equally comprehensive.

String literals should always be enclosed in double quotation marks. While it is possible to use literals without quotation marks, it's bad practice for several reasons:

- It doesn't work if there are spaces or quotation marks in the string.
- ToolBook has to compare the string with variable names to make sure it isn't a reference to a variable rather than a literal. This slows execution.
- You may accidentally use a variable name which is identical to the string. The results in this case are unpredictable.
- Identifying the string literals in a script by visual inspection becomes difficult.

Quotation marks which occur within a string must be set off by a double pair of marks, in addition to those which are required to delimit the entire string, as in Chapter 13's following target example:

```
messageTrack = messageTrack & target & CRLF \
               & "This message comes to you" \
               && "from page 1 of book ""working.tbk""" & CRLF
```

The three quotation marks at the end of the string literal are simply a reflection of the fact that the quoted portion of the string happens to fall just before the delimiter.

> **Tip**
>
> Use the constant `QUOTE` instead of a quotation mark when desired. Usage includes the concatenation operator `&` before and after the constant.

ToolBook has a number of other built-in constants as well. These are discussed in the next section.

Using OpenScript Constants

When you use a color specifier, `GREEN`, for instance, what you are actually specifying is a color value of 120,50,100 in HSV values. `GREEN`, and other OpenScript constants, are somewhat like macros or definitions for variable values. Declaring a variable of type `COLOR`, naming it, say, `myGreen`, and assigning the HSV values is a more complex method of creating a reference to the standard green:

```
...statements...
local COLOR myGreen
myGreen = 120,50,100
...statements...
```

The color constants are `BLACK`, `BLUE`, `CYAN`, `GREEN`, `GRAY`, `MAGENTA`, `RED`, `WHITE`, `YELLOW`, and `LIGHTGRAY`.

Useful text constants, some of which have been used in this and previous chapters, include `CR` (carriage return), `LF` (line feed) `CRLF` (carriage return/line feed pair), `SPACE`, `FORMFEED`, `TAB`, `LEFTQUOTE`, `RIGHTQUOTE`, `QUOTE` (straight double quote), `NULL` (the empty string), and `EOF` (end-of-file).

Additionally, each key and mouse button has an OpenScript constant associated with it.

Note that since color constants represent values of data type `COLOR` and can therefore be viewed as comma-separated lists, you may perform read-only list operations on them. Enter the following expression into the Command Window to see only the saturation value of ToolBook's standard green:

```
put item 2 of GREEN
```

Use the predefined Openscript constant names in expressions of all kinds rather than the corresponding constant values. If you want to manipulate read-only values for use in calculations, put them into variables.

Using Characters, Strings, and Textlines

ToolBook features a number of operators and functions which deal directly with subsets of text in containers. A text container can be a variable of type `STRING` or `STACK`, a literal string, or the `text` or `richText` properties of an object such as a combo box, field, hotword, or recordfield. Subsets of text are characters, items, words, and textlines (see fig. 15.1).

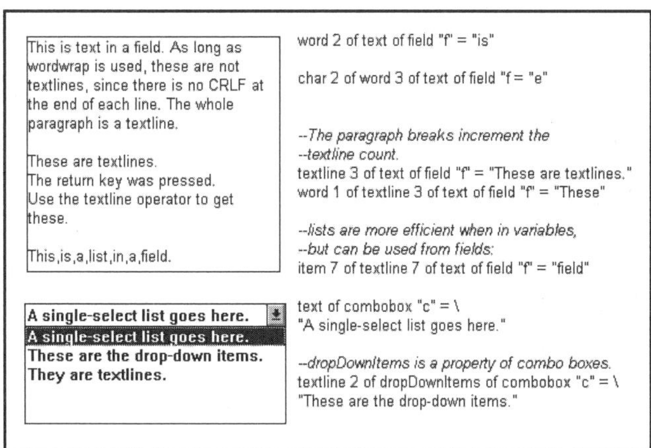

Fig. 15.1

The subdivisions of text in OpenScript are illustrated in a field and in a combo box. The statements to the right of those objects evaluate to `true`.

Strings, Characters, and Words

For practical work with text, you need better-defined, more manageable chunks. OpenScript begins at the beginning with the concept of a `character`, or `char`, plural `characters` and `chars`. This text operator is used to refer to a single character of text. A *character* is usually a letter, numeral, space, or tab, although the carriage return, line feed, and nonprinting ANSI characters above 127 (decimal) are normally included as well. Special characters (punctuation marks and backslashes) may be included in strings also, although you want to make doubly sure that these are delimited by quotation marks. Enter the following expressions, one at a time, into the Command Window.

To extract the second character from a literal string, enter the following:

```
put character 2 of "splunge"
```

The alternate method is as follows:

```
put char 2 of "splunge"
```

To extract characters 3 to 6 inclusive, enter the following:

```
put characters 3 to 6 of "splunge"
```

To demonstrate the use of the `character` operator in the context of a variable, either insert the following into a `buttonClick` handler or enter them into the Command Window separated by semicolons or by Ctrl+Enter:

```
local STRING theString
theString = "splunge"
put chars 2 to 4 of theString
```

Tip

In one of those bursts of formality that sometimes occurs in OpenScript, the number of the operator must match the number of the argument. The following do not compile:

```
put character 3 to 6 of "splunge"
put characters 3 of "splunge"
```

Such a mismatch is simply called a *syntax error*. Look before the point at which the error is highlighted and make sure that the singular and plural operators match their arguments.

You may also use ordinals to extract single characters; remember that they are only defined through `tenth`:

```
put sixth char of "splunge"
```

(These examples may be found on page 3 of `CH15.TBK` included on the enclosed disk. As usual, there is a slight difference in that the result is placed into a field rather than into the Command Window.)

The word text operator acts on strings which are delimited by spaces, tabs, or nonprinting characters:

```
TO HANDLE buttonClick
local STRING x
x = "Paris in the Splunge"
word 4 of x = "spring"
put x
END buttonClick
```

Tip

Don't confuse the WORD data type, which is an unsigned numeric type, with a "word" as applied to text operations. The two have no relationship except for the common name.

The isType() function, used often in Chapter 16, "Statements, Functions, and Expressions, is insensitive to the difference between the two uses of word. Quotation marks are necessary around the parameter word when the data type is meant.

Items and Textlines

There are actually three entities which are referred to by the description "list" at one place or another in ToolBook documentation. One of them is the one-dimensional array. The other two are the item and the textline.

Items are the entries in a comma-delimited list, or stack. A stack may be text in a field or recordfield, or in a variable of type STACK. (Refer to fig. 15.2 for an example of items in a textline of the text of a field.) An example of a literal stack is "cabbage,squid,tuna,snowflake"; although generally speaking, one builds lists by adding items to variables.

The logical operators is in, is not in, and contains work with lists, so it is easy to check for the existence of items:

```
if sysBooks contains "special.sbk"
    caption of button = "Again"
end if
```

If you want the string you want to compare with another to be on the left side of the existence statement, use the alternative keyword in:

```
if "button" is in object of target
    caption of button = "Again"
end if
```

Stack Manipulation. The archtypical method of stack manipulation is based on the commands push and pop. These commands were exemplified in Chapter 13,"OpenScript Fundamentals," in the context of the list (stack) of system books. The same forms of expression work for any item of any stack. To add an item of any data type to the beginning of a list, use the push command, as in the following example:

```
push newSystemBook onto sysBooks
```

To remove the first item of a stack, "pop" it off with the pop command. For instance:

```
pop sysBooks into theVariable
```

The popped item ends up in the variable (or other container). If no container is included in the statement, the popped item goes into the all-purpose variable `It`.

It is also possible to concatenate the popped item with data already in the container. The following syntax places the popped list item before the original contents of `theVariable`:

```
pop sysBooks before theVariable
```

The following form of expression appends the list item onto the end of the original contents:

```
pop sysBooks after theVariable
```

In this manner, it is possible to build up variables or fields containing large amounts of data.

Note

It is possible to push an item onto any position in a stack by using the following syntax:

```
push theItem onto item 2 of theList
```

However, pop always removes the first item of a stack. To remove a specific item from a stack, use the item-based commands, discussed next.

A slower but more flexible and intuitive method of working with list items uses the assignment operator and the `item` keyword. To get a specific list item, use an expression such as the following:

```
theVariable = item 2 of theList
```

If you want `It` to contain the list item, use the following `get` form, as usual:

```
get item 2 of theList
```

Use the following assignment operator to put an item into a specified place in the list:

```
item 2 of theList = theOtherVariable
```

Be aware that the preceding statement destroys the original item 2 of the list and replaces it, while the `push` statement adds the item to the list, preserving the original list but offsetting the positions of the items after the new item by 1.

Working with Textlines. Textlines are strings which end in the Openscript constant `CRLF`, the carriage return/line feed character pair. They may be created in fields or recordfields by pressing the Return key instead of allowing word wrap to occur. The textline in the edit box of a combo box is all that the `text` property of a combo box contains; but another property of the combo box, `dropDownItems`, can be accessed as a set of textlines using the `get` and `put` (or `set`) commands as well as the ubiquitous assignment operator.

The `textline` operators manipulate their argument(s) in a way which is analogous to that of the `character` and `word` operators. Listing 15.4 requires a field, configured as a single-select list box named `f`, another transparent field named `f2`, and a button named `b`. It can be found on page 4 of `CH15.TBK` (supplied on the accompanying disk). The script of the Start Over button is the following initialization handler:

```
TO HANDLE buttonClick
    send enterPage
END buttonClick
```

This is trickery. Clicking the button simply sends the `enterPage` message. The initialization statements are actually in the `enterPage` handler of the script of the page. Because the button is on the page, it is lower in the message hierarchy than is the page. So the message travels upward until it reaches the page's `enterPage` handler. The effect is that that handler is fooled into thinking that the page has just been shown, and initializes the page objects accordingly. Sending a built-in message from another built-in message can, if the book scripts are planned properly, reduce the number of script lines by running handlers which already exist.

The page script is more complex (see Listing 15.4).

Listing 15.4 15LST04.DOC Page Script for Page 4 of *CH15.TBK*

```
TO HANDLE enterPage
    local STACK vs
    local STRING vt
    local LONG i
    hide button "b"
    text of field "f" = NULL
    text of field "f2" = "Select From List"
    if selectedText <> NULL
    selectedText = NULL
    end if
    --This list would typically originate somewhere else
    --as the result of user input or a calculation
    vs = "cabbage,squid,tuna,snowflake"
    textline 1 of text of field "f" = \
    "Which of these has a backbone?" & CRLF & CRLF
    step i from 1 to itemCount(vs)
        textline (I + 2) of text of field "f" = item i of vs
        strokeColor of textline (i + 2) of text of field "f" = red
    end step
END enterPage
TO HANDLE buttonClick
    if target <> field "f"
        break
    end if
    if selectedText = textline 5 of text of field "f"
        text of field "f2" = "Correct!"
        show button "b"
    else
        hide button "b"
        text of field "f2" = "Try Again"
    end if
END buttonClick
```

The statements in the `enterPage` handler are initialization statements. The `buttonClick` handler of the page does the real work. First it checks to make sure the user has clicked inside the field and not somewhere else. Then it compares the position of the choice from the list box with the position of that item of the list defined in the `enterPage` handler. The invisible field text is changed depending on whether a match is found or not.

Note the hierarchy of text operators. You may read or assign (get or put) text directly into a container. To work with smaller entities, the syntax is `textline x of text` of the container, `word y of textline x of text` of the container, and so on (see fig. 15.2 and page 7 of `CH15.TBK`, supplied on the disk accompanying this book).

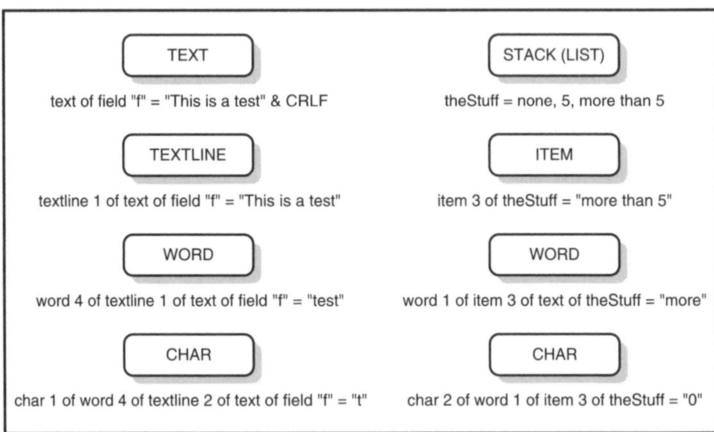

Fig. 15.2

Text operators follow an explicit hierarchy. Put the text of a field into a variable, then use these expressions to manipulate the value of the variable.

Note also that there are many ways in which the functionality of this page could have been achieved. The goal in this instance was to get most of the handlers into one object's script; speed and memory optimization is not usually an issue with such a small book. But, to take one possible variation, the `buttonClick` handler in the page script might more naturally go into the script of the list box field `"f"`.

OpenScript Text Tools

OpenScript is able to get numerals from text strings and use them as numbers in calculations. Conversely, it is able to put numbers into text strings for direct output to variables, fields, or files. It also provides a text parsing capability for assignment of text to an array.

Numerals as Text. As long as a numeral ends up in an untyped variable, a variable of type `STRING`, or a field, you may mix numbers, even if they are typed, with text. Use the Command Window to enter the following handler (as always, when using the Command Window, you specify the line breaks with either a semicolon or Ctrl+Enter):

```
local INT  x; local STRING t
t = "Thou shalt not count to"
x = 4
put x after t
put t
```

The following script, using a button and a field, is included in a button script on page 5 of CH15.TBK (a copy of which is on the accompanying disk). An additional button has been added there to show that the type conversion acts on real numbers as well as integers. For that matter, it works with literal values, and in fact the textual units discussed earlier in this chapter may just as well be taken by numerals:

```
local STRING t
t = "Run away for xxxx seconds"
word 4 of t = 30
put t
```

What will not work is trying to put a numeral into a container which can't hold text.

Text as Numerals. The subject of using numerals occurring in a text string as numbers is very simple and need not be labored much. The basic syntax is similar to other OpenScript expressions. Entering the following statement into the Command Window returns the value 65:

```
put word 4 of "The event happened 35 years ago" + 30
```

An alternate way of expressing this is the following:

```
put chars 20 to 21 of "The event happened 35 years ago" + 30
```

Again, the point is that the number can take the place of any of the aforementioned text units. Additional examples may be found on page 5 of CH15.TBK on the disk supplied with this book.

An issue which has not been addressed yet is the methods of finding out whether a particular word or character is a number. This will be covered in the next chapter.

Text in Arrays. OpenScript implements a parsing scheme to split text based on textlines, words, items, and characters and store the resulting chunks in an array. The array itself must already have been declared, and the size of the array must be sufficient to hold all of the pieces.

The command which accomplishes this is `fill`, the same one which allows you to place a given value in all array elements. To implement text parsing, use the text unit names within brackets (see Listing 15.5, as well as page 6 of CH15.TBK on the disk which accompanies this book).

Listing 15.5 The *[textline][word]* Button Script

```
TO HANDLE buttonClick
    local x[][]
    local LONG a,i,j,y,z
    a = 1
    text of field f1 = NULL
    theText = text of field "f2"
    fill x with theText in [textline][word] order
    y =  item 1 of dimensions(x)
    z =  item 2 of dimensions(x)
    step i from 1 to y
        step j from 1 to z
            textline a of text of field "f1" = x[i][j]
            increment a
        end step
    end step
END buttonClick
```

The line of interest here is the one beginning with the `fill` command. This command takes the textlines you have typed into the field named `f2` and parses it into words. If you type the following:

```
This is a test
of the fill
command parser
```

the array elements are filled as in figure 15.3.

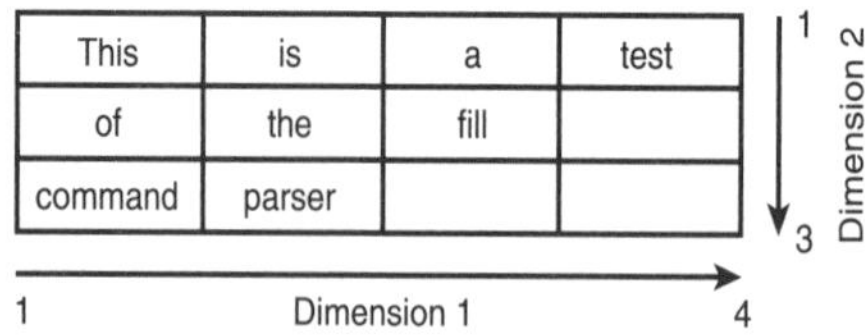

Fig. 15.3

The `fill` command can assign textlines, words, and characters in order to the elements of the array. Unused positions are set to `NULL`.

From Here...

This chapter is an overview of the use of text and numeric variables and literal values within handlers. You learned to assign and retrieve values from containers (starting with variables and ending with text fields), how to work with data types, and how to use arrays. There is much more to know about data types, text subdivisions, arrays, and the evaluation of statements.

For more information on these topics, see the following chapters:

- Chapter 3, "Understanding Objects," teaches you more about text containers.
- Chapter 13, "OpenScript Fundamentals," discusses how to get and set values.
- Chapter 16, "Statements, Functions, and Expressions," shows you how to find out more about calculating values and concatenating strings.

CHAPTER 16

Statements, Functions, and Expressions

The preceding three chapters are concerned primarily with an overview of the structure of OpenScript, with emphasis on handlers, object properties, variables, and messages. Each of those topics is illustrated through example scripts consisting of one or more OpenScript statements. So far, these statements have been defined as expressions, with some control structures being used without further explanation. This chapter examines other types of OpenScript structures that provide values for statements, as well as combinations of expressions that collectively control program flow.

In this chapter, you learn about the following topics:

- Expressions and operators in containers
- Functions and dynamic link libraries
- Control structures

Expressions

Recall that an OpenScript *statement* is one instruction contained within a script. A statement (or group of statements) that produces a result is an OpenScript *expression*. Therefore, the following as a whole is not an expression:

```
go to the next page
```

Although the following is:

```
get the next page
```

It returns the `uniqueName` property of the page in question and places it where all `get` statements go: in the reserved variable `It`.

Containers

Containers have already been defined as those ToolBook components that can hold a value, such as most variables and many properties. An expression must place the value that it produces into a container; using the `get/set` terminology of ToolBook, a container becomes that which can be set to a value. So for a variable:

```
local PAGE p
p = (pageNumber of next page) + (text of field (pageNumberOffset)
```

the calculation to the right of the assignment operator is an expression that is one part of the statement, and `p` is the container that is the other part of the statement.

Operators

The concept of an operator in ToolBook is about the same as that in any other programming language. That concept is a little harder to pin down in a script-based language, such as OpenScript, because word combinations supplement the usual combination of symbols (see Table 16.1 in the "DLLs" section of this chapter). The operator precedence is a ranking of the symbols that indicates which ones are evaluated first within a single expression. This order of precedence is easily overridden through the use of pairs of parentheses, as discussed in the following section.

Overriding Operator Precedence. The operator precedence values, set out in Table 16.1 in the "DLLs" section of this chapter, can be overridden through the use of parentheses. Expressions in parentheses are evaluated before the original operator hierarchy is invoked; in the case of nested parentheses, the expression in the innermost nested pair is evaluated first.

To take the simplest case, the following expression relies on OpenScript's built-in precedence:

```
put 4 * 2 + 3
```

The expression evaluates to 11. The following expression contains a pair of parentheses that override the default precedence:

```
put 4 * (2 + 3)
```

In this case, the Command Window displays `20`.

The following expression:

```
put 4 * ( 2 ^ (5 * (10 - 2)))
```

takes advantage of nested parentheses to give subtraction precedence over multiplication and multiplication over exponentiation. Entering this statement in the Command Window results in a value of `4398046511104`.

Evaluation of Expressions. It is always safe to assume that the right side of a statement whose execution requires evaluation of expressions is evaluated first. A statement in which a variable changes its own value is, therefore, perfectly legal, as you may see by typing this script in the Command Window and pressing Enter:

```
j = 3;j = j + 5; put j
```

The result, 8, is put into the window. Chained operators in OpenScript yield either a logical value or an error (which often is just what you want). For example,

```
put x = 3 = x
```

returns `false` into the Command Window if `x` is not equal to 3 and `true` if it is.

Tip

If an expression is intended to use operators to force a logical return value, setting the various expressions off in parentheses makes the script much more readable:

```
x = 5; put (x = (3 = x))
```

This expression evaluates to `false`.

Functions

A *function* is an OpenScript statement (or group of statements) that returns a value. It's actually an expression that takes the form of a built-in construct or a set of statements in a `TO GET` handler that performs a task.

Structure of Functions

Most, if not all, expressions are functions, under the broadest definition. Certainly, all functions are expressions (usually, groups of expressions). What's the difference? To begin with, there are several typographical restrictions on functions. When a function is used, it is said to be *called*; parameters may or may not be passed to it. Typographically, the parameters are separated by commas; the parameter list as a whole is enclosed in parentheses. For example, the `hypotenuse` function—a ToolBook standard function—can be called from the Command Window as follows:

```
put hypotenuse(3,4)
```

In this case, the parameters are literal values, and the container is the Command Window. Because `hypotenuse` returns the value of the hypotenuse of a right triangle, and because the parameters are the lengths of the other two sides, the Command Window displays `5`.

Note

The `hypotenuse` function, although a good one for introducing function syntax, is very unusual in that it yields the same value regardless of the order in which its parameters are passed (that is, hypotenuse(3,4) = hypotenuse(4,3)). More often than not, the parameters of a function have nothing to do with one another, and the order in which they occur is of extreme importance.

A function always returns a value—that is its purpose. Any function that you write by building a `TO GET` handler must contain at least one `return` statement, which defines the value to be returned. There are libraries of functions, including the Windows modules themselves, that you can *link* in order to call functions that produce results far beyond ToolBook's native capabilities. To use such a library, called a *dynamic link library* (*DLL*), the data types of the parameter values and return value must be defined.

ToolBook Standard Functions. ToolBook contains several functions that are ready for use without further preparation. In addition to several trigonometric functions, such as `hypotenuse`, ToolBook contains functions for calculating algebraic and transcendental values, statistical values, financial operations (some of the most complex built-in functions), and string-manipulation operations, as well as functions that manipulate ToolBook objects and properties. Also included are *viewer functions*, which you use to resolve some of the confusing issues of object placement at various screen resolutions. Most esoteric (and, arguably, clumsy) of all are the *pointer functions*, which allow you to set and get the values of the contents of memory by address. Most native ToolBook and user-written functions are designed to do without the need for pointer functions. Many DLL functions, on the other hand, require their use.

DLLs. Dynamic link libraries (DLLs) are collections of functions in a "wrapper" with specific memory locations in which parameter and return values are stored. Many Windows programs, not to mention Windows itself, carry around a certain amount of baggage in the form of DLLs. Couldn't the functions in these libraries just as well have been included in the program code proper? The short answer is yes, but several other questions arise:

- Are all the functions needed each time the program is run?
- Do you desire to give other programs access to the functions? (This question is especially relevant in the case of Windows, because one reason for Windows' existence is to support function calls from other programs.)
- Are substitute functions required in some cases, and are they likely to be modified frequently?
- Finally, how much more memory is used when each function table has to include every single function in the program?

These considerations normally outweigh just about any amount of inconvenience involved in accessing DLL functions. Actually, accessing such functions from OpenScript isn't difficult. A certain amount of preparation is required, but after that, you can call a DLL function just as easily as a ToolBook function.

The preparation that's needed is using the control structure `linkDLL` to link the library so that its functions are available to OpenScript. Inside the statement block, a function prototype has to be declared for each function desired. This procedure isn't very different from typing a variable (except that it isn't optional). What you're telling ToolBook in a function prototype is the type of parameter(s) passed to the function and the type of value returned by the function. OpenScript data types are a little broader than those in languages such as C, so you have fewer types to worry about. Nonetheless, if the documentation for a DLL specifies a C data type, you have to work out which OpenScript data type corresponds to it, as shown in Table 16.1.

Table 16.1 OpenScript Data Types for Use in DLL Function Prototypes

Data Type	Use for DLL Parameters	Use for DLL Return
BOOL	EMPTY BRACKETS	INT
char, unsigned char, and BYTE	BYTE	BYTE
DOUBLE	DOUBLE	DOUBLE
FLOAT	FLOAT	FLOAT
All handle types	WORD	WORD
INT	INT	INT
unsigned int, UINT, and WORD	WORD	WORD
long	LONG	LONG
unsigned long	DWORD	DWORD
VOID FAR *, CHAR FAR *, LPSTR, LPCSTR	STRING, POINTER, or literal string in quotes	POINTER
STRING	DWORD	not applicable

The DLLs supplied with ToolBook are straightforward; the prototypes are provided in the on-line documentation, and the types used are OpenScript types. Consider three tasks that you almost certainly will perform repeatedly in your career as an OpenScript programmer: determining the screen resolution, in pixels, of a computer on which your application may be run; determining how many colors the video device is capable of displaying at a given time; and determining how many screen units make up one pixel. (One screen unit often is called a *twip*. Standard VGA drivers use pixels of 15 twips in both horizontal and vertical directions. Windows 95 and some high-end video drivers for Windows 3.1 offer several choices for the number of logical units per pixel, however, making the evaluation of twips a very good idea.) You often will want to increase the sizes of your visible objects when the screen resolution, in pixels, changes. If you do so, you usually will want to compensate for the extra magnification, caused by changes in twips per pixel, that can occur as the result of user actions.

Note

So-called large-font video drivers decrease the twips-to-pixel ratio and make the display image appear larger than in standard VGA or SVGA.

The twips-to-pixel ratio is available for the asking in the system property `sysPageUnitsPerPixel`; no function call is required. To determine color depth and screen resolution, you could find functions in the Windows API that provide this information, but it's easier to use the functions provided with the ToolBook DLL TB30WIN.DLL. The functions that you want are `horizontalDisplayRes()` and `verticalDisplayRes()`. Although all VGA and SVGA drivers use the same vertical as horizontal resolution, it doesn't take much more effort to determine both, so call `verticalDisplayRes()` as well. Use `displayBitsPerPixel()` to get the current color depth.

Listing 16.1 shows what the linking and declarations look like. If you want to build the demonstration, make a new book and save it as `CH16.TBK`. The book has one page. Enter Listing 16.1, which is also available at button level of page 1 of `CH16.TBK`, into the script of the page and then return to Reader mode:

Listing 16.1 16LST01.DOC Linking TB30WIN.DLL

```
TO HANDLE enterPage
system POINT p
system WORD colors
    linkDLL "TB30WIN.DLL"
        INT horizontalDisplayRes()
        INT verticalDisplayRes()
        INT DisplayBitsPerPixel()
end linkDLL
```

The handler isn't complete yet; read on.

Some memory overhead is involved in keeping these functions available. Because the screen resolution won't change during the instance of the application, put the returned values into variables or other containers, and free the memory associated with the DLL functions by unlinking the DLL. Continue the page handler started in Listing 16.1 as shown in Listing 16.2.

Listing 16.2 16LST02.DOC Calling DLL funtions

```
item 1 of p = horizontalDisplayRes()
item 2 of p = verticalDisplayRes()
colors = 2 ^ DisplayBitsPerPixel()
unLinkDLL "TB30WIN.DLL"
END enterPage
```

Notice that none of these functions takes a parameter, but each function of course returns a value. In all three cases, the type of value returned is INT. Having declared the functions, you may call them in the same manner as you would native ToolBook functions. Because `displayBitsPerPixel()` returns the color depth in bits, the actual number of colors displayed is 2 bits. For the convenience of those using Runtime TookBook, the example in CH16.TBK uses button captions to display the function returns. To continue using the authoring package, enter the following line in the

Command Window; the displayed result is the number of colors that the display is capable of reproducing at one time:

```
send enterPage;system WORD colors;put colors
```

The first statement simply sends an `enterPage` message, which causes the `enterPage` handler to run, linking the DLL and declaring the functions. Similarly, executing the following line from the Command Window:

```
system POINT p;put p
```

displays the current screen resolution as a list of two numbers expressed as pixels. The `send enterPage` statement is not necessary here, because the variables were set during the original running of the `enterPage` handler. (Recall that system variables persist through a ToolBook book instance.)

DLL functions whose values won't change often during the course of a book's lifetime should be declared in an `enterApplication` or `enterBook` handler as part of the initialization process, and the results should be put into containers for later use. The DLLs containing those functions should then be unlinked as soon as possible to conserve memory and improve performance. If you need the DLL often, keep it linked. An example of a DLL function that you may want to have available throughout the lifetime of an instance of your application is `LockWindowUpdate()`, from the Windows USER module.

But don't forget the "dynamic" part of a dynamic link library. A DLL can be linked at any point in the program and unlinked at any convenient point afterward to conserve memory. The demonstration of the preceding script, as it is implemented in `CH16.TBK`, actually does all its linking and unlinking within the button handlers. The use of a page script in the previous simple illustration makes using the Command Window easier. (Recall that commands keyed into the Command Window enter the system at page level.)

Individual functions can be unlinked by means of the `unlinkDLL function` or `unlinkDLL functions` (for use with multiple functions) commands. For example, to free only the resources associated with the `horizontalDisplayRes()` and `verticalDisplayRes()` functions, first ensure that they're linked and then unlink them, as follows:

```
if "horizontalDisplayRes()" is in DLLFunctions("TB30WIN.DLL")
    unlinkDLL function "horizontalDisplayRes()" from "TB30WIN.DLL"
end if
```

If you're checking for the existence of links, it's best to unlink functions one at a time. If you want to unlink more than one function, though, use this syntax:

```
unlinkDLL functions "horizontalDisplayRes(),verticalDisplayRes" \
                    from "TB30WIN.DLL"
```

Remember that this is one statement; the backslash character simply informs ToolBook that it's written on more than one typographical line. You can write it as one line in the Script editor window, omitting the backslash.

Tip

Don't link a DLL that's already linked; go back to the original link, and add any newly required function declarations there. If a DLL has been linked and unlinked, linking it again is okay. Functions have to be declared each time a link is established.

Caution

Although the `restore system` command unlinks all linked DLLs, it also restores some system properties, destroys system variables, and, in general, is a good thing to avoid until it's time for your program to begin or end. Unlink functions or DLLs explicitly during a program. When an application closes, DLLs are unlinked automatically.

User-Defined Functions. A *user-defined function* is a `TO GET` handler. The function is called by a `get` statement, and any parameters passed to it are enclosed in parentheses at the calling statement. The most telling feature of a function is the fact that it must include at least one `return` statement, which in turn requires one parameter. The value of this parameter is returned to the calling handler. Whenever a `TO GET` handler encounters a `return` statement, the handler is exited immediately.

Caution

A function must always have `return <value>` as its last active statement, whether or not that statement can ever be executed. Even if all of your actual returns are handled by statements earlier in the handler, you must still "return" something at the very end. For a return type of `STRING`, a default return value of `NULL` might be appropriate; for numerical values, return a value that matches the data type of a valid return statement.

As with any handlers, enter each of your function handlers at a level in the message hierarchy that is at or above all objects in the message hierarchy that might call them. Book- or system-book level is best in many cases.

Now it's time to get down to business. The *factorial* of a number `n` is the value of the formula `n = n * (n-1) * (n-2)...*(n-(n-1))`.

Note

Don't be put off by this sort of mathematical definition. Basically, what you're doing is taking a natural number and multiplying it by that number minus 1. Doing this multiplication repeatedly eventually leads to a value of 1 for the number and a potentially huge value for the accumulated product. This value is the factorial of the original number. A factorial is represented by the symbol !, which supposedly represents the startling rate at which the products increase. So `5! = 5*4*3*2*1`, or 120, but `10! = 3628800`. Why pick such an esoteric example? Because it illustrates so many OpenScript concepts, and because it's a good function to implement recursively in the next section.

ToolBook lacks a built-in function for finding the factorial of a number. You can implement this function in a user-defined handler. The following example (with embellishments) is included as page 2 of `CH16.TBK`, supplied on the accompanying disc. If you want to create the example from scratch, create a second page in the copy of `CH16.TBK`, which you built during the exercise using Listings 16.1 and 16.2. The page requires two fields: a single-line field, with typing enabled, named `f`; and a non-wordwrap field, with typing disabled, named `f2`. Implement the function for an input number `n` with the handler, shown in Listing 16.3, placed in the script of the page or book:

Listing 16.3 16LST03.DOC Calculation of Factorial: Iterative Method

```
TO GET iFactorial n
    local REAL result
    local LONG i
    if (not isType ("WORD", n)) or (n = 0)
        return 0
    end if
    result = 1
    step i from 1 to n
        result = result * i
    end step
    return result
END iFactorial
```

The declaration of the variable `result` as type `REAL` is merely to get the relatively huge range of a `REAL` (64 bits). An untyped variable would have worked just as well in this case, because the minuscule gain in efficiency achieved by typing the variable is swamped by the slow algorithm used.

The first thing to do is to ensure that the entered value is a natural number. A ToolBook built-in function, `isType()`, is called to determine whether the entry can be interpreted as type `WORD`. Because a `WORD` cannot contain a fraction or a negative number, the function returns `False` if the entry `n` is one of those. This is a good example of using data typing to prevent an erroneous value from being assigned to a variable.

Note

The `isType()` function returns a `LOGICAL` (`True` or `False`) value. The unary logical operator `not` is used before the function to tell the `if` structure to execute if the function expression is not true.

Type WORD does include the value zero, however, which must be excluded by a further condition in the if statement. (None of the pairs of parentheses in the if statement are necessary, by the way; the parentheses are placed there to set off the conditions for better legibility.) The conditions could have been met by this statement as well:

```
if (not isType(INT, n)) or (n < 1)
```

You may use it if it appeals to you. The exclusion of an INT's negative values, as well as 0, is accomplished here by the expedient of excluding every value below 1. The isType() function is used only to exclude fractional values. (These are, by no means, the only methods of determining whether a number is a natural number.)

Note

If you find the not operator confusing, substitute a statement such as the following:

```
if isType(WORD,n) = false or n = 0
```

As usual, only one or two of many variations of each statement is illustrated.

Tip

Notice the use of quotation marks around isType()'s first parameter, WORD, in the original example. The quotation marks are necessary only when you use isType() to check for type WORD, not for other types or formats.

If the value entered is inappropriate, the return statement inside the if structure executes, forcing the function to terminate and return a value of 0 (which the calling handler, to be discussed later in this section, defines as an error condition that it must deal with).

Note

The keyDown message is forwarded before the return statement causes the function handler to be destroyed. Doing this allows other processes farther up the message hierarchy to intercept the keyDown message, if necessary. A message is forwarded automatically only if no handler exists for it at a given level.

If the value of n passes the tests, the function proceeds to calculate the factorial of n in an iterative manner. First, the result is set to the lowest sensible value (1), as an initialization. Then a step flow structure (to be discussed in the "Control Structures" section of this chapter) runs, using the variable i as a counter. result is its own temporary store, and its value is accumulated by repeated multiplications. When i reaches the value of the user's initial entry, the calculation is complete; the step structure is terminated, and the value of result is returned to the calling handler.

The calling handler is placed in the script of the field named `f`, which is used as the data entry field, as shown in Listing 16.4.

Listing 16.4 16LST04.DOC Calculation of Factorial: Data Validation

```
TO HANDLE keyDown k
local STRING s
if k <> keyEnter
     forward
     break keyDown
end if
get iFactorial (text of self)
if it > 0
    s = It
else
    s = "Invalid Entry. Please try again."
end if
text of field "f2" of this page = s
END keyDown
```

Once again, the entry is tested for inappropriateness at the beginning of the handler; the handler runs only if the parameter in question passes the test. It's actually shorter to test for the appropriateness of a value, putting the entire body of the handler inside the `if` structure. The first method is used here because it keeps related groups of statements close to one another for improved readability.

What you are testing for this time is whether the key value passed with the `keyDown` message (the parameter is called `k` in this case) represents the Enter key. If not, some other key has been pressed; forward the message for possible use by other handlers, and get out quickly with a `break` statement. (The `break` statement, to be discussed in more detail in the "Control Structures" section later in this chapter, causes an immediate exit from a handler from inside an `if` structure.) The message name is optional in this case.

If the key pressed is the Enter key, the handler proceeds to call the `iFactorial` function. Recall that this function returns zero if the entered value is inappropriate. The text of field `f2` is set accordingly by testing the return value; an added measure of safety (probably unnecessary) is provided by having the second `if` statement test whether the value is greater than zero. The value returned by the `iFactorial` function (or an error message) is displayed by taking advantage of OpenScript's automatic numeral-to-text conversion: the value of a numerical variable becomes the text of a field in one case, and a string literal becomes the text in the other case.

The `iFactorial` function could be polished a bit. No provision is made for indicating an overflow condition in field `f2`, for example; the Execution Suspended message box simply informs you that an overflow has occurred. Because growth of the factorial of a number is such that the largest number that can be evaluated within ToolBook is 170 (yielding 7.257415615307994e+306—a 306-digit decimal number), overflow is easy to instigate. This example also exhibits a rather extreme case of roundoff error, because ToolBook displays only 16 of the digits.

Recursive Functions. The factorial calculation also is the classic illustration of the way that recursion can be used in a function. A *recursive function* is one that calls itself at some point in its execution. This type of function seldom is absolutely necessary (it uses additional system resources for each call to itself, and it requires care to prevent the function from attempting to call itself an infinite number of times). A small branch of computer science is devoted to discovering ways of eliminating recursion in every function for which it's considered necessary. Nevertheless, many programmers, especially those involved in artificial intelligence and, by extension, those exploring computer-based training, like recursive functions. The recursive version of the factorial function illustrates the concept.

Duplicate page 2 of your copy of `CH16.TBK`, or use the prebuilt page of that book supplied on the accompanying disc. The same page objects are required for the new page as for page 2; using Edit, Select Page, Edit Duplicate duplicates the page and its objects. The page script entered from Listing 16.3 and the field script from Listing 16.4 are duplicated as well. Change the page script to the one in Listing 16.5.

Listing 16.5 16LST05.DOC Factorial Computation Using Recursion

```
TO GET rFactorial n
    local REAL result
    local LONG i
if (not isType ("WORD", n)) or (n = 0)
        return 0
    end if
if n = 1
        return 1
    end if
    result = rFactorial(n-1) * n
    return result
END rFactorial
```

In this case, input values are winnowed, as in the handler for the iterative version (refer to Listing 16.4) of the function. The second `if` statement is necessary to prevent a *runaway function* (one that attempts to call itself an indefinite number of times); all recursive functions must have an escape hatch of some sort. This one takes advantage of the fact that the function counts down (rather than up, as in the iterative version) and therefore converges to 1. When 1 is reached, that particular copy of the function returns a value of `1`.

Why isn't the result of this function always 1? A newly generated copy of the function doesn't return to the calling handler, but to the copy of `rFactorial` that called it; `result` continues to be updated. Suppose that the entered number is 5. The function `rFactorial` is called by the calling handler; it then proceeds to call itself once during each of four additional loops. In each new copy, `n` is replaced by the expression `((n-1) * n)`. The fifth copy of the function returns `20` to the fourth copy; the fourth returns `12` to the third; and so on until `((n-1) * n)` = 1. At that point, the second `if` structure prevents any further calls to `rFactorial` by itself. But at that top level, the value of `n` is the original value of `n`. The second `if` structure is, therefore, not executed, and the function returns `answer`, which in this example is `5 * 4 * 3 * 2 * 1` (1 stops the process), or 120.

Pointers and Handles. OpenScript uses built-in functions to dereference pointers and handles (see Table 16.2).

Caution

Manipulation of pointers and handles can damage memory locations used by ToolBook, Windows, and other applications. Ensure that you save all work before using any of the functions described in Table 16.2.

Note

A *pointer* is a memory address. A *handle* is a pointer to a pointer. To *dereference* a pointer or handle is to get or set the value of the memory location to which it refers.

Table 16.2 Pointer Functions Allow Getting and Setting of Values by Address

Function	Return and New Value Type	Size
`pointerByte()`	`BYTE`	1 byte
`pointerDouble()`	`DOUBLE`	8 bytes
`pointerDWord()`	`DWORD`	4 bytes
`pointerFloat()`	`FLOAT`	4 bytes
`pointerInt()`	`INT`	2 bytes
`pointerPointer()`	`POINTER`	4 bytes
`pointerString()`	`STRING`	user-determined
`pointerWord()`	`WORD`	2 bytes

Each of the pointer functions takes two or three parameters. The first parameter always is the *offset*: a number of bytes added to the pointer to take you to, for example, a given member of a structure when the pointer contains the address of the beginning of the structure. The second parameter is the pointer itself. The third, optional parameter is a value with which to replace the current value in the memory location "pointer + offset." When you calculate the offset, which always is in bytes, take into account the size of the data that you're passing and returning. To get to an item in an array of `LONG`s, for example, count the offset by fours.

See the example "Using RECT Structures" in the book `\MTB30\samples\library.tbk` (its Program Manager item is named Script Library) for a detailed example of using `pointerInt()`).

One set of handles, or pointers to pointers, which you will use quite a bit in scripts in books with multiple windows and in scripts of media-rich books, is the various window handles necessary to create, control, and maintain multiple windows. A window handle is a number of type DWORD that is assigned by Windows to a window upon creation. If that window is destroyed (as when a digital video window or a viewer closes), that window's window handle is destroyed as well and you must not use it again to refer to the window. (Windows may decide to reassign the number of a previously destroyed window to a newly created window, but that fact does not relate the two windows in any way.)

OpenScript contains many ways of manipulating window handles. You may use expressions such as `windowHandle of viewer "viewer 2"`, `windowHandle of mainWindow`, `windowHandle of targetWindow`, and, using implicit reference, `windowHandle of this window`, where `this window` is generally the target window or the active window (which is usually the same window in any case).

> **Tip**
>
> The system property `sysCientHandle` may be used instead of the full designation `windowHandle of mainWindow`. The system property `activeWindowHandle` is available for identifying the active window.

Sometimes you'll want to find out which window is referenced by a certain window handle. An OpenScript built-in function, `windowRefFromHandle()`, returns a description (in ToolBook object syntax) of a window when passed the window's handle. For example, to assign the play window of a clip to a certain viewer, you may use the clip property `mmDeviceHandle`:

```
parentWindow of windowRefFromHandle(mmDeviceHandle) = viewer id 2
```

As usual in programming, there are several ways of accomplishing the same goal. When changing the parent window of a viewer, for instance, it's easy to simply assign the new parent window's window handle to the value of the viewer property `parentWindow` of the reassigned viewer.

Control Structures

The section, "Structured Programming" of Chapter 13, "OpenScript Fundamentals" pointed out that part of what puts the structure in structured programming is script blocks, which control what data is processed. The synonymous terms *control structure* and *flow structure* were introduced in Chapter 13 without further elaboration, and they have been used when necessary (but without much comment) in the example scripts of Part IV. This section examines the various control structures of OpenScript. Most of these structures have counterparts in other languages, although a special one called `translateWindowMessage` specifically provides for direct processing of messages generated by Windows.

if/then/else

This structure is so basic to programming that its use has been taken for granted in numerous examples. This structure is the basic *conditional* structure, meaning that if a condition is `True`, one task is performed and that if a condition is `False`, another task is performed. The condition can be one of inclusion (`if n = 1; return 1; end if`) or omission (`if not isType(INT,n);return 0;end if`). To use `if/then/else`, follow these steps:

1. Establish the condition. The condition must evaluate to `True` or `False`.
2. (Optional) If you like the natural-language look of the word `then`, include it in the conditional line.
3. Determine the action(s) to be performed if the conditional statement evaluates to `True`.
4. (Optional) Determine the action(s) to be performed if the conditional statement evaluates to `False`. Use the `else` keyword to tell OpenScript that such an optional action exists.

   If no action is desired for an evaluation to `False`, skip to step 6.
5. If `else` is in use, add its action(s); if not, skip to step 6.
6. Close the structure with an `end if` statement. (This step is not optional.)

For illustration, examine the following `if` structure:

```
if n = 0 then
    text of field "f" of this page = "Your entry is out of range."
else
    go to page "Test 32"
end if
```

An `if` structure with no `else` command should be a familiar sight by now:

```
if n = 0
    text of field "f" of this page = "Your entry is out of range."
end if
```

Use the `if/then/else` structure whenever a choice between two courses of action must be made. Often, `if` statements play a crucial role in application initialization and data verification, as in the examples of factorial functions presented in the preceding sections, "User-Defined Functions" and "Recursive Functions."

> **Note**
>
> If your condition relies on a property or value that is set to a logical value automatically, don't use processing time by testing it against literal `True/False` values. Instead of the following:
>
> ```
> if visible of viewer "Stamps" = TRUE
> ...statements...
> ```
>
> use this:
>
> ```
> if visible of viewer "Stamps"
> ...statements...
> ```
>
> Because `visible` always contains a logical value, no reason exists to assign it one explicitly.

`if` statements can be nested. In the `iFactorial` script (refer to Listing 16.4 in the "User-Defined Functions" section of this chapter), the first `if`, rather than relying on two conditions, could have been two nested structures, as shown in Listing 16.6.

Listing 16.6 16LST06.DOC Simple usage of *if* (with *break* and *forward*)

```
if isType("WORD",n)
    if n = 0
        forward
        break
    end if
end if
```

Notice that each `if` statement requires its own `end if` statement.

`if` statements can be nested as deeply as necessary. In most cases, though, deep nesting (which is fairly hard to keep track of, let alone modify) can be avoided through the use of one of the other flow structures, especially `conditions/when/else`.

***break* in *if/then/else* Structures.** `break` is another OpenScript command that so far has been used with little or no explanation.

The purpose of the `break` command is simply to stop execution of the current handler or, in specified cases to be discussed in the following sections, the current control structure. If you use `break` in the body of an `if/then/else` structure, the statement causes the entire handler to end. No further parameters are associated with `break` in an `if` construct, although you can use the command `break to system`.

break to system. `break` normally restores control to the parent handler or, if it is executed in the topmost calling handler, to the ToolBook system. One form of the `break` command, `break to system`, exits the current handler, skips any calling handlers (including the topmost handler, even if it's in a system book), and returns program control to the system. This command can be used as a command statement or as the result of a condition in a flow structure.

conditions/when/else

Closely related to the `if/then/else` control structure is the `conditions/when/else` block. This type of statement block is like a multiple choice `if/else` statement in which an action is taken in response to the logical value of an expression. The conditions actually need not have anything to do with one another. Like the `if` block, an optional else statement can be provided to execute if none of the conditions evaluates to `True`.

Listing 16.7 shows the general form of the `conditions` structure.

Listing 16.7 16LST07.DOC Usage of *conditions/when/else*

```
conditions
--t1 is any expression which returns a logical value
when t1 = TRUE
        go to page "stoats" --or any other valid statements
--t2 is any expression which returns a logical value
when t2 = TRUE
        go to page "goats" --or any other valid statements
--t1 is any expression which returns a logical value
        go to page "cats" --or any other valid statements
    else --optional
--use any valid statements
 go to page "and especially rabbits"
    end conditions --not optional
```

The similarity of this structure to that of the `if/then/else` form is evident. In this case, three choices plus a default choice exist.

Using `conditions`, you can modify the factorial script to return more information about the nature of an erroneous entry. Replace the iterative factorial handler of Listing 16.4 with the one shown in Listing 16.8. This listing is implemented on page 3 of `CH16.TBK`. The `conditions` structure now takes up most of the script and queries the input value several times about what data type it is. Notice that the type specifier `STRING` is useless for excluding numerals, because an OpenScript string can be composed of numerals.

Listing 16.8 16LST08.DOC Using *conditions* to Validate Input Data

```
TO GET iFactorial2 n
    local REAL @result
    local STRING s
    local LONG i
    conditions
        when not isType(REAL,n)
            s = "That's a string."
            break conditions
        when isType(INT,n) and n < 0
            s = "That's a negative number."
            break conditions
        when n = 0
```

(continues)

Listing 16.8 Continued

```
            s = "You have entered zero."
            break conditions
        when not isType("WORD",n)
            s = "That's a fraction."
            break conditions
        else
            @result = 1
            step i from 1 to n
                @result = @result * i
            end step
            return @result
        end conditions
        return s & CRLF & "Please enter a positive integer."
END iFactorial2
```

More importantly, the order in which the `when` statements occur in this `conditions` structure is important. This situation is a blessing, not a curse, if it is understood and used properly. Specifically, the following condition in Listing 16.8:

```
when not isType("WORD",n)
```

must be the final one, because it depends on `n`'s failing all the other tests. You get off pretty easily in this case; you'll find the `conditions` structure to be a useful tool with which to sift statements that depend on one another in much more complex ways.

step

Another flow construct used in the factorial function is the `step` structure. This flow-control method has the advantage that a single statement can be used to initialize the variable that counts the number of steps, to specify how many steps are to be counted, and to evaluate the step limit (if that is a function, variable, or property).

A *step* is an opportunity to execute statements. The statements, of course, appear inside the body of the `step` structure; evaluations are performed by using the current value of the `counter` variable. Each time the statement block encounters an `end step` (or `break` or `continue`) statement, the `step` structure determines whether the value of the counter has reached its maximum. If the counter value has not reached its maximum, the body statements repeat, this time using the new value of the counter to perform calculations. If the counter value has reached its maximum, the `step` process is complete, and the next script statement executes. In other words, a `step` structure is a loop.

The typographical representation of a `step` structure is somewhat different than for an `if` or `conditions` block. Follow this model to write a `step` structure:

1. Establish the starting value of the counter. A variable, often named `i` and of type `LONG`, usually is used as the counter.

2. Establish the ending value of the counter. You can do this by specifying a numeric literal, variable, or function return value. You can count down by making the end value smaller than the start value. You may use a negative number as a start or end value..

3. Establish the span of the steps. You may, for example, be interested in every other item in a list. In such a case, the step value would be 2; the counter is incremented by 2 each time the structure steps. If counting down, you could specify the interval as –2. If the step value is +1, this parameter becomes optional.

4. Determine and enter the OpenScript statements that define action(s) to be performed if the conditional statement evaluates to `True`.

5. Close the structure with an `end step` argument. (This step is not optional.)

To illustrate the full syntax, look at the slightly expanded `step` structure from your factorial function:

```
step i from 1 to n by 1
    @result = @result * i
end step
```

The `by 1` phrase is optional, in this case, because the default is 1.

while

When it's necessary to use a logical value to control a loop, the `while` structure is a good choice. `while` loops through a block of statements until its conditional variable or function evaluates to `False`. The `step` and `while` constructs often are interchangeable. You always can turn a numerical value into a logical value by using a comparison operator and turn a logical value into a number by using an `if` block.

To create a `while` loop, follow these steps:

1. Establish and initialize the logical variable or function.

2. Determine the logical condition necessary to get out.

3. Close the structure with an `end while` statement.

4. Determine the block statements. Unlike the `step` loop, `while` doesn't manipulate a counter automatically; you must do this in the main statement block. Initialization of the counter also is your responsibility; this occurs before the `while` loop is entered. If the counter is initialized in the while loop, unpredictable performance and the opportunity for a possible infinite loop result.

5. Close the structure with an `end while` statement. (This step is not optional.)

Listing 16.9 hauls out the factorial loop again, this time to show what it looks like as a `while` loop:

Listing 16.9 16LST09.DOC Factorial Engine Using a *while* Loop

```
i = 1
while i <> n
@result = @result * i
i = i + 1
end while
```

Notice the manual initialization and updating of the counter `i`.

do...until

As mentioned earlier, the `step` and `while` structures have many properties in common. One common characteristic is the fact that the statement block requires an input value that is within the range that causes the handler to run. In a `while` structure, for example, the loop won't run if the value of the conditional variable is `False` to begin with. Although such a scenario is possible as a result of poor initialization and out-of-range entries as well as in normal program execution, the fact remains that whatever the situation is, the statements in a `while` (or `step`) loop have no chance to act on the input data, even to correct it. The loop statements never see the data at all.

To ensure that your control structure runs at least one time, consider using a `do...until` loop. The handler barges right into this kind of loop, executing the statement block at least once. As in the `while` loop, the conditional statement, which is evaluated at the end of each loop rather than at the beginning as in the other looping structures, must yield a logical value, and counter handling is the programmer's job. Typical uses include replacement of menu and list items, in which failure of a code block to run can lead to visually unsatisfactory results, or worse.

Another good use of the `do...until` routine is to determine the drive or directory that holds a key file; the purpose simply is to make sure that the directory is found. A typical use of this technique is to set the `CDMediaPath` property manually.

Tip

Use the code shown in Listing 16.2 to bypass the Media Packager if you want to know whether files originally supplied on a CD-ROM are on any mounted drive of any kind.

The operation of the handler described in Listing 16.2 should be fairly clear by now. The handler searches drive letters `c` through `z` for a file that you'll have to create. Try a Windows Notepad file named `KEY.TXT` and save it in the same directory with your media files. (If you think that nobody has a `z` drive, think again. `z` is a good mnemonic letter and is used.) If all the letters have been searched without success, the next letter is "`.`"—an invalid drive specification that causes an error message to pop up. The key file must be searched for at least one time, making the search task a good candidate for a `do...until` loop.

break and *continue*

`break` was discussed earlier in the context of the `if/then/else` structure. Recall that in that structure, the `break` command breaks out of the entire handler, and the `continue` command is not used.

Things are different with the other flow constructs. In these constructs, the `break` command can be used to break out of the entire handler or simply out of the control structure. Here's where structured programming really comes up to speed and starts being fun.

The `continue` command serves as a complement to the `break` command. Each command is an instruction for a loop to stop processing at a point before the control structure nominally completes its tasks. Instead of exiting the structure of the handler, however, the command returns control to the beginning of the loop, as though the loop had completed normally. For `step` loops, this situation means that the counter is adjusted normally, although statements that directly manipulate the counter variable can be used to override the default stepping. The manual counter indexing of `do` and `while` structures require the programmer to write the statements that increment, decrement, or ignore the counter's value. You can add the name of the loop type after a `break` or `continue` to help in visually tracing nested loops. In the case of the `step` loop, you also can add a variable reference as a parameter to `continue`, so that a loop other than the innermost loop runs.

To use the `continue` command, create a page containing a field in which typing is enabled; then enter the statements shown in Listing 16.10 in the script of the field. (This example is on page 4 of `CH16.TBK`.) The handler converts the double spaces that sometimes appear between sentences to single spaces, which are more suitable for use with variable-pitch fonts. In this case, you must type the entry text (possibly including double spaces) in the field and then press Enter.

Listing 16.10 16LST10.DOC Using *continue* and *break*

```
TO HANDLE keyDown k
local LONG i, cc
    if k <> keyEnter or text of self = NULL
        forward
        break
    end if
    cc = charCount(text of self)
    step i from 1 to cc
        if char i of text of self = SPACE
            if char(i + 1) of text of self <> SPACE
                continue step
            else
                clear char i of text of self
                cc = cc - 1
            end if
        end if
    end step
END keyDown
```

translateWindowMessage

A completely different kind of control structure, the `translateWindowMessage` structure, is the one through which you can process messages from Windows directly. This structure is rather dangerous to your application's health if it is improperly used; make sure that you are familiar with Windows messaging, work on a copy rather than the original of your book, and remember to save your work often. The basic steps in using this structure are:

1. Establish the Windows message(s) that you want to intercept. The on-line Windows API help file or any Windows programming manual contains most of the message numbers and names. Use the message number, as OpenScript does not automatically recognize any Windows message names.
2. Establish the OpenScript message(s) that you want to send or the property that you want to get upon reception of the Windows message(s). You can send only one message from a single statement but can include several statements in one control structure. You can call a function or get a user property (that is, you can call a `TO GET` handler).
3. (Optional) If you're calling a function or getting a property, determine the desired ToolBook object target. If no target is specified, the message is sent to the page.
4. If you're calling a function or getting a property, determine the data type of the return value. This step is, of course, irrelevant if you are just sending a message.
5. Establish which window will be processing the messages. If you intend to use the main window, which is the default, the window need not be specified.
6. Close the structure with an `end translateWindowMessage` statement. (This step is not optional.)

The `translateWindowMessage` structure is illustrated in its message-sending form in the mouse scroll example on page 4 of `CH16.TBK`. If you really want to build the example from scratch, you must first switch to Author level if necessary and create a book with one page. This is all you need, except for the page's script and an external bitmap file which, when displayed, is larger than the ToolBook window. The bitmap `STOATS8.BMP`, supplied in the same directory as the book `CH16.TBK`, should suffice if you are running your video card at a resolution of 640 × 480. Put the script, whose text is Listing 16.11, at page level.

Listing 16.11 16LST11.DOC Translating Windows Messages

```
TO HANDLE EnterPage
    system LOGICAL scanning
    system INT xs,ys
    system DWORD hWnd
--use the system property sysPageUnitsPerPixel for screen unit
--to pixel conversions. You can also use the various conversion
--functions.
--Assign variables just to avoid having to key in so many
--characters as you enter the handlers
```

Listing 16.11 Continued

```
    xs = item 1 of sysPageUnitsPerPixel
    ys = item 2 of sysPageUnitsPerPixel
--Initialize the "scanning" flag so that scrolling is off:
    scanning = FALSE
--Establish the path to the bitmap. In this case, the bitmap
--is assumed to be in the same folder as the book.
get last word of name of this book
while last char of it <> "\"
    clear last char of it
end while
--Open bitmap and set the parent window of its display window.
get imagecommand("open" && it & "stoats8.bmp alias bmp1 style" \
    && "child parent" && sysClientHandle && "wait")
get imagecommand("window bmp1 state maximized")
hWnd = imagecommand("status bmp1 window")
get imagecommand("play bmp1")
--Translate messages from the Windows operating system
--and send OpenScript messages to the ToolBook system:
translateWindowMessage for hWnd
    on 513 send bDown     --513 is sent on left button down
    on 514 send bUp       --513 is sent on left button up
end translateWindowMessage
--Forward the enterPage message so higher levels receive it:
    forward
END EnterPage
TO HANDLE leavePage
    unTranslateAllWindowMessages
    get imageCommand("close all")
    forward
END leavePage
TO HANDLE bDown
    system LOGICAL scanning
    system POINT location
    system DWORD hWnd
--This is the handler called by the translated Windows message 513.
--It sets "scanning" so that the scroller operates
--and establishes the initial mouse position.
    scanning = TRUE
    location = mousePosition of this window
END bDown
TO HANDLE bUp
    system LOGICAL scanning
    system DWORD hWnd
--This is the handler called by the translated Windows message 513.
--It resets "scanning" so that the scroller does not operate.
--the idle handler will restore the appropriate
--cursor when idle messages resume.
    sysCursor = 4     --"wait" cursor (hourglass)
    scanning = FALSE
END bUp
TO HANDLE idle
    system LOGICAL scanning
    system POINT location
    local POINT bmpOffset
```

(continues)

Listing 16.11 Continued

```
    local POINT bmpSlop
    local POINT bmpLoc,newPos,currentLoc
    system INT xs,ys
--the idle handler will restore the appropriate
--cursor when idle messages resume after Windows message 514
--is translated and handled.
--exit handler without processing and restore normal cursor
--if "scanning" is not TRUE:
    if not scanning
        if sysCursor <> 44
            sysCursor = 44
        end if
        break
    end if
--idle is a repeating message, so prevent flicker and
--slowdown by setting the cursor only if needed. Use the
--four-pointed cursor to indicate when scrolling is available:
    if sysCursor <> 7
        sysCursor = 7
    end if
--bmpOffset is how much the mouse has been moved since
--the previous idle message:
    get mousePosition of this window
    item 1 of bmpOffset = (item 1 of It - item 1 of location)
    item 2 of bmpOffset = (item 2 of It - item 2 of location)
--bmpSlop is the amount of motion available.
--Each of the 2 items, which represent width and height,
--are computed from the full size of the bitmap. The
--screen size is subtracted so the picture doesn't move
--offscreen, and each item is multiplied by the number
--of twips per pixel. However, no stretching or shrinking
--actually occurs when the resolution changes.
    get imageCommand("where bmp1 source wait")
    item 1 of bmpSlop = (item 3 of It - 640) * xs
    item 2 of bmpSlop = (item 4 of It - 480) * ys
--bmpLoc is the present position of the bitmap, in
--pixels multiplied by twips per pixel.
    bmpLoc = curLoc()
--Calculate the points at which scrolling must
--stop because the edge of the picture meets the
--edge of the window:
    conditions
        when (item 1 of bmpLoc + item 1 of bmpOffset ) <= 0 \
             and (item 2 of bmpLoc + item 2 of bmpOffset) <= 0 \
             and (item 1 of bmpLoc + item 1 of bmpOffset) > \
                 -item 1 of bmpSlop \
             and (item 2 of bmpLoc + item 2 of bmpOffset) > \
                 - item 2 of bmpSlop
            break conditions
        else
            break idle
    end conditions
--Update the bitmap position to account for scrolling:
    item 1 of curLoc = (item 1 of bmpLoc + item 1 of bmpOffset)
    item 2 of curLoc = (item 2 of bmpLoc + item 2 of bmpOffset)
```

Listing 16.11 Continued

```
--Update the location of the cursor:
    location = mousePosition of this window
--Update the position of the bitmap:
--"self" is the page and is just a placeholder
    set bmpLoc of self to curLoc
END idle
TO GET curLoc
    system INT xs,ys
    local POINT z
    get imageCommand("status bmp1 position wait")
    item 1 of z = (item 1 of It) * xs
    item 2 of z = (item 2 of It) * ys
    return z
END curLoc
TO SET bmpLoc to curLoc
    system INT xs,ys
    get imageCommand("window bmp1 position" \
        && (item 1 of curLoc)/xs & "," \
        & (item 2 of curLoc)/ys && "wait")
END bmpLoc
```

In use, pressing and holding the left mouse button within the bounds of the picture changes the mouse pointer to a four-pointed arrow and allows the user to push a Windows bitmapped image around the screen, using the ToolBook client window as a clipping rectangle. Releasing the button ends push-around functionality and restores the mouse pointer to its original state.

From the script's perspective, pressing the left button causes Windows to send message 513, which is translated by the `translateWindowMessage` structure into the custom message `bDown`. The `bDown` message is sent to the `bDown` handler, which simply sets `scanning` (a flag to switch push-around scrolling on and off) to `True` (on) and shows the four-pointed cursor. When the mouse button is released, 514 is translated into `bUp`, whose handler turns off scrolling and restores the pointing-hand cursor.

The push-around functionality is provided by an `idle` handler. If `scrolling` is `True`, each time an `idle` message is received by the page, the `idle` handler checks for mouse movement. If there has been any movement, the handler then checks to make sure that the bitmap hasn't scrolled off the screen. If the bitmap is in a position to be moved, it is moved. Finally, the new position of the bitmap is stored for use when the next `idle` message arrives.

This script is more a template than a usable tool. Specifically, you can use the `buttonDown`, `buttonUp`, and `buttonStillDown` messages to create a scrolling picture, though not without using a stage object. The reason that translating Windows messages is necessary is that there is no stage object to receive the button messages; the displayed image of the bitmap is not a ToolBook object and cannot receive OpenScript messages. But it is a Windows object, so it generates and responds to Windows messages. Nevertheless, nearly everything that's been discussed in this chapter is represented in the script. Notice, in particular, the `break` statement with no parameter; such a break exits the entire handler. Contrast this usage of `break` with the `conditions` block that determines screen limits; this structure was written specially to illustrate the difference between a `break conditions` statement, which merely causes an exit from the control structure, and a break from a handler statement. In the first case, the statements following the `conditions` structure execute; in the second case, they don't.

Also of interest is the call to a user-defined `TO SET` handler, `TO SET bmpLoc to curLoc` and a user-defined function, `TO GET bmpLoc()`. The function also serves as the `TO SET` handler's `TO GET` handler, demonstrating that, in a practical sense, a `TO GET` handler can always be viewed as a function, which sometimes happens to be written to return the value of a property that has been set by a `TO SET` construct. The `TO SET` and `TO GET` handlers are actually superfluous as used because they contain only one to three statements each, but features are easy to add to such handlers. Another advantage of using custom handlers is that one functional unit may be called by other handlers as needed.

The sequential `if` structures in the `idle` loop are not a result of poor optimization. In an `idle` or `buttonStillDown` handler, it's important to check each possible combination of property states separately, because the idea is to prevent screen flicker and severely degraded performance caused by repeated redraws. To check a value for such a purpose, the behavior for each possible result must be evaluated and handled.

The main illustration in the code listing is of the `translateWindowMessage` structure. The messages translated are Windows messages 513 and 514, which correspond to left button down and up, respectively. A user-defined message is sent each time a message of one of those values is sent by Windows. The message translation continues until translation of one or more of them is canceled by an `untranslateWindowMessage` statement or, as in Listing 16.11, an `untranslateAllWindowMessages` statement.

To send a Windows message directly to the ToolBook system for default processing by Windows, include a `forward to system` statement in the called handler.

If you're translating the Windows `ActivateApp` message, OpenScript provides several parameters automatically. Refer to the ToolBook on-line help system for details.

start spooler

When you are printing from a script, you can invoke the `print` command only from within a `start spooler` structure. To set up printing, follow these steps:

1. Establish the first page to be printed, and navigate to that page, if you're not already on it.
2. Establish how many pages are to be printed. This number can be a positive integer for a range of pages, or `ALL` for all pages.
3. Establish other properties of the printed material, such as more complex page and background selection and formatting. This procedure often requires loops or other structures in the body of the `start spooler` structure.

4. Include a `print` command. The number of pages to be printed is passed to this command as an argument.
5. Close the structure with an `end spooler` statement. (This step is not optional.)

To print the first three pages of a book, use the following format:

```
start spooler
    go to page 1
    print 3
end spooler
```

in

The `in` control structure specifies the viewer in which a block of statements is to be executed. Recall that viewers are not in the main message hierarchy. If one viewer is the target window and you want to manipulate objects in a different viewer, you must do so explicitly. Follow these steps:

1. Establish the name or ID of the desired viewer.
2. Insert your statement(s). Remember that viewers show pages, so page and background object references have to be expressed in terms of what's displayed in the viewer.
3. Close the structure with an `end in` statement. (This step is not optional.)

You can use the `in` structure to send statements from the main window to a pop-up or child viewer, or the other way around, as follows:

```
in viewer "Display 2"
    hide menubar
end in
```

Use functions and control structures freely in your scripts. Become especially familiar with the `in viewer...` structure. You will be unable to define or trace message flow among windows unless you're comfortable with the means of modifying the normal message hierarchy.

From Here...

You've learned in this chapter about the structure of expressions, which are about the building blocks of statements, and about functions, which can be built-in to OpenScript, written by you, or utilized by linking to a function library. Expressions and functions return values; containers such as variable and properties receive values. Directing this movement of information are the various control structures. You now have at your disposal the tools of programming in OpenScript.

- To find out more about using DLLs, see Chapter 11, "Working with Text."
- To find out more about the `TO HANDLE`, `TO SET`, and `TO GET` control structures, see Chapter 13, "OpenScript Fundamentals."

- To find out more about the `NOTIFYBFORE` and `NOTIFYAFTER` control structures, see Chapter 14, "Messages, Objects, and Properties."
- To find out more about using DLLs, see Chapter 19, "Using Dynamic Link Libraries (DLLs) and Dynamic Data Exchange (DDE)."
- To find out more about the `in` control structures, see Chapter 8, "Working with Viewers."

CHAPTER 17

Data and File Management

Understanding file management in any programming language is one of the keys to creating usable programs. There are a variety of file types that you will want to use with Multimedia ToolBook. These include:

- Text files (ASCII, Rich Text)
- ToolBook files (book and system books)
- Windows initialization files (INI files)
- Data files (database files, and so on)
- Multimedia elements (sound, graphics, video, animation)

External file access is handled in a variety of ways, depending on the type of information that is incorporated in the file. And, to make things just a bit more confusing, there is always more than one way to handle the same basic task in Multimedia ToolBook (MTB). Your decision of the best means of handling any file operation is going to depend on your particular application. At times, you may choose one method over another because of the ease of programming. In other cases, you will be more interested in speed considerations. And, in still other cases, your main consideration might be providing an interface for your user that is similar to other Windows applications that they use. The exact nature of the your application will determine exactly what programming techniques you use.

Organizing data for effective and efficient delivery to the end user is an important consideration for the application developer. This chapter offers guidance to help you do the following:

- Use low-level file functions for managing data
- Import and format text
- Create custom indexes to support full text searches

Importing and Exporting Text

MTB is an extremely full-featured programming environment that offers so many features it is difficult to imagine how they were all thought up! One of these handy features, data import, makes it very easy to set up record fields from raw data. In most cases, when you use Windows programs you would use DDE or OLE to share information. But there are still a great many applications that are commonly used that do not support DDE or OLE. For example, the popular accounting package PeachTree does not support DDE, but does have a means of exporting data—PeachTree Data Query. Other examples include many of the popular statistics programs like Systat and some of the older spreadsheet programs, such as Reflex.

If the application you want to share information with writes out a delimited-field text file (that is, the data is written out with commas or tabs between entries), then follow these steps to create a ToolBook file that contains the data:

1. Open your book (or better yet, test it in a new, empty book).
2. Choose File, Import from the menu bar and select `.TXT` as the Import Type.
3. Choose Text/Delimited fields and enter the delimiter. Use `^t` for tabs or the character that is used in the file.
4. Choose OK and then the name of the text file.

Caution

Quotation marks are used to set off strings. Do not use a quote for a delimiter!

Now, sit back and watch! ToolBook will import the data, creating a record for each data field. The record delimiters (usually carriage returns in your file) are translated to new pages. Thus, if you have five fields (such as `name`, `age`, `marital status`, `address`, and `phone`) there will be five record fields on each page, and each page will contain the name and other information from each record in the file. If this was your customer database and there were 5,000 customers, 5,000 pages would be created.

As is always the case in ToolBook, you can get the same effect by writing a script. The following command would do essentially the same process as the previously described steps:

```
import "mydata.txt" as delimited using ","
```

This is assuming, of course, that your data is in the file `mydata.txt` and items are separated by commas.

ToolBook also supports fixed field files. This is especially useful when interfacing with scientific codes that stream out data in fixed formats. When specifying the Reading Format for fixed fields, you must tell ToolBook the length of each field. These are specified in the Text - Fixed Fields Field Lengths box in the Text Format dialog box (see fig. 17.1).

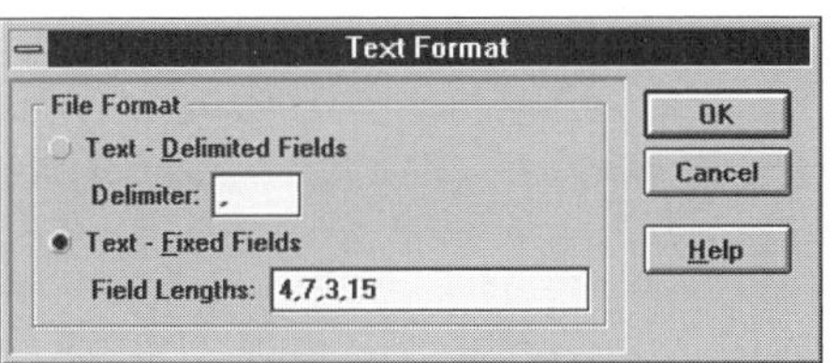

Fig. 17.1

Fixed field lengths are specified in the Text Format dialog box.

The example in the figure is for a text file that has four fields of lengths 4, 7, 3, and 15, respectively. This implies that the length of each line in the file will be 29 characters long. An OpenScript example that accomplishes the same thing is the following:

```
import "mydata.txt" as fixed using 4,7,3,15
```

In a similar way, you can use ToolBook to export record fields to fixed-length field or delimited field text files for other applications. The Export command will write out data from each page in the specified background, with fields in layer order and records in page order. The Export command can be accessed through the File menu, or through OpenScript using the following format:

```
export <fileName> as <fixed¦delimited> using <field-lengths¦separator>
```

In fixed-length records, some output formatting is possible; use a negative number to align data on the right (with blanks used to fill the left), a positive number to left align, and a number less than the number of characters in a field to truncate. Thus, if record fields `a`, `b`, and `c` contained `dog`, `cat`, and `mouse`, the following command:

```
export "junk.dat" as fixed using 5,-5,3
```

would result in the following data being written to the file `junk.dat`:

```
dog    catmou
```

The next section discusses general practices used for opening, reading, writing, and closing text files with MTB.

Reading and Writing Text

ToolBook provides a variety of text file commands; these include `createFile`, `openFile`, `readFile`, `writeFile`, and `closeFile`.

The command `createFile` is used to open a new file. It takes the argument `fileName`, which is the full pathname of the file to be created. If the file already exists, the existing file will be deleted, so be careful if this is not your intent! If the file exists and is read-only, the `sysError` variable will be set to `read-only`, and the file will not be deleted.

The command `openFile` opens a file that is already in existence. Up to ten files can be opened simultaneously in ToolBook. If the file does not exist, `sysError` will be set to `no such file`.

The command `readFile` can be used to either read to a specified character or for a specified number of characters. In theory, these features could be very useful. In practice, however, there is almost always an easier and/or faster way to get information into and out of a ToolBook file. The command is included because it is a standard feature of ToolBook and also because you might find it useful for "small" jobs, like temporary storage on disk of the contents of a field. When you need to perform quick data access, you will find it easier to store data in a database file format. (This topic is discussed in detail in Chapter 19, "Using Dynamic Link Libraries (DLLs) and Dynamic Data Exchange (DDE).")

The two formats for the `readFile` command are as follows:

```
readFile <fileName> to <character>
```

where `fileName` is any valid DOS filename and `character` is a literal character (such as `dog`) or a constant (such as `EOF`, which means "end-of-file"). The other format is the following:

```
readFile <fileName> for <number of characters>
```

where `number of characters` is the number of characters that are to be read.

The `readFile` command will read an ASCII file, initially positioning the `read` at the beginning of the file and then moving the pointer to the end of the text currently read (no surprises here). The results of the `read` are put into the `it` variable. When the end-of-file is reached, it is set to `null` and `sysError` is set to `end of file`.

> **Note**
>
> The end-of-file (EOF) constant is not read into `it`, so you cannot use a `while it is not EOF` sort of structure to read in data from a file—doing so will result in an infinite loop!

You can read the entire contents of an ASCII file into `it` with the following statement:

```
readFile fileToRead to EOF
```

Of course, doing so may lead to memory limitation problems if the file contains a lot of text! (For more information about the memory limitations in MTB, see the section "Multimedia ToolBook and Memory Management" in Chapter 20, "Fundamentals of Multimedia.")

When you have completed the `read` process, you need to explicitly close the file using the `closeFile` command. Listing 17.1 illustrates how you might use these commands to write a button handler to read data from a field `textBox` to a file that the user chooses. Notice that if the file already exists, the user will be given a choice to append or overwrite the existing file.

Listing 17.1 This Handler Exports Text from a Field to an ASCII File

```
to handle buttonUp
     -- save data from a field to a file
     clear sysError
     sysErrorNumber = 0
     sysSuspend=false
     ask "File name to save field data in?" with "data.tmp"
     if sysError is not "cancel" then
          put it into fileToOpen
          openFile fileToOpen
          put sysErrorNumber into openStatus
          conditions
               when openStatus = 0
                    --file successfully opened
                    request "File already exists! " & \
                    "Do you want to append data or overwrite?" \
                    with "append" or "overwrite" or "cancel"
                    conditions
                         when it is "overwrite"
                              closeFile fileToOpen
                              createFile fileToOpen
                         when it is "append"
                              --do nothing, already positioned at end
                         else
                              break buttonUp
                    end conditions
               when openStatus = 559
                    --no such file
                    createFile fileToOpen
               else
                    --some other file opening problem...
                    request "Cannot open file:" & fileToOpen with "OK"
                    break buttonUp
          end conditions
          clear sysError
          writeFile text of field "textBox" to fileToOpen
          if sysError is not null
               request "Could not write to file" && fileToOpen & "."
          end if
          closeFile fileToOpen
     end if
end buttonUp
```

After the contents of the field have been written to a disk file, you will want to use the `readFile` command to retrieve it. This could be accomplished by using the script in Listing 17.2.

Listing 17.2 This Handler Imports Text From an ASCII File Into a Field

```
to handle buttonUp
     clear sysError
     sysErrorNumber = 0
     sysSuspend=false
     ask "File name where data is stored?" with "data.tmp"
     if sysError is not "cancel" then
          put it into fileToOpen
          openFile fileToOpen
          put sysErrorNumber into openStatus
          conditions
               when openStatus = 0
                    --file successfully opened
                    break conditions
               when openStatus = 559
                    --no such file
                    request "File not found! Specify the full path name."
                      with "OKAY"
                    closeFile fileToOpen
                    break buttonUp
               else
                    request "File not found!" && \
                       "Specify the full path name." with "OKAY"
                    closeFile fileToOpen
                    break buttonUp
          end conditions
          clear sysError
          readFile fileToOpen to EOF
          if sysError is not null
               request "Problem reading file!" with "OKAY"
               break buttonUp
          end if
          closeFile fileToOpen
          put it into text of field "textBox"
     end if
end buttonUp
```

These examples are provided in the ToolBook file `CH1701.TBK` contained on the CD-ROM that was included in this book. These examples are intended as a starting point for creating your own scripts. In a usable application, you would either hide the operation from the user altogether—that is, you as the programmer would make the choice of the temporary filename, whether to append or overwrite, and so on—or you would provide the path to the filename for the user (for example, setting it and reading it from the `WIN.INI` file), or you would use the standard Windows file interface, discussed in Chapter 19, "Using Dynamic Link Libraries (DDLs) and Dynamic Data Exchange (DDE)."

Importing Books and Pages

Another very powerful feature of MTB is that it permits you to import other books and pages into a book. This is useful when you want to make use of viewers or resources from another book. To import pages from another book, you can use the menu interface. Choose File import type ToolBook files, and choose the format that you want to import (see fig. 17.2).

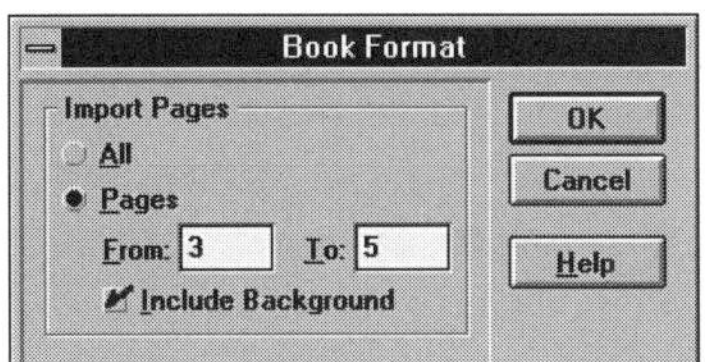

Fig. 17.2

The Book Format dialog assists in the process of importing pages (with or without their backgrounds) into the current book from another book.

Be sure to check Include Background if you want the background for the pages copied. The pages you import will be placed after the current page. The OpenScript equivalent for this is the following:

```
import pages 3 to 5 of book "junk.tbk"
```

If you want the pages, but not the background, use the following command:

```
import pages 3 to 5 of book "junk.tbk" without background
```

Importing an entire book is similar to the following:

```
import book "goodbook.tbk"
```

It is important to realize that importing a book will change that book's page numbers and page IDs. This is another good reason for explicitly naming all objects in your applications, rather than referencing the ID numbers assigned by ToolBook.

Importing pages with record fields is a little more complicated when you do not also import the background. ToolBook follows a hierarchy of preferences for placement of the imported text. First, it matches the record field name, looking for a record field with the same name. If the same record field name cannot be found, ToolBook attempts to match record ID numbers. If those do not match, then layer order is used, placing text in a field that has the same layer number.

Note

If a page is imported without its background and has data in record fields, and the background on which it is placed has fewer record fields than the source, the extra records are discarded by ToolBook.

Validating Entries

ToolBook provides many features that make it an ideal environment to use when creating applications that require a lot of interactivity; you would be hard-pressed to find any other programming environment easier to use for this purpose than

ToolBook. You can use ToolBook to create text or numeric entry fields that are self validating to provide an interface for users to input their responses to your questions.

The validation or checking of entries can be accomplished during the entry phase itself or after the user exits the field. The script in Listing 17.3 could be placed into the field that is being tested, limiting the user to the lowercase characters *a* through *z*.

Listing 17.3 Handlers to Check Entries Into a Field Are Easy to Construct

```
to handle keyUp key
     if key > 64 and key < 91 then
          -- this key is okay
          forward
     else
          request "please use lower case characters only"
     end if
end keyUp
```

This script uses the `keyUp` keyboard event message, which tests for the key that is released. Of course, this script has the problem that the disallowed character will still be placed in the text field. An example of a solution to this difficulty is to use the script in Listing 17.4.

Listing 17.4 An Improved Example Handler to Check for Data Input in a Field

```
to handle keyChar keyPressed
     if (keyPressed < 97 or keyPressed > 122) then
          break
     else
          forward
     end
end
```

In this example, the `keyChar` keyboard event message is used. This returns the ANSI value of the character pressed. The `keyChar`, `keyUp`, and `keyDown` events take the following general form:

```
keyXXX key,<isShift>,<isControl>
```

The optional returned value `isShift` returns `true` if the Shift key is held down while the other key is struck, while `isControl` returns `true` for a depressed Ctrl key.

There are times that you will want to prevent the user from entering more than a specific number of characters into a field—for example, in the case when you have the user entering his or her two-character state code. This can be accomplished by using the script in Listing 17.5 in the field.

Listing 17.5 Handler Prevents User From Entering More Than Two Characters Into the Field

```
to handle keyChar keyPressed
     local INT maxChar
     local INT curCount
     maxChar = 2
     curCount = charCount(my text)
     if (curCount >= maxChar) \
      or (keyPressed = keyEnter and curCount >= maxChar - 1)
          --don't do anything
     else
          forward
     end
end
```

In this example script, placed in the field itself, you prevent the user from entering more than two characters. After the user has entered the state code and leaves the field, you might want to check to see if the code that he or she entered is a valid state code. This could be done by using a `leaveField` event message placed in the script of the field (see Listing 17.6).

Listing 17.6 Handler Checks a Two-Character Entry in a Field

```
to handle leaveField
     put my text into stateName
     get USAState(stateName)
     if it is false then
          request "Invalid state code. " &\
          "Please enter two letter state code."
          select my text
          send clear
     else
          forward
     end if
end
```

In this example, the user is told that the state code is invalid (using the request statement), and the bad state code is cleared. The needed routine for checking the state name, `USAState`, could be placed in the script of this field (or at a higher level if it will be used for more than one field). There are any number of ways to write this script, such as that shown in Listing 17.7.

Listing 17.7 Function Checks for a Valid Two-Letter State Code

```
to get USAState state2Char
     put "." & state2Char & "." into checkMe
     if checkMe is in \
     "xALxAKxAZxARxCAxCOxCTxDExDCxFLxGAxHIxIDxILx"&\
     "IN.IA.KS.KY.LA.ME.MD.MA.MI.MN.MS.MO.MT.NE.NV."&\
```

(continues)

Listing 17.7 Continued

```
        "NH.NJ.NM.NY.NC.ND.OH.OK.OR.PA.RI.SC.SD.TN.TX."&\
        "UT.VT.VA.WA.WV.WI.WY." then
            return true
        else
            return false
        end
end
```

The preceding code examples can be found in the file `CH1702.TBK` in the `\EXAMPLES` subdirectory on the CD-ROM disk packaged with this book.

Formatting Data

ToolBook provides some built-in features for formatting entries in specific ways. For example, if you had a field that was used to store a list of dollar amounts, you would probably want the data formatted as currency. This is accomplished using the format command, which takes the following form:

```
format [<type>] <container> as [<new format>] [from <old format>]
```

`type`, an optional argument, is number, date, or time (default is number), `container` is the string specifier (such as a local variable or text of field xxx), and `new format` and `old format` are the formatting strings, described in Tables 17.1 and 17.2. The examples in the tables assume that the local variable `sDate` contains the date January 8, 1996, the variable `sTime` contains 7:05 p.m., and the variable `myNum` is 56.87.

Table 17.1 Quick Reference for Date and Time Format Strings

Format	Meaning	Example	Returns
M	Month's name	Format date sDate as M	January
MMM	Month 3 letter abbreviation	Format date sDate as MMM	Jan
m	Month's number	Format date sDate as m	1
d	Day's number	Format date sDate as d	8
dd	Day's number with leading zeros for 1–9	Format date sDate as dd	08
y	Year's number	Format date sDate as y	1996
yy	Year's last two digits	Format date sDate as yy	96
h	Hour on 12-hour clock	Format time sTime as h	7
hh	Hour on 12-hour clock, leading zeros	Format time sTime as hh	07
h24	Hour on 24-hour clock	Format time sTime as h24	19

Format	Meaning	Example	Returns
hh24	Hour on 24 hour clock, leading zeros	Format time sTime as hh24	19
min	Minute	Format time sTime as min	05
sec	Second	Format time sTime as sec	22
AMPM	AM or PM	Format time sTime as AMPM	PM
seconds	Date in seconds since 00:00:00 GMT on January 1, 1970	Format date sDate as seconds	821059200
seconds	Time in seconds since 00:00:00 of the current day	Format time sTime as seconds	68722

Table 17.2 Quick Reference for Numeric Format Strings

Format	Meaning	Example	Returns
e+	Scientific notation, positive exponents show + sign, lowercase e	format myNum as #.##e+, format myNum as ###.###e+	5.69e+1 568.7 e-1
E+	Scientific notation, positive exponents show + sign, uppercase e	format myNum as #.####e+	5.687 E+1
e-,E-	Scientific notation, no positive exponent sign	format myNum as #.####e-	5.687 e 1
null	Displays number as precisely as possible	format myNum as null	56.87
?	Uses default value of sysNumberFormat	format myNum as ?	(varies)
0	Displays a zero if there are fewer digits or rounds decimals if less	format myNum as 000.0	056.9
@H or @h	Hexadecimal	format myNum as @H0000	0038
@D or @d	Decimal	format myNum as @D0000	0070
@O or @o	Octal	format myNum as @o0000	57
@B or @b	Binary	format myNum as @B00000000	00111000

Sorting Information

Many times when you are creating applications, you may need to sort items. There are a number of routines in ToolBook that facilitate these tasks.

The `sortItems` `comboBox` property specifies that the elements in the `comboBox` are to be sorted into alphabetical order. This can be set by selecting the Sort Items checkbox in the Combo Box Properties dialog box, which can be displayed by double-clicking the combo box (see fig. 17.3).

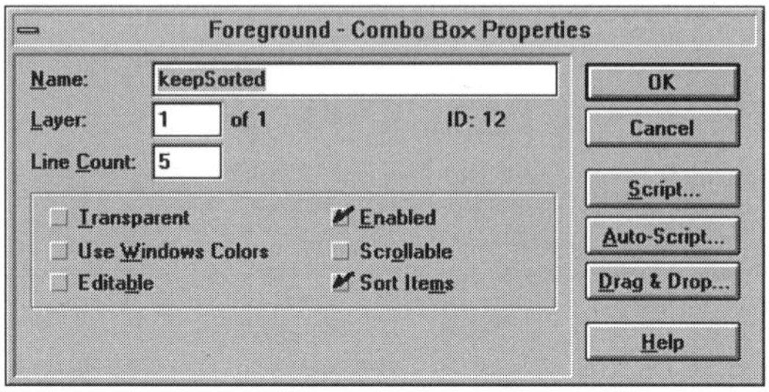

Fig. 17.3

Use the Sort Items checkbox in the Combo Box Properties to create a sorted list.

To set the property using OpenScript coding, you would use the following script:

```
sortItems of comboBox "keepSorted" = true
```

When the `comboBox` `sortItems` property is `true`, any items inserted into the drop-down list of the `comboBox` will automatically be sorted into alphabetical order. Figure 17.4 shows such a drop-down list in sorted order.

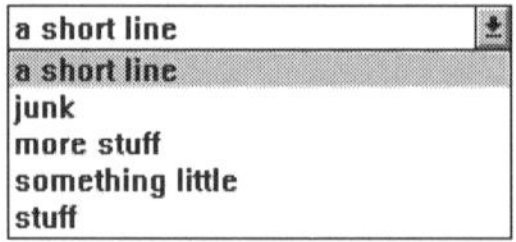

Fig. 17.4

Items placed in the drop-down list of a combo box are sorted in alphabetical order.

The rest of this section provides you with an in-depth look at some complex sorting routines that you might find useful. Unfortunately, there are no “quick-and-dirty” solutions to these kinds of programming problems; so you can use these complete examples as a starting point for creating your own routines. Asymetrix has kindly provided examples of methods for sorting arrays to cut-and-paste from its sample scripts into your application. One such script (in the sample file `LIBRARY.TBK` supplied with MTB) demonstrates how to use a quick `sort` routine to create a sorted field such as the one displayed in figure 17.5.

Sort by:
Text Number Date

a	3	5/23/91
b	2	3/11/92
c	4	4/1/06
d	9	11/13/66
e	0	7/4/76
f	6	7/7/64
g	7	4/1/23
h	1	2/9/55
i	5	3/1/29

Fig. 17.5

Obtain sample sorting routines from the Script Library supplied with Multimedia ToolBook.

This example consists of a single, tab-delimited field with two vertical lines drawn over it. Each of the three radio buttons contains a handler that loads the field's text into a 2D array and then passes it to a handler in the page. The script for the `text` button is shown in Listing 17.8.

Listing 17.8 Loading an Array from a Field

```
to handle buttonclick
      local retval
      local x[][]
      set fref to field "sortField"
      fill x with text of fref in [textline][word] order
      -- this calls the sorting routine. Note the first column
      -- of the array is specified, to be sorted as "text:
      send twoDquickSort x,1,"text"
      -- this part loads the sorted array back into the field
      set d to dimensions(x)
       step i from 1 to item 1 of d
            clear ln
            step j from 1 to item 2 of d
                 put x[i][j] after ln
                 if j < item 2 of d
                      put tab after ln
                 end
            end
            put ln after retval
            if i < item 1 of d
                 put crlf after retval
            end
       end
       put retval into text of fref
end
```

In the second and third lines, two local variables are declared, the second as a dynamic 2D array. In the next line, the local variable `fref` is set as a reference to the field that will be sorted. In line four, the local array is filled with the text of the field; the first dimension of the array is the number of rows and the second dimension is the columns. If in doubt, a quick "debug" of the button will show you the filling order of the array, as shown in figure 17.6.

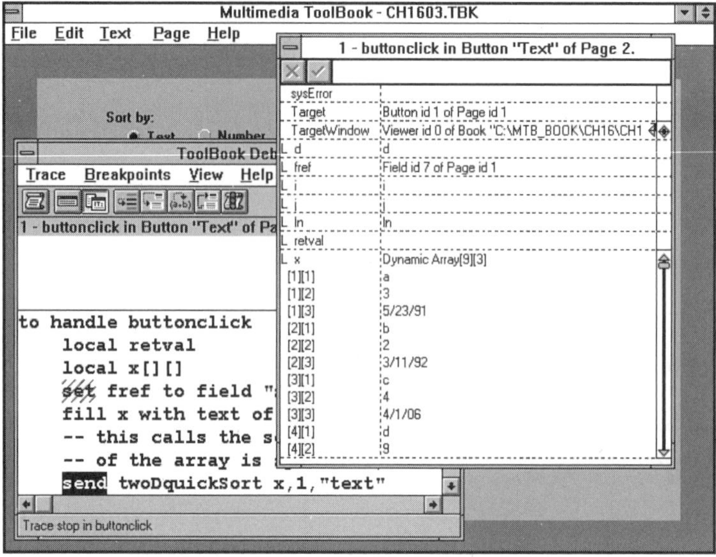

Fig. 17.6

Review the fill order of an array using the Debugger.

Line eight of the button script calls the sort routine, passing the filled array (x), the column to be sorted on (1), and the format for the sort (text). In the step I loop, the returned array values are placed into a local variable, retval, with tabs after each value and carriage-return line-feeds (CRLF) after each. The second-to-last line puts this formatted data back into the field.

For the number and date sort, or radio buttons, the script is essentially the same as the text sort, with the call specifying the appropriate column (2 and 3) and data type (number and date, respectively).

Let's discuss the scripts used to create this example. A "generic" sort routine was created and placed at the appropriate level in the application. If you are going to do a lot of sorting, you would place such a script at the book level, or either the page or background levels. The quick sort routines are provided in the following scripting examples. The first one is the main calling script in Listing 17.9.

Listing 17.9 A Sorting Routine

```
to handle twoDquickSort fArray[][] by reference,sortColumn,dtype
     --keep in mind that arrays are passed by reference, not by value
     system stbk_noSwap
     set stbk_noSwap to 0
    send twoDquicksrt fArray, 1, item 1 of dimensions(fArray), \
        sortColumn,dtype
end
```

The script example in Listing 17.10 is the sort routine.

Listing 17.10 The "Guts" of the 2D Sort Routine

```
to handle twoDquicksrt fArray[][] by reference, lo, hi,sortColumn,dtype
    system  stbk_noSwap
    if hi > lo
          send swap  fArray, lo, ((lo+hi) div 2)
          set lst to lo
          step i from (lo+1) to hi
              conditions
                   when dtype is "text"
                        set test to fArray[i][sortColumn] \
                         < fArray[lo][sortColumn] as text
when dtype is "date"
                        set test to fArray[i][sortColumn] \
                         < fArray[lo][sortColumn] as date
else
                        set test to fArray[i][sortColumn] \
                         < fArray[lo][sortColumn] as number
end
             if test
                  increment lst
                  send swap fArray, lst, i
             else
                  increment stbk_noswap
             end if
        end step
        send swap fArray,lo,lst
         send twoDquicksrt fArray, lo, lst-1,sortColumn,dtype
         send twoDquicksrt fArray, lst+1,hi,sortColumn,dtype
        end
end
```

The format of this routine should look familiar to you if you are a programmer; if not, the algorithm can be found in any beginning programming book. The remaining routine in Listing 17.11 is for swapping variables.

Listing 17.11 Providing the Simple Swap Needed by a Quick Sort Routine

```
to handle swap fArray[][] by reference, a, b
     local temp
     step i from 1 to item 2 of dimensions (fArray)
          set temp to fArray[a][i]
          set fArray[a][i] to fArray[b][i]
          set fArray[b][i] to temp
     end
end
```

Searching for Information

A subject closely related to sorting is indexed searching. Indexing text in your MTB application is surprisingly easy and extremely powerful. If your application has specific text that is never modified by the user (such as many interactive help and tutorial programs), you may want to create the index for the user and ship it with your application. To do this, choose Index, Index Settings from the main menu. You use the Index Settings interface to set up the options for the index—such as files, pages, objects, hotwords, and keywords for the indexing process.

Indexing Files

In the Index Settings dialog box, under the first tab heading, Files, you indicate the books to include in the search (see fig. 17.7). MTB will allow you to create a reference that spans multiple books.

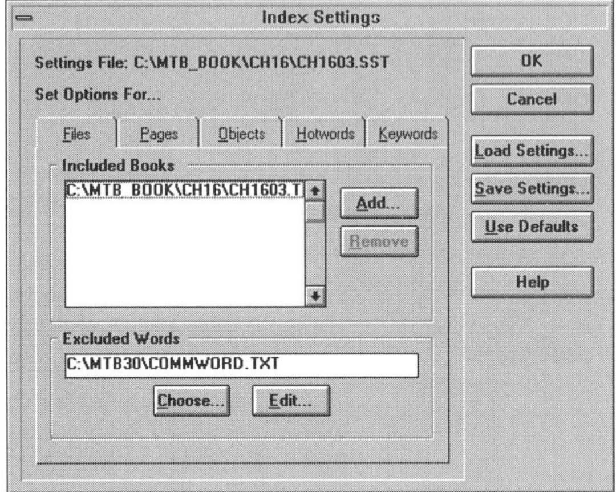

Fig. 17.7

Establish index search parameters under the Index Settings Files tab.

The Excluded Words field allows you to select an ASCII file that consists of common words—one per line with a carriage-return line-feed after each word—that will be excluded during the indexing operation.

Indexing Pages

Under the second tab heading, Pages, you indicate the way that the pages should be identified in the index. Often it is convenient to use the title of the page as the index. At other times, you will have a field or record field that contains the title that you want to display in your index.

The Page Contexts combo box provides a means of grouping like pages in ToolBook. Each page in a ToolBook file can be assigned a context. For example, suppose you are creating a multimedia history educational title. You might assign the context "war" to any page that discusses wars. This provides a way to speed up the search process. To use contexts, carefully choose a set of words or phrases that classify groups of pages in your application. Enter these in the list by clicking New in the Page Contexts section of the Pages tab (see fig. 17.8). Next, navigate to each page that you want to include in your context searches. Choose Page Settings from the Index menu, and then select the Page Context from the list.

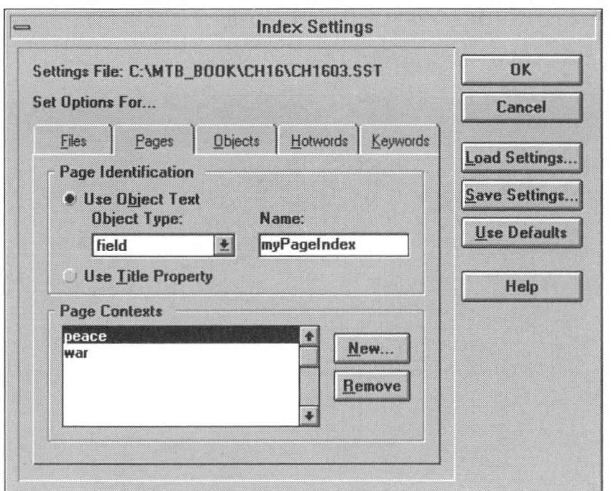

Fig. 17.8

Make the search process more efficient by assigning a context to like pages of your application.

Indexing Objects

Use the Objects tab heading to indicate the objects that you want to have included in the search. This allows you to easily customize your searches. For example, you can specify that you want the search to include fields and record fields but not buttons or combo boxes. You can also specify exclusion if the object is hidden or on the background (see fig. 17.9).

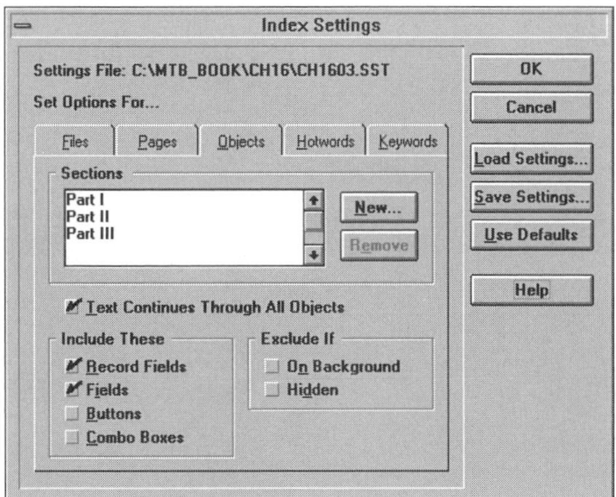

Fig. 17.9

Customize search parameters for objects under the Index Settings Objects tab.

In addition to the Context feature of specifying subselection in searching, MTB provides a feature that lets you subselect groups of items on a page. This is the Sections feature. Sections consist of objects that you want to logically group for searching operations. For example, you may have designed your application so that there are header fields, main body text record fields, and footnote fields on each page. You could set up three sections (header, body, and footnote) and then choose the fields that are part of the header and associate them with the header section, and so on.

This is accomplished by first selecting the object (button, field, record field, or combo box) on the page and then choosing Index, Object Settings from the main menu. Now, choose the section name from the combo box (see fig. 17.10).

> **Note**
>
> If you do not specify a section name for an object, it will automatically be assigned to the section default—which is a section with no name.

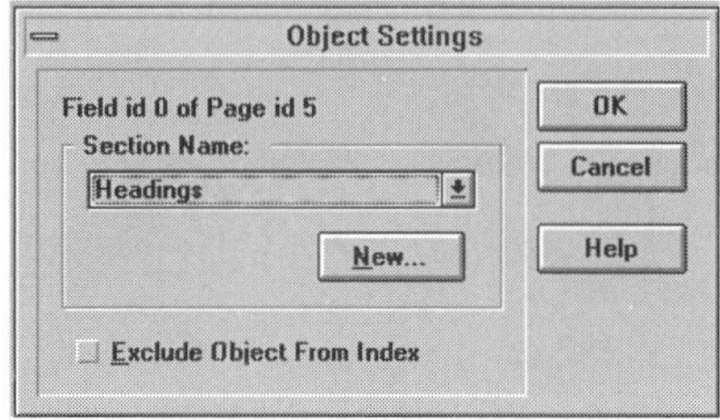

Fig. 17.10

Use the Object Settings dialog box for grouping related objects into sections.

Indexing Hotwords

The fourth tab heading, Hotwords, allows you yet another method for choosing indexes based on features of the text (see fig. 17.11). You can create hotwords within the text regions (as described in Chapter 7) and then assign the hotword tags a data type (integer, real, date, character). Then, you can specify a search on the hotword using a range, such as `DateOfBirth < 01/12/1915`.

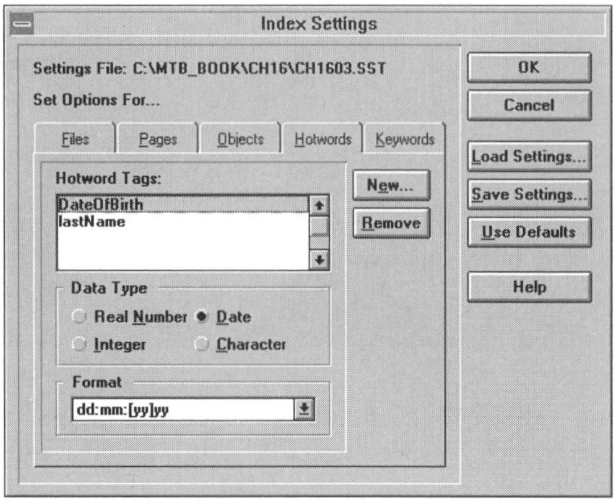

Fig. 17.11

Text used as a hotword tag becomes a nonactive hotword.

The steps involved in setting up hotword tags start with choosing a list of hotwords that you want to associate with words or phrases in the text of your application. From the Hotword tab of the Index Settings, choose New and enter the hotwords and their associated data type (this is required) and format (this is optional). Now, you are ready to mark the words or phrases as hotword tags.

Go to the page on which the text you want to mark appears. Select the text, and from the Index menu, choose Hotword Settings. From the Choose Tag drop-down list, select the tag you want to associate with the selected text (see fig. 17.12). Repeat the process for each word or phrase on each page that you want to index in this manner.

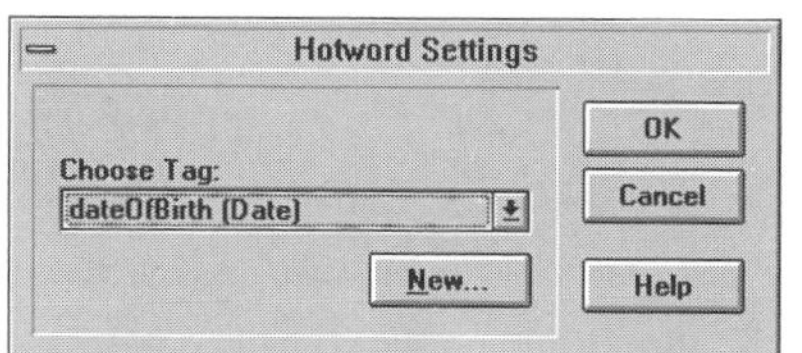

Fig. 17.12

Select hotword tags to be indexed under the Hotword Settings dialog box.

Indexing Keywords

You can specify keywords for your search index in the Keywords tab in the Index Settings dialog box. This is one of the most powerful features of MTB indexing, and is similar to keyword indexes in most books. The basic procedure used is to first choose a list of words to include in your keyword index and enter these in the Keyword list (see fig. 17.13).

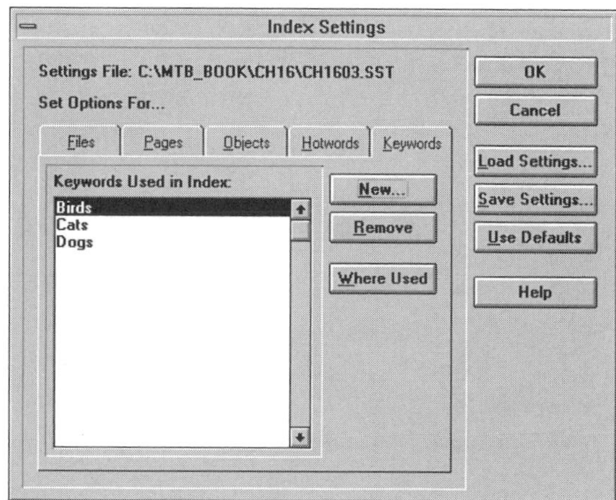

Fig. 17.13

Establish keywords for use in full-text searches through the Index Settings Keywords tab.

Next, you navigate to each page in your application and choose the words from your index list that describe the contents of the page (see fig. 17.14).

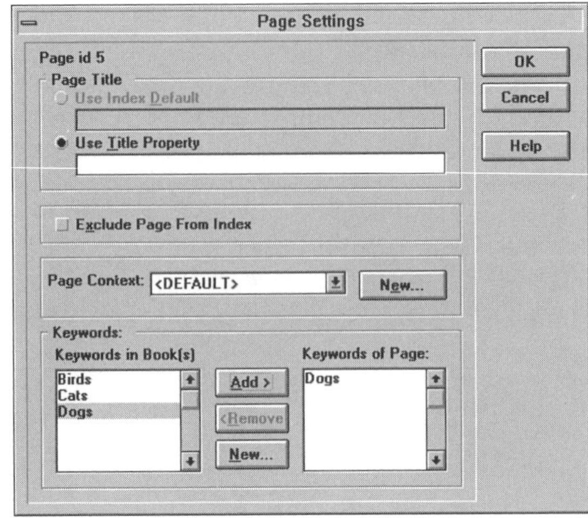

Fig. 17.14

Context names for pages are created through the Page Settings dialog box.

Searching the Index

All of the index building activities that you perform in the steps outlined in the previous sections will create an index that is searchable by the end users of the application. The product can be searched by word, partial word, phrase, keyword, section, hotword tag, multiple search terms, or words in proximity. By default, the search menu is not added at Reader mode, and will need to added (for examples, see Chapter 9, "Creating Custom Menus").

An example of a search is shown in figure 17.15. In this example, the query words `dog* + famous` were used. This will find any occurrences of `dog`, `dogs`, `dogbreath`, and any words beginning with `dog` that occur along with `famous`. The proximity search limits the closeness of the search to words that are plus or minus the specified number of words from the specified word.

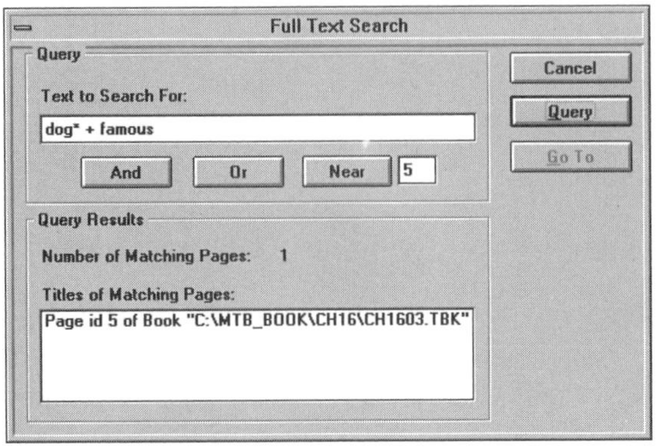

Fig. 17.15

Initiate custom searches of an application using the Full Text Search dialog box.

In a similar way, you can choose Keyword Search from the Index menu and perform keyword searches.

Using OpenScript Commands to Create Indexed Searching

While the built-in features of MTB indexing are not difficult to master, you might find a few occasions where you want to avoid using these menus. One case is where you need to be very selective about the text that you want to include, perhaps including the script of some buttons on some pages and not on others. Another case is when the user is typing in text or importing text into the application, and you want to create indexing for this data at runtime. These cases can be handled by writing OpenScript code to do the indexing.

There are a number of Dynamic Link Library (DLL) functions provided with MTB that allow you to do this kind of searching. The script example in Listing 17.12 creates a full-text search index for a book. This example was provided by Asymetrix in its `LIBRARY.TBK` file. It is broken into chunks with commentary to explain how it works.

Listing 17.12 Method of Automating the Building of an Index

```
-- this handler builds a full-text search index of the current book.
to handle buildIndex
      -- display an hourglass cursor... this can take a while.
      sysCursor = 4
      -- link the DLLs required to build an index
      linkDll "fts30mtb.dll"
           STRING ftsRemoveIndex   (STRING)
           DWORD  ftsInitIndex     (STRING,STRING,WORD)
           LONG   ftsAddContext    (DWORD,STRING)
           STRING ftsAddPage       (DWORD,STRING,STRING,STRING,LONG)
           STRING ftsAddTextToSection      (DWORD,STRING,STRING)
            STRING ftsAddSectionsToPage    (DWORD)
            STRING ftsBuildIndex           (DWORD)
       end
       -- get the name of the index to use
       indexName = name of this book
       if indexName = NULL
            request "You must save this book before building" & \
                     "an index for it."
            send cleanExit
       end
       while "." is in indexName
            clear last char of indexName
       end
       -- remove any existing index of that name
       get ftsRemoveIndex(indexName)
       -- initialize the index
       indexHandle = ftsInitIndex(indexName, \
           sysToolBookDirectory&"default.sst",sysWindowHandle)
       if it = 0
            -- if there is an error stop this process
            request "Error initializing index"
            send cleanExit
       end
```

The first section (the first 13 lines) of Listing 17.12 links in the needed functions from the FTS30MTB.DLL. For more information on linking DLLs, see the "Declaring and Linking DLLs" section in Chapter 19.

In the second section of Listing 17.12 (lines 14 through 19), the name for the index is set to the name of the book, and an exit routine is called if the user has not named the book (standard practice for Windows programs).

The while loop in lines 20 through 22 will strip off the file extension part of the name.

Line 23 removes any preexisting index of the same name, and line 26 initializes the index. The file sysToolBookDirectory&"default.sst" is the default settings file for initialization settings for the indexing. You may want to change this to indicate a particular set of setup options. The default options will be something like that shown in Listing 17.13.

Listing 17.13 Sets the Default Options for Searching

```
;This file defines global options for generating a Search Index.
[CREATE]
MANAGER=aapi
TXFSIZE=1000
CWDFILE=
SPECIALS=
TITLE_SECTION=TITLE,YES
CONC_SECTION=
NON_CONC_SECTION=
DEFAULT_SECTION=OTHER,YES
MAXP_PER_SECT=500
MAXCHP=65534
MAXART=65534
MAXPAR=65534
MAXWRD=65534
KEYFIELDS=3
KF1=#HANDLE C
KF2=#ARTREF A
KF3=#KEYWORD C
FIRST_CHAP=default

[Options]
includeBooks=
includedObjects=recordField,field
excluded=
textFlow=true
NewSet=FALSE

[Keywords]
Lines=0

[Contexts]
Lines=0
```

The easiest way to create a special SST file for a particular application is to switch to reader mode and choose Index, Index Settings from the main menu, select the index options you are interested in, and then save the resulting settings file. Generally, you would place this file in the same directory that the application resides in rather than the `sysToolBookDirectory`.

Listing 17.14 Building an Index by Adding Objects in the Background and Page

```
   -- step through the pages of this book
   step i from 1 to pageCount of this book
        pageRef = page i of this book
        bgRef = parent of pageRef
        -- if this background is different than the previous one
        -- get a list of objects on this background
        if bgRef <> curRef
             curRef = bgRef
             bgObs = getObjectList(bgRef,"field,recordField",FALSE)
        end
        -- get a title to associate with this page
        title = name of pageRef
        if title = NULL
             title = pageRef
        end
        -- add the page to the index
        get ftsAddPage(indexHandle,pageRef,title,"",1)
        if it = NULL
             request "Error Adding Page"
             send cleanExit
        end
        -- step thru the fields, recordFields on this background
        -- and add their text to the default section of the index
        step j from 1 to itemCount(bgObs)
             curObj = item j of bgObs
             if object of curObj = "recordField"
                  -- to get the text of a recordField we have to
                  -- refer to a page rather than the background
                  -- words 1 to 4 of a recordField reference
                  -- are:  "recordField id X of"
                  curObj = words 1 to 4 of curObj && pageRef
             end
             textExp = "richText of"&&curObj
             get ftsAddTextToSection(indexHandle,textExp,"")
        end
        -- get a list of fields on this page and add their text
        -- to the default section of the index
        pgObs = getObjectList(pageRef,"field",FALSE)
        step j from 1 to itemCount(pgObs)
             curObj = item j of pgObs
             textExp = "richText of"&&curObj
             get ftsAddTextToSection(indexHandle,textExp,"")
        end
        -- add the text placed into sections to the index
        get ftsAddSectionsToPage(indexHandle)
```

(continues)

Listing 17.14 Continued

```
        end
        --build the index
        get ftsBuildIndex(indexHandle)
        if it = NULL
             request "Failed to build index."
        else
             request "Index successfully built."
        end
        send cleanExit
end buildIndex
```

The previous lines step through the pages in the book, first obtaining a list of the objects in the background, then adding the page to the index. Next, the records and record fields have their text added to the default section of the index. After the background objects have been added, the objects on the page are added. Finally, the index is built (see Listing 17.15).

Listing 17.15 Method for Cleanly Exiting the Build Process

```
-- this process will exit the build process cleanly
-- (removing the DLLs, etc.)
to handle cleanExit
     sysCursor = 1
     unlinkDLL "fts30mtb.dll"
     break to system
end cleanExit
```

The routine `cleanExit` is used to exit the routine, unlinking the DLL that was linked in lines four through 12 and returning the cursor to its default state.

From Here...

In this chapter, we discussed ways to enhance ToolBook applications using low-level file functions, import and format techniques, and custom index creation to support full-text searches.

For information on more ways to enhance your books, refer to the following chapters:

- Chapter 7, "Adding Multimedia Elements," offers details for integrating audio and video with your application.
- Chapter 9, "Creating Custom Menus," describes how to customize ToolBook's Reader level menu for your own purposes.
- Chapter 10, "Using Graphics," deals with the use of images and color palettes.
- Chapter 11, "Working with Text," provides additional details on text formatting.
- Chapter 18, "Using Special Effects," talks about how to add wipes, fades, and animation features to your book.

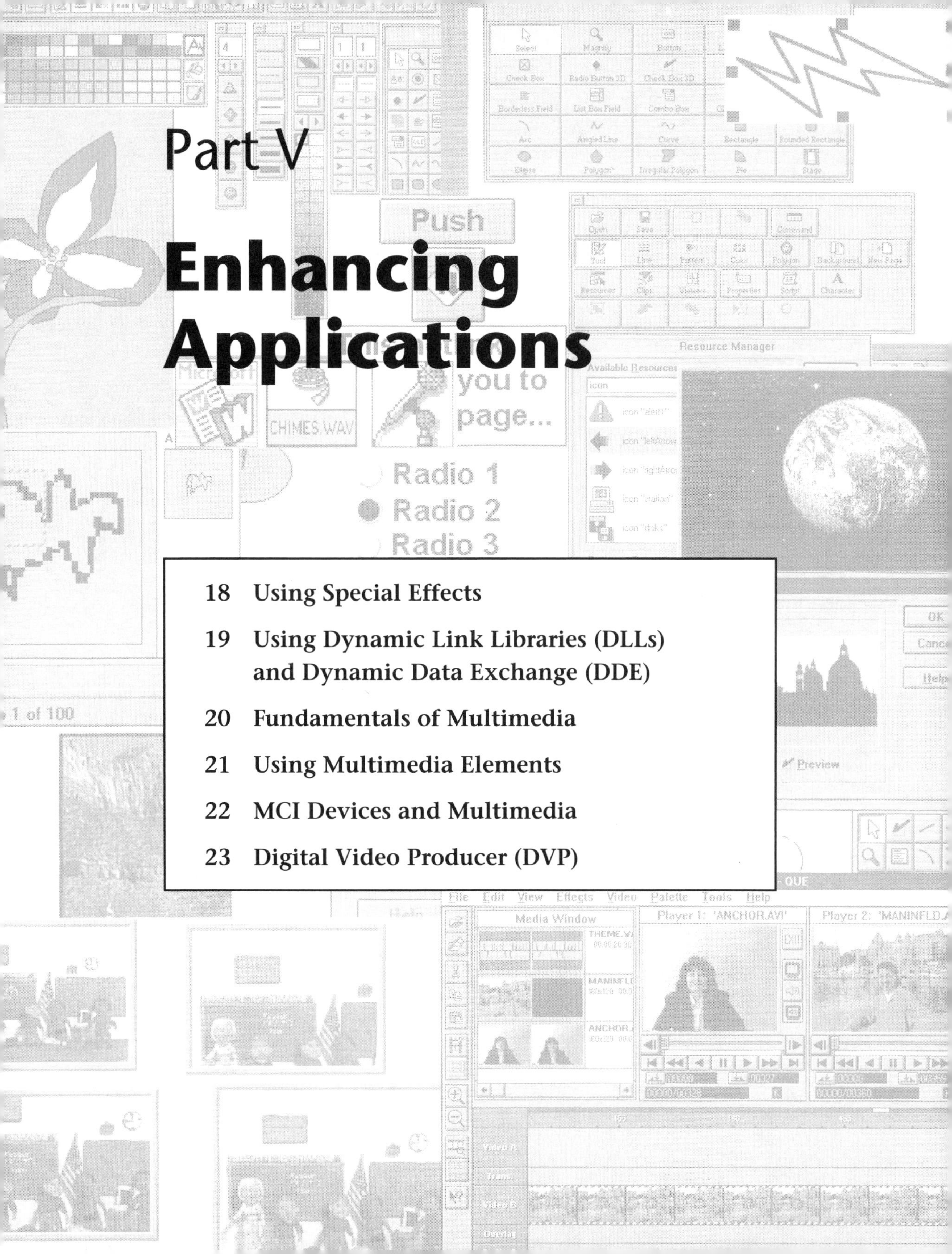

Part V

Enhancing Applications

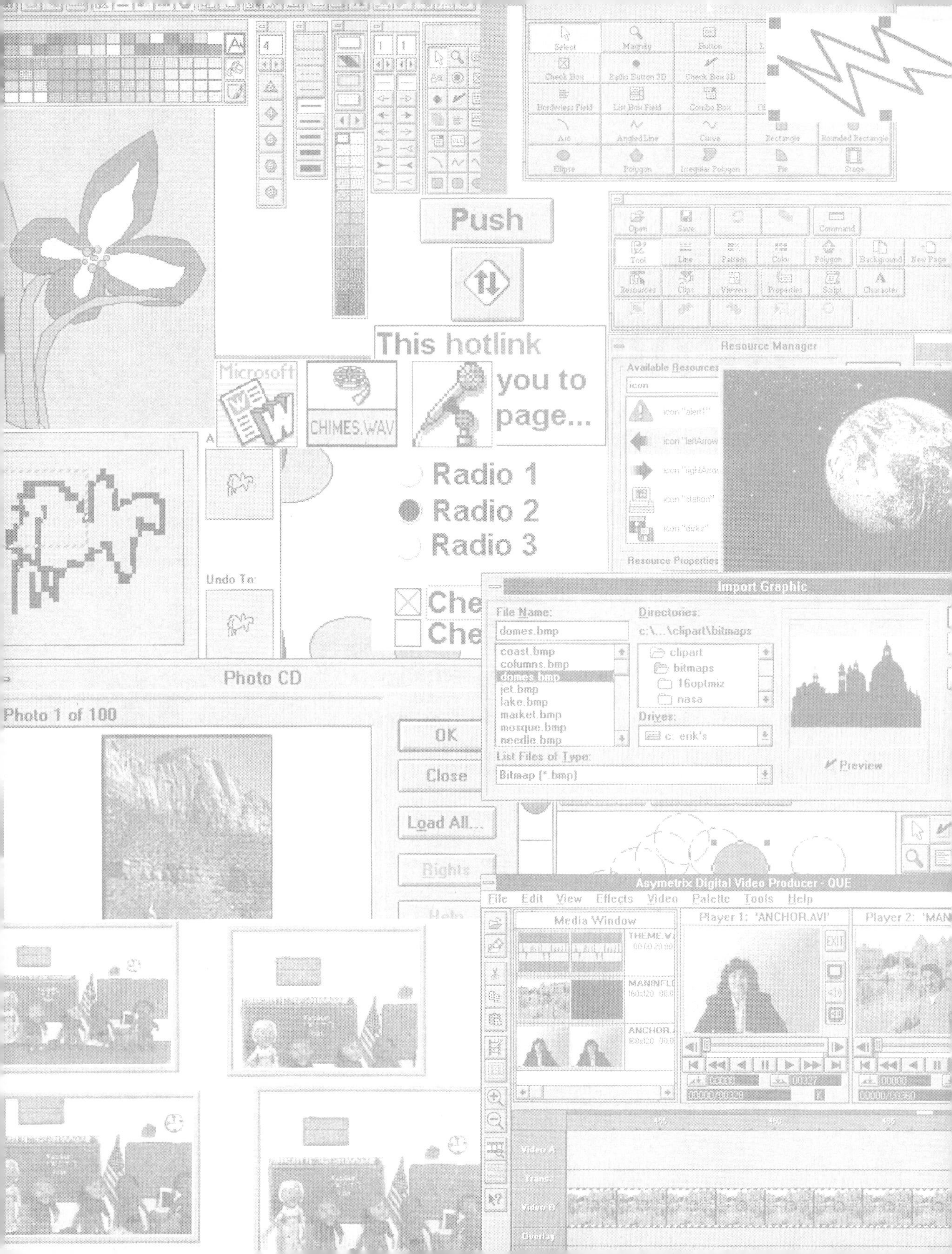

Select
Magnify
Button
Check Box
Radio Button 3D
Check Box 3D
Borderless Field
List Box Field
Combo Box
Arc
Angled Line
Curve
Rectangle
Rounded Rectangle
Ellipse
Polygon
Irregular Polygon
Pie
Stage
Push
Open
Save
Command
Tool
Line
Pattern
Color
Polygon
Background
New Page
Resources
Clips
Viewers
Properties
Script
Character
This hotlink
you to
page...
Microsoft
CHIMES.WAV
Resource Manager
Available Resources
icon
Radio 1
Radio 2
Radio 3
Undo To:
Resource Properties
Import Graphic
File Name:
domes.bmp
Directories:
c:\...\clipart\bitmaps
coast.bmp
columns.bmp
domes.bmp
jet.bmp
lake.bmp
market.bmp
mosque.bmp
needle.bmp
clipart
bitmaps
16optmiz
nasa
Drives:
c: erik's
List Files of Type:
Bitmap (*.bmp)
Preview
Photo CD
Photo 1 of 100
OK
Close
Load All...
Rights
Asymetrix Digital Video Producer - QUE
File
Edit
View
Effects
Video
Palette
Tools
Help
Media Window
Player 1: 'ANCHOR.AVI'
EXIT
Video A
Trans.
Video B
Overlay

CHAPTER 18

Using Special Effects

This chapter discusses some of the special effects that are commonly used in multimedia applications. ToolBook provides a simple interface to support a number of useful special effects, including drag-and-drop operations, page-turning operations, and a range of different kinds of animations. In this chapter you'll discover how to do the following:

- Create and apply drag-and-drop operations
- Assign and set page transition effects
- Produce both simple and complex animation

Using Drag-and-Drop

The drag-and-drop operation is used often in Windows programs. This feature of GUI interfaces is easily understood by users, and ToolBook provides programming tools that make creating these easy-to-use interfaces relatively simple. During the interface design process, it is important to consider what operations users will find to be most "natural" in an interface. If the interface involves positioning objects, grouping objects, or rearranging items, there is a good chance that the drag-and-drop operation might be a good candidate for a simple interface.

Some examples of commonly-used Windows programs that have drag-and-drop capability include the Windows File Manager, which allows you to drag a filename from one drive and drop it on another to initiate a file copy. Another example is the Solitaire game, which allows you to drag a card from one area of the window and drop it on any other location in the window. In the former case, the drag image icon is represented as a file, and the image changes to the "no-drop" symbol (red circle with a diagonal line) when the drag image is positioned over a "no-drop" zone. In the latter case, the drag image is represented as the card being moved; and when it is dropped onto an unallowed position, the card slides back to its pre-drag location.

This section describes the basic techniques used for creating a drag-and-drop interface.

Understanding Drag-and-Drop

Drag-and-drop operations require you to define a source, one or more destinations, a drag icon or image, and a no-drop image or icon. You will need to set the properties of the draggable object and the destination objects, and define the drag-and-drop events.

Any object that can be placed on a page can be set up to be dragged. Destination objects can be any object or page. You can design your application so that objects can be dragged from one viewer to another.

An object is indicated as "draggable" by setting its `defaultAllowDrag` property to `true`. Destination objects are designated by setting their `defaultAllowDrop` properties to `true`. For example, figure 18.1 shows a simple drag-and-drop application, allowing the user to drag the circle, triangle, diamond, or oval onto the white rectangle.

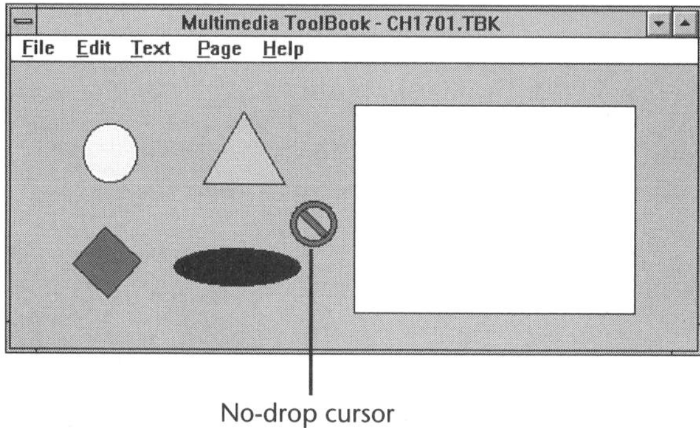

Fig. 18.1

Drag-and-drop operations use Source and Destination objects.

This example was created by drawing five graphic objects: two ellipses, two polygons (one three-sided and one four-sided), and a rectangle. To make the four objects on the left side draggable, follow these steps:

1. Set their properties by right-clicking each object in reader mode. The dialog box in figure 18.2 appears.

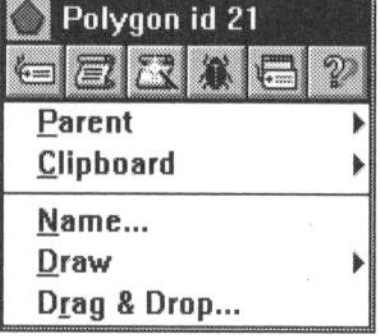

Fig. 18.2

Access the Drag & Drop dialog box through an object's right-click menu.

2. Choose Drag & Drop in this dialog box. The Drag & Drop dialog box appears (see fig. 18.3).

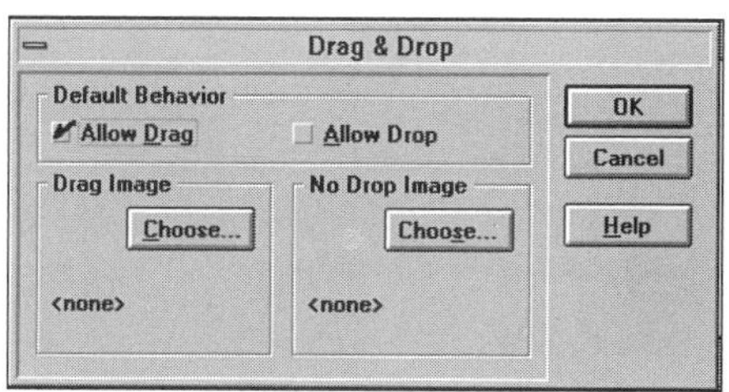

Fig. 18.3

Select the Choose button in the Drag Image area to invoke the Choose Drag Image dialog box.

3. Select the Allow Drag checkbox.

At this point, running the application will show the no-drop icon (crossed-out circle) when you drag one of the draggable items, unless the cursor is over a draggable item; in which case, it will turn into the default drop icon (an arrow on a page.) However, dropping the object will not initiate any action; the actions must be scripted.

Defining a Drag Image

When you drag an item, the cursor changes according to whether it is positioned over a no-drop zone or an area that allows drop. By default, objects you create in Multimedia ToolBook (MTB) have their `defaultAllowDrop` property set to `false`; when a drag operation is over these regions, the cursor is set to the no-drop icon. The default drag cursor over areas that have their `defaultAllowDrop` property set to `true` is an arrow on top of a page.

There are often cases where you will want to change these images to something more appropriate for your application. For example, suppose you are scripting a drag-and-drop of subdirectory names (for example, in a program that allows the user to reorganize his or her disk drives). In this case, you might want the drag image to be a folder, and the no-drop image to be a crossed-out folder. To do this, first add these icons to the Resource Manager dialog box (see fig. 18.4). From the Author level menu, select Resources (Ctrl+F10), choose Select Icons, and then choose Import for each of the icons you want to use. (More information on resource management is available in Chapter 5, "Understanding the Media Management Tools.")

Next, in author mode, right-click each drag object and change the drag image to the folder with an arrow and the no-drop image to the crossed-out folder (as shown in fig. 18.4.) Now, when you drag these objects over the white rectangle, they will display the folder icon, while everywhere else they will display the no-folder icon.

> **Note**
>
> MTB ships with a set of icons (including these shown), which are installed in the `MTB30\CLIPART\CURSORS\` subdirectories. The set supplied is extensive, but Murphy's law of computer clip art states that "no matter how complete your set of clip art is, you will not have the one item you really need." You can create your own icons and cursors using the Icon/Cursor editor supplied with MTB (select Resources, Icons, New), or you can purchase icons by the thousands on CD-ROM.

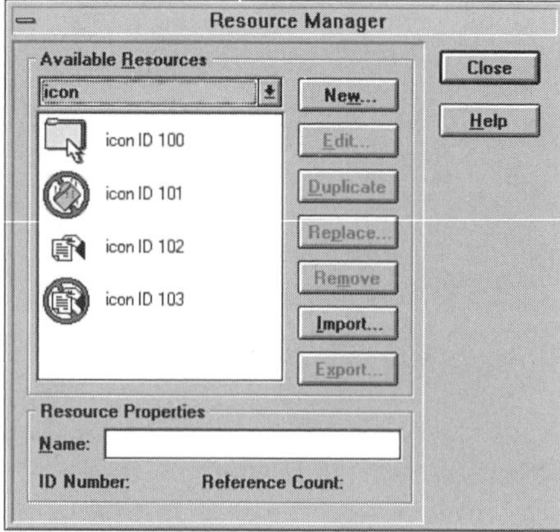

Fig. 18.4

Drag-and-drop icons are added to a ToolBook application using the Resource Manager.

You are not limited to the use of icons and cursors for the drag-and-drop image. If you want, you can use a bitmap image for these operations. The file `CH1801.TBK`, used for the previous examples, has been modified to show an example of this. A green triangle was drawn in BITEDIT (select Resources, select Bitmaps, select New) and then chosen as the drag image for the green triangle object; the effect which results makes it appear that the drag operation creates a *copy* of the triangle that can be dragged by the user around the screen.

Receiving a Dropped Item

At this point, we have discussed how to define the zones for drag-and-drop and how to specify the drag images. These two operations give the visual effect of the drag-and-drop, but we have not yet defined the actual operation. There are a number of OpenScript messages that are relevant. These are described in Table 18.1.

> **Note**
>
> The only essential message that you must define for the drag-and-drop action is the `endDrag`.

Table 18.1 Drag-and-Drop Messages

Message	Description	Uses
`drag <sourceObj> [within <rec bounds>] [silently]`	Starts the drag-and drop action as though initiated by the user with the mouse.	Used when a drag command cannot be initiated directly, such as for a group or for a right-click. The `silently` parameter is used when you don't want drop messages sent.

Message	Description	Uses
`beginDrag`	Is sent to the dragged object when the drag event begins.	Frequently used in list box cases to initiate the drag of lines of text.
`endDrag <destObj>, <loc>, <target window>`	Is sent to the dragged object when the drag event ends.	Used to specify what will happen when the mouse button is released at the end of the drag.
`enterDrop <sourceObj>`	Is sent to an object (if it allows drop) when the mouse cursor enters its bounds.	Used to specify some other action (like a blinking color, status line text).
`leaveDrop <sourceObj>`	Is sent to an object when the mouse cursor leaves its bounds.	Used to specify some other action (like a blinking color, status line text).
`objectDropped <sourceObj>, <loc>`	Is sent to an object when a dragged object is released within its bounds.	Used to place an object or initiate an action based on the location where the object is dropped.
`stillOverDrop <sourceObj>, <loc>`	A continuous message sent to the object while the mouse cursor is within its bounds.	Especially useful for drag-and-drop in fields when used in conjunction with the `textFromPoint()` function.
`to get allowDrag`	Is sent to a source object to determine if it is draggable.	Useful for conditional drag-and-drop operations (e.g. allow only rectangles to be dragged after the user clicks a "move rectangles" button.)
`to get allowDrop <sourceObj>`	Sent to a source object to determine if it allows drop.	Useful for conditional drag-and-drop operations.

Expanding on the previous section's example of the drag-and-drop of the triangle from the left of the window into the white rectangle, you would next define the drop action. In this example, let's suppose that you want a copy of the triangle or other dragged object to appear at the `endDrag` position. First, you define the `objectDropped` handler so that you can get the name of the object that has been dragged:

```
to handle objectDropped iobj
    system objToCopy
    put iobj into objToCopy
end
```

This script is placed in the page script, and sets the value of the system variable `objToCopy` to a reference to the object dropped (e.g. `Polygon id 21 of Page id 0`). Now, we will set up the `endDrag` operation, placing this script in the page:

Listing 18.1 Setting up *endDrag*

```
to handle endDrag pObject, pLoc
     system objToCopy
     sysLockScreen = true
     if objToCopy <> null then
          select objToCopy
          send duplicate
          move selection to pLoc
     end
     objToCopy = null
     sysLockScreen = false
end endDrag
```

This code specifies that, at the end of the drag operation, a copy of the dragged object is placed at the current location. This allows multiple copies of the dragged object to be placed in the drop region. Also, the objects that are dropped retain the properties of the original (that is, they can be dragged and will generate a new copy of themselves when dropped in the drop area). This simple example provides all of the essential elements for the drag-and-drop operation.

Another common use for drag-and-drop is the draggable text lines from a list box. The next example shows you how you might use this feature to simulate the drag-and-drop actions of filenames onto the trash can icon from the Macintosh operating system (see fig. 18.5).

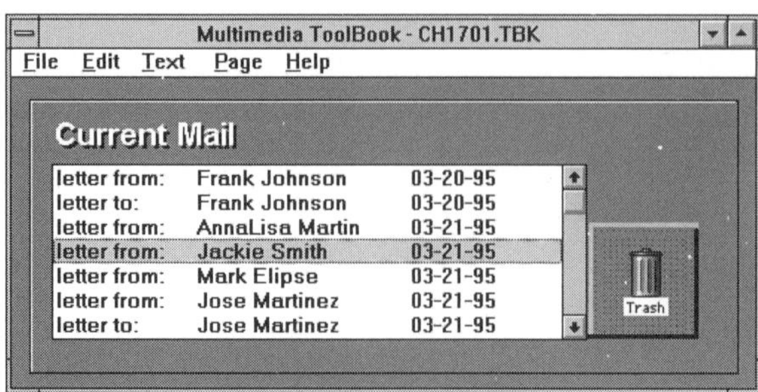

Fig. 18.5

Use drag-and-drop with a list box to simulate the Macintosh trash can feature.

Assuming that you have already written the interface script for retrieving the "current mail" information (which is beyond the scope of this example), we will demonstrate the scripting techniques used to create the drag-and-drop action.

In the script of the single-select text field containing the mail information, the script from Listing 18.2 is placed.

Listing 18.2 The Dragging Script

```
to get allowDrag
     get textFromPoint(sysMousePosition) of self
     -- make sure edge was not clicked
     if it is not "-1,-1"
          set selectedTextLines of self to item 1 of it
          return TRUE
     else
          return FALSE
     end
end
```

This script replaces the standard `allowDrag` handler, allowing the textline clicked to be selected (without this handler, you will not be able to both select the textline and initiate a drag operation). In this example, the trashcan icon consists of two pictures that have been grouped—one, named `trashEmpty`, is an empty trashcan; and the other, `trashFull`, is a bulging trashcan. The drop behavior is specified in Listing 18.3.

Listing 18.3 The Dropped Script

```
to handle objectDropped pTarget
     if my trashFull is false then
          put true into my trashFull
          send sendtoback paintObject "trashEmpty"
     end if
     if object of pTarget is field and text of pTarget is not null
          clear textline (selectedTextLines of pTarget) of text of pTarget
     end
end
```

This script makes use of a few advanced techniques. A *user property*, `trashFull`, is being checked in the `if` statement to determine which paint object to show (`trashEmpty` or `trashFull`). If the property is `false`, then the `trashEmpty` paint object is sent behind the `trashFull` paint object. (User properties are explained more fully in Chapter 14, "Messages, Objects, and Properties.") After the object (a textline) has been dropped, it should be removed from the text of the field. This is accomplished by the `clear textline` command.

The script of the `enterPage` handler should contain script to fill the field and set the user property of the trash to `false` (so the can appears empty). If you were to use this example in an application, you would probably also write a handler to empty the trash and retrieve items from the trash.

Adding Page Transitions

Another feature of MTB that provides some visual interest to your applications are *page transitions*. Page transitions, though relatively new to computer interfaces, are nevertheless very familiar to users because of the many digital transitions that are used in television programming. MTB provides page transitions that are easy to program and use.

The general format of the transition command is the following:

```
transition <effect string> [at <point>] to <page | color>
```

The `effect string` is composed of the effect, duration, destination, and speed (`fast`, `slow`, `normal`, or `speed <milliseconds>`), the `point` is the transition effect point in page units (supported only by the `zoom` effect), `page` is the destination page to transition to, and `color` is the destination color to transition to.

Table 18.2 lists the effects, direction, destination, and notes for transitions.

Table 18.2 Transition Effects

Effect	Direction	Destination	Notes
blinds	n/a	n/a	Uses "venetian blinds" (vertical stripes)
dissolve	n/a	n/a	A "blocky" dissolve with one image showing over the other
drip	n/a	n/a	The image is revealed in a drip pattern down the screen
fade	n/a	n/a	A smoother version of the dissolve
iris	n/a	n/a	An iris opening effect, with somewhat aliased edges
push	n/a	left, right, top, bottom	A smooth "this image pushes that image off the screen" effect
puzzle	n/a	n/a	One image replaces the other puzzle piece by puzzle piece
rain	n/a	left, right	Fills the screen vertical bar by vertical bar (more like blinds than rain)
slide	in, out	left, right, top, bottom	Current image slides over the stationary other image—either slide it in, or slide it out
spiral	in, out	n/a	Somewhat aliased spiral effect
split	in, out	horizontal, vertical	Image splits in middle and new image is revealed (either in or out)
tear	n/a	left, right, top, bottom, horizontal, vertical	Jagged edge tearing effect (like torn paper)

Effect	Direction	Destination	Notes
turnPage	n/a	left, right,	Somewhat aliased page turning effect
wipe	n/a	left, right, top, bottom	Like a slide, but neither image moves (both stationary and the effect is to reveal new image)
zoom	in, out	left, right, top, bottom, `lowerLeft`, `lowerRight`, `upperLeft`, `upperRight`	Rectangular zoom in or out from a point. This is the only effect which takes an argument for the effect location `<point>`

Transition effects can add dynamic impact to your multimedia software, adding artsy effects to the screen changes (see fig. 18.6). For example, if you were making a slide show application that displayed pictures in the middle of a frame, you might alternate between the push effects (push top, push left, and so on) using a script such as the following:

```
transition "push left fast" to next page
```

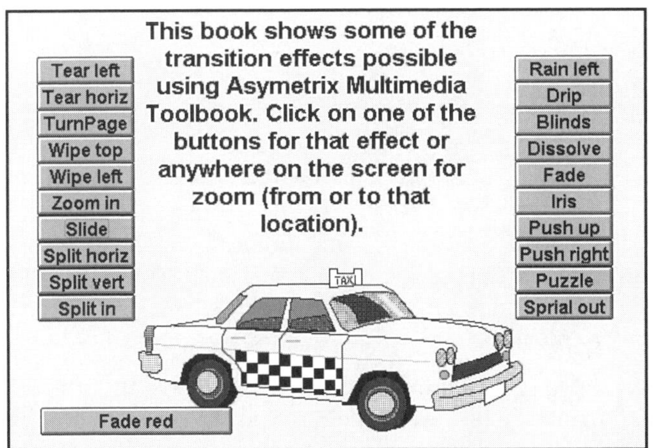

Fig. 18.6

Pre-effect transitions are used before a media clip is played.

You can use transition effects as you navigate between pages, or within the page itself, transitioning to another color. Transition effects are also used within stages. (For more information on this, see Chapter 7, "Adding Multimedia Elements.")

The examples shown in this section can be found in the file `CH1802.TBK` which is included on the CD-ROM packaged with this book. This example contains button examples for each of the transition effects.

Object Animation

The use of animations in a multimedia application makes the product appealing to the customer. MTB has many built-in features that make creating animations relatively simple. The following sections discuss some of the ways that you can use animation to spice up your program, providing a number of different techniques that can be used to create effective animated sequences.

Simple Animations Using Hide and Show

One of the simplest means of creating animation in MTB is to use the "hide" and "show" commands. You can hide and show bitmaps, items, or groups to create an effective animation. For example, to generate an animation of a person yawning, you might create the images in figure 18.7.

Fig. 18.7

Simple animations are created using the hide and show commands.

These faces were created in ToolBook with the drawing tools (mostly the irregular polygon). One image was created, then copied, and then modified. The modified image was copied, modified, modified again, and so on for the six images. Next, the images were lined up, one on top of the next, and each group was named.

Here's a hint. If you have trouble getting things lined up in ToolBook, turn the object transparent, line it up with the image below it, and then turn the transparency off. This makes the process of aligning images much easier!

Now, a simple script, like the one in Listing 18.4, was written (and in this example, placed in a button).

Listing 18.4 Modifying Images

```
to handle buttonUp
     show group "yawn1"
     pause 20
     show group "yawn2"
```

```
hide group "yawn1"
pause 20
show group "yawn3"
hide group "yawn2"
pause 20
...
```

The blocks of show and hide are repeated, showing each of the six faces in order, and then in reverse order. This gives the effect of a yawn. The `pause` statement was used to provide a moment (actually, 20 ticks or about 1/5 of a second) of time for each picture to display. This example can be found in the file `CH1804.TBK` included on the CD-ROM.

Another powerful way to use the hide and show method of animation is to create a picture in another program, such as a paint program or a video digitizer. Then, use the ToolBook chromakey feature to create areas that show as clear, displaying the underlying background.

Displaying Animation Files

The use of animation files that have been created in other animation programs, such as Autodesk 3D Studio, can add another dimension of quality to your applications. Although there are many different methods you can use to display such files, the most straightforward means is through the use of stages, which is discussed in detail in Chapter 7, "Adding Multimedia Elements." Note that the playback of animation files requires the use of appropriate MCI drivers for the file type being displayed, which must be installed on the system in use.

In short, the steps you use to play an external animation file in a stage are the following:

1. Create the stage by selecting the stage tool and clicking and dragging to define the stage area.
2. Modify the stage to meet your needs, select Object, then Stage Properties from the Author level menu, then set the options for frame, display, pre-effect, and post-effect as desired in the Stage Properties dialog box.
3. Define the animation clip. First select Object, Clips from the Author level menu. This presents the Clip Manager dialog box.
4. Click the New button. This displays the Choose Source Type dialog box.
5. Click the Animation File button.
6. Choose the animation file (`*.fli`, `*.flc`, `*.mmm`) using the Choose Source File dialog box.
7. Script the button or other item (for example, the enterPage handler) used to launch the animation so that it plays. You can use an animation Auto-Script for the stage, such as shown in Listing 18.5.

Listing 18.5 OpenScript Auto-Script for Animation

```
TO HANDLE buttonClick
--{Cue the first frame of an animation or video}
     if mmIsOpen of clip id 100 -- not necessary, but nice
          mmClose clip id 100 wait
     end if
     mmOpen clip id 100 wait
     mmCue clip id 100 wait
     forward
END
```

To use this Auto-Script, replace the clip ID 100 with the name of your clip (for example, clip `goodBoy`).

Path Animation

As in the show and hide animation example, you will begin a path animation by creating the individual cels that make up your animation. In the example that was shown, we have created a simple "stained-glass" butterfly using the MTB draw tools. The first position was created and then the items were copied, modified to a new position, copied and modified, copied and modified (see fig. 18.8). This resulted in four butterflies, each consisting of a group of draw objects. These four groups were then grouped, and the path animation was defined for the group.

> **Note**
>
> You can create a path animation for a single object or for a group of objects; use a group of objects to create an animation that changes as it moves along the animation path (such as a man walking.)

Fig. 18.8

Path- and cel-based animation is created using ToolBook's Path Animation feature.

A path animation consists of a series of segments that are defined by vertices (see fig. 18.9). Once you have created the object(s) you want to animate, define the animation path and write the script for moving the object along the path. The vertices define the positions that the object will take (the steps). The more vertices in your path, the smoother the animation will appear. The rate of an animation depends on how far apart the vertices are as well as the number of steps between each display.

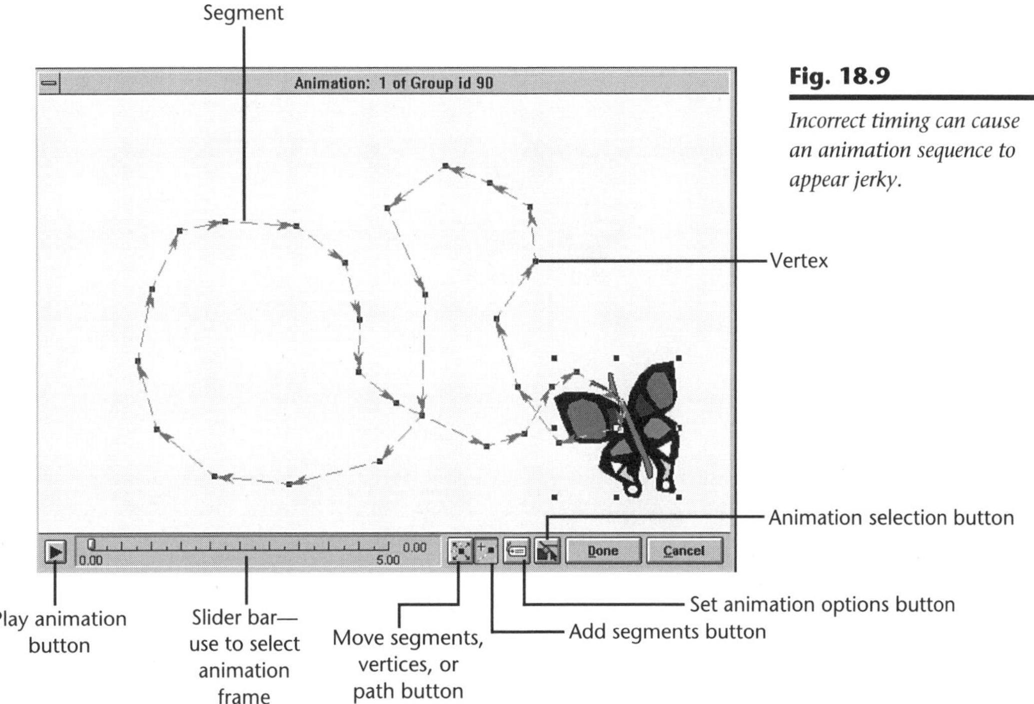

Fig. 18.9

Incorrect timing can cause an animation sequence to appear jerky.

This path was created with the following steps:

1. Select the object or group of objects to be animated.
2. From the main menu, select Tools, Path Animation. A screen similar to that in figure 18.9 is shown.
3. The cursor will have changed to an arrow with a crosshair. Click, in sequential order, each spot that you want to include as a vertex in your animation. (Don't worry if you make a mistake! You can always fix it later.)
4. When you have finished creating the path, use the Select button to modify the segments, vertices, or path. Click a vertex and drag it to move its position. Double-click a vertex to change the segments from a straight line to a curve (see fig. 18.10). Click and drag on any segment to move the entire path.
5. Click the Done button to save the animation.

You can have more than one animation defined for an object. This is accomplished by clicking the Animation Selection button. This brings up the animation Select Object dialog box permitting selection of the animation path to be edited (see fig. 18.11). This feature can be useful when you want to choose the path based on some criteria (for example, in an educational software title, you might want the butterfly to fly to a flower when the child clicks the correct vocabulary word, and fly out of the frame when they click the wrong word).

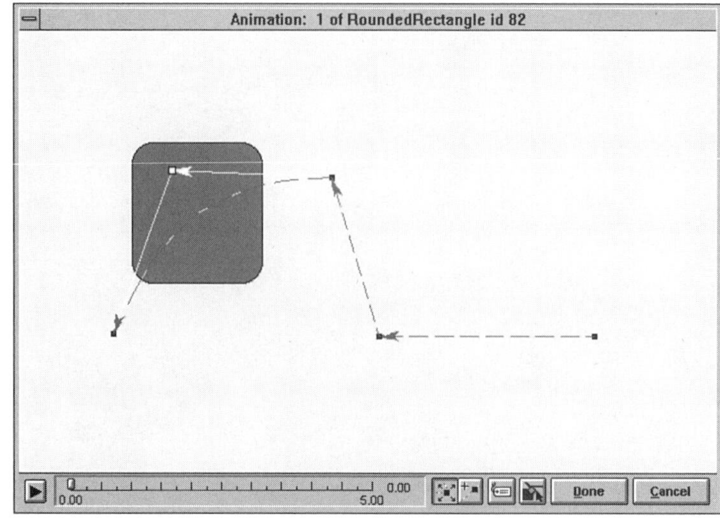

Fig. 18.10

Changing from a straight line to a curve in the Path Animation window.

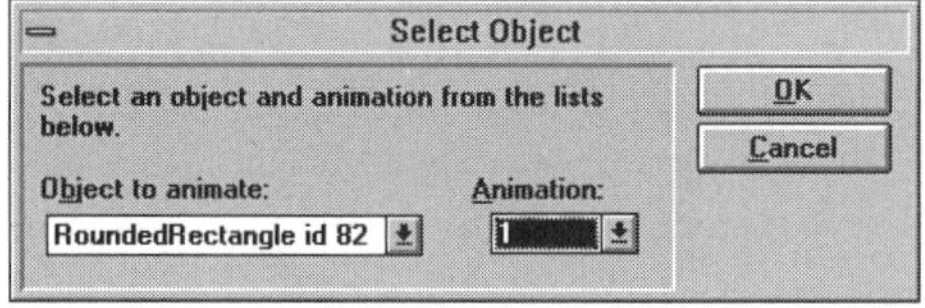

Fig. 18.11

Define multiple animations for an object via the Animation Select Object dialog box.

In the sample file `CH1804.TBK` that is on the CD-ROM included with this book, the animation of the butterfly has been completed by adding a few other screen elements for it to fly through (see fig. 18.12). The butterfly can fly between the layers of the elements on the screen. This was accomplished by placing some items in front of the butterfly and some behind (that is, their layer numbers are higher than the butterfly groups and some are lower).

Fig. 18.12

The completed butterfly animation screen consists of multiple layers.

Another feature of the MTB path animations that is useful in many cases is its ability to resize an item as it is animated. You can only specify an object size at the endpoints of the path, but it is a simple matter to create more than one path for an object if you want to have the object change sizes more than once. The example shown in figure 18.13 shows this method in use. First, move the object to the path beginning point and resize it with the resize handles. Then, move it to the end of the path and resize with the handles. Now the object will shrink or grow at an even pace along the path.

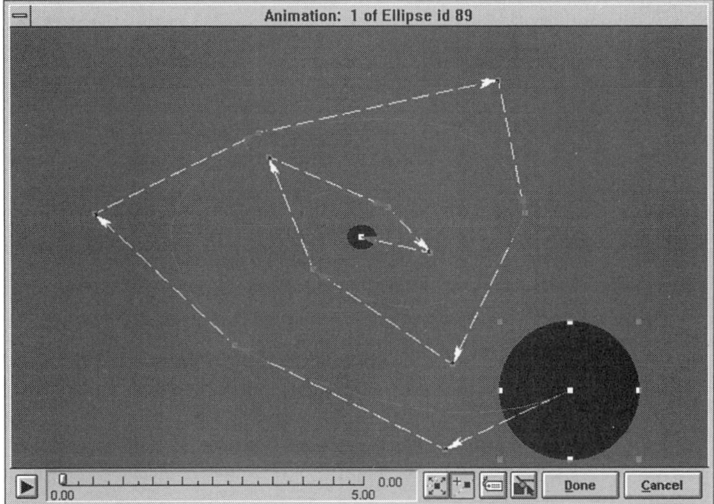

Fig. 18.13

Path animations like the shrinking ball may be resized in the process of being animated.

Even more fine-tuning of the animation can be done using the Animations button on the path animation screen. Clicking this button brings up the Animation Settings dialog box (see fig. 18.14).

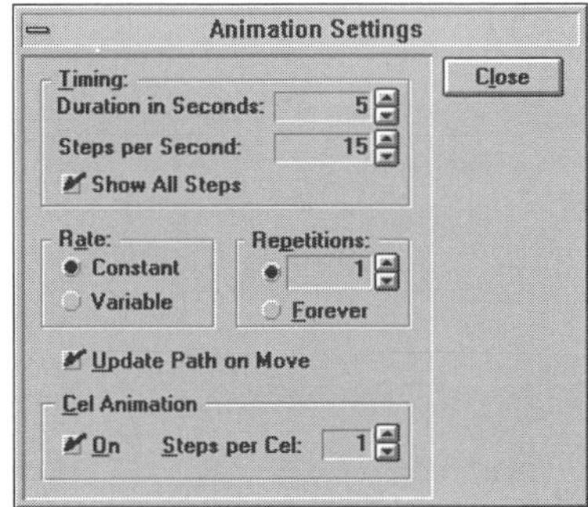

Fig. 18.14

Control the duration of an animation sequence via the Animation Settings dialog box.

Here you have the option to set the following parameters for your animation:

- **Duration in Seconds** sets the number of seconds (you can use decimal values for fractions) for the entire animation.

- **Steps per Second** sets the number of increments that the animation moves each second (up to 30). MTB will skip steps if the machine is not capable of playing the animation at this rate in order to finish the animation within the time specified. The larger the number of steps, the smoother the animation.
- The **Show All Steps** checkbox, when selected, forces MTB to show all of the specified steps, effectively overriding the duration setting for computers that cannot complete the animation in the specified time.
- The **Constant** and **Variable** radio buttons provide you with a choice between keeping the animation moving along the path at a fixed rate (Constant) versus moving at the same rate for each segment (Variable), causing the animation to be slower on shorter segments.
- The **Repetitions** setting sets the number of times that the object travels along the path when the animation is played. If you click **Forever**, the animation will continue playing until you press the Escape key or send the `stopAnimation` message to the object.
- The **Update Path on Move** checkbox, when selected, specifies that if you move the object at author level, the animation path will be repositioned. When unchecked, the animation will start at the point you fixed in the animation window.
- When **Cel Animation** is turned on, it creates the effect of a cel animation, hiding and displaying the objects in the group (in layer order) as it moves along the animation path. You must first group the items to be displayed in this manner.
- **Steps per Cel** indicates the number of cels that MTB moves before hiding one cel and displaying the next. Be careful how you set this in combination with the timing settings. Make sure you test the resulting application on a variety of machines that you might target for your final application before release.

All of the path animation settings can (of course) be set with OpenScript commands. The appropriate commands are described in Table 18.3.

Table 18.3 Animation Messages and Properties

Property or Message	Description	Arguments	Passed, Returned Values
`playAnimation` message	Send to an object to begin the animation	`<anNum>, [<notifyObj>, <wait>]`	The animation to play, the object to notify when done, wait flag for control
`playStep` message	Sent by MTB to an object currently running an animation to move to next step	`<anNum>`	The animation playing

Property or Message	Description	Arguments	Passed, Returned Values
`restoreAnimation` message	Send to an object to reset the object to the starting point of the animation	`<objList>`, `<animList>`	A list of animation objects to reset, a list of animations corresponding to the animations
`stopAnimation` message	Send to an object to stop the animation and leave object where it is	`<status>`	`successful` or `aborted`
`doneAnimatingNotify` message	Sent when an object finishes its animation	`<status>`, `<object identifier>`	`successful` or `aborted`, object that finished
`jumpToPercent` message	Send to an object to move it to a point in the animation path	`<%complete>`, `<animNumber>`	How far along an animation path to jump to (as a percent), the animation number
`anim_AnimationSettings` permanent property	Property of the animated object containing paths and settings	(See Table 18.4)	
`anim_CelAnimation` property	Determines if the animation cycles through the cels	`<anNum> of <objRef>`	Requires animation number and the object reference, returns True or False
`anim_CurrentTime` runtime property	Contains elapsed time since Windows was started	`<anNum> of <objRef>`	Requires animation number and the object reference, returns time in `ms`
`anim_CurrentStep` runtime property	Contains the current step of the animation	`<anNum> of <objRef>`	Requires animation number and the object reference, returns number of the current step
`anim_Duration` permanent property	Specifies the duration time for the animation (may not be accurate if `anim_ShowAllSteps = TRUE`)	`<anNum> of <objRef>`	Requires animation number and the object reference, returns duration in seconds
`anim_ElapsedTime` runtime property	Contains the elapsed time for the animation	`<anNum> of <objRef>`	Requires animation number and the object reference, returns elapsed in `ms`

(continues)

Table 18.3 Continued

Property or Message	Description	Arguments	Passed, Returned Values
`anim_EndSize` permanent property	Indicates the size of the object at the end of the animation	`<anNum> of <objRef>`	Requires animation number and the object reference, returns object size in page units (x, y)
`anim_NumRepetitions` permanent property	Indicates the number of times the objects will repeat the animation	`<anNum> of <objRef>`	Requires animation number and the object reference, returns positive integer
`anim_NumSteps` permanent property	Indicates the number of steps in the path	`<anNum> of <objRef>`	Requires animation number and the object reference, returns positive integer
`anim_Offset` runtime property	Contains the amount to offset the step positions, used to move the path during an animation	`<anNum> of <objRef>`	Requires animation number and the object reference, returns X,Y offset values in page units
`anim_StartPosition` permanent property	Contains the start position of an animation	`<anNum> of <objRef>`	Requires animation number and the object reference, returns X,Y values in page units
`anim_StartSize` permanent property	Indicates the size of the object at the start of the animation	`<anNum> of <objRef>`	Requires animation number and the object reference, returns object size in page units (x, y)
`anim_StartTime` runtime property	Indicates the start time of the object's current animation	`<anNum> of <objRef>`	Requires animation number and the object reference, returns time in `ms`
`anim_StepsPerCel` property	Determines how many steps the animation takes before showing the next cel	`<anNum> of <objRef>`	Requires animation number and the object reference, returns the number of steps.
`anim_ShowAllSteps` permanent property	Determines whether to skip steps when the animation is behind	`<anNum> of <objRef>`	Requires animation number and the object reference, returns True or False

These various animation messages and properties make it easy to create OpenScript commands to control your path animations. An example of such coding is provided below in Listing 18.6, which was provided by Asymetrix in their Path Animation Help file.

Listing 18.6 Example of Path Animation Scripting

```
to handle buttonClick
system numSteps
     --Variable to share with playStep handler
     numSteps = anim_NumSteps of self
     send playAnimation 1 to self
end

--Monitors animation, using animation properties to
--calculate percentage complete
to handle playStep
     system numSteps
     curStep = anim_CurrentStep of target
     if now <> null then
          percent = ceiling((curStep/numSteps)*100)
          caption of statusBar = percent & "%"
     end if
     forward     --Always forward playStep message
end playStep
```

This sample script shows how you could use OpenScript to show the status of an animation in the window's status bar.

One additional permanent property for path animations that you might find very useful when controlling these animations is `anim_AnimationSettings`. This property contains a table of the animation paths of the object and their settings in the format of a two-dimensional dynamic array. These values can be read and modified by creating `to get` and `to set` handlers. The `[n]` dimension is the number of arrays created for the object.

Table 18.4 Elements in the *anim_AnimationSettings* Array

Value	Description
[n][1]	Path; list of page unit coordinates for the vertices in the path
[n][2]	Curved vertices; list of `true` or `false` corresponding to each vertex (defines a curve if `true`)
[n][3]	Rate type; `constant` or `variable`
[n][4]	Cel animation; `true` if the animation plays cels
[n][5]	Show all steps; determines whether to skip steps if the animation gets behind
[n][6]	Start position; a list in page units of the animation's starting position

(continues)

V

Enhancing Applications

Table 18.4 Continued

Value	Description
`[n][7]`	Repetitions; integer representing number of times the animation will repeat
`[n][8]`	Duration; the time the animation will take to complete one repetition
`[n][9]`	Number of steps; total number of steps in the animation
`[n][10]`	Compiled path; list of bounds of the object at each step of the animation
`[n][11]`	Steps per cel; how many steps along the path the object moves before the cel is shown
`[n][12]`	Step rate; how many steps the animation will move per second
`[n][13]`	Fixed path; `false` if the path moves when the object is moved at the author level
`[n][14]`	Row number; the number of the current animation
`[n][15]`	Start size; the size of the object in page units at the first step of the animation
`[n][16]`	End size; the size of the object in page units at the last step of the animation

Note

To distribute a ToolBook that has an animation path, you must include the `MTB30ANM.SBK` file as part of the application. Do not use the `MTB30.SBK` file, because it also includes other (author) routines that you will not need for your finished application. You can either push the book onto your system books:

```
push "MTB30ANM.SBK" onto sysBooks
```

Or, you can put it into the system startup books in the `MTB30.INI` file:

```
startupSysBooks=MTB30ANM.SBK.
```

From Here...

The animation methods discussed in this chapter should get you started in creating full-featured animations for your applications. For more information on the topics discussed in this chapter, refer to the following chapters:

- Chapter 7, "Adding Multimedia Elements," gives you more information on using animations in stages. It also discusses stages, hotwords, and OLE.
- Chapter 10, "Using Graphics," provides you with information on creating the drawings that are useful when creating animations.
- Chapter 15, "Understanding Variables, Values, and Text," gives you a better understanding of arrays and how they can be used.

CHAPTER 19

Using Dynamic Link Libraries (DLLs) and Dynamic Data Exchange (DDE)

Asymetrix ToolBook supports the use of *dynamic link libraries* (DLLs) and *dynamic data exchange* (DDE), features that make the OpenScript programming language completely open-ended. These extensions allow you to call Windows functions from within ToolBook, pass information to other software programs on your system, and receive data from other applications.

If there is a programming task you would like to accomplish within ToolBook that you find awkward in OpenScript, you have the following alternatives:

- You can find another program that performs the same function, and use DDE.
- You can use MCI calls to perform the function—usually for hardware control. (See Chapter 22, "MCI Devices & Multimedia.")
- You can link a DLL that includes subroutines for performing the function.
- You can create a specialty DLL in C++ and link it within MTB.

DLLs and MTB40

Dynamic link libraries (DLLs) are libraries of routines that perform specific tasks. They are stored external to any calling programs and are available to any program on the system. There are many Windows DLLs that can be called from OpenScript to perform low level tasks, and MTB supplies users with a few very useful DLLs (discussed in this chapter).

Programming has changed drastically over the years; now it is common practice to purchase distribution licenses for DLLs supplied by software vendors, saving thousands of hours of development time. For example, you can purchase DLLs that will automate the process of accessing the Internet, support scanning devices, do image manipulation (such as dithering), sort data, or plot data in three dimensions. A good programmers' software catalog, such as the Programmers Shop (800-421-8006), can supply you with information on purchasing DLLs.

Besides commercial DLLs, there are thousands of public domain, manufacturer supplied, and Windows DLLs available. When researching the best way to accomplish a programming task, start by seeing what functions are available from Windows DLLs; by using Windows DLLs, you save disk space since they are already in place on the systems. There are many good books on this topic, and Microsoft is very supportive in providing programmers with their Software Developer's Kit (SDK).

To find out about specific DLL functions, visit the multimedia forum on CompuServe and ask other programmers for advice on where to find the DLL you need. Also, visit related forums. Diligent searching and inquiry will usually provide answers within days or even hours.

Declaring and Linking DLLs

The first step in linking a DLL in MTB is to find out the details about the functions it includes. Commercial DLLs will have detailed documentation and examples of the links. Windows DLL linking information can be obtained from Microsoft or through a myriad of Windows programming books available on the market. You are provided with some examples of useful Windows DLL links in this book, but no attempt has been made to be comprehensive on this subject.

In general, you use a DLL by linking it, declaring the functions and their return variables, calling the functions as needed, and (optionally) unlinking the DLL when you have completed the calls.

To link a DLL, use the `linkDLL` control structure:

```
linkDLL <DLL file>
    <return type> <function name> [= <DLL function>]
 (<parameter type list>)
end linkDll
```

`<DLL file>` is the name of the DLL file you want to link, such as `TB30WIN.DLL` or `USER.EXE`. Of course, if the DLL file is not in the computer's path, you must specify its location. If you are using a built-in Windows library, specify the module name instead of the file name in case the file names have been changed. For example, use `KERNEL` not `KRNL386.EXE` and `USER` not `USER.EXE`.

`<return type>` is the literal data type returned by the function. These are `BYTE`, `DOUBLE`, `DWORD`, `FLOAT`, `INT`, `LONG`, `POINTER`, `STRING`, and `WORD`.

`<function name> = <DLL function>` is the name or alias of the function that you are calling. If you use an alias, follow it with the literal function name, `DLL function`. You will need to use aliases when there are OpenScript commands that have the same names as the functions you are calling in the DLL, as shown in the following example:

```
linkDLL "KERNEL"
     INT winOpenFile = openFile(STRING, POINTER, WORD)
end linkDLL
```

`<parameter type list>` is the list of data types for the function's parameters. The allowed types are `BYTE`, `DOUBLE`, `DWORD`, `FLOAT`, `INT`, `LONG`, `POINTER`, `STRING`, and `WORD`.

Data Types for DLL Functions

Table 19.1 provides a correspondence between the Windows C data types and the ToolBook data types.

Table 19.1 Data Types for DLL Functions

Windows C Data Type	DLL Parameter Type	DLL Return Type
int	INT	INT
BOOL	INT	INT
void	none	INT
unsigned char, BYTE	BYTE	BYTE
UNIT, unsigned int, WORD	WORD	WORD
HANDLE, HWND, HBMP, HDC, etc.	WORD	WORD
long	LONG	LONG
unsigned long	DWORD	DWORD
FLOAT	FLOAT	FLOAT
DOUBLE	DOUBLE	DOUBLE
VOID FAR *, CHAR FAR *, LPSTR, LPCSTR	STRING or POINTER	POINTER
STRING	DWORD	Returns a handle to the string in the LOWORD and a value for sysErrorNumber in HIWORD

You can pass constant strings as input to a DLL function using a constant (a string in quotes) or a property or variable. To pass a null string from ToolBook, use empty quotation marks (""). To pass a null pointer to the DLL, use the value null, not an empty string.

If the function you're linking to modifies a string or returns data in a buffer, declare the data type as POINTER, not STRING, and pass the pointer to Windows memory.

If you have a DLL that returns a long pointer to a string (LPSTR) or a CHAR FAR *, declare it as a POINTER and then convert the returned value to ToolBook data type, as shown in the following example:

```
linkDLL "TSTLPSTR.DLL"
     POINTER iReturnLPSTR()
end
to handle callIt
     get iReturnLPSRT()
     strVarBack = pointerString(0,It)
     request "Value is: " & strVarBack
end
```

Tips for Linking DLLs

You will often want to link the DLLs that your program needs at the time the book is opened (such as in the `enterBook` handler). However, there are many times that you will not want to do it this way. If, for example, you have a large application with a lot of DLLs being linked, doing the links on `enterBook` can create a slow starting book. In this case, it may be better to move the link to somewhere later in the application, such as right before the first time it is required. You can provide the user with some kind of distraction at this point, such as a popup graphic or information panel to read, to give the effect of a faster application.

Another reason to link DLLs elsewhere in the application is that if you need the function only temporarily, you may be better off linking it, using it, and then unlinking it to free up system resources.

> **Note**
>
> When you link a DLL, you must be certain that you know the arguments. Incorrect linkages are not detected by MTB during the link, and an erroneous call can cause a dreaded General Protection Fault (GPF) in your application. Be careful!

The usual method for linking DLLs is demonstrated in Listing 19.1.

Listing 19.1 Linking DLLS

```
to handle enterBook
     clear sysError
     sysSuspend = true
     linkDLL "USER"
          INT showWindow(WORD,INT)
          WORD setActiveWindow(WORD)
     end linkDLL
     sysSuspend = false
     clear sysError
     linkDLL "TBKFILE.DLL"
          INT fileExists(STRING)
          STRING getFileList(STRING)
     end linkDLL
     if sysError is not null
     request "TBKFILE.DLL not found."
          break
     end if
end
```

This example shows the usual `linkDLL` practices: begin by clearing `sysError` and setting `sysSuspend` to `false` (to suppress `Execution Suspended` error messages if the link cannot be made). Next, link the DLL. In non-Windows DLL calls, the `sysError` flag is checked and an appropriate message indicating the difficulty is constructed.

Unlinking DLLs

When you have finished with a DLL, you can either explicitly unlink it, or you can allow it to automatically unlink when the application is exited. You would want to unlink a DLL when it is no longer needed to free up the resources that it uses. The command for unlinking is as follows:

```
unlinkDLL <DLL file>
```

For example, to unlink `TBKFILE.DLL` in Listing 19.1, use the following command:

```
unlinkDLL "TBKFILE.DLL"
```

Be aware that if you use the command `restore system`, you will unlink *all* currently linked DLLs.

Tip

You cannot free up the resources needed for Windows DLLs, so you do not save anything by unlinking these routines.

Using DLLs

The use of DLLs allows unlimited expansion in your ToolBook coding. Many functions that are not practical to code in OpenScript can be found ready to use in the shipped DLLs. Described in this section are the following ToolBook DLLs:

- `TB30DLG.DLL`—This displays Windows style dialog boxes.
- `TB30WIN.DLL`—This determines the characteristics of devices, determines fonts, and provides access to the WIN.INI file.
- `TB30DOS.DLL`—This allows you to perform file functions, such as delete, copy, and get files lists.
- `TB30PDX.DLL`—This provides access to Borland Paradox database functions.
- `TBKDB3.DLL`—This allows you to access dBASE III functions.

TB30DLG.DLL

The `TB30DLG.DLL` functions allow you display and get information from Windows style dialog boxes. These functions include means of controlling the display of combo boxes, list boxes, color dialog boxes, file and directory dialog boxes, and other miscellaneous functions.

Table 19.2 and many of the remaining tables in this chapter provide you with the arguments and syntax for the links and calls, each followed by a single-line example of the function's usage. This format will allow you to quickly look up and reference the calls as you need them while scripting. For more detail on any of these calls, see the online help files from Asymetrix, the Asymetrix OpenScript manual, or your Microsoft Windows' Developer Kit.

Table 19.2 *Combobox TB30DLG.DLL* Functions

Funct. Declar-ations	Function	Description	Declarations	Parameters
get addComboBoxItem(hDlg,"comboBox sounds","Play MIDI",-1,1)				
INT	addComboBoxItem	Adds a new item to the drop-down list of the combo box control	WORD, STRING, STRING, INT, INT	<hDlg>, <control name>, <new item>, <index>, <sort flag>
get deleteComboBoxItem(hDlg,"comboBox styles","Jazz")				
INT	deleteComboBoxItem	Deletes an item from the drop-down list of a combo box control	WORD, STRING, STRING	<hDlg>, <control name>, <item>
get setComboBoxItems(hDlg,"ComboBox items","Sounds" & CRLF & "videos")				
INT	setComboBoxItems	Sets the text for one or more items in the drop-down list box control	WORD, STRING, STRING	<hDlg>, <control name>, <new items>

The DLL functions used in Table 19.2 are useful for the cases in which you want to be able to create dialog boxes "on the fly," based on other things going on at that time. In many cases, however, it is easier (and preferable) to create your dialog boxes as viewers using standard OpenScript commands. An example of the use of some of the combo box calls is as follows:

```
to get TBKDialogInit hDlg, hWndFocus
     get setComboBoxItems(hDlg,"ComboBox items", \
          "Play sounds"&CRLF&"Play video")
     get setControlText(hDlg,"ComboBox items","Play sounds")
     return 0
end
```

Table 19.3 provides some additional functions found in `TB30DLF.DLL` for list boxes in the dialog box.

Table 19.3 ListBox *TB30DLG.DLL* Functions

Funct. Declar-ations	Function	Description	Declarations	Parameters
get addListBoxItem(hDlg,"listbox items","Sounds",-1,1)				
INT	addListBoxItem	Adds a new text line item to a list box control	WORD, STRING, STRING, INT, INT	<hDlg>, <control name>, <new item>, <index>, <sort flag>
get deleteListBoxItem(hDlg,"listBox items","misc.")				
INT	deleteListBoxItem	Deletes a text line item from a list box control	WORD, STRING, STRING	<hDlg>, <control name>, <item>
get deletenListBoxItem(hDlg,"listBox items",nItem)				
INT	deletenListBoxItem	Deletes a text line item, based on its index number, from a list box control	WORD, STRING, INT	<hDlg>, <control name>, <item>
put getListBoxItems(hDlg,"listBox items")				
STRING	getListBoxItems	Returns the text of the selected text line or text lines in a list box control	WORD, STRING	<hDlg>, <control name>
put getListBoxSelection(hDlg,"listBox items")				
STRING	getListBoxSelection	Returns the text of the selected text line or text lines in a list box control	WORD, STRING	<hDlg>, <control name>
put getnListBoxSelection(hDlg,"listBox items")				
STRING	getnListBoxSelection	Returns the index number or numbers representing the selected text line or text lines in a list box control	WORD, STRING	<hDlg>, <control name>

(continues)

Table 19.3 Continued

Funct. Declar-ations	Function	Description	Declarations	Parameters
get setListBoxItems(hDlg,"listbox items","Frogs" &CRLF& "Mice")				
INT	setListBoxItems	Sets the text for a text line or a list of text lines in a list box control	WORD, STRING, STRING	<hDlg>, <control name>, <new items>
get setListBoxSelection(hDlg,"listbox items","A" & CRLF & "B")				
INT	setListBoxSelection	Selects a text line or list of text lines, in a list box control	WORD, STRING STRING	<hDlg>, <control name>, <selection>
get setnListBoxSelection(hDlg,"listBox items","5,3,2")				
INT	setnListBoxSelection	Selects a text line or list of text lines in a list box control by index number	WORD, STRING, STRING	<hDlg>, <control name>, <selection index>

An example of the usage of one of these functions is provided in the following example, which will select lines six, one, and three in the specified list box:

```
to get DCommand hDlg
        get setnListBoxSelection(hDlg,"listBox items","6,1,3")
        return 0
end
```

Table 19.4 provides a reference to the TB30DLG color functions: controlling palette display and color conversions.

Table 19.4 Color Palette *TB30DLG.DLL* Functions

Funct. Declar-ations	Function	Description	Declarations	Parameters
get chooseColorDlg(255,255,255)				
STRING	chooseColorDlg	Displays the standard Windows color dialog box	BYTE, BYTE, BYTE	<red value>, <green value>, <blue value>
get colorPaletteDlg(0,0,0)				
STRING	colorPaletteDlg	Displays the standard Windows color dialog box	BYTE, BYTE, BYTE	<red value>, <green value>, <blue value>

Funct. Declar-ations	Function	Description	Declarations	Parameters
currColors = getCustomColors( )				
STRING	getCustomColors	Returns a CRLF-delimited list of the 16 colors that represent the current custom color palette	none	
get setCustomColors(1,"255,0,0" & CRLF & "0,255,0")				
INT	setCustomColors	Sets the colors for the custom color palette	INT, STRING	<index>, <colors>

The color dialog box functions of the TB30DLG.DLL are simple to access, and they provide a simple means of using color palettes in your applications. The script in Listing 19.2 shows how you might link to one of these functions to provide an interface in your application (see fig. 19.1).

Listing 19.2 Linking *chooseColorDlg* in *TB30DLG.DLL*

```
to handle buttonUp
     linkDll "TB30DLG.DLL"
          STRING chooseColorDlg(BYTE,BYTE,BYTE)
     end
     get chooseColorDlg(255,255,255)
     if it is not null then
          rgbFill of irregularPolygon "hair" = it
     end
end
```

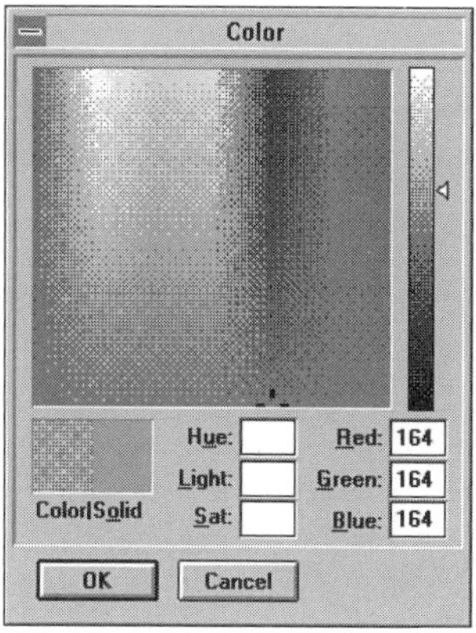

Fig. 19.1

The result of using chooseColorDlg is a color dialog box.

A few simple changes in the script (see Listing 19.2), as follows, produce an alternative color dialog box (see fig. 19.2):

```
to handle buttonUp
     linkDll "TB30DLG.DLL"
          STRING colorPaletteDlg(BYTE,BYTE,BYTE)
     end
     get colorPaletteDlg(0,0,0)
     if it is not null then
          rgbFill of irregularPolygon "hair" = it
     end
end
```

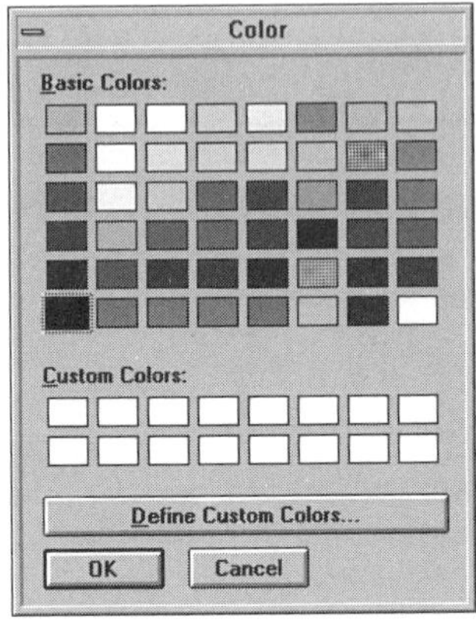

Fig. 19.2

A different dialog box is created by substituting colorPaletteDlg for chooseColorDlg in Listing 19.2.

Both of these scripts allow the user to choose a color from a standard Windows dialog box and then assign it to an item in the page. These examples are contained in the file `CH1901.TBK` on the CD-ROM included with this book.

Table 19.5 provides a list of the `TB30DLG` functions that are related to file and directory access and usage.

Table 19.5 File and Directory *TB30DLG.DLL* Functions

Funct. Declar-ations	Function	Description	Declarations	Parameters
newDir = ChooseDirectoryDlg("new directory:",null)				
STRING	ChooseDirectoryDlg	Displays the choose directory dialog box	STRING, STRING	<caption text>, <default path>
get openDlg(".","*.TXT","Text file:","Open File")				
STRING	openDlg	Displays the Windows open dialog box	STRING, STRING, STRING, STRING	<directory>, <extension>, <prompt>, <caption>

Funct. Declar-ations	Function	Description	Declarations	Parameters
get openFileDlg("Next animation:",defBook,defPath,"*.fli",1)				
`STRING`	`openFileDlg`	Displays the Windows open file dialog box	`STRING, STRING, STRING, STRING, INT`	`<caption>, <default file>, <default path>, <filters>, <index>`
get saveAsDlg("Save as",null,null,"*.txt",1)				
`STRING`	`saveAsDlg`	Displays the Windows save as dialog box	`STRING, STRING, STRING, STRING, INT`	`<caption>, <default file>, <default path>, <filters>, <index>`

The following is an example of using the `chooseDirectoryDlg`:

```
to handle buttonUp
     linkDLL "TB30DLG.DLL"
          STRING chooseDirectoryDlg(STRING,STRING)
     end
     newDir = chooseDirectoryDlg("new directory",null)
     request "New directory:" && newDir
end
```

The resulting dialog box is shown in figure 19.3.

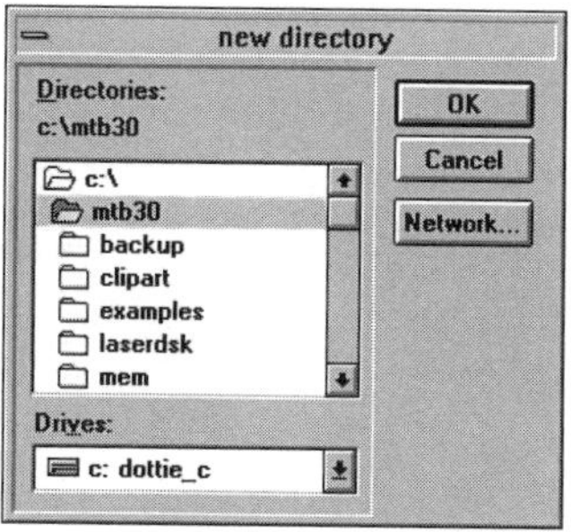

Fig. 19.3

A dialog box is created with chooseDirectoryDlg.

V

Enhancing Applications

Note

Other functions in the `TB30DLG.DLL` include: `chooseFontDlg()`, `controlIDtoName()`, `controlNameTohWnd()`, `controlNameToID()`, `dialog()`, `dialogCallBack()`, `getDialogFocus()`, `getOpenFileDlgFilterIndex()`, `getSaveAsDlgFilterIndex()`, `enableControl()`, `endTBKDialog()`, `enterWaitState()`, `getControlText()`, `getValue()`, `isButtonChecked()`, `isControlEnabled()`, `leaveWaitState()`, `setBitMapData()`, `setButtonCheck()`, `setControlText()`, `setDialogFocus()`, `setGroupedButtonCheck()`, `setIconData()`, `setValue()`.

TB30WIN.DLL

The TB30WIN.DLL functions are used when you need to find out more about the capability of the machine that is currently running. You can use the functions to discover details of the graphic card and how it displays, get and change the values for Windows variables from WIN.INI, convert display units, and find out about the fonts on a system.

The functions in TB30WIN.DLL that report features of the graphics display can be essential when you are targeting a wide variety of display devices for your final distribution of an application. This is especially true if your application requires more than 640×480 pixel resolution. The difficulty is that the "standards" for graphic display beyond the VGA resolution are not very "standard" and have been interpreted by different graphics card manufacturers in different ways over the years.

Unless you have complete control over the final display device for your application, you should consider either creating your application in such a way that the user can resize viewers and palettes as needed, or keeping the main viewer within the 640 by 480 pixel limits. If this is not possible, then you will need to write routines that use the functions from Table 19.6 to determine the output resolution of the display device.

For example, if you want to announce the current display resolution capability in pixels *x* and *y*, use the following code:

```
request "Current graphics mode X,Y:" && \
horizontalDisplayRes() && "by" && verticalDisplayRes()
```

Examples of these functions are provided in the example ToolBook file CH1902.TBK.

Table 19.6 Display Device *TB30WIN.DLL* Functions

Funct. Declarations	Function	Description	Declarations	Parameters
get clientFromPage(pageScroll of mainWindow, magnification of mainWindow, bounds of rectangle "frame" of this page)				
STRING	clientFromPage	Converts set of coordinates in ToolBook page units to pixels relative to the upper-left corner of the client area of ToolBook window	STRING, INT, STRING	<page scroll>, <magnification>, <point¦rectangle>

Funct. Declar-ations	Function	Description	Declarations	Parameters
get clientFromScreen(windowHandle of this window,"0,0")				
STRING	clientFromScreen	Converts point or rectangle in pixels relative to the upper-left corner of the screen into point or rectangle in pixels relative to the upper-left corner of client area	WORD, STRING	<windowHandle>, <point¦rectangle>
get displayAspectX( )				
INT	displayAspectX	Relative pixel width for the display device	none	
get displayAspectXY( )				
INT	displayAspectXY	Diagonal pixel width for the display device	none	
get displayAspectY( )				
INT	displayAspectY	Height of the pixel for the display device	none	
get displayBitsPerPixel( )				
INT	displayBitsPerPixel	Number of color bits for each pixel	none	
get displayColorPlanes( )				
INT	displayColorPlanes	Number of color planes for the device	none	
get displayLogPixelsX( )				
INT	displayLogPixelsX	Number of pixels per inch along the width of the display device	none	
get displayLogPixelsY( )				
INT	displayLogPixelsY	Number of pixels per inch along the height of display device	none	

(continues)

Table 19.6 Continued

Funct. Declar-ations	Function	Description	Declarations	Parameters
theColor=HLStoRGB(275.95,75.21,23)				
STRING	HLStoRGB	Converts the specified HLS color value into RGB color value	DOUBLE, DOUBLE, DOUBLE	<hue>, <lightness>, <saturation>
get horizontalDisplayRes( )				
INT	horizontalDisplayRes	Returns screen's horizontal resolution in pixels	none	
get horizontalDisplaySize( )				
INT	horizontal-DisplaySize	Returns screen's horizontal size in millimeters	none	
get pageFromClient (pageScroll of mainWindow, magnification of mainWindow, bounds of mainWindow)				
STRING	pageFromClient	Converts set of coordinates in pixels relative to the upper-left corner of the client area of a ToolBook window into ToolBook page units	STRING, INT, STRING	<pageScroll>, <magnification>, <point¦ rectangle>
get pageFromScreen(windowHandle of mainWindow, pageScroll of mainWindow, magnification of mainWindow, bounds of mainWindow)				
STRING	pageFromScreen	Converts a set of coordinates in pixels relative to the upper-left corner of the display screen into coordinates in ToolBook page units	WORD, STRING, INT, STRING	<windowHandle>, <pageScroll>, <magnification>, <point¦ rectangle>
myHLScolor=RGBtoHLS(RGBfillColor of selection)				
STRING	RGBtoHLS	Converts the specified RGB color value into HLS color value	WORD, WORD, WORD	<red>, <green>, <blue>

Funct. Declar-ations	Function	Description	Declarations	Parameters
get screenFromClient(windowHandle of this window,"0,0")				
STRING	screenFromClient	Converts a point or rectangle in pixels relative to the upper-left corner of the ToolBook client area into pixels	WORD, STRING	<windowHandle>, <point¦rectangle>
get screenFromPage(windowHandle of mainWindow, pageScroll of mainWindow, magnification of mainWindow, bounds of rectangle "bigBox")				
STRING	screenFromPage	Converts a set of coordinates in ToolBook page units to coordinates in pixels	WORD, STRING, INT, STRING	<windowHandle>, <pageScroll>, <magnification>, <point¦rectangle>
request "Screen (vertical) in pixels:" && verticalDisplayRes()				
INT	verticalDisplayRes	Returns physical display's vertical resolution in pixels	none	
request "Vertical screen size in mm:" && verticalDisplaySize()				
INT	verticalDisplaySize	Returns physical display's vertical size in millimeters	none	
numPix = xPixelsFromUnits(screenU)				
INT	xPixelsFromUnits	Converts horizontal dimension in pixels into dimension in ToolBook page units	INT	<xdimension>
scrUnits = xUnitsFromPixels(numPix)				
INT	xUnitsFromPixels	Converts horizontal dimension in Tool-Book page units into dimension in pixels	INT	<xdimension>
numPix = yPixelsFromUnits(screenU)				
INT	yPixelsFromUnits	Converts a vertical dimension between pixels and ToolBook page units	INT	<ydimension>

(continues)

Table 19.6 Continued

Funct. Declar-ations	Function	Description	Declarations	Parameters
scrUnits = yUnitsFromPixels(numPix)				
INT	yUnitsFromPixels	Converts a vertical dimension between ToolBook page units and pixels	INT	<ydimension>

Table 19.7 contains other useful TB30WIN functions. For example, the popText() function is a useful "quick" programming feature that allows you to create a popup text box without going through the trouble of creating a viewer. Simply link the DLL, and script the object as follows:

```
get popText("Bold header","This is the text that will be \
displayed...", mousePosition of this window)
```

Another useful TB30WIN function is printerFonts(<typeface>), which returns a list of the available type faces when passed a null and the available sizes for a font when passed the font name.

Some examples of these functions are provided in the ToolBook file CH1902.TBK.

Table 19.7 Miscellaneous *TB30WIN.DLL* Functions

Funct. Declar-ations	Function	Description	Declarations	Parameters
get displayFonts("Arial")				
STRING	displayFonts	Returns sizes of characters available for specified type-face or names and sizes of all available typefaces	STRING	<typeface name>
get IniVar ("ToolBook","startupSysBooks","ToolBook.ini")				
STRING	getIniVar	Returns value of specified item in specified section of any INI file	STRING, STRING, STRING	<section name>, <item name>, <file name>
get getModuleList( )				
STRING	getModuleList	Returns list of Windows modules currently loaded on the system	none	

Funct. Declar-ations	Function	Description	Declarations	Parameters
request getModulePath("MTB30RUN.EXE")				
`STRING`	`getModulePath`	Returns the path of any specified Windows module currently loaded on the system	`STRING`	`<module name>`
getWinIniVar ("COOP", "startupModule")				
`STRING`	`getWinIniVar`	Returns value of specified item in the specified section of WIN.INI file	`STRING,` `STRING`	`<section name>,` `<item name>`
get papMenu (windowHandle of mainWindow, pageScroll of mainWindow, magnification of mainWindow, position of rectangle "myMenu", menuList, null)				
`INT`	`popMenu`	Displays a popup menu and returns the number of the item chosen	`WORD,` `STRING,` `INT,` `STRING,` `STRING,` `STRING`	`<windowHandle>,` `<pageScroll>,` `<magnification>,` `<position>,` `<menuItems>,` `<spare>`
get popText("Mouse","Small rodent.", mousePosition of this window)				
`INT`	`popText`	Displays text in a read-only popup window with a shadowed border	`STRING,` `STRING,` `STRING`	`<title>,` `<text string>,` `<point>`
get popTextGetBounds("Title","Happy Days", mousePosition of this window)				
`STRING`	`popTextGetBounds`	Returns the bounds of the popup window to be displayed by the `poptext()` function	`STRING,` `STRING,` `STRING`	`<title>,` `<text string>,` `<point>`
get printerFonts("")				
`STRING`	`printerFonts`	Returns size of characters available for printing with a typeface	`STRING`	`<typeface name>`

(continues)

Table 19.7 Continued

Funct. Declar-ations	Function	Description	Declarations	Parameters
get sendKeys("%{keyEnter}",1)				
`INT`	`sendKeys`	Sends the specified keys to an active application as though typed	`STRING`, `INT`	`<key string>`, `<return>`
if setIniVar("MyApp","defBook", "TEMPLATE.TBK", "MYAPP.INI") = 1				
`WORD`	`SetIniVar`	Sets the value of the item in the specified section of any INI file to a new value	`STRING`, `STRING`, `STRING`, `STRING`	`<section name>`, `<item name>`, `<new value>`, `<file name>`
if setWinIniVar("PlayBook","allLevels","false") = 1				
`WORD`	`setWinIniVar`	Sets the value of the item in the specified section of WIN.INI file to a new value	`STRING`, `STRING`, `STRING`	`<section name>`, `<item name>`, `<new value>`
get yieldApp()				
`INT`	`yieldApp`	Yields execution to any waiting task		

Tip

Perhaps the most often used function in `TB30WIN.DLL` is `setINIVar()`, which allows you to set the value of a variable in any section of an INI file.

TB30DOS.DLL

`TB30DOS.DLL` allows you to access functions that deal with files, disk drives, and system settings. The functions are described in Table 19.8.

Table 19.8 *TB30DOS.DLL* Functions

Funct. Declarations	Function	Description	Declarations	Parameters
get copyFile(oldFile,newFile)				
INT	copyFile	Copies the source to the destination file name	STRING, STRING	<source file>, <destination file>
get createDirectory(newDir)				
INT	createDirectory	Creates a new directory	STRING	<dir name>
get fileExists("coophelp.tbk")				
INT	fileExists	Determines if the file exists	STRING	<file name>
get getCDDriveList( )				
INT	getCDDriveList	Returns a string of CD drives on the system	none	
get getCurrentDirectory("C")				
INT	getCurrentDirectory	Gets the current working directory on the drive	STRING	<drive letter>
request "Sorry! That file is not on drive:" & getCurrentDrive( )				
INT	getCurrentDrive	Gets the current drive	none	
fileList = getDirectoryOnlyList("C:*.*","N")—returns all dirs in name order				
INT	getDirectoryOnlyList	Returns a list of files matching the path and file name	STRING, STRING	<path>, <sort order>
DOSPath = getDosEnvironmentString("path")				
INT	getDos-EnvironmentString	Returns the DOS environment flag for the tag name	STRING	<tag name>
if getDriveKind("D") is not "CDROM" then				
INT	getDriveKind	Returns the drive type	STRING	<drive letter>

(continues)

Table 19.8 Continued

Funct. Declar-ations	Function	Description	Declarations	Parameters
get getDriveList( )				
INT	getDriveList	Gets a list of valid drives	none	
get getFileAttributes("test.tbk")				
INT	getFileAttributes	Gets the file attributes	STRING	<file name>
get getFileDate("test.tbk")				
INT	getFileDate	Gets the date and time for the file	STRING	<file name>
get getFileList("*.txt")				
INT	getFileList	Returns the list of matching files	STRING	<file name>
dontDelFiles = getFileOnlyList("C:\","HS","E")—all root level system & hidden				
INT	getFileOnlyList	Returns list of matching files	STRING, STRING, STRING	<path>, <file attributes>, <sort order>
get getFileSize(fileToRemove)				
INT	getFileSize	Gets the file size	STRING	<file name>
get getFreeDiskSpace("C")				
INT	getFreeDiskSpace	Gets the number of free bytes	STRING	<disk drive>
request "Your drive label is" && getVolumeName("C")				
INT	getVolumeName	Returns the volume label for the drive	STRING	<disk drive>
if isCDDrive("D") then				
INT	isCDDrive	Indicates if the drive is a CD	STRING	<drive name>
get moveFile("c:\temp\junk.tbk","c:\goodstuf\real.tbk")				
INT	moveFile	Moves and renames a file	STRING, STRING	<file spec>, <destination>

Funct. Declar-ations	Function	Description	Declarations	Parameters
get removeDirectory("c:\mtb30")				
INT	removeDirectory	Deletes the specified empty directory	STRING	<path name>
get removeFile("c:\temp\junk.tmp")				
INT	removeFile	Deletes the specified file	STRING	<file name>
get setCurrentDirectory("c:\test")				
INT	setCurrentDirectory	Makes the specified directory the current working directory	STRING	<dir name>
get setCurrentDrive("D")				
INT	setCurrentDrive	Makes the specified drive the current drive	STRING	<drive letter>
get setFileAttributes("c:\test\hideme.tbk","RH")—readonly, hidden				
INT	setFileAttributes	Sets the file attributes	STRING, STRING	<file name>, <attributes>
get setFileDate("c:\temp\junk.txt",00:00:00","01/01/99")				
INT	setFileDate	Sets the date and time stamp for a file	STRING, STRING, STRING	<path>, <time>, <date>
get setSystemDate(1,1,96)				
INT	setSystemDate	Sets the system date	INT, INT, INT	<month>, <day>, <year>
get setSystemTime(13,00,00)				
INT	setSystemTime	Sets the system time	INT, INT, INT	<hour>, <minute>, <seconds>

An example of a code fragment that uses some of these functions is provided in the listing that follows: the local variable `toDrive` consists of a drive letter (such as *E*), the variable `fromFile` contains the full path name of a file (such as `c:\temp\junk.txt`), and the variable `fName` is the path and file name for the new file (such as `newdir\newjunk.txt`):

```
if isCDDrive(toDrive) then
     request "Cannot move this file to a CD ROM disk!" with "okay"
else
     toFile = toDrive & ":\" & fName
     get moveFile(fromFile,toFile)
end if
```

TBKDB3.DLL and *TB30PDX.DLL*

If you are creating an application that manipulates large amounts of data, you will find the functions contained in the Asymetrix `TBKDB3.DLL` and `TB30PDX.DLL` files extremely useful. The functions found in these DLLs will allow you to do the following:

- Initialize records and set record and block sizes, record types, etc.
- Open, close, and copy data from one table or record to another
- Create, read, and write *BLOBs* (*Binary Large Objects*)
- Create and use index keys for tables

These functions allow you access to all of the functions needed for creating and maintaining databases from within ToolBook. One advantage of using database files with ToolBook, over other ways of maintaining information, is that you can easily update information externally to the ToolBook environment in which the data will be used. In other words, you can create special "tools" used outside of your application to keep the data files current. This is especially helpful in codes that are data driven (such as multimedia encyclopedias).

Another excellent use of database functions is in creating a code that will interact with data written by another application. A user-friendly interface that allows management at a large company to query the corporate accounting files to obtain current financial information, or a program that allows a secretary to easily enter information into a file that can be read directly by the payroll accounting software are two examples.

`TB30PDX.DLL` and the Paradox engine are very powerful and have an advantage over the dBASE III functions of `TB30DB3.DLL` in that they support BLOBs. BLOBs are large blocks of binary data, such as graphics, video clips, and sound files. The BLOB itself is not contained inside the database file; instead, a reference to the location (its *handle*) is stored in the table.

In Table 19.9 through Table 19.18, the functions that can be found in these DLLs are outlined and grouped by subject: Paradox password functions; Paradox data and function initializing; Paradox sorting and retrieving values; Paradox tables; Paradox BLOB functions; Paradox keying and indexing; Paradox data searching; miscellaneous Paradox functions; dBASE indexing; and other functions of dBASE.

Table 19.9 *TB30PDX.DLL* Password Functions

Funct. Declar-ations	Function	Description	Declarations	Parameters
get addPXPassword(myPassWord)				
`INT`	`addPXPassword`	Enters a password	`STRING`	`<password>`
get decryptPXTable("c:\data\temp\temp.db")				
`INT`	`decryptPXTable`	Decrypts a table	`STRING`	`<table file name>`
get deletePXPassword(oldPW)				
`INT`	`deletePXPassword`	Removes a password	`STRING`	`<password>`
get encryptPXTable("c:\data\mydb", newPW)				
`INT`	`encryptPXTable`	Encrypts a table	`STRING`, `STRING`	`<table file name>`, `<password>`
get isPXTableProtected("myData.db")				
`INT`	`isPXTableProtected`	Tests if a table is encrypted	`STRING`	`<table file name>`

Table 19.10 *TB30PDX.DLL* Data and Function Initializing

Funct. Declar-ations	Function	Description	Declarations	Parameters
get exitPX()				
`INT`	`exitPX`	Closes the Paradox environment	none	
put getPXMaxFiles into maxPXfiles				
`INT`	`getPXMaxfiles`	Gets the maximum number of file handles that can be used	none	
get getPXMaxLocksFromINI()				
`INT`	`getPXMaxFilesFromINI`	Gets the maximum number of files from WIN.INI	none	

(continues)

V Enhancing Applications

Table 19.10 Continued

Funct. Declar-ations	Function	Description	Declarations	Parameters
maxLocks = get getPXMaxLocks( )				
INT	getPXMaxLocks	Gets the maximum number of record locks that can be used	none	
maxLocks = get getPXMaxLocksINI( )				
INT	getPXMaxLocks-FromINI	Gets the maximum number of locks from WIN.INI	none	
maxTableHND = getPXMaxTables( )				
INT	getPXMaxTables	Gets the maximum number of Table handles that can be used	none	
get getPXMaxTablesFromINI( )				
INT	getPXMaxTables-FromINI	Gets the maximum number of tables from WIN.INI	none	
get getPXMaxTablesFromINI( )				
INT	getPXSwapSize	Gets the internal swap buffer size	none	
get getPXSwapSizeFromININ( )				
INT	getPXSwapSize-FromINI	Gets the swap size from the WIN.INI file	none	
get getPXUserInfo( )				
STRING	getPXUserInfo	Gets user informa-tion from WIN.INI	none	
get initializePX(name of this book)				
INT	initializePX	Initializes Paradox Engine for concurrency operations	STRING	<client name>
get savePX( )				
INT	savePX	Saves swap buffer to disk	none	

Funct. Declar-ations	Function	Description	Declarations	Parameters
get setPXINIMaxFiles(10)				
INT	setPXINIMaxFiles	Sets MaxFiles entry in the [Paradox Engine] section of WIN.INI	INT	<maximum files>
see getPXMaxocks( )				
INT	setPXINIMaxLocks	Sets MaxLocks entry in the [Paradox Engine] section of WIN.INI	INT	<maximum locks>
get setPXMaxTables(10)				
INT	setPXINIMaxTables	Sets MaxTables entry in the [Paradox Engine] section of WIN.INI	INT	<maximum tables>
get setPXINISwapSize(4*num tables of this book)				
INT	setPXINISwapSize	Sets SwapSize entry (KB) in the [Paradox Engine] section of WIN.INI	INT	<swap size>
get setPXSortOrder("a")—sort in ascii order				
INT	setPXSortOrder	Sets the sort order	STRING	<sort order>
get setPXTableCreateMode(1)—Paradox 4.0 compatible files				
INT	setPXTable-CreateMode	Sets the mode for creating tables	INT	<mode>
get setPXMaxTableSize (64)				
INT	setPXTableMaxSize	Sets the maximum block size (MB) for new tables	INT	<size>
get setPXUserInfo("Dall Fern,f:\,2,No,No"—don't share, don't lock				
INT	setPXUserInfo	Sets user information in WIN.INI	STRING	<list of values>

Table 19.11 *TB30PDX.DLL* Sorting and Retrieving Values

Funct. Declar-ations	Function	Description	Declarations	Parameters
get addPXKey("bigDB", "Last Name First", 1)				
INT	addPXKey	Creates primary or secondary index on table	STRING, STRING, INT	<table alias>, <field names>, <mode>
get dropPXKey("bigDB", "Last Name", idIndex)				
INT	dropPXKey	Deletes primary or secondary index	STRING, STRING, WORD	<table alias>, <field name>, <index ID>
get mapPXKey("bigDB", "Last Name, First Name", "Last name First", 1)				
LONG	mapPXKey	Obtains field handle for composite or case-insensitive, single-field index	STRING, STRING, STRING, INT	<table alias>, <field names>, <key field name>, <mode>
get queryPXKey(item i of fileList)				
STRING	queryPXKey	Gets information about an index	STRING	<index file name>
get searchPXField("bigDB", "Last Name", In, 0)				
INT	searchPXField	Searches a table on a specified field	STRING, STRING, WORD, INT	<table alias>, <field name>, <index ID>, <mode>
get searchPXKey("clients", "2", "Doe, Jane", 0)				
INT	searchPXKey	Searches a table for a key match	STRING, INT, STRING, INT	<table alias>, <number of fields>, <field values>, <mode>

Table 19.12 *TB30PDX.DLL* Table Functions

Funct. Declar-ations	Function	Description	Declarations	Parameters
get addPXTable("c:\data\new.db","c:\data\old.db")				
INT	addPXTable	Copies records from one table to another	STRING, STRING	<source table>, <destination table>
get closePXTable("new")				
INT	closePXTable	Closes a table	STRING	<table alias>
get copyPXTable("d:\data\viewDB", it)				
INT	copyPXTable	Copies one table family to another	STRING, STRING	<source table>, <destination table>
get createPXTable("c:\data\newtabl", "Title, author, journal", "A25, A25, A40")				
INT	createPXTable	Creates a table	STRING, STRING, STRING	<table name>, <field names>, <field types>
get decryptPXPassword("c:\data\private")				
INT	decryptPXTable	Decrypts a table	STRING	<table file name>
get deletePXTable("c:\data\olddb")				
INT	deletePXTable	Deletes a table family	STRING	<table file name>
get doesPXTableExist("c:\data\temp")				
INT	doesPXTableExist	Tests if a table exists	STRING	<table name>
get emptyPXTable("c:\data\temp")				
INT	emptyPXTable	Removes all records from a table	STRING	<table file name>
get encryptPXTable("c:\data\temp", psswrdnew)				
INT	encryptPXTable	Encrypts a table	STRING, STRING	<table file name>, <password>
request getPXErrorString(prevErr)				
STRING	getPXErrorString	Gets the error message for an error number	INT	<error number>

(continues)

Table 19.12 Continued

Funct. Declar-ations	Function	Description	Declarations	Parameters
dbFields = getPXFieldCount("tempdb")				
INT	getPXFieldCount	Returns the number of fields in a table	STRING	<table alias>
get getPXKeyFieldCount("tempdb")				
INT	getPXKey-FieldCount	Returns the number of key fields in a table	STRING	<table alias>
get getPXMaxLocksFromINI( )				
INT	getPXMaxLocks	Gets the maximum number of record locks per table	none	
if getPXMaxTables() > myMaxCount then				
INT	getPXMaxTables	Gets the maximum number of tables that can be open at one time	none	
recHere = getPXRecordCount("myData")				
LONG	getPXRecord-Count	Gets the number of records in a table	STRING	<table alias>
get openPXTables("myTable","tempDB",0,0)				
INT	openPXTables	Opens a table	STRING, STRING, INT, INT	<table alias>, <table filename>, <index ID>, <save every change>
get packPXTable("myDb")				
INT	packPXTable	Packs the database (removes space occupied by deleted records)	STRING	<table alias>
get renamePXTable("curtbl", "oldtbl")				
INT	renamePXTable	Changes the base name of a table family	STRING, STRING	<source table>, <destination table>

Funct. Declar-ations	Function	Description	Declarations	Parameters
get setPXTableCreateMode(1)				
INT	setPXTable-CreateMode	Sets the mode for creating tables	INT	<mode>
get setPXMaxTableSize(64)—64 mb				
INT	setPXTable-MaxSize	Sets the maximum block size for new tables	INT	<size>
get upgadePXTable("myData")				
INT	upgradePXTable	Upgrades an older Paradox table (Paradox 3.5 or later) to the latest table format	STRING	<table alias>

Table 19.13 *TB30PDX.DLL* BLOB Functions

Funct. Declar-ations	Function	Description	Declarations	Parameters
hBlobClone = clonePXBlob("tempdb", "myField")				
INT	clonePXBlob	Creates private BLOBs from public BLOBs in current record	STRING, STRING	<table alias>, <field name>
get closePXBitmapWindow(hWndBMP)				
INT	closePXBitmap-Window	Closes a bitmap window	WORD	<window handle>
get closePXBlob(hModifiedBlob, 1)				
INT	closePXBlob	Closes a BLOB	INT, INT	<BLOB handle>, <accept>
get dropPXBlob("tempdb", "BLOBfield")				
INT	dropPXBlob	Drops a BLOB from current record of table	STRING, STRING	<table alias>, <field name>

(continues)

Table 19.13 Continued

Funct. Declar-ations	Function	Description	Declarations	Parameters
get freePXBlobMemory(hndlBinData)				
INT	freePXBlob-Memory	Frees global memory referenced by BLOB handle	WORD	<handle>
get freePXGraphicBlob(hBitmap)—hBitmap is handle returned from				
INT	freePXGraphic-Blob	Frees GDI memory referenced by a bitmap handle	WORD	<hBitmap>
get freePXGraphicBlobPalette(hPal)				
INT	freePXGraphic-BlobPalette	Frees GDI memory referenced by Windows color palette	WORD	<hPalette>
BMPSize = getPXBitmapSize(hBitmap)				
LONG	getPXBitmapSize	Gets the size of a bitmap	INT	<bitmap handle>
hMeta = getPXBlob(hBlob, getPXBlobSize(hBlob), 0)				
LONG	getPXBlob	Reads data from a BLOB	INT, WORD, LONG	<BLOB handle>, <size>, <offset>
hFileName = getPXBlobQuick("tempdb", "binData", 10)				
LONG	getPXBlobQuick	Reads BLOB leader directly from current record of table	STRING, STRING, INT	<table alias>, <field name>, <size>
set bSize to getPXBlobSize(hBlob)				
LONG	getPXBlobSize	Gets the size of a BLOB	INT	<BLOB handle>
bmpSize = getPXFileSize("xmap.bmp")				
LONG	getPXFileSize	Gets file size for BLOB operations	STRING	<file name>

Funct. Declar-ations	Function	Description	Declarations	Parameters
hBitmap = getPXGraphicBlob(hBlob)				
LONG	getPXGraphic-Blob	Returns handle to a Windows bitmap	INT	<BLOB handle>
hBitmap = getPXGraphicBlob(hBlob)				
LONG	getPXGraphic-BlobPalette	Returns handle to standard Windows color palette	INT	<BLOB handle>
text of field "review" = getPXMemoBlob(hBlob)				
STRING	getPXMemoBlob	Returns memo BLOB as a ToolBook string	INT	<BLOB handle>
hWndBMP = openPXBitmapWindow (hBMP, hPal, clientHandle of mainWindow, pageUnitsToClient(position of ellipse "Center"), 2, rgbFill of ellipse "Center")				
INT	openPXBitmap-Window	Opens child window for displaying a bitmap	WORD, WORD, WORD, STRING, INT, STRING	<bitmap handle>, <palette handle>, <parent handle>, <position/bounds>, <mode>, <background color>
hBlob = openPXBlobRead("tempdb", "ReviewText")				
LONG	openPXBlobRead	Opens a BLOB for reading operations	STRING, STRING	<table alias>, <field name>
hBlob = openPXBlobWrite("tempdb", "bits", 10240, 0)				
LONG	openPXBlobWrite	Opens BLOB for writing operations	STRING, STRING, LONG, INT	<table alias>, <field name>, <size>, <save current>
get setPXBitmapWindowInfo(hWndBitmap, hBitmap, hPalette, 2, rgbfill of this page)				
INT	setPCBitmp-WindowInfo	Sets display attributes for bitmap window	INT, INT, INT, INT, STRING	<window handle>, <bitmap handle>, <palette handle>, <mode>, <background color>

(continues)

Table 19.13 Continued

Funct. Declar-ations	Function	Description	Declarations	Parameters
get setPXBlob(hBlob, bSize,0, hBits)				
INT	setPXBlob	Writes data to a BLOB	INT, DWORD, LONG, WORD	<BLOB handle>, <size>, <offset>, <buffer>
get setPXBlobFromFile(hBlob, fSize, 0, 0, fName)				
INT	setPXBlob-FromFile	Converts a file in BLOB format	INT, DWORD, DWORD, DWORD, STRING	<BLOB handle>, <size>, <file offset>, <offset>, <file name>
get setPXGraphicBlob(hBlob,hBitmap,hPal)				
INT	setPXGraphic-Blob	Copies Windows bitmap handle into a graphic BLOB	INT, WORD, WORD	<BLOB handle>, <hBitmap>, <hPalette>
get setPXGraphicBlobFromFile(hBlob, "bright.bmp")				
INT	setPXGraphic-BlobFromFile	Converts a bitmap file in BLOB format	INT, STRING	<BLOB handle>, <file name>
get setPXMemoBlob(hBlob, text of field "dateLine")				
INT	setPXMemoBlob	Copies a string into a memo BLOB	INT, STRING	<BLOB handle>, <text>
get writePXBlobToFile(hBlob, "music.wav", 2)—overwrite file if it exists				
LONG	writePXBlob-ToFile	Writes a BLOB to a file	INT, STRING, INT	<BLOB handle>, <file name>, <mode>
get writePCGraphicBlobToFile(hBlob, "bright.bmp", 1)—write as read-only				
LONG	writePXGraphic-BlobToFile	Writes a graphic BLOB as a bitmap file	INT, STRING, INT	<BLOB handle>, <file name>, <mode>

Table 19.14 *TB30PDX.DLL* Locking and Unlocking Functions

Funct. Declar.	Function	Description	Declarations	Parameters
request getPXNetErrorUser( ) && "has the record locked."				
STRING	getPXNetError-User	Reports name of the user causing a locking error	none	
get getPXNetUserName( )				
STRING	getPXNetUser-Name	Obtains the name of a user	none	
get gotoPXNetRecordLock("tempdb", lockHandle)				
INT	gotoPXNet-RecordLock	Returns to a previously locked record	STRING, INT	<table alias>, <lock handle>
get isPXNetRecordLocked("tempdb")				
INT	isPXNetRecord-Locked	Determines if the current record has been locked	STRING	<table alias>
get isPXNetTableChanged("tempDB")				
INT	isPXNetTable-Changed	Tests if a table has been changed	STRING	<table alias>
get lockPXNetFile("db.cfg", 1)—full lock, no concurrency				
INT	lockPXNetFile	Locks a file	STRING, INT	<file name>, <lock type>
lockHandle = lockPXNetRecord("tempdb")				
LONG	lockPXNetRecord	Locks the current record of a table	STRING	<table alias>
get lockPXNetTable("tempdb", 1)				
INT	lockPXNetTable	Locks a table	STRING, INT	<table alias>, <lock type>
get refreshPXNetTable("tempdb")				
INT	refreshPXNet-Table	Resynchronizes a shared table	STRING	<table alias>

(continues)

Table 19.14 Continued

Funct. Declar.	Function	Description	Declarations	Parameters
get unlockPXNetFile("netfl.cfg",1)				
INT	unlockPXNetFile	Unlocks a file	STRING, INT	<file name>, <lock type>
get unlockPXNetTable("tempdb", 1)				
INT	unlockPXNe-tRecord	Unlocks the current record of a table	STRING, INT	<table alias>, <lock handle>
get unlockPXNetTable("tempDb",1)				
INT	unlockPXNet-Table	Unlocks a table	STRING, INT	<table alias>, <lock type>

Table 19.15 *TB30PDX.DLL* Searching Functions

Funct. Declar.	Function	Description	Declarations	Parameters
get searchPXField("clients", "Last Name", In, 0)				
INT	searchPXField	Searches a table on a specified field	STRING, STRING, WORD, INT	<table alias>, <field name>, <index ID>, <mode>
get searchPXKey("clients", "2", "Doe, Jane", 0)				
INT	searchPXKey	Searches a table for a key match	STRING, INT, STRING, INT	<table alias>, <number of fields>, <field values>, <mode>

Table 19.16 *TB30PDX.DLL* Miscellaneous

Funct. Declar.	Function	Description	Declarations	Parameters
get appendPXRecord("tempdb")				
INT	appendPXRecord	Adds an empty record to a table	STRING	<table alias>
get deletePXRecord("tempdb")				
INT	deletePXRecord	Deletes the current record from a table	STRING	<table alias>

Funct. Declar.	Function	Description	Declarations	Parameters
get emptyPXRecord("tempdb")				
INT	emptyPXRecord	Clears the current record of a table	STRING	<table alias>
get firstPXRecord("tempdb")				
INT	firstPXRecord	Moves to the first record of a table	STRING	<table alias>
hRawData = getPXRaw("tempdb", sizeofData)				
LONG	getPXRaw	Gets raw data from the current record of a table	STRING, INT	<table alias>, <size>
rSize = getPXRawDataSize("myTable")				
INT	getPXRawData-Size	Gets the size of the raw data in a record	STRING	<table alias>
get getPXRecordNumber("tempdb")				
LONG	getPXRecord-Number	Gets the current record number of a table	STRING	<table alias>
get gotoPXRecord("tempdb", it)				
INT	gotoPXRecord	Moves to a specified record of a table	STRING, LONG	<table alias>, <record number>
get insertPXRecord("tempdb")				
INT	insertPXRecord	Inserts an empty record into a table	STRING	<table alias>
get lastPXRecord("tempdb")				
INT	lastPXRecord	Moves to the last record of a table	STRING	<table alias>
while nextPXRecord("tempdb") >= 0				
INT	nextPXRecord	Moves to the next record of a table	STRING	<table alias>
get previousPXRecord("tempdb")				
INT	previousPX-Record	Moves to the previous record of a table	STRING	<table alias>

(continues)

Table 19.16 Continued

Funct. Declar.	Function	Description	Declarations	Parameters
get setPXRaw("tempdb", hdlData, sizeofData)				
INT	setPXRaw	Writes raw data to the current record of a table	STRING, INT, INT	<table alias>, <data handle>, <size>
get updatePXRecord("tempdb")				
INT	updatePXRecord	Updates the current record in a table	STRING	<table alias>

Table 19.17 *TBKDB3.DLL* Indexing Functions

Funct. Declar.	Function	Description	Declarations	Parameters
get checkDBindex(dbPath&"lastnm.ndx")				
INT	checkDBIndex	Checks the specified index file against the current dBASE file	STRING	<file name>
get closeDBIndexFile(fileName)				
INT	closeDBIndexFile	Closes the specified dBASE index file	STRING	<file name>
if createDBIndexFile("lastnm.ndx","LASTNAME + FIRSTNTL",1,0)				
INT	createDBIndexFile	Creates and opens a dBASE index file	STRING, STRING, WORD, WORD	<file name>, <sort expression>, <unique key>, <preserve existing>
get deselectDBIndexFile()				
INT	deselectDBIndexFile	Deselects the currently selected index file so it is no longer the current index file	none	
get getDBIndexExpression()				
STRING	getDBIndexExpression	Returns the expression used to form the keys of the current index file for the current dBASE file	none	

Funct. Declar.	Function	Description	Declarations	Parameters
get getDBIndexFileName( )				
STRING	getDBIndexFileName	Returns the name of the currently selected index file	none	
get getDBKeyType( )				
INT	getDBKeyType	Returns the type of the current key in the current index file	none	
get getDBKeyValue( )				
STRING	getDBKeyValue	Returns the value of the current key for the current index file	none	
get openDBIndexFile("lstnm.ndx")				
INT	openDBIndexFile	Opens the specified index file and makes it the current index file for the current dBASE file	STRING	<file name>
get reindexDBFile(currData)				
INT	reindexDBFile	Reindexes the specified index file	STRING	<file name>
get selectDBIndexFile(ndxFileName)				
INT	selectDBIndexFile	Makes the specified file the index file	STRING	<file name>

Table 19.18 *TBKDB3.DLL* Miscellaneous Functions

Funct. Declar.	Function	Description	Declarations	Parameters
get closeALLDBFiles( )				
INT	closeAllDBFiles	Closes all open dBASE and index files		none
get closeDBFile(fileName)				
INT	closeDBFile	Closes the specified dBASE file	STRING	<file name>

(continues)

Table 19.18 Continued

Funct. Declar.	Function	Description	Declarations	Parameters
put createDBFieldTag(nfs) into tagNumber				
INT	createDBFieldTag	Creates a field tag that specifies the number of fields in a dBASE file to create	WORD	<number of fields>
get createDBFile(dbFileName,tagNumber,1)				
INT	createDBFile	Creates and opens a dBASE file	STRING, WORD, WORD	<file name>, <field tag number>, <preserve existing>
get deleteDBFile(tempFile)				
INT	deleteDBFile	Deletes the specified file and any currently open associated index files	STRING	<file name>
get findDBKey("lastn")				
INT string>	findDBKey	Searches the current index file to find the closest key that matches the specified string	STRING	<search
get firstDBKey( )				
INT	firstDBKey	Makes the first key in the current index file the current key and makes the record referenced by the first key the current record	none	
get firstDBRecord( )				
INT	firstDBRecord	Makes the first record the current record	none	
get freeDBFieldTag(tagNumber)				
INT	freeDBFieldTag	Frees memory used by the field tag	WORD	<field tag number>

Funct. Declar.	Function	Description	Declarations	Parameters
get getDBDateFormat( )				
STRING	getDBDateFormat	Gets the date format currently in use by the DLL	none	
request "ERROR: " & getDBErrorString(it)				
STRING	getDBErrorString	Returns a string describing the error	INT	<error code>
get getDBFiledCount( )				
INT	getDBFieldCount	Returns the number of fields in the current dBASE file	none	
get getDBFieldName(i)				
STRING	getDBFieldName	Returns the name of the field of the specified column number	WORD	<field position>
get getDBFieldPrecision("age")				
INT	getDBFieldPrecision	Returns the number of decimal places for the specified numeric field	STRING	<field name>
if getDBFieldTYpe(nextFLD) is 5—a memo field				
INT	getDBFieldType	Returns the field type for the specified field	STRING	<field name>
get getDBFieldValue(item i of fieldName)				
STRING	getDBFieldValue	Returns the value of the specified field for the current dBASE record and file	STRING	<field name>
get getDBFieldWidth(fName)				
INT	getDBFieldWidth	Returns the width of the specified field in the current dBASE record and file	STRING	<field name>

(continued)

Table 19.18 Continued

Funct. Declar.	Function	Description	Declarations	Parameters
get getDBFileName( )				
STRING	getDBFileName	Returns the name of the current dBASE file	none	
get getDBNavigateToDeleted( )				
INT	getDBNavigate ToDeleted	Returns the state of the switch that controls navigation to records marked as deleted	none	
get getDBRecordCount( )				
LONG	getDBRecordCount	Returns the number of records in the current dBASE file	none	
get getDBRecordDeleted( )				
INT	getDBRecordDeleted	Determines if the current record is marked for deletion	none	
get getDBRecordNumber( )				
Long	getDBRecordNumber	Returns the number of the current record	none	
get gotoDBRecord(nextRec)				
INT	gotoDBRecord	Navigates to the specified record number in the data file and makes it the current record	DWORD	<record number>
get lastDBKey( )				
INT	lastDBKey	Makes the last key in the current index file the current key and makes the record referenced by the last key the current record	none	

Funct. Declar.	Function	Description	Declarations	Parameters
get lastDBRecord( )				
INT	lastDBRecord	Makes the last record in the current dBase file the current record	none	
get nextDBKey( )				
INT	nextDBKey	Makes the next key the current key and the record referenced the current record	none	
get nextDBRecord( )				
INT	nextDBRecord	Makes the next record the current record	none	
get openDBFile(dbNew)				
INT	openDBFile	Opens and initializes the specified file and makes it the current dBASE file	STRING	<file name>
get packDBFile( )				
INT	packDBFile	Compacts the current dBASE file by reclaiming space occupied by the records marked for deletion	none	
get previousDBKey( )				
INT	previousDBKey	Makes the key before the current key in the current index file the current key	none	
get previousDBRecord( )				
INT	previousDBRecord	Makes the record before the current record in the current dBASE file the current record	none	

(continues)

Table 19.18 Continued

Funct. Declar.	Function	Description	Declarations	Parameters
get removeDBRecords(i,i+10)				
INT	removeDBRecords	Removes from the current dBASE file the records in the specified range, inclusive	DWORD, DWORD	<start number>, <end number>
get selectDBFile(theDBFile)				
INT	selectDBFile	Makes the specified file the current dBASE file and opens the file if needed	STRING	<file name>
get setDBDateFormat("MM/DD/YY")				
INT	setDBDateFormat	Sets the date format for transactions	STRING	<format string>
get setDBFieldTag(tagNumber,i,item i of fieldNames, item i of the fieldType, item i of fieldWidth, 0)				
INT	setDBFieldTag	Sets the specified field in the specified field tag to the specified field name, type, width, and decimal precision	WORD, WORD, STRING, STRING, WORD, WORD	<field tag number>, <field item>, <field name>, <field type>, <field width>, <field decimals>
get setDBFieldValue("lastN",newLN)				
INT	setDBFieldValue	Sets the contents of the specified field in the current record to the specified new value	STRING, STRING	<field name>, <new value>
get setDBNavigateToDeleted(1)—turn on the feature				
INT	setDBNavigate➥ ToDeleted	Sets a switch to allow navigation to records marked for deletion	INT	<option>

Funct. Declar.	Function	Description	Declarations	Parameters
get setDBRecordDeleted(1)—mark for deletion				
INT	setDBRecord➥ Deleted	Marks the current record for deletion	WORD	<delete value>
get writeDBRecord(i)				
INT	writeDBRecord	Writes the contents of the record buffer into the specified record and updates all open index files	DWORD	<record number>

A detailed example of how some of these database functions can be used in an application is provided in the final section of this chapter, "Example Application: The Multimedia Part Store Ordering System," where the development of a multimedia database application is discussed.

Windows API Functions

The linking of MTB with DLLs is certainly not limited to those that are supplied by Asymetrix with the shipped version of Multimedia ToolBook. You can link to *any* DLL that you can find documentation for! Do exercise caution, however—do not assume that the DLLs that you have on your system will be available to your end user (even if they are part of the Windows operating system). Also, keep in mind the copyright issues: be sure that you have the legal right to distribute the DLL that you are using with the application. Finally, be sure you know what you are doing; incorrectly calling a DLL is a sure way to crash your system (or, more likely, the system of the user you distribute the application to!).

These cautions aside, you will find that some of the most useful DLL links that you can make are to the Windows application programming interface (API) functions. In particular, the User module controls everything in Windows that involves window creation, communications, hardware, and messaging; the Kernel module controls memory management, multitasking, and resource management; and the GDI module controls painting, drawing, plotting, and color functions of Windows.

Although it is beyond the scope of this book to explain in detail the many features of the Windows operating system that you can access this way, you will find some useful examples in this section (see Table 19.19). For more information about using the Windows API functions, visit your local computer book store and pick up one of the many books on the subject. Also, contact Microsoft and request the Software Developer's Kit, which contains a wealth of detailed information about programming for the Windows platform.

Table 19.19 Some Useful Windows API Functions

Funct. Declar.	Function	Description	Declarations	Parameters
hWnd = findWindow(0,"Media Player—CD Audio (playing)")				
WORD	findWindow (in USER.DLL)	Gets the window handle of another window	DWORD, STRING	<window class>, <caption>
if isIconic(hWnd)> 0 then get showWindow(hWnd,3) — maximize the window end if				
INT	isIconic (in USER.DLL)	Determines if the window is minimized	WORD	<hWnd>
get postMessage(hWnd,16,0,0)—tells the app to exit				
INT	postMessage (in USER.DLL)	Displays the Windows open file dialog box	WORD, WORD, WORD, DWORD	<hWnd>, <msg type>, <wParam>, <IParam>
get setActiveWindow(hWnd)				
WORD	setActiveWindow (in USER.DLL)	Makes another window the active window	WORD	<hWnd>
get postMessage(hWnd,16,0,0)—tells the app to exit				
INT	postMessage (in USER.DLL)	Displays the Windows open file dialog box	WORD, WORD, WORD, DWORD	<hWnd>, <msg type>, <wParam>, <IParam>
get showWindow(hWnd,3)—maximize this window				
INT	showWindow (in USER.DLL)	Changes display state of a window (0=hide, 1=show, 2=minimize & activate, 3=maximize, 6=minimize and activate next, 7=minimize)	WORD, INT	<hWnd>, <function>
WORD	globalAlloc (in KERNEL.DLL)	Allocates a block of memory from the global heap	WORD, DWORD	
WORD	getParent (in USER.DLL)	Returns the parent window of a specified child	WORD	

Listing 19.3, which is a code fragment from the file WWWALKER.TBK (written by Paolo Tosolini, tolsolini@psicosun.univ.trieste.it), finds out if Mosaic (World Wide Web browser) is running.

Listing 19.3 Using USER.DLL Functions to Find out if Mosaic is Running

```
to get getMosaicHandle
     linkDLL "user"
          INT  GetWindowText(WORD,STRING,INT)
     end
     -- get first window in the window manager's list
     set wH to GetWindow(sysWindowHandle,0) -- 0 returns the first
window
     -- Step through all remaining windows, and retrieve information
     -- on the windows that are at the top level.
     do
          -- test if the window is a top-level window.
          if GetParent(wH) = 0
               set FileName to nameOfFile(wH)
               set WindowCaption to nameOfWindow(wH)
               if WindowCaption contains "NCSA Mosaic" -- Check if it
is Mosaic
                    return wH
               end
          end
          -- Get the next window handle in the window manager's list.
          -- The parameter value "2" causes getWindow to return either
          -- the handle of the next window in the list or "0" if you
          -- are already on the last window.
          set wH to GetWindow(wH,2)
     until wH = 0
     return 0
end
```


Writing DLLs in C

The art of creating DLLs may take some time to master, but for a serious programmer, the skills obtained will be well worth the investment. DLLs provide a convenient means of encapsulating functions that are useful for many different applications and can be easily called. The ToolBook programming environment supports advanced features of the DLL interface. MTB passes the address of a string to a DLL as a far pointer into ToolBook's memory space (and for this reason you should declare the string parameters in your DLLs as LPSTRs).

To simplify the format of your ToolBook calls, you can use the STRING return variable type to set the ToolBook `sysError` flag and specify a value for `sysErrorNumber`. The following listing demonstrates this concept:

```
#define    TESTFUNCT_ERROR      -1
#define    INVALIDPARAM_ERROR   -9
DWORD _export FAR PASCAL  getTestFunct(LPSTR oneEntry, int err_value)
{
    HANDLE   something;
    DWORD    dwResult = (DWORD) MAKELONG(NULL, TESTFUNCT_ERROR);
     if (!oneEntry || !*oneEntry)
    {
        //Put the coding for the function here
        //On error, remember to set the result
        dwResult = (DWORD) MAKELONG(something, err_value);
    }
    return (dwResult);
}
```

In this example, if `something` is set to any value except NULL, then ToolBook sets the `sysErrorNumber` to the value stored in the HIWORD (`err_value`). Thus, in OpenScript programming, you need only check the `sysErrorNumber` value for error checking after calling the function.

Not only can you call DLL functions from OpenScript, you can also call OpenScript commands from a DLL! This is accomplished using the `TBM_EXECUTE` and `TBM_EVALUATE` messages, which are registered by ToolBook at startup. These are accessed through the Windows API function `registerWindowMessage()`. Use the following `sendMessage()` function to execute these commands:

```
sendMessage(hWnd, wMsg, wParam, (LONG)lParam)
```

where `hWnd` is the window handle, `wMsg` is the registered Windows message, `wParam` is nonzero if `sysSuspend` is set to false during command execution. For `TBM_EXECUTE`, `lParam` is a pointer (LPSTR) to a zero-terminated string containing the OpenScript commands to be executed. For `TBM_EVALUATE`, `lParam` is a FAR pointer to an evaluation buffer containing the expression to be evaluated and a buffer for the result, as defined in the following code listing:

```
typedef struct tagTBMEval {
   LPSTR lpExpression;
   //null-terminated string containing the OpenScript expression
   //to evaluate
   WORD  wRetType;
   //identifies type of return value:
   //0 => CHAR,   1=> BYTE,    2=> INT,
   //3 => WORD,   4=> LONG,    5=> DWORD,
   //6 => FLOAT,  7=> DOUBLE,  8=> POINTER,
   //9 => LPSTR (zero-terminated)
   LPVOID lpRetVal;
   //FAR pointer to memory block where return value is stored
   WORD nRetValueLength;
   //length of return value memory block if wRetType is STRING
} TBMEVAL;
```

Using MTB30 as a DDE Client or Server Application

The Windows environment provides a communications protocol known as dynamic data exchange (DDE), which allows programs running under Windows to exchange information and execute commands. Programs that are communicating using DDE act as *client* (the initiator of the conversation) and *server* (the responder to the conversation).

A DDE is initiated by the client by addressing an open server through its server name. The client can request data from a server, send data to a server, or request a server to execute a command. Of course, both the client and the server must support DDE for this to work! ToolBook supports DDE as do most of the popular Windows programs.

In order to know what commands are available in the client or server application that you are interfacing with ToolBook, you must find the information in the documentation provided with the software. ToolBook supports DDE using the OpenScript messages `executeRemote`, `getRemote`, `remoteGet`, `remoteSet`, `setRemote`, `closeRemote`, `keepRemote`, and `remoteCommand`. Table 19.20 provides a correspondence between the Windows message and ToolBook calls.

Table 19.20 Correspondence Between Windows Message and ToolBook DDE Calls

Windows Message	ToolBook Call
WM_DDE_INITIATE	executeRemote, getRemote
WM_DDE_REQUEST	remoteGet, getRemote
WM_DDE_POKE	remoteSet, setRemote
WM_DDE_ACK	respondRemote
WM_DDE_EXECUTE	remoteCommand

Each of the ToolBook OpenScript commands that are used in DDE are explained below.

The OpenScript `executeRemote` command sends the `WM_DDE_EXECUTE` message to the server application, first sending a `WM_DDE_INITIATE` message (when necessary). After the ToolBook command has been executed, the `WM_DDE_TEMINATE` message is sent to the server. When the command has executed successfully, `sysError` is set to `OK`. The syntax for the command is the following:

```
executeRemote <command> [application <server name>] [topic <server topic>]
```

where `<command>` is an expression that the server application can understand as a command (see the DDE documentation for the application you are using). The `<server name>` is the name of the application, such as `toolbook` or `excel`. If more than one instance of the application is running, the instance that responds first becomes the server. The `<server topic>` parameter is a topic recognized by the server, usually a file name. For ToolBook (and some other Windows applications) the topic `system` allows any instance of the server application to respond to the request. Table 19.21 lists some Windows applications and their topics and commands.

The `getRemote` command sends the `WM_DDE_REQUEST` message to the server application, first sending a `WM_DDE_INITIATE` message (when necessary). After the ToolBook command has been executed, the `WM_DDE_TEMINATE` message is sent to the server. When the command has executed successfully, `sysError` is set to `OK`. The syntax for the command is the following:

```
getRemote <item> [application <server name>] [topic <server topic>]
```

where `<item>` is any expression understood by the server application, such as a ToolBook property, a cell range for Excel, or a folder item for Ecco.

The `remoteGet` command is sent to the current ToolBook page of the DDE server through a `WM_DDE_REQUEST` message by the client application. ToolBook will return the result in `IT` after executing the following statement:

```
set it to evaluate <item>
```

where `<item>` was sent with the following syntax:

```
remoteGet <item>
```

The `remoteSet` command is sent to the current ToolBook page of the DDE server by the client application when it executes a `WM_DDE_POKE` Windows message. By default, ToolBook executes the following statement:

```
set it to evaluate <item>
```

and automatically sends a `respondRemote` message to the client (corresponding to the `WM_DDE_ACK` Windows message). If you create a handler to explicitly handle the `remoteSet`, you will also need to include a `respondRemote` command so that the client does not receive a `Failed: Denied` response to the request.

The `setRemote` command sends the `WM_DDE_POKE` message to the server application. After the ToolBook command has been executed, the `WM_DDE_TEMINATE` message is sent to the server. When the command has executed successfully, `sysError` is set to `OK`. The syntax for the command is as follows:

```
setRemote <item> to <value> [application <server name>] [topic <server topic>]
```

where `<item>` is an expression that can be set in the server application and `<value>` is a legal value for that expression.

The `closeRemote` command is used to close a DDE channel that was explicitly kept open with the `keepRemote` command. Normally, ToolBook closes a DDE channel as soon as the calling script returns to the top level. The syntax for the command is the following:

```
closeRemote application <server name> topic <server topic>
```

The `keepRemote` command keeps a DDE channel open between ToolBook and a server application. The syntax for the command is as follows:

```
keepRemote application <server name> topic <server topic>
```

The `remoteCommand` command is sent to the current ToolBook page of the DDE server by the client application when it executes a `WM_DDE_EXECUTE` Windows message. ToolBook executes the command that was passed.

Table 19.21 Examples of DDE Server Commands

Application	Server Name	Topic	Command
getRemote "text of field ""allData""" application "toolbook" topic "ch19ex.tbk"			
Asymetrix ToolBook	toolbook	open books, system	OpenScript commands (separated by semicolons)
getRemote "AOR_Total" application "excel" topic "acctng.xls"			
Microsoft Excel	`excel`	open files, system	Excel macro commands (in square brackets)
executeRemote "[FileOpen""c:\mtb_book\ch19\ch19.doc"",0]" application "winword" topic "system"			
Microsoft Word	`winword`	open documents, system	Word Basic for Windows commands (in square brackets)
getRemote "GetFolderType, 1,2,3" application "Ecco"			
Arabesque Ecco Professional	`ecco`	system	Wide range of supported commands
executeRemote "&Capture:&Freehand:&Area:&Window:F&ullScreen" & \application "Capture" topic "system"			
Delta Point Freeze Frame	`capture`	system	Menu string separated by colons

Examples for a variety of other applications, including Lotus AmiPro, Lotus 1-2-3, Microsoft Visual Basic, Borland ObjectVision, Software Publishing Corporation's

SuperBase 4, Blyth Omnis 5, DCA Crosstalk, and Future Soft DynaComm, can be found in the Asymetrix OpenScript Reference Manual under the `executeRemote` keyword section.

Example Application: The Multimedia Part Store Ordering System

This chapter concludes with a sample application that demonstrates how you can use some of the concepts described in this section. The example application uses dBASE III DLL links to a database that stores the names, description and prices of products, and the names of graphic clips of the items (see fig. 19.4). This sample application can be used as a starting point for your own applications.

The multimedia parts ordering system demonstrated in figure 19.4 relies on the `TBKDB3.DLL` routines for storage and retrieval of the information used. This provides a quick and easy way to access information.

The button at the top of the screen, create empty dataBase file, would certainly not be included in a shipped application! It is used to show the general practices for setting up the external file used to store the data for the application. Normally, the functions contained in this button would be incorporated into either a stand-alone book that is used externally to the application to maintain the database, or as an advanced user setup screen tucked away on another page of the application and reached by navigating through a menu item. The script in this button is provided in Listing 19.4.

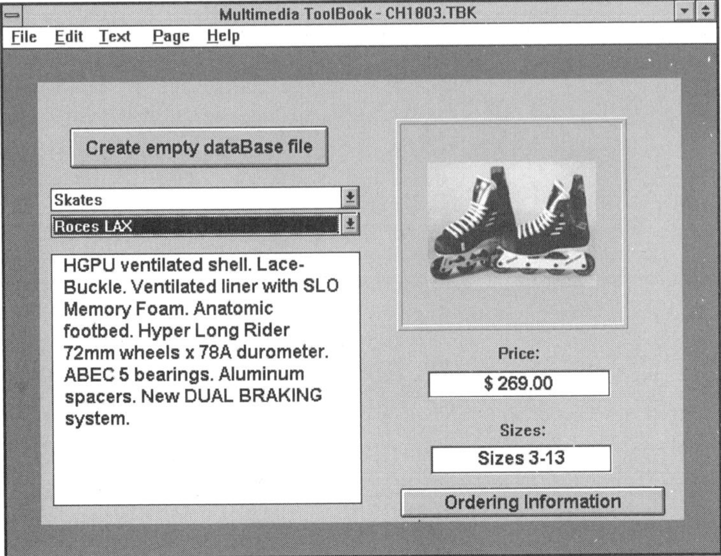

Fig. 19.4

The multimedia Part Store Ordering System provides information about, and pictures of, inventory items.

Listing 19.4 Steps for Setting Up a New Database File with *TBKDB3.DLL* Functions

```
to handle ButtonUp
     clear syserror
    get closeAllDBfiles()
--   set up the field tags
     ftn = createDBFieldTag(126)
--  set field type for product Types
     clear syserror
     a = setDBFieldTag(ftn,1,"prodT","c","50",0)
---- set field type for each of the 25 product fields
     clear syserror
     step g from 1 to 25
          zz = g + 1
          fielType = "Prod" & g
          c = setDBFieldTag(ftn,zz,fielType,"c","25",0)
     end step
-- set field type for each of the 25 product description fields
     step g from 1 to 25
          zz = g + 26
          fielType= "prodD" & g
          d = setDBFieldTag(ftn,zz,fielType,"m",0,0)
     end step
-- set field type for each of the 25 product size fields
     step g from 1 to 25
          zz = g + 51
          fielType= "prodS" & g
          d = setDBFieldTag(ftn,zz,fielType,"c",25,0)
     end step
-- set field type for each of the 25 product price fields
     step g from 1 to 25
          zz = g + 76
          fielType= "prodP" & g
          d = setDBFieldTag(ftn,zz,fielType,"4",10,0)
     end step
     step g from 1 to 25
          zz = g + 101
          fielType= "p" & g
          d = setDBFieldTag(ftn,zz,fielType,"c",35,0)
     end step
--  create the Database file
     clear syserror
     e = createDBFile("c:\product.dbf",ftn,0)
     if e <> 1 then
          get getDBErrorString(e)
          request "Error creating DB file: " & it
     end if
--  pre-loading some data to test the creation process
     temp = "Skates"
     f = setDBFieldValue("prodT",temp)
     temp = "Roces Barcelona BCN"
     f = setDBFieldValue("prod1",temp)
```

(continues)

Listing 19.4 Continued

```
     temp = "HGPU ventilated shell. 3 buckles. HGPU tongue. Ventilated
liner with SLO memory foam. Anit-shock footbed. Tartaruga rocerable
frame. Hyper Long Rider 76mm wheels × 78A durometer. ABEC 5 bearings.
Aluminum spacers. New DUAL BRAKING system."
     f = setDBFieldValue("prodD1",temp)
     temp="Sizes 3-13"
     f = setDBFieldValue("prodS1",temp)
     tempNum=26900
     f = setDBFieldValue("prodP1",tempNum)
     temp="pic1"
     f = setDBFieldValue("p1",temp)
     temp = "Roces LAX"
     f = setDBFieldValue("prod2",temp)
     temp = "HGPU ventilated shell. Lace-Buckle. Ventilated liner with
SLO Memory Foam. Anatomic footbed. Hyper Long Rider 72mm wheels ×
78A durometer.  ABEC 5 bearings. Aluminum spacers. New DUAL BRAKING
system."
     f = setDBFieldValue("prodD2",temp)
     temp="Sizes 3-13"
     f = setDBFieldValue("prodS2",temp)
     temp=23900
     f = setDBFieldValue("prodP2",tempNum)
     temp="pic2"
     f = setDBFieldValue("p2",temp)
     g = writeDBRecord(1)
     temp = "Wheels"
     f = setDBFieldValue("prodT",temp)
     temp = "Superlite"
     f = setDBFieldValue("prod1",temp)
     temp = "Light weight wheels"
     f = setDBFieldValue("prodD1",temp)
     temp="72mm × 78A, 82A, 85A"
     f = setDBFieldValue("prodS1",temp)
     tempNum=495
     f = setDBFieldValue("prodP1",tempNum)
     temp="pic3"
     f = setDBFieldValue("p1",temp)

     temp = "Superlite (2)"
     f = setDBFieldValue("prod2",temp)
     temp = "Light weight wheels"
     f = setDBFieldValue("prodD2",temp)
     temp="76mm × 78A, 82A, 85A"
     f = setDBFieldValue("prodS2",temp)
     tempNum=550
     f = setDBFieldValue("prodP2",tempNum)
     temp="pic4"
     f = setDBFieldValue("p2",temp)
     temp = "X-360 Cross-Fit"
     f = setDBFieldValue("prod3",temp)
     temp = "Light weight wheels"
     f = setDBFieldValue("prodD3",temp)
```

```
        temp="72.5mm × 78A, 82A"
        f = setDBFieldValue("prodS3",temp)
        tempNum=550
        f = setDBFieldValue("prodP3",tempNum)
        temp="pic5"
        f = setDBFieldValue("p3",temp)
        g = writeDBRecord(2)

        h = closeAllDBFiles()
        request "All done!!!!" with "Ok"
    end
```

As you see in Listing 19.4, each record is set up for a different type of product. For each product category, up to 25 different objects can be entered into the inventory. In a practical sense, this is not the best way to set up this kind of application. (It will create problems if a product line has more than 25 different items in it!) But for purposes of illustration, it makes the rest of the coding simple to explain. To expand on this example, you would most likely use one record per product and key on product type.

The fourth line in the code sets up the total number of fields that will be used in the database. In this example, the first field, `ProdP`, is the general class for the product (Skates or Wheels). Up to 25 products can be stored under each product's general class (a total of 1 + 5×25 = 126 fields). For each product, there are five informational items stored. They are as follows:

- Product name (saved as `prod1`, `prod2`, etc., through `prod25`) with the data type "character" and allowing 25 characters for storage:

  `setDBFieldTag(ftn,zz,fielType,"c","25",0)`

- Product description, stored as a memo field (`prodD1`, `prodD2`, etc., through `prodD25`):

  `setDBFieldTag(ftn,zz,fielType,"m",0,0)`

- Product size, stored as a character field (`prodS1`, `prodS2`, etc., through `prodS25`) with 25 characters:

  `setDBFieldTag(ftn,zz,fielType,"c",25,0)`

- Product price, stored as a numeric (`prodP1`, `prodP2`, etc., through `prodP25`):

  `setDBFieldTag(ftn,zz,fielType,"4",10,0)`

- Product clip name for the image file, stored as a character with 25 characters (`P1`, `P2`, etc., through `P25`):

  `setDBFieldTag(ftn,zz,fielType,"c",35,0)`

Note that the names of the field variable are actually constructed in the step loops used in the example script.

Now, the database file is created. Again, for simplicity, an example that is actually bad coding practice has been used. Normally, you would never hard wire a reference to a particular path (`c:\product.dbf`), but would instead have the code installation routine prompt for an installation subdirectory, put the path in the `WIN.INI` file, and then reference the appropriate path from this variable:

```
createDBFile("c:\product.dbf",ftn,0)
```

At this point, the basic structure of the database has been defined. Now, for this example, begin filling in some of the data for the database. In practice, you might want to write a similar script as a beginning point for a larger application and then generalize and expand it so that you have access to easy routines for adding new records, replacing outdated information, and adding new information to fields. Perhaps you will even want to provide the capability to add new fields to your database file as needed. In this simple example, you add two records. (The first record, for the product category "skate," has two products entered, while the second record, for "wheels," has three products listed.)

You will, no doubt, have noticed that this code example is incomplete, as the actual `LinkDLL` call was not included. The script for the link and declarations was placed in the `enterBook` handler (see the book script of `CH1903.TBK` for the details). The code for displaying the appropriate values (as obtained from the database file) is contained in the `enterPage` handler in Listing 19.5.

Listing 19.5 Linking the *TBKDB3.DLL* Functions for the Multimedia Parts Store Example

```
to handle enterPage
     system rc
     put null into tempVar
     put "product.dbf" into fName
     clear syserror
     get openDBFile(fName)
     if it <> 1
          request "Error opening Database File. I will create this
              for you..."
          if it is "cancel" then
               break to system
          else
               send buttonUp to button "newDB"
               put "c:\product.dbf" into fName
               clear syserror
               get openDBFile(fName)
          end if
     end if
     rc = getDBRecordCount()
     get firstDBRecord()
     clear tempVar
     clear tempProd
     get getDBFieldValue("ProdT")
     put it into tempVar
```

```
--  go ahead and put the first product information into the boxes
     get getDBFieldValue("prod1")
     put it into text of field "descript"
     get getDBFieldValue("prodD1")
     put it into text of field "descript"
     get getDBFieldValue("prodS1")
     put it into text of field "sizes"
     get getDBFieldValue("prodP1")
     put it/100 into text of field "price"
     step i from 1 to 25
          temp = "prod" & i
          get getDBFieldValue(temp)
          put it & CRLF after tempProd
     end step
     if rc > 1 then
          step w from 2 to rc
               get nextDBRecord()
               get getDBFieldValue("ProdT")
               put CRLF & it after tempVar
          end step
     end if
     get closeDBFile(fname)
     put tempVar into dropdownItems of comboBox "category"
     put tempProd into dropdownItems of comboBox "types"
     put item 1 of tempProd into text of comboBox "types"
end
```

Because the sample application will be sent without the actual database, the file will be generated when the page is entered (if it was not found) using the `openDBFile` command. In most of your applications, you would either quietly create the file for the user (e.g., for new installations) or loudly complain to the user that the file has been deleted and needs to be restored. In this case, merely give a message and generate the file.

Next, look through the file for the first product type and first example of that product, and then display the information for that product. The combo box for the product types is filled with the types found in the database. (In this example, there are only two: skates and wheels.) The remaining coding for this example is found in the combo boxes. As the user selects a different product within the category (e.g., a different skate), the corresponding information should be displayed. This is accomplished using the script in the product `comboBox` in Listing 19.6.

Listing 19.6 Coding for Choosing Fields from a Specified Record

```
to handle selectChange
     system currentRecord
     put my selectedItem into toGet
     put "c:\product.dbf" into fName
     clear syserror
     get openDBFile(fName)
     if it <> 1
          request "Error opening Database File."
```

(continues)

V Enhancing Applications

Listing 19.6 Continued

```
          end if
          get goToDBRecord(currentRecord)
          clear tempProd
          temp = "prodD" & toGet
          get getDBFieldValue(temp)
          put it into text of field "descript"
          temp = "prodS" & toGet
          get getDBFieldValue(temp)
          put it into text of field "sizes"
          temp = "prodP" & toGet
          get getDBFieldValue(temp)
          put it/100 into tempValue
          format tempValue as "#.00"
          put "$" && tempValue into text of field "price"
          temp = "P" & toGet
          get getDBFieldValue(temp)
          put it into picFile
          mmOpen clip picFile
          mmShow clip picFile in stage "displayPic"
          get closeDBFile(fname)
     end
```

The logic is quite straightforward. Because all 25 possible products for each category were put in the same record as the category name, you need to reference only one record:

```
get goToDBRecord(currentRecord)
```

The chosen product is displayed when the user changes the selection. The "number" (the variable `toGet`) that is used to reference the product details is the same as the line that was chosen in the `comboBox`.

All that is left is to be sure that, as the user changes to a different category of product (skates versus wheels), the appropriate data is displayed. In this example, I choose to display the first of the products in the category, as demonstrated in the `comboBox` script in Listing 19.7.

Listing 19.7 Displaying the First Record in the Field

```
to handle selectChange
     system currentRecord
     put my selectedItem into currentRecord
     put "c:\product.dbf" into fName
     clear syserror
     get openDBFile(fName)
     if it <> 1
          request "Error opening Database File."
     end if
     get goToDBRecord(currentRecord)
     clear tempProd
```

```
        get getDBFieldValue("prod1")
        put it into tempProd
        step w from 2 to 25
             temp = "prod" & w
             get getDBFieldValue(temp)
             if it is null then
                  break step
             end if
             put CRLF & it after tempProd
        end step
        put tempProd into dropdownItems of comboBox "types"
        put item 1 of tempProd into text of comboBox "types"
        get getDBFieldValue("prodD1")
        put it into text of field "descript"
        get getDBFieldValue("prodS1")
        put it into text of field "sizes"
        get getDBFieldValue("prodP1")
        put it/100 into tempValue
        format tempValue as "#.00"
        put "$" && tempValue into text of field "price"
        get getDBFieldValue("P1")
        put it into picFile
        mmOpen clip picFile
        mmShow clip picFile in stage "displayPic"
        get closeDBFile(fname)
   end
```

This simple example should be a useful jumping off point for you to create more complex examples. The data itself is displayed in text fields and in a stage (for graphics data).

From Here...

This chapter provides a starting point for using DLLs, DDE, and Windows API functions in your ToolBook applications. The advent of Windows 95 and its impact on the use and integration of the Windows 3.x API functions, and the prevailing use of OLE over DDE is sure to mark another phase in the extension of Multimedia ToolBook's capabilities. For more information about controlling devices, see the following chapters:

- Chapter 5, "Understanding the Media Management Tools," discusses the Resource Manager dialog box in detail and shows you the ins and outs of the Clip Manager.
- Chapter 22, "MCI Devices and Multimedia," teaches you about MCI command syntax and how to assign an alias.

CHAPTER 20

Fundamentals of Multimedia

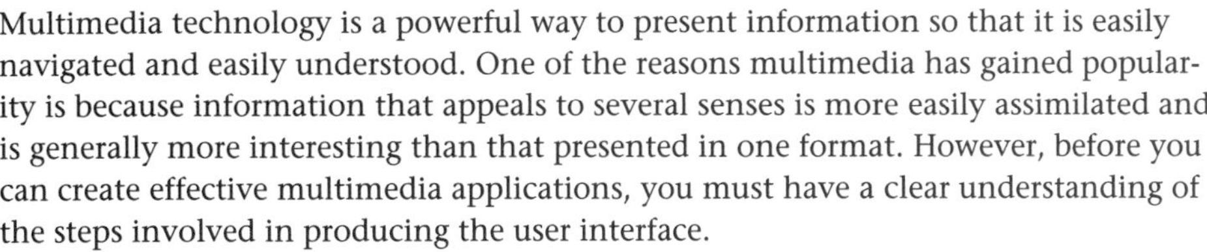

Multimedia technology is a powerful way to present information so that it is easily navigated and easily understood. One of the reasons multimedia has gained popularity is because information that appeals to several senses is more easily assimilated and is generally more interesting than that presented in one format. However, before you can create effective multimedia applications, you must have a clear understanding of the steps involved in producing the user interface.

In this chapter, you'll learn the following:

- Fundamental aspects of multimedia technology
- Key elements in user interface design
- Techniques for establishing and troubleshooting a multimedia development environment

Multimedia System Requirements

If you are creating a simple application with few multimedia features, then a 386 with a minimum 33MHz processor, 4 MB RAM, and a double-speed CD-ROM drive (if delivering on this media) are sufficient. However, MTB requires a fair amount of the available RAM (up to 3 MB, depending on the routines that have been linked), and, in practice, it is best to use 8 MB RAM and accelerated graphics as your recommended base system.

If you are creating an application that absolutely must run on low-end systems, then you must strongly consider your options before beginning the project. MTB is a wonderful tool for quickly creating fully functional applications, but its power comes with a price: memory and speed overhead. As a non-compiled program, the resulting application can run considerably slower than a similar program written in a compiled language and will probably require more RAM. In many cases, this overhead is not a problem. If you design your application carefully, these drawbacks of MTB may be irrelevant. But, if you must run on low-end systems, only applications that do not push the RAM limitations are appropriate.

MTB contains some easy-to-use functions that make testing the system that is currently running easy. When creating an application, it is often useful to have certain information about the system, as detailed in Table 20.1.

Table 20.1 ToolBook Functions Used to Query the Current System

System Feature	MTB Functions	Location	Use
Graphics mode	displayBitsPerPixel()	TB40WIN.DLL	Choosing whether to display 8- or 24-bit color graphics images. Choosing color depth of video files.
	displayAspectX(), displayAspectY(), displayLogX(), displayLogY()	TB40WIN.DLL	Finding the relative width and height of a pixel for the device (both X and Y) and the number of pixels per inch (X and Y) in order to calculate the overall size of a window or graphic.
CD-ROM	getCDDriveList(), getDriveKind(), isCDDrive()	TB40DOS.DLL	Finding out how many CD-ROM drives are installed on the system and what the drive letters are.
Disk drives	getDriveList(), getCurrentDrive(), setCurrentDrive(), getFreeDiskSpace(), getVolumeName()	TB40DOS.DLL	Finding out what drives are on the system and how much free disk space is available on the drives (e.g., to create backup directories or temp files).
File and directory details	copyFile(), fileExists(), getFileAttributes(), getFileDate(), getFileList(), getFileSize(), moveFile(), removeFile(), setFileAttributes(), createDirectory(), getCurrentDirectory(), removeDirectory()	TB40DOS.DLL	Commands for finding out information about files and directories. Moving or deleting files and directories. Checking and changing file attributes (e.g., to manage data files created by your application).

System Feature	MTB Functions	Location	Use
System settings	`setSystemDate()`, `setSystemTime()` `sysDate`, `sysTime`	`TB40DOS.DLL` System property	Setting the system date and time. Getting the system date and time.
INI variables	`getIniVar()`, `SetIniVar()`, `getWinIniVar()`, `setWinIniVar()`	`TB40WIN.DLL`	Getting and setting variables in the WIN.INI or other INI files.
Memory	`percentFreeSpace`	System property	Finding out how much memory is available on a page or background.

For those programmers who are proficient at interfacing with Windows functions, there are also a number of useful flags that can be accessed to set features of your running application. For example, to find out the currently running system, you can use the `GetWinFlags()` Windows function, for which returns are shown in Table 20.2.

Table 20.2 Returns for the *GetWinFlags()* Function

Function	Return
`WF_80x87`	`math coprocessor found`
`WF_CPU286`	`8286 processor found`
`WF_CPU386`	`8386 processor found`
`WF_CPU486`	`8486 processor found`

Another feature of Windows that you might want to access provides the Windows and DOS versions currently running. This information is from the kernel. The ToolBook script in Listing 20.1, supplied by Asymetrix as an example script, shows how to access these functions.

Listing 20.1 Accessing the Kernel

```
to handle buttonClick
    linkDLL "kernel"
        DWORD GetVersion()
    end linkDLL
    set verNum to GetVersion()
    set WverNum to verNum mod 65536
    set DverNum to verNum div 65536
    set majorNumber to WverNum mod 256
    set minorNumber to WverNum div 256
    set dmajorNumber to DverNum div 256
```

(continues)

Listing 20.1 Continued

```
    set dminorNumber to DverNum mod 256
    request "Windows version:" && majorNumber & "."  \
     & minorNumber & CRLF & \
      "DOS version:" && dmajorNumber & "." & dminorNumber
    unlinkDLL "kernel"
end buttonClick
```

Placing this script into a button and running it will result in a dialog box, as shown in figure 20.1.

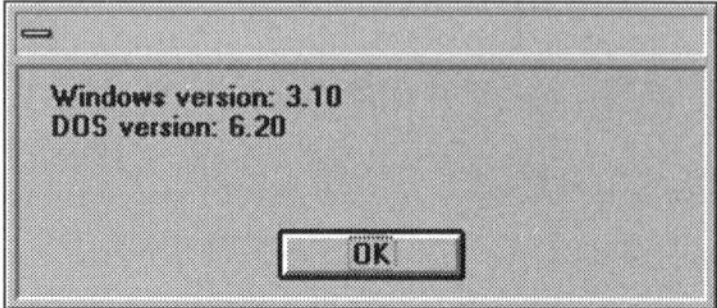

Fig. 20.1

This dialog box shows which Windows and DOS versions are running.

Palettes and Colors

Unfortunately, just because the MTB application you create displays nicely on your own system, that is no reason to assume that it will display in a similar way on another system. Unless you have complete control over the equipment that your end user will use to display the application, there are certain design and programming issues that need to be resolved before you get too far into the production process.

When you are working on 256-color machines (8-bit color), you can run into problems if you do not carefully manage your color palettes. As a new palette is called up, the images that are still displayed change from their current palette to the new palette, sometimes resulting in unsightly color shifts (a human face turns from tan to green, for example). The best way to avoid these problems is to understand a little bit about how the Windows Palette Manager handles color. The Palette Manager is a part of the Windows graphic device interface (GDI).

The Palette Manager reserves the first and last 10 colors (numbered zero–nine and 246–255) as standard colors. The remaining 236 colors are available on a priority basis. When a window becomes active (such as a ToolBook viewer), the Palette Manager matches each color in the newly activated window with the palette. If an exact match isn't available, the Palette Manager finds an unused palette entry, sets it to the color, and marks it as used. If there are no unused palette entries, the color gets mapped to the closest available color in the currently active palette.

After the current window's colors have all been mapped, the colors from other open windows are mapped into the palette, following the same process. The order of precedence leaves the desktop last. (If the colors of the current wallpaper are not a good match for the currently displayed image, you can experience some unpleasant visual effects with the wallpaper!)

When a window is displayed, it might take a moment for the palette to be calculated. As soon as the new palette is constructed, the screen will "flash" as the new palette is realized. This is one of the effects that programmers find unacceptable when constructing a multimedia application.

In ToolBook, the background and the foreground of a page are assigned separate palettes. The background palette retains precedence over the foreground palette, and whatever object is placed *last* on the background takes precedence over what was placed before. Thus, you can have an application that looks just fine, switch into the background and place just one more little picture to round out your composition, and *voilà*—your previously beautiful page turns into an ugly mixture of colors!

How can you solve these problems? Now that you understand the nature of the problem, the solutions become obvious. First of all, when creating images to import into ToolBook, be sure to retain the standard Windows colors as the first and last 10 colors in all of your palettes; most Windows graphics programs do this by default. Choose from these colors to fill your backgrounds, text boxes, buttons, and other screen objects. When you are displaying photographs, artwork, videos, or animation, always create your scripts so they close any objects that have a different color palette before opening the new object. This technique will help avoid the unpleasant color shifts that you might otherwise encounter. Of course, if the target machine is true color (24-bit), you will not have these problems.

> **Note**
>
> If you are doing your development on a 24-bit color machine, *do not wait* until late in the development cycle to test your colors in an 8-bit environment if these machines are your target configuration! Palette management must be part of the design of each and every screen.

To edit the palette of a picture, you can use Microsoft's `PALEDIT.EXE` program (included with ToolBook) or the palette editor in your graphics program (such as Fractal Design Painter or Photoshop). `PALEDIT` enables you to take a picture's current palette and change it to an "identity" palette (a palette that includes the 20 standard Windows colors) by choosing Make Identity Palette from the Palette menu. This process forces the current picture colors into the middle 236 colors and places the 20 system colors in the first and last 10 spaces of the palette.

Other solutions include creating a common color palette for all the pictures that will be displayed on one page. If your application is displaying similar types of pictures, this is a viable solution. You can "dither down" all the images for a page into a common palette, often with excellent results. Another solution is to purposefully enhance these shifts, add a little sound effect, and call it art (what I like to call the MTV look). If this is not suitable for your application, you can use transitions, such as fade to black, before changing to a new picture. This will eliminate the palette flash as Windows switches palettes.

Note

Sticking to the 20-color standard Windows palette for your backgrounds, buttons, and fields allows you to create an application that will likely look similar on most machines. However, be careful about the color combinations that you use. Do not rely on subtle color shade differences on a machine for effect because it might not look quite the same on all monitors or with all graphics cards.

The best bet for widespread applications is to use solid, contrasting colors and to test the resulting application on as many different graphics cards as you can before releasing the application.

You may want to keep two versions of video and graphics files on your delivered CD-ROM—one 8-bit and one 24-bit—and choose the image to display according to the target machine's capability. The code example in Listing 20.2 does just that; it gives an error message if the machine cannot support 256 colors, and it chooses between two images for the 8-bit and 24-bit machines.

Listing 20.2 Supporting More Than One Version

```
linkDLL "tb40win.dll"
     INT DisplayBitsPerPixel ()
     pixelDepth = displayBitsPerPixel()
end linkDLL
conditions
     when pixelDepth = 4
          request "Sorry! Your system is not configured properly \
           to play color video!" with "OK"
     when pixelDepth = 8
          mmPlay clip "ocean scene 256"  in stage "demoView" autoclose
     else
          mmPlay clip "ocean scene full" in stage "demoView" autoclose
     end
```

In summary, keep the following palette issues in mind when designing an interface that must run in 256-color mode:

- Either design and test for the lowest common denominator system on which your product will run, or write branching code that uses specific images for specific graphics modes.
- Reserve the first and last 10 colors in the palette for standard Windows colors (the "identity" palette).
- Before a new palette is loaded into your application, minimize the "flashing" by closing or hiding all objects displayed that are not composed of the 20 standard colors, fade to black or white, or create an "arty" effect with the palette change.

Resolution and Page Size

If you are creating an application that runs in a nonstandard video graphics mode, you must consider the issues of resolution and page size. These issues are discussed in this section.

Image Resolution. The only standards for graphic drivers for the Windows platform are VGA (640 x 480 pixels, 16-color mode) and super VGA (640 x 480, 256 colors). However, a 640 x 480 full-color mode is also safe to use, as most drivers are now relatively consistent. Once you move into resolutions higher than 640 x 480 pixels, you must take special precautions to be sure that your application will display properly on all targeted systems. If you are creating a title that will be mass-marketed, then you should seriously consider staying away from screen dimensions greater than 640 x 480, as the graphic drivers for the different competing cards do not adhere to a standard. Such products will sometimes display full screen and sometimes larger or smaller than full screen (depending on the system and how the application was created).

> **Note**
>
> A good rule of thumb: unless it will impact your market negatively in other ways, design for the lowest common denominator machine. Assume your users will not be very technically sophisticated (and may not know how to change color modes on their systems), and design your product to work in 640 x 480 graphics mode with 256 colors.

Page Size. For some obscure reason, MTB background (page) size is measured in inches or centimeters, not pixels. This feature of MTB causes untold amounts of confusion. The next section gives you more information about the units of measurement used in MTB and how to convert between them. A safe figure to use for background size in 640 x 480 graphics mode is 6.5 x 4.5 inches. This creates an application that almost fills the entire screen, but leaves a little room around the edge of the window for the desktop. If you are going to provide other open windows on the desktop, you might want your application's main window to be smaller than this.

Understanding MTB's Units of Measure

As you get deeper into programming applications with MTB, you will find that you need to understand ToolBook's units of measurement. Table 20.3 provides a convenient reference for the most commonly used object properties and the units of measurement that are used by the properties.

Table 20.3 Commonly Used Object Size Properties and Their Units of Measurement

Property	Objects	Returns	Units
`bounds`	buttons, combo boxes, fields, record fields, groups, graphic objects, hotwords, OLE objects	A list of four numbers: x-top-left, y-top-left, x-bottom-right, y-bottom-right.	For draw objects, in page units. For viewers, in pixels relative to the client area of the parent window. For a popup window, bounds are relative to the desktop.
`position`	buttons, combo boxes, fields, record fields, graphic objects, groups, OLE objects, windows, palettes	A list of two numbers: x-top-left, y-top-left.	For buttons, combo boxes, fields, record fields, groups, OLE objects, or graphic objects, the coordinates are in page units relative to the upper-left corner of the page. For viewers, the coordinates are in pixels from the top-left corner of the screen.
`size`	all objects except pages	A list of two integers representing width and height.	For viewers, the coordinates are in pixels. For all other objects, coordinates are in page units.
`vertices`	draw objects, graphic objects, groups, viewers	A list of points that define the particular object's shape, in X,Y pairs.	For viewers, the units are in pixels. For all other objects, the units are page units.

To convert between the different units, which is sometimes necessary when you are trying to position an object exactly within a page, you must use the conversion routines provided. These include `xPixelsFromUnits()` and `yPixelsFromUnits()`. These are from the `TB40WIN.DLL` and convert a dimension in pixels (screen units) to ToolBook page units. These calculations can be essential for computing the actual display device capabilities when trying to support a wide variety of machines, as the value can and will vary between graphics cards.

Conversely, the routines `xUnitsFromPixels()` and `yUnitsFromPixels()` convert from page units to pixels.

Getting viewers to display just where you want them can be a little confusing at first because the units used for viewers is different than for other objects (refer to Table 20.1).

The function `clientFromPage()` in `TB40WIN.DLL` converts a set of ToolBook page units to coordinates in pixels relative to the upper-left corner of the client area of the ToolBook window. The function `pageFromClient()` does the conversion in the other direction.

> **Note**
>
> The client area begins below the menu bar and does not include the scroll bars.

For example, suppose you have a page, `mainMenu`, that has a draggable rectangle `bigBox` that could be positioned by the user anywhere on the screen. You want to display a viewer, `newView`, at the coordinates of this rectangle. You would use the script in Listing 20.3.

Listing 20.3 Display a View at Rectangle Coordinates

```
to handle buttonUp
     linkDLL "tb40win.dll"
          STRING clientFromPage(STRING, INT, STRING)
     end linkDLL
     --find location of rectangle "bigBox" relative to upper-left
     --corner of Toolbook window
     get clientFromPage(pageScroll of mainWindow, \
          magnification of mainWindow, \
          bounds of rectangle "bigBox" of page "mainMenu")
     put it into recPos
     open viewer "newView"
     --now, put the viewer at this position (top-left coordinates)
     set position of viewer "newView" to item 1 of recPos, \
      item 2 of recPos
     show viewer "newView"
end
```

This example is contained in the button of the book `EXAMPLES\20FIG2.TBK` supplied on the CD-ROM. The sample also provides a simple example of drag-and-drop scripting techniques (see fig. 20.2).

Although you could have easily used a shadowed text field to get nearly the same effect as the viewer popup in this example, there will be many cases in which you will find using a viewer preferable. For example, if you are already nearing the limits of the page or background memory, adding another field to the page may not be feasible. Also, the viewer has the advantage that it can extend past the edges of the current window—a feature that can be very useful in your application as it is "user-friendly" and allows the user the freedom to position a viewer anywhere on the desktop.

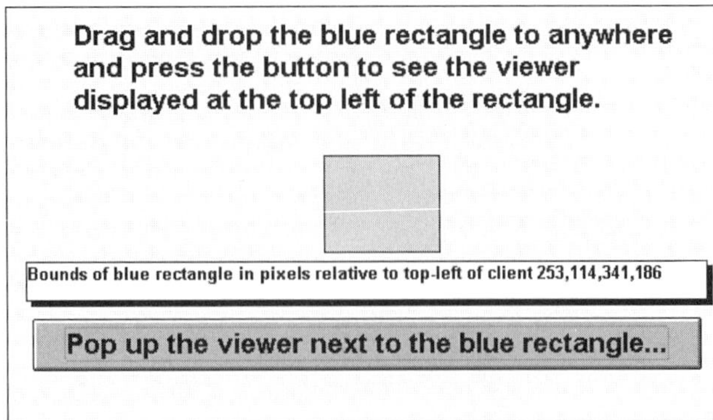

Fig. 20.2

This is an example of drag-and-drop and using clientFromPage to place a viewer.

Multimedia ToolBook and Memory Management

As many ToolBook programmers can testify, memory management issues can be a major problem with ToolBook. Part of the problem has been caused by memory "leaks" in the various versions of ToolBook, memory that gets taken and not released by a process. Sometimes the leak can be traced to a simple programming error, especially if routines are called outside of ToolBook.

Other memory problems occur when the programmer is stepping over the limit of some resource within ToolBook. And still other problems have proven almost impossible to trace, even by the Asymetrix technical staff. It is possible, even likely, that you will never be plagued by memory problems. But, if you do have these difficulties, the only course of action is to carefully trace the routine that is causing the problem until you resolve the issue.

This section introduces you to the limitations of ToolBook memory, explains the error messages that result when exceeding different types of available memory, discusses common programming errors that cause memory leaks, and shows you some advanced techniques for handling memory problems.

Field Memory

Fields are capable of holding no more than 32K characters. If this limit is exceeded, your application will generate an error, as shown in figure 20.3.

If you have more than one field on the page and they both get close to the maximum number of characters permissible in the field, your page memory may fill up prior to exceeding the field character limits. In this case, your application will generate an error message similar to that shown in figure 20.4.

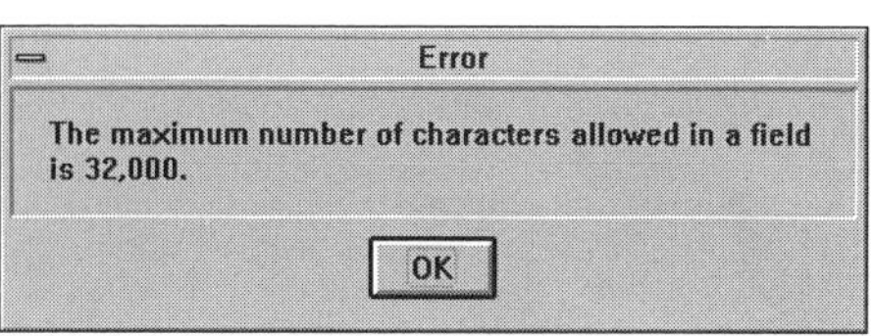

Fig. 20.3

You have gone beyond the field memory limit.

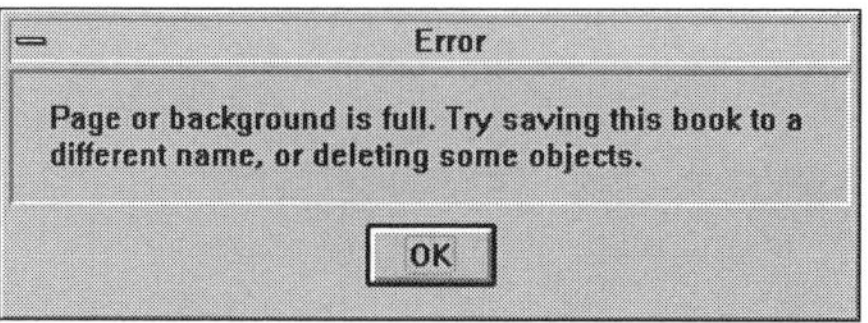

Fig. 20.4

You have gone beyond the page memory limit.

If you are in control of the text that is placed within the field, then you can avoid these problems by keeping the field information within the limits. On the other hand, if the user is filling the field (for example, with a list of file names or by reading in or typing in text), then you must protect the field from becoming overfilled and generating an error message. If the user is typing text into the field, you could handle this with the script shown in Listing 20.4, which would be placed in the script of the field itself.

Listing 20.4 Limit the Amount of Text Placed in a Field

```
to handle keyDown key
     --allowing the field to get almost full but not completely full
     if charcount(text of field "textBox") > 31900 then
          --allow some keys through so user can delete text
          if key < 9 or key = 12 or key = 16 or (key >32 and key \
           < 48) then
               forward
          else
               request "This field is full! Please delete some \
                text " & "before attempting to add more!" with "ok"
          end if
     else
          forward
     end if
end
```

If the user is entering the text by other methods, you would want to place a handler for the overflow in the script that is controlling the field filling process rather than in the field itself.

Page and Background Memory

If you put too many draw objects or other items on a page, you will exceed the space available for storing information on that page, and the page memory will create an

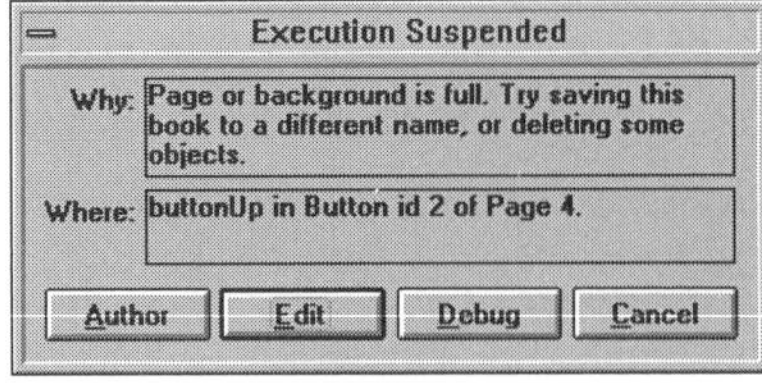

Fig. 20.5

Execution has stopped because the limit of page memory has been exceeded.

execution suspended message (see fig. 20.5).

Each draw object (such as rectangles and circles) requires somewhere between 30 and 140 bytes. These requirements can go up if user-defined properties are assigned to the drawn objects or the objects contain scripts. The object definitions, scripts, and user-defined properties come out of the memory allocated to the page. The background memory is handled in exactly the same way as the page.

A script that is part of an object on a page or background also uses the memory of the page or background *unless* the script gets larger than 1.2K. Once the script becomes larger than this, it gets its own 34K section of memory.

> **Note**
>
> If you have an object script near the limit of 1.2K, it is sometimes better to push it past the limit so that it gets its own memory allocation, as this might make your scripts run faster!

A bitmap that is under 1K uses the memory of the page or background section (depending on where it is placed). If it is larger than 1K, it is given its own area of memory.

If you are running out of page memory and your page contains a large number of small draw objects, you might consider creating a bitmap of the entire page (by using a screen capture program, for example). This frees up some of the page memory. Or, you might try reducing the user-defined properties of the objects or the scripts.

Sometimes saving the book to a new name purges the page of extraneous memory requirements, allowing the page to fit within the available memory.

If you want to write a handler for page or background memory overflows, you can determine the current memory demands for a page or background with the `percentFree` function:

```
request percentFreeSpace of this page
```

Local Memory

Local and system variables share the *instance local memory*. When this has been exhausted, the message `Not enough local memory...` is displayed. Both local and system variables store their contents in instance local memory, including the `it` variable.

Caution

To retain as much instance memory as possible, be careful to use system variables *only* where absolutely necessary.

There are a few useful techniques for avoiding too many system variables. One of these techniques requires you to think a little differently than you do with many other programming languages. Ask yourself: Do I really need to store that variable as a system variable? Or, is the value of the variable available to me in other ways? For example, if the user has made a selection from a combo box, the value of the variable is available to you globally by examining the `text of comboBox "xxx" of page "xxx"`.

Another technique that is useful if the page or background memory is not a problem in your application is to store information needed globally in the user-defined property of an object. And still another alternative is to save the values in a field, either hidden on the page or on another page, that the user cannot navigate to.

Other Memory Management Techniques

At times, you might have persistent memory problems with page or background memory that do not go away when you have corrected the original problem. For example, you may get a "page full" error, remove objects from the page, and then get a "page full" memory when trying to add back one of the elements previously deleted. The following are some suggestions for ways to solve these problems:

- Have you done a lot of editing without doing a *save as*? ToolBook only cleans up after itself when you save the book under a new name.
- Try using CD-ROM optimization options—this forces MTB to check the objects in the book.
- If all else fails, run the `MTBXFER.TBK` program from Asymetrix (included on this CD-ROM in the `UTILITIES` subdirectory).

Another, but less preferable, means of controlling memory issues is to use Windows programming techniques. A number of memory flags and messages are available, including the following *global memory flags:*

- `GMEM_FIXED`
- `GMEM_MOVEABLE`
- `GMEM_NOCOMPACT`
- `GMEM_NODISCARD`
- `GMEM_ZEROINIT`
- `GMEM_MODIFY`
- `GMEM_DISCARDABLE`
- `GMEM_NOT_BANKED`

- GMEM_SHARE
- GMEM_DDESHARE
- GMEM_NOTIFY

Also available are the following *local memory flags:*

- LMEM_FIXED
- LMEM_MOVEABLE
- LMEM_NOCOMPACT
- LMEM_NODISCARD
- LMEM_ZEROINIT
- LMEM_MODIFY
- LMEM_DISCARDABLE

There are also some ToolBook functions that allow you to directly manage global variables. These include: `setGlobalVar()`, `getGlobalVar()`, `clearAllGlobalVars()`, and `globalVarCount()`.

An example of how these functions can be used is contained in the ToolBook files `EXAMPLES\20FIG06a.TBK` and `20FIG06b.TBK` on the CD-ROM. These files provide you with a useful technique for sharing a variable between two books.

The script in Listing 20.5 is used in the button that sets the value for a global variable. Notice that there is an explicit link to the `MTB40BMP.DLL` that is needed only if the system book `MTB40.SBK` is not in the `sysBooks` stack.

Listing 20.5 Setting a Value For a Global Variable

```
to handle buttonUp
     --link the function if MTB40 is not loaded
     if "MTB40" is not in sysBooks then
          sysSuspend = false
          clear sysError
          linkDLL "MTB40BMP.DLL"
               STRING setGlobalVar(STRING,STRING)
               STRING getGlobalVar(STRING)
          end linkDLL
          if sysError is not null
               request "MTB40BMP.DLL not found."
               break
          end if
     end if
     ask "Name for new global variable: "
     put it into newGlobal
     ask "Value for " & newGlobal & ":"
     put it into globVal
     get setGlobalVar (newGlobal,globVal)
     if "MTB40" is not in sysBooks then
          unlinkDLL "MTB40BMP.DLL"
     end if
end buttonUp
```

Memory Leaks in MTB

One of the problems that has plagued ToolBook users since the first release of the software is *memory leaks:* a process allocates a memory block but fails to completely deallocate (free up) the memory when finished. To be perfectly fair to Asymetrix, it should be pointed out that there are many other programs that have similar difficulties. Even the original Window's Program Manager (version 3.0) had problems freeing system resources; it loaded the program icons but did not release them when the window was closed.

The solution to the problems can only be found through very careful research. First, you must recognize that there is a problem! As you are scripting, you may only activate some feature of your application a few times each time you are working on it. However, your end user may need to perform the same function hundreds of times. To see if there are memory leaks (or any other problems), you should occasionally take a break from development and test the code, running it through the paces that your end user might perform.

You don't need to wait for the program to crash before detecting a memory leak. There are commercial, shareware, and freeware programs available to help you detect these problems. One of my favorites is ResGauge, written by Richard Albury and included in the `UTILITIES` subdirectory of the CD-ROM bundled with this book. (Thanks, Richard!) This freeware utility enables you to monitor the System, Graphics Device Interface (GDI), and the User (interface) memory modules (see fig. 20.6). This and other similar utilities allow you to watch what is happening to your memory as you step through the procedures that your end user might perform.

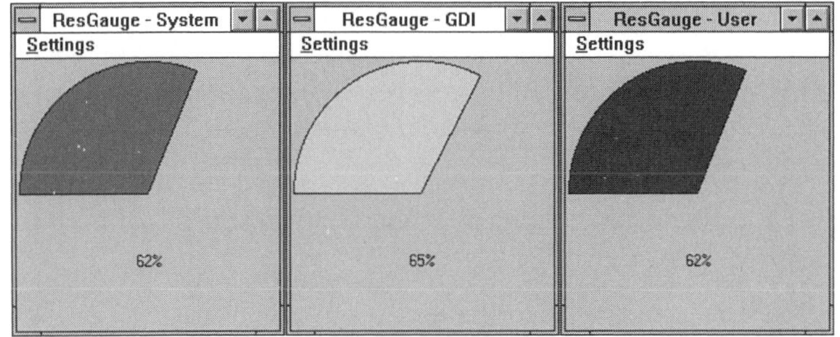

Fig. 20.6

ResGauge memory checker detects memory problems, and it's free!

What do you do if you find a memory leak in your program? The following checklist will provide you with some ideas for handling the problems:

- Are you running the latest version of Multimedia ToolBook? The most recent release may fix your problem.
- Are you coding cleanly? Check your coding very carefully. If, for example, you are using MCI multimedia device calls, you should follow the protocol of `OPEN`, perform actions, `CLOSE`. If you do *not* follow protocol, you'll find that your script appears to work correctly, but when the function is called repeatedly, you run out of memory.

- Are you using bitmap graphics? Try deleting the graphics and regenerating them from the original program. Often a bad header record in the graphic itself is to blame.
- Shut down Windows and reboot the computer.
- Try using CD-ROM optimization options—this forces MTB to check the objects in the book.
- Run the `MTBXFER.TBK` program from Asymetrix (included on this CD-ROM in the `UTILITIES` subdirectory).

Of course, tracking down the leak is not always easy. You can begin by making a copy of your book and deleting major portions of it that you think have no bearing on the problem. Through this process, you can sometimes close in on the culprit. Often you will find that the problem is located outside of ToolBook directly (say, through the call to a faulty DLL). Once you have the problem isolated, it can sometimes be solved by rewriting the script, using a different means of calling a function, finding a different way of accomplishing the task, or asking for help.

The Asymetrix Forum on CompuServe is a good place to look for help; many of the "regulars" have gone through the same problems you are experiencing and can point you in the right direction. Asymetrix technical support is also very active on the forum and provides quick feedback on your difficulty after you have done the work of tracking it down to the lines of code causing the problem.

From Here...

The process of creating a multimedia application is often larger than first expected. In this chapter, the process that is used for designing the interfaces is discussed in some detail. An overview of the entire development process is contained in Chapter 1, "Overview," in the section "Overview of the Application Development Life Cycle."

Also in this chapter, you learned some of the issues surrounding the use of graphics, especially the problems associated with creating multimedia applications that need to run on a variety of platforms.

Refer to the following chapters for related information:

- Chapter 3, "Understanding Objects," gives a larger overview of the application of color in your program.
- Chapter 10, "Using Graphics," provides the "how to" details of getting graphics into your book and using them effectively.

CHAPTER 21

Using Multimedia Elements

Previous chapters have discussed many different multimedia elements that you will use in your MTB applications. This includes using the Clip Manager to define media clips, and using stages to display multimedia elements. However, you may find there are times when you will want to use other methods for displaying multimedia elements. Why is this?

Although ToolBook does an excellent job of displaying multimedia elements, the program was not designed as a multimedia display engine—its "claim to fame" is its ease of use for prototyping interactive multimedia applications—and there will be times these methods will not meet your needs. For example, if you have numerous pictures to display, you may run out of space in the Clip Manager prior to adding all of the pictures. Other limitations have to do with the priorities established during the development of MTB as a tool. For example, MTB 3.0 is not optimized for response to changing large bitmaps while maintaining a continuous flow of music, and doing so may result in "skips" in the audio.

In this chapter, you'll learn the following:

- Types of multimedia elements and their uses
- Limitations encountered using multimedia elements in ToolBook
- Techniques for overcoming multimedia integration problems
- How to configure an application for the end user's system

Understanding Sound

Appropriate use of sound in an application can add immensely to its impact and effect. In order to program sound into your application, it is important that you have a basic understanding of the types of sound files that are used in Windows, along with the pros and cons of their usage in different contexts.

Sound files can be used in a variety of ways. These include playing short bursts of sound for sound effect, using narration tracks along with pictures for effect, and playing background "mood" music while displaying animations or other graphics. Some details and suggestions for using sound in these ways are provided in a following section, "Using Sound Files."

Types of Sound Files

Currently, there are three basic types of sound files that you will be concerned with when creating multimedia elements for your programs:

- Digitized sound files—which are created by using digital recording equipment to produce a sound file that can be played back through the sound card of a computer system.
- MIDI sound files—which is produced using a music keyboard or other means of entering computer "formulas" for sound. These are turned into music to be played back on the computer through special chips included on the sound card.
- CD Audio sound files—which are music files stored in the CD Audio format, the same format used by the music industry for all of the music CDs on the market today.

Digitized Sound Files. Digitized sound files can be easily created on most computers with a sound card and a "line-in" or "microphone-in" jack. The quality of the sound file will vary considerably, depending on such factors as the following:

- the quality of the sound card
- the quality of the sound being input (background noise, professional narrator, type of microphone, etc.)
- the settings for the recording (recording rate, recording resolution, and mono versus stereo)
- the quality of the mixing of the sound (after it has been captured)

In general, the best practice is to first record the sound that you want to digitize in a sound studio on high quality recording equipment. This will minimize background noise. Next, this sound should be fed into the sound card and digitized at the settings most appropriate for the final application.

Music is usually recorded and stored at 22 kHz with stereo sound, while narration is often stored at a lower rate (11 kHz) and in mono. The settings you use will depend on the target machine (how fast is it? what kind of sound card will it have?) and on the space limitations of your application. You must also consider whether to digitize in an 8-bit or 16-bit resolution; many old sound cards only support 8-bit sound.

On a PC, sound files are almost always saved in the `.WAV` format. Digitized sound files from the Macintosh are usually saved in an AIFF format. There are utilities that will allow you to convert between the file types. ToolBook does not support AIFF sound files directly at this time.

A benefit of using digitized sound over MIDI sound for music is that with digitized sound, you know exactly what the resulting music will sound like. With MIDI, the output varies with the quality of the sound chips on the end users' machine. A major drawback to using digitized sound is that the resulting files are usually very large, requiring a great deal of storage space and system resources to play back, while MIDI files are small and compact.

MIDI Sound Files. *MIDI* is an acronym for *Musical Instrument Digital Interface.* MIDI sound is produced from a "formula" for music stored in a compact format on the computer. These files can be generated by MIDI instruments—such as musical keyboards or electrical drums—and then recorded on the computer; or they can be produced directly in software.

Virtually all of the sound cards that are currently being produced contain the hardware to interpret the MIDI files as music. In the past, there was a certain level of difficulty in standardizing the way that the different instruments were encoded on the sound cards, preventing MIDI from being useful except in specific contexts. Now, most sound cards have fairly good approximations of the "key" instruments, such as piano, harpsichord, music box, flute, and violin.

Virtually all sound cards supporting MIDI install MIDI as an MCI device under Windows. The MIDI Mapper directs software that plays a MIDI file to the correct instruments by mapping the channels and maintaining a standardized set of instruments, simplifying the programming task of incorporating this type of music in the application.

MIDI sound is ideally suited for cases where you want to play background mood music and don't want the overhead of storing large digitized sound files or cannot tolerate the impact playing digitized files will have on the resources of the computer. However, if the music is a key feature of the software and you do not have control over the sound card used on the target system, MIDI is not a good choice.

CD Audio Sound. CD Audio sound is the most familiar format for music files today; it is the primary format used by the music industry for distributing music to consumers. CD Audio disks can contain up to 75 minutes worth of full spectrum music, and can be easily controlled from Windows.

CD Audio is best used in cases where sound is a critical element of the application and must be of high fidelity. Drawbacks to using CD Audio include the following:

- Many consumer systems are not properly set up to use CD Audio; use may necessitate more customer support.
- There is no way to preload CD Audio, thus requiring constant access to the CD-ROM drive while the sound is playing.
- CD Audio files are not very compact.
- Integrating CD Audio with ToolBook and other Windows files to produce "hybrid" CD-ROM disks is more difficult (sometimes they cost more to master).

One option for using CD Audio with ToolBook is to create the ToolBook files and store them on the local hard drive, using the CD-ROM drive to play back the sound.

This is the approach taken by HyperGlot Software Company in its "Think and Talk" Berlitz series of language acquisition software programs. The main ToolBook routines are installed on the hard drive. The text and graphics for each lesson can be loaded from the first CD in the set as needed, and the sound is stored on the additional CDs in CD Audio format. In the "Think and Talk German" program, for example, disk one contains the routines and the text and graphics, while the remaining eight CDs store the audio tracks.

Using Sound Files

Now that you know the basic types of sound available, you get to learn some of the techniques that you can use to add sound to your application. The exact method that you use will depend on the nature of the application that you are creating. This section provides some examples of "typical" uses of sound.

Playing Short Sound Bursts for Effect

Often times, you will want to have a sound effect associated with some action, such as an "illegal" mouse click. An example of this is provided in the file CH21EX01.TBK, as shown in figure 21.1.

Fig. 21.1

Use short sound bursts as user alerts.

Clicking the red background activates the following script:

```
to handle buttonUp
     get playSound("systemDefault")
end buttonUp
```

This will activate the system default sound (usually a beep) whenever the user clicks on the background. Clicking the left mouse button activates the following script:

```
to handle buttonUp
     get playSound("wow.wav")
end buttonUp
```

This is a reference to a particular sound file, stored somewhere within the search path for this book. If the file cannot be found, no sound will play, and `sysError` will be set to `The media resource is not open`. In general, you will want to use a path-specific technique for specifying the location of the file so that it can be found, such as setting a system variable for file locations or using the `HDMediaPath` property of the book, as discussed in previous chapters.

> **Note**
>
> This technique is useful for short sound files only (less than 100k). Longer sound files will not only work properly with this command, but also will not provide graceful error messages indicating the problem.

Creating Narration or Timed Music Tracks

At times, you may want to use a narration or music track with a series of pictures to describe the actions that are occurring. Perhaps the most obvious solution to this would be to create a long digitized sound file and then start it playing, changing the pictures at certain key moments.

This solution can prove to be faulty in MTB, which is not optimized for this type of playback. What will happen if you approach the problem this way is that the sound can be interrupted as the bitmap is replaced by the next bitmap in the sequence, producing an undesired effect. Some potential solutions to this are listed as follows:

- Compose each page as a separate unit with its own sound, and put the sound playing commands into the `enterPage` script (for examples of this technique, see files `CH21EX01.TBK` and `CH21EX02.TBK`).
- Call an external program, such as Asymetrix Compel, to play the sequence.
- Create a digitized video file for the sequence, using a program such as Asymetrix's Digital Video Producer or Adobe Premiere, which allow you to interleave sound into the graphics and maintain control of timing (for an example of this technique, see file `CH21EX03.TBK`).
- Use MCI calls from within ToolBook to control the sound and then use a timer to handle the timing of the images (for an example of this technique, see file `CH21EX04.TBK`).
- Have the narration track controlled by an interface with play, pause, stop, and rewind buttons. This turns control over to the user, who is then empowered to use these tools to alleviate any problems caused by a slow down of the computer system (see file `CH21EX05.TBK` for an example).

Synchronizing Sound and Pictures by Playing a Narration File on *enterPage*. An example of the first technique, embedding each narration sequence into a page, is provided in the sample book `CH21EX02.TBK` where each page contains a script similar to that shown in Listing 21.1.

Listing 21.1 CH21EX01.TBK A Script to Play a Sound Clip on *enterPage*

```
to handle enterPage
     if sysLevel = "reader" then
          sysCursor = 4
          mmOpen clip "narr1" wait
          mmPlay clip "narr1" wait
          mmClose clip "narr1"
          go to next page
     end if
end enterPage
```

In this example, the cursor is turned into an hourglass (`sysCursor = 4`) to indicate to the user that he or she does not have control over the activity. The sound clip is opened, played, and then closed before the next page is displayed.

This technique can be useful in cases where you need to retain control over the way a clip is played and can afford to wrest control away from the user. However, the resulting application will not be perceived as user-friendly if you overuse this technique. In general, a rule of thumb you can use is that you should never keep control for more than 10 seconds.

You can create more interactivity by having a menu from which users can choose clips, or by allowing the user to interrupt the playing process. This former is easily accomplished by creating a combo box, single-select list box, or multi-select list box containing the available clips; navigating to the appropriate page using the basic script for the page supplied in Listing 21.1; and, then navigating back when a clip is selected. The latter can be accomplished by changing the listing as demonstrated in the ToolBook file `CH21EX03.TBK` and Listings 21.2 and 21.3.

Listing 21.2 CH21EX02.TBK Another Script for Playing a Sound Clip on *enterPage*

```
to handle enterPage
     if sysLevel = "reader" then
          sysCursor = 4
          mmOpen clip "narr1" wait
          mmPlay clip "narr1" notify self
          sysCursor = 1
     end if
end enterPage

to handle mmNotify
     go to next page
     sysCursor = 1
     forward
end
```

The first section of the script is similar to that in Listing 21.1, changing the cursor and the opening and playing the clip. However, unlike the previous example, the `wait` parameter is not used on the `mmPlay` line. This results in the control being returned to the user. A Next Page button has been added to the page with the script in Listing 21.3. This is where the clip is closed, and the close notification is then sent to the page. The handler for the notify is taken care of in the page script (the lower part of Listing 21.2), navigating to the next page.

Listing 21.3 CH21EX03.TBK Script for Next Page Button to Interrupt the Playing Clip

```
to handle buttonUp
     sysCursor = 4
     mmClose clip "narr1" wait notify this page
end
```

In summary, you will want to use this means of synchronizing sound and pictures when the following is true:

- The images are to be displayed all in one page.
- A wave file can be associated with a page in the book.

The benefits of this approach include the following:

- Ease of implementation
- Control over what images are displayed with what sounds
- Control over when the user can turn the page
- Ability to automate a "slide show" type of presentation

The drawbacks to this approach include the following:

- Difficult to use this technique when a series of pictures is to be played
- Not very interactive

Synchronizing Sound and Pictures Using an External Program. The technique discussed previously can be very effective when you have a sound clip that you want to play with a static screen. However, if you are attempting to synchronize a single sound file with a series of pictures, this technique is not very useful. Because ToolBook supports OLE and DLLs, in many cases you can extend your application by linking to or embedding players from other multimedia applications. Many other programs, such as Microsoft's PowerPoint presentation software, provide runtime modules and permit you to freely distribute your presentation with the player module.

ToolBook can be combined with other Asymetrix products, such as Compel or MediaBlitz, to create multimedia sequences of slides. This is accomplished by exporting a `.CPL` (clip definition library) file from Compel or MediaBlitz and then importing this file into the ToolBook Clip Manager.

The benefits to using a program external to ToolBook for playing back sequences of sound and pictures is that this approach permits a great deal of flexibility. You can use a program that is designed specifically for this purpose to create the non-interactive presentation parts of the program and then allow ToolBook to do what it does best—interactivity.

Another benefit is speed of development; in general, it is fastest to use tools specifically designed for the task at hand. The primary drawbacks to this approach occur when the title you are creating is going to be distributed to a wide audience. You must first, of course, be certain that your audience owns the program you are linking to or obtain license to link (this is often no problem). The distributed disks (or CD-ROM) will then carry the burden of the extra code for the playback engine of the program you are linking to or embedding. This can create large installation files, which can be a problem. In addition, it can create more need for complex product support after the title is distributed. If the final product is destined for a kiosk application or other location in which you have control over the hardware and software, this approach will not pose a significant problem and the benefits may far outweigh the potential problems.

In summary, you will want to use this means of synchronizing sound and pictures when:

- You need to have control over elements that are difficult to control in ToolBook.
- You want to make use of presentations that you have created in other programs, such as PowerPoint.

The benefits of this approach include the following:

- Flexibility, allowing use of output from a variety of other programs
- Speed of development

The drawbacks to this approach include the following:

- Potential distribution problems
- Possible additional user support needed after release
- More potential for conflicts on systems
- Possibly larger and more complex distribution codes and files

Synchronizing Sound and Pictures using Digital Video. Another option is to create a digitized video file (an `.AVI` file) that contains the stills and music that you want to use. This can be accomplished using the Asymetrix Digital Video Producer (see Chapter 23 for information on how to use this program) or a similar product such as Adobe Premiere. In essence, you will create a video that consists of a series of stills repeated for a number of frames, and tied to the sound track.

Benefits of this approach include that the final product is a single file that can added to the clip editor and easily referenced and controlled from ToolBook. This method permits ultimate control over the timing of the images and the pictures.

The major drawback is the draw on resources required to play such videos back on a system. On some of the older or slower systems, special effects between frames may become distorted as the computer attempts to update the frames. This can be alleviated by using a compression algorithm (such as Cinepak by SuperMatch or Intel Indeo), but compression will also reduce the resolution of the images. Another way to reduce the impact on resources is to play the image at a smaller size; but this, of course, also reduces the resolution.

The benefits of using a digitized video may outweigh the drawbacks in your application, and there are some ways you can almost avoid the penalties discussed here. Some tips include the following:

- Set your frame rate low (for example, five frames per second).
- Do not use transitions between frames, but instead rely on straight cuts.
- Make sure each picture is shown for at least three seconds so that none just quickly "flash" onto the screen.
- Use the lowest resolution sound that you can use and still maintain the quality that you want.

In summary, you will want to use this means of synchronizing sound and pictures when timing is a key element in the linking of the picture and sound.

The benefits of this approach include the following:

- Ultimate control over playback rate and synchronization is possible.
- Setting up the synchronization of sound and images is much easier with this method than any other methods discussed.
- The resulting file can be used in multiple applications.
- The resulting file can easily be called from various places in the application.

The drawbacks to this approach include the following:

- Playback rates may be slow on many systems.
- Resulting files can be very large.

Synchronizing Sound and Pictures Using MCI Commands. Still another useful technique for timing pictures with sound is to call MCI commands from within ToolBook and then display the pictures on the page. In Listing 21.4, which is the book `CH21EX04.TBK`, a series of still image clips were added to the clip editor and then called from the idle loop.

Listing 21.4 CH21EX04.TBK Using an MCI Call and the Idle Loop to Synchronize Sound and Graphics

```
to handle enterPage
     system myTimer,pictNumber
     get callMCI("open song1.wav alias moodMusic wait")
     get callMCI("play moodMusic")
     sysTimeFormat = seconds
     pictNumber = 0
     myTimer = sysTime
end

to handle idle
     system myTimer
     system pictNumber
     if myTimer < sysTime then
          increment pictNumber
          if pictNumber > 6 then
               get callMCI("close moodMusic")
               go to next page
          else
               pName = "p" & pictNumber
               mmOpen clip pName
               mmShow clip pName in stage "pictures"
          end if
          myTimer = sysTime + 6
     end if
end
```

In the `enterPage` handler, the sound file is started using `callMCI` commands `open` and `play`. Next the system time format is set to seconds. Finally, system variables for the picture number and the current value of the time are initialized.

The `idle` handler is used to check the current system time and display the pictures. In this example, the time increment used is six seconds, but the code could be easily modified to permit different time increments for each displayed picture. A system variable, `myTimer`, is compared to the system time, `sysTime`. For ease in scripting, all of the picture clips that were added in the Clip Manager were named as the character p followed by a number, in sequential order (`p1`, `p2`, etc.) This permits a simple means of constructing the name of the next clip to play:

```
pName = "p" & pictNumber
```

For this example, there were six pictures being displayed, and when the time has elapsed for the final clip to display, the `callMCI` command `close` is executed and the application displays the next page in the book.

To modify the script so that different pictures are displayed for different lengths of time, this line

```
myTimer = sysTime + 6
```

could be changed to something like the following:

```
conditions
     when pictNumber = 1
          myTimer = sysTime + 6
     when pictNumber = 2
          myTimer = sysTime + 12
          -- etc for each picture number
end conditions
```

In summary, you will want to use this means of synchronizing sound and pictures when:

- You are having difficulty keeping the sound from "skipping."
- You have a large number of sound files and do not want to add them to the Clip Manager (for example, because you have exceeded the maximum permissible number of clips).
- You do not know ahead of time what sound files the user might choose from the local disk drives.
- You want to start the sound file, leave it running, and then control the display of the pictures.

The benefits of this approach include the following:

- Sound files do not need to be added to the Clip Manager.
- Sound files will play "in the background" permitting you to use the idle loop or other system resources to attend to other tasks.

The drawback to this approach is that exact timing of sound and pictures is difficult.

Synchronizing Sound and Pictures with a User Controlled Interface. In cases where the exact timing of sound and picture is not important, use a technique that permits the user to control the interface using a "next picture" type of button. This technique will not necessarily alleviate the problem of the sound skipping during playback, but instead poses the skip as a direct result of the button being pressed by the user. This situation is less frustrating to the user than an unexplained skip, uncontrollable by the user.

This technique can be especially useful for displaying a series of still pictures that are not known ahead of time, such as an interface where the user can add their own pictures, or a display program for Kodak CDs. A sample of this technique is provided in the example file `CH21EX05.TBK`, where four pictures and one sound file have been added as clips to the clip editor. The `enterPage` handler disables the `previous picture` and enables the `next picture` buttons. The next picture button contains the script provided in Listing 21.5.

Listing 21.5 CH21EX05.TBK Script for Demonstrating How to Play Sound and Pictures

```
to handle buttonUp
     system currPict, lastPict
     -- this variable indicates # of pictures
     lastPict = 4
     sysCursor = 4
     if currPict = null then
          currPict = 0
          mmOpen clip "song1" wait
          mmPlay clip "song1"
     end if
     increment currPict
     if currPict = lastPict then
          enabled of button "nextPict" = false
     end if
     if currPict > 1 then
          enabled of button "prevPict" = true
          pName = "p" & currPict - 1
          mmClose clip pName
     end if
     pName = "p" & currPict
     mmOpen clip pName
     mmPlay clip pName in stage "picturePlay"
     sysCursorsysCursor = 1
end
```

A system variable, `lastPict`, is used to store the number of the last picture in the sequence. (For this sample, the variable is set in the button; but in practice, it would be more typical to set such a variable in the book script.) The cursor is turned into the hourglass while the picture loads. Then, the variable containing the current clip number, `currPict`, is examined to see if it has been set. If not, it is initialized. (Again, typical programming practice has not been followed to provide an easier to follow script—normally, such a variable would be initialized in the `enterPage` or `enterBook` handler.) At the same time, the music clip is started. Of course, you could create separate buttons for starting and stopping the music clip, which provides a better sense of control for the user.

Each previously opened picture clip is closed when the next clip is opened; in some cases it might be better to open all of the clips on the `enterPage` and then close them on `leavePage` rather to open and close each picture as needed. When the last picture in the sequence has been reached, the `next picture` button is disabled.

Figure 21.2 shows the completed interface. The `previous picture` button contains a similar script to the `next picture` script, decrementing the picture counter and disabling itself when the first picture has been reached.

Fig. 21.2

Mitigate synchronization problems between sound and pictures with user controls.

In summary, you will want to use this means of synchronizing sound and pictures when you want the user to have control over the pictures that are displayed while a sound file is playing.

The benefits of this approach include the following:

- Sound files do not need to be added to the Clip Manager.
- Sound files will play "in the background."

The drawback to this approach is that exact timing of sound and pictures is difficult.

Understanding Animation

There are a variety of forms of animation that are supported by Multimedia ToolBook. These include the following:

- Displaying a series of bitmap images, one after the next, in rapid sequence
- Using the path animation tools that are part of Multimedia ToolBook
- Playing back an AutoDesk Animation file (`.FLI` or `.FLC`)
- Playing back a Director Movie (`.MOV`) file
- Using OLE to play animation from another application
- Playing a digitized video animation
- Using MPEG hardware to play a digitized video

Most of these techniques are discussed in detail in different sections of this book. Displaying bitmap images and path animations are discussed in Chapter 18, "Using Special Effects." Playing animation files and using OLE are discussed in Chapter 7, "Adding Multimedia Elements."

Synchronizing Sound and Animation

The various types of animations are discussed in the following sections, with typical uses, benefits, and drawbacks discussed.

Synchronizing a Sequence of Bitmaps

One means of animating in ToolBook is to display a series of bitmap or drawn images in sequence. This technique is essentially the same as the techniques described in the previous section discussing synchronizing sound and pictures, and the same sorts of solutions apply.

The largest difficulty is the timing issue. If timing of images and sound is important to your application, this means of animating is `not` the recommended solution. Unless you have complete control over the speed of the end user's system, you are likely to run into problems in synchronization of the final sequence.

In summary, you will want to use this means of synchronizing sound and animation when:

- Synchronization of sound and image is not important
- Use of bitmaps or pictures created in ToolBook are important

The benefits of this approach include the following:

- The animation can be created completely within ToolBook, with resorting to use of other software.
- Smooth, effective animations can be created that will play back on any system that supports ToolBook files.

The drawbacks to this approach include the following:

- Animations may play back at different rates, depending on how you implement the scripts.
- Sound and animation will not be perfectly synchronized.

Synchronizing Sound and Path Animations

Another method of animation used in ToolBook is the path animation technique discussed in Chapter 18, "Using Special Effects." This method provides timing for images and can be used effectively with sound files that have been timed to match. The sound files can be any of the types discussed previously—MIDI, digitized sound, or CD Audio—and can be played using any of the previously discussed means.

The trickiest part of the operation might be getting the animation and the sound file to begin at the same moment in time. The best practice is to have the animation and sound only loosely associated, so that the timing is not critical. Obviously, lip-synched sound will not do here!

In summary, you will want to use this means of synchronizing sound and animation when you want to make use of ToolBook's handy path animation tools.

The benefits of this approach include the following:

- You can use MIDI or CD Audio files for sound synchronization.
- You can synchronize the sound and animation rather easily.
- The resulting application will play on any system supporting MTB.

The drawback to this approach is that getting the timing perfected is not easy.

Synchronizing Sound and AutoDesk Animation Files

MTB also supports playback of AutoDesk animation files (`.FLI` and `.FLC`). The current drivers for these types of animation are designed to play back the animations at whatever rate the system can support. Every frame is displayed. This makes exact timing impossible. Keep in mind that even if you have complete control over the system, say for a kiosk application, there can be factors that might make the animation play slower at some later date (such as disk fragmentation.) Thus, if exact timing is important to you, this is not the perfect solution. However, if you want the best resolution display of a three-dimensional animation, this is currently your best option.

In summary, you will want to use this means of synchronizing sound and animation when:

- Synchronization of sound is not important
- Quality of animation playback image is important

The benefit of this approach is that animations can be used "as is" from the application that created them. The drawback to this approach is that timing will be very inaccurate.

Creating a Digital Video File from an Animation File

In cases where timing of sound and animation; is critical, you should consider creating a digital video from the animation. There are many tools available on the market today that will allow you to do this, including Microsoft Video For Windows Video Editor. The digital video format is designed to keep picture and sound synchronized by interleaving the two sources. Of course, the drawback to this method can be the loss of resolution in image quality from compression techniques.

In summary, you will want to use this means of synchronizing sound and animation when:

- Synchronization of sound is critical.
- Quality of animation playback image is not as important.

The benefit of this approach is the complete control over timing. The drawback to this approach is that the image will lose some of its original quality.

Using MPEG Compression Hardware for Animation Playback

The only currently available means of maintaining smooth playback and sound synchronization for full screen video or animation is through proprietary MPEG decompression cards. There are many of these on the market today, and the use of these cards is easy to achieve in ToolBook. For use in kiosks or other places where these cards are currently installed, this is a perfect solution.

Keep in mind that as of the publication date of this book, the user base of MPEG decompression cards is quite small and the cost of MPEG compression of video and animation is quite high (about $200 per minute). This status is expected to change rapidly in the near future as more and more graphics cards incorporate advanced processing chips and as the market for image compression hardware and software broadens (and force a drop in price from competition.) The motion picture industries' move into the multimedia market is expected to drive these changes at an accelerated pace as the need for ways to display full screen "movies" on the computer is voiced.

The ability to productively re-package Hollywood's titles in a multimedia format will hinge on the ability of computer graphic cards to support these high data rate images as well as the ability for CD-ROM drives to supply the throughput (faster drives) and greater storage (higher density disks.) Expect to see rapid changes in these areas in the near future.

In summary, you will want to use this means of synchronizing sound and animation when:

- Synchronization of sound is very important.
- The animation is already created and is in high quality video format, ready to be transferred.
- Quality of animation playback image is important.

The benefit of this approach is that animations are very high quality, will play back full screen, and have high quality sound.

The drawbacks to this approach include the following:

- Not many customers have this equipment yet.
- Some of the currently shipping equipment is difficult to interface with.
- The standards for hardware, software, and drivers for these devices is still emerging.

Understanding Video

There are different types of video supported in MTB. These include video overlay, external control of video devices (laser discs, VCRs, and so on), digital video, and MPEG digital video playback.

Video Overlay

Video overlay is supported by video overlay hardware that is installed in the end user's machine. For software that is intended for wide audience distribution, video overlay is not a useful feature as it is dependent on hardware that is unlikely to be installed. However, for some applications, video overlay can be very useful—such as specialty kiosks that use a video camera, and display the live video on the screen through the overlay card. The essential steps in using video overlay are as follows:

1. Define the area to display the overlay video using the stage tool.
2. Set the page property `overlayOpen` to `True`.

Now, the current video source being fed into the video of the video overlay card will display in the stage (provided you have the proper hardware). You can, of course, combine this with MCI calls to control an external device (such as a laser disc player or VCR) to control the video clip being displayed.

External Video Device Control

External control of video devices, whether for playback in a video overlay window or on an external monitor, can be affected through the clip editor by defining the clip start and stop points, or through MCI calls to the device. Note that not all VCRs and laser disc players are controllable. Most controllable devices use a serial cable for the control, and most come with MCI drivers that are installed into Windows. If you have a controllable device that is supplied without the necessary drivers, you can get the current drivers from the BBS services of the company (such as Sony, Pioneer, and Panasonic), or on the support forums on CompuServe or the Internet. More detail for controlling MCI devices is found in the next chapter of this book.

Digital Video Files

Digital video files consist of files that have been digitized from an analog source and now reside on the computer. They can be an effective means to provide information to users. As of the writing of this book, there are basically two types of digitized video that are used for multimedia applications—Video for Windows (`.AVI` files) and Apple QuickTime Video. Both types of files can use a variety of compression techniques, known as *codecs* (compression/decompression codes). These include Cinepak by SuperMatch and Intel Indeo. It is beyond the scope of this book to provide a detailed discussion of the different video compression algorithms or details of creating digitized video; but for an excellent discussion read *How to Digitize Video* by Nels Johnson, 1994, John Wiley & Sons, Inc.

Examples of working with video have been provided throughout the book in various sections. Normally, you will want to add the video clip to the Clip Manager and then play it back in a stage. Chapter 7, "Adding Multimedia Elements," provides details on using media widgets, providing an easy means to control the digitized video clips.

Checklist for Multimedia Elements

As you develop a multimedia application, you may find that there are a series of trade-offs that you must consider that stem from the limitations of today's computer systems. If you don't take the proper perspective, you might find these limitations frustrating.

The "proper perspective" means keeping in mind the bigger picture, beginning with a historical perspective. Recall that it has only been very recently that computers have been able to do digital video at all. And, in a few years, they will be doing it quite well. But, by then, you may not be at all satisfied with the state of the art. Instead, you may be grumbling because "this darn computer can hardly do virtual reality at all... look how slow it is updating and rendering new images... and I'm only asking it to read half-gigabyte files from the quad-density CD-ROM!"

Keeping your project in perspective also means thinking through the bottlenecks and pitfalls of the project before you begin storyboarding, producing elements, and coding. What elements are going to be limiting? How can you get the same information to your end user in a less consumptive method? Could you use a smaller image, a voice-over with stills instead of a video, a shorter animation?

As you develop your application, you must keep in mind that your end user may not have as much RAM, as fast a hard drive, or as powerful of a graphics card as you do on your development system. These limitations need to be taken into account early in the development process. Ask yourself these questions about the end target machine:

- What rate of playback of graphics will the end user have? The rate of playback of graphic images (stills, video, animation) will vary from system to system; if you are targeting a wide market, you will need to support both slower and faster graphic cards and systems.
- What graphics modes are the users going to have? Keep in mind the different graphics modes of the targeted systems as you develop your application; a small video frame with 256 colors may not be very effective for some elements, and may be better displayed in a different manner.
- What kind of sound card will the end user have? Remember that there are still many systems out there that are using 8-bit mono sound, perhaps without MIDI chips. Are these users in your target audience?
- How much disk space will be required to install this application? If you are planning to place the graphics on the disk, for example, to speed access to CD-Audio clips, then be sure that the amount of disk space your application will request is not excessive for the typical end user of the product.
- What CD-ROM access rate will the user need? If you are developing a CD-ROM based product, be sure that it will run on the systems that you are targeting.

In general, you will want to test your application throughout the development process in order to make certain that it will work properly on all targeted machines. And the final application must be tested on a wide range of machines to be certain that the multimedia elements and controllers install and display correctly. Waiting until the end of the project to begin this testing process is a sure recipe for disaster!

From Here...

This chapter has discussed the range of multimedia elements that you may want to incorporate into your application. For details of adding multimedia elements, refer to these other chapters of the book:

- Chapter 5, "Understanding the Media Management Tools," discusses the Clip Manager and how to add multimedia clips to the application.
- Chapter 7, "Adding Multimedia Elements," teaches you more about multimedia elements including stages and OLE.
- Chapter 18, "Using Special Effects," discusses creating animations using hide and show commands with bitmaps and using the path animation tools.
- Chapter 22, "MCI Devices and Multimedia," talks about using MCI to control multimedia devices.

CHAPTER 22

MCI Devices and Multimedia

Although the clip and stage metaphors are useful simplifications of the processes for playing sounds and for displaying and sizing pictures and video, you can have more control over all these procedures by using the `imageCommand()` and `callMCI()` functions. These are wrapper functions to even lower-level calls to Windows MCI API functions. Using them can improve performance and allow use of all features provided by drivers. They may be used along with, or instead of, clips and stages.

In this chapter, you learn about the following topics:

- Understanding MCI devices
- Controlling MCI devices in Multimedia ToolBook
- The `imageCommand()` functions
- Mixing clips and low-level calls

Understanding MCI Devices

A problem that plagues almost every aspect of programming for Windows is the fact that any specific machine on which Windows runs is one of countless hardware and firmware variations on the original PC compatible/DOS operating system. In the realm of multimedia systems, it's not going too far to say that each system has a unique combination of BIOS, processor, memory, sound and video hardware (each with its associated drivers), and interrupt configurations.

The plug-and-play technology that is beginning to spill over into the PC world doesn't change the way a program sees a given system. Windows provides a relatively consistent environment within which programmers can write device drivers for graphics and sound cards that protects the programmer from the variations in the target systems (and vice versa!).

Media Control Interface (MCI) is the environment for device drivers that control what are nominally physical devices: audio compact disc players, videodisc players, videocassette recorders, and related machines. MCI provides no assistance with the electrical connections to the serial or parallel communications protocols of such devices. The target PC's configuration must have the proper hardware, MCI drivers, and connectors to control the desired machines. MCI commands are relatively simple function calls that send commands to the drivers. Their arguments are strings.

Simple and Compound MCI Devices

Formally, there is a distinction made between *simple devices,* which MCI drivers control directly (such as disc or tape players), and *compound devices* whose media information resides in files. In practice, the distinction is not very important aside from the greater complexity of the commands' arguments.

If your application is meant to control mechanical devices or processing cards whose characteristics are not precisely known in advance (or when a different model of a device is substituted for the original), you normally ask the device about its capabilities. Digital video and animation drivers generally have capabilities that are known from the outset and generally will not vary among target machines, so there is not much need to ask for them (although it certainly doesn't hurt to do so, as some devices may acquire unforeseen capabilities in the future).

MCI can also control the recording and playing of sound and MIDI files—capabilities that you may already have in the form of utilities provided with your sound card, but that require MCI drivers and function calls to manipulate directly.

MCI System, Device, and Required Commands

Perhaps a more important distinction in everyday use of MCI is among the different commands that you can be sure are available to you. The MCI *system commands* (not to be confused with ToolBook system commands) that you may find useful are:

- The `break` command, which specifies which key combination overrides the `wait` parameter that may be included in some MCI strings.
- The `sound` command, which plays a single Windows system sound.
- The `sysinfo` command, which returns information pertaining to the MCI layer of Windows.

> **Note**
>
> The `break`, `sound`, and `sysinfo` commands can be used directly, but it's much simpler to use their equivalent OpenScript constructs. The `sysMediaBreakKey system` property and `playSound()` functions are available for issuing the MCI `break` and `sound` commands, the first two tasks. System information is available through individual OpenScript calls and properties such as `sysSupportedMedia`.

Each type of MCI-controllable device has its own MCI driver, usually provided by the device's manufacturer. The available or relevant MCI command set is therefore different among device types, among different manufacturers' drivers, and even among drivers for different models of a single manufacturer's product. The command set will always include the MCI *required functions*, which are supported by every MCI-controllable device. For instance, all machines, physical or virtual, are required to have the ability to return information about themselves. The required functions are not MCI system commands because their arguments are device-dependent, but they are available in some form for every device. Table 22.1 summarizes the required command set.

Table 22.1 MCI Required Commands

Command	Description
can eject	Reports whether media can be ejected from the device
can freeze	Reports whether freeze-frame capability is available
can lock	Reports whether device has provision for locking
capability	Obtains the capabilities of a device
close	Closes the device; closes file if necessary
info	Obtains information from a device in ASCII text
open	Initializes the device; opens file if necessary
status	Obtains status information in ASCII text

Table 22.2 is the set of *basic commands*. The use of these messages by a device is optional, but omission of a basic command from a device's command set is usually an indication that the command has no meaning in the context of the device. For instance, the `save` command is meaningless in the context of a controller for CD audio. You may expect to find a sensible subset the basic commands in the command set of every device.

Tip

Support of the basic commands is not absolutely required by MCI. Always check the device's documentation for supported functions.

Table 22.2 MCI Basic Commands

Command	Description
load	Recalls data from a disk file
pause	Pauses playing or recording

(continues)

Table 22.2 Continued

Command	Description
play	Starts transmitting output data
record	Starts recording input data
resume	Resumes playing or recording on a paused device
save	Saves data to a disk file
seek	Seeks forward or backward
set	Sets the operating state of the device
status	Obtains status information about the device
stop	Stops playing or recording

If a device supports a basic command, it must also support a standard set of options for the command. For a complete description of the basic commands and options, search the Windows help file "MCI Commands" (supplied with ToolBook) for the command names in Tables 22.1 through 22.3 and refer to the documentation supplied with the device you wish to control.

Note that the `status` command appears in both Table 22.1 and Table 22.2. The `status` command as used in the group of basic commands includes options for use with devices which have identifiable timecode addresses, frame numbers, or other *timeline* features. Animation, wave audio, and digital video are examples of devices which use timelines.

For capabilities that are beyond those defined by the required and basic commands, any particular MCI driver may have its command set extended to include commands peculiar to its device or device type.

Some MCI devices have additional commands to add options to existing commands. While some extended commands only apply to a specific device driver, most of them apply to all drivers of a particular device type. For example, the sequencer command `set` extends the set command to add time formats that are needed by MIDI sequencers.

Unless you are certain that the specific MCI driver you use during development will be available on the target system, you should not assume that the device supports the extended commands or options. You can use the `capability` command to determine whether a specific feature is supported, and your application should be ready to deal with "unsupported command" or "unsupported function" return values.

Table 22.3 shows some extended commands. The list of extended commands is subject to growth as new device types appear.

Table 22.3 Selected List of MCI Extended Commands

Command	Device Types	Description
cue	waveaudio	Prepares for playing or recording
delete	waveaudio	Deletes a data segment from the MCI element
escape	videodisc	Sends custom information to a device
freeze	overlay	Disables video acquisition to the frame buffer
put	visual types	Defines the source, destination, and frame windows
realize	visual types	Tells the device to select and realize its palette into the display context of the displayed window
spin	videodisc	Starts/stops disc spin
step	visual types	Step the play one or more frames forward or reverse
unfreeze	overlay	Enables the frame buffer to acquire video data
update	visual types	Repaints the current frame into the display context
where	visual types	Obtains the rectangle specifying the source, destination, or frame area
window	visual types	Controls the display window

The term "visual types" refers to MCI visual devices, such as animation and digital video drivers, and video overlay cards; but these commands are also usable where appropriate for the ToolBook `imageCommand()` function set.

Many MCI commands take further parameters that determine what kind of information they return. While a comprehensive list would soon be outdated, not to mention very large, Table 22.4 shows typical parameters available for use with the capability command (a required command). This particular subset of parameters applies primarily to animation drivers.

Table 22.4 Some Parameters of the *capability* Command

Parameter	Return Value
can eject	TRUE if the device can eject physical media
can play	TRUE if the device can play
can record	FALSE as applied to animation. Such devices cannot record
can reverse	TRUE if the device can play in reverse
can save	FALSE as applied to animation. Such devices can't save
can stretch	TRUE if the device can stretch frames

(continues)

Table 22.4 Continued

Parameter	Return Value
compound device	TRUE if the device supports an element name
device type	Animation devices return "animation"
fast play rate	Fast play rate in frames per second
has audio	TRUE if the device supports audio playback
has video	TRUE as applied to animation
normal play rate	Normal play rate in frames per second
slow play rate	Slow play rate in frames per second
uses files	TRUE if the element of a compound device is a file
uses palettes	TRUE if the device uses palettes
windows	Number of windows the device can support

Of course, each device type has its own set of supported parameters for its own set of supported commands. Don't try to memorize them all; there is a Windows Help file named "Windows MCI API Help" that is supplied with Multimedia ToolBook. This file is the best reference guide, aside from information from the manufacturer or publisher of the device.

Controlling MCI Devices in Multimedia ToolBook

Multimedia ToolBook, in addition to the commands that implement its clip/stage model of multimedia programming, also supports a set of lower-level calls to the MCI. These are the `callMCI()` functions. It comes as a surprise to many OpenScript programmers that MCI commands can be mixed with standard clip and stage operations, but it's important to understand that the clip/stage metaphor is implemented through calls to the MCI system and the Windows API (look forward to Listing 22.4). The low-level calls to the MCI system are only slightly more complicated than the ones used by the ToolBook MCI interface. Once this concept is grasped, some of the esoteric system, clip, and stage properties that are scattered throughout the OpenScript documentation become very useful, and you will be able to take advantage of the device-specific feature control available through MCI without sacrificing the ease of use of stages.

callMCI() and *imageCommand()*

Multimedia ToolBook supports MCI devices through the `callMCI()` functions. It also provides a set of functions, the `imageCommand()` functions, that support bitmap manipulation. Though bitmap display is not directly addressed by MCI proper, the syntax of Multimedia ToolBook's `imageCommand()` set is exactly analogous to that of the callMCI() functions and will be included in this discussion. Keep the two distinct in your mind, though, as discussions with programmers in other environments may otherwise get confusing.

MCI Command Syntax in Multimedia ToolBook

MCI functions as implemented in Multimedia ToolBook have one required argument, a string (and/or a combination of variables that evaluate to a string), and one optional argument, an object reference. The former is the actual command, the latter is the object that receives MCI notification messages, if any. The return value may be a number or a string, depending on the device and the command. A return value of NULL indicates that an error occurred in execution.

The basic syntax of a callMCI() function is simple. Type the following three lines into the Command window and press Enter (after checking that the path to this Windows system sound is correct for your PC and modifying the path in the script line if necessary):

```
get callMCI("open c:\windows\chimes.wav alias w wait");get callMCI
("play w wait");get callMCI("close w")
```

If the system sound chimes.wav has not been removed from your Windows directory, this command line will play it. This is an example of using a compound MCI device.

> **Note**
>
> Internal and virtual devices, which are often compound devices, such as waveform audio cards and digital video drivers, receive the lion's share of the discussion in this chapter. This is simply a reflection of the fact that a sound or video file can be supplied on the accompanying disk, but a video overlay card can't.

There are a couple of peculiarities involved in building arguments to MCI functions as compared with other OpenScript functions. First, notice that the entire command string is quoted; the path does not need to be included in its own quotes (and in fact must not be, unless concatenation is used to build the path from variables combined with strings). Also, the parameters of the argument string are simply space-delimited words.

Assigning an Alias. Very well, but what if the reference to the sound is needed elsewhere in the program? The previous script fragment sets up a system variable that must then be declared within each handler in which it's used. MCI, though not usually known for its elegance, provides a very clean way of dealing with media references: the *alias*.

An alias is in fact a lot like a system variable except that it can be used in callMCI() functions anywhere in the application (even in other books) without further declarations. Extend the simple sound example to use an alias, as on page one of the example book, CH22.TBK which is included on the disk accompanying this book (see Listing 22.1).

Listing 22.1 22LST01.DOC Playing Wave Audio Via the MCI

```
TO HANDLE buttonClick
    get callMCI("open c:\windows\chimes.wav alias cwav")
    get callMCI("play cwav")
END buttonClick
```

Try executing the command `get callMCI("play cwav")` from anywhere else in the book; a buttonClick handler, a mouseEnter handler at any level, and so on. You may enter the statement into the Command window. The sound will still play.

> **Note**
>
> Be sure to close the sound file with a `get callMCI("close cwav")` or `get callMCI("close all")` call after experimenting with the alias. It's bad practice to leave media files open, as they use memory and other system resources..

Notice that the alias is part of the MCI command string; there is no need to concatenate it. Note also that the alias is an argument to an `open` command; you can't directly assign an alias in a `play` or other command. So, if you have only one `play` command to execute, you could skip the alias. Usually it's advantageous to open a file and assign it an alias early in a handler in preparation for quick manipulation later. Since MCI generally deals with relatively low-level commands, it's not uncommon to use several in succession.

> **Tip**
>
> Use OpenScript's built-in `mmDeviceAlias` property when working with clips rather than files.

Several aliases may be in use simultaneously if more than one media file is open.

Simple Devices. Simple MCI devices include CD players, audio and video tape players and recorders, and other devices that are controlled directly. They either do not return data or supply their own data without the need to manipulate files. MCI control of such machines requires that the target computer have the appropriate control card (or serial/parallel port driver) installed in addition to the appropriate (software) MCI driver.

The command set for a given simple device is usually small, but a command that bears the same name in more than one driver (for example, that for controlling an audio CD, which is commonly a playback-only device, and that for controlling a VCR) usually has different arguments for each device.

Given the differences in the command sets for different devices, it's a requirement that an MCI "open..." command (or any other command that opens the device) includes the device type:

```
get callMCI("open videodisc")
```

Compound Devices. Compound devices control the manipulation of data stored in files.

There are a couple of problems with this basic form of `callMCI()` as used to play from files. The most obvious is that the path is fixed. This issue is partially dealt with by MCI itself.

To avoid keying the path and file name into each MCI command, use MCI's ability to assign an alias to a file. An alias is used very much like a variable. Why not use a system variable? The short answer is, No reason. The variation of the sound example could run like that shown in Listing 22.2.

Listing 22.2 16LST02.DOC Accessing a Path and File Using a System variable

```
TO HANDLE buttonClick
    local STRING s
    s = "c:\windows\chimes.wav"
    get callMCI("play" && s)
    get callMCI("close" && s)  -- or, get callMCI("close all")
END buttonClick
```

Note that the MCI command string is in no way different from any other literal string and may be built up from OpenScript expressions in the usual manner.

The script in Listing 22.3 plays a digital video file, specified by a full path name, when the page is entered. The return value is unused.

Listing 22.3 16LST03.DOC Accessing a Path and File Using an Alias

```
TO HANDLE enterPage
    get callMCI("open c:\mtb30\samples\asym01.avi alias mm")
    get callMCI("play mm wait")
    get callMCI("close mm")
END enterPage
```

Tip

Use aliases that are short and memorable, as the very reason for their existence is to make it possible for mnemonic references to be used.

Manipulation of size, position, start and end times, track numbers, and so forth, are fairly straightforward using MCI commands. Unfortunately, there is no required command for setting the screen coordinates of the window in which the video plays; in fact, it always plays in a popup window (with caption bar) at 0,0. This is usually not what you're after. (But see the discussion of the `put` and `window` commands in the sections named "The `put` Command" and "The `window` Command.")

Caution

> Position values in arguments to `callMCI()` and `imageCommand()` functions must be passed as pixels. It's necessary to use the system variable `sysPageUnitsPerPixel` or the function `screenToPageUnits()` to convert such values to ToolBook page units. Call `pageUnitsToScreen()` to pass positions specified in page units to `callMCI()` and `imageCommand()`.

Normally, a video item is intended to play within the bounds of the current window. What is wanted, then, is a child window. Specify it as part of the `open` command using the `style` argument:

```
get callMCI("open c:\mtb30\samples\asym01.avi \
alias mm style child")
```

If you were to execute this function call as is, you might or might not see the picture. It will, as often as not, appear as a child of another window, perhaps one belonging to another application. This call would work if MCI knew which window is the child's parent window. This involves getting a window handle. OpenScript provides a few ways of getting the window handles of its own windows. If the current window is the main window, then `sysClientHandle` or `windowHandle of mainWindow` are appropriate. More generally, use the following:

```
get callMCI("open c:\mtb30\samples\asym01.avi alias mm style \
child" && parent" && windowHandle of this window)
```

It's very good practice to add `wait` parameters to media commands (MCI or clip) whenever possible. Some unpredictable and annoying crashes may occur if the script is allowed to continue to execute while Windows is still processing a media command. Such errors include, but are not limited to, GDI memory errors. The `wait` parameter is simply appended to the text string that comprises the command:

```
get callMCI("open c:\mtb30\samples\asym01.avi alias mm style child" \
          && "parent" && windowHandle of this window && "wait")
```

As always, the backslash line break simply indicates to OpenScript that multiple lines are to be treated as a single expression.

You may not want to use the `wait` parameter with the `play` command, as you may intentionally run other processes concurrently with the playing of media. For instance, you may want to turn pages while a wave audio file is playing. This is usually OK given a target system that can keep up with the concurrent tasks.

When using a compound device, you're opening a file. How does MCI know which MCI driver to use for opening a given file in a compound device? The following are three ways you can accomplish this:

- Specify the driver type with the "type" parameter.
- Map the file extension to the appropriate player.
- Specify the driver type with the "!" operator.

The most direct method is to specify a driver using the "type..." parameter:

```
get callMCI("open c:\mtb30\samples\asym01.avi alias mm" \
        && "type digitalVideo style child parent" && windowHandle \
        of this window && "wait")
```

> **Note**
>
> If there are two or more drivers of a given type on s single system, Windows can sometimes select an incorrect driver, causing the "Execution Suspended" alert to appear. A better way of specifying the driver type is to use the driver manufacturer's own reference. As an illustration, Video for Windows' specification would be "type AVIVideo", while QuickTime for Windows' reference is "type QTWVideo".

Why did the wave file in the example by which you played chimes.wav play with no driver type specified? Because an assumption was made about your Windows configuration, and the second mehod mention previously of assigning the driver was used based on that assumption. The [MCI] section of the WIN.INI file in your WINDOWS directory associates driver types with file extensions. The .WAV extension is mapped to a driver on almost all machines equipped for sound. The installers for most digital video drivers, such as Video for Windows and QuickTime for Windows, register the appropriate file types, as do those for most animation drivers. You cannot rely on an unspecified target computer's having the extensions mapped for anything but wave audio and MIDI files, though; you can either assume that it does, as in the chimes example, or you can specify the driver.

The third method of specifying the driver type of a compound device is to put the ! symbol between the type specification and the filename:

```
get callMCI("open digitalVideo!c:\mtb30\samples\asym01.avi alias mm" \
    && "style child parent" && windowHandle of this window && "wait")
```

This method is exactly equivalent to the first method, though many programmers prefer method three because it results in a shorter statement.

The digital video command has become so lengthy that it's useful to take it apart again as a summary:

```
get callMCI("open c:\stuff\mymovie.avi...
```

Open the following digital video file:

```
...alias mm...
```

The alias is a reference to the file that may be used anywhere in the program. It's most convenient to keep it short and mnemonic, as "mm" for "Main Movie."

```
...type digitalVideo...
```

See the list of driver types at the end of this chapter. Sometimes the file extension makes this phrase unnecessary.

```
...style child...
```

This is part one of making sure the movie window shows up in the correct window. Setting the style to `child` means the movie window is constrained within the bounds of a clipping window (although you haven't yet specified which one).

```
...parent" && windowHandle of this window...
```

This phrase tells MCI which window is the `parentWindow` of the child (movie) window. A built-in viewer property, `windowHandle`, is used to specify the window handle instead of specifying it within the string literally. In this case, the movie will play in a window that appears to be inside the current window. If the window is the main window, the system property, `sysClientHandle`, would do as well as the viewer property, `windowHandle`, of this window.

```
&& "wait")
```

This command causes the function not to return until it's finished executing, so that further script statements do not execute while MCI is processing its command.

Moving and Sizing Visual Media Windows

Next, the child window needs to be positioned and sized. Several MCI commands affect the window properties, and a handy function from the Windows API USER module, `MoveWindow()`, is useful for both positioning and sizing.

The *put* command. The `put` command is used to place and size a window for a visual medium. The use varies with the specific animation, video overlay, or digital video driver. Basic usage for Video for Windows is as follows:

```
get callMCI("put mm window at 100 150 240 180 wait")
```

In this case, the first two numerical parameters specify the position (in pixels, as always) of the display window with respect to the upper-left corner of its parent window. The second two numerals specify the width and height, respectively, of the window. When using Video for Windows, the second pair of numerals may be set to `"0 0"` to specify that the window is not to be resized when its position is changed:

```
get callMCI("put mm window at 100 150 0 0 wait")
```

Note that the position and size values are space-delimited, not comma-delimited as are ToolBook points. A simple comma insertion routine is included in the Play button script on page two of CH22.TBK, although the need for conversion to a ToolBook-style comma-separated list is removed if you simply retrieve "words" one through four rather than "items" one through four. See Listing 22.4 for more information on getting the points returned by MCI functions. QuickTime for Windows users should be aware that the `put` function, as used with the QuickTime MCI driver, can actually size a window all the way down to zero width and height, so the width and height values must always be entered as positive numbers.

`Put` specifies a scaling window when used with the source parameter and a clipping window when the destination parameter is included. Usage varies with the driver, but generally the `source` argument acts on the video image as contained in the file or as received from the video playback machine; that is, the bounds of the original image. The command `"put source"`, followed by the coordinates for a window, shows the entire image reduced or stretched to fit that window. See the note concerning playback window size below; video performance depends critically on it.

The command `"put destination"` followed by window coordinates, on the other hand, specifies a *clipping window*. A clipping window doesn't affect the size of the source material, but defines which portion is visible on-screen. In short, it crops the image. It's useful in eliminating extraneous material from the visual image, or for limiting the visible action to a single object.

Displaying Video in a Viewer. The short `buttonClick` handler in the script of the Play in Viewer button on page three of `CH22.TBK` illustrates the use of a viewer as a media display window. The advantage of using a viewer is that, as a native ToolBook object, its size and position can be set by standard OpenScript commands. However, a viewer does not automatically stretch or shrink the video image when resized. `"open..."` is the only MCI command from the previous example that needs modification to attach the window of a .AVI file to a viewer:

```
get callMCI("open c:\mtb30\samples\asym01.avi alias mm style child" \
          && parent" && windowHandle of viewer "dv" && "wait")
```

This form lets the file extension take care of selecting the proper driver as before.

The *window* Command. The MCI command `window` can be followed by a valid window handle that specifies the window to be used for display. Normally use this form to play visual media in an existing window. It's up to you to make sure the window handle is valid.

This command is probably the most straightforward way of positioning and sizing the visual image if it's not on a stage. (You may use MCI functions with clips, including clips in stages. Use the `mmDeviceHandle` clip property to get the window handle of the clip.) Simply assign a viewer's window handle as the display window handle, then use the standard viewer properties and functions to size and move the image. Append the following lines to the script of the digital video player exercise:

```
get callMCI("window mm" && (windowHandle of viewer "pix"))
```

`"mm"` is the alias of the file. If a clip has been created from the file, use the form:

```
get callMCI("window" && (mmDeviceAlias of clip "p1") \
    && (windowHandle of viewer "pix"))
```

The `handle default` parameter tells the MCI video driver to display its pictures in the window created during `open` as in the original digital video player example. `state` modifies `window` in a driver-dependent manner. It's generally used to maximize, minimize, normalize, hide, or show the window. `text` specifies the text of the destination windows caption bar, if any.

The *MoveWindow()* Function. QuickTime users may want to define a window that allows the movie controller to be shown and hidden. A way of simultaneously positioning and scaling a window directly is to call the `MoveWindow()` Windows API function. It's in the Windows module `USER.EXE`, so `USER` must be linked by a `linkdll` structure and the function prototype defined. What makes the `MoveWindow( )` function so easy to use from OpenScript is that each of its six arguments, except for the window handle, corresponds to an OpenScript data type, but the media window `"mm"`. `MoveWindow()` can simultaneously size a window (normally a stretching, not a clipping, window) and position it on the screen. Link the module in the usual way. You may place these statements in an enter message handler or a button message handler:

```
linkdll USER —Don't use quotes when linking named Windows modules
    INT MoveWindow (WORD,INT,INT,INT,INT,INT)
end linkdll
```

The arguments are passed as follows:

- Window handle of the window being manipulated
- Top-left horizontal coordinate in pixels
- Top-left vertical coordinate in pixels
- Width of the window in pixels
- Height of the window in pixels
- Repaint flag: Set this to `1` if you want the window updated after the move or resize operation (the usual case), `0` if you don't.

The position reference is the upper-left corner of the media window's parent window. The function returns a non-zero value if it is successful. A zero return value indicates an error condition.

Video Window Sizing and Performance. Page four of `CH22.TBK` illustrates an important point about sizing and scaling file-based visual media windows, following "optimal performance rules:"

- The best performance is obtained when the window is at the source picture's natural size or an even integral multiple of the linear dimensions of it (plus one pixel; see point number three).
- Changing the aspect ratio of a window degrades performance.
- The best performance is obtained when the display (destination) window is exactly one pixel taller and one pixel wider than the nominal size, assuming the aspect ratio is correct. The worst performance results when the destination window is one pixel shorter and one pixel narrower than the nominal size.

If you notice no performance degradation while playing a media element which has been sized slightly smaller that its normal width and height, you have a fast machine. Still, you should take into account target machines which may be much slower and optimize your window sizes accordingly.

If you wish to reconstruct page four of CH22.TBK yourself, you will require one page; three buttons; a field named file, drawn long enough to accept the pathname to a Video for Windows file; and the video file itself.

The script of one of the three buttons on page four of CH22.TBK brings together some of the salient points of this chapter (see Listing 22.4).

Listing 22.4 22LST04.DOC Performance Degradation of Video in Windows of Inappropriate Size

```
TO HANDLE buttonClick
    local WORD hWnd
    get text of field "file"
    get callmci("open" && it && "alias mm style child parent" \
        && sysClientHandle && "wait")
    hWnd = callMCI("status mm window handle")
    get callMCI("where mm source max")
    linkDLL "USER"
        INT MoveWindow(WORD,INT,INT,INT,INT,INT)
    end linkDLL
    get MoveWindow(hWnd,word 1 of it, word 2 of it, \
        (word 3 of it) - 1, (word 4 of it) - 1, 1)
    get callmci("play mm",self)
END buttonClick

TO HANDLE MCINotify
    get callMCI("close mm")
    unlinkDLL "USER"
END MCINotify
```

This listing is for the button labeled `Subtract 1 Pixel From Size`. It does just that. You must enter the path to the video file in field `file`, then press the button. The button script takes care of everything, including:

- Declaring a local variable of type WORD to hold the media window's window handle.
- Getting the filename from the field.
- Using the filename in a `callMCI()` function which opens the file, if valid, and assigns an alias and parent window to it.
- Using `callMCI()` again to issue a `status` command with the appropriate parameter to obtain a window handle.
- Using `callMCI()` once more to issue a `where` command with the appropriate parameter to obtain the original size of the media element. This value is returned as a space-delimited list of four numbers. The first pair of numbers

represents the position of the media window's upper left corner; the second pair represents the position of the lower right corner of the window. All values are in pixels.

- Linking the Windows `USER` module to gain access to the function `MoveWindow()`.
- Passing the window handle of the media window and the window's size (the four numbers obtained in step six and contained in `It`) to `MoveWindow()`. Note that since the window position values are separated by spaces, use of "word" rather than "item" is the easiest way to access members of the list. Recall that an integer can be a text entity in OpenScript. One pixel is subtracted from each of the horizontal and vertical dimensions of the window, to make the window slightly smaller than the media element played in it.
- Playing the video file with an instruction to notify self (the button) when the element has finished playing.
- Performing cleanup in an `MCINotify` handler. The media file is closed and the Windows `USER` module unlinked at this time.

Actually, using MCI calls rather than API calls reduces the impact of rule "optimal performance rule" three, but the demo book illustrates that at least you shouldn't size a digital video window slightly smaller than its natural size. You will, of course, do what you must to get the visual effect you desire, but be sure to take performance degradation into account. If possible, digitize your pictures at the correct size for your application to begin with.

Notification

The optional second argument to a `callMCI()` function specifies the object to be notified when the function has completed its task. If you want notification, do the following:

1. Enter an object reference for which you want to receive the notification.
2. Write a handler for the `MCINotify` message in the script of the notified object or higher.

In addition to the standard multimedia notification, there is, for some devices, a command called `signal`. Paired with `signal` is a notification message, `MCISignal`, whose sole purpose is to respond to messages sent by `signal`. These messages and responses are explained in this section.

MCINotify. In order to receive a notification that an MCI command has reached some point in its processing, usually the end, you may add a second parameter to many `callMCI()` functions. The second argument is the identifier of the ToolBook object which is to receive OpenScript's `MCINotify` message. (Keywords such as `self` are allowed in this argument.) The parameters automatically sent along with the `MCINotify` message are the same as those passed with `mmNotify`: the result of the function; the command that started the process; and the device for which the MCI executed the command. The "play..." command in the script of the Play button on pages two and four of CH22.TBK use an MCINotify handler in the script of each button which plays a video file.

The imageNotify message provides notification of the return of a call to an imageCommand() function.

***signal* and *MCISignal*.** The signal command is used when notification is required once or many times as an MCI process runs. Its usage follows normal callMCI() syntax:

```
get callMCI("signal mm at 2000 uservalue 1,this page")
```

This is an example of a signal command which instructs the device instance represented by the alias mm to return the value 1 when the media position reaches 2000 milliseconds. (Times are entered and returned in the current time format.) The report is made to the page object because of the second argument's value, this page. Perhaps a more common usage is to tell signal to return a value repetitively, and perhaps to return the position of the media rather than a single user-defined value. Follow this model to have signal send its position repetitively every 5 seconds:

```
get callMCI("signal mm every 5000 return position,self")
```

The parameter every specifies this function as one which repeatedly reports a position or value to the object, in this case, in whose script the command string resides (self). As with other callMCI() functions, the second argument to the function is the ToolBook object to which the signal command returns user values or positions.

What kind of handler is necessary to intercept these value or position reports? There is a special OpenScript message, MCISignal, which is sent along with appropriate parameters to the ToolBook object specified in the signal command function's second argument. You may use a user value or position to trigger some other event, such as a page turn. Another common use of the MCISignal handler is to display media position or move the thumb of a progress indicator. To report media position in a field, you may use an idle handler to ask for the position at intervals. You may choose instead to use a signal command and an MCISignal handler instead. For example, to respond to the position reported every 5000 milliseconds by the preceding script line, you could use the following handler, entered into the script of the same object from which the signal command originated:

```
TO HANDLEMCISignal theStatus, theDevice, theValue
    textoffield "elapsedTime" = theValue
END MCISignal
```

Note

The parameters to the MCISignal message do not arrive in the same order as those for an MCINotify message. MCISignal brings three paramters with it—status, device; and uservalue (or position). MCINotify also bears three parameters, but they are in the order status, operation, device.

Also, recall that the names you give function parameters are relatively unimportant, but the order of the parameters is. In the simple MCISignal handler just described, the third parameter (theValue) is the only one used; but each of the other two parameters have to be given some name to hold the first and second places.

The *imageCommand()* Functions

OpenScript supplies a number of MCI-like functions for dealing with bitmapped graphics. The syntax for these commands is analogous to MCI's animation or digital video commands. Be aware that these commands, listed in Table 22.5, are not part of the MCI set. They are peculiar to Multimedia ToolBook.

Tip

Certain video drivers fail when media is in a format other than uncompressed bitmap. Use uncompressed BMP files whenever possible.

Table 22.5 *imageCommand()* Calls Compared to MCI Calls

callMCI() **Function**	imageCommand() **Function**
get callMCI ("capability <device or alias>",<object to notify upon completion>)	get callMCI ("capability <device or alias>",<object to notify upon completion>)
get callMCI ("close <device or alias>")	get callMCI ("close <device or alias>")
get callMCI ("info <device or alias><parameters>")	get callMCI ("info <device or alias><parameters>")
get callMCI ("open <device or alias><window type><parent window>", <object to notify upon completion>)"	get callMCI ("open <device or alias><window type><parent window>", <object to notify upon completion>)
get callMCI ("play <device or alias> (from (position) to (position)",<object to notify upon completion>)	get callMCI ("play <device or alias><effect>",<object to notify upon completion>)
get callMCI (""status <device or alias><parameters>"",<object to notify upon completion>)	get callMCI ("status <device or alias><parameters>",<object to notify upon completion>)

callMCI() **Function**	imageCommand() **Function**
get callMCI ("where <device or alias><parameters>",<object to notify uponcompletion>)	get callMCI ("where <device or alias><parameters>",<object to notify upon completion>)
get callMCI ("window <device or alias><parameters>",<object to notify upon completion>)	get callMCI ("window <device or alias><parameters>",<object to notify upon completion>)

These functions have identical syntax to MCI animation commands in almost every respect, except that a transition effect may be specified in the `imageCommand("play...")` string. Of course, another difference in the `play` command is the bitmap's lack of a timeline, so that `"from"` and `"to"` have no meaning.

Mixing Clips and Low-Level Calls

Listing 22.5, implemented in three variants on pages five, six, and seven of CH22.TBK, demonstrates a program that allows Photoshop-style scrolling of a very large bitmap in a clipping window. The script is a revision and refinement of the script presented as Listing 16.11 in the section, "`translateWindowMessage`" of Chapter 16, "Statements, Functions, and Expressions". The large bitmap is now displayed in a stage, so it must be made into a clip, but the scrolling function is closely tied to the availability of window handles and the features of `imageCommand()`. Listing 22.5 is the script of page five of CH22.TBK. To see the slight variations in the scripts of pages six and seven, open the Script Editor and view or print the scripts for those pages. If you want to build page five of this book yourself, you need one page and a stage on the page. The stage's behavior should be set to Stretch Media to Stage. You'll also require a bitmap of greater width and height than that of the stage.

Tip

Use online Help for precise documentation of individual `imageCommand()` functions.

Enter Listing 22.5 into the script of the page.

Listing 22.5 22LST05.DOC The Script of Page 5 of CH22.TBK Uses Mixed Clips and Low-Level Functions

```
TO HANDLE EnterPage
    system LOGICAL scanning
    system INT xs,ys
--use the system property sysPageUnitsPerPixel for screen unit
--to pixel conversions. You can also use the various conversion
--functions. Assign x and y twips/pixel to system variables:
```

(continues)

Listing 22.5 Continued

```
    xs = item 1 of sysPageUnitsPerPixel
    ys = item 2 of sysPageUnitsPerPixel
--Initialize the "scanning" flag so that scrolling is off:
    scanning = FALSE
--Play a clip in the stage.
    mmPlay clip "stoats" in stage "scrl" of this page
--Forward the idle message so higher levels receive it:
    forward
END EnterPage

TO HANDLE leavePage
    if sysOpenMedia <> NULL
        mmClose all
    end if
    forward
END leavePage

TO HANDLE buttonDown
    system LOGICAL scanning
    system POINT location
    scanning = TRUE
    location = mousePosition of this window
    forward
END buttonDown

TO HANDLE buttonUp
    system LOGICAL scanning
--the idle handler will restore the appropriate
--cursor when idle messages resume.
    sysCursor = 4
    scanning = FALSE
END buttonUp

TO HANDLE buttonStillDown ploc,isShift,isCtrl,isRight
    system LOGICAL scanning
    system POINT location
    local POINT bmpOffset
    local POINT bmpSlop
    local POINT bmpLoc
    system INT xs,ys
--the idle handler will restore the appropriate
--cursor when idle messages resume.
--exit handler without processing if the cursor is an hourglass
--or if the control key, shift key, or right button is pressed:
    if (sysCursor = 4) or isShift or isCtrl or isRight
        break
    end if
--buttonStillDown is a repeating message, so prevent flicker and
--slowdown by setting the cursor only if needed.
--Use the four-pointed cursor:
    if sysCursor <> 7
        sysCursor = 7
    end if
    get mousePosition of this window
```

```
    item 1 of bmpOffset = (item 1 of It - item 1 of location)
    item 2 of bmpOffset = (item 2 of It - item 2 of location)
--mmVisualSize of a clip is a built-in clip property
-- representing the "actual" size of the source image.
-- The page unit conversion is done by getting the value of
-- sysPageUnitsPerPixel. The viewer unit conversion functions could
-- have been used instead. The items of sysPageUnitsPerPixel are
-- assigned to system variables in the enterPage handler:
    get (mmVisualSize of clip "stoats")
    item 1 of bmpSlop = (item 1 of It - 640) * xs
    item 2 of bmpSlop = (item 2 of It - 480) * ys
    bmpLoc = thePos("stoats")
    conditions
        when (item 1 of bmpLoc + item 1 of bmpOffset ) <= 0 \
             and (item 2 of bmpLoc + item 2 of bmpOffset) <= 0 \
             and (item 1 of bmpLoc + item 1 of bmpOffset) \
             > -item 1 of bmpSlop \
             and (item 2 of bmpLoc + item 2 of bmpOffset) \
             > -item 2 of bmpSlop
--exit the conditions structure only
            break conditions
        else
--exit the entire handler
            break buttonStllDown
    end conditions
    increment item 1 of bmpLoc by item 1 of bmpOffset
    increment item 2 of bmpLoc by item 2 of bmpOffset
--Update the location of the cursor:
    location = mousePosition of this window
--Update the position of the bitmap:
    send newPos bmpLoc, "stoats"
--Clear temporary stores and let Windows take over for a bit
--to attend to other needs, as the repeating messages can
--clog it up:
    mmYield
END buttonStillDown

--This is a custom function which uses imageCommand()
--to get the position of the bitmap in page units.
--The clip name is passed to it.

TO GET thePos @clip
    system INT xs,ys
    local POINT temp
    get imageCommand("status" \
            && mmDeviceAlias of clip @clip \
            && "position wait")
    item 1 of temp = item 1 of It * xs
    item 2 of temp = item 2 of It * ys
    return temp
END

--This is a custom handler which uses imageCommand()
--to set the position of the bitmap.
--The position and clip name are passed to this handler.
```

(continues)

Listing 22.5 Continued

```
TO HANDLE newPos q, @clip
    system INT xs,ys
--The argument to this function is one string, but it's made up
--of literals,variables,and a property.. Don't forget to
-- separate items of a list with a literal "," (comma).
    get imageCommand("window" \
           && mmDeviceAlias of clip @clip \
           && "position" && (item 1 of q)/xs \
           & "," & (item 2 of q)/ys && "wait")
END newPos

TO HANDLE idle
system LOGICAL scanning
--Restore cursor if and only if it
--isn't already the current cursor (to prevent flicker):
        if sysCursor <> 44
            sysCursor = 44
        end if
--Forward the idle message so higher levels receive it:
    forward
END idle
```

In use, a left-button press-and-hold on the picture changes the mouse pointer to a four-pointed arrow and allows the picture to be pushed around using the main window as a clipping rectangle. Left-button release stops the pusharound and restores the mouse pointer.

The bitmap is a clip, and you may need to check the media path to the file, `STOATS8.BMP`. This is a 256-color picture. It is displayed on a stage.

Stages are movable objects. Why isn't the stage simply moved without all of these calls to `imageCommand()`? You may try it and see; change the `TO GET` handler to the following

```
TO GET thePos @clip
    return position of stage "scrl" of page "Stage Page"
END
```

Change the `newPos` handler to the following

```
TO HANDLE newPos q, @clip
    position of stage "scrl" of page "Stage Page" = q
END newPos
```

The result is available on page six of `CH22.TBK`. The position of the stage does not update until the calling handler is finished, and as long as the button is down, the handler is not going to finish. So the screen doesn't update until the mouse button is released. If this is the effect you want, there's no problem with the script.

In the `buttonDown` handler, variables are initialized. The action is mostly in the `buttonStillDown` handler. The current position of the mouse pointer is calculated;

the difference between that and the original mouse pointer position (obtained from buttonDown or from the update that occurs each time buttonStillDown is run) is computed. The difference is then added to the current position of the bitmap with respect to 0,0 of the main window (in this case, page five shows a viewer used as the clipping window) and the result checked against the horizontal and vertical limits of the bitmap. If the picture can move in the desired direction, it does so; otherwise, the conditions structure terminates handler execution.

The getPos() custom function and the newPos message handler do the actual work. getPos() uses the imageCommand query for window position and returns that value converted into ToolBook page units. The newPos handler takes a new position in pixels and sets the position of the image in the clipping window.

Then the whole loop starts over again as soon as the next buttonStillDown message arrives.

The buttonUp handler sets the scanning variable to False to stop the scrolling and sets the mouse pointer to the hourglass in preparation for the next event. When idle messages resume, the first one sets the mouse pointer back to normal, which in this case is the pointing finger.

Notice that a clip on a stage is being manipulated through low-level calls whose parameters can be ToolBook built-in properties (such as mmDeviceAlias of the clip) to achieve a result that would be difficult through other means.

What is the reason for the stage's presence in the first place? Everything necessary to do the pusharound scrolling example is available through imageCommand() calls. One reason for the stage's presence is to scale the bitmap when logical units per pixel change (for instance, to the popular 12 twips/pixel of 800×600 screen resolution using so-called large fonts).

It may well be argued that stretching a bitmap simply should not be allowed, or that two bitmaps should be provided: one for use at 15 twips/pixel and another for use at 12 twips/pixel. Aside from the question of available space for bitmaps, though, this solution begs the question of what to do when one of the newer, continuously variable resolution drivers are in use on the target machine.

Note

The classic method of stretching a single bitmap *is* to make it the normal graphic of a button (sometimes a huge one). This is in fact how the backdrops are represented. A button won't do in this example because its graphic has no window handle.

Another, more important use of the stage is to receive the mouse click messages. If a ToolBook object were not there to receive the messages, a translateWindowMessage structure becomes necessary. The stage object can receive button messages "through" the picture. (Remember, the picture itself is not a ToolBook object.)

The nested `if` structures in the `idle` loop are not a result of poor optimization. In an `idle` or `buttonStillDown` handler, it's important to check each possible combination of property states separately, as the idea is to prevent screen flicker and severely degraded performance caused by repeated redraws.

A variant of this script is the script of page six of `CH22.TBK`. The alternate script places the scrollable picture in a viewer, where is may be pushed around independently of the main window.

Page seven of `CH22.TBK` shows another variation on the picture-scrolling theme. This time, an attempt is made to move the stage object itself through pure OpenScript messages in the hope of using a simpler script. The attempt fails. The position of the stage doesn't update until the mouse button is released, so the picture doesn't move with the mouse movement (though you may want such a discontinuous visual effect for some purposes). To have full control over the image, you must go to the low-level calls of `callMCI() and imageCommand()`.

From Here...

You have conned, and hopefully digested, a concentrated dose of multimedia manipulation in this chapter. After an introduction to a portion of the flexible and changeable MCI command set, you worked with three compound devices: wave audio, digital video, and bitmaps. You have been introduced to the concept of assigning windows to media in different ways, one of which involves a call directly to the Windows API. Finally, you've worked with mixed clips and low-level media handling calls. If you have a video overlay board, MCI-controllable CD or videodisc player, or the like, you should try controlling the device.

- For further information about media and clips, see Chapter 21, "Using Multimedia Elements."
- For further information about messages, see Chapter 13, "OpenScript Fundamentals."
- For more information about functions and arguments, control structure, and `translateWindowMessage`, see Chapter 16, "Statements, Functions, and Expressions."

CHAPTER 23

Digital Video Producer (DVP)

One of Multimedia ToolBook's greatest strengths is its capability to import multimedia files, such as digital video and sound. Have you ever wondered how these files are created? This chapter helps answer this question by introducing Digital Video Producer (DVP).

Digital video is a great multimedia tool to use in your work. You can have someone on-screen explaining something as only a human can. You can shoot a video of that widget to show it from all angles. Try doing that with still photos, let alone text.

Digital video can add excitement to your presentations, life to your sales, and spirit to everything. These videos don't create themselves, however. You need some way to get the pieces of video from the VCR, laserdisc, and animation software into a coherent form; mix in some sound; and then put the finished product into your application. This chapter shows you the tools that DVP provides for this purpose.

This chapter covers the following topics:

- The basics of the DVP interface
- Mixing two or more videos
- Adding sound
- Titling and special effects
- Capturing video from a VCR

Note

Throughout this chapter, you'll find sections with the word *Example* in the heading. These sections take you through a real-world example of using DVP to create your own video by using the tools and techniques described in this chapter.

What Is DVP?

Digital Video Producer (DVP) is a stand-alone piece of software that ships with Multimedia ToolBook. DVP allows you to create, edit, capture, and convert multimedia files. The files that you work with and create in DVP can be used on their own or within another application, such as Multimedia ToolBook.

Video-Editing Tool

Editing digital video is the heart of DVP and where you can be really creative. You take the raw video and sound—a home movie of your Aunt Martha, the sound of the car next door revving like mad, or the animation that you created frame by frame—and put everything together with great intros, wipes, dissolves, and other effects.

Media-Conversion Tool

Media conversion is a rather small portion of DVP, but it is extremely useful. DVP comes with import and export filters for all major video and graphic formats. You can take a series of bitmaps and output them as an AVI file. Then you take that AVI file and convert it to an FLI file. Going even further, you can mix GIF, BMP, TIFF, AVI, FLC, and WAV files to create a single video. When you need to convert multimedia files from one form to another, you can do it with DVP.

Video-Capture Tool

One necessary step in creating a video is acquiring your images. You can get images from several places. You can use files that you find on CD-ROMs or other sources. You also can acquire images from some video source, such as a VCR, television set, laserdisc, or camcorder. With a camcorder, you can go out into the world, shoot up a storm, bring the tape back, stick it into your VCR, and capture the video to a digital file.

Digital Video Producer has a separate program, called DVP Capture, that captures video for you if you have a capture board that is compatible with Windows. This program eliminates the extra step of capturing the video with another application and then bringing it into DVP. It also simplifies your life because you won't have to learn another piece of software. As a matter of fact, some capture-board manufacturers have licensed DVP to ship with their products.

Installing DVP

Digital Video Producer is not installed by default when you install ToolBook. Installation is very simple. Follow these steps:

1. Insert the CD-ROM into your CD-ROM drive.
2. From Program Manager, choose File, Run.

3. Type **x:\dvp\disk1\setup**, where *x* is the letter of your CD-ROM drive.
4. Choose OK.
5. Follow the prompts in the installation program.
6. Restart Windows when prompted.

After DVP is installed, double-click the DVP icon in Program Manager to get it working.

The Video Preproduction Process

Any project—writing a book, making home improvements, or producing digital video—requires a great deal of work before you ever get around to writing, hammering nails, or building the video. This work is called planning, and it is the biggest time-saving tool in the digital-video process. Many people say that they don't have time to plan—that they need to have the project done next week. This type of production, however, is fraught with danger. Pieces that are vital to the project may be missing, or the project may have to be redone from scratch because something was not fully considered.

The real estate profession has a saying that three things make a property valuable: location, location, and location. Something similar can be said about making a video: success calls for planning, planning, and planning.

Storyboard and Script Basics

Storyboarding is the start of the decision-making process in your video production; it's putting your brainstorm on paper. Draw rough pictures of what each piece of the video will look like, and pretend you are actually producing the video. How long do you want each video segment to be? What type of transition do you want? What sort of sounds do you want?

Great drawing ability certainly is not a prerequisite; stick figures are sufficient. The object is not to make a beautiful drawing but to clarify your ideas and to be able to show someone else your dream.

Figure 23.1 shows the storyboard for the project described in this chapter. The storyboard indicates what video will be shown, what transitions will take place, and any notes that will be needed.

Another decision that you will have to make is whether a script is necessary. A script is nothing more than what is going to be said in your video. If you'll be using actors and shooting your own video, a script could be important. If you aren't shooting any of your own video and just using video from other sources, a script may not be necessary. There is nothing magical about a script, but it can make your life a great deal easier.

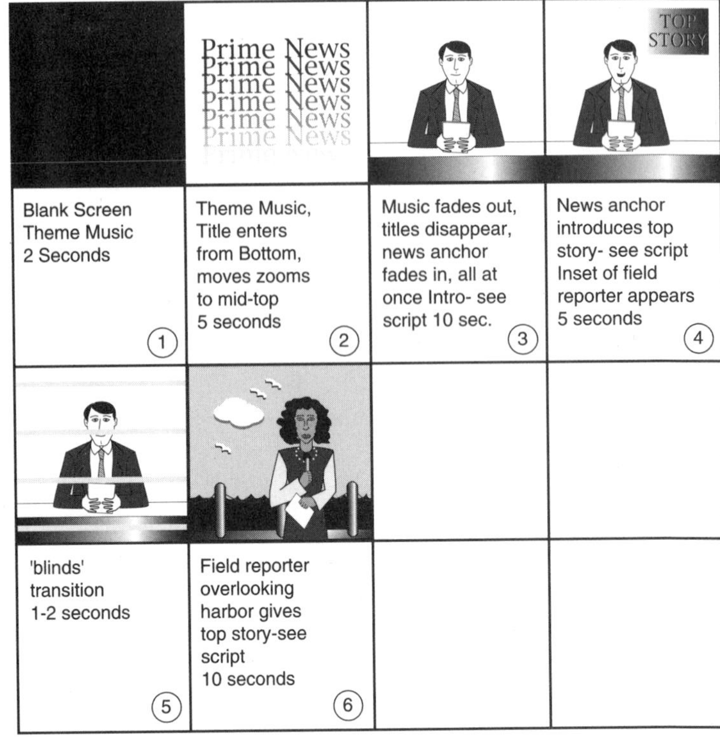

Fig. 23.1

This example of simple storyboards can be used to ease your video production.

Listing 23.1 shows the script I used when I created the example video for the project in this chapter. You'll notice, when you play the video, that the script doesn't exactly match what was said in the video. The idea of a script is not to lay down the law, but to make sure that everything that needs to be said is said and that everything goes along smoothly. How strictly you stick to your script is a decision you'll have to make depending on your own personal circumstances.

Listing 23.1 Storyboard Example

```
Storyboard 3
    News Anchor: Good evening, and welcome to the six o'clock edition
    of Prime Time News. I am Myra Petersen.

Storyboard 4:
    News Anchor: Our man in the field Michael Labelle is standing by
    to bring you our top story tonight, the busy day at the inner harbour.
    Michael...

Storyboard 6:
    Man in the Field: Thank you Myra. Yes, as you can see, it has been
    a busy day here at the Victoria Inner Harbour where everyone is
    getting ready for the Victoria Day parade tomorrow. Everyone is
    predicting sun. This has been Michael Labelle reporting for Prime
    Time News.
```

A script and storyboards are strongly interconnected. You can reference the storyboard in the script, and vice versa. When the storyboards and script are finished, the next step is to collect the source material that you will use to make them come to life on-screen.

Media Collection

Media collection can involve many things, but it essentially means finding all the bits and pieces of videotape, animation files, and sounds that you will need. Use your storyboards to determine what you need. The third storyboard in figure 23.1 shows a person sitting at a desk, looking into the camera, and introducing the news and the first story. This shot will take approximately ten seconds.

> **Note**
>
> Media collection doesn't mean that you have to shoot your own video. It can mean getting clips from CDs or from the Internet. Or it can mean creating your own animation in an animation program. One thing to be careful of when you're collecting media for use in your project is to make sure that you have the proper rights to use the media. A lot of photos and videos out in the world can be used only if the copyright holder gets paid. There are many different types of licensing, so it requires diligence on your part.

The Interface Basics

This section introduces DVP's interface. Figure 23.2 shows the main interface of Digital Video Producer, and figure 23.3 is a close-up of the toolbar.

Fig. 23.2

An example of the major elements of the DVP main window.

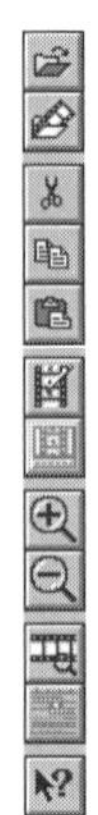

Fig. 23.3

You can use the DVP toolbar to accomplish a number of tasks.

Importing Media into the Media Window

The Media window holds all the diverse *clips* that you collected earlier until you are ready to use them. A clip, in this context, is simply another name for *multimedia file*. It could be a sound, a video, or a bitmap. The Media window is shown in figure 23.2 with a number of clips already imported. To import a clip into the Media window, choose File, Import Media. By default, all the file types that DVP is able to import are displayed in the Import dialog box.

Once the file has been imported, it will show up in the Media window ready to be used. Each type of clip is easy to distinguish. A video file looks like a series of pictures, side by side, showing the first few frames of the video, while a sound file looks like a soundwave. In addition, depending on the type of clip, some details will appear beside it, including the length of the clip, the height and width of a video, and the name of the clip with any comments that are embedded in it.

If these statistics are not sufficient, double-click any of the clips to bring up a window showing much more information. You can also select the video in the Media window and choose File, Media Statistics to do the same thing. The Media Statistics dialog box appears (see fig. 23.4). If the sound or video portion of this dialog box is shaded, then the selected media type either does not support or does not contain the shaded item.

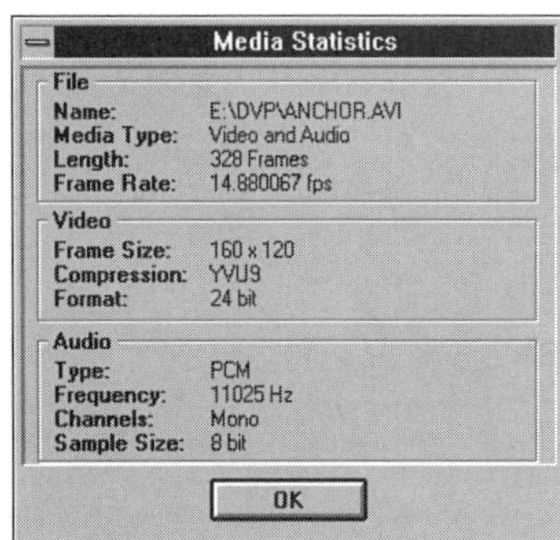

Fig. 23.4

The Media Statistics dialog box shows many details about the clips in your media tray.

Example: Importing

During the rest of this chapter, you will come across sections like this one that have the word *Example* in the heading. These sections describe the steps needed to create the video outlined in the storyboards and script in figure 23.1 and Listing 23.1. All of the clips that you will be using are available on the CD. If you want to follow along with the exercises in this chapter, import all the media clips in the `/CH23` directory on the CD except `FINISH.AVI`.

Tip

You can easily import a number of clips at the same time by selecting several items in the Open dialog box. Use the Shift key to select a range of items and the Ctrl key to select individual items, then click the OK button.

Placing Media on the Timeline

You can't do much with the clips in the Media window. To do anything fun with them, you have to move them to the timeline. There are several ways to do this, and all require you to drag the clip from the Media window or Player and drop it on the timeline. The quickest and simplest method is to drag and drop it on the *tick bar*. You will notice that when you do this, the entire timeline is shaded. This means that the media will be placed on the timeline automatically.

If the clip you are dragging is an AVI, the video portion will be placed on the Video A track and the sound portion will be placed on the Audio A track. You can also drag the clip directly to any appropriate track: video, audio, or overlay. DVP will prevent you from putting a clip in the wrong place, such as a sound file on a video track.

Using the Player

One of the most important tools in DVP is the Media Player. DVP provides two of them, so you can work with two clips at the same time. The Player is very similar to a VCR in that it allows you to play, fast forward, rewind, or pause clips. In addition, you can move a clip frame by frame and mark the start and stop points. The controls of the Media Player are shown in figure 23.5.

Fig. 23.5

The Media Player is used extensively during a project to preview and cut video clips.

Loading the Media Player is easy: you drag a clip from the Media window or the timeline and drop it on the Media Player.

Using the Media Player as a tool to view clips is useful in itself, but it has another function. You can use the Player to select a portion of a clip, called a *clip section,* and then place that section onto the timeline. You mark the beginning of the clip section by using the Player controls to move to the frame that you want, and then click the Mark In button. The display beside the Mark In button changes to reflect the current frame. Also, the yellow bar in the clip indicator moves to reflect the new starting point. Marking the end of the clip section uses the same process except you click the Mark Out button.

Once the Mark In and Out points of the clip have been set, drag the clip from the Preview window to the timeline and position it where you like. You'll notice, once the clip is on the timeline, that only the section you marked by using the Mark In and Mark Out buttons has been placed on the timeline.

Example: Player and Timeline

Let's try and add some video to the project. Use the Player to cut out a section of a clip and place that clip section on the timeline. Follow these steps:

1. Drag the video `anchor.avi` from the Media window to either Player.
2. Use the Next Frame button to move to frame 10.
3. Click the Mark In button to set frame 10 as the Mark In point.
4. Now move to frame 317 with a combination of the Jump Forward, Play, and Next Frame buttons.
5. Set the Mark Out point by clicking the Mark Out button.
6. Drag the clip section from the Player, and drop it on the tick bar at frame 75.

If you miss, you can drag the clip around in the timeline to place it where you want, but be sure to move the audio track as well so the audio will be synchronized with the video.

Tip

If you are having difficulty aligning two clips on the timeline, click once on the tick bar where you want the alignment point to be. You will notice a bar that crosses all the tracks on the timeline. Use this as a visual reference for alignment.

Filters and Transitions

This section deals with two of the tools that you will use to create your own video: *filters* and *transitions*. Filters and transitions are similar in appearance but have very different uses.

Applying a Filter

A *filter* is a tool that makes modifications to either an entire video or selected portions. These changes can be as simple as fading the screen to black or as complex as making the video appear to be reflected in rippling water. DVP comes with a selection of filters that can be applied separately or in combination to create some really nice or really awful effects, depending on what you want.

One of the ways that I often use filters is for adjusting the color balance, brightness, and contrast of videos. The first video capture board I used was of rather poor quality, and all the videos it captured had a very strong green color. One project I worked on involved a man named Phil, and he came to be known as "chloroPhil" in the captured clips because of the green shade of his skin.

To apply a filter, follow these steps:

1. Select the area where the filter will be applied.
2. Choose the filter, or filters, to use.
3. Adjust the options for the filters.

To select an entire clip on the timeline, all you need to do is click it. You will see that the selection border (a black and white barber pole affair) surrounds the entire clip. To select a smaller area of a single clip, or to select more that one clip, requires a slightly more complex process. You hold the Ctrl key down and drag from the start of the area you want selected to the end. To make this selection process easier, you can use the Zoom Out button on the toolbar to see more of the timeline at once; or you can hold the Ctrl key down, click the beginning of the selection, move to the end using the scroll bar, and then hold the Ctrl and Shift keys down and click the end of the selection.

Example: Filters

You will probably note that `anchor.avi` is rather green. I used my old video capture card to capture this clip because I needed an example of how to correct the color balance using a filter. Click the green clip to select it and then choose Effects, Filters. The Filters dialog box appears (see fig. 23.6). Select the Color Balance filter and click Add; then select the Brightness and Contrast filter and click Add again.

> **Note**
>
> Unfortunately, the only way to find out the name of a filter and what it does—aside from the not-so-descriptive icon—is to select it and see its description. Depending on your hardware, there might be a short delay in switching descriptions after you select a filter, so be patient.

Click the Options button to expand the Filters dialog box, and use the controls presented to adjust the video to be less green. Click either of the filters at the right of the dialog box in the Selected list box to change from the Color Balance filter controls to the Brightness and Contrast controls. Use the preview control as a guide to the changes you are making. You can use the scroll bar under the Preview control to move to different parts of the selection and see what the changes will look like.

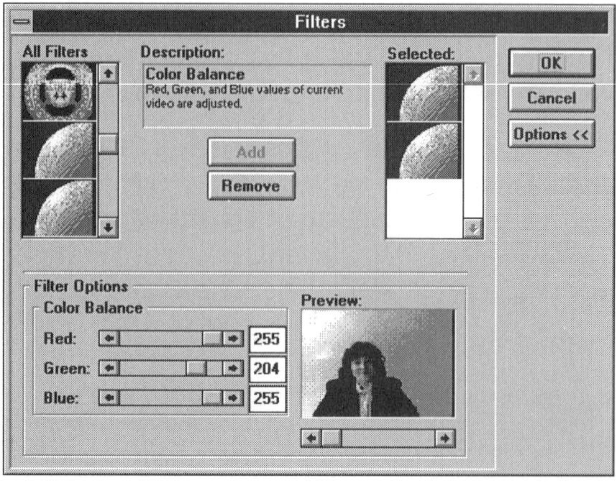

Fig. 23.6

Use the Filters dialog box to set the options for different filters, such as the Color Balance filter.

> **Caution**
>
> The preview control in the Filters dialog box shows only a close approximation of what your final video will look like. The compression options, the size of the video, and whether you use 8-bit color all have an impact on the final outcome. Building a large video can take a long time; sometimes it can be hours before you have your final product. If you are doing a large video build, it might be prudent to try out the filters on a small representative sample of your video before going ahead with the final build.

Once you are done adjusting the filters, click OK to close the Filters dialog box. You should see a thin blue or green line appear at the top of the video clip on the timeline. This gives you a visual reference for the location of the filters on the timeline.

One more filter needs to be added to this clip. Select frames one through 30 of the clip on the timeline, and open the Filter dialog box again. Select the Fade to Black filter and click the Options button. Make sure that the In From Black option is chosen, and click OK.

Adding the Second Video

Up to now, you have only been working with a single video clip on the timeline. Now it is time to add another clip and set the transition between the two. There are six places on the timeline for a second video clip, and each produces a different effect. You can drag it to the tick bar or one of the video tracks. You can place it so that it overlaps with the first video or is in a clear area of the timeline. The placement of video and sound, whether there's a transition, and whether the original video is overwritten or moved, depends on where the video is dropped. Table 23.1 shows the relationship among these different factors.

Table 23.1 The Effect of Dragging a Second Video to Various Places on the Timeline

Destination	Overlap	Video	Audio	Transition	Overwrite/ Move
Tick bar	Yes	First available	First available	Yes	No
Tick bar	No	First available	First available	No	No
Video track	Yes	Same as destination	No	No	Yes
Video track	No	Same as destination	No	No	No
Audio track	Yes	No	Same as destination	No	Yes
Audio Track	No	No	Same as destination	No	No

- *Destination* is the place on the timeline where you will drag the video.
- *Overlap* is whether the position to which you are dragging the video overlaps the placement of another video already on the timeline.
- *Video* describes where the video portion will be placed on the timeline. It will be placed in the first available video track, in the same track as the destination track, or no video will be placed on the timeline.
- *Audio* describes where the audio portion of the video will be placed in the two audio tracks. It will be placed in the first available audio track, in the same audio track as the destination, or no audio will be placed on the timeline.
- *Transition* describes whether a video will be placed on the timeline as a result of your placement of the video.
- *Overwrite/Move* details whether an existing video on the timeline will be moved or overwritten as a result of your placement of a clip. Whether the video will be overwritten or moved can be determined by choosing Tools, Options. If Delete/ Insert is selected, your existing clip will be moved to the right. If Erase/Overwrite is selected, your existing clip will be deleted.

Example: Second Video

Drag `maninfld.avi` onto the Media Player, and set frame 142 as the Mark In point and the end of the clip as the Mark Out point. Drag the clip from the Player onto the tick bar so that the beginning of the clip starts at frame 368. Notice that the clip has been placed in the Video B track, the sound for the clip shows up in Audio B track, and a transition shows up in the transition track.

If you take another look at Table 23.1, you can see that this makes sense. You dragged the clip to the tick bar so that you find the tick bar in the first column. There was an overlap between the clip and a clip that was already on the timeline, so find the line that says yes in the second column. Then read the rest of the columns. The video was placed in the first available video track—in this case, the Video B track. The audio, as well, was placed in the first available audio track. A transition was placed on the timeline, just as the table predicted. Finally, the table predicted that the existing video wouldn't get moved or overwritten, and that is the case here.

Working with a Transition

Any time that there is overlap between Video A and Video B, a transition shows up in the transition track. You see transitions all the time on TV or in the movies: one scene will fade into another, or the screen will appear to wipe from one side to another to change the scene. DVP comes loaded with a number of different transitions, from a simple wipe, to a dissolve, to the effect of a set of blinds closing.

Transitions on the timeline cannot be dragged around as other items can. Their size and position is controlled solely by the amount and position of overlap between the two video tracks. To change a transition, double-click the transition or select the transition and choose Effects, Transition. The Transitions dialog box opens (see fig. 23.7).

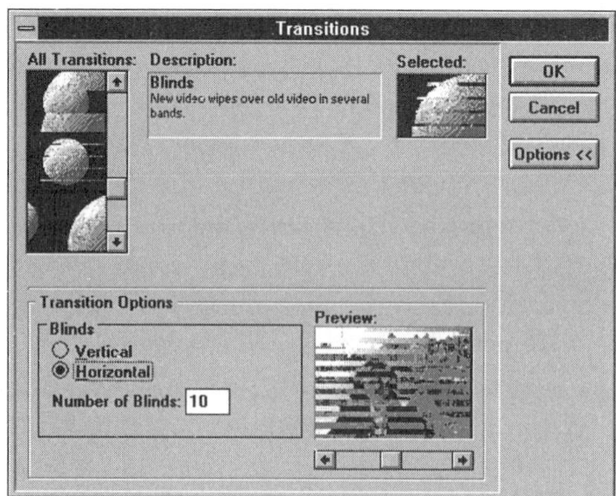

Fig. 23.7

The Transitions dialog box controls the type of transition used as well as the different option.

The operation of the Transitions dialog box is very similar to the Filters dialog box, except that only one transition can be used at a time. Select a transition from the choices on the left, and then you can set any options that are available for that transition by selecting the Options button.

Example: Transition

Double-click the transition in the transition track to open the Transitions dialog box. Select the Blinds transition and click the Options button. Change the Number of

Blinds from five to ten and click OK. The text in the transition on the timeline will change from Wipe to Blinds.

Working with Sound

Until now, I have dealt with sound as a secondary item. Now it's time to take a closer look at sound, an essential element of a successful video. Sound is a powerful stimulus in this world (just look how talkies overtook silent movies many years ago). You can use this stimulus to make your videos more persuasive and enjoyable.

Using the Media Player for Sound

DVP can deal with sound in two formats—as the audio portion of an AVI file or in the WAV format. Sound is handled just the same as video in DVP. It can be imported into the Media window, played in the Media Player, dragged onto the timeline, and moved around in the timeline. Also, the start and end points of the sound can be marked in the Player and dragged onto the timeline. When dealing with sound in the Media Player, DVP considers all WAV files as if they were at 30 frames per second while the audio portion of an AVI file is treated at the same frame rate as the AVI.

Normally a sound clip is time-dependent. This means that a ten second sound clip will always take ten seconds to play. Giving the sound a frame rate allows you to work with it like frame-based video and frees you from having to convert between time and frames. Trying to figure out how many frames it would take to play a 1.23-second sound clip or how long it would take to play 11 frames at 18 frames per second is easy enough with a calculator, but rather tedious. When the sound clip is on the timeline, any size portion of the sound can be selected and manipulated. There is no false frame rate attached to the clip.

Example: Sound in the Player

`theme.wav` is the theme music for the project. Using the Player, set the Mark In point as frame zero and the Mark Out point as frame 180. Drag the clip from the Player to the first frame of the Audio B track.

Working with Sound on the Timeline

Placing sound on the timeline is no different than placing video. The only significant difference between the two is that when two audio clips overlap, there is no transition track between them. There are, however, a couple of ways to make a transition between two audio tracks.

The first of these can be toggled on or off by choosing Video, Audio Cross Fade. This means that where any two audio tracks overlap, the first track will slowly lose volume until it is silent and the second track will start silently and slowly gain volume until it is at full volume. This creates the effect of a smooth change from one track to another. The limitation of automatic cross fading is that either all overlaps are cross-faded or none are.

The second way to create transitions is also a way to adjust the volume of either a part of a track or a whole track. This is accomplished by selecting some portion of an audio track and choosing Effects, Audio Level. The Audio Level dialog box appears (see fig. 23.8). This dialog box allows you to set the volume at the beginning and end of the selection. It will then adjust the volume along the length of that selection, creating a smooth fade. In addition to custom cross fades, this can be used to fade the volume out at the end of a video or to raise the volume of a clip that is too quiet.

Fig. 23.8

The Audio Level dialog box is used to create custom fades.

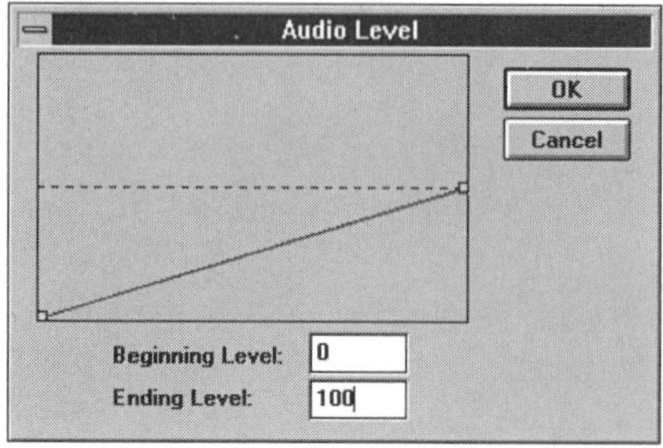

> **Note**
>
> The automatic Audio Cross Fade will override the manual audio level. If you have the Audio Cross Fade toggled on and have the audio level set to maximum for the clip, the clip will still fade out to nothing from maximum volume or in from nothing to maximum volume.

Example: Cross Fading

Your video will use a combination of the automatic cross fading and the manual audio levels. The automatic cross fades will be used to control the transition from theme music to News Anchor and from News Anchor to Man in the Field, so make sure that this is toggled on. Also, you will use the audio level to fade the theme music in, so the music doesn't start suddenly.

Select the equivalent of the first 15 frames of the theme music and open the Audio Level dialog box. Set the beginning level to zero and the ending level to 100, and click OK. To get an indication of the volume of a clip, you will need to show just the Audio track in the timeline by selecting the track and clicking the Show Current Track Only button on the toolbar or by choosing View, Display Current Track Only. A thin line runs below the sound wave and above the clip statistics, showing a visual representation of the volume.

Using Titles and Overlays

Titles and overlays are very powerful tools in DVP. The only limits to the effects that you can create with them are your own imagination and creativity. These tools create the effect of putting a visual item over the top of your main video. This can produce, for example, titles that scroll across your video or an animation of a devil that you superimpose sitting on your brother's shoulder.

Caution

DVP limits you to using either titles or video overlay; you can't use both. It will warn you when you try to put titles over the top of a video overlay, but will not warn you of the consequences when you drag a video sequence onto the timeline over the top of a title.

Adding Titles

Titles are a crucial feature of any video or film. They tell you the name of the work at the beginning, appear as subtitles in the middle to translate foreign languages, and scroll the credits at the end. There is a lot more that you can do with titles to jazz up a video. You could film a family gathering and use titles to put names with faces or create the effect of the guests actually eating their words.

Choose Effects, Titling to bring up the controls for adding titles to your video. Depending on whether or not you made a selection on the timeline, one of two things will happen. If you did not make a selection, a dialog box will open prompting you for the start frame and the number of frames you want the titles to appear on. Clicking OK at this point will bring up the Titling dialog box (see fig. 23.9). If you did make a selection, you will see the Titling dialog box immediately.

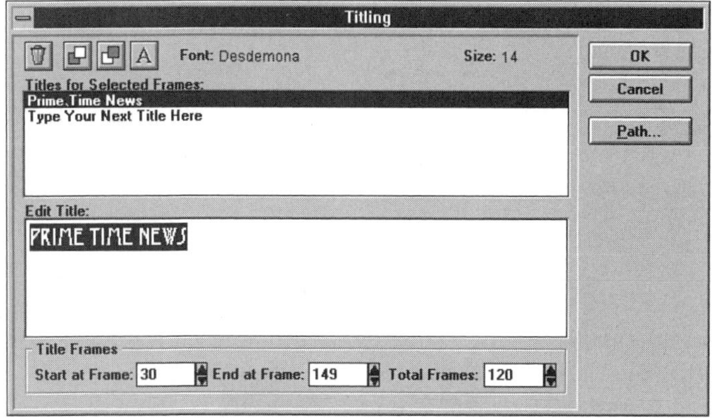

Fig. 23.9

The Titling dialog box gives you the controls needed to add titles to your video.

Type the text of the title in the Edit Title control. As you enter the titles, they appear in the Titles for Selected Frames control. There can be any number of titles at once, but each one must be a single line. If you have more than a single line of titling at a time, you will need to adjust the placement of each using the Path feature described later in this section; otherwise, all the titles will appear on top of one another, making them unreadable.

You use the Font Attribute button to set the font and font style of a title and the Foreground and Background color buttons to set the title's color. Black, by default, is the background color of all titles and will not appear in the video. Rather, it will appear invisible, allowing just the text to show.

Unlike other items, titling cannot be moved on the timeline by dragging it with the mouse. To move or edit a title, you must either select it and choose the Titling option under the Effects menu or double-click the clip to bring up the Titling dialog box.

Example: Adding Titles

The only title that you will be using in this project is the opening title, as shown in Storyboard 2 in Listing 23.1. Make sure that there is no selection in the timeline, and open the Titling dialog box. Set the first frame to 30 and the number of frames to 120, and click OK. The title that you want to use is *Prime Time News*. Type this into the Edit Text control and click OK. You will be coming back to this title to set the Path or animation of the title a little later in this section.

Adding Video Overlay

Video overlay is added to the timeline by dragging a clip from either the Media window or the Player to the overlay track. You can then select some, or all, of the clips and choose Effects, Overlay Options to bring up the Overlay dialog box (see fig. 23.10).

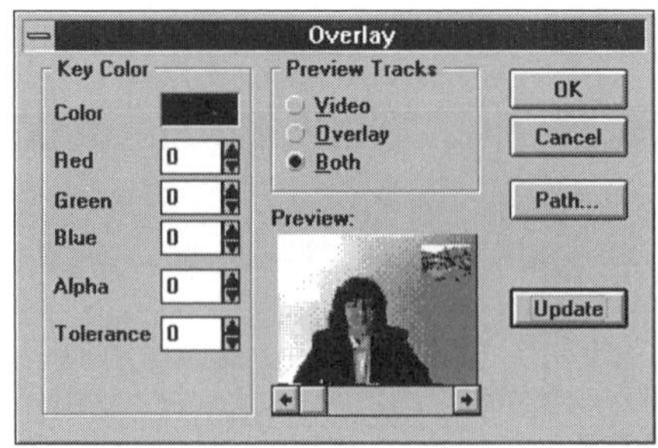

Fig. 23.10

The Overlay dialog box controls the different settings for the various overlays in your video.

The key portion of this dialog box controls two things—which color in the overlay clip will be invisible and how transparent the clip will be. Setting a single color to be invisible allows you to mask out portions of your overlay. For example, an animation that you created has a black background. You don't want that background to show up when you use that animation as an overlay. You only want the actual animation to appear, so you choose black to be the key color. You can choose the key color by setting the red, green, and blue components manually or you can click the appropriate color in the preview control.

Setting the Tolerance will use a range of colors as the key instead of just one. This is particularly effective with live video in which the background has slightly different shades or tints.

The Alpha setting controls how transparent the overlay is. This allows the main video to show through the overlay to create nice effects.

Example: Adding Overlay

The overlay that you will be using is a portion of `maninfld.avi`. The following steps will set up the overlay options for the overlay. Later, this chapter goes over and sets the Path options for this overlay. If you want to jump there now, go to the section titled "Example: Title and Overlay Paths." Otherwise, follow these steps:

1. Drag the file to the Player and set the Mark In point as five.
2. Set the Mark Out point as 157.
3. Drag the clip to frame 230 of the Overlay track.
4. Double-click the overlay to bring up the Overlay dialog box.

For this overlay, you don't want to mask out any color, so you won't be using a key color. You also don't want the background video to show through the overlay, so keep the Alpha setting at zero.

The Title and Overlay Path

With the path function of DVP, you can animate titles and overlays by moving, sizing, and rotating them. Bring up the Path dialog box by clicking the Path button in either the Titling dialog box or the Overlay dialog box described earlier. The example shown in figure 23.11 has already been expanded to show the additional controls by pressing the Options button.

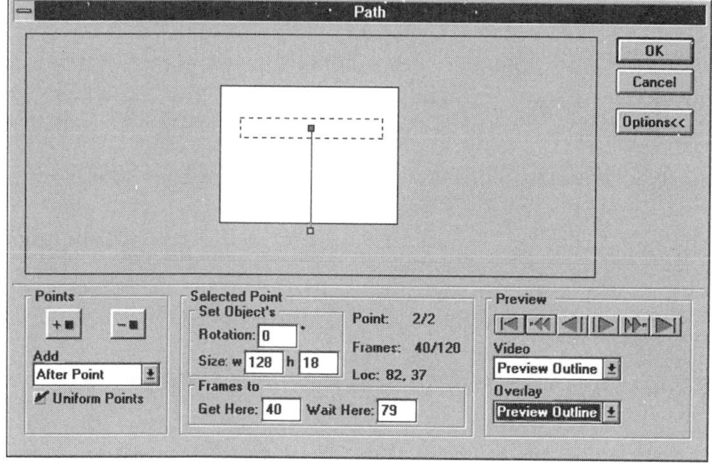

Fig. 23.11

The Path dialog box lets you animate titles and overlays.

When you first bring up the Path dialog box, there will be a dotted outline showing where the overlay or title will sit in the video and a red point in the center of that outline. By dragging the red point, you are able to move the outline around in the dialog box. By clicking in the dialog box, you will see another red point appear. Several other things will happen at the same time. The original point will turn green, the outline will move to be centered around the new point, and a line will connect the two points. This line shows the path that the title or overlay will move along in the video.

You can add as many points to the path as you want by clicking in the dialog box or clicking the Add Point button and then dragging the new point into position. New points created with the Add Point button will appear directly on top of the *active point*. The active point is indicated by the red point, and any green point can be made active by simply clicking it. Points can be added just before the active point, splitting the last line, or after the active point that extends the path. This behavior is controlled by the Add drop-down list box. Points can be deleted by making a point active and then pressing the Delete key or the Remove Point button.

The options in the Selected Point group can be set for each individual point. This gives you many alternatives for animating your title or overlay. The following list describes each of the elements:

- *Get Here* is the number of frames that the title or overlay will take to move to the selected point from the last point. The larger this number is, the slower the animation will be.
- *Wait Here* is the number of frames that the title or overlay will stay at the selected point without moving. Once this number of frames has passed, it will move on to the next frame.
- *Rotation* is how much the title or overlay will be rotated at the selected point. If the rotation set for the selected point is different than the rotation set for the previous point, DVP will interpolate the rotation over the number of frames set in Get Here to create a smooth rotation. This number is given in degrees—zero is upright and going clockwise until it reaches 360 degrees, which is again upright.
- *Size* is the size of the title or overlay in pixels at the selected point. If the size at this point is different than the previous, DVP will adjust the zoom smoothly over the number of frames set in Get Here.
- *Point* tells you what point number is the active point as well as the total number of points. This cannot be directly set.
- *Frames* tells you your current frame number as well as the total number of frames in the entire path. This cannot be directly set.
- *Loc* gives you the location of the active point. This cannot be directly set.
- The *Uniform Points* checkbox controls the number of frames that is set for Get Here when a point is created. If this is checked, Get Here will be equal for every point created. DVP will adjust the Get Here for all the points to make them even. This means that the overlay will take the same amount of time to move between each point, slowing down between short segments and speeding up between longer ones. If you turn this option off, you will have to manually set Get Here for every point.

Example: Title and Overlay Paths

Let's continue on with the creation of a video. In this example, you will try to set the paths for the title and overlay that were set up in the earlier sections "Example: Adding Titles" and "Example: Adding Overlay." Start out by creating a path for the titling that you worked on:

1. Double-click the titling in the Overlay track of the timeline to bring up the Titling dialog box; then click the Path button.
2. Drag the outline of the title down until it's outside of the white square. The white square shows you the area of the video. Anything outside of this area will be off-screen when the video is built.
3. Click in the center of the white screen to create another point, and drag it up slightly so that it's centered horizontally in the white area and about one quarter of the way down from the top.
4. Set the Get Here value of this new point to 40 and the Wait Here value to 79. This way, the title will come in from off-screen in about three seconds and then wait for a bit as the News Anchor fades in before disappearing.
5. Click the lower point to make it active, and set the Size to 1 by 1. This will make the title appear to grow from very small to full size as it moves up the screen.
6. Close this Path dialog box by clicking OK and then close the Titling dialog box.

Next, you need to set the path for the overlay. Follow these steps:

1. Bring up the Overlay dialog box by double-clicking the overlay or selecting the overlay and choosing Effects, Overlay Options.
2. Click the Path button to bring up the Path dialog box again.
3. Set the size to 40 by 30 and then drag the overlay to just inside the upper-right corner of the white area.
4. Close both the Path dialog box and the Overlay dialog box, and you are done.

Building Your Video

Now that you've set up the video to your satisfaction, you'll need to build the video. There are a number of choices that you need to make at this point before you can click the button that starts the build. You need to decide the format for the output, the type of compression to use, the size of the video, and the type of device for playing the video. These options are spread out among several different dialog boxes and menus.

Fun with Palettes

Palettes in a video can be a rather challenging and confusing aspect of digital video. As with any confusing topic, understanding a little about the workings of the topic will remove some of the challenge. This section will try to give you that understanding with respect to palettes. This challenge will also disappear if you use videos with 16-bit or greater color because palettes are only used for videos with 8-bit or lower color. The rest of this chapter is based on that fact and written as though 8-bit color is being used.

A *palette* is a table attached to a video that contains color information. A palette is also called a *color look-up table*. Each pixel in a video has a number between one and 256 attached to it. When that pixel is displayed, the system looks at that number and then goes to the palette and figures out which color is in that spot in the palette and displays it. All the color information is stored in the palette. Each pixel only stores a position. Windows, when it is in 256-color mode, stores a palette that is made up of all the color requests that have come in so far.

The problem comes when more than 256 colors need to be displayed at one time. This causes Windows to make a decision about which colors stay and which colors go. Generally, it will choose to use the colors in the active window or process over any background colors. It will then load the new colors into its palette. The net result is called a *palette shift*, or *palette flash*; the colors in a video, bitmap, or Windows itself change into different and wild colors that look as though a paint store has exploded on-screen. This happens because the information stored in each pixel now points to a color that is completely wrong. The process in the foreground will flash as the palette changes, but will look okay once the new palette is in place.

A video can contain many palettes in its length as the colors change. This can cause palette shifting as the video is played. To combat this problem, DVP has several ways of *optimizing* the palette in a video. It can do this by creating a single palette that matches the various colors in the video as closely as possible. It can bring in a palette of your own creation or from some other source. It can also use a combination of these processes at once.

The choice whether to use 8-bit color or not depends on many factors: the type of machine the video will be played back on, the size of the file needed, and the quality. If the machine that will play the video is only capable of displaying 8-bit color, it is a good idea to do your video in 8-bit color. Doing it in 8-bit color gives you control over exactly which colors will be used. When 16-bit videos are shown on an 8-bit display, they will be dithered to display the greater number of colors. This can result in poorer detail and color in some cases.

Some codecs, such as Video 1 and RLE, can use only 8-bit color, so your choice might depend on that. Videos created using 8-bit color will generally take up less hard drive space and require a lower data rate to be displayed, but there is always the risk of palette shifts.

There are two places that you can optimize a palette. The first is during the building of the video, which is discussed in the section "Doing the Build" later in this chapter. The second is by using the tools provided under the Palette menu. The one that you will probably use the most is Create Palette. This option will go through some or all of the clips on the timeline and create a single optimized palette for the video.

To create this kind of optimized palette, use the following steps:

1. Choose Palette, Create Palette to open the Create Palette dialog box, and enter the range of frames that will be included in the optimization. If you have time, optimize the whole video rather than a small portion of it. Otherwise, you could compromise the quality and usefulness of the optimized palette.
2. Click OK in the Create Palette dialog box to start the optimization process.
3. Select Project Palette in the Build dialog box, which is discussed later in the section "Doing the Build."

There's always the possibility that you'll want to do some fine-tuning on your palette to remove some colors that you don't like. Perhaps you want to merge a few colors to make things look a little better. This can be done by choosing Palette, Edit Palette. Doing this will bring up a little utility that ships with ToolBook called PalEdit.

Example: Palettes

In this project, you will be using the Indeo 3.2 *codec* or compressor/decompressor, which only supports 24-bit color. Therefore, you can move on without worrying about this.

Setting Output Options

To access the Output Format dialog box, choose Video, Output Format (see fig. 23.12).

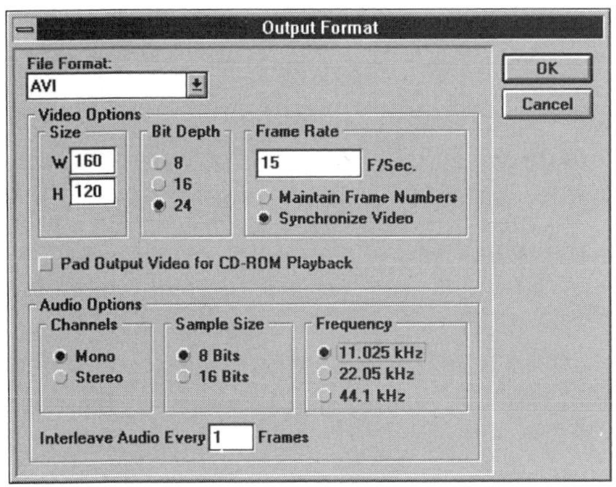

Fig. 23.12

The Output Format dialog box controls the types and format of the final video.

Most of the options are self-explanatory, with a few exceptions. The File Format drop-down box allows you to select the format of your output. If you select a still-motion format, such as DIB or GIF, your video will be output as a series of files, one per frame. This is useful if you want to edit something out of the video. Each frame can be edited in a paint program and then re-imported into the video. Each format can support different types of data: AVI supports both sound and video, WAV only supports sound, and FLI only supports video. AVI is the only option that supports compression in DVP, so the Compression option under the Video menu will be grayed out if you select anything other than AVI here.

> **Note**
>
> When you select a bitmap format, such as DIB or GIF, each of the frames written to the hard drive will be numbered sequentially. You must name the output file with a number at the end, such as `edit1.dib` or `mine1.bmp`, to accomplish this. To import the entire sequence, you need only select the first item. DVP will pick up the rest.

The size of the video is usually either 160 × 120 or 320 × 240, though you can select any size you want. Be aware that if you increase the size of a 160 × 120 video, it will appear blocky. Changing the ratio of height to width will result in a black bar on either the top or the side of your video to compensate for the change.

The *Frame Rate* is the speed of the video expressed as the number of frames per second. Most digital video is created at 15 frames per second since that keeps the size down, and most hardware is able to support it. More recently, with newer compression schemes and newer hardware, 30 frames per second is becoming more popular. 30 frames per second is very smooth animation. The movies you see in a theater are only shown at 24 frames per second, and the frame rate of North American television is 29.97. 15 frames per second is acceptable for most applications and is the frame rate that all of your clips were captured at.

The *Maintain Frame Numbers* and *Synchronize Video* radio buttons affect how DVP deals with differences between the frame rate of the source file(s) and the selected frame rate of the output file. Maintain Frame Numbers will neither drop a frame to reduce the frame rate nor duplicate a frame to increase the frame rate. Synchronize Video will cut out or add the necessary number of frames to accomplish this.

If you have a 30 frame per second source file and you want the output file to be at 15 frames per second, Synchronize Video will chop out every second frame of the source file to reduce the frame rate. Maintain Frame Numbers will double the length of the video to reduce the frame rate, thereby making the video appear to be going in slow motion and doubling the time it takes to show it. Maintain Frame Numbers is quicker during the build but, because sound is time-based not frame-based, the sound from the previous second example will not be slowed and will not be synchronized with the video; it will stop halfway through the video.

Pad Output Video for CD-ROM Playback is a way of optimizing the output file to be more efficient for playback from a CD. If you are planning to put this video on a CD-ROM, select this option. If you are not sure where the file will be played from, select this option anyway as it does not visibly affect playback from a hard drive. Selecting this option also forces the Interleave Audio Every option to 1.

The thing to remember about sound is that you can't make the source file sound better by changing the options. If the source file is mono, 8-bit, and 11.025 kHz, changing the output format to Stereo, 16-bit, and 44.1 kHz will do nothing but make the output file much larger. You can, however, make the sound worse by doing the opposite.

Use Format from First Video Input is a very simple option to use. If this option is selected, the Frame Rate, Frame Size, and Compression Type is taken from the first clip in the timeline and used to build the final video. If this option isn't selected, the settings for Frame Rate and Size are taken from the Output Format dialog box and the Video Compression dialog box.

Example: Output Format

Your video will use the AVI format, 16-bit color, 15 frames per second, and Synchronize Video. The size should be 160 × 120 and the sound should be mono, 8-bit, and 11.025 kHz.

Setting Compression Options

Once you have set the output options to your satisfaction and you have selected AVI as your output format, you need to decide how you are going to compress the final video. You do this by choosing Video, Video Compression. You will be presented with a dialog box similar to the one shown in figure 23.13. The only difference will be that the preview control doesn't show by default. Choose the Preview button to expand the dialog box.

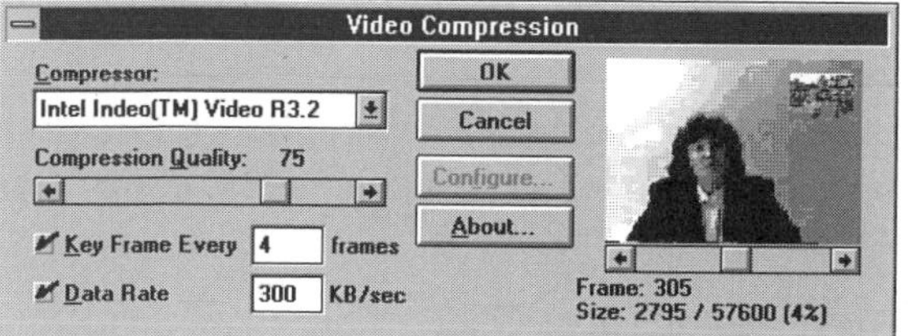

Fig. 23.13

The Video Compression dialog box is where you set the type of Codec you will use.

You're presented with several compression options. First, select which codec you'll use to do the compression from the Compressor drop-down list. Each codec has advantages and disadvantages, and you'll need to choose the one that best suits your project and your preferences.

Tip

My favorite codec is Intel Indeo v3.2. I like this one because it compresses more than a lot of the others do; it's as fast at compressing as any of the others; it uses a 24-bit color format, so I don't have to worry about palettes; and it's fast when it's played back. However, when I'm working on animation, which has many fewer colors than live video and the colors are quite consistent, I'll use Microsoft RLE because it's fast to compress and display and produces very small file sizes.

The next option is the Compression Quality. Most codecs use a type of compression called *lossy compression.* Lossy compression throws away some information in the file in order to achieve a better compression ratio. As the file size drops, more information is thrown away and the quality of the video diminishes. Setting the compression quality allows you to determine the tradeoff between compression ratio and quality. You can use the Preview control to see what the file size and quality will be; but remember, the preview is only a close approximation of the final product.

> **Note**
>
> Try to avoid compressing a video more than once. If you compress a video using a lossy compression method and then recompress it with the same or another lossy compression method, the quality will deteriorate. DVP is smart enough not to recompress video that has not changed unless you tell it to do so. The best option is to use non-compressed video as your source material whenever possible.

The Key Frame Every control determines how often a complete frame of video is placed in the file. Frames that are not key frames only contain the changes since the last key frame.

The Data Rate is the target for the amount of data that will be needed per second to play your video. If you plan to play this video on a CD-ROM, set it to a maximum of 150 for a single-speed CD and 300 for a double-speed CD.

Example: Compression Options

As mentioned before, you will be using the Indeo 3.2 codec. Select this from the Compressor drop-down list, and set the Key Frame Every to four and the Data Rate to 300. Click OK to dismiss the dialog box.

Doing the Build

The building process is almost complete; you need to set just a few more options in the Build dialog box and put the computer to work. To access the Build dialog box, choose Video, Build or click the Build button on the toolbar (see fig. 23.14).

Only a few options are available in this dialog box, but they can have a great effect on the quality of your video as well as the time needed to build your video. First, choose the name of your new video and the directory where it will be saved. The next two options are references for the people who will be working with the video. The information you put in the Title and Description fields will show up only in applications that support them, so go ahead and put whatever you want in there. It might be to help you organize your clips or perhaps find out what the clip is without having to play it. DVP will display the title and descriptions of a clip next to the clip in the Media window.

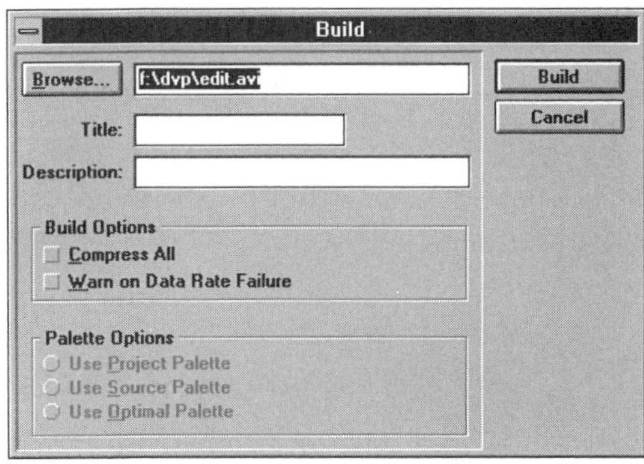

Fig. 23.14

The Build dialog box is the final step in creating your video.

Compress All will recompress the video even if it has already been compressed and hasn't changed. This option is useful if you are changing the frame rate of the movie. If you don't specify this option and you build a video that has not otherwise changed, the frame rate will also not change. You will want to use this option with caution because it could dramatically increase the amount of time needed to build the video as well as possibly degrade its quality.

Warn on Data Rate Failure warns you with a dialog box when the video you are building exceeds the data rate you set in the Video Compression dialog box. If the data rate is exceeded, the video may not play back properly on the chosen hardware.

The palette options are only used for 8-bit color videos. They will either be ignored or will not be available if your output format uses 16- or 24-bit color. The three options are as follows:

- *Use Project Palette*—This option doesn't do any optimization at all. It will take the Project palette and use that for the entire video. It's up to you to create an optimized palette using the tools under the Palette menu described earlier in the section "Fun with Palettes."
- *Use Source Palette*—This option takes the existing palettes in the source clips and places them in the final video. No optimizations are done, and palette shifting could be a distinct problem because of it.
- *Use Optimized Palette*—This option takes the longest to build the video. It examines all the colors in the entire video and produces a single palette of 256 colors that matches all the colors as closely as possible. This option is just the same as the Create Palette option discussed earlier in the section "Fun With Palettes."

Now, you're finally ready to build your video. Click the Build button to start the process. A window will appear with a progress bar and a preview area to show you the frame currently being compressed. Sit back and wait. This process could take some time, depending on your hardware. If you have a hot Pentium, it might not take long at all, but it could take an hour or more on a 386 or a low-end 486.

Example: Build

This is it, the final step in creating your first video! Only a few steps are left. Set the output file to a file of your choosing and, if you want, fill in the Title and Description fields. Make sure Compress All is not checked and Warn on Data Rate Failure is checked. You don't need to worry about the palette options because you are using 24-bit color. Press the Build button, and sit back and wait.

Capturing Video

Capturing video is the process of digitizing video taken from videotape or other format so that it can be used with Digital Video Producer. As simple as that may sound, there are a number of things that have to be done to get a satisfactory result. One of the big problems with digital video is its size. Video files can take up huge amounts of hard drive space. The options you choose when doing a capture have a great impact on the size of the final video. Selecting 16- or 24-bit color, capturing at 30 frames a second instead of 15, using 16-bit as opposed to 8-bit sound, will all balloon the size of a video. What this means is that your computer has to somehow keep up with the stream of data coming from the video capture card.

Quite often, frames will get lost or *dropped* because there is just too much data coming down the pipe for the computer to be able to deal with. This problem can be combated by compressing the video using a codec or reducing the data rate. Many video capture boards provide these codecs right in their hardware, which allows them to compress the data stream before it ever reaches the computer.

There are two ways to start DVP Capture: you can use the icon in the Program Manager, or you can choose Tools, Video Capture in Digital Video Producer (see fig. 23.15). If you start it from the DVP menu, the captured video will be imported into the Media window automatically.

Fig. 23.15

The DVP Capture main window is the starting place to capture video.

The first step in doing a capture is, of course, setting a few options. The options that will be available depend greatly on the type of hardware you have. The following are the items that will apply to many setups:

1. Choose Capture, Settings to bring up the first screen. Here you will set the Frame Rate for the capture—whether you will Capture to Memory or to Disk and whether you will capture audio. Capturing to memory is quicker, will drop fewer frames, and, if you don't have enough memory, will still switch to the hard drive when you run out of memory.
2. Choose File, Set Capture File. The capture file is the file on the hard disk where DVP Capture will write the captured data. Every time you do a capture, this file will be overwritten, so save any captures that you want to keep.
3. Choose Options, Video Format to set the size of the video as well as the bit depth and any compression options your capture board supports.
4. Choose Options, Video Source to set any real-time filters that your board supports. Some examples of these are tint, contrast, and brightness.
5. Now that your options are set, queue up your VCR or camcorder and click the Video button on the toolbar, or choose Capture, Video to begin your capture. Press Escape to end the capture.
6. Finally, save the file under a new name. Choose File, Save Captured Video As, and choose a new name and location for your capture.

From Here...

This chapter has covered a great deal of information. If you've been following along and creating your own video, take a look at `FINISH.AVI` in the `/CH23` subdirectory on the CD. This video is the final product I produced.

You might be interested in several things to do with your video once it's created. The following chapters should be able to help you in your quest for knowledge:

- To find out more about importing and using multimedia files in ToolBook, see Chapter 7, "Adding Multimedia Elements," Chapter 20, "Fundamentals of Multimedia," and Chapter 21, "Using Multimedia Elements."
- To find out more about using the MCI interface to control multimedia, see Chapter 22, "MCI Devices and Multimedia."
- To find out more about what needs to be done before delivery, see Chapter 26, "Preparing for Delivery."

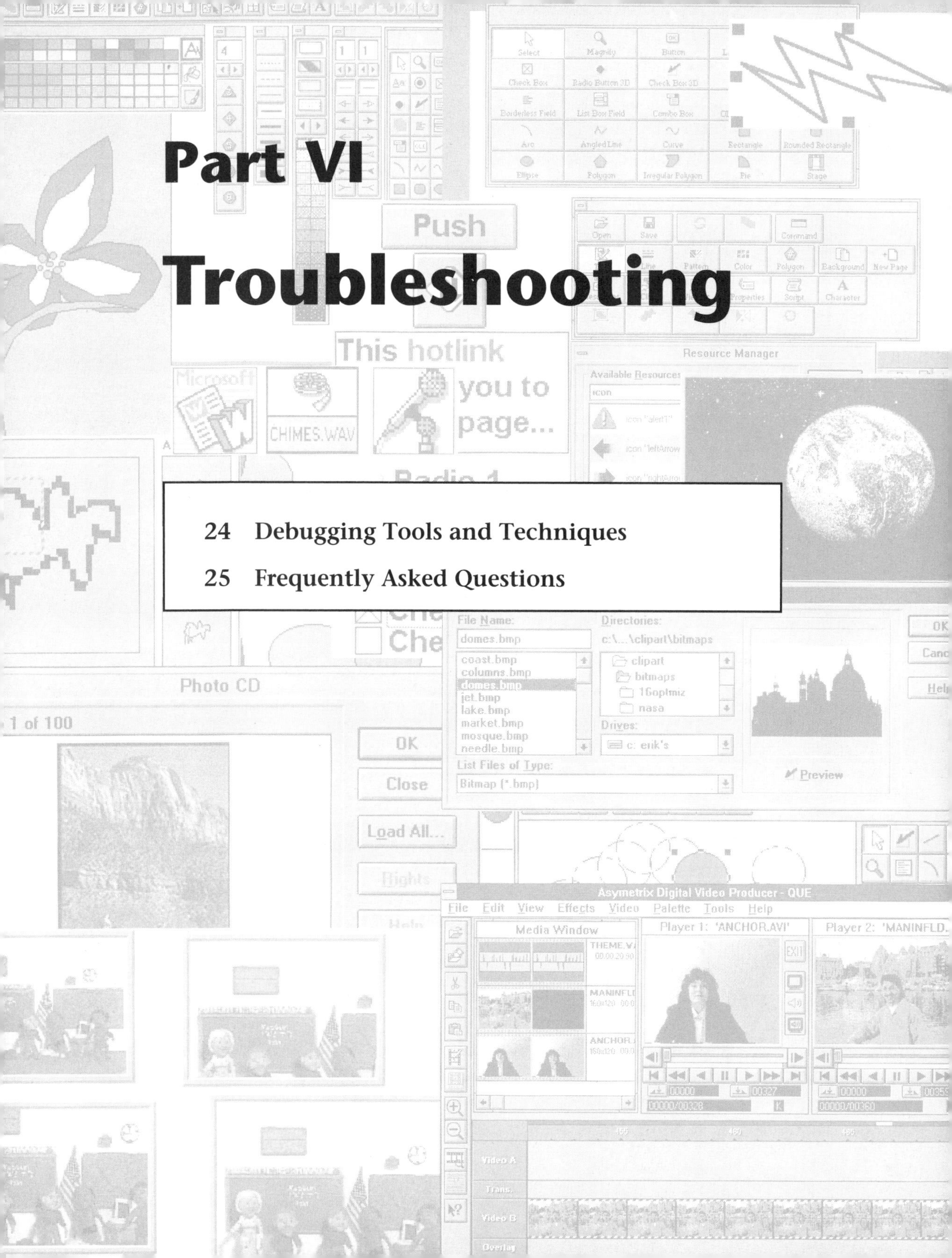

Part VI
Troubleshooting

Push
This hotlink
you to
page...
CHIMES.WAV
Microsoft
Radio 1
Radio 2
Radio 3
Undo To:
Select
Magnify
Button
Check Box
Radio Button 3D
Check Box 3D
Borderless Field
List Box Field
Combo Box
Arc
Angled Line
Curve
Rectangle
Rounded Rectangle
Ellipse
Polygon
Irregular Polygon
Pie
Stage
Open
Save
Command
Tool
Line
Pattern
Color
Polygon
Background
New Page
Resources
Clips
Viewers
Properties
Script
Character
Resource Manager
Available Resources
icon
Resource Properties
Import Graphic
File Name:
domes.bmp
Directories:
c:\...\clipart\bitmaps
coast.bmp
columns.bmp
domes.bmp
jet.bmp
lake.bmp
market.bmp
mosque.bmp
needle.bmp
clipart
bitmaps
16optmiz
nasa
Drives:
c: erik's
List Files of Type:
Bitmap (*.bmp)
Preview
Photo CD
Photo 1 of 100
OK
Close
Load All...
Rights
Help
Asymetrix Digital Video Producer - QUE
File
Edit
View
Effects
Video
Palette
Tools
Help
Media Window
Player 1: 'ANCHOR.AVI'
Player 2: 'MAN
THEME.W
MANINFL
ANCHOR.
EXIT
00000
00327
00000/00328
00000/00360
Video A
Trans.
Video B

CHAPTER 24

Debugging Tools and Techniques

Debugging is a broad term that refers to the correction of errors in every phase of application development—from developing a flow chart to planning a release. The narrow use of the term primarily refers to the correcting of programming (scripting) faults. As the term applies to ToolBook, debugging is the process of assuring the correctness, completeness, and the "executability" of the scripts that comprise your applications. By providing a user-friendly set of syntax and logic-checking tools, MTB helps you achieve zero-defect applications.

In this chapter, you learn about the following topics:

- Debugging basics
- Error trapping
- The OpenScript Debugger

Debugging Basics

This discussion of debugging occurs fairly late, however, the chances are pretty good that you will need to use some debugging techniques at every stage of the development of your application.

Preventive Maintenance of Applications

Debugging starts before scripting starts, as the best debugging tool is a firm conceptual grasp of what is actually going on in the application. As in any building project, construction of a program requires some planning. Ideally, you should consider the following:

- Make flow charts or written descriptions. Start with a document that describes the application as a whole, then supplement with finer divisions of the program: required objects, properties, and extensions; behavior of objects and optimal placement in the object hierarchy of the handlers that manipulate them; and handler behavior.

- Modularize functions to aid in the modification or replacement of specific features. Custom messages and their handlers are usually the building blocks of your modules.
- Use a readable scripting style. One common practice is to use a C-like indentation, heavily commented. It is also common to capitalize a script's handler type and the final `END` statement, but feel free to develop a style that is readable to you.
- Use the fastest method of accomplishing an OpenScript task known to you. Most feature changes are additions, and inefficient scripting can affect an application's performance.

Error Types

The following lists five ways your script can fail:

- *Errors in Compilation*—These are typically errors of omission such as leaving out a script's `END` tag. When this type of error occurs, the Script Editor alerts you that the script will not run. These errors must be corrected on the spot. While you may save a script that fails the compile-time checks, it's very unlikely that its handler or handlers will run at all.
- *Errors in Execution*—Runtime errors occur when the OpenScript interpreter encounters a statement that it can't execute. Your response to such an error depends on the circumstance.
- *Incorrect use of OpenScript statements*—In this case, there is nothing wrong with the script except that you have added or omitted statements inappropriately. For example, the statement `transition blue to next page` is an incorrect use of an OpenScript statement. The statement is used incorrectly, even though the syntax is correct, because `blue` is not a valid special effect. This sort of mistake is not an error to ToolBook, but it almost always causes your application to malfunction.
- *Poor selection of algorithms*—It's up to you to determine whether the underlying process that your handlers are designed to implement is valid. Even in this case, though, a debugging program that can be used to analyze evaluation order and changes in variable values may prove useful—even if it shows that a new algorithm should be chosen.
- *Failures of the ToolBook system*—These may or may not be caused by malfunctions of ToolBook proper. Video drivers and disk fragmentation are examples of external, seemingly irrelevant issues that can cause problems.

Compilation Errors. Although OpenScript is an interpreted language in the sense that its commands are converted to machine language as the ToolBook system encounters them, the system converts object references and statements of the script into more compact tokens for use by its internal database. It's in this sense that Asymetrix uses the term compiler; so, to avoid confusion, the Asymetrix understanding of the term is used in this discussion.

Common Compile-time Scripting Faults. The OpenScript compiler, as mentioned previously, will fail to compile a handler whose syntax is incorrect. The script is examined for erroneous statements each time syntax is checked and at each attempt to close a Script Editor document. The syntax check halts at the first syntax error it encounters and presents the alert box. Sometimes an appropriate description of the fault appears rather than the generic `Syntax Error`. Once the offending statements are repaired or replaced, additional errors may be encountered further along in the script. The compiler can flag only one at a time.

Note that ToolBook allows you to save the script even if it is faulty. This is a useful feature when you need to close the editor document in order to open others to refresh your memory about what is happening in other scripts; to determine how object properties are set; or just to shut the application down when you can work no longer. Also, be aware that you can minimize the script window. Minimization is of limited use in that navigation is severely restricted when a script window is open in any state. In fact, unless you entered the script directly through the Command Window, bypassing the Properties dialog box, you won't even be able to exit Properties.

However, Alt+Tab task switching (in Windows 3.x) does work while a script window is open, and it's a great help to be able to switch tasks to check the contents of a data file in Notepad, recheck the appearance of a graphic element in a graphics environment, copy script fragments and handlers from your own collection (if you don't use AutoScript), etc.

"Playing Computer" and the Visual Inspection of Scripts. In the excitement, or relief, of finishing the script of an object, it's difficult to resist the temptation to run it immediately to see if it works. Resist it. Put your mind in place of the OpenScript compiler and visually examine each statement, imagining what the result of each expression is and why. If you find this difficult on a monitor, select File, Print to get a hard copy of the object's script.

The importance of catching errors visually will become apparent the first time the compiler fails to catch a syntax error in the correct place. In any case, it's vital that every precaution be taken to predict and perfect a script's behavior before allowing it to act on your hard-won objects and properties. This is especially the case when the script is not a book script, but a temporary script written solely to create or copy objects and modify their properties. Such scripts should save the book often to reduce system resource depletion. However, frequent saving makes operations difficult to undo.

Spelling. You'd think that the compiler would be able to catch errors in spelling of its keywords, and it does. But unlike many lower-level languages in which any spelling error causes the compiler to complain, OpenScript generally will not treat an incorrectly spelled variable or property name as an error because it is not one.

The ability to create new variables, without declaration, makes OpenScript very easy to use, but the inescapable consequence of this capability is that if you misspell the name of a variable, a different variable is created. While this new variable contains the value you intended to place in the original one, that value is inaccessible to the other, correctly spelled instance of it. It's not the same container. The situation is similar when using property names. Misspelling a native or a user property name creates a new user property.

It's actually fairly easy to ferret these out by using the Property Browser—if you know approximately where to start looking. An effective method of checking spelling of specific variables in the script is to search for them (press F5 to view the Search dialog box). If the search fails to hit on a point in the script where the variable or property name should be, something's wrong at that point.

Closure of Parentheses and Quotes. The simplest compile-time problems to fix are those involving failure to balance an opening parenthesis or quote with its complementary closing character. In many cases, the compiler will trap this sort of typographical error correctly. In the case of unbalanced quotes, it advises you that there is an "unterminated string" in your handler and places the mouse pointer where it suspects the closing quote should go.

Tip

The Script Editor can never know with certainty where a complementary closing character belongs, so it does not attempt to repair the error on its own.

In the case of unbalanced parentheses, you will usually be presented with the not-too-helpful message, `Syntax Error`. In this instance, it can be visually confusing to track down an imbalance if you have used parentheses to reorder operator precedence, force evaluation of an expression, or if the expression contains functions as parameters to other functions.

The best (really, the only) way of balancing parentheses is to count them. Start from the innermost pair of parentheses (the ones that are closest together). Work your way out by ensuring that the next most complex expression is correctly parenthesized. Continue this operation until you run across an unbalanced pair. Remember to open and close a function parameter block with a parenthesis (often overlooked when the parameters are made up of complicated expressions).

Termination of Conditionals and Loops. It's easy and common to forget to close control structures, such as `if`, `step`, `in`, `linkDLL`, `translateWindowMessage`, and the rest.

Don't forget that statements following an incorrectly parenthesized expression or open-ended control structure are sometimes perceived as valid by the compiler. In such cases, the mouse pointer is not in the problem area of the script's text after the warning dialog box has been displayed. This kind of problem can be extremely refractory in a long, complex handler.

The means of recovery is pretty much the same as that for the previous problems: painstakingly examine your script until some error reveals itself. This provides a powerful motivation to "play computer." It's an even better motive to use small handlers that run by sending custom messages, and to take advantage of the functions of the Script Editor's `Check Syntax` command to perform incremental compilation (available via File, Check Syntax, Ctrl+Y of the Check Syntax button on the Script Editor toolbar).

> **Note**
>
> The easiest way to incrementally check for syntax errors is to press the Check Syntax button on the toolbar each time a significant statement block has been keyed into the Editor. This technique requires a little preparation. For instance, if your structure contains a loop within a loop, both loops need to be closed with `END` statements before the script will compile. There is no additional work involved; the statements need to be inserted at some time anyway. Better yet, test that inner loop (with made-up, or *dummy*, values if necessary) before ever including it in its parent loop.

Runtime Faults and the Execution Suspended Alert

After your script has compiled successfully, you may attempt to run it. It may or may not perform as desired; the goal at the moment is that it run with no errors. Actual, but non-fatal, errors during execution of basic ToolBook expressions are indicated by the interruption of the program flow and the displaying of the Execution Suspended alert box (see fig. 24.1). The various media commands in Multimedia ToolBook (including MCI commands) do not suspend execution by default, though setting the value of the system property `sysMediaSuspend` to `True` causes media-related errors to suspend execution.

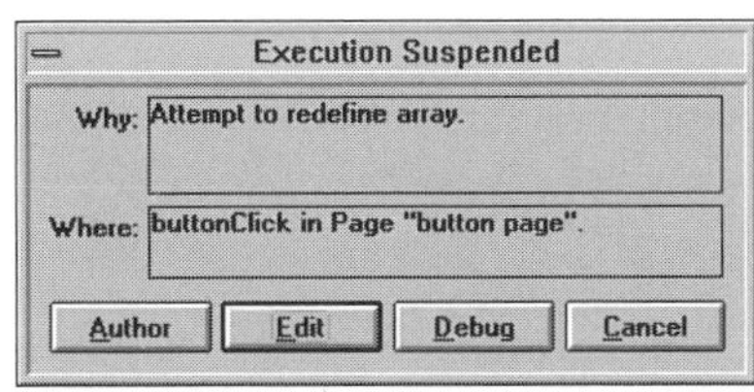

Fig. 24.1

A scripting error stopped the running of the program.

The proper action to take when execution is suspended depends on the active options available under the alert. There are four buttons:

- Author, which switches the system to Author mode (though not in Runtime ToolBook)
- Debug, which enters the Debugger near the statement that suspended execution
- Edit, which opens the Script Editor and allows you to attempt to correct the error on the spot and try running the handler again
- Cancel, which dismisses the alert and leaves the application in its halted state

Certain errors that could compromise system integrity cause ToolBook to gray out the first three buttons. When the Edit button is active, use it first. The position of the caret in the text of the script may help pinpoint the location of the error, and you can get to the Debugger from the Script Editor should you choose to do so.

Exiting the Script Editor after entering it from the Execution Suspended alert causes the message loop to run again, but the remainder of the faulty handler is skipped. The handled message must be sent again before the revised script can be tested.

You may want to suppress the halting of the program and display of the Execution Suspended box. For general OpenScript commands, set the value of `sysSuspend` to `False`. For multimedia command errors, use the property `sysMediaSuspend` instead. For example, you may want to close all open media files, whether they are clips or not. Functions such as `callMCI("close all")` will generate an error if no files are open. While using this function can, and perhaps should, be preceded by testing to see whether any files are open in the first place, it can be used at any time if `sysMediaSuspend` is set to `False` (the default). If you want to close a viewer that may be closed already, though, `sysSuspend` must be explicitly set to `False` beforehand and `True` afterward, as follows:

```
sysSuspend = FALSE
close viewer "Preview"
syssuspend = TRUE
```

Caution

If you must set `sysSuspend` to `False`, set it to `True` again as soon as possible so that ToolBook can continue presenting alerts as errors are encountered.

Note that, at least in this case, an `if` structure that checks whether the viewer is open takes no more statements than the statement block that disables suspension:

```
if isOpen of viewer "Preview"
     close viewer "Preview"
end if
```

The latter is the preferred method for this and related tasks.

The *put* and *request* statements. A debugging method that is sometimes even faster than the Debugger is to set traps that display intermediate results. A significant practical advantage of this method over use of the Debugger is that you can make a trap automatically break out of your handler before that handler has a chance to do any damage. Although this is also true of the Debugger, the latter requires more user intervention and more visual monitoring. It may, therefore, be less safe in some cases.

Basically, the trapping method involves placing one or more `put` (optionally followed by a `pause` or `break` statement) or `request` (optionally followed by a `break` statement) statements at key places within the script. The `put` form is generally more convenient to use, as it does not affect real-time execution of the program (unless a `break` statement is included) and can give you a running visual account of the values of objects and properties.

A slight annoyance is that if the script is entered into the Command Window in the first place, it's erased when the trap value is put there (although the script continues to run). This is fine as long as the script finishes, at which time it will be pushed onto the Command Window history like any other successful command. If the script is halted manually or because of an error, the text of the script is lost. One way of circumventing this problem is to make a temporary button on any page and set the script of the button to the script text containing the "debugging code." Another is to put the trap results into a temporary background field or `recordField` (though this can be inconvenient when the script causes navigation out of the original background).

Finally, you may just store the script as a text file (not only in the Clipboard, in case of a system crash) for copying and pasting back into the Command Window (see fig. 24.2). Page one of `CH24.TBK` illustrates an example of error trapping. Draw two `recordFields` on the background. One should be about 300 page units high and maybe 4800 wide. Name it `fName`. The other should be nearly the size of the remainder of the background with the border set to scrolling. Put a small button on the background. The script of the button is shown in Listing 24.1.

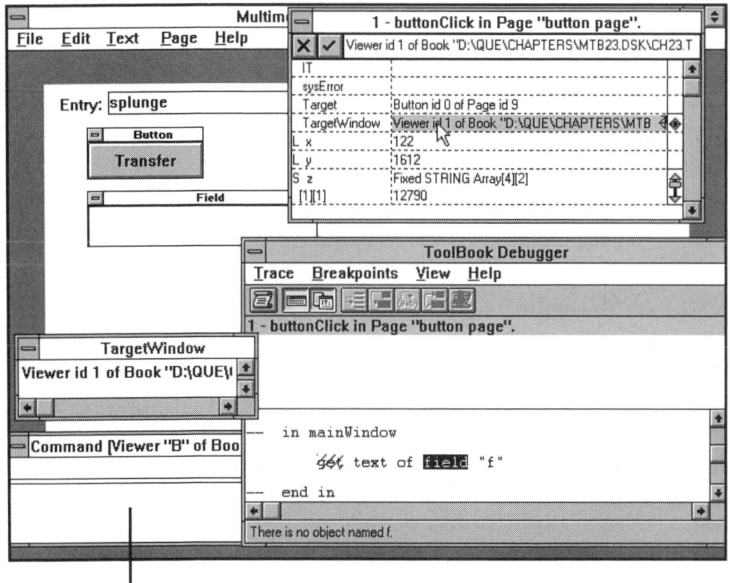

Fig. 24.2

You can use the Command Window to display intermediate results.

VI Troubleshooting

Listing 24.1 24LST01 Button Script for *fname* Example

```
TO HANDLE buttonClick
    local LONG i
    local STRING f,fl,p
    linkDLL "TB30DOS.DLL"
        STRING getFileList(STRING)
    END linkDLL
    linkDLL "TB30DLG.DLL"
        STRING sortTextlines(STRING)
    END linkDLL
    p = "c:\mtb30\samples\"
    f = p & "*.tbk"
    fl = getFileList(f)
    fl = sortTextlines(p)
--put fl;break    --trap
    step i from 1 to textLineCount(fl)
        text of recordfield "fName" = textline i of fl
        text of recordfield "fScript" = script of book \
            (p &(textline i of fl))
        send newpage
    end step
    unlinkDLL "MTB30DLG.DLL"
    unlinkDLL "MTB30DOS.DLL"
END buttonClick
```

The intention is that the handler will return a list of ToolBook files and put its name and the text of its book script into `recordFields`. The path name should be altered to suit your system.

Return to Reader mode and press the button. Apparently, nothing happens. The script doesn't produce the desired results, and you have no idea what it would be doing to data used by other handlers in a more complex application. All you really know is that the handler doesn't crash the system outright and that execution is not suspended because of a statement in the handler (the Execution Suspended alert doesn't appear and there's no immediate reason to think that `sysSuspend` has been set to `False`).

Given the lack of information about data alteration, set your first trap near the beginning of the handler. Place it so that it puts an intermediate value of a variable into the text of the Command Window, then causes a break out of the handler to prevent subsequent statements from executing. In the following example, uncomment the trap line:

```
fl = sortTextlines(fl)
put fl;break    --trap
```

The Command Window appears as expected, but it's empty; the variable `fl` is `NULL`. So that's the first problem in a handler that could have several. Move the trap back, changing the variable appropriately (no change is required in this case):

```
fl = getFileList(f)
--put fl;break    --trap
```

This time, the Command Window has a list of file names. The problem must therefore lie between the statement that gets the file list and the one that sorts it. This is a pretty easy one to solve. Since the sorting line is the next one, the problem must be with it. A brief visual inspection reveals that the text line sort function is trying to sort a path, `p`, rather than a `CRLF`-delimited list of items. This is obviously wrong, and the next line should be altered:

```
fl = sortTextlines(fl)
```

Return to Reader and press the button. The script now gets the book scripts of the files in the list and places them in subsequent new pages as intended. Comment or delete trap lines when they've served their purpose.

The `break` statement after the `put` command causes execution of the handler at that point, as noted. In this case, it's there to prevent the script from running the loop, which could consume time and have unpredictable consequences in a known buggy handler. You won't always want or need the `break` command.

You can also use the `request` command to present a modal dialog box displaying the requested value. The `request` command is useful when you don't know the amount of time you need the program halted with the requested values displayed. If you do use `request`, remember that the command returns a value in `It`, replacing whatever was in `It` to begin with.

Caution

Don't use the `request` command to trap a value contained in `It` that is used in later statements.

`request` should also be avoided in `idle` scripts, even in conditional statements. You may end up with a situation in which the branch is always taken, putting up the alert box each time around the event loop!

Tip

To halt execution of a program that has a `request` statement in an `idle` handler, press Enter or click OK in the `request` box while holding down both shift keys at once.

Using the OpenScript Debugger

The ToolBook Debugger is a part of the programming environment that allows the programmer to step through expressions and statements one at a time, while optionally displaying and updating the values of variables and properties after completion of each step. This is useful in determining whether an expression is evaluated correctly.

It would generally be very cumbersome to manually run the program from the application's start to the statement where the suspected cause of a runtime error executes. The Debugger allows you to define a barrier in the script that halts the program at the specified statement and opens a window that allows you to proceed manually. The barrier is called a *breakpoint* and, in fact, there may be a number of breakpoints set simultaneously in a script, either to stop execution in each of several handlers or to save time by allowing full speed execution of statements that lie between interesting statements within a handler.

Having stepped to the desired script statement, you may change the values of local or global variables, change the values of user properties, or open the Command Window.

The ToolBook Debugger can be called only when the program is not running (either because it was not started or because execution was suspended because of a runtime error). It may be opened from the Script Editor toolbar as described in Chapter 6, "Scripting Tools." You may open it from the Execution Suspended alert box by left-clicking the Debug button. It also appears automatically when you press and hold down both Shift keys simultaneously to halt the program. Ctrl+Alt+SysRq has the same effect, but is perhaps more dangerous in that the SysRq key is uncomfortably close to the Del key.

If you want to set up debugging before attempting to run a script, the Debugger is available at Author level from the Tool palette by holding the Command key down while clicking the Debug button. (Button text and the graphic of the script button change to the Debug symbol while the Command key is held down.)

The Debugger window has the following four subdivisions:

- The menu bar and toolbar make several of the menu commands available via the buttons on the toolbar beneath the menu. The toolbar may be hidden by unchecking View; the status bar by unchecking View, Status Bar.
- The Trace Box is the field that displays the running handler and handlers that called it. The script box contains the script of the handler that is highlighted in the Trace Box.
- The Script Box is where you set breakpoints and monitor the flow of the script. You use various menu commands (with accelerator key equivalents) to run traces of different processes.
- The Status Bar provides in its caption a condensed description of the reason that the Debugger has been entered. If it has been entered via the Debugger button of the Execution Suspended box, the description is similar or identical to the description of the problem given in the Why box of that alert.

Below the menu bar is the toolbar. Its buttons have the following functions.

The Script button opens the Script Editor, whose content is the script that is highlighted in the Trace Box. If this button is pressed after the Debugger is invoked after a runtime suspension of execution, the editor's caret is at (or near) the offending statement. As OpenScript is actually an interpreted language, it follows that execution isn't suspended until the execution of a faulty statement is attempted; therefore, the location of the error is shown at the end of the line that caused it or at the next line.

The Command button opens the familiar Command Window. The standard accelerator for opening the Command Window, Shift+F3, works also. ToolBook documentation lists several limitations of Command Window usage in its discussion of debugging, but in fact, the limitations apply to the use of the Command Window generally. The Command Window is best used for displaying (and, when possible and necessary, setting) the values of system variables and object or user properties, and the running of temporary scripts to modify or interrogate other handlers. A script in the Command Window, although it doesn't have a `TO HANDLE` or `END` statement, follows the other rules of a handler. You must declare system variables before they are known to the system and local variables in other handlers are inaccessible.

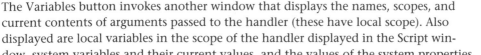

The Variables button invokes another window that displays the names, scopes, and current contents of arguments passed to the handler (these have local scope). Also displayed are local variables in the scope of the handler displayed in the Script window, system variables and their current values, and the values of the system properties `target`, `targetWindow`, and `sysError`. This is also the dialog box in which you edit the values of containers.

The Variables window is accessible only if the Debugger has been opened by an encounter with a breakpoint in a running script. It can't be opened if the Debugger has been called from the toolbar or the Script Editor. Open the Debugger from the toolbar, Script Editor, or Execution Suspended alert to set breakpoints.

Following these toolbar items are buttons for four menu commands that define the OpenScript Debugger's step range.

The Trace Statement button (the equivalent of Trace, Statement or Ctrl+S) defines the step range that you'll usually want to start with if you're completely unsure of the nature of the runtime failure. As the name implies, selecting this command advances the program by one statement and updates the values of variables and properties in the appropriate debug windows as necessary. Note that a statement may take up more than one line if the backslash operator is used; conversely, there may be two or more statements on a line if they are separated by semicolon operators.

The Trace Call button (the equivalent of Trace, Call or Ctrl+C) defines a step that enters a called handler. Use this command when execution actually reaches the line containing the calling statement, as the current line is the next one to execute. The values refreshed while tracing a call include names of local variables and user properties as well as their values (since you're now in a different handler, the local variable containers are not the ones you began with, even if their names are identical). System variables' values are updated, as are the three displayed system properties if any of these have changed.

After using Trace Call, it's very likely that you'll want to return to Trace Statement for a statement-by-statement report from the called handler. If the handler finishes executing, control returns to the calling handler in the usual way, and you may continue to trace steps or additional calls as desired.

The Trace Expression button (the equivalent of Trace, Expression or Ctrl+E) divides a statement into finer steps, updating the appropriate variables and user properties at the completion of each expression. Recall from Chapter 14, "Messages, Objects, and Properties," that an expression is any combination of OpenScript terms that return a value upon execution. While the point at that time dealt with returns from functions, it's actually the case that each time a property (including a name or color, for instance) is retrieved, or a pair of parentheses is used to force evaluation of an arithmetic or logical statement, a value is returned. For example, the following statement contains no fewer than eight evaluations:

```
increment item 1 of my position by (240-y)*15
```

Interpreters need to evaluate constants as well as variables and properties. It's fascinating to watch the evaluation sequence proceed in the following order:

- `1`—(evaluation of a literal)
- `item`—(evaluation of the data type)
- `240`—(evaluation of a literal)
- `y`—(evaluation of a variable)
- `240-y`—(evaluation of the subtraction)
- `15`—(evaluation of a literal)
- `(240-y)*15`—(evaluation of the multiplication)
- `my position`—(evaluation of the current position of the object)

The last term really involves two evaluations: that of the object reference (`my`) and that of the property involved (`position`).

Needless to say, this is the command to use for hard-core examination of suspect string concatenations or mathematical formulas, either of which may boggle the eye. Equally obvious is that evaluating expressions is a lengthy process; after an expression has been traced, you'll probably want to either continue running the application (if your analysis is successful) or return to tracing at the statement level.

The Trace Return button (the equivalent of Trace, Return or Ctrl+R) simply allows a called handler to finish execution at normal speed. The Debugger stops the script at the next unexamined statement in the calling handler. It's a sort of fast forward for skipping over bits of the script that have been debugged.

The Continue Execution button (the equivalent of Trace, Continue Execution or Ctrl+G) sets the program running at normal speed from the point at which it's selected. Use this feature when you're finished examining and modifying your script and want to return to standard operation.

The use of the toolbar buttons, rather than the menu commands, is emphasized here because the extremely repetitive nature of tracing program flow may make selecting menu items irksome. Nevertheless, there's no getting around the fact that the Debugger and its many windows (there are more to come) make finding screen space for them, not to mention for the main window, difficult at best. You may want to hide the toolbar and status bar, as every little gain of screen real estate helps. If you do so, the keyboard equivalents of the toolbar buttons are handy.

Using the Variables Window

The Variables window (shown at the top of figure 24.2) packs a lot of information into a relatively small space. It's designed a bit like a spreadsheet and to some extent works like one. The cells in the first column show the names of the standard items:

- The universal variable `It`—This variable has no scope, as it's not really a single variable. There is an `It` for each handler. However, within a given handler, `It` has local scope. Use a system variable rather than `It` if you want to observe interhandler data manipulation.
- `sysError`—This system property contains a string that is a brief description of the cause of the previous error, unless you have set it to `NULL` as part of an error-handler cleanup.
- `Target`—This system property cannot be set, although its value is editable. When you attempt to save the edit, the save operation fails.
- `TargetWindow`—This system property cannot be set, although its value is editable. When you attempt to save the edit, the save operation fails.

Below the four standard items are the cells that describe your custom variables. They contain one more piece of information about a particular variable. The capital letter `A`, `L`, or `S` appears, separated by a space before the variable name. An `A` variable is an argument (a parameter passed with the message and received by the current handler.) A variable preceded by `L` is local in scope, and one preceded by `S` is a system variable.

There is a separate window that can be shown or hidden (via View, System Variables) that provides only system variables and their values. Another separate window, View, User Properties, displays only the user properties of the object to which the current handler belongs. There is no need for a scope symbol in these windows.

The second column of the Variables window shows the value of the container in the adjacent cell of the first column.

> **Note**
>
> The vertical dividing line between the first and second columns is movable so that their relative widths may be adjusted. The appearance of a two-pointed arrow mouse pointer while the mouse position is over the dividing line means that the line is ready to be moved.

There is a third distinct column in the Variables window. When the continuation symbol appears in a cell in this column, it's an indication that the screen representation of the contents of the container is wider than that of the second column, so that the value extends out of the window to the right. To see the entire value, adjust the width of the second column and/or the entire window. If that doesn't work, double-click the value in the second column. Yet another window appears, this one containing the value only. You may have several value windows open simultaneously.

The value window is useful in viewing lengthy strings and large arrays in a scrolling window. But the Variables window provides a built-in control for examining the values of the elements of arrays whose screen representations are too tall to fit into the Variables window. This control is a tiny scroll bar, located to the left of the main scroll bar of the Variables window, that scrolls the array value representation up and down (refer again to figure 24.2).

Changing Values from the Debugger

The edit box above the variable area of the Variables window is an edit line. When you click the value of a variable, the value appears in the edit line where it may be changed. At this time, the Reject (X) and Accept (checkmark) buttons become active. Enter the new value for the variable or property and press Enter or click Accept if you're satisfied. Press Esc or click Reject to return the text of the line to its original value (no variable or user properties are affected if you reject a change).

When you change a value from the Variables window, the change takes place immediately: the old value is replaced by the new, which is ready for use in expressions of the current statement. Contrast this with changing a value by setting it in the Command Window. In that case, the change doesn't take effect until the next statement. Using the Command Window, however, is the only way of getting and setting object properties such as `bounds`, `position`, `fillColor`, `script`, `text`, etc. Watch out when changing the `script` property of an object in the book you're working on. It's easy to change handlers in such a way that previously sound ones are now dysfunctional. It's especially bad to change the script you're debugging.

But isn't changing the value of a variable or user property also changing the value of the script you're debugging? Well, yes and no—but mostly yes. It can be misleading or even damaging to change certain values in the midst of a series of statements. The change, however, is not permanent; if you restart the book (or send an `enterApplication`, `enterBook`, `enterBackground`, etc. message via the Command Window as appropriate to run the initialization procedures for the script's owner object), the application should be in the state it was before the first value change was made.

Nevertheless, value editing should be done with due care. Every script is different, of course, but generally the values that can stand editing are those that have not been initialized properly. Change the value of the variable or user property to reflect the results of a valid initialization; be sure to add the appropriate initialization statements to the script. Results of algebraic calculations are often OK to change before they're used. Once again, the goal is to fix, add, or remove statements of the script to make it work properly. Once you've found the fault or developed the proper algorithm with the help of the Variables window's editor, the time to fix the script is right away.

To work on the script itself, choose View, Script from the Debugger menu bar, or simply click the Script button on the Debugger toolbar.

Knowledge of the values of values and properties is invaluable in tracing message flow, particularly when using viewers, each of which may or may not be the target window at a given moment. The second page of `CH24.TBK` is an example of how to trace a `buttonClick` message originating in a viewer other than the `mainWindow` to get the text of a field in the `mainWindow` and put it into the text of a field in yet another viewer.

The book needs three backgrounds with one page each. Make a field on the first page, similar to the filename field in the earlier example, and name it `f`. Name the next page `B` and the page after that `F`. Draw a button on page `B`. Select it and, using the Command Window, type the following:

```
size of this background = size of selection
```

Go to the next page (which is on the third background). Draw a field and select it. Run the Command Window script again. Now create two viewers. Name one `B` and the other `F`. Make them any style you like, but make page `B` the default page of viewer `B` and page `F` that of viewer `F`. Put this handler in the script of the button, the button's page, or the background of the first page of the three. There's really no difference in what you'll see, as this script exerts total control over the message path. The `buttonClick` message has to reach it. That is all. In the example book, it's in the script of the page that contains field `f`. A commented-out copy resides in the button script (See Listing 24.2); this doesn't run unless you remove the comment marks.

Listing 24.2 24LST02 Button Script Illustrating Message Path Control

```
TO HANDLE buttonClick
    local x
    system y
    x = 122
    y = (525-x) * 4
--    in mainWindow
        get text of field "f"
--    end in
    if it <> NULL
--        in viewer "F"
            text of field "f2"= it
--        end in
    end if
END buttonClick
```

The comment marks are present because, as there is no simple way to save a breakpoint between application instances, the book is set not to save. The lines you'll have to add are therefore safe and can be present but commented out for the demonstration. They may spoil the feeling of discovery a bit.

Switch to Reader mode and press the button. You'll be informed by an alert box that the field you want to access doesn't exist. You know that it does. Invoke the Debugger by clicking on the page (to make it the target again) and selecting Debug (Ctrl+Script) from the toolbar. The debug window will appear with the start of the script displayed in the lower pane of the display area. Step through the statements using Ctrl+S. You'll see that the value of `targetWindow` doesn't ever change from the viewer showing the button.

Obviously the other objects are not in the current window's message hierarchy. The first step in fixing this is to review what is meant to happen. The field into which you type is in the main window. The button is in another window and the field that receives the transferred text is in another window; so force those windows to be the target windows in turn by using two `in` structures as in Listing 24.3.

Listing 24.3 24LST02 Button Script For Controlling Target Windows

```
TO HANDLE buttonClick
    local x
    system y
    x = 122
    y = (525-x) * 4
    in mainWindow
        get text of field "f"
    end in
    if it <> NULL
        in viewer "F"
            text of field "f2"= it
        end in
    end if
END buttonClick
```

The button now works as expected. Using the Debugger (you'll have to set the breakpoint again), look at the values for `targetWindow`; note that they now switch to the proper window at the proper time. This simple script can be debugged by eye (or written correctly in the first place) once you are used to message passing among windows.

The variables and the values of the expressions are unused except as an illustration of how the Variables window works. Use Trace Expression on the assignment line for the variable `y`. You'll see the various evaluations occurring as in the previous description.

A last note on debugging. If serious problems, such as General Protection Faults and GDI memory errors occur, your script could be the cause. But if you simply can't find anything wrong, try switching your video to standard VGA if you had been using a third-party video driver. Video drivers are notorious for storing information at addresses that belong to Windows or another application. If the video driver is causing a problem, the only real recourse, short of staying with VGA, is to make sure that the driver is the latest revision for the version of Windows you're using.

Another obscure cause of crashes is failure to save onto contiguous blocks of the hard disk. Disk fragmentation seems to seriously confuse Multimedia ToolBook's save mechanism for no apparent reason. One suspects a timing error or a failure to update block information. At any rate, defragmenting the disk (after backing up your work, of course) before an important save can reduce the chances of a crash.

From Here...

This chapter introduced you to the fundamentals of debugging, including basic error trapping, and use of the OpenScript Debugger. Refer to the following chapters for additional details on refining your ToolBook applications:

- For more about text styles that improve script readability, see Chapter 13, "OpenScript Fundamentals."
- For more information about user and object properties, see Chapter 14, "Messages, Objects, and Properties."
- For further information about messages and variables, see Chapter 15, "Understanding Variables, Values, and Text."
- To find out more about statements, arguments, and expressions, refer to Chapter 16, "Statements, Functions, and Expressions."

CHAPTER 25

Frequently Asked Questions

At times, it seems that no matter how much you study a book or work with the software, you will have plenty of questions. While developing with Multimedia ToolBook, you may have many questions. Multimedia ToolBook is a powerful development tool. Of course, with this powerful tool and the different development possibilities comes increased complexity. Multimedia ToolBook does an excellent job of reducing complexity; although as you increase your knowledge of what Multimedia ToolBook can offer, you will increase the depth of your questions.

After completing this chapter, you will be familiar with common issues related to the following areas of Multimedia ToolBook:

- Multimedia
- Viewers
- OpenScript
- Setup
- Optimizing for CD-ROM

Multimedia

Multimedia ToolBook allows you to included a wide variety of media types. In fact, any media that has a Media Control Interface (MCI) driver can be used in Multimedia ToolBook. A driver interprets instructions from Multimedia ToolBook and tells the particular device, such as a sound card, how to respond to various commands, such as play, stop, and rewind.

When you play sound from Multimedia ToolBook, you use the MCI sound driver. Like all MCI drivers, the MCI sound driver allows a wide variety of software, including Multimedia ToolBook, to control the sound card. An MCI driver is required to control any type of media device in Multimedia ToolBook.

Problems Playing Media

Why won't media, such as an audio file, play in Multimedia ToolBook?

First, test the media from the Media Player. Next, make certain that the MCI driver is loaded and set up correctly.

> **Note**
>
> Although this example involves playing sound, you can apply the same troubleshooting techniques to nearly all media playing problems.

Testing the Media. If the driver appears to be loaded and installed correctly, then the media file should be able to play correctly from the Clip Manager within ToolBook. Refer to Chapter 21, "Using Multimedia Elements," for details about creating media clips. However, if no sound plays when testing from the Clip Manager, try testing with the Media Player.

To test the MCI driver from Media Player, follow these steps:

1. Locate the Media Player icon in the Accessories group within Program Manager and double-click the icon.
2. Open the wave file by selecting Device, Sound from the Media Player menu bar and choosing a wave file. If the type of media does not appear in the Device menu, you will need to install the device driver from the Control Panel.
3. Open and Play your wave file in Media Player. If your media file plays correctly, you know that the hardware is set up correctly. However, this doesn't ensure that the MCI driver is loaded correctly, which is the driver that ToolBook uses.
4. Now, display the Send MCI String Command dialog box by pressing Ctrl+F5.
5. Type the command **`play from 1`** in the Send MCI String Command dialog box and press the Send button (see fig. 25.1).

> **Note**
>
> If the media has already played to the end of the file, a simple `play` command will not restart the media.

If the wave file doesn't play when you send the MCI string but does play from regular Media Player, then you do not have the MCI sound driver installed or set up correctly.

Loading the Driver. Microsoft Windows includes an MCI sound driver. You can check whether it's loaded by selecting the driver icon from the Windows Control Panel. If it's not loaded, follow these steps to load it:

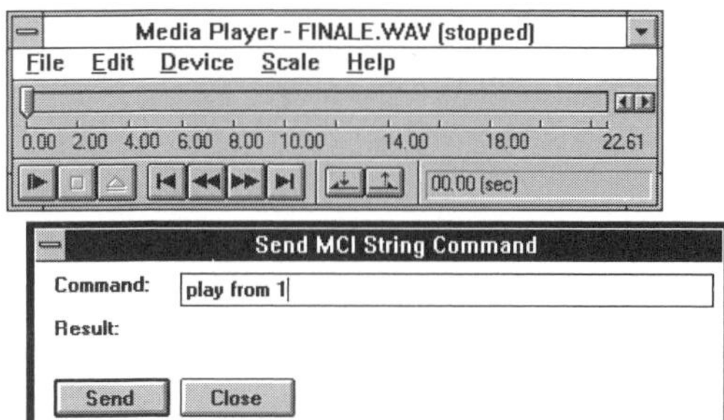

Fig. 25.1

Enter MCI commands into the Send MCI String Command dialog box to test the MCI driver.

1. Double-click the Control Panel icon in the Main group within the Program Manager.
2. Double-click the Drivers icon within the Control Panel. A list of Installed drivers will be displayed.
3. Scroll the list to find the appropriate MCI driver. The list will contain driver references similar to those listed in Table 25.1.
4. If you do not see the appropriate driver installed, select New from the Drivers dialog box.
5. Make sure you have your Windows disks available to locate the MCI driver.

Note

The animation and video driver should be available on your Multimedia ToolBook CD.

There are several common media types, such as Video, Wave Audio, and Animation. Each type of media uses a unique MCI driver. Table 25.1 lists the common media types and their associated drivers as listed in the `WIN.INI` file.

Table 25.1 Media and MCI Drivers

Media Type	MCI Driver
Video (`.AVI`)	[MCI] Microsoft Video for Windows
CD Audio	[MCI] CD Audio
Wave Audio (`.WAV`)	[MCI] Sound
Animation (`.FLI`, `.FLC`)	[MCI] Autodesk Animation
Midi (`.MID`)	[MCI] MIDI Sequence

Each media device uses a unique MCI driver. There are dozens of MCI drivers available; often these are included on a separate disk. Also, the driver may be dependent

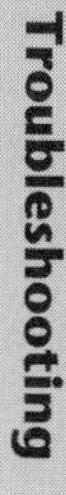

on the type of Windows (Windows NT, Windows 3.1, etc.) that you are using. Therefore, I don't think specifying the driver location would be possible here. Installation of the more commonly selected drivers automatically suggests where to find the driver.

Setting Up the Driver. There are, however, a few additional Windows settings that you can check if sound is not being played with Multimedia ToolBook.

Windows can identify which driver it will need to use for your media file by the name of the file. More specifically, the extension of the filename. `.WAV`, `.AVI`, `.FLC`, and `.MPG` are all examples of file extensions that Windows uses to recognize different media file types.

MCI devices must be set up correctly in your `WIN.INI` and `SYSTEM.INI` files. These two files contain much of your Windows media setup information. The correct setting in your `WIN.INI` file should include an MCI sound reference in the `[mci extensions]` section similar to the following:

```
WAV=WaveAudio
```

Notice that this line does not have spaces. The above reference indicates that when `.WAV` files are notified to be played, the driver associated with `WaveAudio` in the `SYSTEM.INI` file will be used.

Next, you should check the `SYSTEM.INI` file for the appropriate reference in the `[mci]` section.

In this example, the entry in the `[mci]` section of the `SYSTEM.INI` is as follows:

```
WaveAudio=MCISOUND.DRV
```

If the driver is loaded and the media does not play correctly, make certain that you have the latest driver from the device manufacturer.

Playing a Wave File and Allowing Other Actions

How can you play a wave file, and also allow other actions to occur within Multimedia ToolBook?

You can use a notify handler in conjunction with a `clip` command, such as playing a wave audio clip without obstructing the user from interacting with your application.

When you use OpenScript to play a media clip, you state the command and the clip reference, such as the following:

```
mmPlay clip "Video Drum Solo"
```

You can include a parameter to the above line of OpenScript to tell which object to notify when the media command finishes. The parameter can notify any object. Notice that each of the following lines of script notify a different object:

```
mmPlay clip "Video Drum Solo" notify button "Play"

mmPlay clip "Video Drum Solo" notify this page

mmPlay clip "Video Drum Solo" notify background "Chapter1"
```

You can use the `notify` parameter to notify the object from which you send the command as follows:

```
mmPlay clip "Video Drum Solo" notify self
```

Notice that the `mmPlay` command is notifying the same object from which the clip was originally played. Therefore, you must place a notify handler in the script of the same object.

When the `mmNotify` handler is sent, it passes three parameters. The first parameter is the media reference, such as clip `"Begin"`, or clip `ID 5`. The second parameter is the command, which has acted on the media. Examples of commands are `play`, `stop`, and `pause`. The third and last parameter of `mmNotify` is the result. In most cases, you will be looking for a `successful` result. Other results include `failed`, `aborted`, and `superseded`.

To work with the following example, start by placing the script in Listing 25.1 into the script of a button. Also, create a sound clip and name it `Music`. Refer to Chapter 21, "Using Multimedia Elements" for details about creating a media clip.

Listing 25.1 25LIST01.SCR Using a Notify Handler

```
to handle buttonClick
     mmOpen clip "Music"
     mmPlay clip "Music" notify self
end buttonClick

to handle mmNotify clipName, commandName, result
     conditions
          when clipName = clip "Music" and \
          result contains "successful"
mmClose clip "Music"
          when clipName = clip "Music" and result contains "aborted"
               mmClose clip "Music"
               request "Clip Aborted!"
     end conditions
end mmNotify
```

The first handler of the this script opens and plays the clip. The `notify self` parameter of `mmPlay` is a reference to the object that will be notified. In this script, the object to be notified is the same object that sent the message.

> **Note**
>
> Using a `wait` parameter or a `pause` command stops the user from interacting with your application until the media file has finished. Use a notify handler to allow user interaction.

When the object is notified, three values are sent:

- The name of the clip
- The command name
- The result of the clip

The notify handler checks both the clip name and the result to determine when to close the clip.

Repeating Media

How can I loop a media clip so that it repeats automatically?

Not only does a notify handler allow the user to continue to interact with your application while a media file is playing, it also can be used to play a media file continuously.

You can loop a media clip using a notify handler. The notify handler will tell the media clip to play again.

At times, you may need to continue a particular video, sound animation, CD audio, or laserdisc clip until the user is ready to interact with your application. Oftentimes, this type of media control is used for kiosk type applications.

Create a button and add the script from Listing 25.2 to the script of the button. Also, create a wave audio media clip named `Music`. For details about creating clips refer to Chapter 21, "Using Multimedia Elements."

Listing 25.2 25LIST02.SCR Repeating Media Using OpenScript

```
to handle buttonClick
     mmOpen clip "Music"
     mmPlay clip "Music" notify self
end buttonClick

to handle mmNotify clipName, commandName, result
     if clipName = clip "Music" and result contains "successful"
          mmPlay clip "Music" notify self
     end if
end mmNotify

notifyBefore leavePage
     mmClose clip "Music"
end leavePage
```

The script opens and plays a media file in the `buttonClick` handler. The `notify self` parameter identifies that when the clip is finished playing, the `mmNotify` function will be sent along with three parameters.

Refer to the previous section of this chapter, "Playing a Wave File and Allowing Other Actions" for `mmNotify` details.

CD-Audio Doesn't Play

Why won't CD-Audio play in Multimedia ToolBook?

Load the MCI CD-Audio driver. Also, check the CD-Audio cable to be sure it is installed.

To play CD-Audio through your speakers, you must have a sound card installed correctly on your computer. Also, you must have an MCI CD-Audio driver installed correctly. To quickly determine whether you have a sound driver loaded, try playing CD-Audio using the Media Player. To test the audio of your CD-ROM, start by placing an audio CD into your CD-ROM. For more details about testing CD-Audio and loading the CD-Audio MCI driver refer to the "Problems Playing Media" section earlier in this chapter.

If the CD-Audio driver is installed and the Media Player appears to be working correctly, try testing by listening to the audio CD with your headphones. The headphones jack in the front of your CD-ROM is useful for testing. If you can hear sound through the headphones and not the speakers, you need to make sure the cable that links your CD-ROM and the sound card has been installed.

Viewers

A viewer is a window that is displayed as a rectangular area on your screen. Viewers display pages. To display objects within a viewer, you must create objects on the page that the viewer displays. You can use a single viewer to navigate through several pages or display several viewers, each displaying a page.

Displaying the Correct Page in a Viewer

Why is the first page of the book displayed in my viewer rather than the page I expected?

Viewers have a specific property called `defaultPage`. If the `defaultPage` viewer property is not valid, the viewer will display the first page of your application. This problem could occur if you remove the page that a viewer will view.

The `defaultPage` of your viewer must contain a valid page reference or it will default to the first page of your book. Figure 25.2 displays the Viewer Properties dialog box.

Your `defaultPage` value should be a page name or unique page name, such as:

```
page "Contents" of book "Main.tbk"
```

or

```
page ID 2 of this book
```

Referencing a page by page name rather than page ID is best. A different page ID would be assigned to a page when copying, pasting, and importing pages.

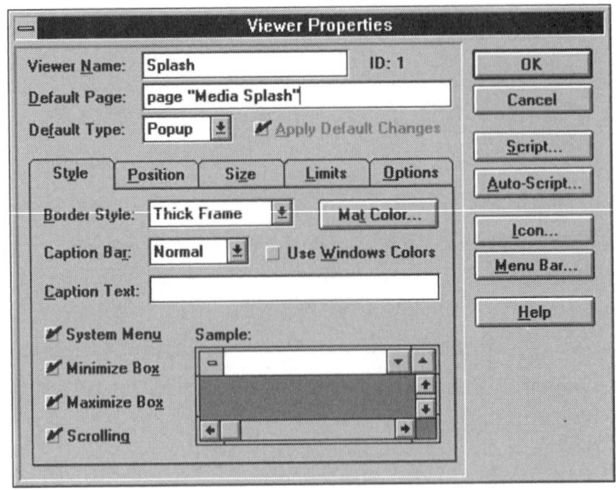

Fig. 25.2

Set the Default Page to a valid page reference to ensure that the correct page is displayed in the viewer.

Viewer Flash

How can I prevent my viewer from flashing when it is displayed?

If objects drawn within your viewer appear to flash when you hide, show, or move them, change the Image Buffers setting in the Options tab of the Viewer Properties dialog box.

An image buffer is a portion of memory set aside to contain an image of the page and/or background. An image buffer is a persistent viewer property that can be one of three settings—0, 1, or 2. If the object that is flashing resides on the page, set the Image Buffers to 1. If the flashing object is on the background, use the 2 setting.

```
imageBuffers of viewer "Media Splash" = 1
```

For more information related to image buffers, refer to Chapter 8, "Working with Viewers."

Creating and Deleting a Viewer Using OpenScript

How can I dynamically create, open, show, and later delete a viewer in my application?

It is possible to completely control a viewer using OpenScript. Use the script in Listing 25.3 to create a new viewer.

Listing 25.3 Create a Viewer Using OpenScript

```
to handle buttonClick
     new viewer
     name of it = "My Viewer"
     open viewer "My Viewer"
     defaultPage of viewer "My Viewer" = this page
     revertFocus of viewer "My Viewer" = true
```

```
    autoClose of viewer "My Viewer" = true
    show viewer "My Viewer"
end buttonClick
```

Use the script in Listing 25.4 to delete the new viewer.

Listing 25.4 Delete a Viewer Using OpenScript

```
to handle buttonClick
    if isOpen of viewer "My Viewer" = true
        close viewer "My Viewer"
    end if
    clear viewer "My Viewer"
end buttonClick
```

The first handler starts by creating a new viewer, naming it `"Media Splash"`, and opening it. Once the viewer is opened, set the `defaultPage` value so that the viewer always opens to the correct page. You can change the page that your new viewer will display by changing the viewer's `defaultPage` value.

OpenScript

Each object that you create with Multimedia ToolBook has specific properties that define how the object reacts to events—such events as `enter` and `leave` messages. You can enhance the way objects react to events by adding OpenScript to any object.

The ability to manipulate objects for your specific need is what makes Multimedia ToolBook extremely powerful. OpenScript is the key used to customize and fine tune the actions of your application.

Stopping the Execution of a Script

How do I stop the execution of script using the authoring version of Multimedia ToolBook?

At times, you may accidentally script your way into an *endless loop*. An *endless loop* is a looping script routine that you cannot easily escape. To stop the execution of script, press and hold both Shift keys.

When you stop the execution of your script in this manner, the ToolBook Debugger is displayed (see fig. 25.3). You have the option to exit the debugger, edit the script, or debug your script.

For more information about using the ToolBook Debugger refer to Chapter 24, "Debugging Tools and Techniques."

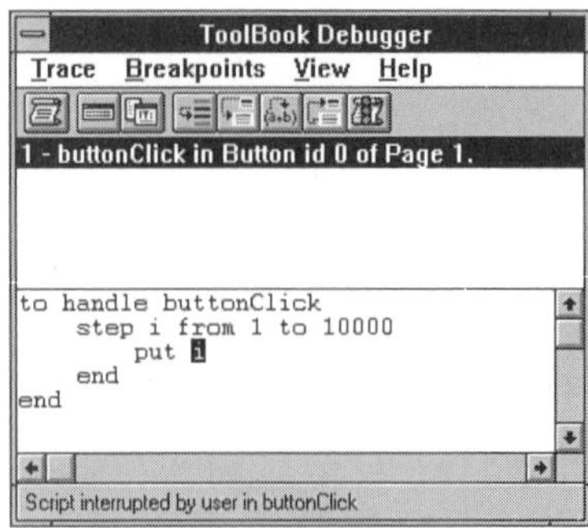

Fig. 25.3

Press and hold both Shift keys to stop the execution of a script.

Hiding the Printing Dialog Box

How can I hide the Printing dialog box?

You can hide the Printing dialog box by preventing the screen from updating. This function should be used with caution because once the screen has been locked, you must unlock it before you can see any changes.

You can freeze the screen in Windows just before printing by using the `lockWindowUpdate()` API function. When printing has concluded, the screen can be unlocked using the same function.

The script in Listing 25.5 is an example of how you can prevent the Printing dialog box from being displayed. Place the following script into the script of a button.

Listing 25.5 Printing Without Displaying the Printing Dialog Box

```
to handle buttonClick
     linkDLL "user"
          INT lockWindowUpdate(WORD)
          WORD getDeskTopWindow()
     end linkDLL
     get lockWindowUpdate(getDeskTopWindow())
     -- make all unseen changes here
     printerStyle = columns
     printerMargins = 1440,1440,1440,1440
     printerGutters = 360,360
     printerScaling = custom
     printerFields = "Info"
     printerFieldWidths = 4005
     printerFieldNames = true
     printerClipText = false
     start spooler
          print 1
     end spooler

     get lockWindowUpdate(0)
end buttonClick
```

> **Note**
>
> This function is used to lock your entire display. Be prepared to test your application when using the `lockWindowUpdate()` function. Before using this function, be sure you understand the benefits of using this function correctly and the dilemmas of using it incorrectly. The screen will not unlock automatically. If you lock the screen without unlocking it later, your screen will not update.

The `lockWindowUpdate()` function is a Windows function that must be linked into your Multimedia ToolBook application from the user DLL within Windows. This function toggles whether a specific window is drawn.

The `getDeskTopWindow()` function must also be linked to from the user DLL. This function allows you to get the reference to the window that covers the entire screen where all other windows are drawn.

Determining the Current Path of Your Book

I need to find and run other books and media based on the current path of my book. How can I find and use the path of my application?

You can find the path of your current book by getting the name of your book. You must save your book before executing the script in Listing 25.6.

Listing 25.6 Determining the Path of Your Book

```
to handle buttonClick
     if name of this book <> null
          bookPath of this book = name of this book
          do
               clear last char of bookPath of this book
          until last char of bookPath of this book = "\"
          request "Your book path is:" && bookPath of this book
     else
          request "Save your book before determining the book path!"
     end if
end buttonClick
```

This script makes use of a user property assigned to the book name `bookPath`. First, set the `bookPath` value to the name of the book, and then clear the characters from this value until you have the path of the book. If the book has not been saved, a request box is displayed.

You can use the `bookPath` value to find files, such as media files. If the file you want to access does not reside in your book's path, you would need to find the file separately. One way of locating a file of your application is to store the location in a `.INI` file. You can use the `getIniVar()` function from the `TB40WIN.DLL` to retrieve INI information.

Preventing a Book from Exiting on Startup

When I start my application, it automatically exits. What can I do?

Edit the script of the book from a new instance of Multimedia ToolBook. Follow these steps:

1. Open a new instance of Multimedia ToolBook.
2. Display the Command Window by selecting View, Command.
3. Display the script of the book you want to edit by entering a command in the Command Window. For example:

```
edit script of book "c:\mtb\mybook.tbk"
```

4. Now modify the script of the book so that you can open the book. For example, comment out the lines that refer to `exit` or `leaveBook`.

You could completely comment out the entire book script by placing two consecutive dashes in front of each line of script. Refer to Chapter 13, "OpenScript Fundamentals" for details on commenting out script.

Differences Between System Variables and Local Variables

What are the differences between system and local variables?

System variables and local variables both contain data; however, they both exist differently in your book.

A system variable holds the information you put into it while you have your current ToolBook instance open. A local variable holds the information you put into it until you finish executing the handler.

Although system variables only need to be set once, they must be recognized in every handler where you want to use a system variable. Local variables must be set in every handler that you want to use the local variable. These variables are automatically cleared at the end of each handler.

Often, an object contains several handlers within its script. Each handler must declare the system variables used within it.

For more information concerning system variables and local variables, refer to Chapter 15, "Understanding Variables, Values, and Text."

Disabling the Save Changes Dialog Box

How can I prevent the user from making changes to the application?

At times, you will find it best to prevent the user of your application from saving changes to the book. You can use the `sysChangeDB` system property to control whether the book is saved.

Use the script in Listing 25.7 to prevent the user from saving changes to the book.

Listing 25.7 Disabling the Save Changes Dialog Box

```
to handle exit
     if sysLevel = reader
          sysChangesDB = false
     else
          sysChangesDB = true
     end if
     forward
end exit
```

This script determines whether the book is at Reader level or Author level. When the book is exited at Reader level, no changes will be saved. Although when the book is exited at Author level, you will have the option to save your book.

Determining the Use of a Large Fonts or a Small Fonts Video Driver

How can I recognize if the user of my application is using a large fonts driver or a small fonts driver?

You may be familiar with the different resolutions that your video card supports. The different resolutions allow you to view all of Windows in greater or lesser detail. Video cards, monitors, software, and the computer itself all contribute to the ability to display information.

To display Windows in a different resolution, you must choose and, in many cases, install a different video driver specific for the resolution you want to view.

Some video drivers allow you to view your text in a larger font. Using a large fonts video driver means larger text for easy reading, while retaining detailed graphics. However, large fonts drivers change or shift how your application appears. For this reason, it is often beneficial to avoid using large fonts drivers.

To check whether the user of your application is using a large fonts driver or a regular small fonts driver, you can use the system property called `sysPageUnitsPerPixel`. `sysPageUnitsPerPixel` specifies the number of page units for each pixel that is displayed both vertically and horizontally.

The script in Listing 25.8 can be used to determine whether you are using a small fonts or a large fonts video driver.

Listing 25.8 Checking for Large Fonts or Small Fonts

```
to handle buttonClick
     conditions
          when item 1 of sysPageUnitsPerPixel = 15 and \
          item 2 of sysPageUnitsPerPixel = 15
               request "Small Fonts Video Driver"
```

(continues)

Listing 25.8 Continued

```
          when item 1 of sysPageUnitsPerPixel = 12 and \
          item 2 of sysPageUnitsPerPixel = 12
               request "Large Fonts Video Driver"
     end conditions
end buttonClick
```

Once you have determined whether the user is using a small fonts or a large fonts video driver, you can have your application react appropriately. For instance, you could simply notify your user that your application may appear differently when using a large fonts video driver. Another option would be to display a completely modified application design that is specified to display correctly when using a large fonts driver.

Preventing Task Switching

How can I prevent the user of my application from switching to other applications?

In Windows 3.1, you can use the API function called `lockInput()`. The `lockInput()` function can be used to prevent the user from switching away from the application that called this function. In effect, this disables two quick and common methods of task switching, Alt+Tab and Ctrl+Esc.

As previously mentioned, when using API calls, care should be used especially when using those API functions that prevent user interaction. Use the script in Listing 25.9 to disable task switching.

Listing 25.9 Preventing Task Switching

```
to handle buttonClick
     linkDLL "user"
          INT lockInput(WORD,WORD,INT)
     end linkDLL
     get lockInput(0,sysWindowHandle,1)
end buttonClick
```

To enable task switching, use the following handler:

```
to handle buttonClick
     get lockInput(0,0,0)
end buttonClick
```

The `lockInput()` function uses three parameters:

- The first parameter is reserved and must remain 0.
- The second parameter is the handle to the window that will receive input.
- The last parameter is a Boolean value that turns the locking flag on and off.

Setup

This section describes specific issues of setting up your application and configuring your authoring environment within Multimedia ToolBook. Multimedia ToolBook developers often ask why their Tools menu has disappeared. Also, developers ask what the dollar sign represents in the Setup Manager. These two issues will be addressed within this section.

Adding the Tools Menu

The Tools menu is not displayed; how can I display it?

The Tools menu includes such authoring functionality as the Property Browser and the Path Animation tool. The Tools menu can be included by including the `MTB30.SBK` system book within your `sysBooks` book property.

If the Tools menu disappears from your menu bar, you can add it back quickly by including it within your `sysBooks` book property. Follow these steps:

1. Display the Command Window.
2. Push the system book onto your `sysBooks` book property. For example:

```
push "C:\MTB40\MTB30.SBK" onto sysBooks
```

To permanently display the Tools menu in Author mode for every new ToolBook instance, you need to modify your `MTB30.INI` file. To do so, follow these steps:

1. Display your `MTB30.INI` file. NotePad works nicely for editing INI files.
2. Change the `startUpSysBooks` reference to include the `MTB40.SBK` file. For example:

```
startUpSysBooks=C:\MTB40\MTB30.SBK,C:\MTB30\MYBOOK.SBK
```

3. Save the changes to `MTB30.INI`.
4. Restart Multimedia ToolBook to see the Tools menu (see fig. 25.4).

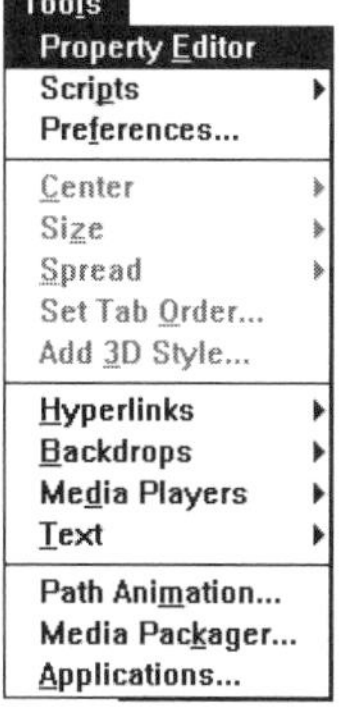

Fig. 25.4

The Tools menu provides special authoring functionality.

If your Tools menu is still not displayed, you need to check the script within your book. Statements to look for are those that clear your `sysBooks` property or reset your Multimedia ToolBook environment, such as `restore system`.

In the Setup Manager, What Does the Dollar Sign Represent?

A directory placeholder is a variable that contains a unique path of a directory on the user's system. This placeholder is used to reference the specific directory during installation of your application. For instance, `$system$` would commonly contain `c:\windows\system`.

The directory placeholder is identified by the dollar signs that surround the placeholder.

Each system that your application is installed on is different. In the Setup Manager, you can specify a particular directory, common to all Windows 3.1 environments, where you can place your files without being required to know the hard coded path. There are five directory placeholders that can be used within the Setup Manager (see Table 25.2).

Table 25.2 Directory Placeholders

Placeholder	Description
`$windows$`	The path of the Windows directory on user's system
`$system$`	The path of the Windows System directory on the user's system
`$install$`	The path of the installation directory where your application will be installed
`$source$`	The path of the directory where `SETUP.EXE` was started
`$common$`	The path of the directory where the Multimedia ToolBook runtime files will be installed

Optimizing for CD-ROM

Although the speed of CD-ROM access is dramatically increasing with each new CD-ROM drive introduced to the market, access to data on a CD is much slower than a hard drive. When you save your application to CD and plan to run it directly from the CD, optimize your application for best performance.

You have the option to change the file format to enhance your application's access and execution speed from CD. To optimize an individual book for CD-ROM, follow these steps:

1. Select File, Save As or Save as EXE from the menu bar. The Save As dialog box appears (see fig. 25.5).

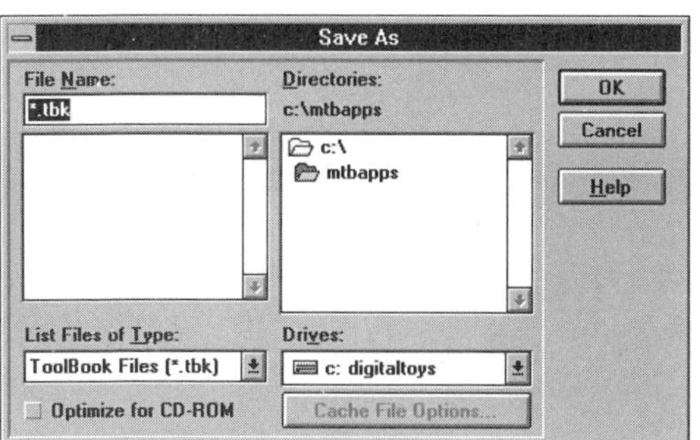

Fig. 25.5

Both the Save As dialog box and the Save As EXE dialog allow you to choose the Optimize for CD-ROM option.

2. Select the Optimize for CD-ROM checkbox and then choose OK.

When you make changes to your book, you must save your book as optimized again. You should use this optimizing option when you have completed the development of your book.

Optimizing Methods

What are the differences in optimizing methods?

There are two major choices to make when determining how to optimize your application. First, if you want to optimize your CD application, you must use a cache file. By default, a cache file is not created. In fact, cache files are not recommended for small applications.

The decision to use a cache file is simple. If your application is large enough to require that you use a CD, then you should use a cache file.

There are two types of cache files that you can use:

- A temporary cache file—which only exists when your application is run. A file is temporarily placed on the user's hard drive and later removed when the application closes.
- A permanent cache file—if you have a very large application with a complete database, full text search, or lots of media and you believe your user will have plenty of hard disk space, use a permanent cache file.

Once you have chosen to use a cache file, you must determine whether to use a minimal, preferred, or extended cache file.

The minimal cache file takes up the least amount of space on the user's hard drive. This type of cache file improves access speed to all of your application's pages.

The preferred cache file takes a larger amount of space on the user's hard drive. It saves page information and references to large objects, bitmaps, and script. This type of cache file will increase access speed beyond the minimal cache file.

The extended cache file is similar to the preferred cache file; however, the extended cache file stores the actual resources that the book uses. The resources include bitmaps, scripts, and objects. Of course, this cache file requires the most amount of disk space on the user's system.

Testing the Cache File

How can I test the cache file I use with my CD-ROM application?

After setting up your cache file, it is possible to test the cache file if you have a network on your system. To do so, follow these steps:

1. Make sure your cache file is on your hard drive.
2. Place your application on a network drive and make certain that the application is read-only. Setting the application to read-only simulates the data on the CD.
3. Make certain that the `MTB30.INI` file points to the cache file. The `MTB30.INI` file should contain a reference to your cache file, such as the following:

   ```
   [cache file]VIDSURF.TBK=C:\VIDSURF\CACHE\VIDSURF.TBC
   ```

4. Now test run your application from the network. The cache file can be accessed on your local hard drive.

From Here...

In this chapter, you have learned about frequently asked questions common to viewers, OpenScript, optimizing, and setup. For further information, see the following chapters:

- Chapter 8, "Working with Viewers," explains information related to image buffers.
- Chapter 13, "OpenScript Fundamentals," provides details on commenting out script.
- Chapter 15, "Understanding Variables, Values, and Text," gives you details on system and local variables.
- Chapter 21, "Using Multimedia Elements," discusses the details of creating a media clips.
- Chapter 24, "Debugging Tools and Techniques," provides an explanation of how to use the OpenScript debugger.

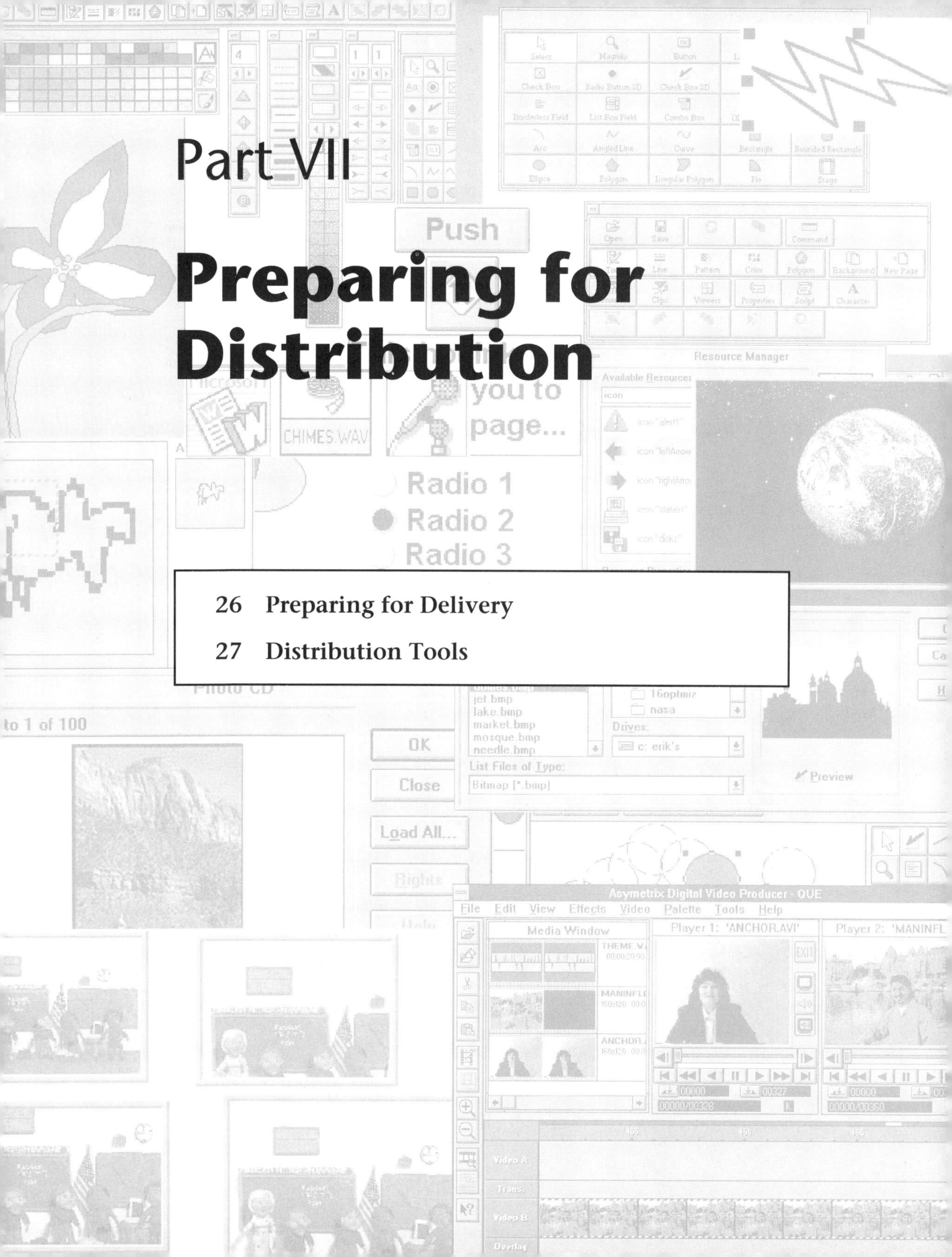

Part VII

Preparing for Distribution

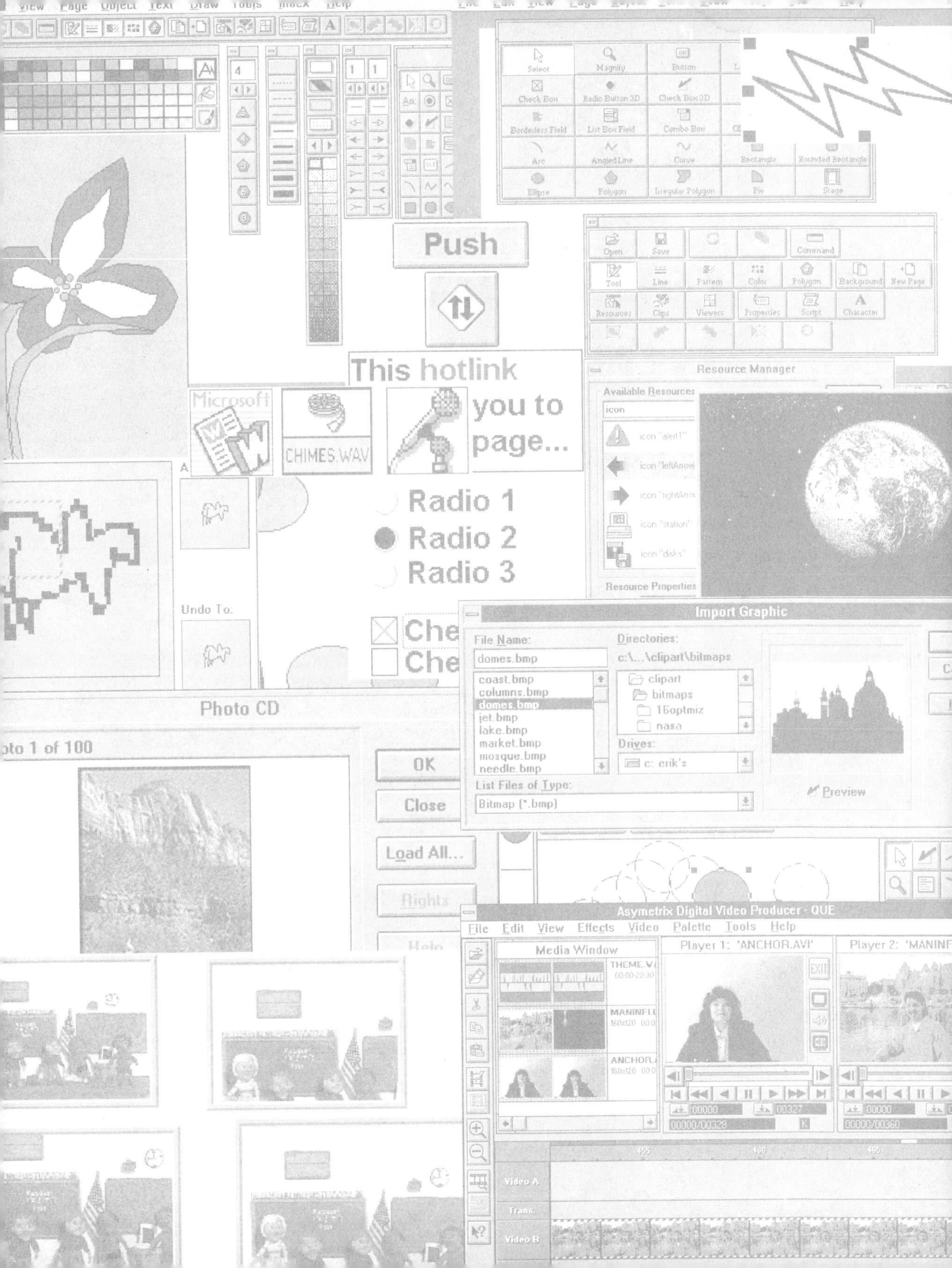

Push
This hotlink
you to
page...
Radio 1
Radio 2
Radio 3
Resource Manager
Import Graphic
Photo CD
OK
Close
Load All...
Asymetrix Digital Video Producer - QUE
Media Window

CHAPTER 26

Preparing for Delivery

Once all the coding is done, the graphics are imported and placed, the video's working, and the buttons are all set, you are still not finished with your job. There are still a number of issues to address and tasks to complete. You need to test your program for bugs and other "nasties." You need to make sure that all the support files, such as fonts, are available. You need to optimize the book and choose a medium for distribution.

Preparing for distribution involves all the finicky and not-so-finicky final steps that must be completed to make a success of your project. Some of the topics covered in this chapter are the following:

- Testing your book
- Preparing your book for the runtime environment
- Distributing the fonts you need with your book
- Working with the runtime version of ToolBook
- Optimizing your book for better performance
- Saving and compressing your book for distribution
- Choosing a distribution method

About Testing

It's happened to everyone: you go and purchase the newest whiz-bang piece of software, bring it home, and find that it can't be used on your machine. It is one of the most frustrating experiences. You want your users to be happy with your product, and you don't want to spend six months taking calls from people who are having problems with your systems when you could be working on something much more profitable. The best way to prevent problems is to apply something called testing.

What Do You Mean *Test?*

The first thing to remember is that there can *never* be enough testing. There may be enough testing from a monetary or timeline point of view, but not from a technical one. There is always one more machine out there that is different from all the ones you tested your program on. There is always one more user who is going to do things just a little bit differently. Of course, you have to stop testing at some point, or you would never get anything out to the users. That point—when you stop testing and start distributing—must be balanced between the need to have a bug-free product and the need to make money and meet a deadline.

There are many ways that testing can be done in today's world. Each of the systems will look slightly different from the others, and each company will tell you that they have the best system. As well, the size of the company creating the project will have an impact on what type of testing is done. If you are a single person, then you don't have all the resources that a company like Asymetrix might have. Despite the differences, the various testing systems have similar core methods that can be scaled to fit into any testing setup. I will go over several of these.

Simulate the Environment. The object of testing is to get rid of the bugs that your users are going to find. How better to do this than by simulating the environment that your users work in? If they all work on 386 machines, it is a good idea to test your product on 386 computers. This is not to say that you should only test in one environment. You should test in as many environments as possible.

I was working at a rather large company a number of years ago, and the people who took care of our mail system installed an upgrade. They tested it, and all seemed well, so they went home for the rest of the weekend. On Monday morning, nobody could access mail and people panicked. It turned out that everybody who tested the mail system had administrator rights to the system. No testing was done by users who had normal rights. Therefore, they had not adequately simulated the environment that their users would be working in.

Test on Many Machines. Testing your product on many different machines is crucial—machines with different processors, different software, different hard drives, different anything. Bugs are capricious little beasts. They sometimes require just the right hardware and software to bring them out of hiding. ToolBook 3 itself brought to light many bugs in some graphics card drivers that didn't show up anywhere else.

Get Many People to Test. Who is it that ultimately finds the weirdest bugs? The people who use your product. Therefore, it makes sense to have many people test your product. Each person works just a little bit differently, possibly finding a unique bug.

One time, a client of mine was having recurring crashes while printing. She worked in an office of 40 or so people and was the only one experiencing the problem. Everybody had a similar computer setup with the same software. So why was only one person having the problem? We reinstalled all the software, swapped out the computer and peripherals in a series of attempts to squash the bug. Nothing worked; the bug would disappear for awhile and then show its ugly head again.

The clue that led us to the answer came when somebody else filled in during my client's vacation. The new person, after about a week, started having the same problem. It turned out that it was the type and flow of the work in that particular position that brought out a bug in the word processor that nobody else experienced.

Be Creative and Silly. There is a lot more to testing than just using the software as it was designed to be used. Using the product in a normal way is important, but finding out how it can handle the mistakes of the end user is equally important. Creativity is the name of the game in testing. If something is too outrageous to try, then that is the perfect thing to do because you never know what your end users are going to do. Pound on the keyboard. Use 200 characters instead of two. Open every single window that you can. Do all the things that you know might break it! Don't be afraid to be silly and have fun doing it. The more problems that can be found at this stage will mean happier customers and fewer support calls.

Make Notes. There is little point in testing a product if the bugs that are found cannot be fixed. One way to ensure that a bug can be fixed is by making it easy for the programmer to reproduce the problem. There is no way to know if a bug is gone if it can't be found in the first place. Depending on the size of the project that you are working on, you could rely on word of mouth to communicate the problem or you could have the tester make notes. Some bigger companies will actually videotape the entire testing session so, if there is a bug, the programmer can see exactly what was happening when the tester found the bug.

One common procedure is to provide the tester with some type of form to fill out. The form can contain all the questions that need to be answered to help the tester give the proper information, such as the following:

- What type of machine is used?
- What type of peripherals are used?
- How much memory is installed?
- What page did the problem occur on?
- What button was pushed last?
- What was the problem?

Each product will require a slightly different form because there will be a different interface and different ways of describing procedures.

The Testing Cycle

The scope and amount of testing that you do depends on your target market. If you plan on sending this product out to 100,000 people, many cycles of testing are in order. If you are using the book for your presentation tomorrow, a much smaller amount of testing should be sufficient.

There are three different stages of testing. One thing to remember is that there are no hard and fast rules governing the different stages of testing. What one person considers to be a *beta* product, another person might consider *alpha*. Some groups might only have a beta and no alpha. It is totally up to you to decide how you want to interpret the different stages.

In-House Testing. In-house testing is the first step in the testing cycle and consists of people, directly connected with the product, doing the testing. This stage usually starts well before the product is finished and well before anyone is happy with it. In-house testing is done as the product is being created to avoid any large missteps that could crop up in the design. For small projects, this is quite often the only testing that is done—the only testers are the people creating it.

The Alpha Stage. The next stage in the cycle is called the alpha. The alpha code is usually distributed to a very limited group of trusted individuals who will test it. Alpha code is the first code to be seen and tested by someone outside of the group or company that created it. It is expected that there will be many bugs in the program, and it is not fit for general release. Depending on the scope of the project, there could be many iterations of the alpha: the product is tested, the bugs are reported, the bugs are fixed, a new version is sent out, and the whole process starts again.

The Beta Stage. One prevalent testing model is called the beta. Beta code is distributed to a wider group of people than the alpha. It is released to increasingly larger groups of people during testing, and each version of the product has more problems fixed than the previous one. Beta code is considered to be quite stable and almost ready for release. The object of beta testing is to get the code out to many people to get a broad range of systems and people testing it. There can also be a number of versions of the beta before the final release of the product.

Embedding Fonts

When using ToolBook, you are able to utilize any of the fonts that are installed on your system. You can use them for any of your text anywhere in your book. When you send that book off to other users, they will need to have access to those fonts as well. If they do not have the appropriate font, windows will substitute a font that looks the closest to the original. This may sound good, but it can look awful. Text will wrap at different positions, text will be cut off, and the look of the application will change. There are two ways that you can avoid this problem. The first is to only use fonts that you know will be installed on all the machines. The second is to embed all the fonts that you are going to need as resources within your book.

Multimedia ToolBook is able to import a copy of many TrueType fonts directly into a book. They are then usable, with certain restrictions, wherever the book may go. Only certain TrueType fonts are licensed to be embedded. This is definitely something you will want to be aware of when embedding fonts.

If, for some reason, you are not able to embed a font into a book, you will need to go through your book and reformat all of your text to use a different font. Select a font that will be available on all the machines or a font that you are able to embed. The following steps show how to do this:

1. Select the field, combo box, and so on.
2. Open the Character dialog box by choosing Text, Character or by pressing F6.
3. Select the appropriate font and click OK.

You can also use OpenScript to accomplish the same thing by setting the `fontFace` property of the object, as shown in the following example:

```
set fontFace of field "test" to "Arial"
```

Caution

If any text is formatted by selecting some of the text inside a field, setting the `fontFace` of the field will have little or no effect on the text. This is because the formatting contained in the `richText` property of a field overrides the other formatting properties. Any time you change individual characters in a field, the `richText` property of the field is used.

Licensing

Every font, like all other software, was created by somebody and is owned by somebody. When you obtain a font, you are generally only purchasing a license that gives you certain rights to use the font. Every font manufacturer, just like every software manufacturer, has a different licensing scheme. There are freeware fonts, shareware fonts, public domain fonts, and commercial fonts. Each gives you different rights to use the font.

With TrueType fonts, there is some licensing information encoded right into it. The information tells programs whether the font can be embedded into an application or document. There are three categories of licensing for embedding fonts.

None. With this level of licensing, the font is not licensed to be embedded in an application or document. If you attempt to embed the font in a ToolBook book, you will receive an error message.

Read-only. Read-only licensing gives you the right to embed a font in your application but with certain limitations. The font can be used only with the application or document it is embedded in. The font cannot be installed permanently on your system. You are not able to edit any text in the document or application. If any of the text using a read-only font is edited, the closest matching font that is permanently installed will be substituted.

When a read-only font is embedded in a ToolBook book, the font will be installed on the user's system at startup, made available to the book, and then deleted when the book is closed. If the system crashes, there will be files left in the system's temporary directory that will need to be deleted at a later time.

Read/Write. This category of licensing gives you full rights to use the font on as many systems as you want. The font can be embedded in an application or document and then permanently installed on any other system. Any read/write fonts embedded in a ToolBook book will be permanently installed on any system that the book is run on.

Importing a Font

ToolBook treats embedded fonts as resources like bitmaps or icons and uses the Resource Manager to work with them. Choose Object, Resources or press Shift+F10 to bring up the Resource Manager. Next, select Font from the Available Resources drop-down box and click Import. The Import Font dialog box shown in figure 26.1 will appear.

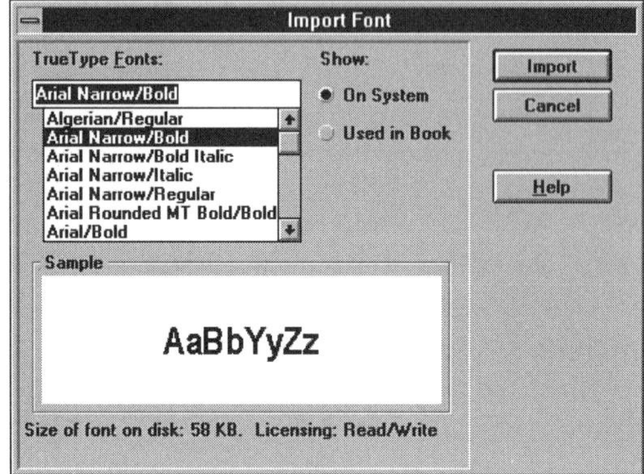

Fig. 26.1

Use the Import Font dialog box to embed fonts in your book.

You will notice that there is a list of fonts shown in the dialog box. This is either a list of all the fonts installed on your system or a list of fonts installed on your system that are also used in your book. The radio buttons labeled On System and Used in Book control which list is shown. Click any of the font names and several things happen: a sample of the font appears in the Sample window and the size of the font in kilobytes appears below the sample window along with the licensing category of the font. Once you have chosen a font, click Import to embed it in your book.

The tedious part of importing fonts is that ToolBook will only import a single font at a time. Once the font is imported, you can give it a name so you can work with the resource using OpenScript. Continue to use the name of the font that appears in the Character dialog box, not the name you give it, when you want to use it to format text.

> **Note**
>
> Despite what the documentation says, the OpenScript command `Import` does not work with fonts. If you attempt to import a font using this command, you will be greeted with the error message `This operation is not supported for this type of resource.`

Working with an Embedded Font

Once a font is imported into your book, you can get some information about it by choosing a font in the Resource Manager and clicking Edit. This will show you the Font Resource dialog box (see fig. 26.2). Some of the same information can be had by looking at the `resourceInfo` property of each font, as follows:

```
get resourceinfo of font id 102
```

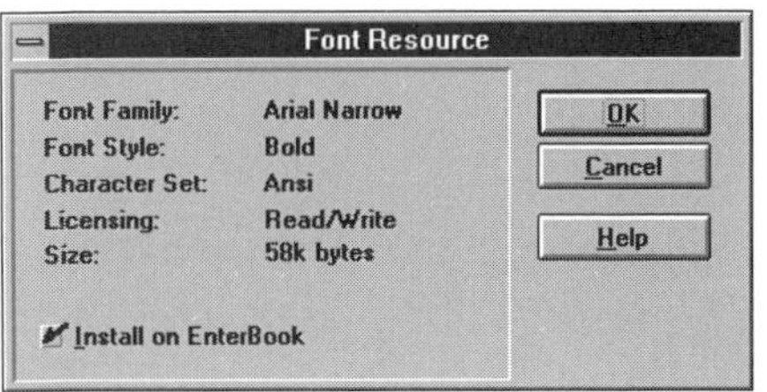

Fig. 26.2

The Font Resource dialog box lets you decide when fonts are installed.

You will notice that there is a checkbox in the Font Resource dialog box labeled Install on EnterBook. This checkbox controls whether the imported font is installed when the book starts up. By default, ToolBook will load all imported fonts when the book starts up. When there is a large number of fonts in your book, this can significantly increase the amount of time needed to start your book. The alternative is to clear this checkbox and load the fonts at another time using OpenScript. The OpenScript command used to do this is `installFontResource`. You can install the font whenever you choose, but it only needs to be installed once. The following example shows how `installFontResource` might be used:

```
to handle getTheFonts
     installFontResource font "Heading"
     installFontResource font "Body Text"
end getTheFonts
```

One big "gotcha" with this technique is that any font used on a particular page must be installed before navigating to that page. The `enterPage` message is sent after the page, with all its text, is displayed. Consequently, if the font was installed on `enterPage`, any text using that font would be displayed using a substitute font.

Preparing for Runtime

There are two environments that a ToolBook book can run in. The first is the normal authoring environment of the full version of ToolBook. The other is the runtime version of ToolBook that you can ship with your book. Runtime ToolBook is a stripped-down version of ToolBook with all the Author level items removed. The ToolBook license gives you the right to ship runtime ToolBook with any of your products. This enables everybody to enjoy your work without having to purchase ToolBook.

Limitations of Runtime ToolBook

The runtime version, due to its stripped down state, is not able to do all the same things that the full version is capable of. This means that there is some preparation required to ensure that your book will function properly with runtime ToolBook:

- The first and most obvious limitation of runtime ToolBook is that you cannot switch to Author level.
- The value of the system property `SysLevel` is always Reader level and cannot be changed.
- The value of the system property `SysRuntime` is always `true`.
- No built-in palettes, windows, or dialog boxes can be displayed. The hot keys for these items do not work, the menus are not available, and if you attempt to use an OpenScript command to access them, an error is generated. Examples are the Command Window, the color tray, toolbars, and Page Properties dialog box.
- Menu Event messages for Author level menus cannot be sent and will cause errors because Author level menus are not available. These messages include all the messages to open an Author level palette or window along with such messages as `align`, `startRecording`, `reshape`, and `author`.
- No direct manipulation by the end user of scripts in a book is possible. Scripts can be modified by setting the `script` property of an object using OpenScript statements.
- Right-click menus are not available.
- Properties of objects cannot be set interactively using the Objects Properties dialog box because these are Author level items and not included in runtime ToolBook. All properties can be set using OpenScript statements with the following exceptions: `startupAutoScriptFile`, `startupReaderRightClick`, `sysReaderRightClick`, `sysShowMRUFiles`, `sysTool`, `sysLevel`, `sysRunTime`, `rulers`, and `sysGrid`. Attempting to set these properties will result in an error.

Getting Around the Limitations

You can work around a good number of the limitations of runtime ToolBook. The main problem with runtime ToolBook is that all the dialog boxes, palettes, and windows that would normally be used to change some aspect of a book are not available. There is no law, however, to prevent you from creating your own palettes, windows, and dialog boxes using viewers and OpenScript. You could copy an objects script into a text field, have the end user edit the script, and then set the objects script property to that text, effectively bypassing the limitation on editing scripts.

A toolbar can be emulated using buttons in a viewer. Right-click menus can be created using the OpenScript command `popMenu()`.

A great place to get some ideas on how to do some of these work-arounds is the `MTB30.SBK` system book shipped with Multimedia ToolBook. There are examples of viewers used as dialog boxes. In fact, the Properties dialog box is implemented in this way.

Optimizing Techniques

There are many ways that you can improve the speed and efficiency of your book. Changing small things can have an impact on the book's overall efficiency. Here are some simple things that you can do to improve the speed of your books.

OpenScript Optimizations

With OpenScript, as with any programming language, there are usually many ways to accomplish the same task. Quite often, one way will run quicker because certain commands or techniques are more efficient:

- Make sure you use quotes around any literal text. For example:

  ```
  Show viewer "mine"
  ```

  When quotes are not used in such cases, ToolBook has to search through all properties of the book or page to see if there is a property with the same name. If there is no match, only then will ToolBook believe it is literal text. By including quotes, ToolBook knows this immediately.
- Use variables instead of properties. Getting the value of a property is slower than getting the value of a variable. If you will be getting the value of a property a number of times, copy the property to a variable and use that instead.
- Whenever possible, use datatypes for variables. When a data type is not specified for a variable, ToolBook will convert the variable into whatever format it thinks is appropriate. This conversion could slow down the script. For example, if an integer number is placed in a variable, ToolBook will cast it as an integer. If that integer is then added to a floating point number, the integer needs to be converted to a floating point number and then added. This conversion can be avoided by setting the datatype of the initial variable to be a floating point number.
- Use arrays instead of comma-delimited text (stacks). ToolBook can access the elements in an array quicker than it can the elements in a stack.
- When you do need to access elements in a stack, and when appropriate, use the `push` and `pop` commands instead of the `item` command.
- When trying to find a single element within a stack, the `in` command is much quicker than moving through the whole list with `pop`.
- Be aware of how much memory your variables take up. If the user's system runs low on memory, your book will become very sluggish. Don't, for example, use a 1000 × 100 element array when a 20 × 100 array will suffice.

Other Optimizations

Along with OpenScript, there are many ways of working with the ToolBook environment and many tools to improve the speed of your book:

- Make the dimensions of your book as small as possible. The smaller the book is, the faster it will display.

- To decrease the amount of time that your book takes to load, use as few statements in the `enterApplication` and `enterBook` handlers as possible. The fewer statements there are in these handlers, the quicker the book will display.
- Delete any unused items on any pages.
- Compact your books by saving the book under a different name using the Save As command. This will remove any objects that have been deleted and make the book as small as possible.
- Use as few backgrounds as possible, and try to reduce the number of times that backgrounds are changed. When ToolBook moves between two pages that share a background, only the foreground has to be loaded, which allows for a quicker transition.
- When placing objects on pages, try to avoid overlapping objects. The more objects that are overlapped, the longer the page will take to display.
- If you have a background that is shared between pages, set the `imageBuffers` to 2. This will increase the speed of ToolBook moving between pages.
- Try to place any object that is the same on multiple pages on the background. This prevents the object from being redrawn when navigating between pages.

Other Details

There are many little details that are quite easy to overlook when you are finishing off your book. Here is a number of things that you can do to give your book that finished look:

- Check the spelling in your book using the spell checker that comes with ToolBook. This is accessed by choosing Edit, Spelling.
- Set the media paths for your book to include the paths of all your clips. Use the Media Packager to replace any explicit path names from your clips with paths that are relative to your media paths. Finally, check to make sure that your clips can be found by choosing Check Links in the Clip Manager.
- If you are using Full-Text Search in your book, it is a good idea to build an index as a final step. This ensures that the index is up-to-date and contains any changes that you have made to your book.
- If you will be saving your book as an EXE, you can choose the icon that your book will use in the Program Manager. You do this by setting the icon of the Main Window viewer from either the Properties dialog box for the Main Window viewer or by using OpenScript, for example:

  ```
  set icon of mainWindow to "icon ID 101"
  ```

  Any time that you change the icon, you will need to save your book again as an EXE.

The Final Save

Once you have optimized your book as much as you can, the final step you need to make is to save your book in its most compact and efficient form. You need to make the decision whether to save your book as a ToolBook book (TBK) or as an executable (EXE). This is also the stage where you decide whether to optimize your book for CD distribution and what sort of cache file you will use. The decisions you make here affect how your users will run your book as well as how your book performs.

Saving the Book as a TBK

The easiest way to save a book is with the Save As command to save your book as a ToolBook book. This is the default method that ToolBook uses to save any book. It has the advantages of being easily recognizable as a ToolBook file and being easy to create. There are disadvantages, however. The book cannot be run from the command line and will have the generic ToolBook icon used by default in the Windows Program Manager. In addition, users will not readily consider your book to be a stand-alone application. This last issue can be important if you are creating a demo for your company or even selling your application on the open market.

A book can be compacted and saved as a TBK by choosing File, Save As, providing a new name and path, and clicking Save. You also have the option to optimize your book to be run from CD and create a cache file. These options will be covered in the section titled "Optimizing the Book for CD."

You are also able to use OpenScript for this in one of two ways. You can open the Save As dialog box by sending the `saveAs` message, or you can bypass the dialog box altogether. For example:

```
save as "D:\MYFILES\GOODBK", true
```

This OpenScript command will save the book under the name `GOODBK` and the true parameter tells the system to overwrite any file with the same name.

Saving the Book as an EXE

Saving a book as an executable file does two things. First, it creates a file that can be executed directly just like any other executable file. Second, it allows you to assign an icon to the application that will be used in the Windows Program Manager. To save a book as an EXE, you follow the same method as saving a TBK, but with one exception: you select Save As EXE from the File menu instead of Save As. You then give it a name and path and click Save. (Figure 26.3 shows an example of the Save as EXE dialog box.)

If you want to use OpenScript to accomplish this task, you can either send the `saveAsExe` message to open the Save as EXE dialog box or use the Save As EXE command. The following example will save a book as an EXE and the false parameter tells the system not to overwrite a file with the same name:

```
save as EXE "D:\MYFILES\GOODBK", false
```

Optimizing the Book for CD

If you will be distributing your book on a CD, this section is for you. CD drives do not operate at nearly the speed that a hard drive does. ToolBook gives you a way to distribute your files on CD and get the best performance that is possible from a CD. It does this in two ways. The first is to organize the data in your book in such a way that it is easily readable from a CD. The second is to give you the option to create a cache file. This cache file will be copied to the user's hard drive when the book is run, giving the advantage of using the much faster hard drive to access frequently needed data in your book. The cache file holds information about the pages in your book, complex bitmaps and scripts, and bitmaps and resources. How much of this data and what types are determined by the options you choose when you optimize your book.

Optimizing for CD can be done with either a TBK or an EXE file. If you want to optimize your book for CD without creating a cache file, all you need to do is click Optimize for CD-ROM in the Save as EXE dialog box (see fig. 26.3). You will notice that the Cache File Options button will no longer be shaded when you do this.

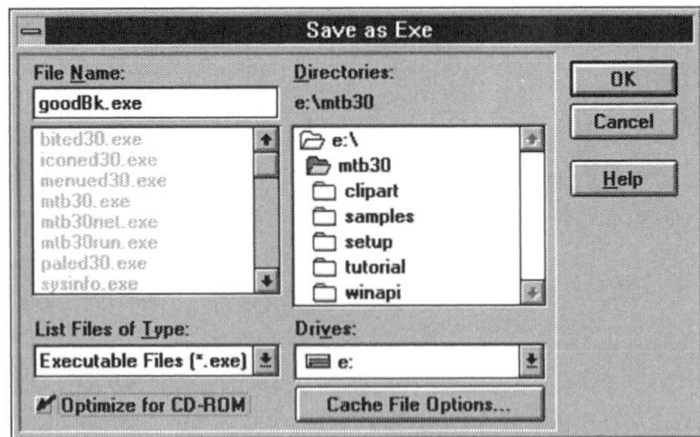

Fig. 26.3

The Save as EXE dialog box can be used to set the Optimize for CD-ROM option.

By clicking the Cache File Options button, the Cache File Options dialog box appears giving you access to the settings for the cache file (see fig. 26.4). There are only two choices that you need to make: whether the file will be installed permanently or temporarily, and what size the file will be.

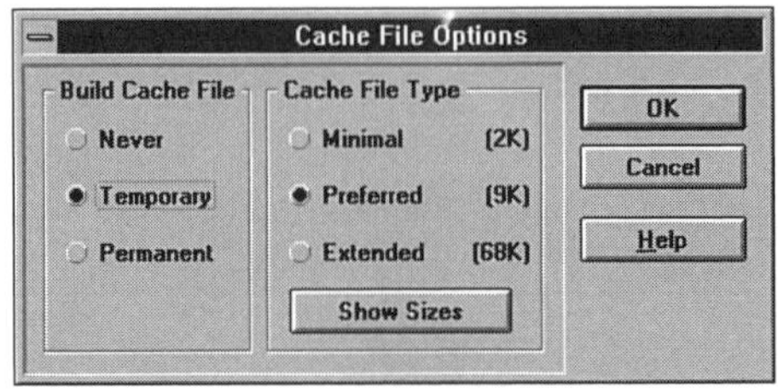

Fig. 26.4

Activate the Cache File Options dialog box to set the parameters for the cache file.

The first choice has three options:

- *Never*—No cache file is built or used.
- *Temporary*—The cache file is built and copied to the hard drive as a TMP file when the book is run. The cache file is deleted when the book is closed.
- *Permanent*—the cache file is built and saved with a TBC extension. This file will need to be copied to the user's hard drive, either by the application or by the installation program. Also, an entry in the `MTB30.INI` file under the `(Cache Files)` section will need to be created so the book can find the cache file. The following is an example entry in the `MTB30.INI` file:

```
(Cache Files)
GOODBK.EXE=C:\MYAPP\GOODBK.TBC
```

The second choice also has three options. The three types of cache files—*Minimal, Preferred,* and *Extended*—all store a different amount of data. They are also different sizes and provide differing levels of speed improvement. Minimal, like its name, holds the least data, is the smallest size, and provides the smallest benefit. Preferred and Extended hold greater amounts of data, are larger in size, and provide greater speed gains.

The biggest concern, when choosing what type of cache file to use, is the size. The larger the cache file is, the larger the amount of hard drive space required. Also, your book will take longer to start when using a temporary cache file because it has to be copied to the hard drive every time. To help you make a better decision about what type of cache to use, you can click the Show Sizes button to calculate approximately how much space each type of cache will take.

Distributing Your Work

Your book is done, all your clips are ready, and you have breathed a big sigh of relief. Now, how are you going to get it to the people who will be using it? Will you send it to them on CD? How about floppy disks? Maybe over the network? Something else? Figuring out how to get your work out to the people that need it is influenced by many things, each one of them pointing to a different way. Each method of distribution has its own details and tasks as well.

Choosing a Distribution Method

How do you decide on a single method of distribution when there are so many options? The answer to that question can be broken down into three elements: cost, amount of time, and hardware. It is worth noting here that choosing a method of distribution is better determined before a project ever begins. That way you are able to custom design your application to suit the distribution.

There may be hundreds of methods, but there are three methods that cover the majority of scenarios. They are floppy disk, CD-ROM, and network. Each of the three has advantages and disadvantages. Some of the questions that you can ask yourself are covered here.

What Type of Hardware Is Available? The first question to ask is what type of hardware is available. You have to determine what the minimum hardware requirements are. If the people that will be using your book have neither CD nor network, the only option left to you is floppy disk. Also, even if they do have these items, they may not be capable of delivering the speed needed for a multimedia application.

Where Will It Run? Is your application going to be run from a central location with only a few files being copied to the hard drive, or is everything going to be copied to the hard drive? If you plan on running your application primarily from one location, floppy disks are out. Your only options are CD and network distribution. Files on both CDs and networks can be executed directly, so they don't necessarily need to be copied to the hard drive, which requires less space on the local hard drive but can be slower.

How Big Is the Book? Attempting to send out an application that is several hundred megabytes in size with floppy disks is rather ridiculous due to the cost and the time involved. Attempting to install such a large application onto a user's hard drive may not work because of lack of hard drive space. Your options as far using networks may also be more limited because there may not be enough hard disk space on the network server itself. Using a CD to distribute large files can work just fine as long as you plan on running the application from the CD or the user has enough hard drive space.

How Many Copies Are You Making? The number of copies that you plan to make will directly effect the cost of reproduction of both floppies and CDs. The initial cost of creating a CD is generally much greater than creating a floppy. However, the cost for each copy of a CD goes down dramatically as the number of copies goes up. The cost per copy for floppies goes down as well, but not as significantly.

How Much Time Do You Have? Using a network to distribute your files generally takes the least amount of time to prepare; all you do is copy the files to the network and you are ready to go. Floppies take more time because the files have to be compressed and copied onto floppy disks and then reproduced. The lead time required for compact discs is the longest due to the fact that there are so many more steps and you will have to rely on a service bureau for reproduction of more than about five or ten CDs.

Steps for CD Distribution

To distribute the CD, follow these steps:

1. Create the directory structure that will be on the CD.
2. Use Setup Manager to create the installation files that will install any necessary files to the user's hard drive as well as runtime ToolBook, if required.

3. Test the installation.

Tip

Use the DOS Subst command to help you test your application by emulating a drive that has only the files for your application on it. For example, if you have created C:\GOOD as the root directory of your application, use the following command to create a W: drive that has C:\GOOD as the root directory:

```
subst W: C:\GOOD
```

4. Burn a one off CD as the premaster. A service bureau can do this, or you can do this if you have the proper equipment. Getting the data to a service bureau can be a difficult task considering the size of the files normally going onto CD. Talk to your bureau and see what sort of removable media devices they support. This could be removable hard drive cartridges, tape backup units, SCSI devices, etc. With the growth of the Internet, there may even be a chance that an electronic transfer could take place. If all else fails, there is always floppy disk.
5. Test installation and the directory structure with the premaster.
6. Duplicate the CD. There are many places that can duplicate CDs for as little as $1 to $2 a copy. The price is coming down as more and more people get into the business and technology improves.

Steps for Floppy Disk Distribution

The following steps can be used when you will be distributing your book on floppy disk:

1. Create the directory structure that will eventually be on the user's hard drive.
2. Use the Setup Manager to create the installation files required.
3. Use the Setup Manager to copy the compressed installation files to floppy.
4. Test the installation.
5. Duplicate the floppies.

Steps for Network Distribution

To distribute a file to a network, follow these steps:

1. Create the directory structure that will eventually be on the user's system.
2. Use Setup Manager to create the installation files that will install any necessary files to the user's hard drive as well as runtime ToolBook if required.
3. Copy the files to a network file server.
4. Test the installation.
5. Ensure that anybody who will install or use this application has read or possibly read/write access to the application.

From Here...

Testing procedures, the runtime ToolBook environment, optimizations, and distribution have all been covered in this chapter. You have learned how to embed fonts in ToolBook books, and some of the decisions that need to be made when selecting a method of distribution. This and other books have more information on these topics. Try out some of the following references:

- More information about resources in ToolBook can be found in Chapter 5, "Understanding the Media Management Tools."
- To find out more about creating and using viewers, see Chapter 8, "Working with Viewers."
- Chapter 27, "Distribution Tools," has more information about using Setup Manager and the Media Packager.

CHAPTER 27

Distribution Tools

The distribution of your application takes thought and some small amount of effort. Multimedia ToolBook provides several tools to aid you in your effort. The two tools that you will learn about in this chapter are the Media Packager and the Setup Manager. Each tool plays a different part in helping you get your application to market.

Using the Media Packager

The Media Packager is a tool that sets up all your media clips so they can be found easily. When you distribute your application, you are distributing a number of files. Many of those files are media files, such as video and sound. Each of these media files needs to be in a directory that the book knows about. If the files are in an unknown directory, they won't be played or displayed.

Understanding Media Search Paths

There are generally two ways that a book can find its media files. The first is to use the `mmSource` property of the clip. The second is to search the media paths of the book in conjunction with the information in the `mmSource` property.

The media search paths are two separate properties of a book that contain any number of directory references. The `HDMediaPath` is for any media files that reside on your hard drive. The `CDMediaPath` is for media files that are on the CD that you distribute your book on. There is no functional difference between the two media search paths except in making your media files easier to manage.

Media search paths are places for your book to search for media files. For example, some of your media files might be contained in the `C:\FILES\MEDIA` directory. You would then put that directory in the `HDMediaPath`, and any clip that references a file in that directory would be able to find it. You can add as many directory references as you like to the media search paths, but the book will take longer to find and play your files as the number increases.

The `mmSource` property works in conjunction with the media search paths to create a full reference to a media file. Each clip in your book has a separate `mmSource` property that must contain at least the name of the file that the clip references and can contain either a partial or complete path reference as well. For example, the `mmSource` property could contain any of the following:

- `VIDEO1.AVI` is the filename of the clip only.
- `MEDIA\VIDEO1.AVI` is the filename along with a partial path reference.
- `FILES\MEDIA\VIDEO1.AVI` is the filename with a longer path reference.
- `C:\FILES\MEDIA\VIDEO1.AVI` is a full reference including drive, directory, and file.

When the `mmSource` property does not contain a full reference to the file, ToolBook will tack the directory references found in the media search paths onto the front to create a full reference. If there are many items in your media search paths, ToolBook will create a full directory reference with each one until it finds the appropriate file. For example, your media search paths contain the following references:

```
C:\MEDIA
C:\DATA
D:\FILES\MEDIA\FUN
```

The `mmSource` of your clip contains:

```
MYFILES\VIDEO1.AVI
```

ToolBook will search for the file in the following places:

```
C:\MEDIA\MYFILES\VIDEO1.AVI
C:\DATA\MYFILES\VIDEO1.AVI
D:\FILES\MEDIA\FUN\MYFILES\VIDEO1.AVI
```

There are several ways that you can set or change the media search paths and the `mmSource` property of your clips. You can use the tools provided in the ToolBook interface described in Chapter 5, "Understanding the Media Management Tools." You can also use OpenScript to directly set the properties. The easiest way, however, is to package your clips using the Media Packager.

The Media Packager

The Media Packager will examine your media search paths and the `mmSource` property of all your clips. It will then attempt to minimize redundancy in these properties by reducing the search paths to the minimum required and removing any explicit references in the `mmSource` property. This process ensures that all clips can be found and reduces the time needed to load clips due to the reduced search paths. If a media file cannot be found, you will be given the opportunity to find the file and either add the path to your search paths or move the file to another directory in your search path. A "before" and "after" comparison might look something like that shown in Table 27.1.

Table 27.1 How the Media Packager Adjusts the Media Search Paths and the Property

Media Search Paths	*mmSource* Property
Before Packaging with the Media Packager	
C:\MEDIA	VIDEO1.AVI
C:\MEDIA\FILES	FILES\VIDEO2.AVI
C:\MEDIA\FILES\ONE	C:\MEDIA\FILES\TWO\GETIT.WAV
C:\MEDIA\FILES\TWO	D:\OTHER\FILES\ZWEEP.WAV
D:\OTHER\FILES	MEDIA\FILES\TEMP\GRRREAT.AVI
After Packaging with the Media Packager	
C:\MEDIA\FILES	ONE\VIDEO1.AVI
D:\OTHER\FILES	VIDEO2.AVI TWO\GETIT.WAV ZWEEP.WAV TEMP\GRRREAT.AVI

You will notice that all explicit references have been changed to path independent references. Also, the media search paths have been pared down to the lowest common path, in this case `C:\MEDIA\FILES`.

Using the Media Packager is a simple process and a very effective way to ensure that your book works as expected. It is used only after all your clips have been created in your book. To start the Media Packager, choose Tools, Media Packager. You will see the dialog box shown in figure 27.1 when you start the Media Packager.

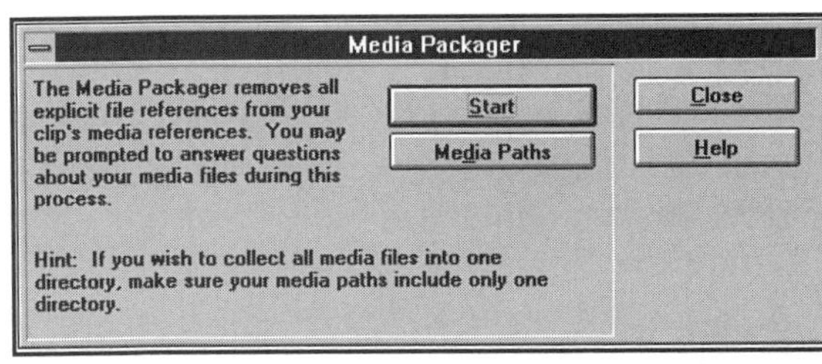

Fig. 27.1

The Media Packager is used to reduce the number of redundant search paths in your book.

> **Note**
>
> If you do not have a Tools item on your menu bar, it could mean that the `MTB40.SBK` file is not defined as a system book. Typing the following line into the Command Window should fix this problem:
>
> ```
> push "mtb40.sbk" onto sysbooks
> ```

The options available to you are to start the packaging process and to edit the media search paths. Editing the search paths will bring up the standard media search path dialog box where you can add or remove path references from either the `HDMediaPath` or the `CDMediaPath`. Once you start the packaging process, ToolBook will go through all the clips defined in your book and attempt to find the source files associated with each one. If one of the files cannot be found, you will be presented with a dialog box asking you to find the file. Next, ToolBook determines if the source files can be found on one of the media search paths. The dialog box shown in figure 27.2 will appear if any of the source files are not on a media search path.

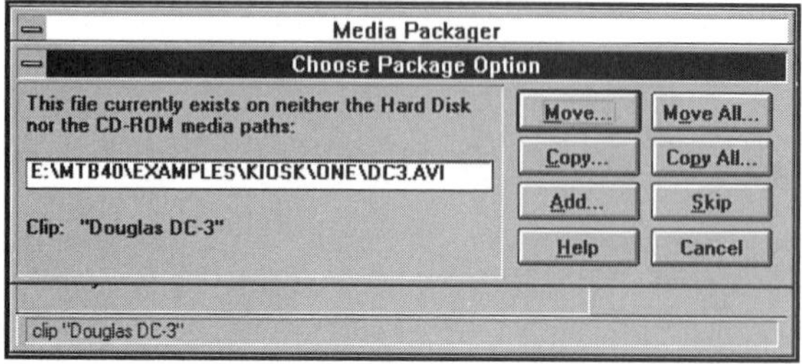

Fig. 27.2

The Choose Package Option dialog box helps you ensure that all your clips can be found.

This dialog box presents you with many options. You can Add the file's path to one of the media search paths, Copy or Move the file to a directory on your search path, or Skip the file. In addition, there is an option to Copy All or Move All of your files to the same directory in one go. Choosing Skip will not remove or otherwise damage your clip; all it will do is set the `mmSource` of that clip to the full directory reference including drive. When any of the Copy or Move options are chosen, you are given the opportunity to select a destination from those defined in the media search paths. If you choose Move All or Copy All, all subsequent files that are not on a search path will be moved or copied to this directory.

Finally, ToolBook will try to relate any entries in your media search paths to the `Bookpath`. The `Bookpath` is a special entry that simply is the path to the current book. If, for example, you have an entry in your `HDMediaPath` that points to a subdirectory of the `Bookpath`, ToolBook will reduce the `HDMediaPath` to the `Bookpath` only, and add the name of the subdirectory to the `mmSource` property of the clip or clips effected.

Using the Setup Manager

The next tool that ToolBook provides is the Setup Manager. This tool helps you set up the installation for your program—from selecting the files to be installed and determining their location, to making changes to the different configuration files and choosing icons to be installed in the Program Manager. Each application you create has different components and installation requirements. By the same token, each system that your application will be installed on has a different setup. Setup Manager has ways of dealing with these differences. An important part of any installation system is how the files will be packaged. This can be taken care of by compressing all or part of your files into a single archive.

The Setup Manager works in conjunction with the `SETUP.EXE` program. Setup Manager creates the installation instructions that `SETUP.EXE` will use when the application is installed; those instructions are stored in a text file with an INF extension.

Start the Setup Manager by double-clicking the Setup Manager icon in the Multimedia ToolBook group within the Windows Program Manager. It can also be started by executing the `SETUPMGR.EXE` program in the `SETUP` subdirectory of your ToolBook directory. The layout of the program uses tabs which run across the top of the main window. Each one corresponds to a different part of the installation process. Clicking any of the tabs brings a new page of setup information to the front, just like pages in a book. Figure 27.3 shows the Setup Manager with the General tab open.

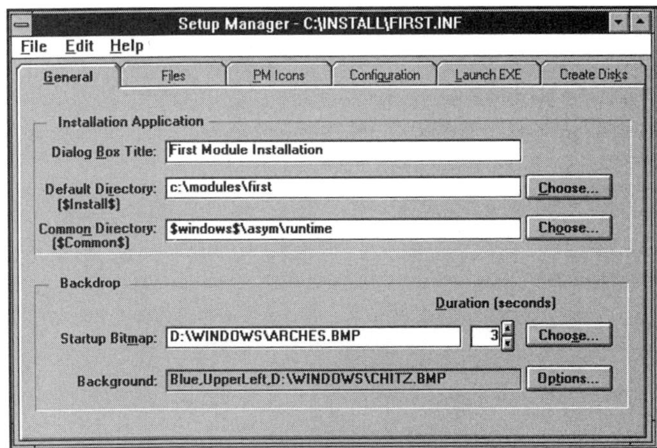

Fig. 27.3

The Setup Manager General tab is the first stop in configuring the setup program for your book.

The General Tab

The General tab is the first stop on the tour. It contains, as its name implies, general information. It is divided into two sections: Installation Application and Backdrop.

Installation Application. You set overall information in this section, as follows:

- *Dialog Box Title*—This is the title of the window that appears when the user starts the `SETUP.EXE` program.
- *Default Directory*—This directory will be the root for all the files that you install. It will be created if it does not already exist. The user will have the option to change this directory at setup time, so this is strictly a default. It is a good idea to leave this pointing to a directory on the `C:` drive unless you are sure that your users will have other drives.

- *Common Directory*—This is the default directory that the ToolBook runtime files will be installed in. If the Setup program finds that a copy of the runtime already exists at the location shown here, new files will only be copied if they are a newer version of the runtime. This field is filled in when you start the Setup Manager, and it is a good idea to leave it at this value so that multiple copies of the runtime are not installed on your users' machines. This value, as well, can be changed by the user at setup time.

Backdrop. This section deals with how the background of the Setup program will look and whether there will be a splash screen. The following list describes the various controls you can use to set the background:

- *Startup Bitmap*—The bitmap specified here will be displayed when the SETUP.EXE is first started, prior to any other activity. It will be displayed for the number of seconds set in the duration field. An example of a Startup Bitmap is the Asymetrix ToolBook logo that flashes on the Screen when you start ToolBook.
- *Duration*—The number of seconds that the Startup Bitmap will be displayed.
- *Background*—This field, unlike the others, cannot be set directly. It simply reports the selections made in the Background Options dialog box that can be brought up by clicking the Options button beside the field (see fig. 27.4).

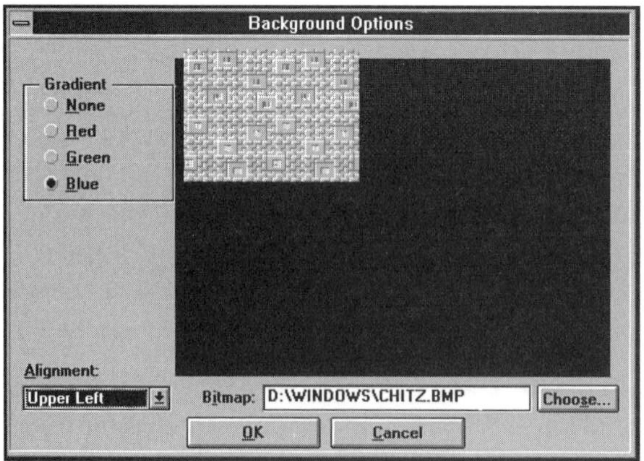

Fig. 27.4

The entries in the Background Options dialog box controls what will appear in the background of your setup.

There are three options on the Background Options dialog box. The large area to the top right of the dialog box is a preview of what your background will look like. The options available are as follows:

- *Gradient*—This is the color that the background will have. It is called a gradient because the color will gradually change from black to the chosen color.

- *Bitmap*—This field contains a path reference and a name of a Windows bitmap. The bitmap chosen here will be shown on the screen throughout the installation process. The file does not need to be added to any of the file components because it is copied to the same directory that the compressed files are created in.
- *Alignment*—This determines where the chosen bitmap will be placed on the screen. If a bitmap is not wanted or needed, No Bitmap can be selected here.

Directory Placeholders. Scattered throughout the Setup Manager are a number of words bracketed by $ characters. These are called directory placeholders and are replaced, at setup time, by various directory paths. There are five different directory placeholders that can be used throughout Setup Manager wherever a directory on the installation machine needs to be specified. The placeholders are valuable because the directories that they point to will change at each installation based on the user's choices and the user's computer configuration. They are as follows:

- *$Common$*—This will be replaced with the path to the common directory.
- *$Install$*—This will be replaced with the default directory or an installation path that the user chooses at setup time.
- *$Windows$*—This will be replaced with the path to the user's Windows directory.
- *$System$*—This will be replaced with the path to the user's Windows system directory.
- *$Source$*—This will be replaced with the path to the directory that the `SETUP.EXE` program was started from.

For example, if I wanted to point to a subdirectory of the installation directory called `MYSTUFF`, I would use the following syntax:

```
$INSTALL$\MYSTUFF
```

When the Setup program is run, the `$INSTALL$` portion of the path will be replaced with a real path.

The Files Tab

The Files tab is the meat of the installation (see fig. 27.5). All the files that are to be copied to the user's system need to be specified here. You have the option of creating several different groups of files called *components*. The end user can choose whether to install each component as a group. Also, changes to configuration files and other installation options can be attached to a single component. This way, you can create a truly customized installation procedure.

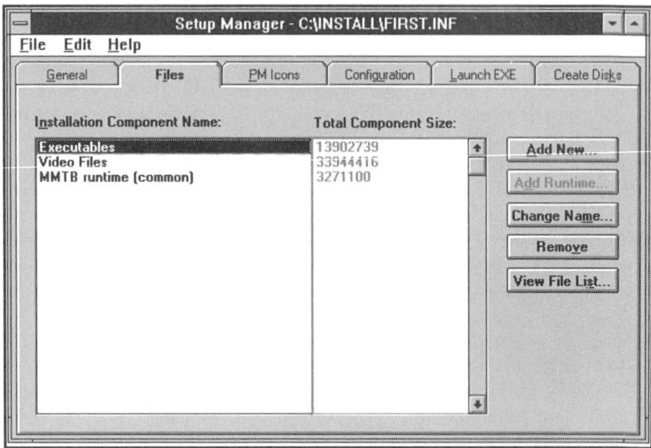

Fig. 27.5

Install components with the Files tab.

The most prominent feature of this tab is the Installation Component Name and Total Component Size windows. These windows list all the components that have been defined for your installation and the total size, in bytes, of all the files in each component. The buttons along the right side of the window work with the component that is selected from this list.

Adding a Component. Obviously, if no components have been created, you will need to do that. Click the Add New button to start this process. A small dialog box will open up asking you to enter the name of the component. Enter a name and click OK. The Component File List dialog box shown in figure 27.6 will appear.

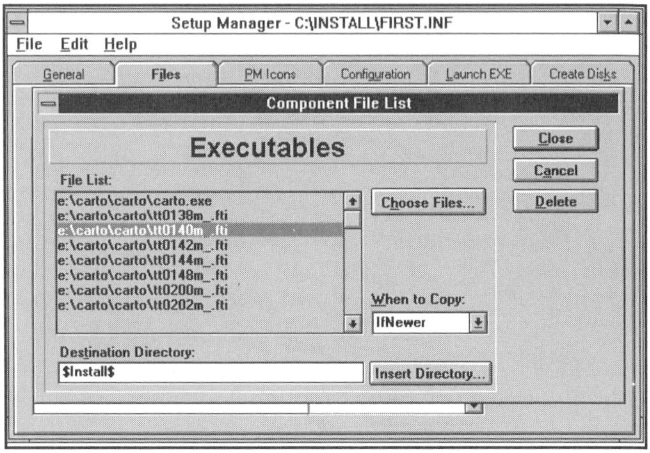

Fig. 27.6

Each of the installation components is listed in the Component File List dialog box.

The purpose of the Component File List dialog box is to enable you to choose the files that will be installed with a particular component. Each file that you select can be installed in a separate directory, and several options become available after installation.

The first step is to click the Choose Files button to select the files that you want installed with this component. Once all your files have been chosen, you need to select where each one will be installed. Select a file from the File List window, and type the installation directory into the Destination Directory field. You can insert a directory placeholder into this field by using the Insert Directory button.

Finally, you need to decide when the file will be installed. The When to Copy drop-down list give you several options, as follows:

- *AlwaysCopy*—The file will always be copied to the destination directory. If a file with the same name exists in that directory, it will be overwritten.
- *AskUser*—The user doing the installation will be asked whether or not to copy the file.
- *IfDoesNotExist*—The file will only be copied to the destination directory if a file with the same name does not already exist in that directory.
- *IfNewer*—This is the same as IfDoesNotExist except the file will also be copied to the destination directory if it is newer than the existing file. The Windows version information will be used first, if it exists, and the DOS time stamp will be used if it doesn't.
- *IfNewerThanSys*—This option is the same as IfNewer except that the user's entire system will be checked for a file with the same name. If a file is found and it is older, the new file will be copied to the destination directory. The old file will only be overwritten if it is in the destination directory.

Once you have finished adjusting the options for all the files, click the Close button to dismiss the dialog box.

Other Options. The remainder of the buttons on the Files tab are generally self-explanatory. However, there are several items that need clarifying; the following is a quick rundown of each:

- *Add Runtime*—This will automatically create a component containing all the files necessary for a runtime environment. A dialog box will open giving you a choice of optional files that might be necessary for your application. The runtime will be installed in the common directory that you specified on the General tab.
- *Change Name*—This changes the name of the component selected in the Installation Component window.
- *Remove*—This removes the selected component.
- *View File List*—This brings up the Component File List dialog box for the selected component.

> **Caution**
>
> Removing a component will also remove any entries on the other tabs that are installed with the component. If you want to preserve any of these other entries, go to the appropriate tab, and change the entry so that it is installed with another component or is always installed.

The PM Icons Tab

You use the PM Icons tab to set up all the icons and program groups that will be installed in the Windows Program Manager(PM). Figure 27.7 shows this section of the Setup Manager.

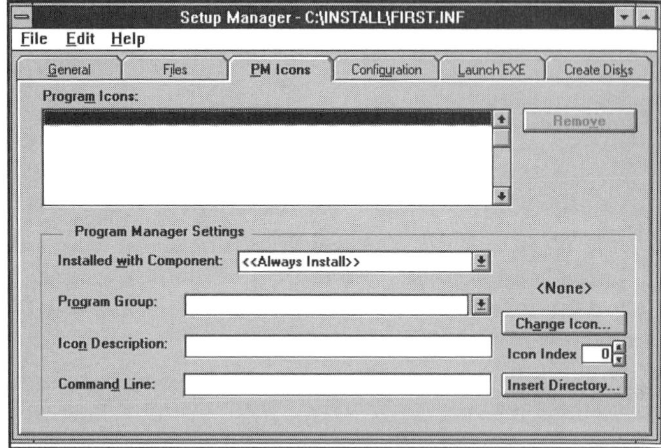

Fig. 27.7

Program manager icons can be setup in the PM Icons tab of the Setup Manager.

The big window at the top of this tab is a listing of all the PM Icons defined so far. You can define as many different icons as you want. To add a new entry, simply click the blank line below the last entry. Also, the order of the entries can be changed by using the mouse to drag them up or down. The different areas to be filled out are the following:

- *Installed with Component*—This drop-down box contains all the components defined in the Files tab as well as an item named Always Install. By selecting any one of the components listed, the icon being defined will only get installed if that component is installed. The Always Install option will install the icon no matter which component is installed, just as long as one is installed.
- *Program Group*—This is the title that will appear under the Program group in the Program Manager or in the title bar of the group when it is opened. If the group name already exists on the user's machine, that group will be used; otherwise, a new group will be created. The drop-down list attached to this field contains all the program groups named on this tab.
- *Icon Description*—This is the name that will appear under the Program Icon in the group specified in the Program Group field above.

- *Command Line*—This is the command line that will actually start the program. For example, `$INSTALL$\MYBOOK.EXE` will start the program `MYBOOK.EXE` in the user's installation directory. Use the Insert Directory button to insert any of the directory placeholders.
- *Change Icon*—If you want to use an icon other than the default icon for your file or application, click this button. You will need to select an ICO file or some other file that has icons within it, such as EXE or DLL. As well as selecting the file here, you must include the file in the component this icon is installed with. You can do this on the Files tab of the Setup Manager. The icon that you choose will appear just above the Change Icon button.
- *Icon Index*—Many files will have more than one icon within them. The number set here is the number of the icon that you want to use within the file. For example, setting this value to zero would use the first icon within the file, while setting it to four would use the fifth icon in the file.

The Configuration Tab

The Configuration tab is where you make all the adjustments to any INI files as well as the `AUTOEXEC.BAT` and `CONFIG.SYS` files (see fig. 27.8). There can be any number of entries in this section.

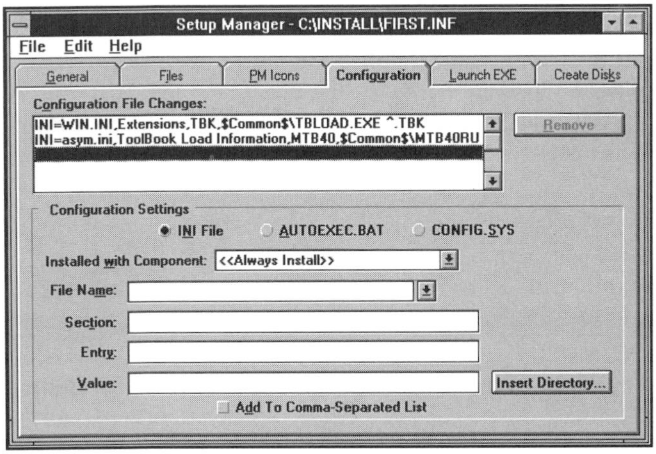

Fig. 27.8

The Configuration tab of the Setup Manager is where you set any adjustments that need to be made to configurations files.

Adding a new configuration entry is as simple as clicking the blank line below the last entry in the Configuration File Changes list box and then filling in the fields in the lower half of the window. Depending on the type of file that you will be changing, there are different fields to fill out. Select the type of file you want to edit by clicking any one of the three radio buttons labeled INI file, AUTOEXEC.BAT, and CONFIG.SYS.

There is one field that is the same between the three options and that is the Installed with Component drop-down box. For any entry in the Configuration File Changes list box, select a component from this list. The change to the configuration file will only be made if the user decides to install that component. Choose Always Install from the list if you want the change to be made no matter which components get installed.

The AUTOEXEC.BAT option has only one other field to fill out. In the AUTOEXEC field, enter the text that you want added to the user's `AUTOEXEC.BAT` file. This could be something from setting an environment variable to running the application at startup.

The CONFIG.SYS option, as well, has only one other field to fill out. The text entered in the CONFIG field will get added to the user's `CONFIG.SYS` file.

The INI file option has the following fields to fill out:

- *File Name*—This is the name of the INI file that you will be working with. The directory placeholders can be used in this field. `$WINDOWS$\WIN.INI` and `$WINDOWS$\SYSTEM.INI` are two examples.
- *Section*—This identifies the section of the INI file you will be working with. Every INI file has different sections. A section is identified by an entry in the INI file surrounded by square brackets. For example, every `WIN.INI` file should have both a `[Windows]` section and a `[Desktop]` section. If the section you enter here does not exist in the INI file, it will be created.
- *Entry*—This identifies the line in the selected section that you will be changing. If the entry does not already exist, it will be created.
- *Value*—This is the actual text that will get entered in the INI file
- *Add to Comma Separated List*—Some entries in INI files have more than one value separated by commas. By checking this box, the text in the Value field will be added to the end of any other values separated by a comma instead of overwriting them.

The Launch EXE Tab

The Launch EXE tab provides you with two things (see fig. 27.9). The first is the ability to launch any program after installing any component. The second is the ability to display a message box when a component is finished installing. Each of these actions can be performed always or only when a certain component is installed. In addition, you can execute any number of programs in a certain sequence and bring up any number of messages. The order of the items in the list determines the order in which they will be executed.

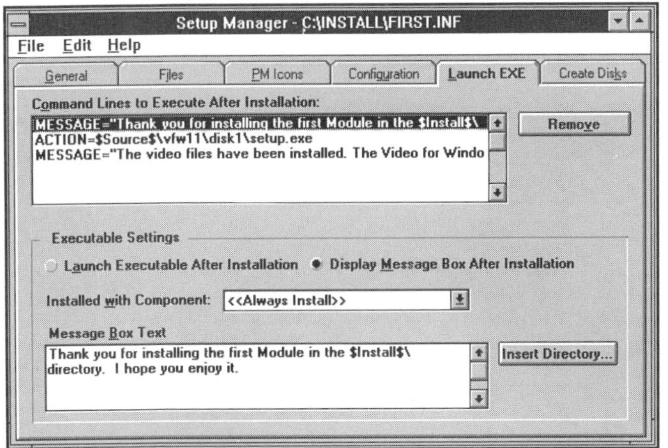

Fig. 27.9

The Setup Manager Launch EXE tab enables you to launch applications after installation of your book.

Defining a command line or a message is an easy four-step process:

1. Click the blank line below the last defined line in the window labeled Command Lines to Execute After Installation. This will start a new entry.
2. Decide whether this entry will launch a program or display a message box by selecting one of the two radio buttons.
3. Select which component this item will be associated with by selecting a component from the Installed with Component drop-down list. Select Always Install if you want the item to execute or display on every installation.
4. Depending on what type of item this is, there will be one of two fields available to you. Type the command line to execute in the Command field or the text of the message in the field labeled Message Box Text. Use any of the Directory placeholders in either of the two options. They will be expanded to a full path at installation time.

The Create Disks Tab

The Create Disks tab is the last stop in setting up your installation (see fig. 27.10). This is where all the files get compressed into a set of installation files. You can create the compressed files on a hard disk to be later copied to your distribution media, or they can go directly to your distribution media. The compressed files will have the same name as the INF file that was created with a sequential number as an extension. For example, if `MYINSTALL.INF` is the name of the INF file, `MYINSTALL.001` will be the first compressed file, `MYINSTALL.002` will be the second, and so on. This means that you will have to save your INF file by using the Save or Save As commands under the File menu prior to creating your compressed files.

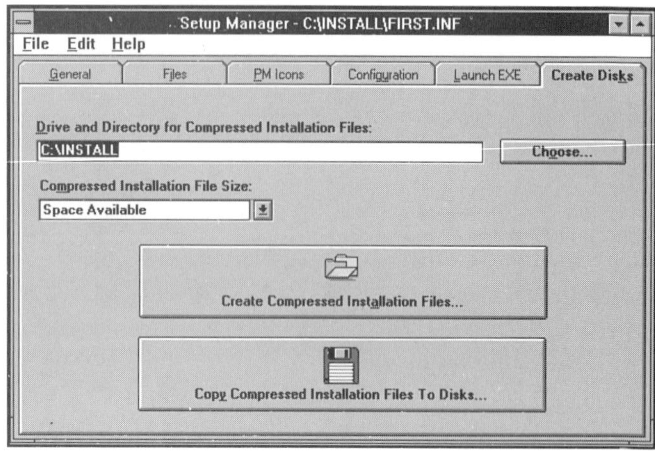

Fig. 27.10

The Create Disks tab is where you compress your book and place it on diskettes.

The controls available to you are as follows:

- *Drive and Directory for Compressed Installation Files*—This is where the compressed files will be created. It could point to a directory on your hard drive or a floppy drive.
- *Compressed Installation File Size*—This determines the size of compressed files that Setup Manager will create. The first compressed file will be smaller than this size to allow room for your INF file, `SETUP.EXE`, and any bitmaps. The Space Available option will write to the selected drive and directory until there is no more room and then ask for another disk. This option is the default. Generally, the only time that you will not use this option is when you are creating files that will be copied to floppy disk at a later time.
- *Create Compressed Installation Files*—This starts the process of compressing your installation files.
- *Copy Compressed Installation Files*—This button will copy a set of compressed installation files created earlier to floppy disk. No compression takes place with this option, so the files need to be of a size that will fit on the selected floppy disk. Compressed files created with the Compressed Installation File Size and set to something other than Space Available work very well.

Modifying the INF File

As mentioned earlier, the instructions that you create with the Setup Manager are stored in a text file with an INF extension. These files can be viewed and edited with any text editor. The `EDIT.EXE` program that comes with Windows is an example. The instructions can be modified in this way without going back into the Setup Manager. In addition, there are several things that can be added to the INF file manually that the Setup Manager can't do for you.

The INF files are separated into different sections just like INI files are. Each component you defined in the Files tab has its own section that contains all the files, PM icons, configuration items, and other items associated with that component. There is also a `[General]` section that contains the information from the General tab of the Setup Manager and a `[DefaultComponent]` section that contains all the items that are always installed.

Additional Options for a PM Icon. There are a couple of items that a PM icon can support, but you cannot set from within Setup Manager. The first is the position of the icon within the program group, and the other is the working directory. These items can be set by editing the INF file directly. Open the file with any text editor, such as the EDIT.EXE program that came with DOS. Find the line in the file that defines the icon you want to change. The line will look something like the following:

```
PMGroupItem0=My Modules,$SOURCE$\MODULE\CARTO.EXE,The First Module
```

Each item in the line is separated by a comma. The different items that can be defined in this line are as follows, in the order that they must appear:

- `PMGroupItem(x)=`—This is the command that tells `SETUP.EXE` what this line is for. Replace the `(x)` with the number of this icon. Each icon that gets installed needs to have a different and sequential number. A comma is not needed after this item.
- Group Name—This is the name of the group that the icon will go in. In the above example, `My Modules` is the group name.
- Command Line—This is the command line for the icon. The example above uses `$SOURCE$\MODULE\FIRST.EXE`.
- Icon Name—This is the name that will appear under the icon. The Icon Name is not defined in the above example.
- Icon File,—This is the name of the file that holds the icon you want to use.
- Icon Index,—This is the number of the icon to use within the icon file.
- xPos,—This is the horizontal position of the icon within the program group.
- yPos,—This is the vertical position of the icon within the program group.
- Working Directory—This is the directory that will be the working directory for the program when it is executed. Go ahead and use the directory placeholders for this.

Each item in this list must appear in the line in the INF file in the same order as shown above. If you need to add an item later in the line and not one of the ones before it, place the comma in the file as a placeholder. For example, I have added a working directory to the example above. Notice that I have used commas as placeholders for the Icon File, Icon Index, xPos, and yPos entries.

```
PMGroupItem0=My Modules,$SOURCE$\MODULE\CARTO.EXE,The First Module
,,,,,$INSTALL$/TEMP
```

Showing Bitmaps During Installation. You have all seen the different installations that display all those screens that talk about the program being installed. They will change a few times during the course of the installation process to keep the user mildly entertained. The SETUP.EXE program is capable of doing this neat little feat with only a slight effort from you. You can add instructions to the INF file to display bitmaps during the installation process based on what percentage of the installation is complete. The instructions are added to the [General] section of the INF file. The syntax for the instruction is as follows:

```
Bitmap(x)=BitmapName,Alignment,StartPercentage,EndPercentage.
```

- `Bitmap(x)=`—This command tells `SETUP.EXE` what this line is for. Replace the `(x)` with a number starting with zero. If you want to have multiple bitmaps in a sequence, insert many lines and replace the `(x)` with sequential numbers.
- `BitmapName`—This is the path to the bitmap that you will be using. Use directory placeholders if necessary.
- `Alignment`—This controls the position of the bitmap on the screen. It can be any of the following: `Centered`, `UpperLeft`, `UpperRight`, `LowerLeft`, `LowerRight`, `CenteredLeft`, `CenteredRight`, `UpperCentered`, `LowerCentered`.
- `StartPercentage`—Once the installation program has completed this percentage of the install the bitmap will be displayed.
- `EndPercentage`—The bitmap will be removed once this percentage of the installation has been completed.

The following is an example of what could be placed in the INF file to display two bitmaps—one for the first half of the installation, the other for the last half:

```
Bitmap0=$SOURCE$/BITMAPS/INSTALL1.BMP,UpperLeft,0,50
Bitmap1=$SOURCE$/BITMAPS/INSTALL2.BMP,UpperRight,51,100
```

Custom Installation Buttons. When SETUP.EXE is run, it presents the user with three options: Full Install, Custom Install, and Exit. The buttons beside these three options are default bitmaps. You can select other bitmaps to replace the defaults. To do this, you will need to change one line in the [General] section of your INF file and add up to two more lines.

- `FullInstallBMP=`—This is the bitmap for the Full Install button. This line is put in the INF file by the Setup Manager with a value of `DEFAULT`. Replace the word default with a path and the name of a bitmap. If this line is removed altogether, the default bitmaps will not be used for the installation and standard radio buttons will be used instead.
- `CustomInstallBMP=`—This is the bitmap for the Custom Install button. Add a path and the name for a bitmap after the equals sign.

- `ExitInstallBMP=`—This is the bitmap for the Exit Install button. Add a path and the name for a bitmap after the equals sign.

Any of these items can contain any of the directory placeholders. For example, the following lines replace the default bitmaps with three of my own:

```
FullInstallBMP=$SOURCE$/BITMAPS/MYFULL.BMP
CustomInstallBMP=$SOURCE$/BITMAPS/MYCUSTOM.BMP
ExitInstallBMP=$SOURCE$/BITMAPS/MYEXIT.BMP
```

Querying the User. When users select Custom Install during an installation, they are able to select which components to install. Sometimes you might want to ask users if they are sure about their selections. This can be done with something called a Query instruction. Each component can have a separate query by placing the query instruction in the component's section of the INF file. The user will be presented with text in a message box with a Yes and No button. The button they select determines whether the associated component is installed or not. This will override any previous setting. The syntax for a query is as follows:

```
query Condition, Text
```

- `Query`—This is the command that tells `SETUP.EXE` what this line is for.
- `Condition`—This can be one of three following options:

  `IfSelected`—The user will only be queried if the component this query belongs to is selected to be installed.

  `IfNotSelected`—The user will only be queried if the component this query belongs to is not selected for installation.

  `Always`—The user will be queried whether or not the component is selected.
- `Text`—This is the text the user will be presented with. The text must be enclosed in quotation marks. It is a good idea to present the text in the form of a yes or no question because that is the choice of buttons the user will have.

A completed query instruction would look something like the following:

```
query IfNotSelected, "You have not selected the Help files for
installation. Do you want to install them now?"
```

I would place this line in the INF file at the bottom of the component that contains the help files.

From Here...

This chapter has covered the two main tools that are provided by ToolBook to help you package your book for distribution. The Media Packager helped you set up your media search paths for greatest efficiency; and by using the Setup Manager, you are able to create an installation system for your Book. The following references will lead you to more information about some topics covered in this chapter:

- More information about dynamic link libraries can be found in Chapter 19, "Using Dynamic Link Libraries (DLLs) and Dynamic Data Exchange (DDE)."
- Chapter 21, "Using Multimedia Elements," goes into more depth about media clips and multimedia elements.
- To find out more about preparing your files for distribution, see Chapter 26, "Preparing for Delivery."

Index

Symbols

A

B

C

D

E

F

G

H

I-J

K-L

M

N

O

P

Q-R

S

T

W

X-Y-Z

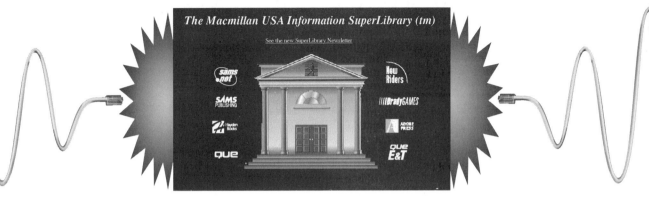

Installation

On this CD-ROM are the setup files that will install the runtime (non-authoring) version of ToolBook on your computer. If you are already running version 4.0 of ToolBook, you do not need to run the install. Users of older versions of ToolBook *will* need to run the install.

To install the files, choose File, Run from the Windows Program Manager and type **X:\SETUP** (where *X* is the letter of your CD-ROM drive).

The install script enables you to install the ScreenCam files onto your hard drive; however, this is not an essential step. You may want to run these from the CD-ROM instead, to save space on your hard drive. Of course, they may run a little slow, depending on your system.

There are three subdirectories on this CD-ROM disk:

- `\EXAMPLES`—This subdirectory contains all of the files from the book chapters. The file `EXAMPLES.TBK` is a table of contents for these examples. To use the file, double-click the filename `EXAMPLES.TBK` from the File Manager, or add it to a program group. (Of course, before these files can be run, you must install the ToolBook runtime files by running the `SETUP`.) Within the `EXAMPLES` application, click an example filename and the `RUN` button to see the example.
- `\SCR_CAM`—The files in this subdirectory contain screen animations of the motions needed to use ToolBook productively. Even veteran ToolBook users will find some of these examples enlightening! You can run any example by double-clicking the filename from within the Program Manager. As these are Lotus ScreenCam executable files, you do not need to install ToolBook to view them. The file `SCRNCAMS.TBK` contains a table of contents for these files. Click the line containing the file that you want to run to launch it from the `SCRNCAMS.TBK` application.
- `\UTILS`—This subdirectory contains some useful utilities discussed in the book.

Many of the examples in the `\EXAMPLES` subdirectory are not very interesting in and of themselves, but rather provide a means for you to play with the scripts from the book without the necessity of typing them in for yourself. We suggest that you take a peak at these as you move through the chapters of the book. The ScreenCam files, on the other hand, may be useful as a "pre-organizer" to the chapter, and may be instructively viewed as you find time.

We hope that you find these files useful and wish you the best as you embark on programming in Asymetrix Multimedia ToolBook!

Licensing Agreement

By opening this package, you are agreeing to be bound by the following:

This software product is copyrighted, and all rights are reserved by the publisher and author. You are licensed to use this software on a single computer. You may copy and/or modify the software as needed to facilitate your use of it on a single computer. Making copies of the software for any other purpose is a violation of the United States copyright laws.

This software is sold *as is* without warranty of any kind, either expressed or implied, including but not limited to the implied warranties of merchantability and fitness for a particular purpose. Neither the publisher nor its dealers or distributors assumes any liability for any alleged or actual damages arising from the use of this program. (Some states do not allow for the exclusion of implied warranties, so the exclusion may not apply to you.)